British Qualifications
011

T EDITION

ide to Professional,
ademic Qualifications
ited Kingdom

LONDON PHILADELPHIA NEW DELHI

Consultant editor: Elizabeth Holmes

Publisher's note

Every possible effort has been made to ensure that the information contained in this book is accurate at the time of going to press, and the publishers and authors cannot accept responsibility for any errors or omissions, however caused. No responsibility for loss or damage occasioned to any person acting, or refraining from action, as a result of the material in this publication can be accepted by the editor, the publisher or any of the authors.

First published in Great Britain in 1966

Forty-first edition published in Great Britain and the United States in 2011 by Kogan Page Limited

120 Pentonville Road
London N1 9JN
United Kingdom
www.koganpage.com

1518 Walnut Street, Suite 1100
Philadelphia PA 19102
USA

4737/23 Ansari Road
Daryaganj
New Delhi 110002
India

British Library Cataloguing-in-Publication Data

A CIP record for this book is available from the British Library.

ISBN 978 0 7494 6235 2
E-ISBN 978 0 7494 6236 9
ISSN 0141-5972

Typeset by AMA DataSet Ltd, Preston
Production managed by Jellyfish
Printed in the UK by CPI Antony Rowe

PUBLISHER'S NOTE

This 41th edition of *British Qualifications* has been considerably revised and updated to reflect the many changes in degree, diploma and certificate courses and to take account of legislative reforms affecting the structure of higher and further education over the past year.

The editor and compilers are most grateful to the academic registrars and the secretaries of the many bodies they have contacted for information and advice. Without their cooperation, the revision and updating of *British Qualifications* would not have been possible.

THE CITY COLLEGE

The City College is an independent institution of further and higher education, catering for local and international students. Established in 1979, the City College was one of the first colleges to have been accredited by the British Accreditation Council (BAC) in 1985 and is an 'A' rated Sponsor approved by the UKBA. Over the years thousands of students have successfully completed their studies at the City College and have progressed to higher studies in British and American universities, or secured successful careers in a variety of fields. As well as maintaining high academic standards and providing quality tuition, the City College is noted for its prompt response to the education and training developments in the global environment.

Studying at the City College has evolved into a truly enlightening experience, given our ethnically diverse student base. Our reputation has been built up upon the academic success of our students and the quality of service we offer.

The City College is located in the City of London, close to the junction of City Road and East Road. The area is well served by public transport, with Old Street Underground and British Rail stations being within five minutes' walk from the college.

Courses Offered

Our faculty is selected on the basis of their academic and professional qualifications as well as on their experience in teaching/lecturing.

The primary focus of study is on Business/Management, Computing, Hospitality and Travel & Tourism Management. The latest addition to our course portfolio is the HND in Health & Social Care.

Facilities

The college occupies a spacious self contained building with purposely built classrooms and offices. It has modern computer facilities allowing students to have free access to the internet and e-mail.

Student Life

The college has a truly international environment, with over 45 different nationalities being represented among the student body. The friendly and welcoming atmosphere within the college encourages students to approach both the academic and administrative staff whenever they are in need of help.

Address: University House, 55 East Road, London N1 6AH

Tel: +44 (0)20 7253 1133

Fax: +44 (0)20 7251 6610

Email: admissions@citycollege.ac.uk

Web: www.citycollege.ac.uk

CONTENTS

KoganPage

REFERENCES

Association of MBAs (AMBA) (annual) *AMBA – Financial Times Guide to Business Schools,* AMBA, London

Committee of Vice-Chancellors and Principals (CVCP) (annual) *University Entrance: The official guide*, CVCP, London

Department for Education and Skills (DfES) (2003) *The Future of Higher Education*, The Stationery Office, London [online] http://www.dfes.gov.uk/hegateway/strategy/hestrategy/foreword.shtml

DfES (2004) *Five-Year Strategy for Children and Learners*, DfES, London

Qualifications and Curriculum Authority (QCA) (2004) *New Thinking for Reform: A framework for achievement*, QCA, London (July)

HOW TO USE THIS BOOK

You may find these notes helpful when using the book.

Part 1 presents an overview of the further and higher educational systems currently in operation in the United Kingdom, including a discussion of the major reforms that have taken place over the past year and their impact.

Part 2 takes a look at the teaching establishments whose qualifications are listed in Part 4 of the book, offering an explanation of the different types of institution, their place in the overall system and the levels of qualification that they award.

Part 3 presents a detailed description of vocational qualifications awarded by many of the professional associations included in Part 5, including an explanation of validating, examining and awarding bodies.

Part 4 is a directory of qualifications awarded by universities in the United Kingdom (ordered by university name). There is a brief introduction detailing admission to degree courses, degree structure and the various categories of degree available.

Part 5 is a directory of qualifications awarded by professional, trade and specialist associations in the United Kingdom (ordered by profession / discipline), including certificates, diplomas, NVQs and SVQs. A short introduction explains the functions of professional associations and how to gain membership.

Part 6 describes various bodies involved in the accreditation of colleges in the independent sector of further and higher education.

Part 7 is a list of study associations and learned societies.

Also included (at the beginning of the book) is a list of all abbreviations and designatory letters used throughout *British Qualifications*.

INDEX OF ABBREVIATIONS AND DESIGNATORY LETTERS

AAB	Associate of the Association of Book-keepers
AACB	Associate of the Association of Certified Bookkeepers
AACP	Associate of the Association of Computer Professionals
AAFC	Associate of the Association of Financial Controllers and Administrators
AAIA	Associate of the Association of International Accountants
AAMS	Associate of the Association of Medical Secretaries, Practice Managers, Administrators and Receptionists
AASI	Associate of the Ambulance Service Institute
AASW	Advanced Award in Social Work
AAT	Association of Accounting Technicians
ABC	Awarding Body Consortium
ABDO	Associate of the British Dispensing Opticians
ABE	Association of Business Executives
ABEng	Associate Member of the Association of Building Engineers
ABHA	Associate of the British Hypnotherapy Association
ABIAT	Associate Member of the British Institute of Architectural Technologists
ABIPP	Associate of the British Institute of Professional Photography
ABMA	Associate of the Business Management Association
ABPR	Association of British Picture Restorers
ABRSM	Associated Board of the Royal Schools of Music
ABS	Association of Business Schools
ABSSG	Associate of the British Society of Scientific Glassblowers
ACA	Associate of the Institute of Chartered Accountants in England and Wales
ACA	Associate of the Institute of Chartered Accountants in Ireland
ACB	Association of Certified Bookkeepers
ACC	Accredited Clinical Coders
ACCA	Associate of the Association of Chartered Certified Accountants
ACCA	Association of Chartered Certified Accountants
ACE	Association for Conferences and Events
ACEA	Associate of the Institute of Cost and Executive Accountants
ACertCM	Archbishop of Canterbury's Certificate in Church Music
ACGI	Associate of City and Guilds of London Institute
ACIArb	Associate of the Chartered Institute of Arbitrators
ACIB	Associate of the Chartered Institute of Bankers
ACIBS	Associate of the Chartered Institute of Bankers in Scotland
ACIBSE	Associate of the Chartered Institution of Building Services Engineers
ACIH	Associate of the Chartered Institute of Housing
ACII	Associate of the Chartered Insurance Institute
ACILA	Associate of the Chartered Institute of Loss Adjusters
ACIM	Associate of the Chartered Institute of Marketing
ACIOB	Associate of the Chartered Institute of Building
ACIS	Associate of the Institute of Chartered Secretaries and Administrators
ACIT	Advanced Certificate in International Trade
ACLIP	Certified Affiliate of CILIP
ACMA	Associate of the Chartered Institute of Management Accountants
ACP	Association of Child Psychotherapists
ACP	Associate of the College of Preceptors

ACP	Association of Computer Professionals
ACPM	Associate of the Confederation of Professional Management
ACPP	Associate of the College of Pharmacy Practice
ACT	Associate of the College of Teachers
ACYW	Associate of the Community and Youth Work Association
ADCE	Advanced Diploma in Childcare and Education
ADCM	Archbishop of Canterbury's Diploma in Church Music
AdDipEd	Advanced Diploma in Education
ADI	Approved Driving Instructor
AECI	Association Member of the Institute of Employment Consultants
AEWVH	Association for the Education and Welfare of the Visually Handicapped
AFA	Associate of the Faculty of Actuaries
AFA	Associate of the Institute of Financial Accountants
AFBPsS	Associate Fellow of the British Psychological Society
AFCI	Associate of the Faculty of Commerce and Industry Ltd
AffBMA	Affiliate of the Business Management Association
AffIManf	Affiliate of the Institute of Manufacturing
AffIMI	Affiliate of the Institute of the Motor Industry
AffIMS	Affiliate of the Institute of Management Specialists
AffInstM	Affiliate of the Meat Training Council
AffIP	Affiliate of the Institute of Plumbing
AffProfBTM	Affiliate of Professional Business and Technical Management
AFIMA	Associate Fellow of the Institute of Mathematics and its Applications
AFISOL	Aerodrome Flight Information Service Officer's Licence
AFPC	Advanced Financial Planning Certificate
AFRCSEd	Associate Fellow of Royal College of Surgeons of Edinburgh
AGCL	Associate of the Guild of Cleaners and Launderers
AGI	Associate of the Greek Institute
AGSM	Associate of the Guildhall School of Music and Drama
AHCIMA	Associate of the Hotel and Catering International Management Association
AHFS	Associate of the Council of Health Fitness and Sports Therapists
AHRIM	Associate of the Institute of Health Record Information and Management
AIA	Associate of the Institute of Actuaries
AIA	Association of International Accountants
AIAgrE	Associate of the Institution of Agricultural Engineers
AIAT	Associate of the Institute of Asphalt Technology
AIBCM	Associate of the Institute of British Carriage and Automobile Manufacturers
AIBMS	Associate of the Institute of Biomedical Science
AICB	Associate of the Institute of Certified Book-Keepers
AIChor	Associate of the Benesh Institute of Choreology
AICHT	Associate of the International Council of Holistic Therapists
AICM(Cert)	Associate Member of the Institute of Credit Management
AICS	Associate of the Institution of Chartered Shipbrokers
AICSc	Associate of the Institute of Consumer Sciences Incorporating Home Economics
AIDTA	Associate of the International Dance Teachers' Association
AIE	Associate of the Institute of Electrolysis
AIEM	Associate of the Institute of Executives and Managers
AIExpE	Associate of the Institute of Explosive Engineers
AIFA	Associate of the Institute of Field Archaeologists
AIFBQ	Associate of the International Faculty of Business Qualifications
AIFireE	Associate of the Institution of Fire Engineers
AIFP	Associate of the British International Freight Association

AIGD	Associate of the Institute of Grocery Distribution
AIHort	Associate Member of the Institute of Horticulture
AIIMR	Associate of the Institute of Investment Management and Research
AIIRSM	Associate of the International Institute of Risk and Safety Management
AIL	Associate of the Institute of Linguists
AILAM	Associate of the Institute of Leisure and Amenity Management
AIMBM	Associate of the Institute of Maintenance and Building Management
AIMC	Associate of the Institute of Management Consultancy
AIMgt	Associate of the Institute of Management
AIMIS	Associate of the Institute for the Management of Information Systems
AIMM	Associate of the Institute of Massage and Movement
AInstAM	Associate of the Institute of Administrative Management
AInstBA	Associate of the Institute of Business Administration
AInstBCA	Associate of the Institute of Burial and Cremation Administration
AInstBM	Associate of the Institute of Builders' Merchants
AInstCM	Associate of the Institute of Commercial Management
AInstM	Associate of the Meat Training Council
AInstPkg	Associate of the Institute of Packaging
AInstPM	Associate of the Institute of Professional Managers and Administrators
AInstSMM	Associate of the Institute of Sales and Marketing Management
AInstTA	Associate of the Institute of Transport Administration
AInstTT	Associate Member of the Institute of Travel and Tourism
AIOC	Associate of the Institute of Carpenters
AIOFMS	Associate of the Institute of Financial and Management Studies
AIP	Associate of the Institute of Plumbing
AIQA	Associate of the Institute of Quality Assurance
AIS	Accredited Imaging Scientist
AISOB	Associate of the Incorporated Society of Organ Builders
AISTD	Associate of the Imperial Society of Teachers of Dancing
AISTDDip	Associate Diploma of the Imperial Society of Teachers of Dancing
AITSA	Associate of the Institute of Trading Standards Administration
AIVehE	Associate of the Institute of Vehicle Engineers
AIWSc	Associate Member of the Institute of Wood Science
ALCM	Associate of the London College of Music
ALI	Associate of the Landscape Institute
ALS	Associate of the Linnean Society of London
AMA	Associate of the Museums Association
AMABE	Associate Member of the Association of Business Executives
AMAE	Associate Member of the Academy of Experts
AMASI	Associate Member of the Architecture and Surveying Institute
AMBA	Association of MBAs
AMBA	Non-Teacher Associate Member of the British (Theatrical) Arts
AMBCS	Associate Member of the British Computer Society
AMBII	Associate Member of the British Institute of Innkeeping
AmCAM	Associate of the Communication Advertising and Marketing Education Foundation
AMCT	Associate of the Association of Corporate Treasurers
AMCTHCM	Associate Member of the Confederation of Tourism, Hotel and Catering Management
AMI	Association Montessori Internationale
AMIA	Affiliated Member of the Association of International Accountants
AMIAgrE	Associate Member of the Institution of Agricultural Engineers
AMIAP	Associate Member of the Institution of Analysts and Programmers

AMIAT	Associate Member of the Institute of Asphalt Technology
AMIBC	Associate Member of the Institute of Building Control
AMIBCM	Associate Member of the Institute of British Carriage and Automobile Manufacturers
AMIBE	Associate Member of the Institution of British Engineers
AMIBF	Associate Member of the Institute of British Foundrymen
AMICE	Associate Member of the Institution of Civil Engineers
AMIChemE	Associate Member of the Institution of Chemical Engineers
AMIED	Associate Member of the Institution of Engineering Designers
AMIEE	Associate Member of the Institution of Electrical Engineers
AMIEx	Associate Member of the Institute of Export
AMIHIE	Associate Member of the Institute of Highway Incorporated Engineers
AMIHT	Associate Member of the Institution of Highways and Transportation
AMIIE	Associate Member of the Institution of Incorporated Engineers
AMIIExE	Associate Member of the Institution of Incorporated Executive Engineers
AMIIHTM	Associate Member of the International Institute of Hospitality Tourism & Management
AMIISE	Associate Member of the International Institute of Social Economics
AMIM	Associate Member of the Institute of Materials
AMIManf	Member of the Institute of Manufacturing
AMIMechE	Associate Member of the Institution of Mechanical Engineers
AMIMechIE	Associate Member of the Institution of Mechanical Incorporated Engineers
AMIMI	Associate Member of the Institute of the Motor Industry
AMIMinE	Associate of the Institute of Mining Engineers
AMIMM	Associate Member of the Institution of Mining and Metallurgy
AMIMS	Associate Member of the Institute of Management Specialists
AMInstAEA	Associate Member of the Institute of Automotive Engineer Assessors
AMInstBE	Associate Member of the Institution of British Engineers
AMInstE	Associate Member of the Institute of Energy
AMInstR	Associate Member of the Institute of Refrigeration
AMInstTA	Associate Member of the Institute of Transport Administration
AMIPlantE	Associate Member of the Institution of Plant Engineers
AMIPR	Associate Member of the Institute of Public Relations
AMIPRE	Associate Member of the Incorporated Practitioners in Radio and Electronics
AMIQ	Associate Member of the Institute of Quarrying
AMIQA	Associate Member of the Institute of Quality Assurance
AMIRTE	Associate Member of the Institute of Road Transport Engineers
AMISM	Associate Member of the Institute for Supervision & Management
AMIStrutE	Associate Member of the Institution of Structural Engineers
AMITD	Associate Member of the Institute of Training and Development
AMIVehE	Associate Member of the Institute of Vehicle Engineers
AMNI	Associate Member of the Nautical Institute
AMPA	Associate Member of the Master Photographers Association
AMProfBTM	Associate Member of Professional Business and Technical Management
AMRAeS	Associate Member of the Royal Aeronautical Society
AMRSH	Associate Member of the Royal Society for the Promotion of Health
AMS	Associate of the Institute of Management Services
AMS(Aff)	Affiliate of the Association of Medical Secretaries, Practice Managers, Administrators and Receptionists
AMSE	Associate Member of the Society of Engineers (Inc)
AMSPAR	Association of Medical Secretaries, Practice Managers, Administrators and Receptionists

AMusEd	Associate Diploma in Music Education
AMusLCM	Associate in Music of the London College of Music
AMusTCL	Associate in Music of Trinity College of Music
AMWES	Associate Member of the Women's Engineering Society
ANAEA	Associate of the National Association of Estate Agents
ANCA	Advanced National Certificate in Agriculture
AOP	Association of Photographers
AOR	Association of Reflexologists
APA	Accreditation of Prior Experience
APC	Assessment of Professional Competence
APCS	Associate of the Property Consultants Society
APMI	Associate of the Pensions Management Institute
APMP	Association for Project Management Professional
AQA	Assessment & Qualifications Alliance
ARAD	Associate of the Royal Academy of Dancing
ARAM	Associate of the Royal Academy of Music
ARB	Architects Registration Board
ARCM	Associate of Royal College of Music
ARCO	Associate of the Royal College of Organists
ARCS	Associate of the Royal College of Science
AREC	Associate of the Recruitment and Employment Confederation
ARELS	Association of Recognised English Language Services
ARELS-FELCO	Association of Recognised English Language Teaching Establishments in Britain
ARIBA	Associate of the Royal Institute of British Architects
ARICS	Associate of the Royal Institution of Chartered Surveyors
ARIPHH	Associate of the Royal Institute of Public Health and Hygiene
ARPS	Associate of the Royal Photographic Society
ARSC	Associate of the Royal Society of Chemistry
ARSCM	Associate of the Royal School of Church Music
ARSM	Associate of the Royal School of Mines
AS	Advanced Supplementary level
ASCA	Associate of the Institute of Company Accountants
ASCT	Associate of the Society of Claims Technicians
ASDC	Associate of the Society of Dyers and Colourists
ASE	Associate of the Society of Engineers (Inc)
ASI	Ambulance Service Institute
ASI	Architecture and Surveying Institute
ASIAffil	Affiliate of the Ambulance Service Institute
ASIS	Accredited Senior Imaging Scientist
ASLC	Advanced Secretarial Language Certificate
ASMA	Associate of the Society of Sales Management Administrators Ltd
ASNN	Associate of the Society of Nursery Nursing
AssCI	Associate of the Institute of Commerce
AssociateCIPD	Associate of the Chartered Institute of Personnel and Development
AssociateIEEE	Associate of the Institution of Electrical and Electronics Engineers Incorporated
AssociateIIE	Associate of the Institution of Incorporated Engineers
AssocIMechIE	Associate of the Institution of Mechanical Incorporated Engineers
AssocIPD	Associate of the Institute of Personnel & Development
AssocIPHE	Associate of the Institution of Public Health Engineers
AssocMIWM	Associate Member of the Institute of Wastes Management
AssocTechIIE	Associate Technician of the Institution of Incorporated Engineers
ASTA	Associate of the Swimming Teachers' Association

ASVA	Associate of the Incorporated Society of Valuers and Auctioneers
ATC	Art Teacher's Certificate
ATCL	Associate of Trinity College of Music
ATCLicence	Air Traffic Controller's Licence
ATCLTESOL	Associate Diploma in the Teaching of English to Speakers of Other Languages, Trinity College
ATD	Art Teacher's Diploma
ATI	Associate of the Textile Industry
ATII	Associate of the Chartered Institute of Taxation
ATPL	Airline Transport Pilot's Licence
ATSC	Associate of the Oil and Colour Chemists' Association
ATSC	Associate in the Technology of Surface Coatings
ATT	Association of Taxation Technicians
ATT	Member of the Association of Taxation Technicians
ATTA	Association of Therapy Teachers Associate
ATTF	Association of Therapy Teachers Fellow
ATTM	Association of Therapy Teachers Member
AWeldI	Associate of the Welding Institute
BA	Bachelor of Arts
BA(Econ)	Bachelor of Arts in Economics & Social Studies
BA(Ed)	Bachelor of Arts (Education)
BA(Lan)	Bachelor of Languages
BA(Law)	Bachelor of Arts in Law
BA(Music)	Bachelor of Music
BABTAC	British Association of Beauty Therapy and Cosmetology Ltd
BAC	British Accreditation Council for Independent Further and Higher Education
BAC	British Association for Counselling
BAcc	Bachelor of Accountancy
BACP	British Association for Counselling Psychotherapy
BADA	British Antique Dealers' Association
BADN	British Association of Dental Nurses
BAE	British Association of Electrolysists Ltd
BAGMA	British Agricultural and Garden Machinery Association
BAgr	Bachelor of Agriculture
BAO	Bachelor of Obstetrics
BAP	British Association of Psychotherapists
BArch	Bachelor of Architecture
BASELT	British Association in State English Language Teaching
BBO	British Ballet Organisation
BChD	Bachelor of Dental Surgery
BChir	Bachelor of Surgery
BCL	Bachelor of Civil Law
BCom	Bachelor of Commerce
BCombStuds	Bachelor of Combined Studies
BComm	Bachelor of Communications
BCS	Bachelor of Combined Studies
BCS	British Computer Society
BD	Bachelor of Divinity
BDA	British Dietetic Association
BDes	Bachelor of Design
BDS	Bachelor of Dental Surgery
BEconSc	Bachelor of Economics

BECTU	Broadcasting, Entertainment, Cinematograph and Theatre Union
BEd	Bachelor of Education
BEng	Bachelor of Engineering
BEng and Man	Bachelor of Mechanical Engineering, Manufacture and Management
BER	Board for Engineers' Regulation
BFA	Bachelor of Fine Arts
BFin	Bachelor of Finance
BHA	British Hypnotherapy Association
BHI	British Horological Institute Ltd
BHS	British Horse Society
BHSAI	British Horse Society's Assistant Instructor's Certificate
BHSI	British Horse Society's Instructor's Certificate
BHSII	British Horse Society's Intermediate Instructor's Certificate
BHSIntSM	British Horse Society's Intermediate Stable Manager's Certificate
BHSSM	British Horse Society's Stable Manager's Certificate
BIA	Beauty Industry Authority
BIAT	British Institute of Architectural Technologists
BIBA	Bachelor of International Business Administration
BIE	British Institute of Embalmers
BIFA	British International Freight Association
BIPP	British Institute of Professional Photography
BIS	British Interplanetary Society
BKSTS	British Kinematograph Sound and Television Society
BLD	Bachelor of Landscape Design
BLE	Bachelor of Land Economy
BLEng	Bi-Lingual Engineer
BLib	Bachelor of Librarianship
BLing	Bachelor of Linguistics
BLitt	Bachelor of Letters
BLS	Bachelor of Library Studies
BM	Bachelor of Medicine
BMA	British Medical Association
BM, BCh	Conjoint degree of Bachelor of Medicine, Bachelor of Surgery
BM, BS	Conjoint degree of Bachelor of Medicine, Bachelor of Surgery
BMedBiol	Bachelor of Medical Biology
BMedSci	Bachelor of Medical Sciences
BMedSci(Speech)	Bachelor of Medical Sciences (Speech)
BMet	Bachelor of Metallurgy
BMid	Bachelor of Midwifery
BMidwif	Bachelor of Midwifery
BMSc	Bachelor of Medical Sciences
BMus	Bachelor of Music
BN	Bachelor of Nursing
BNNursing	Bachelor of Nursing, Nursing Studies
BNSc	Bachelor of Nursing
BNurs	Bachelor of Nursing
BOptom	Bachelor of Optometry
BPA	Bachelor of Performing Arts
BPharm	Bachelor of Pharmacy
BPhil	Bachelor of Philosophy
BPhil(Ed)	Bachelor of Philosophy (Education)
BPL	Bachelor of Planning

BSc	Bachelor of Science
BSc(Archit)	Bachelor of Science (Architecture)
BSc(DentSci)	Bachelor of Science in Dental Science
BSc(Econ)	Bachelor of Science in Economics
BSc(MedSci)	Bachelor of Science (Medical Science)
BSc(Social Science)	Bachelor of Science (Social Science)
BSc(Town & Regional Planning)	Bachelor of Science (Town & Regional Planning)
BSc(VetSc)	Bachelor of Science (Veterinary Science)
BScAgr	Bachelor of Science in Agriculture
BScEng	Bachelor of Science in Engineering
BScFor	Bachelor of Science in Forestry
BScTech	Bachelor of Technical Science
BSocSc	Bachelor of Social Science
BSSc	Bachelor of Social Science
BSSG	Member of the British Society of Scientific Glassblowers
BTEC	Business and Technology Education Council
BTech	Bachelor of Technology
BTechEd	Bachelor of Technological Education
BTEC HC	Business and Technology Education Council Higher Certificate
BTEC HD	Business and Technology Education Council Higher Diploma
BTEC HNC	Business and Technology Education Council Higher National Certificate
BTEC HND	Business and Technology Education Council Higher National Diploma
BTechS	Bachelor of Technology Studies
BTh	Bachelor of Theology
BTheol	Bachelor of Theology
BTP	Bachelor of Town Planning
BVC	Bar Vocational Course
BVetMed	Bachelor of Veterinary Medicine
BVMS	Bachelor of Veterinary Medicine
BVM&S	Bachelor of Veterinary Medicine
BVSc	Bachelor of Veterinary Science
C&G	City and Guilds
CA	Member of the Institute of Chartered Accountants of Scotland
CAA	Civil Aviation Authority
CABE	Companion of the Association of Business Executives
CACHE	Council for Awards in Children's Care and Education
CAE	Certificated Automotive Engineer
CAE	Companion of the Academy of Experts
CAM	Communication Advertising and Marketing Education Foundation
CAS	Certification of Accountancy Studies
CASS	Certificate of Applied Social Studies
CAT	Certificate for Accounting Technicians
CAT	College of Advanced Technology
CATS	Postgraduate Qualification by Credit Accumulation and Transfer
CBA	Companion of the British (Theatrical) Arts
CBAE	Companion of the British Academy of Experts
CBIM	Companion of the British Institute of Management
CBiol	Chartered Biologist
CBLC	Certificate in Business Language Competence
CBSSG	Craft Member of the British Society of Scientific Glassblowers
CCETSW	Central Council for Education and Training in Social Work

CChem	Chartered Chemist
CCol	Chartered Colourist
CCST	Certificate of Completion of Specialist Training
CDBA	Certified Doctor of Business Administration
CDipAF	Certified Diploma in Accounting and Finance
CEE	Extended European Command Endorsement
CeFA	Certificate for Financial Advisers
CEM	Certificate in Executive Management
CeMAP	Certificate in Mortgage Advice and Practice
CEng	Chartered Engineer
CertAMed	Certificate in Aviation Medicine
CertArb	Certificate in Arboriculture
CertBibKnowl	Certificate of Bible Knowledge
CertCIH	Chartered Institute of Housing recognised Housing Qualification
CertCM	Certificate of Cash Management
CertDesRCA	Certificate of Designer of the Royal College of Art
CertEd	Certificate in Education
CertEPK	Certificate of Essential Pensions Knowledge
CertHE	Certificate of Higher Education
CertHSAP	Certificate in Health Services Administration Practice
CertHSM	Certificate in Health Services Management
CertMFS	Certificate in the Marketing of Financial Services
CertOccHyg	Certificate in Operational Competence in Comprehensive Occupational Hygiene
CertRP	Certificate in Recruitment Practice
CertTEL	Certificate in the Teaching of European Languages
CertTESOL	Certificate of Teaching of English to Speakers of Other Languages
CertTEYL	Certificate of Teaching of English to Young Learners
CertYCW	Certificate in Youth and Community Work
CETHV	Certificate of Education in Training as Health Visitor
CEYA	Council for Early Years Awards
CFS	Certificate in Financial Services
CFSP	Certificate in Financial Services Practice
CGeol	Chartered Geologist
CGLI	City & Guilds of London Institute
CHARM	Centre for Hazard and Risk Management
ChB	Bachelor of Surgery
CHD	Choral-Training Diploma
ChM	Master of Surgery
CHP	Certificate in Hypnosis and Psychology
CHRIM	Certified Member of the Institute of Health Record Information and Management
CIAgrE	Companion of the Institution of Agricultural Engineers
CIArb	Chartered Institute of Arbitrators
CIB	Chartered Institute of Bankers
CIBM	Corporate Member of the Institute of Builders' Merchants
CIBS	Chartered Institute of Bankers in Scotland
CIBSE	Chartered Institution of Building Services Engineers
CIC	Construction Industry Council
CIEx	Companion of the Institute of Export
CIFE	Conference for Independent Further Education
CIH	Chartered Institute of Housing
CII	Chartered Insurance Institute
CILA	Chartered Institute of Loss Adjusters

CILIP	Chartered Institute of Library and Information Professionals
CIM	Chartered Institute of Marketing
CIMA	Chartered Institute of Management Accountants
CIMediE	Companion of the Institution of Mechanical Engineers
CIMgt	Companion of the Institute of Management
CIOB	Chartered Institute of Building
CIP	Certificate of Institute Practice
CIPD	Chartered Institute of Personnel and Development
CIPFA	Chartered Institute of Public Finance & Accounting
CIPS	Chartered Institute of Purchasing and Supply
CISOB	Counsellor of the Incorporated Society of Organ Builders
CIT	Certificate in Information Technology
CIWEM	Chartered Institution of Water and Environmental Management
CL(ABDO)	Diploma in Contact Lens Practice of the Association of British Dispensing Opticians
CLAC	Commercial Language Assistant Certificate
CLAIT	Computer Literacy & Information Technology
CLC	Council for Licensed Conveyancers
CLE	Limited European Command Endorsement
ClinPsyD	Doctorate in Clinical Psychology
CMA	Certificate in Management Accountancy
CMathFIMA	Fellow of the Institute of Mathematics and its Applications
CMBA	Certified Master of Business Administration
CMBHI	Craft Member of the British Horological Institute
CMC	Certified Management Consultants
CMet	Chartered Meteorologist
CMIWSc	Certified Member of the Institute of Wood Science
CMS	Certificate in Management Studies
CNAA	Council for National Academic Awards
COA	Certificate of Accreditation
COBC	Certificate of Basic Competence
CoEA	Certificate of Educational Achievement
COES	Certificate of Educational Studies
CofE	Church of England
CofS	Church of Scotland
CompBCS	Companion of the British Computer Society
CompIAP	Companion of the Institution of Analysts and Programmers
CompIEE	Companion of the Institution of Electrical Engineers
CompIGasE	Companion of the Institution of Gas Engineers
CompIManf	Companion of the Institute of Manufacturing
CompIMS	Companion of the Institute of Management Specialists
CompIP	Companion of the Institute of Plumbing
CorporateIRRV	Corporate Member of the Institute of Revenues, Rating and Valuation
COSCA	Confederation of Scottish Counselling Agencies
CPA	Chartered Patent Agents
CPC	Certificate of Professional Competence, the Institute of Transport Administration
CPD	Continuing Professional Development
CPE	Common Professional Exam
CPEA	Certificate of Practice in Estate Agency
CPFA	Member of Chartered Institute of Public Finance and Accountancy
CPhys	Chartered Physicist of the Institute of Physics
CPIM	Certificate in Production and Inventory Management

CPL	Commercial Pilot's Licence
CPM	Certified Professional Manager
CPP	Certificate of Pre-school Practice
CPR	Chartered Professional Review
CProfBTM	Companion of Professional Business and Technical Management
CPS	Certificate in Pastoral Studies and Applied Theology
CPSC	Certificate of Proficiency in Survival Craft
CPsychol	Chartered Psychologist, British Psychological Society
CPT	Continuing Professional Training
CPVE	Certificate of Pre-Vocational Training
CRAeS	Companion of the Royal Aeronautical Society
CRAH	Central Register of Advanced Hypnotherapists
CRCW	Church Related Community Workers
CRNCM	Companion of the Royal Northern College of Music
CSCT	Central School for Counselling Training
CSD	Chartered Society of Designers
CSE	Certificate of Secondary Education
CSM	Certificate in Safety Management
CSMGSM	Certificate in Stage Management (Guildhall School of Music and Drama)
CStat	Chartered Statistician
CSYS	Certificate of Sixth Year Studies
CTABRSM	Certificate of Teaching of the Associated Board of the Royal School of Music
CTextATI	Associate of the Textile Institute
CTextFTI	Fellow of the Textile Institute
CTHCM	Confederation of Tourism, Hotel and Catering Management
CVA	Certificated Value Analyst
CVM	Certificated Value Manager
CVT	Certified Vehicle Technologist
DA	Diploma in Anaesthetics
DAdmin	Doctor of Administration
DAES	Diploma in Advanced Educational Studies
DArch	Doctor of Architecture
DAvMed	Diploma in Aviation Medicine
DBA	Doctor of Business Administration
DBE	Diploma in Business Engineering
DBO	Diploma of the British Orthoptic Society
DBS	Diploma in Business Studies
DCC	Diploma of Chelsea College
DCDH	Diploma in Child Dental Health
DCE	Dangerous Cargo Endorsements
DCE	Diploma in Childcare and Education
DCG	Diploma in Careers Guidance
DCH	Diploma in Child Health
DChD	Diploma of Dental Surgery
DChM	Diploma in Chiropodial Medicine, Institute of Chiropodists and Podiatrists
DCHT	Diploma in Community Health in Tropical Countries
DCL	Doctor of Civil Law
DCLF	Diploma in Contact Lens Fitting
DClinPsych	Doctor of Clinical Psychiatry
DCLP	Diploma in Contact Lens Practice
DCR(R)or(T)	Diploma of the College of Radiographers
DD	Doctor of Divinity

DDH(Birm)	Diploma in Dental Health, University of Birmingham
DDOrthRCPSGlas	Diploma in Dental Orthopaedics of the Royal College of Physicians and Surgeons of Glasgow
DDPHRCS(Eng)	Diploma in Dental Public Health, Royal College of Surgeons of England
DDS	Doctor of Dental Surgery
DDSc	Doctor of Dental Science
DEBA	Diploma in European Business Administration
DEdPsy	Doctor of Educational Psychiatry
DEM	Diploma in Executive Management
DEng	Doctor of Engineering
DES	Department of Education and Science (now the Department for Education)
DETR	Department of the Environment, Transport and the Regions
DFin	Doctor of Finance
DFSM	Diploma in Financial Services Management
DGA	Diamond Member of the Gemmological Association and Gem Testing Laboratory of Great Britain
DGDPRCSEng	Diploma in General Dental Practice, Royal College of Surgeons of England
DGM	Diploma in Geriatric Medicine
DGO	Diploma in Obstetrics and Gynaecology
DHC	Doctorate in Healthcare
DHE	Diploma in Horticulture, Royal Botanic Garden, Edinburgh
DHMSA	Diploma in the History of Medicine, Society of Apothecaries of London
DHP	Diploma in Hypnosis and Psychotherapy
DIA	Diploma of Industrial Administration
DIB	Diploma in International Business
DIC	Diploma of Membership of Imperial College of Science and Technology, University of London
DIH	Diploma in Industrial Health
DipABRSM	Diploma of the Associated Board of the Royal Schools of Music
DipAD	Diploma in Art and Design
DipAdvHYP	Diploma in Advanced Hypnotherapy
DipAE	Diploma in Adult Education
DipAgrComm	Diploma in Agricultural Communication
DipArb	Diploma in Arbitration
DipArb	Diploma in Arboriculture
DipArch	Diploma in Architecture
DipASE(CofP)	Graduate Level Specialist Diploma in Advanced Study in Education, College of Preceptors
DipASSc	Diploma in Arts and Social Sciences
DipAT	Diploma in Accounting Technology
DipAvMed	Diploma in Aviation Medicine
DipBA	Diploma in Business Administration
DipBldgCons	Diploma in Building Conservation
DipBMA	Diploma in Business Management
DipCAM	Diploma in the Communication Advertising and Marketing Education Foundation
DipCD	Diploma in Community Development
DipCHM	Diploma in Choir Training, Royal College of Organists
DipClinPath	Diploma in Clinical Pathology
DipCOT	Diploma of the College of Occupational Therapists
DipCP	Diploma of the College of Teachers
DipCT	Diploma in Corporate Treasury Management
DipDerm	Diploma in Dermatology

DipEd	Diploma in Education
DipEF	Diploma in Executive Finance
DipEH	Diploma in Environmental Health
DipEM	Diploma in Environmental Management
DipEMA	Diploma in Executive and Management Accountancy
DipEngLit	Diploma in English Literature
DipFD	Diploma in Funeral Directing, National Association of Funeral Directors
DipFS	Diploma in Financial Services
DipGAI	Diploma of the Guild of Architectural Ironmongers
DipGrTrans	Diploma in Greek Translation
DipGSM	Diploma of the Guildhall School of Music and Drama
DipHE	Diploma of Higher Education
DipHS	Diploma of the Heraldry Society
DipIEB	Diploma of the International Employee Benefits
DipISW	Diploma of the Institute of Social Welfare
DipLE	Diploma in Land Economy
DipLP	Diploma in Legal Practice
DipM	Postgraduate Diploma in Marketing
DipMedAc	Diploma in Medical Acupuncture
DipMetEng	Diploma in Meteorological Engineering
DipMFS	Diploma in the Marketing of Financial Services
DipMth	Diploma in Music Therapy
DipOccH	Diploma in Occupational Health
DipOccHyg	Diploma of Professional Competence in Comprehensive Occupational Hygiene
DipPDTC	Diploma in Professional Dancers Teaching Course
DipPharmMed	Diploma in Pharmaceutical Medicine
DipPhil	Diploma in Philosophy
DipProjMan	Diploma in Project Management
DipPropInv	Diploma in Property Investment
DipRAM	Diploma of the Royal Academy of Music
DipRCM	Diploma of the Royal College of Music
DipRMS	Diploma of the Royal Microscopical Society
DipSc	Diploma in Science
DipSM	Diploma in Safety Management
DipSurv	Diploma in Surveying
DipSW	Diploma in Social Work
DipTCL	Diploma of the Trinity College of Music, London
DipTCR	Diploma in Organ Teaching
DipTESOL	Diploma in Teaching of English to Speakers of Other Languages
DipTHP	Diploma in Therapeutic Hypnosis and Psychotherapy
DipTM	Diploma in Training Management, Institute of Personnel and Development
DipTransIoL	Diploma in Translation, Institute of Linguists
DipUniv	Diploma of the University
DipVen	Diploma in Venereology, Society of Apothecaries of London
DipWCF	Diploma of the Worshipful Company of Farriers
DIS	Diploma in Industrial Studies
DLang	Doctor of Language
DLit(t)	Doctor of Letters or Literature
DLO	Diploma of Laryngology and Otology
DLORCSEng	Diploma in Laryngology and Otology, Royal College of Surgeons of England
DLP	Diploma in Legal Practice
DM	Doctor of Medicine

DMedRehab	Diploma in Medical Rehabilitation
DMedSc	Doctor in Medical Science
DMet	Doctor of Metallurgy
DMJ(Clin) or DMJ(Path)	Diploma in Medical Jurisprudence (Clinical or Pathological), Society of Apothecaries of London
DMRD	Diploma in Medical Radio-Diagnosis
DMRT	Diploma in Radiotherapy
DMS	Diploma in Management Studies
DMU	Diploma in Medical Ultrasound
DMus	Doctor of Music
DMusCantuar	Archbishop of Canterbury's Doctorate in Music
DNSc	Doctor in Nursing Science
DO	Diploma in Ophthalmology
DO	Diploma in Osteopathy
DocEdPsy	Doctorate in Educational Psychology
DOpt	Diploma in Ophthalmic Optics
DOrth	Diploma in Orthoptics
DOrthRCSEdin	Diploma in Orthodontics, Royal College of Surgeons of Edinburgh
DOrthRCSEng	Diplomate in Orthodontics, Royal College of Surgeons of England
DP	Diploma in Psychotherapy
DPA	Diploma in Public Administration
DpBact	Diploma in Bacteriology
DPD(Dund)	Diploma in Public Dentistry, University of Dundee
DPH	Diploma in Public Health
DPharm	Diploma in Pharmacy
DPhil	Diploma in Philosophy
DPHRCSEng	Diploma in Dental Public Health, Royal College of Surgeons of England
DPM	Diploma in Psychological Medicine
DPodM	Diploma in Podiatric Medicine
DProf	Doctor of Professional Studies
DPS	Diploma in Professional Studies
DPSE	Diploma in Pastoral Studies and Applied Theology
DPsychol	Doctor of Psychology
DrAc	Doctor of Acupuncture
Dr(RCA)	Doctor of the Royal College of Art
DRCOG	Diploma of the Royal College of Obstetricians and Gynaecologists
DRDRCSEd	Diploma in Restorative Dentistry, Royal College of Surgeons of Edinburgh
DRE	Diploma in Remedial Electrolysis, Institute of Electrolysis
DRI	Diploma in Radionuclide Imaging
DRSAMD	Diploma in the Royal Scottish Academy of Music and Drama
DSA	Diploma in Secretarial Administration
DSc	Doctor of Science
DSc(Econ)	Doctor of Science (Economics) or in Economics
DSc(Eng)	Doctor of Science (Engineering)
DSc(Social)	Doctor of Science in the Social Sciences
DScEcon	Doctor in the Faculty of Economics and Social Studies
DSCh(Ox)	Diploma in Surgical Chiropody (Oxon), Oxford School of Chiropody and Podiatry
DScTech	Doctor of Technical Science
DSocSc	Doctor of Social Science
DSSc	Doctor of Social Science
DSTA	Diploma Member of the Swimming Teachers' Association
DTCD	Diploma in Tuberculosis and Chest Diseases

DTech	Doctor of Technology
DTI	Department of Trade and Industry
DTMH	Diploma in Tropical Medicine and Hygiene
DTM&H	Diploma in Tropical Medicine and Hygiene
DTp	Department of Transport
DUniv	Doctor of the University
DVetMed	Doctor of Veterinary Medicine
DVM	Doctor of Veterinary Medicine
DVM&S	Doctor of Veterinary Medicine and Surgery
DVS	Doctor of Veterinary Surgery
DVSc	Doctor of Veterinary Science
ECBL	European Certification Board for Logistics
ECDL	European Computer Driving Licence
ECG	Executive Group Committees (of the Board for Engineers Registration)
EDBA	Executive Diploma in Business Accounting
EdD	Doctor of Education
EDH	Efficient Deck Hand
EdPsyD	Doctor of Educational Psychology
EEAC	European Executive Assistant Certificate
EFB	English for Business
EFL	English as a Foreign Language
EHO	Environmental Health Officer
EIS	Educational Institute of Scotland
EITB	Engineering Industry Training Board
EMBA	European Master of Business Administration
EMBS	European Master of Business Sciences
EMFEC	East Midland Further Education Council
EN	Enrolled Nurse
EN(G)	Enrolled Nurse (General)
EN(M)	Enrolled Nurse (Mental)
EN(MH)	Enrolled Nurse (Mental Handicap)
ENB	English National Board
EngC	Engineering Council
EngD	Doctor of Engineering
EngTech	Engineering Technician
ENS	Electronic Navigational System
ESD	Executive Secretary's Diploma
ESOL	English for Speakers of Other Languages
ESSTL	Engineering Services Training Trust Ltd
EurIng	European Engineer
EuroBiol	European Biologist
FABE	Fellow of the Association of Business Executives
FACB	Fellow of the Association of Certified Bookkeepers
FACP	Fellow of the Association of Computer Professionals
FAE	Fellow of the Academy of Experts
FAFC	Fellow of the Association of Financial Controllers and Administrators
FAIA	Fellow of the Association of International Accountants
FAMS	Fellow of the Association of Medical Secretaries, Practice Managers, Administrators and Receptionists
FAPM	Fellow of the Association for Project Management
FASI	Fellow of the Ambulance Service Institute
FASI	Fellow of the Architecture and Surveying Institute

FASP	Fellow of the Association of Sales Personnel
FBA	Fellow of the British Academy
FBA	Fellow of the British (Theatrical) Arts
FBCS	Fellow of the British Computer Society
FBDO	Fellow of the Association of British Dispensing Opticians
FBDO(Hons)	Fellow of the Association of British Dispensing Opticians with Honours Diploma
FBDO(Hons)CL	Fellow of the Association of British Dispensing Opticians with Honours Diploma and Diploma in Contact Lens Practice
FBEI	Fellow of the Institution of Body Engineers
FBEng	Fellow of the Association of Building Engineers
FBHA	Fellow of the British Hypnotherapy Association
FBHI	Fellow of the British Horological Institute
FBHS	Fellow of the British Horse Society
FBID	Fellow of the British Institute of Interior Design
FBIDST	Fellow of the British Institute of Dental and Surgical Technologists
FBIE	Fellow of the British Institute of Embalmers
FBIPP	Fellow of the British Institute of Professional Photography
FBIS	Fellow of the British Interplanetary Society
FBMA	Fellow of the Business Management Association
FBPsS	Fellow of the British Psychological Society
FCA	Fellow of the Institute of Chartered Accountants in England and Wales
FCAM	Fellow of the Communication Advertising and Marketing Education Foundation
FCB	Fellow of the British Association of Communicators in Business Ltd
FCBSI	Fellow of the Chartered Building Societies Institute
FCCA	Fellow of the Association of Chartered Certified Accountants
FCEA	Fellow of the Institute of Cost and Executive Accountants
FCGI	Fellowship, City & Guilds
FChS	Fellow of the Society of Chiropodists and Podiatrists
FCI	Faculty of Commerce and Industry
FCI	Fellow of the Institute of Commerce
FCIArb	Fellow of the Chartered Institute of Arbitrators
FCIB	Fellow of the Chartered Institute of Bankers
FCIBS	Fellow of the Chartered Institute of Bankers in Scotland
FCIBSE	Fellow of the Chartered Institute of Building Services Engineers
FCIH	Fellow of the Chartered Institute of Housing
FCII	Fellow of the Chartered Insurance Institute
FCIJ	Fellow of the Chartered Institute of Journalists
FCILA	Fellow of the Chartered Institute of Loss Adjusters
FCIM	Fellow of the Chartered Institute of Marketing
FCIOB	Fellow of the Chartered Institute of Building
FCIPD	Fellow of the Chartered Institute of Personnel and Development
FCIPS	Fellow of the Chartered Institute of Purchasing and Supply
FCIS	Fellow of the Institute of Chartered Secretaries and Administrators
FCIT	Fellow of the Chartered Institute of Transport
FCLIP	Chartered Fellow of CILIP
FCLS	First Certificate for Legal Secretaries
FCMA	Fellow of the Chartered Institute of Management Accountants
FCMA	Fellow of the Institute of Cost and Management Accountants
FCMC	Fellow Grade Certified Management Consultants
FCOphth	Fellow of the College of Ophthalmology
FCOptom	Fellow of the College of Optometrists
FCoT	Ordinary Fellow of the College of Teachers

FCPM	Fellow of the Confederation of Professional Management
FCPP	Fellow of the College of Pharmacy Practice
FCSP	Fellow of the Chartered Society of Physiotherapy
FCT	Fellow of the Association of Corporate Treasurers
FCoT	Fellow of the College of Teachers
FCTHCM	Fellow of the Confederation of Tourism, Hotel and Catering Management
FCYW	Fellow of the Community and Youth Work Association
FDSRCPSGlas	Fellow in Dental Surgery of the Royal College of Surgeons of Glasgow
FDSRCSEd	Fellow in Dental Surgery of the Royal College of Physicians and Surgeons of Edinburgh
FDSRCSEng	Fellow in Dental Surgery of the Royal College of Surgeons of England
FE	Further Education
FEANI	Fédération Européene d'Associations Nationales d'Ingénieurs
FECI	Fellow of the Institute of Employment Consultants
FEFC	Further Education Funding Council
FEIS	Fellow of the Educational Institute of Scotland
FFA	Fellow of the Faculty of Actuaries
FFA	Fellow of the Institute of Financial Accountants
FFARCSEng	Fellow of the Faculty of Anaesthetists of the Royal College of Surgeons in England
FFARCSIrel	Fellow of the Faculty of Anaesthetists of the Royal College of Surgeons in Ireland
FFAS	Fellow of the Faculty of Architects and Surveyors (Architects)
FFCA	Fellow of the Association of Financial Controllers and Administrators
FFCI	Fellow of the Faculty of Commerce and Industry
FFCS	Fellow of the Faculty of Secretaries
FFHom	Fellow of the Faculty of Homeopathy
FFPHM	Fellow of the Faculty of Public Health Medicine, Royal College of Physicians of London and Edinburgh and Royal College of Physicians and Surgeons of Glasgow
FFPHMIrel	Fellow of the Faculty of Public Health Medicine, Royal College of Physicians of Ireland
FFRRCSIrel	Fellow of the Faculty of Radiologists, Royal College of Surgeons in Ireland
FFS	Fellow of the Faculty of Architects and Surveyors (Surveyors)
FGA	Fellow of the Gemmological Association and Gem Testing Laboratory of Great Britain
FGCL	Fellow of the Guild of Cleaners and Launderers
FGI	Fellow of the Greek Institute
FGSM	Fellow of the Guildhall School of Music and Drama
FHCIMA	Fellow of the Hotel and Catering International Management Association
FHFS	Fellow of the Council of Health, Fitness and Sports Therapists
FHG	Fellow of the Institute of Heraldic and Genealogical Studies
FHRIM	Fellow of the Institute of Health Record Information and Management
FHS	Fellow of the Heraldry Society
FHSM	Fellow of the Institute of Health Services Management
FHT	Federation of Holistic Therapies
FIA	Fellow of the Institute of Actuaries
FIAB	Fellow of the International Association of Book-keepers
FIAEA	Fellow of the Institute of Automotive Engineer Assessors
FIAgrE	Fellow of the Institution of Agricultural Engineers
FIAP	Fellow of the Institution of Analysts and Programmers
FIAT	Fellow of the Institute of Asphalt Technology
FIBA	Fellow of the Institution of Business Agents
FIBC	Fellow of the Institute of Building Control

FIBCM	Fellow of the Institute of British Carriage and Automobile Manufacturers
FIBCO	Fellow of the Institute of Building Control Officers
FIBE	Fellow of the Institution of British Engineers
FIBF	Fellow of the Institute of British Foundrymen
FIBiol	Fellow of the Institute of Biology
FIBM	Fellow of the Institute of Builders' Merchants
FIBMS	Fellow of the Institute of Biomedical Science
FIBMS	Fellow of the Institute of Medical Laboratory Sciences
FICA	Fellow of the Institute of Company Accountants
FICB	Fellow of the Institute of Certified Book-Keepers
FICE	Fellow of the Institution of Civil Engineers
FIChemE	Fellow of the Institution of Chemical Engineers
FIChor	Fellow of the Benesh Institute of Choreology
FICHT	Fellow of the International Council of Holistic Therapies
FICM	Fellow of the Institute of Credit Management
FICorr	Fellow of the Institute of Corrosion
FICS	Fellow of the Institute of Chartered Shipbrokers
FICW	Fellow of the Institute of Clerks of Works of Great Britain Incorporated
FIDTA	Fellow of the International Dance Teachers' Association
FIED	Fellow of the Institution of Engineering Designers
FIEE	Fellow of the Institution of Electrical Engineers
FIEM	Fellow of the Institute of Executives and Managers
FIEx	Fellow of the Institute of Export
FIExpE	Fellow of the Institute of Explosives Engineers
FIFBQ	Fellow of the International Faculty of Business Qualifications
FIFireE	Fellow of the Institution of Fire Engineers
FIFM	Fellow of the Institute of Fisheries Management
FIFST	Fellow of the Institute of Food Science and Technology
FIGasE	Fellow of the Institution of Gas Engineers
FIGD	Fellow of the Institute of Grocery Distribution
FIGeol	Fellow of the Institute of Geologists
FIHEc	Fellow of the Institute of Home Economics Ltd
FIHIE	Fellow of the Institute of Highway Incorporated Engineers
FIHort	Fellow of the Institute of Horticulture
FIHT	Fellow of the Institution of Highways and Transportation
FIIE	Fellow of the Institution of Incorporated Engineers
FIIHTM	Fellow of the International Institute of Hospitality Tourism & Management
FIIM	Fellow of the International Institute of Management
FIIMR	Fellow of the Institute of Investment Management and Research
FIIRSM	Fellow of the International Institute of Risk and Safety Management
FIISE	Fellow of the International Institute of Social Economics
FIISec	Fellow of the International Institute of Security
FIL	Fellow of the Institute of Linguists
FILAM	Fellow of the Institute of Leisure and Amenity Management
FILT	Fellow of the Institute of Logistics and Transport
FIM	Fellow of the Institute of Materials
FIMA	Fellow of the Institute of Mathematics and its Applications
FIManf	Fellow of the Institute of Manufacturing
FIMarE	Fellow of the Institute of Marine Engineers
FIMatM	Fellow of the Institute of Materials Management
FIMBM	Fellow of the Institute of Maintenance and Building Management
FIMechE	Fellow of the Institute of Mechanical Engineers

FIMechIE	Fellow of the Institute of Mechanical Incorporated Engineers
FIMF	Fellow of the Institute of Metal Finishing
FIMgt	Fellow of the Institute of Management
FIMI	Fellow of the Institute of the Motor Industry
FIMIS	Fellow of the Institute for the Management of Information Systems
FIMM	Fellow of the Institute of Massage and Movement
FIMM	Fellow of the Institution of Mining and Metallurgy
FIMM	International Federation of Manual Medicine
FIMS	Fellow of the Institute of Management Specialists
FIMunE	Fellow of the Institution of Municipal Engineers
FInstAEA	Fellow of the Institute of Automotive Engineer Assessors
FInstAM	Fellow of the Institute of Administrative Management
FInstBA	Fellow of the Institute of Business Administration
FInstBCA	Fellow of the Institute of Burial and Cremation Administration
FInstBM	Fellow of the Institute of Builders' Merchants
FInstBRM	Fellow of the Institute of Baths and Recreation Management
FInstCh	Fellow of the Institute of Chiropodists
FInstCM	Fellow of the Institute of Commercial Management
FInstD	Fellow of the Institute of Directors
FInstE	Fellow of the Institute of Energy
FInstLEx	Fellow of the Institute of Legal Executives
FInstMC	Fellow of the Institute of Measurement and Control
FInstNDT	Fellow of the British Institute of Non-Destructive Testing
FInstP	Fellow of the Institute of Physics
FInstPet	Fellow of the Institute of Petroleum
FInstPkg	Fellow of the Institute of Packaging
FInstPM	Fellow of the Institute of Professional Managers and Administrators
FInstPS	Fellow of the Institute of Purchasing and Supply
FInstR	Fellow of the Institute of Refrigeration
FInstSMM	Fellow of the Institute of Sales and Marketing Management
FInstTA	Fellow of the Institute of Transport Administration
FInstTT	Fellow of the Institute of Travel and Tourism
FInstWM	Fellow of the Institute of Wastes Management
FInstWM	Fellowship of the Institute of Wastes Management
FIntMC	Fellow of International Management Centre
FIOC	Fellow of the Institute of Carpenters
FIOM	Fellow of the Institute of Operations Management
FIOP	Fellow of the Institute of Plumbing
FIOP	Fellow of the Institute of Printing
FIOSH	Fellow of the Institution of Occupational Safety and Health
FIPA	Fellow of the Institute of Practitioners in Advertising
FIPD	Fellow of the Institute of Personnel Development
FIPI	Fellow of the Institute of Professional Investigators
FIPlantE	Fellow of the Institution of Plant Engineers
FIPR	Fellow of the Institute of Public Relations
FIQ	Fellow of the Institute of Quarrying
FIQA	Fellow of the Institute of Quality Assurance
FIR	Fellow of the Institute of Population Registration
FIRSE	Fellow of the Institution of Railway Signal Engineers
FIRTE	Fellow of the Institute of Road Transport Engineers
FIS	Fellow of the Institute of Statisticians
FISM	Fellow of the Institute for Supervision & Management

FISOB	Fellow of the Incorporated Society of Organ Builders
FISTC	Fellow of the Institute of Scientific and Technical Communicators
FISTD	Fellow of the Imperial Society of Teachers of Dancing
FIStrucE	Fellow of the Institution of Structural Engineers
FISW	Fellow of the Institute of Social Welfare
FIT	Foundation Insurance Test
FITD	Fellow of the Institute of Training and Development
FITSA	Fellow of the Institute of Trading Standards Administration
FIVehE	Fellow of the Institute of Vehicle Engineers
FIWM	Fellow of the Institute of Wastes Management
FLAW	Foreign Languages at Work
FLCM	Fellow of the London College of Music
FLCSP	Fellow of the London and Counties Society of Physiologists
FLI	Fellow of the Landscape Institute
FLIC	Foreign Languages for Industry and Commerce
FLS	Fellow of the Linnean Society of London
FMA	Fellow of the Museums Association
FMAAT	Fellow Member of the Association of Accounting Technicians
FMPA	Fellow of the Master Photographers Association
FMR	Fellow of the Association of Health Care Information and Medical Records Officers
FMS	Fellow of the Institute of Management Services
FMusEd	Fellowship in Music Education
FN	Fellow of the Nautical Society
FNAEA	Fellow of the National Association of Estate Agents
FNAEAHon	Honoured Fellow of the National Association of Estate Agents
FNCP	Fellow of the National Council of Psychotherapists
FNI	Fellow of the Nautical Institute
FNIMH	Fellow of the National Institute of Medical Herbalists
FPC	Financial Planning Certificate
FPC	Foundation for Psychotherapy and Counselling
FPCS	Fellow of the Property Consultants Society
FPMI	Fellow of the Pensions Management Institute
FPodS	Fellow of the Surgical Faculty of the College of Podiatrists
FProfBTM	Fellow of Professional Business and Technical Management
FRAeS	Fellow of the Royal Aeronautical Society
FRAS	Fellow of the Royal Astronomical Society
FRCA	Fellow of the Royal College of Anaesthetists
FRCGP	Fellow of the Royal College of General Practitioners
FRCM	Fellow of the Royal College of Music
FRCO	Fellow of the Royal College of Organists
FRCO(CHM)	Fellow of the Royal College of Organists (Choir-training Diploma)
FRCOG	Fellow of the Royal College of Obstetricians and Gynaecologists
FRCP	Fellow of the Royal College of Physicians of London
FRCPath	Fellow of the Royal College of Pathologists
FRCPEdin	Fellow of the Royal College of Physicians of Edinburgh
FRCPsych	Fellow of the Royal College of Psychiatrists
FRCR	Fellow of the Royal College of Radiologists
FRCS(Irel)	Fellow of the Royal College of Surgeons in Ireland
FRCSEd	Fellow of the Royal College of Surgeons of Edinburgh
FRCSEd(C/TH)	Fellow of the Royal College of Surgeons of Edinburgh, specialising in Cardiothoracic Surgery

FRCSEd(Orth)	Fellow of the Royal College of Surgeons of Edinburgh, specialising in Orthopaedic Surgery
FRCSEd(SN)	Fellow of the Royal College of Surgeons of Edinburgh, specialising in Surgical Neurology
FRCSEng	Fellow of the Royal College of Surgeons of England
FRCSEng(Oto)	Fellow of the Royal College of Surgeons of England, with Otolaryngology
FRCSGlasg	Fellow of the Royal College of Physicians and Surgeons of Glasgow
FRCVS	Fellow of the Royal College of Veterinary Surgeons
FREC	Fellow of the Recruitment and Employment Confederation
FRHS	Fellow of the Royal Horticultural Society
FRIBA	Fellow of the Royal Institute of British Architects
FRICS	Fellow of the Royal Institution of Chartered Surveyors
FRIN	Fellow of the Royal Institute of Navigation
FRINA	Fellow of the Royal Institution of Naval Architects
FRIPHH	Fellow of the Royal Institution of Public Health and Hygiene
FRNCM	Fellow of the Royal Northern College of Music
FRPharmS	Fellow of the Royal Pharmaceutical Society of Great Britain
FRPS	Fellow of the Royal Photographic Society
FRS	Fellow of the Royal Society
FRSC	Fellow of the Royal Society of Chemistry
FRSCM	Fellow of the Royal School of Church Music
FRSH	Fellow of the Royal Society for the Promotion of Health
FRTPI	Fellow of the Royal Town Planning Institute
FSAPP	Fellow of the Society of Advanced Psychotherapy Practitioners
FSBP	Fellow of the Society of Business Practitioners
FSBT	Fellow of the Society of Teachers in Business Education
FSCT	Fellow of the Society of Claims Technicians
FSDC	Fellow of the Society of Dyers and Colourists
FSE	Fellow of the Society of Engineers (Inc)
FSElec	Fellow of the Society of Electroscience
FSG	Fellow of the Society of Genealogists
FSG(Hon)	Honorary Fellow of the Society of Genealogists
FSGT	Fellow of the Society of Glass Technology
FSIAD	Fellow of the Society of Industrial Artists and Designers
FSMA	Fellow of the Society of Martial Arts
FSMA	Fellow of the Society of Sales Management Administrators Ltd
FSNN	Fellow of the Society of Nursery Nursing
FSS	Fellow of the Royal Statistical Society
FSSCh	Fellow of the British Chiropody and Podiatry Association
FSSF	Fellow of the Society of Shoe Fitters
FSTA	Fellow of the Swimming Teachers' Association
FSVA	Fellow of the Incorporated Society of Valuers and Auctioneers
FTCL	Fellow of the Trinity College of Music
FTI	Fellow of the Textile Institute
FTII	Fellow of the Chartered Institute of Taxation
FTSC	Fellow of the Oil and Colour Chemists' Association
FTSC	Fellow in the Technology of Surface Coatings
FWeldI	Fellow of the Welding Institute
FYDA	Associate Fellowship of the Youth Development Association
GAGTL	Gemmological Association and Gem Testing Laboratory of Great Britain
GAI	Guild of Architectural Ironmongers
GASI	Graduate Member of the Ambulance Service Institute

GBSM	Graduate of the Birmingham School of Music
GCE	General Certificate of Education
GCE A	General Certificate of Education Advanced Level
GCE O	General Certificate of Education Ordinary Level
GCGI	Graduateship, City & Guilds
GCL	Guild of Cleaners and Launderers
GCSE	General Certificate of Secondary Education
GDC	General Dental Council
GIBCM	Graduate of the Institute of British Carriage and Automobile Manufacturers
GIBiol	Graduate of the Institute of Biology
GIEM	Graduate of the Institute of Executives and Managers
GIMA	Graduate of the Institute of Mathematics and its Applications
GIMI	Graduate of the Institute of the Motor Industry
GInstP	Graduate of the Institute of Physics
GIntMC	Graduate of the International Management Centre
GIS	Graduate Imaging Scientist
GLCM	Graduate Diploma of the London College of Music
GMAT	Graduate Management Admissions Test
GMC	General Medical Council
GMDSS	Global Maritime Distress & Safety System
GMInstM	Graduate Member of the Meat Training Council
GMus	Graduate Diploma in Music
GMusRNCM	Graduate in Music of the Royal Northern College of Music
GNSM	Graduate of the Northern School of Music
GNVQ	General National Vocational Qualifications
GradAES	Graduate of the Royal Aeronautical Society
GradBEng	Graduate Member of the Association of Building Engineers
GradBHI	Graduate of the British Horological Institute
GradDip	Graduate Diploma
GradIAP	Graduate of the Institution of Analysts and Programmers
GradIBE	Graduate of the Institution of British Engineers
GradIElecIE	Graduate of the Institution of Electrical and Electronics Incorporated Engineers
GradIIE	Graduate of the Institution of Incorporated Engineers
GradIISec	Graduate of the International Institute of Security
GradIManf	Graduate of the Institute Manufacturing
GradIMF	Graduate of the Institute of Metal Finishing
GradIMS	Graduate of the Institute of Management Specialists
GradInstNDT	Graduate of the British Institute of Non-Destructive Testing
GradInstP	Graduate of the Institute of Physics
GradInstPS	Graduate of the Institute of Purchasing and Supply
GradIOP	Graduate of the Institute of Printing
GradIPD	Graduate of the Institute of Personnel and Development
GradIS	Graduate of the Institute of Statisticians
GradISCA	Graduate of the Institute of Chartered Secretaries and Administrators
GradMechE	Graduate of the Institution of Mechanical Engineers
GradMIWM	Graduate Member of the Institute of Wastes Management
GradRNCM	Graduate of the Royal Northern College of Music
GradRSC	Graduate of the Royal Society of Chemistry
GradSMA	Graduate of the Society of Martial Arts
GradStat	Graduate Statistician
GraduateCIPD	Graduate of the Chartered Institute of Personnel and Development
GraduateIEIE	Graduate of the Institution of Electrical and Electronics Incorporated Engineers

GradWeldI	Graduate of the Welding Institute
GRC	General Readers Certificate
GRC	Grade Related Criteria
GRIC	Graduate Membership of the Royal Institute of Chemistry
GRSC	Graduate of the Royal Society of Chemistry
GRSM	Graduate Diploma of the Royal Manchester School of Music
GRSM(Hons)	Graduate of the Royal Schools of Music
GSMA	Graduate of the Society of Sales Management Administrators Ltd
GSNN	Graduate of the Society of Nursery Nursing
GTC	General Teaching Council
HABIA	Hairdressing and Beauty Industry Authority
HC	Higher Certificate
HCIMA	Hotel and Catering International Management Association
HD	Higher Diploma
HDCR (R) or (T)	Higher Award in Radiodiagnosis or Radiotherapy, College of Radiographers
HEFCE	Higher Education Funding Council for England
HFInstE	Honorary Fellow of the Institute of Energy
HNC	Higher National Certificate
HND	Higher National Diploma
HonASTA	Honorary Associate of the Swimming Teachers' Association
HonDrRCA	Honorary Doctorate of the Royal College of Art
HonFAE	Honorary Fellow of the Academy of Experts
HonFBID	Honorary Fellow of the British Institute of Interior Design
HonFBIPP	Honorary Fellow of the British Institute of Professional Photography
HonFCP	Charter Fellow of the College of Preceptors
HonFEIS	Honorary Fellow of the Educational Institute of Scotland
HonFHCIMA	Honorary Fellow of the Hotel, Catering and Institutional Management Association
HonFHS	Honorary Fellow of the Heraldry Society
HonFIEE	Honorary Fellow of the Institution of Electrical Engineers
HonFIExpE	Honorary Fellow of the Institute of Explosives Engineers
HonFIGasE	Honorary Fellow of the Institution of Gas Engineers
HonFIMarE	Honorary Fellow of the Institute of Marine Engineers
HonFIMechE	Honorary Fellow of the Institution of Mechanical Engineers
HonFIMM	Honorary Fellow of the Institution of Mining and Metallurgy
HonFInstE	Honorary Fellow of the Institute of Energy
HonFInstMC	Honorary Fellow of the Institute of Measurement and Control
HonFInstNDT	Honorary Fellow of the British Institute of Non-Destructive Testing
HonFIQA	Honorary Fellow of the Institute of Quality Assurance
HonFIRSE	Honorary Fellow of the Institution of Railway Signal Engineers
HonFIRTE	Honorary Fellow of the Institute of Road Transport Engineers
HonFPRI	Honorary Fellow of the Plastics and Rubber Institute
HonFRIN	Honorary Fellow of the Royal Institute of Navigation
HonFRINA	Honorary Fellow of the Royal Institution of Naval Architects
HonFRPS	Honorary Fellow of the Royal Photographic Society
HonFSE	Honorary Fellow of the Society of Engineers (Inc)
HonFSGT	Honorary Fellow of the Society of Glass Technology
HonFWeldI	Honorary Fellow of the Welding Institute
HonGSM	Honorary Member of the Guildhall School of Music and Drama
HonMIFM	Honorary Member of the Institute of Fisheries Management
HonMInstNDT	Honorary Member of the British Institute of Non-Destructive Testing
HonMRIN	Honorary Member of the Royal Institute of Navigation
HonMWES	Honorary Member of the Women's Engineering Society

HonRAM	Honorary Member of the Royal Academy of Music
HonRCM	Honorary Member of the Royal College of Music
HonRNCM	Honorary Member of the Royal Northern College of Music
HonRSCM	Honorary Member of the Royal School of Church Music
HSC	Higher School Certificate
HSE	Health & Safety Executive
HTB	Hairdressing Training Board
HTC	Higher Technical Certificate
IAAP	International Association for Analytic Psychology
IAB	International Association of Book-Keepers
IABC	International Association of Business Computing
IAC	Investment Advice Certificate
IAgrE	Institution of Agricultural Engineers
IAP	Institution of Analysts and Programmers
IAQ	Investment Administration Qualification
IAT	Institute of Asphalt Technology
IBA	Institute of Business Administration
IBC	Institute of Building Control
IBE	Institution of British Engineers
IBF	Institute of British Foundrymen
IBMS	Institute of Biomedical Science
ICAEW	Institute of Chartered Accountants in England and Wales
ICAI	Institute of Chartered Accountants in Ireland
ICAS	Institute of Chartered Accountants of Scotland
ICB	Institute of Certified Book-Keepers
ICE	Institution of Civil Engineers
ICEA	Institute of Cost and Executive Accountants
ICG	Institute of Careers Guidance
IChemE	Institution of Chemical Engineers
ICIOB	Incorporated Member of the Chartered Institute of Building
ICM	Institute of Commercial Management
ICM	Institute of Complementary Medicine
ICM	Institute of Credit Management
ICMQ	International Capital Markets Qualification
ICSA	Institute of Chartered Secretaries and Administrators
ICSF	Intermediate Certificate of the Society of Floristry
IDA	Improvement and Development Agency
IDTA	International Dance Teachers' Association Ltd
IED	Institution of Engineering Designers
IEE	Institution of Electrical Engineers
IEM	Institute of Executives and Managers
IEng	Incorporated Engineer
IETTL	Insulation and Environmental Training Trust Ltd
IEx	Institute of Export
IExpE	Institute of Explosives Engineers
IFA	Institute of Field Archaeologists
IFA	Institute of Financial Accountants
IFA	Insurance Foundation Certificate
IFBQ	International Faculty of Business Qualifications
IFM	Institute of Fisheries Management
IFST	Institute of Food Science and Technology (UK)
IHBC	International Health & Beauty Council

IHIE	Institute of Highway Incorporated Engineers
IHort	Institute of Horticulture
IHT	Institute of Highways and Transportation
IIA	Institute of Internal Auditors
IIE	Institution of Incorporated Engineers
IIExE	Institution of Incorporated Executive Engineers
IIHHT	International Institute of Health & Holistic Therapies
IIHTM	International Institute of Hospitality Tourism & Management
IIRSM	International Institute of Risk and Safety Management
ILAM	Institute of Leisure and Amenity Management
ILE	Institution of Lighting Engineers
ILEX	Institute of Legal Executives
ILT	Institute of Logistics and Transport
IMarE	Institute of Marine Engineers
IMBM	Institute of Maintenance and Building Management
IMC	Institute of Management Consultancy
IMechE	Institution of Mechanical Engineers
IMF	Institute of Metal Finishing
IMI	Institute of the Motor Industry
IMIBC	Incorporated Member of the Institute of Building Control
IMInstAEA	Incorporated Member of the Institute of Automotive Engineer Assessors
IMIS	Institute for the Management of Information Systems
IMM	Institution of Mining and Metallurgy
IMS	Institute of Management Specialists
IncMWeldI	Incorporated Member of the Welding Institute
InstAEA	Institute of Automotive Engineer Assessors
InstAM	Institute of Administrative Management
InstBCA	Institute of Burial and Cremation Administration
InstE	Institute of Energy
InstPet	Institute of Petroleum
IOB	Institute of Brewing
IOC	Institute of Carpenters
IoD	Institute of Directors
IOM	Institute of Operations Management
IOP	Institute of Packaging
IOSH	Institution of Occupational Safety and Health
IOTA	Institute of Transport Administration
IPA	Institute of Practitioners in Advertising
IPD	Initial Professional Development
IPD	Institute of Personnel and Development
IPFA	Member of the Chartered Institute of Public Finance and Accountancy
IPlantE	Institution of Plant Engineers
IPR	Incorporated Professional Review
IPR	Institute of Public Relations
IPSM	Institute of Public Service Management
IQ	Institute of Quarrying
IQA	Institute of Quality Assurance
IRMT	International Register of Massage Therapists
IRRV	Corporate Member of the Institute of Revenues, Rating and Valuation
IRRV	Institute of Revenues, Rating and Valuation
IRSE	Institution of Railway Signal Engineers
IRTE	Institute of Road Transport Engineers

ISEB	Information Systems Examinations Board
ISM	Incorporated Society of Musicians
ISM	Institute for Supervision & Management
ISMM	Institute of Sales and Marketing Management
ISRM	Institute of Sport and Recreation Management
ISTD	Imperial Society of Teachers of Dancing
IStructE	Institution of Structural Engineers
ITEC	International Therapy Examination Council
ITIL	IT Infrastructure Library
ITSA	Institute of Trading Standards Administration
IVehE	Institute of the Vehicle Engineers
IVM	Institute of Value Management
IWSc	Institute of Wood Science
JEB	Joint Examination Board
JET	Jewellery, Education and Training
JP	Justice of the Peace
LA	Library Association
LABAC	Licentiate Member of the Association of Business and Administrative Computing
LAE	Licentiate Automotive Engineer
LAEx	Legal Accounts Executive
LAMDA	London Academy of Music and Dramatic Art
LAMRTPI	Legal Associate Member of the Royal Town Planning Institute
LASI	Licentiate of the Ambulance Service Institute
LASI	Licentiate of the Architecture and Surveying Institute
LBEI	Licentiate of the Institution of Body Engineers
LBIDST	Licentiate of the British Institute of Dental and Surgical Technologists
LBIPP	Licentiate of the British Institute of Professional Photography
LCCI	London Chamber of Commerce and Industry
LCCIEB	London Chamber of Commerce and Industry Examinations Board
LCEA	Licentiate of the Association of Cost and Executive Accountants
LCFI	Licentiate of CFI International (Clothing and Footwear Institute)
LCGI	Licentiate, City & Guilds
LCIBSE	Licentiate of the Chartered Institution of Building Services Engineers
LCP	Licentiate of the College of Preceptors
LCSP	London and Counties Society of Physiologists
LCSP(Assoc)	Associate of the London and Counties Society of Physiologists
LCSP(BTh)	Member of the London and Counties Society of Physiologists (Beauty Therapy)
LCSP(Chir)	Member of the London and Counties Society of Physiologists (Chiropody)
LCSP(Phys)	Member of the London and Counties Society of Physiologists (Physical and Manipulative Therapy)
LCT	Licentiate of the College of Teachers
LDS	Licentiate in Dental Surgery
LDSRCPSGlas	Licentiate in Dental Surgery of the Royal College of Physicians and Surgeons of Glasgow
LDSRCSEd	Licentiate in Dental Surgery of the Royal College of Surgeons of Edinburgh
LDSRCSEng	Licentiate in Dental Surgery of the Royal College of Surgeons of England
LFA	Licentiate of the Institute of Financial Accountants
LFCI	Licentiate of the Faculty of Commerce and Industry
LFCS	Licentiate of the Faculty of Secretaries
LFS	Licentiate of the Faculty of Architects and Surveyors (Surveyors)
LGCL	Licentiate of the Guild of Cleaners and Launderers
LGSM	Licentiate of the Guildhall School of Music and Drama

LHCIMA	Licentiate of the Hotel and Catering International Management Association
LHG	Licentiate of the Institute of Heraldic and Genealogical Studies
LI	Landscape Institute
LicentiateCIPD	Licentiate of the Chartered Institute of Personnel and Development
LicIPD	Licentiate of the Institute of Personnel & Development
LicIQA	Licentiate of the Institute of Quality Assurance
LICW	Licentiate of the Institute of Clerks of Works of Great Britain Incorporated
LIDPM	Licentiate of the Institute of Data Processing Management
LIEM	Licentiate of the Institute of Executives and Managers
LIIST	Licentiate of the International Institute of Sports Therapy
LILAM	Licentiate of the Institute of Leisure and Amenity Management
LIM	Licentiate of the Institute of Materials
LIMA	Licentiate of the Institute of Mathematics and its Applications
LIMF	Licentiate of the Institute of Metal Finishing
LIMIS	Licentiate of the Institute for the Management of Information Systems
LInstBCA	Licentiate of the Institute of Burial and Cremation Administration
LInstBM	Licentiate of the Institute of Builders' Merchants
LIOC	Licentiate of the Institute of Carpenters
LIR	Licentiate of the Institute of Population Registration
LISTD	Licentiate of the Imperial Society of Teachers of Dancing
LISTD(Dip)	Licentiate Diploma of the Imperial Society of Teachers of Dancing
LittD	Doctor of Letters
LIWM	Licentiate of the Institute of Wastes Management
LLB	Bachelor of Law
LLCM	Performers Diploma of Licentiateship in Speech, Drama and Public Speaking
LLCM(TD)	Licentiate of the London College of Music and Media (Teachers' Diploma)
LLD	Doctor of Law
LLM	Master of Law
LM	Licentiate in Midwifery
LMIFM	Licentiate Member of the Institute of Fisheries Management
LMInstE	Licentiate Member of the Institute of Energy
LMPA	Licentiate Member of the Master Photographers Association
LMRTPI	Legal Member of the Royal Town Planning Institute
LMSSALond	Licentiate in Medicine, Surgery and Obstetrics & Gynaecology, Society of Apothecaries of London
LMusEd	Licentiate Diploma in Music Education
LMusLCM	Licentiate in Music of the London College of Music
LMusTCL	Licentiate in Music, Trinity College of Music
LNCP	Licentiate of the National Council of Psychotherapists
LPC	Legal Practice Course
LRAD	Licentiate of the Royal Academy of Dancing
LRAM	Licentiate of the Royal Academy of Music
LRCPEdin	Conjoint Diplomas Licentiate of the Royal College of Physicians of Edinburgh
LRCPSGlasg	Conjoint Diplomas Licentiate of the Royal College of Physicians and Surgeons of Glasgow
LRCSEdin	Conjoint Diplomas Licentiate of the Royal College of Surgeons of Edinburgh
LRCSEng	Licentiate of the Royal College of Surgeons in England
LRPS	Licentiate of the Royal Photographic Society
LRSC	Licentiate of the Royal Society of Chemistry
LRSM	Licentiate Diploma of the Royal Schools of Music
LSBP	Licentiate of the Society of Business Practitioners
LSCP(Assoc)	Associate of the London and Counties Society of Physiologists

LTCL	Licentiate of Trinity College of Music
LTh	Licentiate in Theology
LTI	Licentiate of the Textile Industry
LTSC	Licentiate of the Oil and Colour Chemists' Association
LVT	Licentiate Vehicle Technologist
MA	Master of Arts
MA(Architectural)	Master of Arts (Architectural Studies)
MA(Econ)	Master of Arts in Economic and Social Studies
MA(Ed)	Master of Arts in Education
MA(LD)	Master of Arts (Landscape Design)
MA(MUS)	Master of Arts (Music)
MA(RCA)	Master of Arts, Royal College of Art
MA(SocSci)	Master of Arts (Social Science)
MA(Theol)	Master of Arts in Theology
MAAT	Member of the Association of Accounting Technicians
MABAC	Member of the Association of Business and Administrative Computing
MABE	Member of the Association of Business Executives
MAcc	Master of Accountancy
MACP	Member of the Association of Computer Professionals
MAE	Member of the Academy of Experts
MAgr	Master of Agriculture
MAgrSc	Master of Agricultural Science
MAMS	Member of the Association of Medical Secretaries, Practice Managers, Administrators and Receptionists
MAMSA	Managing & Marketing Sales Association Examination Board
MAnimSc	Master of Animal Science
MAO	Master of Obstetrics
MAP	Membership by Assessment of Performance
MAPM	Member of the Association for Project Management
MAppSci	Master of Applied Science
MAQ	Mortgage Advice Qualification
MArAd	Master of Archive Administration
MArb	Master of Arboriculture
MArch	Master of Architecture
MArt/RCA	Master of Arts, Royal College of Art
MasFCI	Master of the Faculty of Commerce and Industry
MASHAM	Management and Administration of Safety and Health at Mines
MASI	Member of the Architecture and Surveying Institute
MBA	Master of Business Administration
MBAE	Member of the British Association of Electrolysists
MB, BCh	Conjoint Degree of Bachelor of Medicine, Bachelor of Surgery
MB, BChir	Conjoint Degree of Bachelor of Medicine, Bachelor of Surgery
MB, BS	Conjoint Degree of Bachelor of Medicine, Bachelor of Surgery
MB, ChB	Conjoint Degree of Bachelor of Medicine, Bachelor of Surgery
MBChA	Member of the British Chiropody and Podiatry Association
MBCO	Member of the British College of Ophthalmic Opticians
MBCS	Member of the British Computer Society
MBEng	Member of the Association of Building Engineers
MBHA	Member of the British Hypnotherapy Association
MBHI	Member of the British Horological Institute
MBIAT	Member of the British Institute of Architectural Technologists
MBID	Member of the British Institute of Interior Design

MBIE	Member of the British Institute of Embalmers
MBII	Member of the British Institute of Innkeeping
MBioc	Master of Biochemistry
MBKS	Member of the British Kinematograph, Sound and Television Society
MBM	Master of Business Management
MBMA	Member of the Business Management Association
MBSc	Master in Business Science
MBSSG	Master of the British Society of Scientific Glassblowers
MCAM	Member of the Communication Advertising and Marketing Education Foundation
MCB	Mastership in Clinical Biochemistry
MCB	Member of the British Association of Communicators in Business
MCBDip	Member of the British Association of Communicators in Business who hold the Association's Certificate and Diploma
MCC	Master of Community Care
MCCDRCS(Eng)	Member of the Royal College of Surgeons of England, Clinical Community Dentistry
MCD	Master of Civic Design
MCDH	Master of Community Dental Health
MCGI	Membership, City & Guilds
MCGPIrel	Member of the Irish College of General Practitioners
MCh	Master of Surgery
MChD	Master of Dental Surgery
MChem	Master of Chemistry
MChemA	Master of Chemical Analysis
MChemPhys	Master of Chemical Physics
MChemPST	Master of Chemistry Polymer Science and Technology
MChir	Master of Surgery
MChOrth	Master of Orthopaedic Surgery
MChS	Member of the Society of Chiropodists and Podiatrists
MCIArb	Member of the Chartered Institute of Arbitrators
MCIBS	Member of the Chartered Institute of Bankers in Scotland
MCIBSE	Member of the Chartered Institution of Building Services Engineers
MCIH	Corporate Member of the Chartered Institute of Housing
MCIJ	Member of the Chartered Institute of Journalists
MCIM	Member of the Chartered Institute of Marketing
MCIOB	Member of the Chartered Institute of Building
MCIPD	Member of the Chartered Institute of Personnel and Development
MCIPS	Member of the Chartered Institute of Purchasing and Supply
MCIT	Member of the Chartered Institute of Transport
MCIWEM	Member of the Chartered Institution of Water and Environmental Management
MCLIP	Chartered Member of CILIP
MCom	Master of Commerce
MCommH	Master of Community Health
MComp	Master of Computer Science
MCOptom	Member of the College of Optometrists
MCoT	Member of the College of Teachers
MCPM	Member of the Confederation of Professional Management
MCPP	Member of the College of Pharmacy Practice
MCQ	Multiple Choice Question paper
MCSD	Member of the Chartered Society of Designers
MCSP	Member of the Chartered Society of Physiotherapy
MCT	Member of the Association of Corporate Treasurers

MCTHCM	Member of the Confederation of Tourism, Hotel and Catering Management
MCYW	Member of the Community and Youth Work Association
MD	Doctor of Medicine
MDA	Master of Defence Administration
MD; ChM	Conjoint Doctorate in Medicine, Doctorate in Surgery
MDCR	Management Diploma of the College of Radiographers
MDent	Master of Dental Science
MDes	Master of Design
MDes(RCA)	Master of Design, Royal College of Art
MDORCPSGlas	Membership of Dental Orthopaedics, Royal College of Physicians and Surgeons of Glasgow
MDra	Master of Drama
MDS	Master of Dental Surgery
MDSc	Master of Dental Science
MEBA	Master of European Business Administration
MECI	Member of the Institute of Employment Consultants
MEd	Master of Education
MEd(EdPsych)	Master of Education (Educational Psychology)
MEdStud	Master of Educational Studies
MEng	Master of Engineering
MEnv	Master of Environmental Studies
MEnvSci	Master of Environmental Science
MESc	Master of Earth Sciences
MFA	Master of Fine Art
MFC	Mastership in Food Control
MFCM	Member of the Faculty of Community Medicine
MFDO	Member of the Faculty of Dispensing Opticians
MFDS	Member of the Faculty of Dental Surgery
MFGDPEng	Membership in General Dental Practice, Royal College of Surgeons of England
MFHom	Member of the Faculty of Homeopathy
MFM	Master of Forensic Medicine
MFPHM	Member of the Faculty of Public Health Medicine, Royal College of Physicians of London and Edinburgh and Royal College of Physicians and Surgeons of Glasgow
MFPHMIrel	Member of the Faculty of Public Health Medicine, Royal College of Physicians of Ireland
MFTCom	Member of the Faculty of Teachers in Commerce
MGDSRCSEd	Membership in General Dental Surgery, Royal College of Surgeons of Edinburgh
MGDSRCSEng	Membership in General Dental Surgery, Royal College of Surgeons of England
MGeog	Master of Geography
MGeol	Master of Geology
MGeophys	Master of Geophysical Sciences
MHCIMA	Member of the Hotel and Catering International Management Association
MHM	Master of Health Management
MHort(RHS)	Master of Horticulture, Royal Horticultural Society
MHSM	Member of the Institute of Health Services Management
MIAB	Member of the International Association of Book-keepers
MIAEA	Member of the Institute of Automotive Engineer Assessors
MIAgrE	Member of the Institution of Agricultural Engineers
MIAP	Member of the Institution of Analysts and Programmers
MIAT	Member of the Institute of Asphalt Technology
MIBC	Member of the Institute of Building Control

MIBCM	Member of the Institute British Carriage and Automobile Manufacturers
MIBCO	Member of the Institution of Building Control Officers
MIBE	Member of the Institution of British Engineers
MIBF	Member of the Institute of British Foundrymen
MIBiol	Member of the Institute of Biology
MIBM	Member of the Institute of Builders' Merchants
MICB	Member of the Institute of Certified Book-Keepers
MICE	Member of the Institute of Civil Engineers
MIChemE	Member of the Institution of Chemical Engineers
MICHT	Member of the International Council for Holistic Therapies
MICM	Member of the Institute of Credit Management
MICM(Grad)	Graduate Member of the Institute of Credit Management
MICorr	Member of the Institute of Corrosion
MICS	Member of the Institute of Chartered Shipbrokers
MICSc	Corporate Member of the Institute of Consumer Sciences Incorporating Home Economics
MICW	Member of the Institute of Clerks of Works of Great Britain Incorporated
MIDTA	Member of the International Dance Teachers' Association
MIED	Member of the Institution of Engineering Designers
MIEE	Member of the Institution of Electrical Engineers
MIEM	Member of the Institute of Executives and Managers
MIEx	Member of the Institute of Export
MIEx(Grad)	Graduate Member of the Institute of Export
MIExpE	Member of the Institute of Explosives Engineers
MIFA	Member of the Institute of Field Archaeologists
MIFireE	Member of the Institution of Fire Engineers
MIFM	Registered Member of the Institute of Fisheries Management
MIFST	Member of the Institute of Food Science and Technology
MIGasE	Member of the Institution of Gas Engineers
MIGD	Member of the Institute of Grocery Distribution
MIHEc	Member of the Institute of Home Economics
MIHIE	Member of the Institute of Highway Incorporated Engineers
MIHM	Member of the Institute of Healthcare Management
MIHort	Member of the Institute of Horticulture
MIHT	Member of the Institution of Highways and Transportation
MIIA	Member of the Institute of Internal Auditors
MIIE	Member of the Institution of Incorporated Engineers
MIIExE	Member of the Institution of Incorporated Executive Engineers
MIIHTM	Member of the International Institute of Hospitality Tourism & Management
MIIM	Member of the Institute of Industrial Managers
MIIM	Member of the International Institute of Management
MIIRSM	Member of the International Institute of Risk and Safety Management
MIISE	Member of the International Institute of Social Economics
MIISec	Member of the International Institute of Security
MIL	Member of the Institute of Linguists
MILAM	Member of the Institute of Leisure and Amenity Management
MILT	Member of the Institute of Logistics and Transport
MIM	Professional Member of the Institute of Materials
MIMA	Member of the Institute of Mathematics and its Applications
MIManf	Member of the Institute of Manufacturing
MIMarE	Member of the Institute of Marine Engineers
MIMatM	Member of the Institute of Materials Management

MIMBM	Member of the Institute of Maintenance and Building Management
MIMC	Member of the Institute of Management Consultancy
MIMechE	Member of the Institution of Mechanical Engineers
MIMechIE	Member of the Institution of Mechanical Incorporated Engineers
MIMF	Member of the Institute of Metal Finishing
MIMI	Member of the Institute of the Motor Industry
MIMinE	Member of the Institution of Mining Engineers
MIMIS	Member of the Institute for the Management of Information Systems
MIMM	Member of the Institute of Massage and Movement
MIMM	Member of the Institution of Mining and Metallurgy
MIMS	Member of the Institute of Management Specialists
MInstAEA	Member of the Institute of Automotive Engineer Assessors
MInstAM	Member of the Institute of Administrative Management
MInstBA	Member of the Institute of Business Administration
MInstBCA	Member of the Institute of Burial and Cremation Administration
MInstBE	Member of the Institution of British Engineers
MInstBM	Member of the Institute of Builders' Merchants
MInstCF	Master Fitter of the National Institute of Carpet and Floorlayers
MInstChP	Member of the Institute of Chiropodists & Podiatrists
MInstCM	Member of the Institute of Commercial Management
MInstD	Member of the Institute of Directors
MInstE	Member of the Institute of Energy
MInstLEx	Member of the Institute of Legal Executives
MInstMC	Member of the Institute of Measurement and Control
MInstNDT	Member of the British Institute of Non-Destructive Testing
MInstP	Member of the Institute of Physics
MInstPet	Member of the Institute of Petroleum
MInstPkg	Member of the Institute of Packaging
MInstPkg(Dip)	Diploma Member of the Institute of Packaging
MInstPM	Member of the Institute of Professional Managers and Administrators
MInstPS	Corporate Member of the Institute of Purchasing and Supply
MInstPSA	Member of the Institute of Public Service Administrators
MInstR	Member of the Institute of Refrigeration
MInstSMM	Member of the Institute of Sales and Marketing Management
MInstTA	Member of the Institute of Transport Administration
MInstTT	Full Member of the Institute of Travel and Tourism
MInstWM	Member of the Institute of Wastes Management
MIOC	Member of the Institute of Carpenters
MIOFMS	Member of the Institute of Financial and Management Studies
MIOM	Member of the Institute of Operations Management
MIOP	Member of the Institute of Printing
MIOSH	Member of the Institution of Occupational Safety and Health
MIP	Member of the Institute of Plumbing
MIPA	Member of the Institute of Practitioners in Advertising
MIPD	Member of the Institute of Personnel and Development
MIPI	Member of the Institute of Professional Investigators
MIPlantE	Member of the Institution of Plant Engineers
MIPR	Member of the Institute of Public Relations
MIPRE	Member of the Incorporated Practitioners in Radio & Electronics
MIQ	Member of the Institute of Quarrying
MIQA	Member of the Institute of Quality Assurance
MIR	Member of the Institute of Population Registration

MIRRV	Member of the Institute of Revenue, Rating and Valuation
MIRSE	Member of the Institution of Railway Signal Engineers
MIRTE	Member of the Institute of Road Transport Engineering
MISM	Member of the Institute for Supervision & Management
MISOB	Member of the Incorporated Society of Organ Builders
MISTC	Member of the Institute of Scientific and Technical Communicators
MIStrucE	Member of the Institution of Structural Engineers
MISW	Member of the Institute of Social Welfare
MITAI	Member of the Institute of Traffic Accident Investigators
MITSA	Member of the Institute of Trading Standards Administration
MIVehE	Member of the Institute of Vehicle Engineers
MIWM	Member of the Institute of Wastes Management
MIWPC	Member of the Institute of Water Pollution Control
MJur	Master of Jurisprudence
MLA	Master of Landscape Architecture
MLang	Master of Languages
MLangEng	Master of Language Engineering
MLD	Master of Landscape Design
MLE	Master of Land Economy
MLI	Member of the Landscape Institute
MLing	Master of Languages
MLitt	Master of Letters
MLPM	Master of Landscape Planning and Management
MLS	Master of Library Science
MM	Master of Midwifery
MMA	Master of Management and Administration
MMAS	Master of Minimal Access Surgery
MMath	Master of Mathematics
MMedE	Master of Medical Education
MMedSci	Master of Medical Science
MMet	Master of Metallurgy
MML	Master of Modern Languages
MMS	Member of the Institute of Management Services
MMSc	Master of Medical Sciences
MMus	Master of Music
MMus(Comp)	Master of Music (Composition)
MMus(Perf)	Master of Music (Performance)
MMus, RCM	Master of Music, Royal College of Music
MMusArt	Master of Musical Arts
MN	Master of Nursing
MNAEA	Member of the National Association of Estate Agents
MNatSc	Master of Natural Science
MNCP	Member of the National Council of Psychotherapists
MNeuro	Master of Neuroscience
MNI	Member of the Nautical Institute
MNIMH	Member of the National Institute of Medical Herbalists
MNRHP	Full Member of the National Register of Hypnotherapists and Psychotherapists
MNRHP(Eqv)	Full Member (Equivalent) of the National Register of Hypnotherapists and Psychotherapists
MNTB	Merchant Navy Training Board
MObstG	Master of Obstetrics and Gynaecology
MOptom	Master of Optometry

MOrthRCSEng	Membership in Orthodontics, Royal College of Surgeons of England
MPA	Master of Public Administration
MPaedDenRCSEng	Membership in Paediatric Dentistry, Royal College of Surgeons of England
MPC	Master of Palliative Care
MPH	Master of Public Health
MPharm	Master of Pharmacy
MPharmSci	Master of Pharmaceutical Science
MPhil	Master of Philosophy
MPhil(Eng)	Master of Philosophy in Engineering
MPhys	Master of Physics
MPhysGeog	Master of Physical Geography
MPlan	Master of Planning
MPPS	Master of Public Policy Studies
MPRI	Member of the Plastics and Rubber Institute
MProf	Master of Professional Studies
MProfBTM	Member of the Professional Business and Technical Management
MPS	Member of the Pharmaceutical Society of Northern Ireland
MPsychMed	Master of Psychological Medicine
MPsychol	Master of Psychology
MQB	Mining Qualifications Board
MRad	Master of Radiology
MRad; MRad(D)	Master of Radiology (Radiodiagnosis) or (Radiotherapy)
MRAeS	Member of the Royal Aeronautical Society
MRCGP	Member of the Royal College of General Practitioners
MRCOG	Member of the Royal College of Obstetricians and Gynaecologists
MRCP	Member of the Royal College of Physicians of London
MRCP(UK)	Member of the Royal College of Physicians of the United Kingdom
MRCPath	Member of the Royal College of Pathologists
MRCPEdin	Member of the Royal College of Physicians of Edinburgh (superceded by MRCP(UK))
MRCPGlasg	Member of the Royal College of Physicians of Glasgow (superceded by MRCP(UK))
MRCPIrel	Member of the Royal College of Physicians of Ireland
MRCPsych	Member of the Royal College of Psychiatrists
MRCSEd	Member of the Royal College of Surgeons of Edinburgh
MRCSEng	Member of the Royal College of Surgeons of England
MRCVS	Member of the Royal College of Veterinary Surgeons
MRDRCS	Membership in Restorative Dentistry, Royal College of Surgeons of England
MREC	Member of the Recruitment and Employment Confederation
MREHIS	Member of the Royal Environmental Health Institute of Scotland
MRes	Master of Research
MRIN	Member of the Royal Institute of Navigation
MRINA	Member of the Royal Institution of Naval Architects
MRIPHH	Member of the Royal Institute of Public Health and Hygiene
MRPharmS	Member of the Pharmaceutical Society of Great Britain
MRSC	Member of the Royal Society of Chemistry
MRSH	Member of the Royal Society for the Promotion of Health
MRSS	Member of the Royal Statistical Society
MRTPI	Member of the Royal Town Planning Institute
MS	Master of Surgery
MSA	Marine Safety Agency
MSAPP	Member of the Society of Advanced Psychotherapy Practitioners

MSBP	Member of the Society of Business Practitioners
MSBT	Member of the Society of Teachers in Business Education
MSc	Master of Science
MSc(Econ)	Master of Science in Economics
MSc(Ed)	Master of Science in Education
MSc(Eng)	Master of Science in Engineering
MSc(Entr)	Master of Entrepreneurship
MSc(Mgt)	Master of Science in Management
MScD	Master of Dental Science
MScEcon	Master in Faculty of Economic and Social Studies
MSCi	Master of Natural Sciences
MScTech	Master of Technical Science
MSE	Member of Society of Engineers (Inc)
MSF	Member of the SMAE Institute
MSFA	Advanced Financial Planning Certificate
MSIAD	Member of the Society of Industrial Artists and Designers
MSMA	Member of the Society of Martial Arts
MSocSc	Master of Social Science
MSSc	Master of Social Science
MSSc	Master of Surgical Science
MSSCh	Member of the British Chiropody and Podiatry Association
MSSF	Member of the Society of Shoe Fitters
MSt	Master of Studies
MSTA	Member of the Swimming Teachers' Association
MSTI	Certificate of Insurance Work
MSurgDentRCSEng	Membership in Surgical Dentistry, Royal College of Surgeons of England
MSW	Master of Social Work
MTCP	Master of Town and Country Planning
MTD	Master of Transport Design
MTech	Master of Technology
MTh	Master of Theology
MTheol	Master of Theology
MTP	Master of Town Planning
MTPI	Master of Town Planning
MTropMed	Master of Tropical Medicine
MTropPaediatrics	Master of Tropical Paediatrics
MUniv	Master of University (Honorary)
MURP	Master of Urban and Regional Planning
MusB	Bachelor of Music
MusD	Doctor of Music
MVC	Management Verification Consortium
MVM	Master of Veterinary Medicine
MVSc	Master of Veterinary Science
MWeldI	Member of the Welding Institute
MWES	Member of the Women's Engineering Society
MYD	Member of the Youth Development Association
NACOS	National Approval Council for Security Systems
NAEA	National Association of Estate Agents
NAG	National Association of Goldsmiths
NAMCW	National Association for Maternal and Child Welfare
NC	National Certificate
NCA	National Certificate in Agriculture

NCC	National Computing Centre
NCC	Navigational Control Course
NCDT	National Council for Drama Training
NCTJ	National Council for the Training of Journalists
NCVQ	National Council for Vocational Qualifications
ND	Diploma in Naturopathy
NDD	National Diploma in Design
NDF	National Diploma in Forestry
NDH	National Diploma in Horticulture
NDSF	National Diploma of the Society of Floristry
NDT	National Diploma in the Science and Practice of Turfculture and Sports Ground Management
NEBOSH	National Examination Board in Occupational Safety and Health
NEBS	National Examining Board for Supervision & Management
NFTS	National Film and Television School
NICCEA	Northern Ireland Council for the Curriculum, Examinations and Assessment
NID	National Intermediate Diploma
NIM	Northern Institute of Massage
NNEB	National Nursery Examination Board
NRHP	National Register of Hypnotherapists and Psychotherapists
NRHP(Affil)	Affiliate of the National Register of Hypnotherapists and Psychotherapists
NRHP(Assoc)	Associate of the National Register of Hypnotherapists and Psychotherapists
N-SHAP	National School of Hypnosis and Psychotherapy
NTTG	National Textile Training Group
NUJ	National Union of Journalists
NVQ	National Vocational Qualifications
NWRAC	North Western Regional Advisory Council for Further Education
OCR	Oxford, Cambridge & RSA Examinations
ODLQC	Open & Distance Learning Quality Council, formerly CACC, Council for Accreditation of Correspondence Colleges
ONC	Ordinary National Certificate
OND	Ordinary National Diploma
OSCE	Objective Structured Clinical Exam
PBTM	Professional Business and Technical Management
PCN	Personnel Certification in Non-Destructive Testing Ltd
PDP	Professional Development Programme
PESD	Private and Executive Secretary's Diploma, London Chamber of Commerce and Industry
PgC	Postgraduate Certificate
PGCE	Postgraduate Certificate in Education
PGCert	Postgraduate Certificate
PgD	Postgraduate Diploma
PGDip	Postgraduate Diploma
PGDip(Comp)	Postgraduate Diploma in Composition
PGDip(LCM)	Postgraduate Diploma of the London College of Music
PGDip(Perf)	Postgraduate Diploma in Performance
PGDip(RCM)	Postgraduate Diploma of the Royal College of Music
PGDipMin	Postgraduate Diploma in Ministry
PGDipMus	Postgraduate Diploma in Music
PhD	Doctor of Philosophy
PhD(RCA)	Doctor of Philosophy (Royal College of Art)
PIC	Professional Investment Certificate

PIFA	Practitioner of the Institute of Field Archaeologists
PIIA	Practitioner of the Institute of Internal Auditors
PInstNDT	Practitioner of the British Institute of Non-Destructive Testing
PJDip	Professional Jewellers' Diploma
PJGemDip	Professional Jewellers' Gemstone Diploma
PJManDip	Professional Jewellers' Management Diploma
PJValDip	Professional Jewellers' Valuation Diploma
PPL	Private Pilot's Licence
PPRNCM	Professional Performance Diploma of the Royal Northern College of Music
PQS	Professional Qualification Structure
PQSW	Post-Qualifying Award in Social Work
PRCA	Public Relations Consultants Association
PSC	Private Secretary's Certificate
PSD	Private Secretary's Diploma
PTA	Pianoforte Tuners' Association
PVM	Professional in Value Management
QC	Queen's Counsel
QCA	Qualifications and Curriculum Authority
QCG	Qualification in Careers Guidance
QDR	Qualified Dispute Resolver
QICA	Qualification in Computer Auditing
QIS	Qualified Imaging Scientist
QPA	Qualification in Pensions Administration
QPSPA	Qualification in Public Sector Pensions Administration
RA	Royal Academician
RAD	Royal Academy of Dancing
RADA	Royal Academy of Dramatic Art
RAM	Royal Academy of Music
RANA	Royal Animal Nursing Auxiliary
RAS	Royal Astronomical Society
RBS	Royal Ballet School
RC	Roman Catholic
RCM	Royal College of Midwives
RCN	Royal College of Nursing
RCSLT	Royal College of Speech and Language Therapists
RCVS	Royal College of Veterinary Surgeons
REA	Regional Examining Body
REC	Recruitment and Employment Confederation
Ret'dABID	Retired Associate of the British Institute of Interior Design
Ret'dFBID	Retired Fellow of the British Institute of Interior Design
Ret'dMBID	Retired Member of the British Institute of Interior Design
RGN	Registered General Nurse
RHS	Royal Horticultural Society
RHV	Registered Health Visitor
RIBA	Royal Institute of British Architects
RICS	Royal Institution of Chartered Surveyors
RINA	Royal Institution of Naval Architects
RJDip	Diploma for Retail Jewellers
RJGemDip	National Association of Goldsmiths Gemstone Diploma
RM	Registered Midwife
RMN	Registered Mental Nurse
RMS	Royal Microscopical Society

RNMH	Registered Nurse for the Mentally Handicapped
RP	Registered Plumber
RPS	Royal Photographic Society
RSA	Royal Society of Arts
RSBEI	Registered Student of the Institution of Body Engineers
RSC	Royal Society of Chemistry
RSCN	Registered Sick Children's Nurse
RSP	Registered Safety Practitioner
RTO	Recognised Training Organisation
RTPI	Royal Town Planning Institute
SA	Salvation Army Management
SBP	Society of Business Practitioners
SCAA	School Curriculum and Assessment Authority
ScD	Doctor of Science
SCE	Scottish Certificate of Education
SCLS	Second Certificate for Legal Secretaries
SCMT	Ship Captain's Medical Training
SCOTVEC	Scottish Vocational Education Council
SCPL	Senior Commercial Pilot's Licence
SE	Society of Engineers
SEE	Society of Environmental Engineers
SEFIC	Spoken English for Industry and Commerce
SenAWeldI	Senior Associate of the Welding Institute
SEng	Qualified Sales Engineer
SenMWeldI	Senior Member of the Welding Institute
SF	Society of Floristry Ltd
SFA	Securities and Futures Authority
SFInstE	Senior Fellow of the Institute of Energy
SG	Society of Genealogists
SGT	Society of Glass Technology
SHNC	Scottish Higher National Certificate
SHND	Scottish Higher National Diploma
SIEDip	Securities Industry Examination Diploma
SInstPet	Student of the Institute of Petroleum
SITO	Security Industry Training Organisation Ltd
SLC	Secretarial Language Certificate
SLD	Secretarial Language Diploma
SNC	Scottish National Certificate
SND	Scottish National Diploma
SNNEB	Scottish Nursery Nurses Examination Board
SPA	Screen Printing Association
SPRINT	Sport Play and Recreation Industries National Training Executive
SQA	Scottish Qualifications Authority
SRD	State Registered Dietician
SRN	State Registered Nurse
SSC	Secretarial Studies Certificate, London Chamber of Commerce and Industry
STA	Specialist Teacher Assistant (CACHE)
STA	Swimming Teachers' Association
STAT	Society of Teachers of the Alexander Technique
StudentIEE	Student of the Institution of Electrical Engineers
StudentIIE	Student of the Institution of Incorporated Engineers
StudentIMechE	Student of the Institution of Mechanical Engineers

StudIAP	Student of the Institution of Analysts and Programmers
StudIManf	Student Member of the Institute of Manufacturing
StudIMS	Student of the Institute of Management Specialists
StudProfBTM	Student of the Professional Business and Technical Management
StudSE	Student of the Society of Engineers (Inc)
StudSElec	Student of the Society of Electroscience
StudWeldI	Student of the Welding Institute
SVQ	Scottish Vocational Qualification
TC	Technician Certificate
TCA	Technician in Costing and Accounting
TCA	Technician of the Institute of Cost and Executive Accountants
TCert	Teacher's Certificate
TD	Technician Diploma
TDCR	Teacher's Diploma of the College of Radiographers
TechICorr	Technician of the Institute of Corrosion
TechMIWM	Technician Member of the Institute of Wastes Management
TechRICS	Technical Surveyor of the Royal Institution of Chartered Surveyors
TechRMS	Technological Qualification in Microscopy, Royal Microscopical Society
TechRTPI	Technical Member of the Royal Town Planning Institute
TechSP	Technician Safety Practitioner
TechWeldI	Technician of the Welding Institute
TEMOL	Training in Energy Management through Open Learning
TI	Textile Institute
TIMBM	Technician of the Institute of Maintenance and Building Management
TMBA	Teacher Member of the British (Theatrical) Arts
TnIMBM	Technicians of the Institute of Maintenance and Building Management
TOEFL	Test of English as a Foreign Language
TPP	Test of Professional Practice
TVM	Trainer in Value Management
UCAS	Universities and Colleges Admissions Service
UCL	University College London
UEB	United Examining Board
UKCC	United Kingdom Central Council
UKCP	United Kingdom Council for Psychotherapy
UMIST	University of Manchester Institute of Science and Technology
URC	United Reformed Church
VetMB	Bachelor of Veterinary Medicine
VTCT	Vocational Training Charitable Trust
WCMD	Welsh College of Music and Drama
WES	Women's Engineering Society
WJEC	Welsh Joint Education Committee
WMAC	West Midlands Advisory Council for Further Education
WSA	West of Scotland Agricultural College
YHAFHE	Yorkshire and Humberside Association for Further and Higher Education
ZSL	Zoological Society of London

Part 1

Introduction

Since its first publication in 1970, *British Qualifications* has charted a number of fundamental changes in further and higher education provision in the UK. Major advances in technology and more flexible delivery and attendance patterns have created different types of learning opportunity, encouraging an ever more diverse student population to access education at all levels. The range of subjects delivered has grown beyond all recognition. New areas of research have been established and developed into major subject specialisms. Employers and professional bodies have collaborated to develop subject areas aligned to changing industry requirements. Flexibility and choice are the hallmarks of today's system, and anyone new to higher education might well be bewildered by the sheer variety of degree pathways available. The capacity to combine and mix modules and subjects has in fact grown beyond anything that could have been imagined in 1970.

Traditional boundaries between academic and vocational pathways continue to break down, and today most degrees have a vocational slant. Extended industry and professional placements, sponsored research projects, practitioner input and field-based assignments are common features in many degrees, and provide an important link into practice at the early stages of learning. Overall in 20 years, universities have doubled in size and the responsibilities they have taken on have expanded considerably.

Collaboration between further and higher education (HE) institutions has enabled a substantial amount of HE-level provision to be delivered in further education institutions. Clear progression routes have been established for some time.

Considerable breadth of provision is now available in further education. Not only has the sector grown to accommodate sub-degree provision, it has continued to deliver a wide range of pre- and post-18 vocational qualifications, which include technical, occupational and professional awards.

Today, certain types of external qualification cross the boundaries between further and higher education. Several higher education institutions (HEIs) – particularly those that gained university status in the 1990s and more recently in 2005 – deliver advanced professional qualifications and higher national diplomas or certificates awarded by awarding bodies like Edexcel, OCR and SQA. At the same time there has been a significant shift towards further education's involvement in delivery of these types of qualification, and a greater input from private sector colleges.

EDUCATION REFORM

The Higher Education Act 2004 introduced in 2006/07 brought new student support and tuition fee arrangements. For full-time UK and EU undergraduate students, institutions may charge up to £3,290 (2010/11 figures), and this may influence where individuals choose to study. An independent review of higher education funding and student finance was launched in November 2009. At the time of writing, the review is still ongoing. (Further authoritative, official information about universities and colleges in the UK can be found at the Unistats website, www.unistats.com.) Information on student finance can be found at www.direct.gov.uk.

As well as implementing reforms, the further and higher education sectors contribute to UK economic performance and the delivery of the government's policies on HE. As part of this shared responsibility a great deal of effort is being made to increase access to and participation in education, particularly among individuals who have not had much involvement in the past. The general availability of modular study programmes and related credit recognition of units, and greater use of ICT and e-learning resources, have done a lot to create more flexible methods of delivery and attendance requirements in further and higher education.

FOUNDATION DEGREES

Foundation degrees (FDs) were established to give people the intermediate technical and professional skills that are in demand from employers, and to provide more flexible and accessible ways of studying. They are a higher level qualification awarded by universities. The qualification can be 'built up' from a range of relevant learning experiences, to allow for extremely flexible and adaptable qualifications that can be 'tailored' by employers to support their workforce and business development needs. They offer opportunities for employment and career advancement. Progression routes include links with associated professional qualifications and/or direct entry to the final year of a relevant Honours-level degree. FDs are offered by universities, colleges and other providers.

The first FDs in 2001 were studied by 4,000 students. In 2010, there were just over 99,700 enrolled on FDs. Close to 4,000 FD courses were available in 2010, with a further 900 new courses in development. Foundation degree forward (*fdf*) was established in the 2003 Higher Education White Paper; it is the centre of expertise on Foundation degrees and its website www.fdf.ac.uk/ provides up-to-date information and guidance on all aspects of FDs for students, employers and institutions, including the full range of courses and illustrative case study material.

POLICY AND REGULATION

National priorities for further and higher education are now set by the UK and Scottish parliaments and the Welsh and Northern Ireland assemblies, following devolution in 1999/2000. Policy development, planning and implementation rest with the government departments responsible for each national education brief – the Department for Business, Innovation and Skills (BIS), the Department for Employment and Learning Northern Ireland (DELNI), the Scottish Executive, and the Department for Children, Education, Lifelong Learning and Skills (DCELLS) in Wales.

In England, delivery of further education is subject to external audit and public reporting by the Office for Standards in Education, Children's Services and Schools (Ofsted). In Scotland, the Scottish Funding Council (SFC) has overall responsibility for planning, funding and quality assurance of further education through its work with Her Majesty's Inspectorate of Education (HMIE).

DCELLS is responsible for planning, funding and promotion of all post-16 education in Wales. Estyn (the Welsh-language acronym for Her Majesty's Inspectorate for Education and Training in Wales, website: www.estyn.gov.uk) is the appointed authority for audit of the quality of provision and related areas.

The Department for Employment and Learning (DELNI) is responsible for planning and funding of further education provision in Northern Ireland. Inspection and audit are undertaken by the Education and Training Inspectorate on behalf of the Department (www.delni.gov.uk, www.etini.gov.uk).

QUALITY ASSURANCE

A degree of convergence does exist in the area of quality assurance of qualifications at Level 3 and below. England, Wales and Northern Ireland share a common qualifications system, and the regulators in each country (listed below) work together in regulating qualifications for use across the three countries. Scotland has a separate qualifications system, although there is close correlation across all four countries, particularly in the area of vocational qualifications.

The following four bodies are responsible for the accreditation and standards of external qualifications and for curriculum and assessment for ages 3–16:

- England: Ofqual: Office of the Qualifications and Examinations Regulator;
- Northern Ireland: Council for Curriculum, Examinations and Assessment (CCEA*);
- Scotland: Scottish Qualifications Authority (SQA*);
- Wales: Department for Children, Education, Lifelong Learning and Skills (DCELLS).

*CCEA is also an Awarding Body for qualifications in Northern Ireland, which include National Qualifications to A level. SQA is also an Awarding Body that develops and validates SQA-branded qualifications including National Qualifications (Access, Intermediate, Higher and Advanced Higher Levels), Higher National Certificates and Diplomas, Scottish Vocational Qualifications and Scottish Professional Awards.

In higher education the responsibility for standards and quality rests firmly with each institution. All institutions work with the independent Quality Assurance Agency for Higher Education (QAA) for England, Northern Ireland, Scotland and Wales. Institutional audits and subject-level reviews have been undertaken by QAA since 2001. It publishes its findings on its website as publicly accessible information; see www.qaa.ac.uk.

Given the scale and diversity of degree provision in the present-day higher education sector, there has been a need to clarify what can reasonably be expected from undergraduate and postgraduate programmes. QAA has responded to this requirement and developed a code of practice for higher education providers, and subject benchmark statements indicating the expected standards of degrees across a range of subjects.

QUALIFICATION FRAMEWORKS

In further response to the breadth and diversity of qualifications available, a number of national qualification frameworks have been introduced. The framework concept is closely associated with greater transparency and comparability between types of qualification, particularly between those that were traditionally classified as academic or vocational. Common characteristics of all frameworks include universal adoption and understanding of qualification titles, and national tariffs of credits that recognize relevant levels of achievement.

The framework for Higher Education Qualifications in England, Wales and Northern Ireland (FHEQ) applies to degrees, diplomas, certificates and other academic awards by higher education providers (Figure 1.1).

The Scottish Credit and Qualification Framework (SCQF) was developed by SQA, the Scottish Executive, QAA (Scottish Office) and Universities for Scotland. It provides an overview of all levels of national and higher qualifications provision in Scotland (Figure 1.2).

The Qualifications and Credit Framework (QCF) is a new framework for recognizing and accrediting qualifications in England, Wales and Northern Ireland. The intention behind the

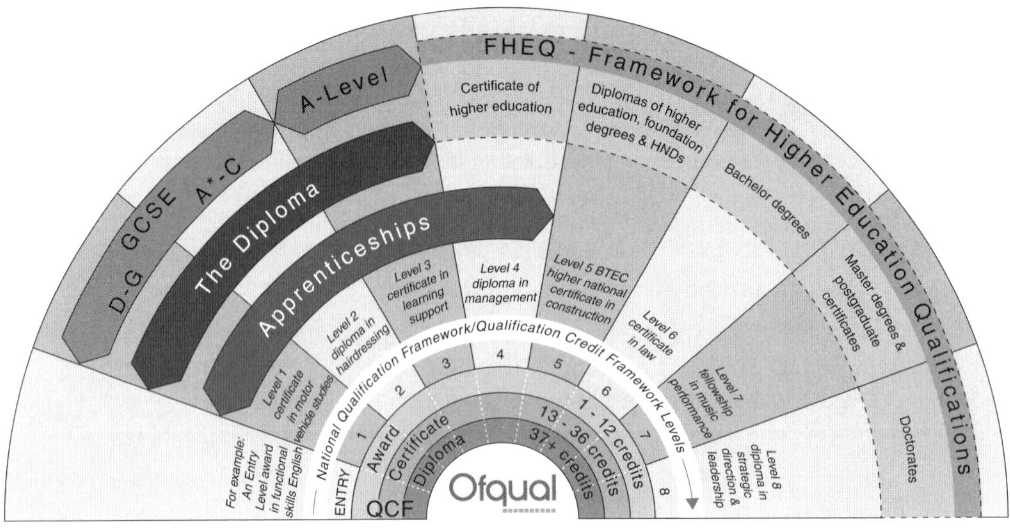

Figure 1.1 Framework for Higher Education Qualifications in England, Wales and Northern Ireland
Source: www.qaa.ac.uk

reform was to make the system and qualifications offered far more relevant to the needs of employers, with more flexibility for learners. Every unit and qualification in the framework has a credit value (where one credit represents 10 hours) and a level between Entry level and level 8. There are three sizes of qualification in the QCF:

Awards: 1–12 credits
Certificates: 13–36 credits
Diplomas: 37 credits or more

This means that each qualification title contains the level (from Entry to level 8), the size (Award/Certificate/Diploma) and the details of the content of the qualification. For a full list of accredited qualifications please visit the National Database of Accredited Qualifications at www.accreditedqualifications.org.uk. This is a fully searchable database of qualifications that are accredited by Ofqual, DCELLS and CCEA.

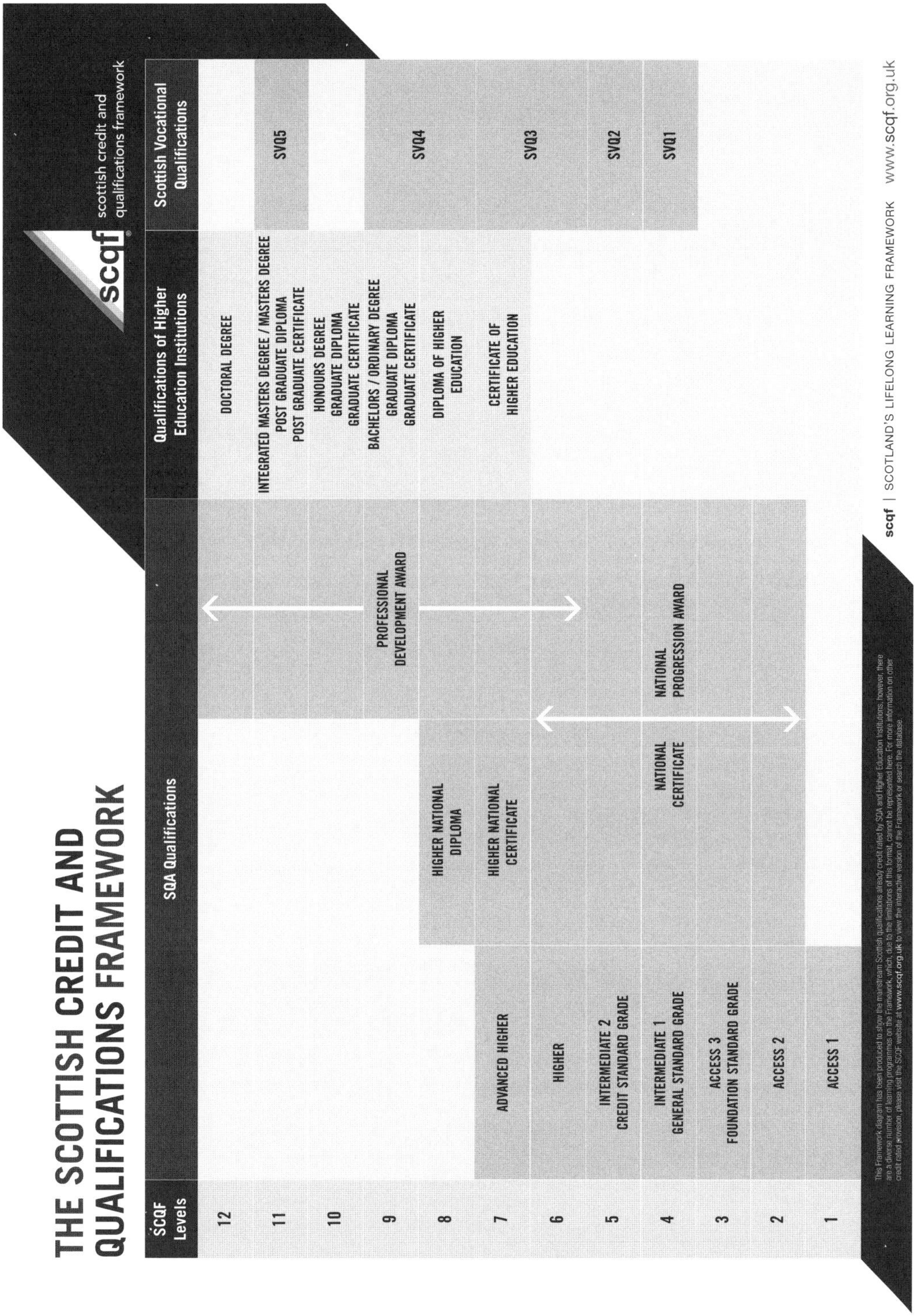

THE SCOTTISH CREDIT AND QUALIFICATIONS FRAMEWORK

scqf scottish credit and qualifications framework

SCQF Levels	SQA Qualifications			Qualifications of Higher Education Institutions	Scottish Vocational Qualifications
12				DOCTORAL DEGREE	
11				INTEGRATED MASTERS DEGREE / MASTERS DEGREE POST GRADUATE DIPLOMA POST GRADUATE CERTIFICATE	SVQ5
10				HONOURS DEGREE GRADUATE DIPLOMA GRADUATE CERTIFICATE	
9			PROFESSIONAL DEVELOPMENT AWARD	BACHELORS / ORDINARY DEGREE GRADUATE DIPLOMA GRADUATE CERTIFICATE	SVQ4
8		HIGHER NATIONAL DIPLOMA		DIPLOMA OF HIGHER EDUCATION	
7	ADVANCED HIGHER	HIGHER NATIONAL CERTIFICATE		CERTIFICATE OF HIGHER EDUCATION	SVQ3
6	HIGHER				
5	INTERMEDIATE 2 CREDIT STANDARD GRADE				SVQ2
4	INTERMEDIATE 1 GENERAL STANDARD GRADE	NATIONAL CERTIFICATE	NATIONAL PROGRESSION AWARD		SVQ1
3	ACCESS 3 FOUNDATION STANDARD GRADE				
2	ACCESS 2				
1	ACCESS 1				

This Framework diagram has been produced to show the mainstream Scottish qualifications already credit rated by SQA and Higher Education Institutions, however, there are a diverse number of learning programmes on the Framework, which, due to the limitations of this format, cannot be represented here. For more information on other credit rated provision, please visit the SCQF website at **www.scqf.org.uk** to view the interactive version of the Framework or search the database.

scqf | SCOTLAND'S LIFELONG LEARNING FRAMEWORK www.scqf.org.uk

Figure 1.2 Framework for Higher Education Qualifications in Scotland

Part 2

Teaching Establishments

The statutory responsibility for the provision of education in the United Kingdom lies with the Department for Education and the Department for Business, Innovation and Skills (BIS) in England, the Welsh Assembly Government's Department for Children, Education, Lifelong Learning and Skills (DCELLS), the Education Department of the Scottish government and the Department of Education and Department of Employment and Learning in Northern Ireland. In the United Kingdom the statutory system of public education has three progressive stages: primary education (up to the age of 11 or 12), secondary education (up to age 16), and further education (post-16).

This section briefly describes further and higher provision and the main types of institution.

FURTHER AND HIGHER EDUCATION

'Higher education' is a generic term that broadly defines any course of study leading to a qualification at level 4 and above in the National Qualifications Credit Framework for England, Wales and Northern Ireland, and level 6 and above in the Scottish Credit and Qualifications Framework.

Higher education incorporates study towards a wide range of qualifications including Foundation, undergraduate and postgraduate degrees, certificates and diplomas awarded by individual universities and other higher education institutions (HEIs) with degree-awarding powers.

It can also include study towards general, technical or occupationally-related diplomas and certificates awarded by the large unitary awarding bodies. Unitary awarding bodies are characterized by their breadth of provision, from GNVQ and A levels through to qualifications at level 5 and above in the national frameworks.

The other category that can be characterized as higher education includes post-experience education above level 4 (and level 7 in Scotland). This includes qualifications available from awarding bodies that represent a particular sector, occupation or technical/craft area, and professional institutions that are also approved as awarding bodies.

Higher education can take place in universities and HEIs (which continue to provide the majority of undergraduate and postgraduate courses). It can also take place in colleges of further education. A significant number of colleges deliver parts of, and in some cases entire, Foundation and undergraduate degree courses in agreement with a selected university partner that is responsible for Quality Assurance and final awards.

In general terms, further education is available for students who are over the age of 16 and still in full-time education, and for adults aged 19 and over. Further education provision includes GCSEs, A levels and other types of general and vocational qualifications below level 4 (and level 6 in Scotland) in the National Qualifications Frameworks.

All qualifications are awarded by approved external awarding bodies that include AQA, City & Guilds, Edexcel, LCCI, OCR, OCN and SQA in Scotland. This also includes qualifications below level 4 (level 6 in Scotland) that have a craft or technical focus or are related to an occupation/sector. At the time of writing, readers who want to find out more about approved qualifications below level 4 will find the National Database of Accredited Qualifications website informative (www.accreditedqualifications.org.uk). It contains details of all those qualifications which are accredited by the regulators of external qualifications in England (Ofqual), Wales (DCELLS) and Northern Ireland (CCEA).

FURTHER AND HIGHER EDUCATION INSTITUTIONS

England and Wales

There is a wide range of further and higher education establishments, including colleges with various titles. There are also a number of independent specialist establishments, like secretarial and correspondence colleges.

According to latest figures available, there were 120 universities, 49 other education institutions and 444 further education colleges (of which 95 were sixth form colleges) in the UK in 2007/2008. Of the universities, 98 are in England (including The Open University), 7 are in Wales, 13 are in Scotland and 2 are in Northern Ireland. Courses include those for first and second degrees, certain graduate-equivalent qualifications, and the examinations of the principal professional associations. These institutions also provide courses leading to important qualifications below degree level, such as Foundation degrees, Higher National Diplomas and Certificates, and Diplomas of Higher Education.

Most colleges of further education specialize in providing courses which lead to qualifications below degree level, such as A levels and BTEC qualifications. Some offer degree courses, including in many cases Foundation degrees.

Students aged 16–18 who have been ordinarily resident in the UK for three years and European Community nationals normally have the right to attend a full-time course without paying tuition fees. Colleges are free to determine fee levels for other students.

Scotland

There are 43 colleges of further education in Scotland which provide a broad mix of courses, many awarded by the Scottish Qualifications Authority (SQA). Most courses of higher education at or near degree level and beyond are provided by the 13 universities, The Open University in Scotland and the 7 other HEIs. These institutions offer a range of vocationally-oriented courses ranging from science, engineering and computing to health care, art and design, music and drama, and teacher training, as well as the more traditional 'academic' courses. All the universities and HEIs are funded by the Scottish Funding Council.

Northern Ireland

Responsibility for the further education sector in Northern Ireland rests with the Department for Employment and Learning (DELNI) which directly funds colleges. There are six further education colleges, and these offer a wide range of vocational and non-vocational courses for both full-time and part-time students.

Queen's University Belfast and the University of Ulster receive funding from the Department for Employment and Learning, Northern Ireland.

Many of the courses in both universities are designed to suit the needs of industry, commerce and the professions. Agricultural, horticultural and food colleges in Northern Ireland are administered through the Department of Agriculture, as in Scotland.

UNIVERSITIES AND HE COLLEGES

Universities are self-governing bodies, largely financed by the government through the Higher Education Funding Councils in the UK. They generally derive their rights and privileges from Royal Charter or Act of Parliament, and any amendment of their charters or statutes is made by the Crown acting through the Privy Council on the application of the universities themselves. The universities alone decide what degrees they award and the conditions on which they be awarded; they alone decide which students to admit and which staff to appoint. However, government policies have started to influence admission criteria, particularly in the area of widening access and participation in higher education. Student fees set by universities are also subject to strict guidelines set by the government.

Institutions receiving funding from Higher Education Funding Council for England (Source: Higher Education Funding Council for England)

The 19 schools and institutes of the University of London which receive funds directly from the HEFCE are marked *.

Anglia Ruskin University; Aston University; University of Bath; Bath Spa University; University of Bedfordshire; Birkbeck College*; University of Birmingham; University College Birmingham; Birmingham City University; Bishop Grosseteste University College Lincoln; University of Bolton; Arts University College at Bournemouth; Bournemouth University; University of Bradford; University of Brighton; University of Bristol; Brunel University; Buckinghamshire New University; University of Cambridge; Institute of Cancer Research*; Canterbury Christ Church University; University of Central Lancashire; Central School of Speech and Drama*; University of Chester; University of Chichester; City University, London; Conservatoire for Dance and Drama; Courtauld Institute of Art*; Coventry University; Cranfield University; University for the Creative Arts; University of Cumbria; De Montfort University; University of Derby; Durham University; University of East Anglia; University of East London; Edge Hill University; Institute of Education*; University of Essex; University of Exeter; University College Falmouth; University of Gloucestershire; Goldsmiths College*; University of Greenwich; Guildhall School of Music and Drama; Harper Adams University College; University of Hertfordshire; Heythrop College*; University of Huddersfield; University of Hull; Imperial College London; Keele University; University of Kent; King's College London*; Kingston University; Lancaster University; University of Leeds; Leeds College of Music; Leeds Metropolitan University; Leeds Trinity and University College; University of Leicester; University of Lincoln; University of Liverpool; Liverpool Hope University; Liverpool Institute for Performing Arts; Liverpool John Moores University; University of London; University of the Arts, London; London Business School*; London School of Economics and Political Science*; London School of Hygiene and Tropical Medicine*; London Metropolitan University; London South Bank University; Loughborough University; University of Manchester; Manchester Metropolitan University; Middlesex University; Newcastle University; Newman University College; University of Northampton; Northumbria University; Norwich University College of the Arts; University of Nottingham; Nottingham Trent University; The Open University; School of Oriental and African Studies*; University of Oxford; Oxford Brookes University; School of Pharmacy*; University of Plymouth; University College Plymouth Marjon; University of Portsmouth; Queen Mary, University of London*; Ravensbourne; University of Reading; Roehampton University; Rose Bruford College; Royal Academy of Music*; Royal Agricultural College; Royal College of Art; Royal College of Music; Royal Holloway, University of

London*; Royal Northern College of Music; Royal Veterinary College*; St George's University of London*; St Mary's University College; University of Salford; University of Sheffield; Sheffield Hallam University; University of Southampton; Southampton Solent University; Staffordshire University; University Campus Suffolk; University of Sunderland; University of Surrey; University of Sussex; Teeside University; Thames Valley University; Trinity Laban Conservatoire of Music and Dance; UCL*; University of Warwick; University of the West of England, Bristol; University of Westminster; University of Winchester; University of Wolverhampton; University of Worcester; Writtle College; University of York; York St John University.

Universities receiving funding from the Department for Employment and Learning in Northern Ireland (source: Higher Education Funding Council for England)

Queen's University Belfast; University of Ulster.

Higher Education Institutions receiving funding from the Scottish Funding Council (Source: Scottish Further and Higher Education Funding Council)

University of Aberdeen; University of Abertay Dundee; University of Dundee; Edinburgh College of Art; University of Edinburgh; Glasgow Caledonian University; Glasgow School of Art; University of Glasgow; Heriot-Watt University; Napier University; The Open University in Scotland; Queen Margaret University, Edinburgh; Robert Gordon University; Royal Scottish Academy of Music and Drama; Scottish Agricultural College; University of St Andrews; University of Stirling; University of Strathclyde; University of the West of Scotland; UHI Millennium Institute.

Institutions receiving funding from the Higher Education Funding Council for Wales (source: Higher Education Funding Council for Wales)

Aberystwyth University; Bangor University; Cardiff University; University of Glamorgan; Glyndwr University; University of Wales, Lampeter; University of Wales, Newport; The Open University in Wales; Swansea Metropolitan University; Swansea University; Trinity University College; UWIC (University of Wales Institute, Cardiff).

OTHER HE ORGANIZATIONS

There are a number of other organizations involved in shaping the Higher Education sector, for example the British Academy, the General Medical Council and Research Councils UK. You can find a full list of these organizations on the Universities UK website, www.universitiesuk.ac.uk.

Part 3

Qualifications

INTRODUCTION

Definition of Common Terms

A number of terms are commonly used as synonyms for qualifications, for example, 'examinations' and 'courses'. This can hide important differences of meaning and lead to confusion and misunderstanding. In some contexts it may be important to make these differences explicit in order to guard against exaggerating or diminishing the level of achievement, which is an essential core of the concept of qualification. It is especially important to clarify the difference in meaning between 'examination', 'course' and 'qualification'.

Examination

An examination is a formal test or assessment. It can focus on one or more of the following: knowledge, understanding, skill or competence. An examination may be set as a written test, an oral test, an aural and oral test (eg, a foreign language test) or a practical test. In the past, most forms of external assessment in FE were based on a model of examination dominated by the psychometric model, designed to discriminate between individuals – normative referencing – and took the form of written tests. There was considerable variation in different kinds of written examination, ranging through essays, question and answer, and 'multiple response'. Today, largely as a result of the introduction of National Vocational Qualifications (NVQs), the purpose and format of many examinations have been reappraised, and criterion-referenced examinations that focus on achievement (and in the case of NVQs, competence) are increasingly common. Many forms of assessment are now an integral part of the learning process, with a formative as well as a summative function rather than a separate, terminal, summative function.

Course

A course implies an ordered sequence of teaching or learning over a period of time. A course is governed by regulations or requirements, frequently imposed by an external awarding body and sometimes by the institution providing the course. An important distinguishing feature between different courses is the length of time allocated to study: it can vary from a few days to several years. Some courses offer a terminal award on the basis of course completion, and these courses are set for a given period of time. Other 'set period' courses may prescribe examinations; these can include continuous assessment, terminal testing or a combination of both. In other courses, the programme of study may be accomplished at a faster or slower rate; such courses normally enjoin continuous assessment or a terminal examination, or both. Many courses require attendance at an institution, while distance learning, correspondence courses, and various forms of flexible-learning courses are usually free of these requirements, although some of these courses may require occasional attendance for residential components or face-to-face tutoring. A successful examination result usually confers a qualification or an award.

Qualification

A qualification is normally a certificated endorsement, from a recognized awarding body, that a level or quality of accomplishment has been achieved by an individual. Qualifications are usually conferred on successful completion of an examination, although not all examinations necessarily offer qualifications. An examination may offer an award that is a part-qualification. For example, an NVQ candidate may acquire a unit of competence that is a part-qualification building towards a full statement of competence – an NVQ. A first-year student on an HND course may be required to pass all first-year examinations in order to be permitted to continue into the second year; in a sense, that student is 'qualified' to continue the course but no qualification is awarded. Some award-bearing examinations may be fully recognized and certificated qualifications in themselves (eg, a BTEC HNC) but only part-qualifications for a profession (eg, Chartered Engineer).

Apparent anomalies do exist. Some professional bodies and trade associations award qualifications that are recognized within the profession or association but that are not obtained by examination. They are usually awarded on the basis of experience, and payment of a fee, and denote membership or acceptance. When the body also offers an examination route to the same qualification, successful examinees are usually known as 'graduate members'.

There are a number of accreditation authorities that approve qualifications. There are also many specialist and general validating, examining and awarding bodies that are responsible for the design and assessment of qualifications.

ACCREDITING REGULATORY BODIES

England

Sector Skill Councils

The Alliance of Sector Skills Councils launched in April 2008 is an organization that supports the network of licensed UK Sector Skills Councils (SSCs). These are employer-led, independent organizations that cover specific work sectors across the UK (currently accounting for approximately 90 per cent of the UK workforce). With the influence granted by licences from the governments of England, Scotland, Wales and Northern Ireland, and with private and public funding, this independent network engages with the education and training supply-side, such as universities, colleges, funders and qualifications bodies, to increase productivity at all levels in the workforce. Details are listed in Table 3.1.

Table 3.1 Sector Skill Councils

Asset Skills
Sector: Property and planning, housing, cleaning sectors and facilities management
Tel: 01392 423399
E-mail: info@assetskills.org
Website: www.assetskills.org

Cogent
Sector: Chemical and pharmaceutical, oil, nuclear, gas, petroleum and polymer
Tel: 01925 515200
E-mail: info@cogent-ssc.com
Website: www.cogent-ssc.com

ConstructionSkills
Sector: Construction
Tel: 0344 994 4400
E-mail: call.centre@cskills.org
Website: www.cskills.org

Creative & Cultural Skills
Sector: Crafts, music, performing, heritage, design and visual arts
Tel: 020 7015 1800
E-mail: info@ccskills.org.uk
Website: www.ccskills.org.uk

Energy & Utility Skills
Sector: Gas, power, waste management and water industries
Tel: 08450 779922
E-mail: enquiries@euskills.co.uk
Website: www.euskills.co.uk

e-skills UK
Sector: Business and information technology
Tel: 020 7963 8920
E-mail: info@e-skills.com
Website: www.e-skills.com

continued

Table 3.1 *Continued*

Financial Services Skills Council
Sector: Financial services, accountancy and finance
Tel: 08452 573772
E-mail: info@fssc.org.uk
Website: www.fssc.org.uk

GoSkills
Sector: Passenger transport
Tel: 01216 355520
E-mail: info@goskills.org
Website: www.goskills.org

Government Skills
Sector: Central Government
Tel: 0207 215 1424
E-mail: info@government-skills.gsi.gov.uk
Website: www.government-skills.gov.uk

Improve Ltd
Sector: Food and drinks manufacturing and processing
Tel: 08456 440448
E-mail: info@improveltd.co.uk
Website: www.improveltd.co.uk

The Institute of the Motor Industry
Sector: Retail motor industries
Tel: 01992 511521
E-mail: imi@motor.org.uk
Website: www.motor.org.uk

Lantra
Sector: Environmental and land-based
Tel: 0845 707 8007
E-mail: connect@lantra.co.uk
Website: www.lantra.co.uk

Lifelong Learning UK
Sector: Community learning education, FE, HE, libraries, work-based learning and training providers
Tel: 0300 303 8077
E-mail: advice@lluk.org
Website: www.lluk.org

People 1st
Sector: Hospitality, leisure, travel and tourism
Tel: 01895 817000
E-mail: info@people1st.co.uk
Website: www.people1st.co.uk

Proskills UK
Sector: Building products, coatings, extractive and mineral processing, furniture, furnishings and interiors, glass and glazing, glazed ceramics, paper and printing
Tel: 01235 833844
E-mail: info@proskills.co.uk
Website: www.proskills.co.uk

SEMTA
Sector: Science, engineering and manufacturing technologies
Tel: 0845 643 9001
E-mail: customerservices@semta.org.uk
Website: www.semta.org.uk

Skills for Care & Development
Sector: Social care, children and young people's services
Tel: 0113 390 7666
E-mail: sscinfo@skillsforcareanddevelopment.org.uk
Website: www.skillsforcareanddevelopment.org.uk

Skills for Health
Sector: Healthcare
Tel: 01179 221155
E-mail: office@skillsforhealth.org.uk
Website: www.skillsforhealth.org.uk

Skills for Justice
Sector: Justice, community safety and legal services
Tel: 01142 611 499
E-mail: info@skillsforjustice.com
Website: www.skillsforjustice.com

continued

Table 3.1 *Continued*

Skills for Logistics
Sector: Freight logistics and wholesaling industries
Tel: 01908 313360
E-mail: info@skillsforlogistics.org
Website: www.skillsforlogistics.org

SkillsActive
Sector: Sport and recreation, health and fitness, outdoors, playwork and caravanning industry
Tel: 020 7632 2000
E-mail: skills@skillsactive.com
Website: www.skillsactive.com

Skillset
Sector: TV, film, radio, interactive media, animation, computer games, facilities, fashion and textiles, photo imaging and publishing
Tel: 020 7713 9800
E-mail: info@skillset.org
Website: www.skillset.org

Skillsmart Retail
Sector: Retail
Tel: 020 7462 5060
E-mail: contactus@skillsmartretail.com
Website: www.skillsmartretail.com

SummitSkills
Sector: Building services engineering
Tel: 01908 303960
E-mail: enquiries@summitskills.org.uk
Website: www.summitskills.org.uk

The Alliance of Sector Skills Councils (ASSC)
Tel: 08450 725600
E-mail: info@sscalliance.org
Website: www.sscalliance.org

The Qualifications and Curriculum Development Agency (QCDA)

53–55 Butts Road, Earlsdon Park, Coventry CV1 3BH, Tel: 0300 303 3010, e-mail: info@qcda.gov.uk

QCDA is a public body, sponsored by the Department for Education, which is currently responsible for the development of the national curriculum, qualifications and delivery of assessment.

Ofqual: Office of the Qualifications and Examinations Regulator

Ofqual's role is to ensure all learners get the results they deserve, standards are maintained, and their qualifications are correctly valued and understood, now and in the future. It regulates exams, qualifications and tests in England and vocational qualifications in Northern Ireland.

In 2009, the government passed legislation in the form of the Apprenticeship, Skills, Children and Learning Act, which established Ofqual as the regulator of qualifications, examinations and tests in England. Ofqual commenced work as a fully independent non-ministerial government department on 1 April 2010. Ofqual is now accountable to Parliament rather than to government ministers.

Scotland

Scottish Qualifications Authority (SQA)

Customer Contact Centre, tel 0845 279 1000, fax 0845 213 5000, e-mail customer@sqa.org.uk

The Scottish Qualifications Authority (SQA) is the national accreditation and awarding body in Scotland. SQA is an executive non-departmental public body (NDPB) sponsored by the Scottish government's Learning Directorate.

SQA works in partnership with schools, colleges, universities and industry to provide high-quality, flexible and relevant qualifications and assessments – embedding industry standards where appropriate. We strive to ensure that SQA qualifications are inclusive, accessible to all, that they provide clear progression pathways, facilitate lifelong learning and recognize candidate achievement.

People take our qualifications at all stages of their lives – at school, at college, at work, and in their leisure time. There are qualifications at all levels of attainment. QA is responsible for three main types of qualification: units, courses and group awards.

Most SQA-awarded qualifications are made up of a combination of units, which can also be used in their own right. Each unit represents approximately 40 hours of teaching with additional study. You achieve a unit by passing an assessment.

Courses consist of Standard Grades and six National Courses levels – Access 2 & 3, Intermediate 1 & 2, Higher, Advanced Higher and the Scottish Baccalaureate. They are mainly taken at school but some colleges may also offer provision at some levels.

National Qualification Group Awards are designed to be taken at college – National Certificates (NCs), Higher National Certificates and Diplomas (HNCs and HNDs) and National Progression Awards (NPAs) – and the workplace: Scottish Vocational Qualifications (SVQs), Professional Development Awards (PDAs) and Customized Awards. A private company or training provider must become an 'approved centre' to deliver SQA qualifications, or work in partnership with a college or training provider.

Standard Grades and National Courses

Standard Grades are generally taken over two years in the third and fourth years of secondary school. The courses are made up of different parts, called elements, usually with an exam at the end of fourth year.

National Courses, with the exception of Access level, are made up of three units plus an external assessment usually an examination. These can be taken in the fourth, fifth and sixth years at school.

There is a comprehensive appeals system for those who do not perform as well as expected.

About Higher National Qualifications

Higher National Certificates (HNCs) and Higher National Diplomas (HNDs) are developed by SQA in partnership with further education colleges, universities, and industry and commerce. They are credible, flexible qualifications that are designed to deliver the skills and knowledge to meet the needs of today's businesses.

National Progression Awards (NPAs)

NPAs are designed to assess a defined set of skills and knowledge in specialist vocational areas. They are mainly used by colleges for short programmes of study.

National Certificates

National Certificates are primarily aimed at 16–18-year-olds and adults in full-time education, normally at a college. They prepare candidates for employment or further study, by developing a range of knowledge and skills.

Scottish Vocational Qualifications (SVQs)

SVQs are based on job competence, and recognize the skills and knowledge people need in employment. SVQs can be attained in most occupations and are available for all types and levels of job.

They are primarily delivered to candidates in full-time employment and in the workplace.

Professional Development Awards (PDAs)

PDAs are qualifications for people who are already in a career and who wish to extend or broaden their skills. In some cases they are designed for people wishing to enter employment. PDAs can be taken at college or the workplace.

Customised Awards

Though these qualifications meet the needs of the majority of organizations, SQA also offers specially designed vocational qualifications at any level to meet an organization's need for skills and expertise.

Scottish Credit and Qualifications Framework

The SQA is a partner in a 'credit' system called the Scottish Credit and Qualifications Framework (SCQF), which helps to understand Scottish qualifications and how they relate to one another by making clear the credit value of each type of qualification available in Scotland.

The framework has 12 levels: from Level 1 for very basic education to Level 12 for doctoral degrees.

More information about SQA and its qualifications can be found at their website www.sqa.org.uk

VALIDATING, EXAMINING AND AWARDING BODIES/ORGANIZATIONS

A large number of external bodies provide qualifications recognized by accrediting and regulatory bodies. Not all qualifications are available across the entire further education sector: some colleges specialize in particular vocational areas, while others are involved in more general adult education provision.

The Federation of Awarding Bodies (FAB) is a trade federation and membership organization for vocational awarding bodies. At the time of writing FAB has 97 Ofqual recognized awarding bodies as full members. It also has associate members. www.awarding.org.uk.

It is important to contact the examining or awarding bodies directly to find which colleges deliver the qualifications desired. However, most colleges deliver courses leading to qualifications awarded by the sample selection of organizations listed in the following section:

ABC Awards

Robins Wood House, Robins Wood Road, Aspley, Nottingham NG8 3NH, Tel: 0115 854 1616, Fax: 0115 854 1617, E-mail: enquiries@abcawards.co.uk, Website: www.abcawards.co.uk

ABC Awards is a vocational awarding organization with accredited QCF qualifications in all sectors. Many of ABC's qualifications are included in the Foundation Learning Catalogue and are recognized as being eligible for apprenticeships and additional and specialist learning for diplomas. ABC Awards is dedicated to working with centres to deliver exceptional and flexible qualifications.

AQA

Stag Hill House, Guildford, Surrey GU2 7XJ, Tel: 01483 506 506, Fax: 01483 300 152, E-mail: mailbox@aqa.org.uk, Website: www.aqa.org.uk

AQA is the largest of the English exam boards currently awarding around 49 per cent of full course GCSEs and 42 per cent of A Levels nationally. As an awarding body AQA offers a broad range of qualifications available through academic or vocational pathways including GCEs, GCSEs, Entry Level Certificates, Basic and Key Skills, Vocationally Related Qualifications and others such as the Diploma, the Extended Project Qualification, and the AQA Baccalaureate among others.

ASDAN

Wainbrook House, Hudds Vale Road, St George, Bristol BS5 7HY, Tel: 0117 9411126, E-mail: info@asdan.org.uk, Website: www.asdan.org.uk

ASDAN is established as a registered charity for 'The advancement of education, by providing opportunities for all learners to develop their personal and social attributes and levels of achievement through ASDAN awards and resources, and the relief of poverty, where poverty inhibits such opportunities for learners.'

ASDAN offers the following qualifications:

- Key Skills (including the Wider Key Skills) Levels 1–4
- Basic Skills (Skills for Life/Adult Literacy and Numeracy/ALAN) Levels 1 and 2
- Diploma in Life Skills Entry Levels 1–3
- Certificate in Career Planning Levels 1–3
- Certificate of Personal Effectiveness (CoPE) Levels 1, 2 and 3
- Award of Personal Effectiveness (AoPE) Levels 1 and 2
- Personal and Social Development (PSD) Entry 1, 2 and 3 and Levels 1 and 2
- Community Volunteering Qualifications (CVO) Levels 1 to 3 and Volunteering at an Event Levels 1 and 2
- Employability Entry 2 – Level 3 including Enterprise and Career Education Pathways
- Personal Progress Qualifications Entry 1

To find out more about ASDAN visit www.asdan.org.uk.

City & Guilds

1 Giltspur Street, London EC1A 9DD, Tel: 020 7294 2800, Fax: 020 7294 2400,
Website: www.cityandguilds.com

City & Guilds is a leading vocational educational organization, offering more than 500 work-related qualifications worldwide. Around 2 million people every year start City & Guilds qualifications, which span from basic skills to the highest level of professional achievement.

With over 130 years of experience, we offer a wide range of qualifications from agriculture to engineering; hairdressing to health and social care; IT to tourism; and photography to catering. They are developed with the help of industry experts and are workplace-relevant, so our qualifications equip people for doing a real job – benefiting them and their employer.

City & Guilds qualifications develop both knowledge and practical skills. They are available at nine levels and are suitable for anyone, whether they are beginners or advanced in their career or area of study. Assessment is based on any combination of examination, projects or coursework.

The organizations which offer City and Guilds qualifications include schools, colleges, training organizations, companies and adult education institutes. Depending on the organization, it is possible to study full-time, part-time or through distance learning.

Edexcel Foundation

190 High Holborn, London WC1V 7BH, Tel. BTEC and NVQ: 0844 576 0026, GCSE: 0844 576 0027, GCE: 0844 576 0025, The Diploma: 0844 576 0028, DiDA and other qualifications: 0844 576 0031, Website: www.edexcel.org.uk

Edexcel is the UK's largest awarding body, operating in over 80 counties and offering a range of international qualifications including GCEs, GCSEs, vocational and business learning and adult literacy and numeracy qualifications that are offered in schools and colleges, through training providers or in the workplace. Edexcel's BTEC qualifications provide a range of widely accessible, high-quality education programmes of study directly related to employment. Edexcel approves nationally recognized qualifications and Certificates of Achievement that equip students both for employment and for further study. These include adult learning qualifications and NVQs. They are delivered through a network of approved centres around the world. It collaborates closely with industry, government and others to ensure that Edexcel programmes serve the interests of individuals, employers and the nations they are taken in.

EDI plc

International House, Siskin Parkway, Middlemarch Business Park, Coventry CV3 4PE,
Tel: 08707 202909, Fax: 02476 516505, E-mail: enquiries@ediplc.com, Website: www.ediplc.com

Education Development International plc (EDI) is a leading provider of education and training qualifications and assessment services.

In the UK, EDI is accredited by government to award a wide range of vocational qualifications, including apprenticeships and diplomas. EDI's expertise is in quality assuring work-based training programmes working closely with employers and over 1,500 private training providers and further education colleges.

Internationally, EDI trades under the London Chamber of Commerce and Industry brand and offers a range of business and English language qualifications which have a history that can be traced back to 1887. LCCI International qualifications are widely used in South East Asia and over 100 countries around the world.

The EDI website has a search facility: www.ediplc.com/Qualifications_Search.asp

NCFE

Citygate, St James' Boulevard, Newcastle upon Tyne NE1 4JE, Tel: 0191 239 8000, Fax: 0191 239 8001, E-mail: info@ncfe.org.uk, Website: www.ncfe.org.uk

NCFE is a national awarding organization and registered educational charity. It currently offers over 400 nationally accredited qualifications from Entry level up to and including Level 4 as well as NVQs, functional Skills, Diplomas, Apprenticeships and Key Skills. Further qualifications are in development. The NCFE website has a qualifications finder search facility at www.ncfe.org.uk/qualfinder.aspx

OCR

1 Hills Road, Cambridge, CB1 2EU, Tel: 01223 553998, Fax: 01223 552627,
E-mail: general.qualifications@ocr.org.uk, Website: www.ocr.org.uk

OCR is at the forefront of developing qualifications for the 21st century. It offers a range of more than 500 general and vocational qualifications, from GCSEs, A levels and Diplomas to OCR Nationals, NVQs and specialist qualifications. You can find a full index of OCR qualifications here: www.ocr.org.uk/ qualifications/index.html

WJEC

245 Western Avenue, Cardiff CF5 2YX, Tel: 02920 265000, E-mail: info@wjec.co.uk, Website: www.wjec.co.uk

WJEC is an examining board offering the following major qualifications: General Certificate of Secondary Education (GCSE); Entry Level (EL) and Advanced (A)/Advanced Supplementary (AS) levels and the Welsh Baccalaureate, a new overriding qualification for Wales available at different levels and incorporating GCSEs, A Levels, GNVQs or NVQs. In addition WJEC provides Key Essential Skills, Functional Skills in England and Project and Principal Learning Plans.

JCQ: Joint Council for Qualifications

Sixth Floor, 29 Great Peter Street, London, SW1P 3LW, Tel: 020 7638 4135/4132, Fax: 020 734 4343, E-mail: info@jcq.org.uk, Website: www.jcq.org.uk

The Joint Council for Qualifications (JCQ) was established in 2004 (supersedes the Joint Council for General Qualifications, 1998–2003) and consists of AQA, City & Guilds, CCEA, Edexcel, OCR, SQA and WJEC, the seven largest providers of qualifications in the UK, offering GCSE, GCE, AEA, Scottish Highers, Welsh Baccalaureate, Entry Level, Vocational and vocationally-related qualifications. The JCQ enables member awarding bodies to act together on a number of issues including providing, wherever possible, common administrative arrangements for the schools and colleges and other providers which offer their qualifications and dealing with the regulators; in responding to proposals and initiatives on assessment and the curriculum.

The National Database of Accredited Qualifications (NDAQ) contains details of qualifications that are accredited by the regulators of external qualifications in England (Ofqual), Wales (DCELLS) and Northern Ireland (CCEA). The website also carries a full alphabetical list of awarding bodies offering qualifications accredited by the regulatory authorities in England, Wales and Northern Ireland. For more information visit www.accreditedqualifications.org.uk.

Part 4

Qualifications Awarded in Universities

ADMISSION TO DEGREE COURSES

Higher Education Institutions (HEIs)

Most institutions have a general requirement for admission to a degree course; special requirements may be in force for particular courses. Requirements are usually expressed in terms of subjects passed at GCE A level and the Higher Grade of the SCE. The universities have a clearing-house to handle applications for university courses, UCAS, www. ucas.ac.uk. All intending students who live in the United Kingdom may obtain information on application procedures from their schools or colleges, or directly from UCAS. The scheme covers all universities and all medical schools. UCAS also has specialist services: the Graduate Teacher Training Registry (GTTR), the UK Postgraduate Application and Statistical Service (UKPASS) and the Conservatoires UK Admissions Service (CUKAS).

HEIs have specific schemes to encourage access and participation in higher education. These can include partnerships with further education colleges that run access to higher education courses.

The Open University

For admission to most first-degree courses, no formal educational qualifications are necessary. However, students who have successfully completed one or more years of full-time study at the higher education level (or its equivalent in part-time study) may be eligible for exemption from some credit requirements of the BA degree. The Open University handles its own admissions.

Business Schools

The degrees awarded by the various university business schools are postgraduate and therefore normally require an honours degree as part of their entrance qualification.

AWARDS

The awards made by the universities may be separated into the following categories: first degrees; higher degrees; honorary degrees; first diplomas and certificates; higher diplomas and certificates.

First Degrees

Nomenclature

Various names are given to the first degrees at British universities. At most universities the first degree in Arts is the BA (Bachelor of Arts) degree and the first degree in Science is the BSc (Bachelor of Science) degree. But at the universities of Oxford and Cambridge and at several new universities, the BA is the first degree gained by students in both Arts and Science. In Scotland the first arts degree at three of the four old universities is Master of Arts (MA). There are numerous variations on the bachelor theme, eg BSc (Econ) (Bachelor of Science in Economics), BCom (Bachelor of Commerce), BSocSc (Bachelor of Social Science), BEng (Bachelor of Engineering), BTech (Bachelor of Technology). The first award in medicine is the joint degrees of MB, ChB (Bachelor of Medicine, Bachelor of Surgery), the designatory letters of which vary from university to university.

Structure of Courses

First-degree courses vary considerably in structure, not only between one university and another but also between faculties in a single university. The degree examination is usually in two sections, Part 1 coming after one or two years of the course and Part II, 'finals', at the end of the course. The first-degree system at some Scottish universities differs substantially from that in English and Welsh universities (see below).

Bachelor Degrees

These degrees, sometimes known as 'ordinary' or 'first' degrees, lead to qualifications such as Bachelor of Arts (BA), Bachelor of Science (BSc) or Bachelor of Medicine (MB).

Each university decides the form and content of its own degree examinations. These vary from university to university.

The first-degree structure in all British universities is based on the Honours degree. Successful candidates in Honours degree examinations are placed in different classes according to their performance, first class being the highest. The other classes given vary from university to university, but the classification most often used is: Class I; Class II (Division 1); Class II (Division 2); Class III. Most graduates who go on to higher academic qualifications, and those entering, for example, the higher grades in the Civil Service or research, normally have an Honours degree of good class.

You can find out more about recognized UK degrees at the BIS website; www.bis.gov.uk.

Number of Subjects Studied

Excluding medicine and dentistry, the broad subject areas are Arts (or Humanities), Social Science, Pure Science and Applied Science. Most students study one main subject selected from one of these areas. It is possible to distinguish many types of degree course according to the number of subjects studied; these types are a variation on three main categories:

- honours course in one to three subjects with or without examinable subsidiary subjects;
- pass or ordinary courses in one to three subjects with or without examinable subsidiary subjects;
- commmon studies for pass and honours in one to three subjects, with or without examinable subsidiary subjects.

Length of Degree Course

First-degree courses may be preceded by a preliminary year, from which students with the appropriate entry qualifications may be exempted. At most universities honours and pass courses in arts, social science, pure and applied science last three or four years, but courses in architecture, dentistry and veterinary medicine usually last five years, and complete qualifying courses in medicine up to six years. Courses in fine arts and pharmacy may last four years; four-year courses exist mainly in double honours schools, especially when they involve foreign languages and a period of study abroad, and in the technological universities, where some courses include a period of integrated industrial training (sandwich courses).

The Scottish First Degree

The distinctive feature of first degrees at some Scottish universities is the Ordinary MA course, which has no counterpart in England and Wales, and the Ordinary BSc course. The function of the Ordinary MA is to provide a broad, general education. Scottish undergraduates are required to show during their first two years of study, over a range of subjects, that they are fit to go on to an honours degree course, which takes a further two years to complete.

Aegrotat Degrees

Candidates who have followed a course for a degree but have been prevented from taking the examinations by illness may be awarded a degree certificate indicating that they were likely to have obtained the degree had they taken the examinations.

Higher Degrees

These comprise:

- some Bachelor's degrees: BPhil, BLitt, etc;
- Master's degrees: MA, MSc, etc;
- Doctor of Philosophy: PhD or DPhil;
- Higher Doctorates: DLitt, DSc, etc.

At Oxford and Cambridge the degree of MA is conferred on any BA of the university without any further course of study or examination after a specified number of years and on payment of a fee. Candidates for a Master's degree at other universities (and at some for the degrees of BPhil, BLitt and BD, which are of equivalent standing) are normally required to have a first degree, although it need not have been obtained in the same university. Master's degrees are taken after one or two years' full-time study. The PhD requires at least two, or more usually three, years of full-time study.

In some universities and faculties students may be selected for a PhD course after an initial year's study or research common to both a PhD and a Master's degree. Candidates for a Master's degree are required either to prepare a thesis for presentation to examiners, who may afterwards question them on it orally, or to take written examination papers; they may be required to do both. All PhD students present a thesis; some may be required to take an examination paper as well. MPhil, MSc and similar degrees are usually awarded at the end of a one- or two-year course in a special topic on the results of a written examination or a thesis. Higher doctorates are designated on a faculty basis, eg DLitt (Doctor of Letters) and DSc (Doctor of Science). Candidates are usually required to have at least a Master's degree of the awarding university. Senior doctorates are conferred on more mature and established workers, usually on the basis of published contributions to knowledge.

Foundation Degrees

Foundation degrees were established to give people the intermediate technical and professional skills that are in demand from employers and to provide more flexible and accessible ways of studying. Increasing opportunities for employment and career advancement is a priority. Foundation degree content and assessment is therefore designed in consultation with employers. Additional progression routes include links with associated professional qualifications and/ or direct entry to the final year of a relevant Honours level degree.

Provision is available across a range of further education colleges and a number of HEIs.

Honorary Degrees

Most universities confer honorary degrees on persons of distinction in academic and public life, and on others who have rendered service to the university or to the local community. Normally degrees awarded are at least Foundation degree level.

Diplomas and Certificates of Higher Education

Courses for first diplomas and certificates are relatively simple in structure; they usually reach a level lower than that required for the award of a degree. There is usually a carefully defined course in a specialized or vocational subject, lasting one or two years, followed by all candidates. Most courses are full time.

Postgraduate Diplomas and Certificates

Diplomas (eg in public health, social administration, medicine and technology) are awarded either on a full-time, or less often part-time, basis according to the subject and the university. Candidates must usually be graduates or hold equivalent qualifications. Diplomas are awarded after formal courses of instruction and success in written examinations. A Certificate or Diploma in Education is awarded to graduates training to become teachers after one year's full-time study and teaching practice.

Postgraduate Courses

A number of courses for graduates or persons with equivalent qualifications are offered in further education establishments. They include short specialist courses in Management and Business Studies and secretarial courses for graduates.

Business Schools

A Master of Business Administration (MBA) is an internationally recognized postgraduate qualification intended to prepare individuals for middle to senior level general managerial positions. Most programmes contain as their core a number of subjects considered essential for understanding the operations of any enterprise. These are: accounting and finance, operations management, business policy, economics, human resource management, marketing, information systems and strategic planning.

Unlike any other Master's programme, the MBA is not only postgraduate, it is also strongly post experience. A minimum of three years' (often more) work experience at an appropriate level of responsibility is generally expected of applicants. The requirement for a first degree (or equivalent) is sometimes waived for those holding an impressive track record of over five years at managerial level. Approximately one-third of MBA students have an engineering or information technology background. Many undertake the qualification to facilitate change from technical or specialist positions to more generalist ones.

The MBA was conceived originally in the United States at the beginning of the 20th century. Introduced in the United Kingdom in the late 1960s, it did not grow in popularity until the late 1980s. The popularity of this degree in the United Kingdom can be seen in the rapid expansion in the number of providers. The Association of MBAs (AMBA) operates a system of accreditation.

The accreditation process, which is internationally recognized for all MBA, DBA and Masters in Business and Management (MBM) programmes, measures individual MBA programmes against specific accreditation criteria.

Further information, including a list of accredited MBA programmes, can be obtained from the Association of MBAs, 25 Hosier Lane, London EC1A 9LQ; Tel: 0207 246 2686, E-mail: info@mbaworld.com, Website: www.mbaworld.com.

The Association of Business Schools (ABS)

137 Euston Road, London NW1 2AA; Tel: 020 7388 0007, Fax: 020 7388 0009, E-mail: abs@the-abs.org.uk, Website: www.the-abs.org.uk

The ABS is the representative body for Management and Business Education. It has all the United Kingdom's leading business schools. The ABS works broadly in three main areas; policy development, promotion and representation and training and development.

The ABS is able to provide general information about the wide range of courses and programmes provided by the United Kingdom's business schools.

First Awards

BA, BEd, BEng, LLB, BSc: with 1st Class, 2nd Class (Divisions 1 and 2), 3rd Class Honours or Pass; or unclassified with or without Distinction.

MEng: awarded to students who successfully complete a course of study which is longer and more demanding than the BEng first degree course in Engineering.

GMus (Graduate Diploma in Music): awarded to those students who complete three years' approved full-time study (or equivalent) in Music and who demonstrate competence in musical performance.

DipHE (Diploma of Higher Education): equivalent in standard and often similar in content to the first two years of an Honours degree course.

Certificates of Higher Education: equivalent to the first year of an Honours degree course.

Higher Awards

MA, MBA, MEd, MSc: for successful completion of an approved postgraduate course of study of 48 weeks' duration (or the part-time equivalent).
MPhil, PhD: for successful completion of approved programmes of supervised research.
DSc, DLitt and DTech: for original and important contributions to knowledge and/or its applications.
Postgraduate Diploma: awarded for the successful completion of an approved postgraduate course of study of 25 weeks' duration (or the part-time equivalent).
Postgraduate Certificate: awarded for the successful completion of postgraduate/post-experience courses of 15 weeks' duration (or the part-time equivalent).
Postgraduate Certificate in Education (PGCE): awarded on completion of a one-year full-time course; candidates must be British graduates or hold another recognized qualification.
Diploma in Professional Studies: available in the fields of education and nursing, health visiting, midwifery and sports coaching. Students normally hold an initial professional qualification. A minimum of two years' experience is normally expected.

UNIVERSITY OF ABERDEEN
www.abdn.ac.uk

College of Arts and Social Sciences; www.abdn.ac.uk/about/social-sciences/php

Aberdeen Business School; www.abdn.ac.uk/business

accounting, economics, enterprise, entrepreneurship, finance, innovation, international relations, macro-economics, management studies, property & real estate management, MBA programmes; MA(Hons), MBA, MRes, MSc, PgCert, PhD

School of Divinity, History and Philosophy; www.abdn.ac.uk/sdhp

cultural history, divinity, history, history of art, philosophy, religious studies, theology, Catholic studies, Jewish studies, ministry, art & business, English & Scottish studies, social anthroplogy, visual culture; BD, BTh, DMin, LicTh, MA(Hons), MLitt, MTh, PgDip, PhD

School of Education; www.abdn.ac.uk/education

early childhood studies, music, primary education, professional development, TQFE, curative education, secondary education, tertiary education, autism, care; BA(Hons), BEd(Hons), MEd, MPhil, MRes, MSc, Mus(Hons), PGCert, PGDE, PGDip, PhD

School of Language & Literature; www.abdn.ac.uk/sll

Celtic, comparative literature, creative writing, English/literature/language, film and visual culture, French, German and Hispanic studies, Irish–Scottish studies, Latin American studies, linguistics, medieval studies, modern thought, the novel, sociolinguistics, European studies, history of Scotland, Gaelic studies, langauge and linguistics; MA, MA(Designated), MA(Hons), MLitt, PhD

School of Law; www.abdn.ac.uk/law

civil, French/German/ Belgian/Spanish law, property law, Roman law; LlB, LlB(Hons), LlM, MPhil, PhD

School of Social Science; www.abdn.ac.uk/socsc

anthropology, gender studies, politics and international relations, social anthropology, ethnology and cultural history, sociology, Latin American studies, realignment and society, globalization, Europolitics, sex & gender, violence; MA(Hons), MA, MLitt, MPhil, MRes, MSc, PGDip, PhD

College of Life Sciences and Medicine; www.abdn.ac.uk/clsm

School of Biological Sciences; www.abdn.ac.uk/biologicalsci

animal ecology, biology, conservation biology, ecology, environmental science, forest conservation/science, forestry, immunology, plant & soil science, plant biology, ecology and environmental sustainability, marine biology, parasitology, tropical environmental, wildlife management, zoology; BSc(Hons), BSc(Hons, Medical Science), MPhil, MSc, MSc/PGDip, MRes, PhD

School of Medical Science; www.abdn.ac.uk/sms

biochemistry, biomedical sciences, biotechnology, clinical pharmacology, drug development, genetics, health & human nutrition, human embryology & development, immunology, medical imaging/physics, microbiology, molecular biology, neuroscience, nursing, midwifery, pharmacology, physiology, primary care sport & exercise science, sports studies, environmental microbiology, applied marine and fisheries ecology; BSc(Hons), MPhil, MSc, MSc/PGDip, PhD

School of Medicine and Dentistry; www.abdn.ac.uk/medicine-dentistry

dentistry, health science, health studies, medicine, applied medicine; BDS, BSc, MA, MBChB, MMedSci, MPhil, MSc, PhD

School of Psychology; www.abdn.ac.uk/psychology

patient safety: clinical human factors, psychology various joint degrees, research methods, social cognition, neuroscience; BSc(Hons), MA, MRes, MSc

Rowlet Institute of Nutrition and Health Studies; www.rowletac.uk

health studies/with education; BSc(Hons), MSc, MSc/PgDip, PhD

College of Physical Sciences; www.abdn.ac.uk/about/physical-sciences.php

School of Engineering; www.abdn.ac.uk/engineering

chemical engineering, civil engineering, electrical & electronic engineering, mechanical engineering, project management, safety engineering, energy futures, subsea engineering, oil and gas structures; BEng(Hons), BScEng, EnD, MEng, MSc

School of Geosciences; www.abdn.ac.uk/geosciences

Dept of Archaeology; www.abdn.ac.uk/archeology

archaeology with anthropology/Celtic civilization/history/geography, archaeology of the north; BSc(Hons), MA(Hons), MPhil, PhD

Dept of Geography & the Environment; www.abdn.ac.uk/geography

geography, geoscience, international relations, management studies, marine & coastal resource management, planning, political economy, property, rural surveying, spatial planning; BSc(Hons), MA(Hons), MSc, PgDip/Cert, PhD

Dept of Geology & Petroleum; www.abdn.ac.uk/geology

gas enterprise management, geology, geology and physics, geoscience and geography, integrated petroleum geoscience; BSc(Hons), MA(Hons), MRes, MSc, PgDip/Cert, PhD

Centre for Planning & Environmental Management; www.abdn.ac.uk/cpem

geographical and spatial planning, property, urban planning, real estate, rural planning & environmental management, sustainable rural development, land economy; BSc(Hons), MA(Hons), MSc

School of Natural & Computing Sciences; www.abdn.ac.uk/sncs

Chemistry; www.abdn.ac.uk/chemistry

chemistry, biomedical materials, chemical science, environmental chemistry, materials, medicinal chemistry; BSc(Hons), MChem, MSc, PgDip, PhD

Computing Science; www.csd.abdn.ac.uk

artificial intelligence, business information systems, computing science, artificial intelligence, business computing/information systems, intelligent software agents, mathematics, psychology, GIS, computing and e-business/education, information systems and management, knowledge technology, natural language generation; BSc(Hons), MA(Hons), MSc, MSci, PhD

Mathematics; www.maths.abdn.ac.uk/

algebraic/differential geometry, functional analysis, engineering mathematics, mathematics, pure mathematics, relativity theory, topology; BSc(Hons), MA(Hons), MSc, PhD

Physics; www.abdn.ac.uk/physics

physical sciences, physics, physics with chemistry/geology/philosophy/engineering/mathematics; BSc(Hons), MSc(Hons)

UNIVERSITY OF ABERTAY, DUNDEE
www.abertay.ac.uk

School of Arts, Media & Computer Games www.abertay.ac.uk/studying/schools/amg

computer arts, computer games/technology, information technology, creative sound production, visual communication and visual design, game arts and animation, game design and production management, computer games, games technology; BA(Hons), BSc(Hons), DipHE, MProf, MSc/PGDip

Dundee Business School; www.abertay.ac.uk/studying/schools/dbe

accountancy, business administration, business studies, enterprise creation, enterprise and design, ethics and sustainability, Europe (law, economy, business law, management), finance and business, HRM, international management, law, marketing, management/studies, oil and gas accounting, retail marketing, tourism; golf management, biotechnology BA (Hons), GradCert, MBA, MSc, PGDip

The School of Contemporary Sciences; www.abertay.ac.uk/studying/schools/ss

bioinformatics, biomedical sciences, biotechnology, civil engineering studies, energy and environmental management, environment and sustainability, food biotechnology, forensic sciences, health sciences, medical biotechnology, policy and security, renewable energy water pollution control; BSc(Hons), DipHE, MSc, MTech, PGDip

The School of Social & Health Sciences; www.abertay.ac.uk/studying/schools/shs

behavioural science, coaching, counselling, criminological studies, forensic psychobiology, media, culture and society, mental health, nursing, psychology, public administration, sexual/reproductive health, social science, sociology, sports, sport and exercise/management/nutrition/psychology, sports development; BA(Hons), BSc(Hons), GradCert, MSc, PGDip, MPA

ABERYSTWYTH UNIVERSITY
www.aber.ac.uk

School of Art; www.aber.ac.uk/art

art, art history, fine art, museum and gallery studies; BA(Hons), MA, MPhil, PhD

Institute of Biological, Environmental & Rural Sciences; www.aber, ac.uk/ibers

agriculture, animal science/zoology, biochemistry, biology, conservation/countryside management, environmental science/management, equine science, genetics, marine & freshwater biology, microbiology, tourism & recreation; BSc(Hons), MPhil, MSc, PhD

Dept of Computer Science; www.aber.ac.uk/en/cs

business information technology, computer graphics, computer science(software engineering), vision and games, intelligent autonomous systems, internet computing/engineering, mobile wearable computing, open source computing, robotics, software engineering; BEng, BSc(Hons), HND, MEng, MSc, PhD

School of Education & Lifelong Learning; www.aber.ac.uk/sell

childhood studies, lifelong learning, education degrees are offered combined with other subjects; BA(Hons), BSc(Hons), MPhil, PGCE, PGD, PhD

Dept of English & Creative Writing; www.aber.ac.uk/en/english

creative writing, English literature, literary /classical studies, postmodern fictions, American studies, ; BA(Hons), MA, PhD

Dept of European Languages; www.aber.ac.uk/eurolangs

French, German, Italian, modern European culture, modern German Studies, romance languages, Spanish; BA(Hons), MA, PhD

Institute of Geography & Earth Sciences; www.ies.aber.ac.uk/

environmental earth/science, geography, GIS and remote sensing, glaciology, human geography, local and regional economic development, physical geography, quaternary environmental change, space, time and/politics/culture; BSc(Hons), MPhil, MRes, MSc, PhD

Dept of History & Welsh History; www.aber.ac.uk/history

economic & social history, European history, medieval /& modern history, contemporary history, politics & modern history, Welsh history, history & media, early British /18th century history, history of medicine, Celtic history; BA(Hons), MA, PhD

Dept of Information Studies; www.dis.aber.ac.uk

business information, historical & archival /information & library studies, records management, information management/systems, records & information management; BA(Hons), BSc(Econ), Dip/Cert, MPhil, MSc(Econ), PhD

Dept of International Politics; www.aber.ac.uk/interpol/en

European politics, intelligence & /strategic studies, international history/politics/strategic studies/third world/military history, international relations, military history, political studies, intelligence studies, peace conflict & security, international politics & the third world; BSc(Econ), MA, MSc, MSc(Econ), PhD

Dept of Law and Criminology; www.aber.ac.uk/law-criminology

business law, criminal law, criminology with applied psychology/law, European law, human rights, law, law with languages; BA(Hons), BSc(Econ), LlB, LlM, PhD

School of Management and Business; www.aber.ac.uk/en/smb

accounting & finance, business, business economics, business finance, economics, entrepreneurship, marketing, international business/finance, management; BSc(Econ), MBA, MSc(Econ), PhD

Institute of Mathematical & Physical Sciences; www.aber.ac.uk/en/maps

applied mathematics, statistics, computer science, pure mathematics, physics, planetary and space physics, space science, theoretical physics, astrophysics, materials science, solar system physics; BSc(Hons), MMath, MPhys, PhD

Dept of Psychology; www.aber.ac.uk/en/psychology

psychology; single Honours or Combined, BSc(Econ), BSc(Hons), PhD

Dept of Sport & Exercise Science; www.aber.ac.uk/sport/exercise

sport and exercise science, equine & human sport exercise, exercise psychology/physiology/ biomedicine; BSc(Hons), PhD

Dept of Theatre, Film & Television Studies; www.aber.ac.uk/en/tfts

drama & theatre, film & television, film studies, performance, media & communication studies, practising performance, scenography & theatre design, scriptwriting, Welsh medium courses; BA(Hons), MA, MPhil, PhD

Dept of Welsh; www.aber.ac.uk/cymraeg-welsh

Breton, Welsh & Celtic languages, Celtic studies, Irish, Welsh 1st language, medieval Welsh literature; BA(Hons), MA

ANGLIA RUSKIN UNIVERSITY
www.anglia.ac.uk

Faculty of Arts, Law and Social Sciences; www.anglia ac.uk/en/home/faculties/alss

Dept of English, Communication, Film & Media; www.anglia.ac.uk/ruskin/en/home/faculties/alss/deps/english.media

art, film & media, communication studies, drama, English language/language teaching & EFL, creative international business English, film studies, television and theatre writing, media studies, journalism, drama, publishing, applied linguistics & TESOL, philosophy, writing; BA(Hons), MPhil, PhD

Anglia Law School; www.anglia.ac.uk/ruskin/en/home/faculties/alss/deps/law

criminology, international business law, law, legal practice, professional legal studies; BA(Hons), LlB, LlD, LlM

Cambridge School of Art; www.anglia.ac.uk/ruskin/en/home/faculties/alss/deps/csoa

animation, children's book illustration, computer games, fashion design, film, television and theatre, fine art, illustration, interior design, photography, printmaking; BA(Hons), FdA, MA, MFA

Dept of Humanities & Social Sciences; www.anglia.ac.uk/ruskin/en/home/faculties/alss/deps/hss.

criminology, forensic science and criminology, history, English, philosophy, psychosocial studies, public service, social policy, sociology, transnational crime; BA(Hons), FdA, MPhil, PhD

Dept of Music & Performing Arts; www.anglia.ac.uk/ruskin/en/home/faculties/alss/deps/music

contemporary theatre, creative music technology, drama/therapy, music, music therapy, performing arts, popular music, film studies; BA(Hons), FdADip, MA, MPhil, PhD

Ashcroft International Business School; www.anglia.ac.uk/ruskin/en/home/faculties/aibs

accountancy, business, business economics, business management, corporate management, enterprise and entrepreneurship, HRM, international business, international management, leadership, marketing, tourism management; BA(Hons), BSc(Hons), MA, MBA, MSc, CertHE, HNC, HND

Faculty of Education; www.anglia.ac.uk/ruskin/en/home/faculties/education

early childhood studies, education, education studies, ESOL, EYPS, furthe, adult, higher education, learning through technology, PGCE primary and secondary courses, primary education/with modern foreign languages, teaching and learning assistants, teaching English (literacy), teaching mathematics (numeracy); BA(Hons), Diplomas, FdA/FdSc Professional Practice, MA, PGCE, UnivCert

Faculty of Health and Social Care; www.anglia.ac.uk/ruskin/en/home/faculties/hsc

children and young people's nursing, case management, children and family, community public health nursing, health care, management and leadership in health and social care, midwifery, nursing (adult, child, learning disabilities, mental health), operating department practice, perioperative care, physiotherapy, public health, radiotherapy & oncology practice, registered nurse (adult, child, learning disabilities, mental health), social work, social policy, youth and community work; BSc(Hons), Cambridge FdSc, Cert HE, Dip HE, MSc, PGDip/Cert

Faculty of Science and Technology; www.anglia.ac.uk/ruskin/en/home/faculties/fst

Dept of Built Environment; www.anglia.ac.uk/ruskin/en/home/faculties/fst/departments/builtenv

architecture, architectural technology, building surveying, civil engineering, construction management, environmental planning, project management, quantity surveying, real estate management, structural engineering, sustainable construction, town planning; BSc(Hons), FdSc, MSc, PGCert, PGDip

Dept of Computing & Technology; www.anglia.ac.uk/ruskin/en/home/faculties/fst/departments/comptech

animation technology, audio technology, audio, video and music technology, business information systems/technology, computer games, computer networking, computer science, computing, creative music technology, electronics, engineering management, forensic computing, information security, integrated engineering, mechanical engineering, mobile telecommunication, multimedia, network management, network security; BEng(Hons), BSc(Hons), HND

Dept of Vision and Hearing Science; www.anglia.ac.uk/ruskin/en/home/departments/vision-hearing

ophthalmic dispensing, ophthalmics, optometric clinic assistants, optometry, hearing aid technology; BOptom(Hons), BSc(Hons), FdSc, UnivCert

Dept of Psychology; www.anglia.ac.uk/ruskin/enhome/departments/psychology

cognitive neuroscience, clinical/child psychology; BSc(Hons), MSC

Dept of Life Sciences; www.anglia.ac.uk/ruskin/en/home/faculties/fst/departments/lifesciences

animal behaviour, animal welfare, applied biomedical science, biomedical sciences, cell and molecular biology, coaching science, conservation, ecology, equine studies, forensic science, marine biology, microbiology, sports coaching & PE sports science, wildlife biology, zoology; BSc(Hons), FdSc, MSc, PGDip

Degrees validated by Anglia Ruskin University offered at:

COLCHESTER INSTITUTE
www.colchester.ac.uk

Art, design and media
art, fashion textiles, fine art, graphic design, media/video production; BA(Hons), FdA, HNC, MA

Business and management
accountancy, business, e-business, hospitality, logistics & transport, public services, sport, tourism; BA(Hons), DipMan, Foundation degree, HNC, HND, PgDip/Cert

Computing and administration
computing, business administration, systems support, web design; Bsc(Hons), BTEC, Dipl Man, Nat Cert

Construction
brickwork, construction management, electrical installations, plumbing, site supervision/management, woodcraft/carpentry/joinery/cabinet making; BSc(Hons), Foundation degree, HNC, NVQs 4 & 5

Education
lifelong learning, literacy & ESOL, continuing education, TESOL teacher training; BA(Hons), Cert in Education, EFT, ESOL, Foundation degree, PGCE, PGCE and CertEd

Engineering
acoustics & noise control, electrical/electronic engineering, mechanical engineering; C&G Certs, Dipl in Acoustics, Foundation degree, HNC

Health & care
counselling, health, social care; BA(Hons), Foundation degree, DipHE

Hospitality and food studies
food & drink service, food preparation & cooking, hospitality supervision; Dips, Nat Dip, NVQs

Music and performing arts
acting, jazz and popular music, music, musical theatre, technical theatre; BA(Hons), Foundation degree, MA

ASHRIDGE
www.ashridge.ac.uk

executive coaching, management, organization consulting, sustainability & responsibility; Doc Orgn Consulting, ExecMBA, MBA, MSc

ASTON UNIVERSITY
www.aston.ac.uk

Aston Business School; www.aston.ac.uk/aston-business-school
accounting, business & management/social science, business computing & IT, business research & consultancy, economics & management, finance, HRM, international business & management/economics/modern language, international commercial law, investments, IT project management, law, management/ and administration, administration, marketing, mathematics with economics, management & strategy; BSc(Hons), DBA, Foundation degree, LlB, LlM, MBA, PhD

Centre for Learning, Innovation and Professional Practice; www.aston.uk.ac/clip

curriculum & learning development, learning & teaching, media & learning technologies; Foundation Degree Centre, MA, PG Cert

School of Engineering and Applied Science; www.aston.uk.ac/eas

Chemical Engineering & Applied Chemistry

applied chemistry, biological chemistry, chemical engineering, chemistry; BE Eng, MEng, MChem

Computer Science, BSc

computing science, computing for business, multimedia computing

Electronic Engineering

communications engineering, computer science, electrical & electronic engineering, internet systems; BSc, BEng

Engineering Systems & Management

construction management/project management; BSc

Technology & Enterprise Management

technology & enterprise management

Logistics & Transport Management

logistics, transport management; BSc

Mathematics

mathematics, mathematics with computing; BSc

Mechanical Engineering & Design

electromechanical engineering, mechanical engineering, design engineering; BEng, MEng

Product Design

industrial/ medical product design, engineering product design, medical product design, product design & management, sustainable product design; BSc

School of Life and Health Sciences; www.aston.uk.ac/life-health-sciences

applied & human biology, audiology, biomedical science, cell and molecular biology, cognitive neurosciences, health psychology, hearing aid audiology, human biology, infection and immunity, optometry, pharmacy, psychiatric pharmacy/ therapeutics, psychology; BSc(Hons), GradDip, FD MPharm, MRes, MSc, PGCert/Dip, PhD

School of Languages and Social Sciences; www.aston.uk.ac/ls

Modern Languages & Translation studies

French, German, Spanish, translation studies, international business and modern languages studies course combinations

International Relations, Politics & European Studies

European studies and European languages: politics with international relations/business/management, sociolgy/politics and other, politics with international relations and business/politics/public policy & management/sociology

English Language

English language, English language and range of subjects for combined honours

Modern Languages & Translation Studies

French, German, Spanish, translation studies, international business and modern languages and numerous subjects for joint honours

Sociology & Public Policy

social sciences, sociology, sociology and business/computer science/international relations/politics, public policy & management and business/international relations/politics/sociology;
BA(Hons), BSc(Hons), MA, MPhil, MRes, MSc, PhD

BANGOR UNIVERSITY
www.bangor.ac.uk

College of Arts and Humanities; www.bangor.ac.uk/cah

Creative Studies & Media; www.bangor.ac.uk/creative.industries

creative studies, film studies, journalism, media studies, theatre, professional writing, media /creative practice/writing

English; www.bangor.ac.uk/english

creative writing, English literature/language, journalism, publishing, theatre studies, Arthurian legend, medieval and early modern literature

History, Welsh History & Archaeology; www.bangor.ac.uk/history
archaeology, contemporary history, history, medieval & early modern history, Welsh history, heritage, Celtic archaeology

School of Linguistics & English Language; www.bangor.ac.uk/linguistics
creative writing, English language, English literature, applied/ linguistics, cognitive linguistics, anthropological linguistics

School of Modern Languages; www.bangor.ac.uk/ml
French, German, Italian, Spanish (with another subject), mid European languages and cultures, translation studies

School of Music; www.bangor.ac.uk/music
music, music technology, composition, elecroacoustics

Theology & Religious Studies; www.bangor.ac.uk/trs
religious studies, theology, study of religion

School of Welsh; www.bangor.ac.uk/ ysgolygymraeg; details of courses provided in Welsh language
bilingualism; BA(Hons), BD, BMus, Diploma, MA, MMus, MPhil, MTh, PgDip, PhD

College of Business, Social Sciences and Law; www.bangor.ac.uk/cbss

Bangor Business School; www.bangor.ac.uk/business
accounting, banking, business studies, economics, finance, leisure management, management, marketing, administration, ICT, social authority law, Islamic justice, information management

School of Social Sciences; www.bangor.ac.uk/so
criminology and criminal justice, health and social care, social policy, social work, social studies, sociology, social research

School of Law; www.bangor.ac.uk/law
law, criminal justice, commercial law, law & devolved goverments, company law, consumer law, family & welfare law, media law, intellectual property; BA(Hons), DBA, HND, LlB, LlM, MA, MBA, MSc, MPhil, PGDip, PhD

College of Education and Lifelong Learning; www.bangor.ac.uk/cell

childhood studies, design & technology, secondary education, education, design and technology, secondary education, post-11 learning support studies, early childhood and learning support studies, primary education, product design PGCE primary/secondary lifelong learning; range of subjects (combined studies) offered at BA Degree, Certificate, Diploma, FdA, HNC/HND levels

Academic Development Unit; www.bangor.ac.uk/adu
Welsh for adults;
BSc(Hons), EdMed, FdA, MA, MEd, MMusD, MPhil, MTh, PGCE, PhD

College of Natural Sciences; www.bangor.ac.uk/cns

CNS School of Biological Sciences; www.bangor.ac.uk/biology
natural sciences, medical /molecular biology, biology, biomedical science, cancer biology, ecology, molecular biology, zoology, zoology with animal behaviour/ animal ecology/conservation/marine zoology; BSc(Hons), Dipl, MA, MBiol, MPhil, MRes, MSc, MZool, PhD

School of Environment, Natural Resources, & Geography; www.bangor.ac.uk/senrgy
agriculture, conservation, environment, environmental conservation/management, science, countryside management, environmental planning and management/science, forest ecosystems, forestry, geography, sustainable development, terrestrial and marine ecology; BA/BSc(Hons), BSc(Hons), MA, MEnvSci, MPhil, MSc, PhD

School of Ocean Sciences; www.bangor.ac.uk/sos
coastal/geological oceanography, marine biology/ and geology/environmental studies/science/vertebrate zoology, oceanography, marine science, ocean science, geological oceanography; BSc(Hons), MMBiol, MMSci, MOcean, MPhil, MSc, PhD

Welsh Institute for Natural Resources; www.bangor.ac.uk/wnr

College of Health & Behavioural Sciences; www.bangor.ac.uk/cohabs

School of Healthcare Sciences; www.bangor.ac.uk/healthcaresciences
health studies, health science, critical care, midwifery, nursing, occupational therapy, pharmacology, operating department practice, public health, radiography & allied health professions, social care practice; BN(Hons), BSc(Hons), BMidw, DipHE, GradCert/Dip, MPhil, PhD,

School of Medical Sciences; www.bangor.ac.uk/sms
behavioural neurology, clinical and functional brain imaging, molecular science for medicine, sport science, exercise physiology; MSc, PGDip/Cert(HE), BMed Sci, BSc PhD

School of Psychology; www.bangor.ac.uk/psychcology
child & language development, clinical & health psychology, neuropsychology, psychology, applied behavioural analysis, neuroimaging, consumer psychology, mindfulness; BSc(Hons), MSc, PhD, MRes, MA

School of Sport, Health & Exercise Science; www.bangor.ac.uk/sport
sport science, sport, health and exercise, physical education, exercise science, physiology, exercise rehabilitation; BSc(Hons), MPhil, MSc, PhD

Institute of Medical & Social Research; www.bangor.ac.uk/imscar
dementia & ageing, health economics, public health; PhD

College of Physical and Applied Sciences; www.bangor.ac.uk/copas

School of Chemistry; www.chemistry.bangor.ac.uk/
analytical chemistry, chemistry, chemistry with biomolecular sciences, environmental chemistry, marine chemistry, molecular science for medicine; BSc, MChem, MSc, PGDip, PhD, MPhil

School of Electronics; www.eng.bangor.ac.uk/
computer systems engineering, electronic engineering, electronics (hardware systems/software programming), electronics for business (banking and finance/business law/business management), music technology, broadband communications, optoelectronics, nanotechnology; BEng(Hons), BSc(Hons), MEng(Hons), MSc, PhD

School of Computer Science; www.cs.bangor.ac.uk
computer science/animation, internet systems and e-commerce, creative technologies, information and communications technology, computer systems engineering, electronic engineering, visualization; BA(Hons), BEng(Hons), MEng(Hons), MPhil, MRes, MSc, PhD

UNIVERSITY CENTRE BARNSLEY
www.barnsley.hud.ac.uk

Art & Design
contemporary crafts design/visual arts, interdisciplinary art & design; BA(Hons)

Construction
construction, project management; BSc(Hons), FdSc, HNC

Business Management
business administration, business management; BA (Hons), FdA, MBA

Computing
animation, digital film, film, multimedia, music and enterprise; BA(Hons), FdSc

Early Years & Childhood Studies
early years, leading in the children's workforce; FdA, BA(Hons)

Education & Training
early years, education & training, numeracy for teachers, post-compulsory education and training, professional development; BA(Hons), CertEd, FdA, MA/PGDip/PGCert, PGCE

Film
digital film & visual effects, film, animation, music; BA(Hons)

History
history, English literature, humanities; BA(Hons)

Journalism & Media
journalism, media production; FdA

Multimedia
multimedia/computing; BSc(Hons), FdSc

Music
music production & sound recording, popular music and promotion; BA(Hons)

Professional Development for Staff in Education
Education and training, literacy and numeracy, professional development; BA, MA, PGDip/Cert

Psychology
psychological studies; BSc(Hons)

Sciences
resource and waste management; Dip

Social sciences
social sciences; BSc(Hons)

Teaching
post compulsory Education and training; CertEd, PGCE

UNIVERSITY OF BATH
www.bath.ac.uk

Faculty of Engineering and Design; www.bath.ac.uk/engineering

Architecture & Civil Engineering; www.bath.ac.uk/ace
architectural engineering: environmental design, construction management, architecture, civil engineering, conservation of historic buildings/historic gardens & cultural landscapes, facade engineering, internation construction management; BEng, BSc, EngD, MArch, MEng, MPhil, MSc, PGCert, PhD

Chemical Engineering; www.bath.ac.uk/chem-eng
biochemical engineering, chemical and bioprocess engineering, chemical engineering, environmental management; BEng, EngD, MEng, MPhil, MSc, PhD

Electronic & Electrical Engineering; www.bath.ac.uk/elec-eng
communication engineering, communications, computer systems engineering, digital communications, electrical & electronic/electrical power engineering, electrical power systems, power transmission & motion control systems electronics, mechanical engineering, mechatronics, space science & technology, wireless systems; BEng, EngD, MEng, MPhil, MSc, PhD

Mechanical Engineering; www.bath.ac.uk/mech-eng
aerospace engineering, automotive engineering, dynamics and control, innovation & engineering design, fluid power systems, mechanical, manufacturing, mechatronics, medical engineering, power transmission & motion control systems, technology management; EngD, MEng, MPhil, MSc, PhD

Faculty of Humanities and Social Science; www.bath.ac.uk/hss

Dept of Economics; www.bath.ac.uk/economics
economics/and finance, international development, politics, international money & banking, economics (development); BSc(Hons), MPhil, MRes, PhD

Dept of Education; www.bath.ac.uk/education
childhood, youth & education studies, coach education, sport, sports development, sports performance, TESOL; BA(Hons), EdD, FdSc, MA, MPhil, MRes, PGCE, PhD, ProfPGCE

Dept of European Studies & Modern Languages; www.bath.ac.uk/esml
contemporary European politics, European cinema studies, international politics/security, interpreting and translating, modern languages & European studies, politics/ and economics/international relations; BA(Hons), BSc(Hons), MA, MPhil, PGDip, PhD

Dept of Psychology; www.bath.ac.uk/psychology
health/ psychology, science, risk and health communication, applied cognition, social processes; BSc(Hons), MPhil, MSc, PhD

Department of Social and Policy Sciences; www.bath.ac.uk/soc-pl
business & community, death & society, European social policy/research/ sciences, social work & applied social studies, sociology, wellbeing & human dev; BSc, MPhil, MRes, MSc, PhD

Faculty of Science; www.bath.ac.uk/science

Dept of Biology & Biochemistry; www.bath.ac.uk/bio-sci
biology, biochemistry, biosciences, molecular biology, developmental biology, evolution & population biology, medical bioscience, molocular plant science, industrial biotechnology & enterprise; BSc(Hons), MPhil, MRes, PhD

Dept of Chemistry; www.bath.ac.uk/chemistry
chemistry/for drug discovery; BSc(Hons), MChem, MSci, PhD

Dept of Computer Science; www.bath.ac.uk/comp-sci
advanced computer systems, computer information systems, computer science; BSc(Hons), EngD, MComp, MSc, PhD

Dept of Mathematics; www.bath.ac.uk/math-sci
mathematical biology/sciences, mathematics, modern applics of mathematics, statistics; BSc(Hons), MMath, MSc, PhD

Dept of Natural Sciences; www.bath.ac.uk/nat-sci
biology, chemistry, pharmacology, physics; BSc(Hons), MSci

Dept of Pharmacy & Pharmacology; www.bath.ac.uk/pharmacy
pharmaceutical practice and therapeutics, pharmacology, pharmacy; MPharm, MPharmacol, PhD

Dept of Physics; www.bath.ac.uk/physics
mathematics and physics, physics/with computing, nanoscience, medical physics, photonics; BSc, MSc, MPhil, MPhys, PhD

School of Management; www.bath.ac.uk/management

accounting & finance, international management, management, advanced management practice, marketing, innovation & technology management; BSc(Hons), DBA, EngD, MBA, MPhil, MRes, MSc, PhD

School for Health; www.bath.ac.uk/health

health practice, health care/ informatics, information governance, sport and exercise science, sports physiotherapy, sport and exercise/medicine; BSc(Hons), MD, MPhil, MS, PGDip, PhD

BATH SPA UNIVERSITY
www.bathspa.ac.uk

Bath School of Art and Design; www.artbathspa.com
art, art & design, ceramics, fine art, graphic communication, fashion design, ceramics, digital design, 3D design, interactive multimedia, media communication, textile design studies, fine art; BA(Hons), FdA, MFA, MPhil, PhD

Development and Participation; www.bathspa.ac.uk/schools/development-and-participation; QTLS
lifelong learning, student study skills

School of Education; www.bathspa.ac.uk/schools/education
early years education, FE management, global citizenship, international education, primary education studies/for teaching assistants, PGCE (primary (3–11)/middle years (7–14)/ secondary (11–16); range of subjects), professional studies, TESOL; FD, GradCert, MA/MTeach, PGCE, PGCert/Dip

School of Humanities & Creative Industries; www.bath-spa.ac.uk/schools/humanities-and cultural-industries
broadcasting, creative media practice and publishing production, creative writing, cultural studies, film & screen skills, media communications, English

literature, script writing, publishing; study of religions, philosophy & ethics, history, Irish studies, media communications; BA(Hons), MPhil, PhD.MA

Music and the Performing Arts; www.bathspampa.com

commercial music, creative arts, creative music technology, dance, drama, and performing arts, music, theatre production, arts management, composition; BA(Hons), FdA, FdMus, MA, PhD

School of Science, Society and Management; www.ssmbathspa.com

biology, business & management, development geography, diet and health, environmental science, food & nutrition, GIS, geography, health studies, heath and social care management, human nutrition, management and management systems, psychology, sociology, tourism management, ecological impact assessment; BA(Hons), BSc (Hons), BA/BSc, MPhil, MSc, PhD, FDA, DipHE

UNIVERSITY OF BEDFORDSHIRE
www.beds.ac.uk

Faculty of Creative Arts, Technologies & Science; www.beds.ac.uk/departments/cats

Bedfordshire Institute of Media and the Creative & Performing Arts; www.beds.ac.uk/departments/bim

Div of Art & Design

advertising design, animation, art and design, fashion design, fine art, graphic design, illustration, interior architecture, digital photography & video art, art design & internet technologies

Div of Journalism & Communication

creative writing, journalism, media arts, media practices, PR, sport /broadcast journalism, media performance

Div of Media Arts & Production

documentary, media arts, media, culture and technology, music technology, media production, new media and internet technologies, television production, radio production, script writing

Div of Performing Arts & English

children's literature & culture, contemporary theatre/dance and professional practice, education studies, English studies, performing arts, theatre & profession practice; BA(Hons), FdA, MA, MRes, PhD

Dept of Computer Science & Technology; www.beds.ac.uk/departments/computing

computer science/ networking, information systems, mobile computing, computer games development, software engineering, AI and robotics, computer security and forensics, applied computing & IT, computer animation, business info systems, computer and internet applications, computing and entrepreneurship, telecommunications management BSc(Hons), FdSc, MSc

Div of Science

biomedical science, biotechnology, biological sciences environmental sciences, forensic science, medical science, nutritional sciences, nutritional therapy; BScHons, FdSc, MSc, PgCert, PgDip, MPhil, PhD

Faculty of Health and Social Sciences; www.beds.ac.uk/departments/healthsciences

Dept of Acute Health Care; www.beds.ac.uk/departments/acute

Dept of Community Services

Dept of Midwifery & Child Health

midwifery, nursing, learning disabilities, mental health, operating dept practice, osteopathy, social work, sports therapy, care management, complementary therapy, dental nursing/practice management, clinical science, health studies, leadership, medical education, psychological intervention, sexual health, public health; BSc(Hons), FdA, FdSc, MSc, PGDip/Cert, DipHE

Dept of Applied Social Studies; www.beds.ac.uk/departments/appliedsocialstudies

applied social studies, criminology, early years studies, child and adolescent studies, counselling health and social care, social work, sociology, young people's services, youth and community studies, youth justice; BSc(Hons), FdA, FdSc, MSc, ProfDoc

Div of Psychology; www.beds.ac.uk/departments/psychology

applied psychology, counselling and therapies, criminal behaviour, criminology, health/social psychology, psychology, crime/ criminal behaviour; BSc(Hons), CertHE, FdA, MSc, PhD

Div of Sports Therapy; www.beds.ac.uk/departments/spoth
sports therapy; BSc (Hons)

Bedfordshire & Hertfordshire Postgraduate Medical School; www.beds.ac.uk/departments/bhpms
clinical science/clinical science (diabetes), dental / medical education, public health, sexual health; MA, MSc, PGDip, PGCert

Institute for Health Research; www.beds.ac.uk/researchir
psychological approach to health & management, public health, research & evaluation; MSc, PhD

Institute of Applied Social Research; www.beds.ac.uk/research/lasr
child & family welfare, crime, vulnerable young people, youth justice; ProfDoc

University of Bedfordshire Business School www.beds.ac.uk/departments/ubbs

Depts of Accounting & Finance, Marketing, Strategy & HRM, Business Systems, Law (School of), Language & Communication
accounting, advertising, applied natural sciences, applied linguistics, creative and innovative development, Islamic finance and banking, international commercial law, public services, air management, sport studies, arts management, beauty therapy and spa management, business decision/management/studies (e-business/finance/business studies/marketing), commercial law, entrepreneurship, event management, finance and business management, football studies, retail management, HRM, information systems, intercultural communication, international business and management/finance and banking/HRM/tourism, international finance, international tourism management, law/with criminology/management, leisure and business management, logistics and supply chain business management, marketing communications, marketing and business management, marketing, media practices, PR, project management, sport development/management/tourism, strategic leadership and management, travel and tourism; BA(Hons), BSc(Hons), DBA, FdA, LlB, LlM, MA, MBA, MSc, PGCErt, LLM

Faculty of Education and Sport; www.beds.ac.uk/departments/ecs

School of Education; www.beds.ac.uk/departments/schoolofeducation
applied education studies, disability studies, early years education, education studies/practice, mathematics enhancement course/education key stage 2/3 middle years/primary education with Italian, Spanish/secondary, lifelong learning, post-compulsory education, qualified teacher status primary education, PGCE primary education; BA(Hons), PGCert, MA, FdA, PGCE

THE QUEEN'S UNIVERSITY OF BELFAST
www.qub.ac.uk

School of Biological Sciences; www.qub.ac.uk/schools/schoolofbiological sciences
agricultural biochemistry, biological sciences, environmental biology, food quality, safety and nutrition, genetics, land use & environmental management technology, land environmental sustainability, marine biology, microbiology, molecular biology, rural sustainability, zoology; BSc(Hons), MSc, PGDip, PhD

School of Chemistry and Chemical Engineering; www.ch.qub.ac.uk
chemistry, medicinal chemistry, chemistry with forensic analysis, chemical engineering, chemical enzymology, process engineering; BSc(Hons), MSci, BEng, MEng, MSc, PGDip, PhD

School of Education; www.qub.ac.uk/schools/school of education
applying psychology to education, arts, culture and society, autistic spectrum disorders, coaching and mentoring, education, e-learning, diversity and inclusion, guidance and counselling, initial teacher education, leadership and management in education, management, management and business studies, personal and civic education business and HR, primary school experience, lifelong learning, social and community development, TESOL; AdvCertEd,

DASE, EdD, MA, MEd, MSc, MSSc, PGCE, PGDip/Cert, UnivCert, BA(Hons)

School of Electronics, Electrical Engineering and Computer Science; www.qub.ac.uk/schools/eeec

business information technology, computing and IT, computer & electronic security, computer games design and development, computer science, creative multimedia, educational multimedia, electrical and electronic engineering, electronics, telecommunications, software & electronic systems engineering, advanced wireless technology; BEng, BSc, MEng, MSc, MPhil, PhD

School of English; www.qub.ac.uk/schools/SchoolofEnglish

creative writing, English language & linguistics, Irish writing, linguistics, medieval studies, modern literary studies, modern poetry, reconceiving the Renaissance; BA(Hons), MA, PhD

School of Geography, Archaeology and Palaeoecology; www.qub.ac.uk/schools/gap

archaeology, dating and chronology, geography, landscape, heritage & environment, palaeoecology; BA(Hons), BSc(Hons), MSc, PhD

School of History and Anthropology; www.qub.ac.uk/schools/SchoolofHistoryandAnthroplogy

ancient history, anthropological studies, ethnomusicology, Irish history, modern history, social anthropology, cognition & culture; BA(Hons), GradDip, MA, MPhil, PhD

School of Languages, Literatures and Performing Arts; www.qub.ac.uk/schools/SchoolofLanguages Literatures andPerformingArts

drama studies, film studies, French/German/Irish & Celtic/ Spanish & Portugese studies, visual studies, linguistics, Irish translation studies, translation; BA(Hons), MA, PhD

School of Law; www.law.qub.ac.uk/law/with politics

law/with politics, common & civil law, legal science, criminology, governance, international commerce, human rights; LlB, LlM, MSSc, MLSc, PGdip, MPhil, PhD

Queen's University Management School; www.qub.ac.uk/schools/mgt

accounting, accounting & finance, actuarial science and risk management, business economics, economics, finance, management, international business, environmental management, financial regulation management & information systems, new ventures, sustainable management; BSc(Hons), MSc, MScs, eratiMBA, PhD

School of Mathematics and Physics; www.qub.ac.uk/schools /Schoolof MathematicsandPhysics

applied mathematics, computer science and physics, pure mathematics, operational research, statistics, physics with astronomy, physics with medical applications, theoretical /plasma physics, vacuum technology; BSc(Hons), GradDip, MSc, MSci, PhD

School of Mechanical and Aerospace Engineering; www.qub.ac.uk/schools/SchoolofMechanicaland AerospaceEngineering

aerospace engineering, internal combustion engines, mechanical and manufacturing engineering, product design and development aerospace – integrated aircraft technologies, engines, polymers; BEng, MEng, MSc

School of Medicine, Dentistry and Biomedical Sciences; ww.qub.ac.uk/schools/mdbs

medicine, biomedical science, clinical dentistry, dentistry, human biology, surgery, molecular medicine, mental health, obstetrics, public health; BCh, BAO, BSc(Hons), BDS, DAO, Diploma, MB, MD, MSc

School of Music and Sonic Arts; www.mu.qub.ac.uk

music, acoustics and psychoacoustics, composition, creative practice, electro-acoustic composition, Irish traditional music, musicology, music technology, performance, sound design, sound engineering; BMus, BSc(Hons), MA, PhD

School of Nursing and Midwifery; www.qub.ac.uk/schools/SchoolofNursingandMidwifery

nursing sciences – adult branch/children's branch/ learning disability branch /mental health branch, maternal and child health, midwifery sciences/ studies, continuing professional development, evaluation of complex healthcare interventions, clinical practice; BSc(Hons) Diploma, MPhil, PhD, DNursingPractice

School of Pharmacy; www.qub.ac.uk/schools/SchoolofPharmacy

clinical pharmacy, community pharmacy, pharmacist prescribing, pharmacy; MPharm, MSc, PGCert/Dip

School of Planning, Architecture and Civil Engineering; www.qub.ac.uk/schools/SchoolofPlanningArchitectureand CivilEngineering

architecture, civil engineering, durability of structures, environmental engineering, environmental planning, management, spatial regeneration, urban and rural design, water resources; BSc(Hons), MSc, MArch, MPhil, PhD

School of Politics, International Studies and Philosophy; www.qub.ac.uk/schools/SchoolofPoliticsInternationalStudies andPhilosophy

cognitive science, comparative ethnic conflict, European gender and society, union policies, international relationsinternational studies, Irish politics, law with politics, legislative studies and practice, philosophy, political philosophy, politics, politics, economics & philosophy, violence, terrorism and security; BA(Hons), LlB, MA, MRes, MPhil, PhD

School of Psychology; www.psych.qub.ac.uk

atypical child development, educational child and adolescent applied psychology BSc(Hons), MSc, DocClinPsych, PhD DocEducational

School of Sociology, Social Policy and Social work; www.qub.ac.uk/schools/SchoolofSociologySocialPolicy SocialWork

criminology, gender studies, social policy, social work, social research methods, sociology; BA(Hons), BSW, MA, MSc, DChild Stud

UNIVERSITY OF BIRMINGHAM
www.bham.ac.uk

College of Arts and Law; www.colleges.bham.ac.uk/artslaw

Institute of Archaeology and Antiquity; www.iaa.bham.ac.uk

antiquity, archaeology/and heritage management, classical archaeology, Egyptology, anthrolopology, ancient history, Byzantine, Ottoman, and modern Greek studies, classics, classical literature and civilization, Roman history, eastern Mediterranean history, Greece and the Greeks; BA(Hons), MA, MPhil, diploma, PhD

Birmingham Law School; www.law.bham.ac.uk

law, commercial law, criminal law & criminal justice, European law, international commercial law, English law, law, legal studies (GradDip); LlB, LlM, MPhil/MJur/PhD

English, Drama and American & Canadian Studies; www.weblearn.bham.ac.uk

American studies, Canadian studies, English & American literature & film history, applied linguistics, art history and music, creative writing, cultures, directing and dramaturgy, playwriting studies, drama and theatre arts, English language, English linguistics, English literature, Shakespeare studies, film studies, history, film & television, history and cultures, intelligence studies, languages, literary/linguistics, medieval English and history, philosophy, theology and religion, transAtlantic studies, US foreign policy; BA(Hons), BSc(Hons), MPhil, PhD

School of History and Cultures; www.historycultures.bham.ac.uk

African studies, ancient & medieval, archaeology and anthropology, Caribbean literature, contemporary history, cultural heritage of Shakespeare's England, early modern history, economic & social history, history, history and social science, history of Christianity, modern European history, Reformation and early modern studies, Shakespeare, Stratford-upon-Avon and the cultural history of Renaissance England, social research (economic & social history), 20th-century British history, war studies, West Midlands history, air power, world war studies; BA(Hons), MA, MPhil, PGDip, PhD

School of Languages, Cultures, Art History and Music; www.about.bham.ac.uk/colleges/artslaw/lcam

Centre for European Languages & Culture

modern languages, film studies, cultural enquiry, culture, society & communication, European studies, French, gender studies, German, Hispanic, humanities, Italian, modern European cultures, translation studies

Centre for Modern Languages

Japanese

Dept of History of Art

history of art

Dept of Music

composition, editing, musicology, performance, performance practice; BA, MA, BMus, MA, MPhil, PhD

The School of Philosophy, Theology and Religion; www.about.bham.ac.uk/colleges/artslaw/ptr

biblical studies, electronic scholarly editing, global ethics, history of Christianity, inter-religious relations, icognitive science, Islam and Christian–Muslim relations, Islamic studies, Jewish and holocaust studies, philosophy of language and linguistics/ of mind and psychology/of religion and ethics, pentecostal and charismatic studies, politics and religion, practical theology, Quaker studies, religion and culture, Sikh studies, theology and religion, ethics; BA(Hons), BMus, MA, MPhil, PhD

College of Engineering and Physical Sciences; www.about.bham.ac.uk/colleges/eps

School of Chemistry; www.chem.bham.ac.uk

chemical biology, chemistry and/with analytical science/bioorganic chemistry/pharmacology, materials chemistry, molecular processes and theory, molecular synthesis

School of Chemical Engineering; www.eng.bham.ac.uk/chemical

chemical engineering, air pollution management and control, biochemical engineering, energy engineering, formulation engineering, food safety, hygiene and management, hydrogen fuel cells

School of Civil Engineering; www.eng.bham.ac.uk/civil

civil engineering, energy engineering, geotechnical engineering, railway systems engineering and integration, road management and. engineering, transport technology, construction management, water resources technology and management

School of Computer Science; www.cs.bham.ac.uk

artificial intelligence, computer science with business software engineering, computer security, electronic and software engineering, intelligent systems engineering, internet software systems, mathematics and computer science, natural computation

School of Electrical, Electronic and Computer Engineering; www.eece.bham.ac.uk

communications engineering (satellite and mobile), computer interactive systems, communications networks, computer and communications systems engineering, electronic and electrical engineering, software engineering, electromagnetic sensor systems, radio frequency engineering, computer engineering, embedded systems, interactive digital media, satellite and mobile communication

School of Mathematics; www.mat.bham.ac.uk

analysis, fluid dynamics, combinatorics, finite group theory, mathematical engineering, mathematical logic, mathematics, mathematics with business management/psychology/philosophy, mathematics and sport science, pure mathematics and computer science, theoretical physics and applied mathematics

School of Mechanical Engineering; www.eng.bham.ac.uk/mechanical

mechanical engineering/(biomedical), automotive engineering, engineering , engineering management, operations management, project management, materials and mechanical engineering

School of Metallurgy and Materials; www.eng.bham.ac.uk/metallurgy

materials, materials engineering/science & technology, materials for sustainable energy technologies, metallurgy, biomaterials, engineered materials for high performance applications/in aerospace and related technologies, science and engineering of materials , sports science and materials technology

School of Physics and Astronomy; www.ph.bham.ac.uk

medical and radiation physics, physics, physics and astrophysics/ tehnology of nuclear reactors/nanoscale physics/ particle physics and cosmology, theoretical physics, theoretical physics and applied mathematics, radioactive waste management and decommissioning; BEng, BNatSci, BSc(Hons), DEng, MEng, MPhil, MRes, MSc, MSci, PGDip/Cert, PhD

College of Life and Environmental Sciences; www.about.bham.ac.uk/colleges/les

School of Biosciences; www.biosciences.bham.ac.uk

analytical genomics, biochemistry, biology, molecular biotechnology, conservation and utilization of plant genetic resources, genetics, human biology, molecular mechanistic toxicology

School of Geography, Earth and Environmental Sciences; www.gees.bham.ac.uk

air pollution management & control, applied meteorology & climatology, earth sciences, enterprise, environment and place, environmental geoscience/health/ management/planning, geography, geology with biology, archaeology, hydrotechnology, public & environmental health science, safety & the environment, science of occupational health, resource and applied geology, urban regional planning,

School of Psychology; www.psychology.bham.ac.uk

psychology, brain injury, clinical criminology/psychology, cognition and computational neuroscience, cognitive behaviour therapy/neuropsychology and rehabilitation, criminological psychology, forensic psychology, neuroscience

School of Sport and Exercise Sciences; www.sportex.bham.ac.uk

mathematics and sports science, sport and exercise, sports science and materials technology; PG Studentships available, BSc(Hons), Clin, ForenPsyD, MPhil, MRes, MSc, PhD, PsyD, PGDip, PhD, PGDips

College of Medical and Dental Sciences; www.about.bham.ac.uk/colleges/mds

The Five Schools of the College are: Cancer Sciences, Clinical and Experimental Medicine, Dentistry, Health and Population Sciences, Immunity and Infection; biomedical materials science, cancer, cardiovascular sciences, dental hygiene and therapy, dental surgery, dentistry, health sciences, hormones & genes, immunity & infection, medical science, medicine, surgery, neuroscience, nursing, physiotherapy; BDS, BMedSci, BSc(Hons), BNurs, DDS, MBChB, MD

College of Social Sciences; www.about.bham.ac.uk/colleges/socialsciences

Birmingham Business School; www.business.bham.ac.uk

accounting and finance, business and American studies, business management, business management with communications, development economics, economic development research and policy, economic policy, economics, environmental and natural resource economics, European business management, geography and urban and regional planning, geography, HRM, international accounting and finance, international business/economics/marketing/money and banking, investments, management, marketing, marketing communications, mathematical economics & statistics, mathematical finance, money, banking & finance, planning with economics, political science, social policy, urban and regional planning, urban and regional studies, urban governance; BSc Economics, BSc(Hons), Dip, MSc, MBA, DBA, MPhil, PhD PGCert, PGDip, UCert

School of Education; www.education.bham.ac.uk

applied golf management studies, autism/spectrum disorders, bilingualism in education, childhood, culture and education, dyslexia studies, education and learning, education for health professionals, educational psychology, English language and literature in education, hearing impairment, inclusion and special educational needs, international studies in education, IT and education, leadership in education, learning and learning contexts, learning difficulties/disabilities (severe, profound and complex), multisensory impairment (deafblindness), sport, physical education and coaching science, social, emotional and behavioural difficulties, speech and language difficulties, sports coaching, teacher training (early years, general primary, secondary subject courses) – (English, geography, history and citizenship, mathematics, modern foreign languages, physical education, religious education, biology, chemistry, physics), TEFL, visual impairment; AdCert, BA(Hons), BPhil, ChildPsyD, EdD, EdPsychD, MEd, MPhil, PGCE, PGCert/Dip, PhD

School of Government and Society; www.about.bham.ac.uk/colleges/socialsciences/governmentsociety

aid management, central and east European studies, conflict, security and development, ethnicities and culture, European politics, governance and democratic participation, governance and development management, health services management, health care policy and management, international development/ political economy of development/ relations/ studies, leading public service change and organizational development, local government studies, local policy and politics, media, culture and society, political economy, politics and religion, poverty reduction and development management, public administration, public service commissioning, Russian studies, society and economics, social and political theory, social policy, social research, social work, sociology; BA(Hons), BSc(Hons), GradDip/ Cert, MA, MPhil, MSc, PhD

The School of Social Policy (The Health Services Management Centre; Institute of Applied Social Studies); www.hsmc.bham.ac.uk; www.iass.bham.a.uk

health and social care, health care policy and management, improvement, leadership for health services, leading public service change and organizational development, public service commissioning, social policy, social work; MA, MSc, PGDip

Degrees validated at the University of Birmingham offered at:

SCHOOL OF EDUCATION, SELLY OAK
www.education.bham.ac.uk

applied golf management studies, autism, bilingualism in education, childhood, culture and education, dyslexia studies, education for health professionals, English language and literature in education, educational psychology, hearing impairment, inclusion and special educational needs, international studies in education, IT and education, leaders and leadership in education, learning and learning contexts, learning difficulties/ multisensory impairment, sports coaching, teacher training – primary courses; early years, general primary/secondary subject courses (English, geography, history and citizenship, mathematics, modern foreign languages, physical education, professional development religious education, biology, chemistry, physics), TEFL, visual impairment; AppEd, BA, ChildPsyD, EdPsychD, MPhil, PhD, PGCE

UNIVERSITY COLLEGE BIRMINGHAM
www.ucb.ac.uk

business & marketing, childhood and education, hospital, food and events management, recreational sport and tourism, sports therapy, sales management; BA(Hons), BSc(Hons), FdA Dip HE, FdSc, MA, MSc, PGCE, PGDip/Cert

BIRMINGHAM CITY UNIVERSITY
www.bcu.ac.uk

Birmingham Institute of Art and Design; www.bcu.ac.uk/bid

animation, architecture, architectural practice administration, art /and education, project management, fashion promotion/styling, interior design, stage management, art practice and education, contemporary curatorial practice, design, fashion design, fashion retail management, fine art, gemmology/horology/jewellery & silversmithing, graphic design, history of art & design, landscape architecture/ studies, textile design, theatre, performance and event design, product design, queer studies in arts and culture, surface design, visual communication, urban design; BA(Hons), BTEC, CertHE/DipHE, HND, MA, MPhil, PgCert/PgDip, PhD

Birmingham City Business School; www.bcu.ac.uk/business-school

accounting, advertising, business and management, business law/psychology/information technology, clinical risk, internal audit practice, risk management, business studies, economics, finance, HRM, international business, international marketing, management, marketing, PR, combined studies in audit management and consultancy, business, business management, international HRM; BA(Hons), DBA, HND, MBA, MPhil, MSc, PhD

Faculty of Education, Law and Social Sciences; www.bcu.ac.uk/elss

Education & Teacher Training; www.bcu.ac.uk/education
children and integrated professional care, early childhood, early childhood education studies, early years, post-compulsory education and training, art and education, secondary art and design/drama, mathematics, music, primary education /with QTS, secondary education, subject enhancement in mathematics; BA(Hons), FoundD, FoundC, CA, MPhil, PGDip/Cert, PGCE, PhD

The School of Law; www.bcu.ac.uk/law
corporate and business law, international human rights, legal studies, law, law with American legal studies/criminology/legal practice/business law/ human rights, legal practice; criminological investigation policy security studies, GradDip, MPhil/PhD, HND, LlB(Hons), PGCert/PGDip/LLM

School of Social Sciences; www.cu.ac.uk/ social sciences
criminal investigation, criminology /& security studies, housing practice, integrative counselling and psychotherapy, forensic psychology, crime research, integrative psychotherapy, psychology, public sociology, social sciences, sociology; BA(Hons), BSc(Hons), CertHE, FdA, MA, MPhil, MSc, PGCert, PGDip, PhD

Faculty of Health; www.bcu.ac.uk/ health

advanced health care, child care, health and social care, health and wellbeing (exercise science/nutrition science/individuals and communities), health promotion and public health, management / long-term conditions, medical ultrasound, mental health, midwifery, nursing/RN, operating department practice, pain management, perioperative specialist practice, diagnostic radiography, rehabilitation work (visual impairment), social work, speech and language therapy, strategic leadership; BSc(Hons), DipHE, FdA, MPhil, MSc, PgCert, PGDip, PQ, PhjD

Faculty of Performance, Media and English; www.bcu.ac.uk/pme

Birmingham Conservatoire; www.conservatoire.bcu.ac.uk
jazz, digital arts in performance, music, music technology, popular music studies; AdvPGDip, BMus(Hons), HND, MA, MMus, MPhil, PGCert, PhD

Birmingham School of Media; www.bcu.ac.uk/mediacourses
journalism, freelance photography, music industries, PR, radio production; broadcast journalism, online journalism, event and exhibition management, international broadcast journalism, media & communication, creative enterprise, social media, television & interactive content; BA(Hons), PGDip, MA, MPhil, PhD

Birmingham School of Acting; www.bsa.bcu.ac.uk
acting, community and applied theatre/dance theatre, physical theatre, professional voice practice acting: the British tradition, stage management; BA(Hons), MA, PgDip

School of English; www.lmds.bcu.acuk/ English
English, English and media/drama/psychology/creative writing, English literature/language studies/ linguistics, writing, philosophy; BA(Hons), Diploma, MA, MPhil, PhD

Faculty of Technology, Engineering and the Environment; www.bcu.ac.uk/tee-landing

business information and business systems technology, computer games technology, computer networks/and security, computer science/ technology, computing and electronics, electronic engineering, forensic computing, information & communications technology, telecommunications & networks;
creative game animation and development, film production and technology/special effects, multimedia technology, music technology, sound engineering and production, sound & multimedia technology, television technology & production; automotive engineering, computer-aided automotive design, engineering foundation, management of manufacturing systems, mechanical engineering, motorsports technology, architectural technology, building surveying, construction management & economics, construction quantity surveying, construction, estate management practice, planning and development,

property & construction, quantity surveying, real estate; BSc, HNC, FdSc, MSc, PgCert, PgDip

BISHOP GROSSETESTE COLLEGE
www.bgc.ac.uk

children's services (early childhood/children and youth work), continuing professional development, drama in the community, early childhood studies, education (non-QTS), primary education with QTS, heritage studies, education studies in art and design / drama/English/geography/history/mathematics/ music/sport/theology, PGCE in education (primary/ secondary), English literature, learning practitioners; BA(Hons), FdA, GradDip, MA, PGCE

EAST LANCASHIRE INSTITUTE OF HIGHER EDUCATION AT BLACKBURN COLLEGE
www.blackburn.ac.uk

Vocation qualifications (BTEC, City & Guilds etc) offered in: business, care and health, childhood studies, construction, computing, creative arts, essential studies, hair and beauty, hospitality, motor vehicle, public services

Courses offered at University Centre, Blackburn College: applied psychology – counselling and health, business accounting, business studies, business, care practice, complementary medicine, design (contemporary textiles/graphic communication/illustration and animation/interiors/moving image/new media, digital communication systems, digital media design, early years childcare, educational studies, electrical/electronic engineering, history, English language and literary studies, financial services, fine art (integrated media), hospitality management, housing studies, criminology, HRM, information and internet technology, journalism, law, law with psychology, marketing, mechanical engineering, neighbourhood management, photographic media, politics and English/ history, public services management, social sciences, sociology and English/history, sustainable construction, sustainable engineering, working with children and young people; BA(Hons, Ord), BEng(Hons, Ord), BSc(Hons, Ord), DMS (validated externally), Foundation degree, HNC, HND, LlB (validated by Lancaster), LlM, MBA, MSc

BOURNEMOUTH UNIVERSITY
www.bournemouth.ac.uk

The Business School; www.business.bournemouth.ac.uk

accounting, business, business law, business studies with economics/enterprise/finance/human resource, management/law/marketing/operations and project management, business & management, economics, entertainment law, finance, finance with risk management, international business studies/ finance/management, international business with economics, international commercial law, intellectual property, intellectual property management, law, law and taxation, management, marketing/human resources, operations project management, taxation; BA(Hons), LlB(Hons), LlM, MA, MBA, MPhil, MSc, PhD

School of Conservation Sciences; www.bournemouth.ac.uk/conservation

animal behaviour & welfare, applied architectural stonework and conservation, applied biology, arboriculture, archaeology, archaeological and forensic sciences, archaeology and prehistory, biological sciences, biodiversity conservation, building conservation, crime scene and international investigations, cultural services (libraries/museums), ecology & wildlife conservation, equine behaviour & welfare, field archaeology, forensic anthropology & crime scene investigation, biological anthropology, forensic archaeology/science/geoinformatics, heritage conservation management/and tourism, human osteoarchaeology, maritime archaeology, marine ecology, museum studies, outdoor management, recovery and identification of human remains, timber building conservation, world heritage resource management, zooarchaeology; BSc(Hons), CertHE, FdA, FdSc, MSc, PhD

School of Design, Engineering & Computing; www.dec.bournemouth.ac.uk

architectural visualization/modelling and animation/ technical illustration, applied art & design, business / business information technology, computer-aided design – graphics & packaging, computer games design/networking/security, computing, design engineering/visualization, digital media development, electronics and computer technology, engineering (manufacturing management/mechanical design/ engineering/electrical technology), entertainment technology, fashion and textiles, digital music, industrial design, forensic computing & security, games technology, information technology management, internet communication systems/communication systems, music and sound technology, network systems management, product design, project management, psychology, smart systems and technology, software engineering/management/product design, sound design technology, sustainable graphics & packaging, sustainable product design, web systems, wireless and mobile networks; BSc(Hons), Foundation degrees, HNC, HND, MA, MPhil, MSc, PhD

School of Health and Social Care; www.bournemouth.ac.uk/hsc

advanced nurse practitioner, children & family studies, urgent care practice, leadership & management, midwifery, psychosocial interventions, vulnerable adults, advanced mental health practice/ practice, nursing, public health; AdvDip, BA(Hons), BSc(Hons), DipHE, FdA, FdSc, MPhil, PGDip/Cert, PhD, Dr Prof Practice

The Media School; www.media.bournemouth.ac.uk

advertising, marketing communications, communication & media, 3D computer animation arts, computer visualization, digital cinematography, English, film production & cinematography, global computer animation practice, interactive media production, marketing, media production, multimedia, multimedia journalism, music, music technology, performing arts: contemporary theatre performance/ dance/ music/theatre, photography, film and television, popular music, PR, radio production, software design for games, scriptwriting for film and television, soundtrack production, television and film production, writing for media, video production; BA(Hons), BSc(Hons), FdA, MA, MBA, MPhil, MSc, PhD

School of Services Management; www.bournemouth.ac.uk/services/ management

applied animal/countryside management, golf and sports turf /events/hospitality/ international hospitality and tourism management, international retail marketing/tourism/European tourism management, landscape design, leisure marketing, retail management, sports coaching & athlete development, tourism & spa management, sports development & coaching/management, sports psychology & coaching sciences; BA(Hons), FdA, FdSc/Cert HE, MPhil, MSc, PhD

UNIVERSITY OF BRADFORD
www.bradford.ac.uk

School of Computing, Informatics and Media; www.scim.brad.ac.uk

Computing; www.computics.brad.ac.uk advanced computer science, artificial intelligence for games computing, business computing, computer science for games, multimedia computing, forensic computing computer science, ICT with business/law/marketing/media/psychology, informatics, information systems, intelligent systems and robotics, internet computing, mobile computing, networks and performance engineering, software development applications, software engineering

Media: digital arts and media, digital and creative enterprise, digital cinema, digital media /& technologies, film studies, informatics, media studies with/ cinematics/computer animation/digital imaging/ music technology/television/web design, media

technology and production, television production, web design and technology, web technologies
Mathematics; www.maths.brad.ac.uk applied mathematics, computational mathematics, informatics, space science
Creative technology: advanced computer animation and special effects, computer animation, graphics for games, informatics, interactive systems and video games design, visual computing; BA(Hons), BSc(Hons), MAMSc, FdSc

School of Engineering, Design and Technology; www.eng.brad.ac.uk

advanced materials engineering, automotive design technology, automotive engineering quality improvement, civil & structural engineering, clinical technology, computer-aided engineering, e-business technology & management, electrical & electronic engineering, power electronics, electromechanical technology, telecommunications & internet engineering, engineering and management, information technology management, industrial engineering, manufacturing engineering/management, mechanical/ & automotive engineering, mechanical & vehicle technology, medical engineering, personal, mobile & satellite communications, plant and process engineering, product design, technology management, wireless sensor & embedded systems; BEng, BSc, FD, MEng, MPhil, MSc, PhD

School of Health Studies; www.brad.ac.uk/acad/health

cancer care, dementia care, diagnostic radiography, health, wellbeing and social care, midwifery, nursing (adult branch/mental health branch/child branch), nursing practice (acutely ill adult/cancer and palliative care/pain management/tissue viability) nursing studies (adult, child, mental health), occupational therapy, physiotherapy; AdvDip, BSc(Hons), CertHE, DipHE, FD, MSc, MPhil, PGDip/Cert, PhD

School of Life Sciences; www.brad.ac.uk/acad/lifesci

Div of Archaeological Geographical & Environmental Sciences

archaeological prospection/sciences, archaeology, bioarchaeology, environmental management/science, forensic and archaeological sciences, forensic archaeology and crime scene investigation, human osteology and palaeopathology, physical and environmental geography; BA, BSc, CertHE, MA, MSc, MPhil, PhD

Div of Biomedical Sciences

applied/ biomedical science, cellular pathology, medical biochemistry, medical microbiology, pharmacology; BSc(Hons), MSC, PgD

Bradford School of Pharmacy

clinical pharmacy, pharmacy, pharmaceutical services and medicines control; DPharm, MSC, MPharm

Dept of Chemical and Forensic Sciences

chemistry; chemistry for analysis/drug discovery/medicines development/chemistry with pharmaceutical and forensic science, clinical sciences, forensic sciences, medical sciences; BSc(Hons), MPhil, PhD

Div of Optometry

optometry; BSc, MPhil, PhD

Institute of Cancer Therapeutics

cancer pharmacology, drug discovery, safety pharmacology; MPhil, MSc, PhD

The School of Lifelong Education and Development; www.brad.ac.uk/admin/conted/cfa

employability and entrepreneurship, integrated emergency management, regeneration project management, TESOL and linguistics, training and development, community regeneration and development, community justice, public sector administration; Foundation degrees, Certs, MA, MSc, PGDip/Cert

The School of Management; www.brad.ac.uk/acad/management

accounting, business studies, finance, financial, business and management studies, HRM, international business and management, law, management, financial management, European management marketing; BA(Hons), BSc(Hons), DBA, LlB, GradDip(Law), Int Masters MBA, MRes, PhD

The School of Social and International Studies; www.brad.ac.uk/acad/ssis

applied criminal justice, business economics, conflict resolution, creative writing, criminology, development and peace studies, development studies, diversity and social policy, economics, English, financial economics, history, interdisciplinary human studies, international development/ economics/relations, international relations and security studies, mental health practice, peace studies, philosophy, politics/ and law, psychology, social policy, social work, sociology; BA(Hons), BSc(Hons), MA, MPhil, PhD, PGDip

Degrees validated by University of Bradford offered at:

BRADFORD COLLEGE
www.bradfordcollege.ac.uk

Art & Design: 3D design (interior design), advertising and fine art, arts for the creative industries, contemporary surface design and textiles, engineering illustration and digital media, fashion design, fine art, multimedia & design graphic design, photography (editorial, advertising and fine art), visual arts
Accountancy and Law: accountancy, advertising and campaign management marketing, business administration, business (finance), business management, business studies, financial services, HRM, information technology, international business management, law/ legal practice, management, marketing and sales, project management
Interior Design: beauty therapy, beauty therapy sciences, creative hairdressing, make-up effects and artistry
Education Studies: culture, ICT citizenship, identity and learning, early years practice, graduate and registered teacher programme early years, inclusive education, leadership & management in education, PGCE primary/French, PGCE secondary (11–18, age ranges) science, physics, chemistry, maths), post-compulsory education and training foundation degree, primary education with qualified teacher status (QTS), supporting and managing learning in education, teaching
Law and Social Welfare: counselling and psychology, creative practice in community settings, health and social welfare, person centred community development work, public services management, social & community care, social work, supported & community housing, youth and community development
Computing: business computing solutions, computing computing (general, ICT systems support, software development), network infrastructure technologies, software applications development
Construction (architecture, quantity surveying and construction management): construction design, construction engineering management, electrical, electronic, mechanical and manufacturing engineering, metallurgy and materials
Diet, Nutrition and Health: health-related exercise and fitness, hospitality and travel management, ophthalmic dispensing with management, outdoor adventurous activities, pharmacy, sports coaching, sports science, travel and tourism management; BSc(Hons), CertHE, DipHE, Foundation degrees, HNC, HNDBA(Hons), LlB(Hons), MA, MEd, PGDipCert

UNIVERSITY OF BRIGHTON
www.brighton.ac.uk

Faculty of Arts; www.arts.brighton.ac.uk

School of Architecture and Design, School of Arts and Media, School of Humanities

architectural design, architecture; English language, linguistics, media; textiles/fashion with business studies; critical fine art practice, inclusive arts practice, painting, printmaking, sculpture; film and screen studies, history of decorative art and crafts, history of design, culture, history of design and material culture, museum and heritage studies, visual culture; applied ethics, conflict, culture, cultural and critical theory, globalization, histories /and cultures, history, humanities and critical studies, literatures, modernity cultures, politics, war; architectural and urban studies, interior architecture, interior design; English language teaching studies, media-assisted language teaching, TESOL/TEFL; broadcast /creative media, English language, English literature, English studies, media; media studies; radio production, television production; dance performance visual art, music performance visual art theatre performance; 3D design, 3D materials practice, digital music and sound art, moving image, film and screen studies, photography/ & sound, sustainable design: arts and design by independent project, digital media arts (lighthouse), graphic design, illustration, sequential design/illustration; BA(Hons), FdSA, Grad Dip, MA, MDes, MFA, MPhil, PGDip/ Cert, PhD

Faculty of Education and Sport; www.brighton.ac.uk/fes

Chelsea School; www.brighton.ac.uk/chelsea

education in dance, exercise and health science, exercise physiology, fitness, international sport policy, PE, initial teacher education, physical education with QTS, sport and exercise science, /leisure management, sport coaching /& development, sport, culture and media/ society, sport development/journalism studies,

School of Education; www.brighton.ac.uk/education

early years care and education, early years professional status, learning and development, English literature and education, information technology education, key stage 2/key stage 3 English education/ICT education/mathematics /science education, design and technology education, mathematics education, PGCE-primary education 5–11 years/3–7 years, numerous subjects, primary education 3–7 years/5–11 years, post-compulsory education, professional education studies, professional studies in learning and development/primary education, RE, science education, working with young people, youth work

Centre for Learning and Teaching; www.brighton.ac.uk/clt

learning and development; learning and teaching in HE; BA(Hons), BSc(Hons), CertEd, EdD, FdA, MA, MPhil, MPhil/PhD, MSc, PGCert, PGCE, PhD

Faculty of Health and Social Science; www.brighton.ac.uyk/fhss

School of Applied Social Science; www.brighton.ac.uk/sass

applied psychology, community psychology, counselling and psychotherapy, criminology, health and social care, mental health, politics, psychology, psychosocial studies, social policy, social science, social work, sociology, substance misuse; BA(Hons), MA, MPhil, MSc, PGDip/Cert, PhD

School of Health Professions; www.brighton.ac.uk/sohs

clinical education, health through occupation, neuromusculoskeletal physiotherapy, occupational therapy, physiotherapy/and education/management, podiatry, rehabilitation science, sports injury management; BS(Hons), MSc, PGDip/Cert, PhD, Prof Doc

School of Nursing and Midwifery; www.brighton.ac.uk/snm

acute and critical care, acute clinical practice, adult/child/mental health nursing, children, family and public health, community specialist practice, health studies nurse practitioner, mental health and psychosocial care, midwifery, paramedic practice, professional practice, specialist community public health nursing, supporting long-term care; BSc(Hons), FdSc, MPhil, MRes, MSc, PGDip/Cert, PhD

Faculty of Management and Information Sciences; www.brighton.ac.uk/mis

Brighton Business School; www.brighton.ac.uk/bbs

accounting, business administration, business management, business management with finance, business studies, change management, economics, finance, general management, international business, investment, logistics and supply chain management, management, management (entrepreneurship/human resources/public service), personnel and development, professional accounting, public service management; ACCA, BA(Hons), LlB, MBA, MSc

School of Service Management; www.brighton.ac.uk/ssm

culinary arts, food and culinary arts, hospitality and event management, international event management/event marketing/ hospitality management/ tourism management/travel management, retail management/ enterprise/ marketing, tourism and international development, tourism and social anthropology, travel and tourism management, travel and tourism marketing; BA(Hons), FdA, MA, MSc, PhD

School of Computing, Mathematical and Information Sciences; www.brighton.ac.uk/cmis

business computer systems, business information systems, computer games development, computer science/ (games), computing, computing with business, digital media, digital television management and production, e-learning design, enterprise systems, European computing, information managemen/(health), information studies, information systems, interactive technology design, internet and distributed systems, internet computing/systems architecture, learning technologies, mathematics, mathematics & computing, mathematics with business, networked systems, software engineering; BA/

BSc(Hons), FdSc, MA, MComp, MPhil, MSc, PGDip, PGCert

Faculty of Science and Engineering; www.brighton.ac.uk/scieng

School of Environment and Technology; www.brighton.ac.uk/set

Built Environment: architectural technology, building studies, building surveying, construction management, environmental assessment and management, facilities management, project management for construction, sustainability of the built environment, town planning; civil engineering, civil with environmental engineering; automotive electronic engineering, computing & communications, digital electronics, electrical and electronic engineering; environmental/hazards/management and assessment/sciences, environment and media studies, GIS sustainability of the built environment, town planning, water and environmental management; geography, GIS and environmental management; earth and ocean science, environmental geology, geology; aeronautical engineering, automotive electronic engineering, automotive engineering, mechanical engineering, manufacturing engineering; product design/ product design technology/sports product design/ sustainable product design with professional experience; BA/BSc(Hons), BEng(Hons), BSc(Hons), FdSc, FdEng, MEng, MPhil, PGDip/Cert, PhD

School of Pharmacy and Biomolecular Sciences; www.brighton.ac.uk/pharmacy

analytical chemistry with business, applied/ biomedical science, biological sciences, biomedical science (cellular pathology), bioscience, pharmacy and biomolecular sciences clinical biochemistry, medical microbiology, haematology and transfusion science, ecology and biogeography, clinical pharmacy practice, community pharmaceutical health care, industrial pharmaceutical studies, pharmaceutical and biomedical sciences, chemical sciences, pharmacy; BSc(Hons), MSc, MPharmHons, MPhil, MRes, PGDip, PhD

Brighton and Sussex Medical School; www.bsms.ac.uk

cardiology, clinical education, diabetes, health or social care, leadership and management in health care, medicine, nephrology, public health, surgery; BM, BS, MD, MPhil, MSc, PGDip/Cert, PhD

Institute of Postgraduate Medicine

UNIVERSITY OF BRISTOL
www.bris.ac.uk

Faculty of Arts; www.bris.ac.uk/arts

School of Arts; www.bris.ac.uk/arts

Dept of Archaeology; www.bris.ac.uk/archanth;

ancient history, anthropology, archaeological and anthropological sciences/studies, conflict archeology, historical and landscape archeology, maritime archeology, social anthropology

Dept of Drama, Theatre, Film, Television; www.bris.ac.uk/drama

documentary practice, cinema studies, composition of music for film and television, drama, film and television production, performance research

Dept of Music; www.bris.ac.uk/music

British music, composition/ for film and television, medieval music, music, music theory, musicology, performance, Russian music

Dept of Philosophy; www.bris.ac.uk/philosophy

philosophy and French/German/Italian/Portugese/ Russian/Spanish/classical studies/English/economics/ politics/psychology/mathematics/physics/sociology/ law/the history of science; BA(Hons), BSc(Hons), MA, Mlitt, MMus, MSci, PGDip, PhD

School of Humanities; www.bris.ac.uk/humanities

Dept of Classics & Ancient History; www.bris.ac.uk/classics

ancient history, ancient history & archaeology classical studies, classics, history

Dept of English; www.bris.ac.uk/english

English, English and philosophy/classical studies/ drama, English literature and community engagement, modern and contemporary poetry, romanticism, Shakespeare and English literature

Dept of History; www.bris.ac.uk/history

colonialism, contemporary history, histories, peoples, cultures, history, medieval and early modern history, Russian history, ancient history

Dept of Art History; www.bris.ac.uk/arthistory

art histories and interpretations, history of art

Dept of Theology and Religious Studies; www.bris.ac.uk/thrs
biblical studies, theology and religious studies, Buddhist studies, interfaith studies, modern theology, New Testament archaeology of early Christianity, philosophy and ethics, reception of the bible: tradition, theology and politics/sociology/philosophy

School of Modern Languages; www.bris.ac.uk/sml
French, German, Hispanic, Portuguese and Latin American studies, Italian, Russian, Russian studies (includes Czech); Mandarin, translation, European literatures, modern languages, Russian history, literary and cultural studies, linguistics; BA(Hons), MA, MLitt, MPhil, PGDip, PhD

Faculty of Engineering; www.bris.ac.uk/engineering

Dept of Aerospace Engineering; www.bris.ac.uk/aerospace
aerospace systems design/engineering, aeronautical engineering

Dept of Civil Engineering; www.bris.ac.uk/civilengineering
civil engineering, water and environmental management

Dept of Computer Science; www.cs.bris.ac.uk
computer science/and electronic/mathematics, internet technologies with multimedia, security machine learning and data mining/ advanced microelectronic systems, computer resources

Dept of Electrical and Electronic Engineering; www.bris.ac.uk/eeng
optical communications, communications and multimedia engineering, communication networks and signal processing, computer science and electronics, electrical and electronic engineering, electronic and communications engineering, image & video communications, wireless communication systems and signal processing

Dept of Engineering Mathematics; www.enm.bris.ac.uk
advanced computing (machine learning) applied nonlinear mathematics, artificial intelligence, engineering mathematics

Dept of Mechanical Engineering; www.bris.ac.uk/mecheng
advanced/ mechanical engineering, solid mechanics; BSc(Hons), BEng, EngDPGCert MEng, MSc, PhD,

Faculty of Medical and Veterinary Science; www.bris.ac.uk/mvs

Dept of Anatomy; www.bris.ac.uk/anatomy
anatomical science, anatomical science with veterinary anatomy, human musculoskeletal science, neuroscience,

Dept of Biochemistry; www.bris.ac.uk/biochemistry
biochemistry/with molecular biology and biotechnology, medical biochemistry, quantitative cell imaging

Dept of Cellular and Molecular; Medicine; www.bris.ac.uk/cellmolmed
cancer biology, immunology, medical /microbiology, pathology, transfusion and transplantation science, virology

Dept of Clinical Veterinary Science; www.vetschool.bris.ac.uk/
animal behaviour & welfare, meat science and technology, veterinary cellular and molecular science, veterinary nursing and bioveterinary science, veterinary parasitology, veterinary science

Dept of Physiology and Pharmacology; www.bris.ac.uk/phys-pharm
cardiovascular science, cell signalling & cell biology, neuroscience, pharmacology, physiological science; BSc(Hons), BVS, MD, MSc, MSci, PhD

Faculty of Medicine and Dentistry; www.bris.ac.uk/fmd

medicine, surgery, child and adolescent health, clinical sciences, dental implantology, dental studies (lingual orthodontics), ethics in medicine, medicine, health care ethics and law, molecular neuroscience, obstetrics & gynaecology, oral and dental science, palliative medicine, premedical programme, primary health care, psychiatry, reproduction and development, stem cells and regeneration, social medicine; MB, BDS, BSc(Hons), ChB, ChM, DDS, Diploma, DPDS, MClinDent, MD, MMedEd, MSci, PhD

Faculty of Science; www.bris.ac.uk/science

School of Biological Sciences; www.bris.ac.uk/biology

biology, botany, ecological & evolutionary processes, ecology and management of the natural environment, geology and biology, psychology and zoology, zoology

School of Chemistry; www.chm.bris.ac.uk/

chemistry, chemical physics, inorganic and materials chemistry, law with chemistry, organic and biological chemistry, physical and theoretical chemistry, chemical synthesis

School of Earth Sciences; www.gly.bris.ac.uk/

archaeological and anthropological sciences, biology, earth system science, earth sciences, environmental geoscience, geology, palaeobiology, science of natural hazards

Dept of Experimental Psychology; www.psychology.psy.bris.ac.uk/

biological psychology, cognition, computational neuroscience, neuropsychology, psychology and zoology, research methods, vision sciences

School of Geographical Sciences; www.ggy.bris.ac.uk/

geography, human geography, physical geography, society and space, science of natural hazards

Dept of Mathematics; www.maths.bris.ac.uk/

applied/pure mathematics, biology and mathematics, economics and mathematics, mathematics, mathematics and computer science/philosophy/physics/statistics, statistics

Dept of Physics; www.phsy.bris.ac.uk/

astrophysics, correlated electron systems, mathematics and physics, micro- and nanostructural materials, nanophysics and soft matter, particle physics, physics, physics with astrophysics, physics and philosophy, quantum photonics, theoretical physics; BSc(Hons), DSc, LlB, MRes, MSci, MSc, PhD, UGCert

Faculty of Social Science and Law; www.bris.ac.uk/fss

Centre for East Asian studies; www.bris.ac.uk/ceas/
East Asian studies/development and the global economy

Dept of Politics; www.bris.ac.uk/politics;
politics, international relations

Dept of Sociology; www.bris.ac.uk/sociology
advanced clinical audiology, economics, economics and econometrics/ finance/ public policy, education, educational research, ethnicity and multiculturalism, European governance, family therapy and systemic practice, gender and international relations, inclusive theory and practice (empowering people with learning disabilities), international development/relations/security, management learning and change, nutrition, physical activity and public health, policy research, politics, public policy, quantitative development economics, rehabilitative audiology, sign linguistics, social work, social work with children and young people, social and cultural theory, social science research methods (politics/international relations/sociology), society and space, sociology, strategic management, technology and society

Graduate School of Education; www.bris.ac.uk/education
education, educational research, science and education, teaching English to speakers of other languages

School for Policy Studies; www.bristol.ac.uk/sps

childhood studies, early childhood studies, international health, social policy/and politics/sociology

School of Applied Community and Health Studies; www.bris.ac.uk/sachs

Centre for Deaf Studies
audiology, deaf studies, deafhood studies

Dept of Exercise, Nutrition and Health Sciences
nutrition, physical activity and public health

audiological rehabilitation

Norah Fry Research Centre
educational psychology, inclusive theory and practice: empowering people with learning disabilities

Centre for Personal and Professional Development
counselling, creative writing for therapeutic purposes

School of Law; www.bris.ac.uk/law

law, law with chemistry, law and French/ German, socio-legal studies, adv studies legal system; BA(Hons), BSc(Hons), DSocSci, EdD, LlB, LlD, LlM, MEd, MPhil, MSc, MSci, PCGE, PhD

Degrees validated by University of Bristol offered at:

WESLEY COLLEGE BRISTOL
www.wesley-college-bristol.ac.uk

theological studies, theology/mission and ministry; BA(Hons), Diplomas and Certificates, MA, foundation degree

UNIVERSITY OF THE WEST OF ENGLAND, BRISTOL
www.uwe.ac.uk

Bristol Business School; www.uwe.ac.uk/bbs

applied social research, business enterprise, business studies/law, coaching and mentoring, economics/(international business), accounting, banking and finance, entrepreneurship, finance, finance and global operations, financial management (/professional learning and development), HRM, international HRM, international management, leadership and management in health and social care, leadership and organization of public services, management, marketing, marketing communications, social marketing, tourism development, sustainabilty for small businesses; BA(Hons), BSc(Hons), MA, MBA, MSc, PhD

School of Creative Arts; www.uwe.ac.uk/sca

animation, art and visual culture, art, media and design by project, creative practices, design: process, drama, drawing and applied arts, fashion design, fashion/textile design, film studies, fine art, graphic design, journalism, material, media (animation/photography); BA(Hons), FdA, MA, MPhil, PhD

Faculty of Environment and Technology; www.uwe.ac.uket

School of the Built and Natural Environment; www.uwe.ac.uk/bne

architecture and environmental enginering planning, applied social research (built environment), architectural technology and design, architecture, building surveying, built and natural environments, applied GIS, built environment studies/(urban design), climate and energy management, civil engineering, community safety and crime prevention, construction/commercial management, construction project management, countryside conservation and management, environmental engineering, geographical and environmental management, geography, geography and tourism, housing, housing development and management, integrated catchment management, law for construction professionals, planning, property, property development and planning, property management and investment, quantity surveying, real estate mnagement, river and coastal engineering, spatial planning, tourism and environmental management/sustainability, town and country planning, transport planning, urban and rural regeneration, urban design; BArch, BEng(Hons), BSc(Hons), DBEnv, FdSc, HNC, MA, MPlan, MPhil, MSc, PGDip/Cert, PhD

Bristol Institute of Technology; www.uwe.ac.uk/cems

electronics, aerospace/design engineering, audio and music technology, business information systems, computer science, digital media, electrical and electronic engineering, games technology, health informatics, information and library management, information technology, IT for business, manufacturing engineering, systems engineering, mathematics and statistics, mechanical engineering, music technology, product design, robotics, computer science for games, computer security, smart products, motor sport engineering software engineering, statistics and management science; BEng, BSc(Hons), FdSc, MEng, MPhil, MSc, PGDip/Cert, PhD

Faculty of Health and Life Sciences; www.uwe.ac.uk/hls

School of Life Sciences; www.uwe.ac.uk/hls/ls

applied/biochemistry and molecular biology/biological sciences/biomedical science, (clinical)/genetics/microbiology/physiology and pharmacology, biotechnology, cellular pathology, clinical chemistry, conservation biology, environmental biology/environmental health/science, forensic biology/chemistry/ science, counselling psychology, environmental consultancy/ health, forensic genetics, haematology, health psychology, health, safety and the environment, human biology, immunology, medical microbiology, molecular biotechnology, pharmaceutical sciences, psychology/ and forensic science/sports biology, science communication, sports biology, sports biomedicine; BSc(Hons), DBMS, MPhil, MSc, PGDip/Cert, PhD, ProfDocs

School of Health and Social Care; www.hsc.uwe.ac.uk

adult nursing, child and adolescent mental health, children's nursing, clinical research, community practice, diagnostic imaging, leadership and management in health and social care, leadership and organization of public services, learning disabilities/ mental health nursing, mental health/psychosocial interventions, midwifery, music therapy, nuclear medicine, occupational therapy, paramedic science, physiotherapy, specialist community/ public health, sports therapy and rehabilitation /advanced practice, substance misuse, veterinary physiotherapy, BSc(Hons) BSc, DipHE, FD, MSc, PhD, MPhil, PGCert/Dip, ProfDoc, ResDip

Faculty of Social Sciences and Humanities; www1.uwe.ac.uk/ssh/

Bristol Law School; www.law.uwe.ac.uk

commercial law, criminal justice, criminology, environmental law, criminal law, contract law, public law, European business law, European and international law, international economic law/human rights/trade law, industrial law, law; LlB, LlM, PhD

School of Education; www.uwe.ac.uk/ssh/education

applied social research, business and education, drama and education, early childhood studies, early years education, education in professional practice, English/ psychology, guidance (vocational/educational), HE learning support, initial teacher education, leadership and organisation of public services, mental health nursing, music therapy, PGCE lower primary – early years (3–7)/post-16 training post-compulsory education and training/secondary art and design/business education/design and technology/English/geography/history/mathematics/modern languages/science/upper primary (7–11), primary education, learning and skills, special education, vocational education; ASR, BA(Hons), CertEd, DipHE, MA, MPhil, MSc PGCert/Dip, PhD,

School of Languages, Humanities & Social Science www.uwe.ac.uk/lhss

English, history, international history with international politics, regional histories; European business, English language, linguistics, translation, intercultural communication; criminology, human rights, international relations, peace and conflict studies, politics, philosophy, sociology, psychosocial studies; BA, MA, PGDip/Cert, PhD

Hartpury College (Associate Faculty); www.hartpury.ac.uk

agricultural business management, amenity horticultural management, animal behaviour and welfare, animal management, animal science, bioveterinary science, conservation and countryside management; equine/business management/dental science/performance/sports science; food and drink manufacturing; coaching science, golf management, outdoor adventure / sport and exercise management, sport/events/ management/studies/business management/coaching performance

Veterinary Nursing; equine veterinary nursing science, veterinary nursing science, veterinary practice management; BA(Hons), BSc(Hons), FdSc, FdA, MA, MSc

BRUNEL UNIVERSITY
www.brunel.ac.uk

School of Arts; www.brunel.ac.uk /about/ acad /sa

contemporary literature and culture/music/performance making, creative writing, digital games theory and design/performance, documentary practice, drama, cult film & TV, games design, journalism, modern drama studies, music, musical composition/ performance, the novel, sonic arts, TV studies; BA(Hons), BMus, MA, MMus, MPhil, PhD

Brunel Law School; www.brunel.ac.uk/about/acad/bls

law, legal practice, consumer affairs, European and international commercial law, intellectual property/ economic/international economic and trade/international human rights law, public international law and world order; CPE, European Masters, GradDip, LlM, LLB, MPhil, PhD

School of Engineering and Design; www.brunel.ac.uk /about/acad /sed

advanced manufacturig systems, engineering management, packing technology, design and branding, integrated product design, multimedia design & 3D technologies, data communication systems, engineering, sustainable electrical power, wireless communication systems, advanced engineering design/ mechanical engineering, aerospace engineering, automotive and motorsport engineering, biomedical engineering, building services engineering/management/ with sustainable energy, sustainable energy technologies; BA(Hons), BEng, BSc(Hons), EngD, MEng, MPhil, MSc, PhD

Brunel Business School; www.brunel.ac.uk /about/acad/bbs

business and management, accounting, marketing, business studies, international business, corporate brand management, e-business systems, global supply chain management, HRM, human resource and employment relations, international business management; BSc, MSc, MBA, PhD

School of Health Sciences and Social Care; www.brunel.ac.uk/about/acad/health

biomedical sciences, biochemistry/forensics/genetics/ human health/immunology), occupational therapy, physiotherapy, social work, specialist community public health nursing, specialist social work (adults)(children and families), health promotion and public health, neurorehabilitation, occupational health and safety management, occupational therapy, molecular medicine, cancer research, urgent care, social work; BSc, BA, MSc, MA, PGDip, PGCert

School of Information Systems, Computing and Mathematics; www.brunel.ac.uk/about/acad/siscm

artificial intelligence, computational mathematics with modelling, computer science, computing, digital media and games, enterprise systems architecture, financial computing, information and communication technology, information systems (business/e-commerce/human–computer interaction/social web), mathematics, modelling and management of risk, network computing, software computing, financial mathematics, statistics, systems integration; BSc, MSc, MTech, PhD

School of Social Sciences; www.brunel.ac.uk/about/acad/sss

accounting, economics, finance, social anthropology, anthropology and psychology/sociology, business economics/ finance/management, governance, health, history, international money, international politics, international relations, investment, media and communications, media studies, medical anthropology, politics, psychoanalysis, psychology, public affairs and lobbying, public policy, social and cultural research, sociology, intelligences and security, child welfare; BA, BSc, MRes, MSc, PhD

School of Sport and Education; www.brunel.ac.uk/about/acad/sse

secondary education, sport science (coaching, human performance, management, PE & youth sport), youth and community studies/work, child welfare and protection in sport, PGCE (secondary) English, physical education, science (primary with QTS, sport and exercise psychology, human performance, sport psychology), BA, BSc, EdD, MA, MPhil, MSc, PGCert, PhD

University Specialist Research Institutes offer postgraduate degree opportunities

UNIVERSITY OF BUCKINGHAM
www.buckingham.ac.uk

Buckingham Business School; www.buckingham.ac.uk/business/about/bbs

accounting, business, business enterprise, communication, communication studies, economics, finance, financial management, information systems, management, marketing, media communications, service; BSc(Econ)(Hons), BSc(Hons), CMS, MBA, MSc/ Diploma

Dept of Education; www.beds.ac.uk/departments/schoolofeducation/education

Teacher Training; independent PGCE, PGCE with QTS, educational leadership, performance management; MEd

School of Humanities; www.buckingham.ac.uk/humanities

Dept of Economics & International Studies; www.beds.ac.uk/international

biography, business journalism, business, communication studies, business/economics, EFL, English literature, EFL/ESL, English studies/for teaching, French, global affairs, history, information systems, international business and trade, international studies, journalism, law, decorative arts, media studies/communication, military history, politics, psychology, security and intelligence studies, Spanish, TESOL; BA(Hons), BSc(Econ)Hons, DPhil, MA, MPhil, MSc

Buckingham School of Law; www.buckingham.ac.uk/law

access to law, common law, international and commercial law, law; Certificate, Diploma, LlB, LlM

School of Medicine; www.buckingham.ac.uk/medicine

graduate entry/postgraduate schools medical school; Clinical MD, MBBS, MSc

School of Science; www.buckingham.ac.uk/science

applied computing, computing, innovative computing; BSc, Cert Comp, MSc, PGDip, Phd

Psychology; www.buckingham.ac.uk/psychology

psychology, obesity, cognition & perception, developmental/educational/music psychology; BSc(Hons), MPhil, MSc, PhD

Clore Laboratory

diabetes, obesity and metabolic research, bioinformatics; DPhil, MPhil, MSc

BUCKINGHAMSHIRE NEW UNIVERSITY
www.bucks.ac.uk

Faculty of Design, Media & Management; www.bucks.ac.uk/about/structure/academic/faculties/design-media-management

School of Applied Management & Law; www.bucks.ac.uk/about/structure/academic-schools/applied-management-law

business, international management, sports management and science, music and entertainment industries, advertising, HRM, accounting and finance, events and festival management, law, commercial pilot training

School of Design, Craft & Visual Arts; www.bucks.ac.uk/about/structure/academicschools/design-craft-visual-arts

conservation and interpretation of cultural artefacts, new media, internet technologies, creative industries, visual imagery

School of Applied Production & New Media; www.bucks.ac.uk/about/structure/academicschools/music-entertainment-image

commercial music, film and television production, music and entertainment, art management, music management, creative industries, new media, production, journalism, scriptwriting, performance

Faculty of Society and Health; www.bucks.ac.uk/about/structure/faculties/society-and-health

School of Social Sciences, Primary Care & Education; www.bucks.ac.uk/about/structure/academicschools/social-care-education

community health care, public health practice, community health care, mentorship/practice teacher/practice education, social work, mental health nursing, education, psychology/cognitive behavioural therapy, criminology/police studies

School of Advanced and Continuing Practice; www.bucks.ac.uk/about/structure/academicschools/advanced-continuing-practice
cancer and palliative /critical/respiratory care, nurse practitioner (acute care/emergency care/primary care), advanced practice

School of Pre qualifying Nursing; www.bucks.ac.uk/about/structure/academicschools/pre-registration-nursing
BA(Hons), BSc(Hons), Certs, DMS, GradDip, FD, HNC, HND, LlB(Hons), LlM, MA, MBA, MCommunMan, MSc, PhD, FD

UNIVERSITY OF CAMBRIDGE
www.cam.ac.uk

School of Arts and Humanities; www.csah.cam.ac.uk

Faculty of Architecture and History of Art; www.aha.cam.ac.uk
architecture, environmental design, design in the built environment, history of art, medieval art and architecture, Renaissance art & architecture, 20th-century art & theory, western & non-western cultural exchange; BA, MPhil, MSt, PhD

Faculty of Asian & Middle Eastern Studies; www.ames.cam.ac.uk
Chinese studies, Hebrew and Semetic studies, Japanese studies, Middle Eastern and Islamic studies, Korean studies, Arabic & Persian studies, East Asia, Southern Asia studies, Assyriology, Egyptolgy; BA, MPhil, PhD

Faculty of Classics; www.classics.cam.ac.uk
art and archaeology, classics, Greek and Latin literature, history, philology and linguistics, philosophy; BA, MPhil, PGCE

Faculty of Divinity; www.divinity.cam.ac.uk
biblical studies, church history, historical and systematic theology, religious studies and the philosophy of religion, the Christian tradition; BA, MPhil, PhD, PGDip

Faculty of English; www.english.cam.ac.uk
American literature, Anglo-Saxon, Norse & Celtic, English & applied linguistics, medieval/English literature, European languages and literatures, English studies: criticism and culture/18th-century and romantic studies; language for literature; BA, MLitt, MPhil, PhD

Faculty of Modern and Medieval Languages; www.mml.cam.ac.uk
Depts of French, German & Dutch, Italian, Spanish and Portuguese, European literature, Linguistics, Modern Greek, neo-Latin, Russian studies, screen & media cultures, Slavonic studies; BA, MPhil, PhDE

Faculty of Music; www.mus.cam.ac.uk
ethnomusicology, historical musicology, music/with education studies, analysis, practical musicianship, tonal compositions and analysis and repertoire, musical composition, science and music, choral studies; BA, MPhil, Ph, MMusD

Faculty of Philosophy; www.phil.cam.ac
ethics, experimental psychology, history of philosophy, logic, metaphysics, philosophy of science, political philosophy, aesthetics, mathematical logic, ancient philosophy; BA, MPhil, PhD

School of Humanities and Social Science; www.cshss.cam.ac.uk

Faculty of Archaeology and Anthropology; www.archanthcam.ac
archaeological heritage & museum, archaeology, archaeology of the Americas, biological anthropology, Egyptian archaeology, European prehistory, human evolutionary studies, medieval archaeology, Mesopotamian studies, palaeolithic and mesolithic archaeology, social anthropology, south Asian archaeology; BA, MPhil, PhD

Faculty of Economics; www.econ..cam.ac.uk
asset pricing, behavioural economics, British industrialisation, economics of networks, economics of poor countries, industrial organisation, microeconomics, politics, quantitative methods, microeconomics, macroeeconometricsconomics; BA, Diploma, MPhil, PhD

Faculty of Education; www.educ.cam.ac.uk
arts culture and education, child and adolescent counselling, citizenship and wellbeing in schools, critical approaches to children's literature, education,

educational leadership and school improvement, inclusive and special psychology and education, mathematics, PGCE; early years, primary, secondary, second language education; BA, MEd, PGCE, PGDip/Cert, PhD

Faculty of History; www.hist.cam.ac.uk

American history, British political and constitutional history, economic history, European history, extra-European history, medieval history, political thought; BA, MPhil, PhD

Faculty of Law; www.law.cam.ac.uk

criminological research, criminology, international law, law, legal studies, large range of legal topics at Master level; BA, Diploma, LLD, LLM, MLitt, MPhil, PhD

Institute of Criminology; www.crim.cam.ac

applied /criminology, penology and management, applied criminology and police management; MPhil, MSt, PhD

Faculty of Politics, Psychology, Sociology and International Studies; www.ppsis.cam.ac.uk

Politics and International Studies; www.ppsis.cam.ac.uk

history of political thought, international relations, modern world politics, the political theorists, politics, representative democracy; BA, MPhil, MSt, PhD

Dept of Social and Developmental Psychology

psychology, social and developmental psychology

Dept of Sociology

sociology, modern society and global transformations; BA, MPhil, PhD

Centre for Family Research

bioethics & the family, early social development & the family, genetics, health & families, non-traditional families, parent, children & family relationships; MPhil, PhD

History and Philosophy of Science; www.hps.cam.ac.uk

history, philosophy and sociology of science, technology and medicine, classical traditions in science, natural philosophy, science in society; BA, MPhil, PhD

Land Economy; www.landecon.cam.ac.uk

environmental policy, land economy, planning, growth and regeneration, real estate finance; BA, MPhil, PhD

Centre of Latin American Studies; www.latin-america.cam.ac.uk

economic issues in contemporary Latin America, history of South American external relations, Latin American literary culture/film and visual arts, race and ethnicity/anthropology/sociology and politics in Latin America; MPhil, PhD

Centre of African Studies; www.africa.cam.ac.uk

African studies; MPhil

Centre of South Asian Studies

modern South Asian studies; MPhil

Development Studies Committee; www.devstudies.cam.ac.uk

development studies; MPhil

School of Biological Sciences; www.cam.ac.uk/sbs

Faculty of Biology; www.cam.ac.uk

agriculture, biochemistry, biotechnology and pharmacological industries, experimental psychology, genetics, genomes and gene products, health, integrated functional systems, pathology, pharmacology, physiology, development and neuroscience, plant sciences, zoology; BA, MPhil, PhD

Faculty of Veterinary Medicine

Department of Veterinary Medicine; www.vet.cam.ac.uk/

Clinical Course: veterinary science, preclinical course; MPhil, VetMB

Wellcome Trust Centre for Stem Cell Research; www.cscr.cam.ac.uk

stem cell biology; PhD

Wellcome Trust/Cancer Research UK Gurdon InstituteTechnolog; www.gurdon.cam.ac.uk

cellular and molecular biology, developmental, cell and cancer biology; PhD

Post Doc School of Technology; www.tech.ac.uk

Faculty of Engineering; www.eng.cam.ac.uk

engineering (aerospace & aerothermal,) civil, electrical & electronic, engineering for sustainable development, environmental, industrial systems, information & computer, instrument & control, manufacture and management, manufacturing, mechanical, structural; BA(Hons), MEng, MPhil, PhD

Faculty of Business & Management (Judge Business School); www.jbs.cam.ac.uk
business & management economics, energy & environment, finance & accounting, information systems, international business, management science & operations, organizational analysis, management, institutional relations, creating customer loyalty; MBA, MFin

Computer Laboratory; www.clcam.ac.uk
advanced computer science, computer science, computer speech, text and internet technology; BA, MPhil, PhD

Department of Chemical Engineering & Biotechnology; www.ceb.cam.ac.uk
advanced chemical engineering, bioscience enterprise, biotechnology, chemical engineering; BA/MEng, MPhil, PhD

Cambridge Programme for Sustainability Leadership; www.cpi.cam.ac.uk
cross-sector partnership, sustainable business, sustainability leadership; sustainable cities biodiversity & ecostem services, climate leadership; MSt, PGCert

School of Physical Sciences; www.cam.ac.uk/about/physsci

Faculty of Earth Sciences & Geography; www.esg.cam.ac.uk
conservation leadership, earth sciences, environment, environmental science, geography, geological science, minerals science, society & development; BA, MPhil, PhD

Scott Polar Research Institute; www.spri.cam.ac.uk
glaciology, polar studies, ocean geoplitica, climate change; MPhil, PhD

Faculty of Mathematics; www.maths.cam.ac.uk
applied mathematics and theoretical physics, computational bilology, mathematics, mathematics with physics, pure mathematics and mathematical statistics, statistical science; BA, MPhil, PhD, MMath, MAdvStud

Statistical Laboratory Faculty of Physics & Chemistry; www.statslab.cam.ac.uk
astronomy, astrophysics, materials science and metallurgy, nanoscience & technology, physical, theoretical inorganic, organic chemistry, physics, statistical science, mathematical statistics; BA, MPhil, MSci, PhD

School of Clinical Medicine; www.medschl.cam.ac.uk

Dept of Clinical Biochemistry (Metabolic Research Laboratories); www.clbc.cam.ac.uk
biomedical research, diabetes, molecular cell biology of membrane traffic pathways, obesity and other related endocrine and metabolic disorders; PhD

Dept of Clinical Neurosciences (Cambridge Centre for Brain Repair; Neurology Unit; Neurosurgery; Wolfson Brain Imaging Centre); www.neurosciences.medschl.am.ac.uk
cognitive brain science, dementia, genetics of multiple sclerosis, glial cell biology unit, haemorrhagic stroke, hydrocephalus, memory and semantics group, movement disorders, stroke research; MB/PhD

Dept of Haematology; www.haem.cam.ac.uk
transfusion medicine diagnostics development; PhD

Dept of Medical Genetics; www.cimr.cam.ac.uk/medgen
eye diseases, genetics of inflammatory disorders, juvenile diabetes; BChir, MB, MD, PhD

Dept of Medicine
anasthesia, clinical pharmacology

Obstetrics & Gynaecology

Oncology

Paediatrics

Psychiatry
brain mapping, developmental psychiatry

Pubic Health & primary Care
general practice & primary care research, clinical gerentology

Radiology

Surgery
orthopaedic research

CAMBRIDGE INTERNATIONAL COLLEGE
www.cambridgecollege.ac.uk

business and economics, financial management, marketing and management, human resource administration; BA, Diplomas

CANTERBURY CHRIST CHURCH UNIVERSITY
www.canterbury.ac.uk

Faculty of Arts and Humanities; www.canterbury.ac.uk/arts-humanities

access to music, American studies, applied linguistics, art, commercial music, digital media, English language and communication/language studies, film, radio and television studies, film production, fine and applied arts, history, history with archaeology, media, media and cultural studies, multimedia journalism, music, music production, music technology, performing arts, religious studies, theology, visual art; BA(Hons), BA/BSc, Foundation Degree, MA, MMus, MPhil/PhD, PGDip

Faculty of Business and Management; www.canterbury.ac.uk/business-management

The Business School; www.canterbury.ac.uk/business-management/business-school

accounting and finance, advertising management, business & management, business management, business studies, culinary business, economics, entrepreneurship, human resources management, logistics, management studies, managerial finance, marketing, music industry management, retail management

Centre for Leadership & Management; www.canterbury.ac.uk/business-management/CLMD

coaching, leadership development, organizational development, personal effectiveness, project management, recruitment and selection, team dev, management studies; BSc(Hons), MA, MBA, MPhil/PhD, MSc, PGDip/Cert

Faculty of Education; www.canterbury.ac.uk/ education

childhood/early childhood studies, early years/professional status/ studies, educational studies, enabling learning, inclusion and institutional development, leadership and management for learning, lifelong learning, literacy and learning, religion in education, school development, teaching skills for life – numeracy, literacy/ESOL, PGCE; primary teaching, 7–14, 11–16 (iteach), 11–18, 14–19, post-compulsory primary education, teaching & learning, modular (primary/secondary), ICT research; post-compulsory education, post-graduate initial teacher education, primary education, professional development; BA(Hons), EdD, EYPS, FDA, MA, MPhil/PhD

Faculty of Health and Social Care; www.canterbury.ac.uk/health/home

Department of Allied Health Professions; www.canterbury.ac.uk/health/allied-health-professions

advanced occupational therapy practice, clinical reporting, diagnostic radiography, health and social care, medical imaging, occupational therapy, radiography, speech language therapy, dispensing opticians

Centre for Health and Social Care Research; www.canterbury.ac.uk/health/health-social-care-research

Dementia Services Development Centre South East; www.dementiacentre.canterbury.ac.uk/

mental health, public health

Dept of Health, Well-being & the Family; www.canterbury.ac.uk/health

dance movement, midwifery, child nursing, health and social care, health studies (health promotion, public health, maternal and child health, practice based play therapy), health-wellbeing-family, interprofessional health & social care (midwifery, nursing, psychotherapy

Department of Nursing and Applied Clinical Studies; www.canterbury.ac.uk/health/nursing-applied-clinical-studies
adult nursing, advancing nursing practice, cancer care, cardiac nursing, ethics of health care delivery. gerontology and dementia related studies, iinterprofessional health & social care, nursing competence, practice development, practice education, public and community health, workforce analysis and development

Department of Social Work, Community and Mental Health; www.canterbury.ac.uk/health/social-work-community-mental-health
children and families, health and social care, mental health and learning disabilities, nursing studies (mental health), social work, specialist social work with adults/in mental health services, young children, their families and carers; Adv Dip, BSc(Hons), DipHE, Foundation Degree, GradCert, MA, MPhil/PhD, MRes, MSc

Faculty of Social and Applied Sciences; www.canterbury.ac.uk/social applied-science

Dept of Applied Psychology; www.canterbury.ac.uk/social-applied-sciences/aspd
applied social & psychological development, clinical psychology, cognitive behavioural therapy and psychological wellbeing practice, psychology, sport & exercise psychology

Dept of Applied Social Science; www.canterbury.ac.uk/social-applied-sciences
global governance/politics, politics and governance/international relations, sociology and social science

Dept of Computing; www.canterbury.ac.uk/social-applied-sciences/computing, internet computing
business computing, computing, cybercrime forensics, forensic computing

The Department of Law and Criminal Justice Studies; www.canterbury.ac.uk/social-applied-sciences/crime-and-policing
law & legal studies, applied criminology, crime & policing, crime & policing studies, forensic investigation, police studies

Dept of Geographical and Life Sciences; www.canterbury.ac.uk/social-applied-sciences/geographical-and-life-sciences
animal science, biosciences, ecology and conservation, environmental biology, environmental science, geography, integrated science, urban and regional studies

Dept of Sports Science, Tourism and Leisure; www.canterbury.ac.uk/social-applied-sciences/sport-science-tourism-and-leisure
event management, sport and exercise science/exercise psychology, leisure management, sport science, tourism and leisure studies, tourism management, physical education & sport, event management; BA/BSc, MBA, MSc, MA, Adv Dip, Grad Cert, PGDip

CARDIFF UNIVERSITY
www.cardiff.ac.uk

Welsh School of Architecture; www.cardiff.ac.uk/archi
architecture, environmental designs of buildings, sustainable energy & environment, urban design, theory & practice of sustainable development; BSc, DipProfStudies, MA, MArch, MPhil, MSc, PhD

School of Biosciences; www.cardiff.ac.uk/bios
biochemistry, biology, biomedical science – anatomy/neuroscience/physiology, dental hygiene/therapy, medical pharmacy, genetics, microbiology, molecular biology, zoology; BSc(Hons), MRes, MSc, PhD, BDS, MBBCh

Cardiff Business School; www.cardiff.ac.uk/carbs
accounting, banking, business economics, business management – human resources/international/logistics & operations/marketing, economics, finance, financial economics, HRM, international economics, international transport, lean operations, management

studies, marine policy, marketing, port and shipping administration, public /policy/administration, strategic marketing; BSc, BScEcon, MBA, MPA, MSc, PhD

School of Chemistry

chemical biology, chemistry, chemistry with physics/ industrial experience, inorganic chemistry, organic synthesis, physical organic chemistry, solid state and materials chemistry, molecular modelling, sustainable chemistry, theoretical and computational chemistry; BSc, MChem, MPhil, PhD

School of City & Regional Planning; www.cardiff.ac.uk/c/plan

city & regional planning, geography (human) & planning, geography/planning, international planning, regeneration studies, sustainability, planning and environmental policy, transport, urban design, housing, regeneration studies; BSc, MSc, PhD

School of Computer Science & Information; www.cardiff.cs.cf.ac.uk

computer science, information systems/computer vision and computer graphics/knowledge and information systems/distributed and mobile systems/ computing/computer systems engineering, strategic information systems, information security and privacy, computer systems & maths; BSc, MSc, PhD

School of Dentistry; www.cardiff.ac.uk/ denti

dental surgery, dental therapy & hygiene, implantology, oral diseases, orthodontics, tissue engineering; BDS, BSc(Hons), MClinDent, MD, MPhil, MSc, PhD

School of Earth and Ocean Sciences; www.cardiff.ac.uk/earth

earth sciences, environmental geoscience/hydrogeology, exploration and resource geology, geobiology, geology, marine geography, geoscience; BSc, MESc, MPhil, MSc, PhD

School of Engineering; www.cardiff.ac.uk/ engin

architectural/civil/environmental/clinical engineering, communication engineering and signal processing, computer systems/electrical and electronic engineering, electronic and communications/environmental/geoenvironmental/integrated engineering, mechanical/medical/orthopaedic/structural engineering, sustainable energy and environment, electroenergy engineering hydroenvironmental engineering, magnetics; BEng, EngD, MEng, MPhil, MSc, PhD

School of English, Communication & Philosophy; www.cardiff.ac.uk/encap

applied linguistics, communication, creative writing, critical & cultural theory, analytic mid-European philosophy, English language/literature, ethics & social philosophy, forensic linguistics, language and communication, philosophy, analytic mid-European philosophy; BA, Diploma, MA/Dip, MPhil, PhD

School of European Studies; www.cardiff.ac.uk/euros

French, German, Spanish, Italian, European/European Union studies, international relations, political theory, law, politics translation studies, politics & public policy, Welsh politics & government; BA, BScEcon, LlB, MA, MScEcon, MPhil, PhD

School of Healthcare Studies; www.cardiff.ac.uk/sohcs

healthcare science, intra & perioperative practice, medical illustration, neurorehabilitation, neuro-musculoskeletal physiotherapy, occupation & health, occupational therapy, operating department practice, physiotherapy, radiography & imaging, radiotherapy & oncology, sports physiotherapy, surgical care practice; CertHE, DipHE, MPhil, MSc, PGDip/Cert, PhD

School of History and Archaeology; www.cardiff.ac.uk/hisar

ancient and medieval warfare, ancient history, archaeology, care of collections, conservation, early Celtic studies, early medieval society and culture, European neolithic, history and archaeology of the Greek and Roman world, medieval/history, Byzantine studies, medieval British studies/history, Welsh history; BA, BSc, MA, MPhil, MSc, PhD

Journalism Media and Cultural Studies; www.cardiff.ac.uk/jomec

international journalism/PR /political communications, science, media and communication, journalism, media & cultural studies; BA, MA, MPhil, MSc, PGDip, PhD

School of Law; www.law.cf.ac.uk

canon law, commercial law, European legal studies, human rights, medical practice, law, linternational commercial law, law & criminology/politics/sociology/French/German/Welsh, social care, governance development, law; LlB, LlM, MPhil, PhD

Centre for Lifelong Learning

languages, business & management, computer studies, law, science & environment, social studies

School of Mathematics; www.cardiff.ac.uk/maths
analysis, computing in the physical sciences, mathematics/& its applications, numerical analysis, operational research and statistics and risk; BSc, MMath, MPhil, MSc, PhD

Manufacturing Engineering Centre; wwwmec.cg.ac.uk
industrial engineering and systems engineering, manufacturing engineering; MPhil, PhD

School of Medicine; www.cardiff.ac.uk/medic
advanced surgical practice, bioinformatics, child health, critical care, dermatology, diabetes, anaesthesia, geriatric medicine, intensive care medicine, learning disabilities, geriatric medicine, public health, genetics, medicine, obstetrics & gynaecology, occupational health, oncology, paediatrics, pain management, palliative medicine, primary care & public health, psychiatry, therapeutics, wound healing; MBBCh, MD, MPH, MPhil, MSc/PGDip/Cert, PhD

School of Music; www.cardiff.ac.uk/music
composition, ethnomusicology, music, musicology, performance studies; BA/BMus, MA, MMus, PhD

School of Nursing & Midwifery Studies; www.cardiff.ac.uk/sonims
adult nursing, advanced practice, child nursing, community public health nursing, health studies, independent prescribing, mental health, non-medical prescribing, nursing children and young people with cancer; BMid, BN, BSc(Hons), DipHE, DNurs, DocProf, MPhil, MSc, PGDip/Cert, PhD

School of Optometry & Vision Sciences; www.cardiff.ac.uk/optom
clinical investigation, vision sciences, optometry, visual neuroscience & molecular biology, structural biophysics ; BSc, MPhil, PhD

School of Pharmacy; www.cardiff.ac.uk/phring
clinical pharmacy, clinical research, community pharmacy, non-medical prescribing for pharmacists and nurses, pharmaceutical medicine, pharmacy, international pharmacological economics; Dipl, MPharm, MPhil, MSc, PhD,

School of Physics and Astronomy; www.astro.cardiff.ac.uk
astrophysics, biophotonics, physics, medical physics, astronomy, theoretical and computational physics; BSc, MPhil, MPhys, PhD

Postgraduate Medical and Dental Education; www.cardiff.ac.uk/pgmde
dental /medical education, general/ hospital practice, IM & T

School of Psychology; www.cardiff.ac.uk/psych
clinical psychology, educational psychology, psychology; BSc, DEdPsych, DClinPsych, GradDip, PhD

School of Religious and Theological Studies; www.cardiff.ac.uk/relig
chaplaincy studies, Christian doctrine/ethics, church history, religious & theological studies, Indian religions, Islam, practical theology; BA, DipD, MA, MPhil, MTh, PhPG

School of Social Sciences; www.cardiff.ac.uk/socsci
criminal justice, criminology, social sciences, education, equality and diversity, social policy/work, social science research methods, sociology; BA, BSc, DHS, DSW, EdD, MA, MSc, PGCE

School of Welsh; www.cardiff.ac.uk/welsh
Welsh, Welsh ethnological studies, Welsh history, early Celtic studies, medieval British studies; BA, MA, PhD

UNIVERSITY OF CENTRAL LANCASHIRE
www.uclan.ac.uk

Faculty of Arts, Humanities and Social Sciences; www.uclan.ac.uk/ahss

School of Creative & Performing Arts; www.uclan.ac.uk/ahss/creative.performing.arts
acting, art & design, contemporary theatre, dance, music practice/ performance, fine art, contemporary visual arts, drawing, brand promotion, digital design for fashion, Eastern fashion, fashion design/ promotion, marketing management, retail management (fashion), styling; BA(Hons), MA, MBA, MPhil, PGCert/Dip, PhD, UniCert

Northern School of Design; www.uclan.ac.uk/ahss/design

3D design, advertising, animation, antiques, ceramics, children's book illustration, computer games, consumer product design, contemporary visual arts, design, digital graphics, games design, graphic design, illustration, interior design, product design, textiles; BA(Hons), BSc(Hons), MA, PGDip/Cert, MPhil, PhD

School of Education and Social Sciences; www.uclan.ac.uk/ahss/education_social_sciences

Criminology: criminal justice, law and criminology
Deaf Studies: British sign language/English interpreting & translation/communication, deaf studies
Education; children, schools & family, children & young people
History: history, history of medicine and education/popular culture, labour history, local history, family and community history, modern world history, museums and heritage
Social Sciences: ethnicity & human rights, politics, religion, culture & society, sociology; BA(Hons), BSc(Hons), MA, Mhil, PGCE, PhD, UnivCert, PGCert

School of Journalism, Media and Communication; www.uclan.ac.uk/ahss/journalism_media_communication

journalism, film and media studies, TV screenwriting, infographics, interactive digital media/production, media practice/technology, modern & contemporary literature, language & linguistics, culture, news graphics, play writing, publishing; BSc(Hons), BA(Hons), MA, MPhil, PGDip, PGCert, PhD

Lancashire Law School; www.uclan.ac.uk/ahss/lancashire_law_school

advanced legal practice, employment /European commercial law, forensic and legal medicine, human rights, international business law, law, criminology, senior status, legal practice medical law and bioethics; BA(Hons), BA/BSc, LlB, LLM, MA, MPhil, PGDip

School of Languages and International Studies; www.uclan.ac.uk/ahss/languages_and_international/

Asia Pacific studies, Arabic, Chinese, French/business French, German/business German, Japanese, Spanish, TESOL with applied linguistics, business English, English for foreigners; BA(Hons), MPhil, PhD

Faculty of Health and Social Care; www.uclan.ac.uk/health

School of Dentistry, & Institute for Postgraduate Dental Education; www.uclan.ac.uk/health/schools/dentistry_at_uclan/

aesthetic dental implantology, clinical periodontology, dental surgery, dentistry, endodontology, oral surgery, orthodontic therapy, restorative cosmetic dentistry; BDS, CertHE, MSc

School of Nursing and Care Science; www.uclan.ac.uk/health/schools/school_of_nursing/

prereg nursing, mental health nursing, professional practice – acute, operative and critical care, children, family and community health, complementary therapies, continuing and long-term care, counselling and psychological therapies, emergency and unscheduled care, mental/ health care, stroke care; Advanced Certificate, BSc(Hons), GradCert, MPhil, MSc, PGDip, PhD

School of Public Health and Clinical Sciences; www.uclan.ac.uk/health/schools/sphcs/

asymptomatic/cervical screening, clinical care & health informatics, epidemiology and statistics, exercise referral, general practice, group leadership in primary care, gynaecological care, hazard analysis, health and social care (clinical imaging), health improvement/informatics/promotion within sexual health/protection, health service management, health training, rheumatoid arthritis, maternal and infant nutrition, medical practice, men's sexual health, midwifery, neonatal care/practice, occupational therapy, ophthalmology, pain management, physiotherapy, public health/ informatics, rehabilitation studies, rheumatoid arthritis, sexual health/ transmitted infections, sport, health and fitness, sports therapy, substance use, working with people with acquired brain injury; AdvCert, BSc(Hons), DipHE, FdA, FdSc, MA, MPhil, MSc, PGDip/Cert, PhD

School of Social Work; www.uclan.ac.uk/health/schools/school_of_social_work/

care, community and citizenship, child health & social care, safeguarding children, social policy/work; BA(Hons), MA, PGCert

Faculty of Management; www.uclan.ac.uk/management

Lancashire Business School; www.uclan.ac.uk/lbs

accounting/information, finance, business, business administration, business and management/marketing, business information management/project management/studies/systems, communication management, economics, European business management, financial management, global business, HRM, international business/finance, investment, logistics and supply chain management, advertising & marketing, operations, PR, retail management, sustainable business; BA(Hons), DBA, MA, MBA, MSC, PGDip/Cert

School of Sport, Tourism and the Outdoors; www.uclan.ac.uk/management/ssto

leisure (management), sport/management, sports coaching/development/event management/PR studies, sports policy & community development, adventure coaching/leadership/management, international/tourism management, hospitality, sports/event management, international festivals; BA(Hons), FdA, MA/PGDip/PGCert

Faculty of Science and Technology; www.uclan.ac.uk/sc.tech

School of Built and Natural Environment; www.uclan.ac.uk/scitech/built_natural_environment/

architecture, architectural conservation/technology, building services, building surveying, construction/law/management/project management, environmental hazards, environmental management, facilities management, geography, project management, quantity surveying, sustainable regeneration engineering/waste management; BA(Hons), BSc(Hons), FdSc, BEng, MSc, PGDip/Cert

School of Computing, Engineering and Physical Sciences; www.uclan.ac.uk/scitech/computing_engineering_physical

Computing: computer games, computer network, forensic computing, information systems, internet software development, mobile interactive technology, multimedia development, systems management, software engineering

Software Engineering: agile software projects, computing, database systems, interaction design, multimedia computing, network computing

Motor Sports & Electronic Engineering: computer-aided engineering, digital signal & image processing, computer engineering, electronic design automation, electronic engineering, motor sports/engineering, robotics and mechatronics, mechanical technology, electronic design automation

Physics & Maths: astronomy, astrophysics, computational physics, mathematical physics, mathematics, physics; BEng(Hons), BSc(Hons), FdSc, MEng(Hons), MPhil, MSc, PhD

School of Forensic and Investigative Sciences; www.uclan.ac.uk/scitech/forensic_investigative/

archaeology, chemistry, fire engineering/leadership studies/investigation/safety/engineering, forensic chemistry/genetics, police and criminal investigation, risk management, DNA profiling, disaster victim investigation; BA(Hons), BEng, BSc(Hons), FdSc, MPhil, PhD

School of Pharmacy and Pharmaceutical Sciences; www.uclan.ac.uk/scitech/pharmacy

biological sciences, biomedical science, cancer biology and therapy, independent prescribing, pharmacy, physiology and pharmacology, non-medical prescribing; BSc(Hons), MPharm, MSc, PGDip/Cert, PhD

School of Psychology; www.uclan.ac.uk/scitech/psychology/

applied psychology, forensic psychology, child development, social psychology, sport & exercise psychology, health psychology, neuropsychology, forensic psychology, psychology; BSc(Hons), GradDip, MSc

UNIVERSITY OF CHESTER
www.chester.ac.uk

Dept of Biological Sciences; www.chester.ac.uk/biology

animal behaviour, animal/zoo management, biomedical sciences, biology, diabetes management, forensic biology, human nutrition, nutrition dietetics, public health nutrition; BSc, MSc, PhD

Chester Business School; www.chester.ac.uk/chester-business-school

business administration/management/studies, information systems, international business, finance, HRM, management, marketing, tourism & events management, tourism management, strategy; BA(Hons), BA/BSc, FdA, MBA, MPhil, PhD

Computer Science and Information Systems; www.chester.ac.uk/csis

agile development, computer studies, computing, artificial intelligence, emergent systems, e-learning, mobile computing and multimedia-based music promotion; BSc(Hons), MPhil, PhD

Centre for Exercise and Nutrition Science; www.chester.ac.uk/cens

cardiovascular rehabilitation, exercise and nutrition science, weight management; MSc, PhD.MPhil

Centre for Public Health Research; www.chester.ac.uk/cphr

public health, research methods; MSc

Centre for Science Communication

Centre for Research into Sport and Society; www.chester.ac.uk/scicom

sociology of sport and exercise; MSc, PhD

Education & Children's Services; www.chester.ac.uk/education

children and young education studies, early childhood studies, continuing professional development, early years practice, education, PGCE secondary/primary/early years, teaching assistance, working with children, young people and families; BA(Hons), BEd, EdD, FdA, MA, MEd, PGCE

English; www.chester.ac.uk/english

creative writing, English, English language, 19th-century literature and culture; BA, MA, PhD

Art & Design; www.chester.ac.uk/art & design

art and design, fine art, graphic design, photography; BA(Hons), MA, MSc

Geography and Development Studies; www.chester.ac.uk/geography

geography, international development studies, natural hazard management; BA(Hons), MA, MSc, PhD

Health and Social Care; www.chester.ac.uk/health

community and child health, mental health and learning disability, midwifery and reproductive health, professional development and allied health care, pre-registration nursing, social work; BA(Hons), BSc(Hons), MA, MSc, PGCert, PhD

History and Archaeology; www.chester.ac.uk/departments/history-and-archeology

archaeology, military history; BA(Hons), MA, MPhil, PhD

Languages; www.chester.ac.uk/languages

European languages and cultures, French, German and Spanish; BA(Hons), MA, PGCert/Dip

Law; www.chester.ac.uk/law

law, law (combined), law with journalism or criminology; BA(Hons), LlB, LlM

Leadership and Management; www.chester.ac.uk/

MBA, MSc

Marketing, Tourism & Events Management; www.chester.ac.uk/events

Mathematics; www.chester.ac.uk/mathematics

applied statistics, computational applied mathematics, mathematics; BSc(Hons), MPhil, PhD

New Technology Initiative; www.chester.ac.uk/nti;

IT, project & programme management, professional development

Centre for Exercise & Nutrition Sciences; www.chester.ac.uk/sport;
sport and exercise sciences/sociology, sports coaching and fitness, sports development/sciences; BA(Hons), BSc(Hons), FD, MPhil, PhD, MSc

Social & Communication Studies; www.chester.ac.uk/scs
clinical counselling, communication studies, counselling skills/studies/supervision, crime and justice, criminology, politics, psychological trauma, PR, sociology; BA(Hons), BSc(Hons), MA, PhD

Theology & Religious Studies; www.chester.ac.uk/trs
Christian youth, community evangelism, Muslim youth work, religious studies, theology; BA(Hons), BTh, Dip HE, FdA, MA, MPhil, MTh, PhD

UNIVERSITY OF CHICHESTER
www.chiuni.ac.uk

Faculty of Business, Arts & The Humanities; www.chiuni.ac.uk/ Faculties.cfm
applied language studies, dance, drama, English, fine art, history, media, music, performing arts, theology; BA(Hons), MA, Dip

School of Enterprise, Management and Leadership
accounting, business studies, event management, finance, HRM, IT management for business, marketing, tourism management; BA(Hons), FD, MA, MPhil, PhD

Faculty of Sport, Education & Social Sciences; www.chiuni.ac.uk/ Faculties.cfm#sportEducation
continuing professional development, teacher & learning support, teacher education; graduate teacher programme; primary PGCE, primary/secondary, primary education & teaching, modern langs, English, Maths, physical/religious education
Childhood and Youth: childhood studies, early childhood education, mathematics education, teaching and learning support, teaching assistants
psychology, counselling: social work and social care; sport; adventure education, physical education, sports, exercise and health sciences, sport & exercise psychology; BA(Hons), BSc(Hons), FD, GradDip/ Cert, MAPGCE, MSc, MSW, TESOL

CITY UNIVERSITY LONDON
www.city.ac.uk

School of of Arts; www.city.ac.uk/arts

Centre for Adult Education; www.city.ac.uk/cae
creative industries; FD

Cultural Policy and Management; www.city.ac.uk/cpm
culture, policy and management, cultural leadership programme, creative industries, information in the cultural sector, innovation, creativity, leadership; FD, MA

Faculty of Journalism; www.city.ac.uk/ journalism
broadcast/television/investigative/magazine/newspaper/science/international/financial journalism, creative writing, electronic publishing, journalism, publishing studies; BA(Hons), MA, MSc, PhD

Dept of Music; www.city.ac.uk/music
film music and multimedia studies, Mediterranean and Middle Eastern music studies, music composition (electroacoustic/instrumental and vocal), music performance studies, musicology/ethnomusicology, popular music studies, culture studies, creative practice; BMus, DMA, MA, MMA, MPhil, PhD

Centre for Translation Studies; www.city.ac.uk/
audiovisual translation, legal translation, principles and practice of translation, translation skills; Dip, MA, PGCert

Cass Business School; www.cass.city.ac.uk

Faculty of Actuarial Science and Insurance; www.cass.city.ac.uk/facact
actuarial management, actuarial science, insurance

Faculty of Finance; www.cass.city.ac.uk/facfin
accounting, corporate finance, econometrics, investment & risk management, mathematical finance, asset management

Faculty of Management; www.cass.city.ac.uk/facmana
accounting and finance, actuarial management/science, banking & international finance, business studies, energy, trade & finance, European business, finance and investment, financial mathematics, investment analysis and insurance/ management, investment & financial risk management, international accounting & finance, management, mathematical trading, quantitative finance, real estate, real estate finance and investment, shipping, supply chain and energy courses, voluntary sector management, charity accounting/marketing/fundraising, NGO management; BSc(Hons), MBA, MEb, MPhil, MSc, PGDip, PhD

School of Engineering and Mathematical Sciences; www.city.ac.uk/sems
aeronautical engineering, air safety management/transport engineering/transport operations/management, aircraft maintenance management, analysis and design of structures for hazards, architecture, artificial intelligence, automotive & motorsport engineering, biomedical engineering, business computing systems, civil engineering, civil engineering structures, clinical engineering with healthcare technology management, computer science, computer systems engineering, construction management, electrical engineering, electronic computer systems energy and environmental technology and economics, energy engineering, finance and risk, games technology, information engineering, maritime operations, mathematical science, mathematics & finance, mechanical & automotive engineering, mechanical engineering, media communication systems, multimedia & internet systems engineering, power systems and energy management, professional civil engineering, project management, software engineeringstatistics, surveying, systems and control, telecommunications /and networks, electrical and electronic engineering; BEng, BSc(Hons), MEng, MMath, MPhil, MSc, PgDip, PhD

Centre for Mathematical Science; www.city.ac.uk/sems/mathematics; mathematical science with statistics/computer science/finance/economics; BSc, MMath

School of Community and Health Sciences; www.city.ac.uk/communityandhealth
adult nursing, anatomy, applied biological sciences, biochemistry, genetics, microbiology, nutrition, pathophysiology, pharmacology, physiology; BSc, DipHE, PGDip

City Health Research Centre; Education Development Unit;
interdisciplinary studies in professional practice; MSc, PhD

Interdisciplinary Studies in Professional Practice; www.city.ac.uk/communityandhealth/spp;
interprofessional practice, health management, clinical leadership, disabilty & social inclusion, disabilty studies; MPhil, PhD

Investigative, Security and Police Sciences; www.city.ac.uk/cisps/pdp
applied investigation, economic crime and fraud investigation, intelligence and security, policing; degree pathway

Language and Communication; www.city.ac.uk/lcs
human communication, joint professional practice, speech & language therapy; BSc(Hons), MSc,

Mental Health and Learning Disabilities; www.city.ac.uk/sonm/nursing/mental-health-nursing
mental health nursing, BSc, DipPG, Dip

Midwifery and Child Health; www.city.ac.uk/sonm/midwifery-child-health
child health, midwifery, child nursing; BSc, DipHE, PGDip

Optometry and Visual Science; www.city.ac.uk/optometry
advanced/ophthalmic dispensing, applied vision research, imaging and instrumentation, optometry, visual neuroscience, visual psychophysics and perception; BSc, MSc, FD, PGDip

Public Health, Primary Care and Food Policy; www.city.ac.uk/communityandhealth/phpcfp
education, food policy, practice development, primary care (district nursing, practice nursing), public health; specialist nursing (health visiting, school nursing), MSc, PGDip, Dip

Radiography; www.city.ac.uk/radiography
nuclear medicine technology, radiography, oncology/diagnostic imaging; BSc(Hons), FD, GradDip Cert, MSc, PhD

School of Informatics; www.soi.city.ac.uk

Centre for Health Informatics; www.soi.city.ac.uk/organisation/chi
health care technologies, health informatics; MSc

Centre for Human Computer Interaction Design; www-hcid.soi.city.ac.uk
human-centred systems; MSc, PhD

Centre for Software Reliability; www.csr.city.ac.uk
Safety critical systems, modelling, software dependability (safety and reliability), software fault tolerance/metrics and quality assurance, resilience, assurance and risk management in computer systems; MSc, MPhil, PhD

Department of Information Science; www.soi.city.ac.uk/business
systems analysis, e-business systems, human-centred systems, information leadership

Department of Computing; www.soi.city.ac.uk
artificial intelligence, business computing systems, computer science, electronic publishing, games technology, health informatics, human computer interaction, information management in the cultural sector, information systems, library science, music technology, software development, software engineering; BSc(Hons), MA, MScMIl, MInnov

City Law School; www.city.ac.uk/law

law, law and property evaluation, energy law, competition law, crime & justice, European law, media communucations & IP law, economics and international trade, professional skills & practice; LIB, LlM, MPhil, PhD

School of Social Sciences; www.city.ac.uk/social

Department of Economics; www.city.ac.uk/economics
accountancy, business economics, economics, economic evaluation in health care, economic regulation and competition, financial economics, health economics, international business economics; BSc, MSc, PhD

Department of International Politics; www.city.ac.uk/intpol
international politics/and sociology; BSC, MA, PhD

Department of Psychology; www.city.ac.uk/psychology
counselling psychology, clinical supervision, health psychology, organizational psychology/ organisational behaviour, psychology, psychology and health, specialist educational intervention; BSc, MSC, PhD

Dept of Sociology; www.city.ac.uk/sociology
criminology, global migration, human rights, international communications and development, media communication systems/ studies, international politics, race and ethnicity, refugee studies, social research methods, sociology, surveillance studies, political communication, transnational media & communication; BEng, BSc(Hons), DPsych, GradDip/Cert, MA, MSc, PhD, ProfDoc

Degrees validated by City University offered at:

GUILDHALL SCHOOL OF MUSIC & DRAMA
www.gsmd.ac.uk

acting, training actors, costume supervision, music, music composition, music therapy, performance, range of musical instruments taught, singing, electronic music, technical theatre arts, stage management; BA(Hons), BMus, MA, MMA/DMA, MMP, MMus, MPerf, PGDip

---

LABAN
www.laban.org

choreography, dance, dance studies/theatre/performance; BA(Hons), MA, MPhil, MSc, PGDipls, PhD

SCHOOL OF PSYCHOTHERAPY & COUNSELLING PSYCHOLOGY AT REGENT'S COLLEGE
www.spc.ac.uk

counselling, psychology, psychotherapy; DCounsPsy, MA, MPhil/PhD, PGDip

THE NORDOFF-ROBBINS MUSIC THERAPY CENTRE
www.nordoff-robbins.org.uk

music therapy; MMusTherapy, PGDip

COVENTRY UNIVERSITY
www.coventry.ac.uk

Coventry School of Art & Design; www.coventry.ac.uk/artanddesign

Dept of Design & Visual Arts
fashion/accessories, art, graphic design, illustration; BA(Hons)

Dept of Industrial Design
automotive/bike/boat/computer-aided product/consumer product/transport/industrial product/sports product/sustainable transport/toy/transport/vehicle design, rehabilitation engineering; BA(Hons), BSc(Hons), MA, MDes

Dept of Media & Communication
advertising, culture, English, journalism, media/production, photography, film & vision culture; BA(Hons), MA, PGDip/Cert

Dept of Performing Arts
dance theatre/making, e-music, music, music technology/composition, theatre, performance, performing arts innovation & enterprise, professional practice; BA(Hons)

School of Lifelong Learning; www.coventry.ac.uk/SOLL

advanced management techniques, enterprise & global entrepreneurship, leadership career development, management practice, multimedia & technology, project management, metrology; FD, BA(Hons), MA, PGdip/Cert, Msc

Faculty of Business, Environment & Society; www.coventry.ac.uk/bes

Coventry University Business School; www.coventry.ac.uk/bes/cubs
accountancy, advertising, banking & finance, business, biotechnical technology, economics, engineering/project management, enterprise & entrepreneurship, environmental/European business management, finance, financial/international business economics, global business, HRM, information technology, international business/law/management/marketing/sport management/tourism management, investment, law, leisure management, logistics, management information systems, management for construction, marketing, risk & disaster/sport business management, sport & exercise therapy, strategic marketing, supply chain management; BSc(Hons), MA, MSc, MBA, LlM

Coventry University Law School; www.coventry.ac.uk/besl/aw
law and business/French/international studies/Spanish, diplomatic law and global change, global development and international law, international business law; LlB, LlM, MSc

Department of Geography, Environment & Disaster Management; www.coventry.ac.uk/bes/ged
climate & environmental, international security GIS, international crisis management, disaster management & emergency planning/engineering/management, reconstruction & development, environmental management, geography, global sustainability, natural hazards, tourism management, risk & disaster

management; Prof Doc, BA, BSc, MA, MSc, MBA, MPhil, PhD

School of International Studies & Social Science; www.coventry.ac.uk/bes/isss
community & social action, criminology/psychology, global security, history, international crime & global security, terrorism, international relations, politics, sociology; MA, PhDMPhil

Faculty of Engineering & Computing; www.coventry.ac.uk/engineeringandcomputing

aerospace systems engineering/technology, architecture, architectural design technology/engineering, automotive engineering/design, aviation management, avionics technology, building/services engineering/surveying, business decision management/information systems/technology, civil engineering/design, computer hardware & software, computers, networking & communications technology, construction/management, control engineering, creative computing, security/media production, e-commerce, electrical systems, electronic engineering, engine design & development, mathematics, project management, enterprise systems development, ethical hacking & network security, European construction engineering studies/industrial entrepreneurship/information technology management/logistics, financial mathematics, forensic computing, games technology, health informatics, information & systems architecture, internet & enterprise computing, IT, logistics, management, manufacturing systems engineering, mathematical sciences, mathematics, computing/statistics, mechanical engineering/design, media computing, microelectronics & wireless systems, modelling simulation & control, multimedia/network & mobile computing, operational communications, purchasing & supply, software engineering/developmentstructural engineering/with architecture, supply chain management, vehicle dynamics, vehicle structures & safety, virtual engineering; BEng, BSc(Hons), MEng, MSc

Faculty of Health & Life Sciences; www.coventry.ac.uk/hls

Dept of Clinical Psychology; www.coventry.ac.uk/HLS/ClinPsych
clinical psychology, parapsychology; DocClinPsych

Dept of Nursing, Midwifery & Health Care
adult/children & young people nursing, contemporary health care (cancer care for teenagers & young adults), health studies, learning disability/mental health nursing, midwifery, paramedic science, social & health care management, health & lifestyle, operating dept practice, substance misuse; BSc(Hons), DipHE, FdSc, MSc, PGDip/Cert

Dept of Physiotherapy & Dietetics
acupuncture, dietetics, manual therapy, neurological physiotherapy, physiotherapy, sports nutrition; BSc(Hons), MSc

Dept of Psychology; www.coventry.ac.uk/psychology
applied forensic studies, applied/clinical/forensic psychology, crime, health/sport psychology, parapsychology, psychology, criminology, reading development, sociology; BSc(Hons), MSc

Dept of Social & Community Studies
applied community & social studies/health & social care, mental health studies, practice education, social & health care management, social work, youth work, criminology and law/sociology/psychology, career guidance

Dept of Occupational Therapy; www.coventry.ac.uk/OT
Occupational therapy, neurological occupational OT, assistance techniques; BSc, MSc, Dip

Dept of Biomolecular & Sports Sciences; www.coventry.ac.uk/HLS/BSS;
analytical chemistry & forensic sciences, biomedical science/technology, environmental health, forensic & investigative science, human bioscience, medical and pharmacological science, nutrition & food science, sport, exercise, health science, sports therapy, biomolecular & sport science, strength & conditioning, translational medicine; BSc(Hons), HNC, HND, MSc

CRANFIELD UNIVERSITY
www.cranfield.ac.uk

School of Applied Sciences; www.cranfield.ac.uk/sas

manufacturing, materials & nanotechnology, motorsport, business & IS, economics and management, engineering, environment & water, offshore, welding; EngD, MPhil, MSc, MTech, PhD

Cranfield Defence and Security; www.cranfield.ac.uk/cds

defence acquisition/leadership/sensors & data fusion/ simulation & modelling and logistics, explosives ordnance, forensics, global security, guided weapons, information operations/management, international HRM, military aerospace/electronic systems/OR/ vehicle technology, project management, resilience, scientific computation, security, weapon & vehicle systems; EngD, MSc, PGDip/Cert, PhD

School of Engineering; www.cranfield.ac.uk/soe

aerospace, air transport, astronautics, applied mechanics, automotive engineering, computation, engineering, energy, human factors, safety, power and propulsion, process and systems engineering; EngD, MSc, PhD

Cranfield Health; www.cranfield.ac.uk/health

bioinformatics, analytical biotechnology, medical medicine, nanomedicine, translational medicine, clinical research bioscience and diagnostics, environment and health, food chain systems, medical technology regulation; DM, MSc

Cranfield School of Management; www.cranfield.ac.uk/som

business performance, complex systems, economics, enterprise, entrepreneurship, finance and management, information systems, international HRM, managing organizational performance, logistics and supply chain management, management development, management knowledge and strategic change, marketing and sales management, operations management, organization studies, marketing; DBA, MBA, MSc, PhD

UNIVERSITY OF CUMBRIA
www.cumbria.ac.uk

Faculty of the Arts; www.cumbria.ac.uk/about us/faculties/faculty of the arts

School of Media and Performing Arts

games design, media production, multimedia design and digital animation, music, performing arts, scriptwriting

School of Art and Design

ceramics, crafts, drawing, fine art, furniture, graphic design, illustration, jewellery, metalwork, photography

School of Humanities

American studies, art, contemporary culture, creative writing, drama, English language/literature, film studies, geography, history; BA(Hons), DipHE, MA, MPhil, PhD, TESOL

Faculty of Business, Social Sciences and Sport; www.cumbria.ac.uk/aboutus/faculties/facultyofbsss

School of Applied Social Sciences

applied psychology, counselling, policing and criminal justice studies, social science, youth and community development; AdvUnivDip, BA(Hons), BSc(Hons), DipHE, PdAMA, PdSc, PgDip/Cert

Faculty of Education; www.cumbria.ac.uk/aboutus/faculties/education

graduate teacher programme, mathematics development for teachers, science specialism, student associates scheme, subject knowledge enhancement; FD, BA/BSc(Hons), GTS, PGCE

Faculty of Science and Natural Resources; www.cumbria.ac.uk/aboutus/faculties/facultyofscienceandnaturalresources

National School of Forestry

forest and woodland management/ecosystem management

School of Outdoor Studies

adventure, environment, integrated land management, wildlife

School of Construction, Engineering & Technology

applied chemistry, applied science and technology, construction management, engineering, environmental engineering, forensic science, mechanical engineering, renewable energy, sustainable engineering; BA(Hons), BEng(Hons), BSc(Hons), FdEd, FdSc, MA, MSc, PGDip

Faculty of Health, Medical Science & Social Care; www.cumbria.ac.uk/about us/faculties/facultyofhealth

School of Nursing & Midwifery

community and public health nursing, family planning and sexual healthcare, learning disabilities, nursing and children's nursing, medical imaging science; radiography, medical imaging, mental health nursing, midwifery, nurse practitioner, occupational therapy, physiotherapy, public health and complementary therapy; BSc(Hons), CPD, DipHE, FdSc, MSc, PGC, PGD, PhD, Rad

DEMONTFORD UNIVERSITY
www.dmu.ac.uk

Faculty of Art and Design; www.dmu.ac.uk/faculties/art_and_design

architecture, dance, design, fashion, fine art, graphics design, media studies, photography, product design, textiles; BA(Hons), BArch(Hons), BSc(Hons), DipHE, FoundStud, MA, MA/MSc, MPhil, PGDip, PhD

Faculty of Business and Law; www.dmu.ac.uk/faculties/business_and_law

advertising, business, economics, finance, HRM, law, leadership, marketing, public policy; BA(Hons), BSc(Hons), DipHE, GDL/CPE, HND, LlBHons, LLM, LPC, MA, MPhil, MBA, MSc, PGDip/Cert, PhD

Faculty of Health and Life Sciences; www.dmu.ac.uk/faculties/his

audiology, biomedical science, criminology, dental tech, enviroment, forensic science, human community, psychology, social work, youth work; BA(Hons), BSc(Hons), DipHE, FdA, MA, MPharm(Hons), MSc, PGDip, RSHDip

Faculty of Humanities; www.dmu.ac.uk/faculties/humanities

arts management, creative writing, dance, drama, education, English, history, international relations, journalism, media studies, music; BA(Hons), MA, PGDip

Faculty of Technology (Computer Science and Engineering); www.dmu.ac.uk/faculties/technology

audio recording/technology, business information technology, computers, computers/security/science, creative technology, digital video, electronic engineering, electronic games, electronics, engineering design, forensic computing, info/commtech, mechatronics, media production/technology, mutilmedia computing, music, music technology, radio, software engineering; BEng, BSc(Hons), HND, MPhil, MSc, PGDip, PhD

UNIVERSITY OF DERBY
www.derby.ac.uk

Faculty of Art, Design, and Technology; www.derby.ac.uk/adt

American studies, applied art & design, architecture, built environment, commercial photographic fashion, creative writing, film/video history, fine art, English, media, motorsport, music and media technologies, product design, textiles, theatre, visual commerce; BA(Hons), MDes, PhD, Univ Cert/Dip

Faculty of Business, Computing and Law; www.derby.ac.uk/bcl

Derbyshire Business School

accountancy & finance, business, coaching, enterprise, HRM, leadership, marketing, purchasing & supply

Law & Criminology

law, business, international, social and public, law; criminology, crime & justice

Computing

computing forensics/games/networks, security, information science/technology, software, games; BA(Hons), BSc(Hons), FD, LlBHons, LlM, MA, MPharm, MPhil/PhD, MSc, PGDip/Cert

Faculty of Education, Health and Sciences; www.derby.ac.uk/ehs

Education

education studies, teacher education, early/childhood studies

Health

mental health, nursing studies, occupational therapy, art therapy, public health, health care practice, radiography, sport & exercise

Science

biological science, geography and environmental science, forensic science, psychology; Adv Dip, BA(Hons), BEd, BSc(Hons), EdD, FdA, HNC/HND, jtHons, MA, MSC, PGCert/Dip, PGCE, PhD, Univ Cert/Dip

DONCASTER BUSINESS SCHOOL
www.don.ac.uk/dbs

business administration/management, strategic personnel & management, leadership & management, learning & development, construction, HRM, information and communication technology, marketing; CIM, CIPD, CIPS, HND/BA(Hons), MBA, MSc

UNIVERSITY OF DUNDEE
www.dundee.ac.uk

College of Art, Sciences and Engineering; www.dundee.ac.uk/case

School of Architecture; www.architecture.dundee.ac.uk

architecture, advanced sustainability of the built environment, adv practice management & law

School of Computing; www.computing.dundee.ac.uk

applied computing, artificial intelligence, business intelligence, computing science, e-commerce, design ethnography, information technology, interactive media design, IT, vision and imaging

Duncan of Jordanstone College of Art and Design; www.djcad.dundee.ac.uk

animation, art and design/ digital film, art philosophy/imaging, contemporay practice, design – graphics/interior and environmental/innovative product/interactive media/jewellery and metal/textile/ technology, exhibitions, fine art, graphics, illustration, media arts and imaging, forensic/medical art

School of Engineering, Physics and Mathematics; www.dundee.ac.uk/eps

applied physics, biomedical engineering, civil engineering, concrete design and environmental management, electronic & electrical engineering/microcomputer systems/management, physics, environmental engineering, earthquake and offshore engineering, mathematics, mechanical engineering & mechatronics, product design, renewable/structural engineering, sustainabilty; BA(Ord/Hons), BEng, BSc, CertHE, DipHE, MArch, MEng, MRes, MSc, MSci, PhD

College of Arts and Social Sciences; www.dundee.ac.uk/artsoc

School of Accounting & Finance; www.dundee.ac.ukaccountancy

accounting, finance, business management, international accountancy, international finance, Islamic accounting and finance, strategic financial management

Continuing Education; www.dundee.ac.uk/conted;

CPD, communication and languages, community outreach; MA

School of Education, Social Work and Community Education; www.dundee.ac.uk/eswce

Teaching; community education (learning & development), education, educational psychology, PGCE primary/secondary, primary education, professional development, childhood studies, teaching qual (further education/higher education), social work

Interdisciplinary Disability Research Institute (IDRIS)

Institute for Research and Innovation in Social Services (IRISS)

School of Humanities; www.dundee.ac.uk/humanities

Centre for Archive and Information Studies; www.dundee.ac.uk/cias

archives and records management/information rights, family and local history digital appl

Communication and Language Studies; www.dundee.ac.uk/language studies;

French, German, Spanish

English; www.dundee.ac.uk/English

English, English and film studies, women culture & society

History; www.dundee.ac.uk/history

early America, European history Greater Britain in the twentieth century, history, Scottish history, urban and cultural history, church history

Philosophy; www.dundee.ac.uk/philosophy

European philosophy, philosophy/and literaure, continental philosophy

Politics; www.dundee.ac.uk/politics

European politics, international relations & politics/geoplitics, international politics & security

Women, Culture & Society

School of Law; www.dundee.ac.uk/law

commercial & international commercial law, company law & corporate governance, criminal justice & evidence, English law, environmental law, European law, family law, healthcare law and ethics, human rights, property, contract, tort & delict, private international law, public international law, public law, Scottish law, international crime & justice

Graduate School of Natural Resources Law, Policy and Management; www.dundee.ac.uk/postgradschool

Centre for Energy, Petroleum and Mineral Law and Policy

energy law and policy, international and comparative nuclear law and policy, international dispute resolution and management, mineral law and policy, natural resources law and policy, petrol, energy law & taxation

UNESCO Centre for Water Law, Policy and Science

international water management, water law, water governance and conflict resolution

School of Psychology; www.dundee.ac.uk/psychology

psychological research methods, psychological therapy in primary care, psychology, development psychology

School of Social and Environmental Sciences; www.dundee.ac.uk/social science

Economic Studies: business economics with marketing, economics, financial economics, spatial economics and development, numerous joint degrees with economics, energy studies, international business
Environmental Science: environmental science/with geography
Geography: applied population and welfare geography, environmental management, remote sensing, social research methods, sustainable catchment management, town and regional planning

MA(Hons), MLitt/MSc, MSc, LlB, LlM, PhD, PGCert, BAcc, BIAcc, BIFin, BSc(Hons)

College of Life Sciences; www.lifesci.dundee.ac.uk

anatomical sciences, biochemistry, biomedical sciences, drug discovery, crops for the future, drug design and mechanisms, environmental biology/ science, forensic anthropology/ art, human anatomy, medical art, microbiology, molecular biology, molecular genetics, neuroscience, pharmacology, physiological sciences, physiology, sports biomedicine, zoology

School of Research

Centre for Anatomy and Human Identification; www.lifesci.dundee.ac.uk/CAHId
Div of Biological Chemistry and Drug Discovery; www.lifesci.dundee.ac.uk/bcdd
Biological Services (CLS); www.lifesci.dundee.ac.uk/biolservices
Div of Cell and Developmental Biology; www.lifesci.dundee.ac.uk/cdb
Div of Cell Biology and Immunology; www.lifesci.dundee.ac.uk/cbi
CRUK Nucleic Acid Structure Research Group; www.lifesci.dundee.ac.uk/nasg
gene regulation and expression
Molecular and Environmental Microbiology; www.lifesci.dundee.ac.uk/mmb
Div of Molecular Medicine; www.lifesci.dundee.ac.uk/mm
Div of Molecular Physiology; www.lifesci.dundee.ac.uk/mp
MRC Protein Phosphorylation Unit; www.lifesci.dundee.ac.uk/mrccpu
Div of Plant Sciences; www.lifesci.dundee.ac.uk/pl
Div of Signal Transduction Therapy; www.lifesci.dundee.ac.uk/dstt
TMRC Research Lab
BSc(Hons), MRes, MSc, PhD

College of Medicine, Dentistry and Nursing; www.dundee.ac.uk/cmdn

School of Dentistry; www.dundee.ac.uk/dentalschool

dentistry, oral health science, prosthodontics

School of Nursing and Midwifery; www.dundee.ac.uk/medden

advanced practice nursing and palliative care, adult/ child nursing and midwifery, health nursing, infection prevention and control, nursing and midwifery, health studies

School of Medicine; www.dundee.ac.uk/medschool

anaesthesia, cardiovascular lung biology cancer, diabetes, health skills, immunology, medical science, medicine, molecular medicine, neuroscience, oncology, orthopaedic and trauma surgery, orthopaedic and rehabilitation technology, palliative care, primary care, psychiatry cognitive behavioural psychotherapy, psychological therapy in primary care, public heath, surgery; BDS, BHealthN, BM, BMSc, BN, BSc, DDSc, DipCert, MA, MBChB, MChOrth, MD, MDSc, MFM, MMAS, MMSc, MNurs, MPH, MPhil, MSc, MSSc

Biomedical Research Institute

Div of Clinical & Population Sciences & Education

Centre for Primary Care & Population Research

Dental Health Services & Research Unit (DHSRU)

Institute for Health Skills & Education

Dundee Epidemiology and Biostatistics Unit

Institute of Cardiovascular Research Centre for Neuroscience

Centre for Oncology & Molecular Medicine

DURHAM UNIVERSITY
www.dur.ac.uk

Faculty of Arts and Humanities; www.dur.ac.uk /arts.humanities

Dept of Classics and Ancient History; www.dur.ac.uk/classics
ancient epic/historiography/philosophy, ancient history, ancient history and archaeology, classical past, classical tradition, classics, Greece, Rome and the Near East

Dept of English Studies; www.dur.ac.uk/ english.studies
English literature and philosophy/history, medieval and renaissance literary studies, romantic and Victorian literary studies, poetry, 20th-century literary studies, education studies

Dept of History; www.dur.ac.uk/history
history, medieval history, early modern history, modern history, research methods (economic and social history)

Dept of Music; www.dur.ac.uk/music
music (ethnomusicology/composition/electroacoustic studies/performance), musicology, education studies

School of Modern Languages and Cultures; www.dur.ac.uk/mlac
Arabic translation and interpreting, culture and medieval and renaissance studies, French, German, Hispanic studies, Italian, Russian, the photographic image, seventeenth-century studies, translation studies, culture & difference

Dept of Philosophy; www.dur.ac.uk/ philosophy
history and philosophy of science and medicine, philosophy, philosophy, politics and economics (PPE), philosophy and politics/ psychology, theology/English literature/education studies

Dept of Theology and Religion; www.dur.ac.uk/theology.religion
biblical studies, Christian theology (Anglican, Catholic studies), religion and society, theology & philosophy/religion/European studies; BA(Hons), GDip, MA, MLitt, MMus, MTh, PhD

Faculty of Science; www.dur.ac.uk/ science.faculty

School of Biological and Biomedical Sciences; www.dur.ac.uk/ biological.sciences
biology, biomedical sciences, cell biology, ecology, evolution & behaviour, molecular biology & biochemistry, natural sciences, zoology

Dept of Chemistry; www.dur.ac.uk/ chemistry
chemistry, bio-organic chemistry, catalysis, organometallic, coordination and supramolecular chemistry, inorganic materials, photonic and electronic materials, physical organic chemistry, polymer chemistry, structural chemistry, synthetic methodology, theoretical chemistry and simulation

Dept of Engineering and Computer Science; www.dur.ac.uk/ecs/computing.science
advanced software engineering, aeronautics, civil/ electronic/mechanical engineering, communications/ computer engineering, computer science, design, general engineering, internet and distributed systems technologies, internet systems and e-business, new and renewable energy, software engineering, software engineering management, design & operations engineering

Dept of Earth Sciences; www.dur.ac.uk/ earth.sciences
earth science, environmental, geology, geophysics, geosciences

Dept of Mathematical Sciences; www.dur.ac.uk/mathematical.sciences
mathematics, biomathematics, elementary particle theory, mathematical sciences

Dept of Physics; www.dur.ac.uk/physics
elementary particle theory, physics, physics and astronomy, theoretical physics

Dept of Psychology; www.dur.ac.uk/ psyhology
cognitive neuroscience, developmental psychopathology/ psychology, psychology, psychology (applied); BA(Hons), BEng, BSc(Hons), MA, MChem, MEng, MMath, MPhil, MPhys, MSc, MSci, PhD

Faculty of Social Science and Health; www.dur.ac.uk /science.health

School of Applied Social Sciences; www.dur.ac.uk/sass

crime, violence and abuse, children & young persons, criminology, policy, professions and communities, social policy, social work, society & politics, social research, sport and community and youth work, sociology, sport

Dept of Anthropology; www.dur.ac.uk/ anthropology

anthropology, development/evolutionary anthropology, health and human sciences, human sciences, medical anthropology, research methods (anthropology), sociocultural anthropology

Dept of Archeology; www.dur.ac.uk/ archeology

archeology/& ancient civilizations, ancient history conservation of archaeological and museum objects, museums and artefacts studies, palaeopathology (human)

Durham Business School; www.dur.ac.uk/ dbs

accounting & finance, business, business finance, corporate & international finance, economics, business economics accounting, decision science, entrepreneurship, financial management, HRM and organizational behaviour, international banking, international money, investment, marketing psychology, modelling & analysis for management, public management, strategy and organization, strategy management

School of Education; www.dur.ac.uk/ education

educational assessment, education studies, history of art, PGCE primary/secondary, practice of education, primary education, research methods (education),

Dept of Geography; www.dur.ac.uk/geo

risk & environmental hazards/security, health & public policy

School of Government and International affairs; www.dur.ac.uk/sgia

Arab world studies, international relations, international studies, Islamic finance, politics, international theory & history, international security, interdependance & organization, globalization; BA(Hons), DBA, EdD, MA, MA(Ed), MBA, MSc, PGCE, PGCert, PhD

Faculty of Social Science and Health; www.dur.ac.uk/science.health

Dept of Anthropology; www.dur.ac.uk/ anthroplogy

anthropological medicine, anthropology, biological anthropology, development anthropology, evolutionary anthropology, health and human sciences, human sciences, medical anthropology, research methods (anthropology), sociocultural anthropology

School of Applied Social Sciences; www.dur.ac.uk/sass

criminology, community and youth work, education studies – sociology, managing community practice, social research methods, social work/with children and young people, their families and carers, sociology, sociology and anthropology/law/politics, sport; BA(Hons), BSc(Hons), MA, MProf, MSc, PhD/MPhil, PGDip/Cert

Durham Law School; www.dur.ac.uk

European trade & commercial law, international trade & commercial law, law, society & law, legal studies

School of Medicine & Health; www.dur.ac.uk/school.health

clinical management, health research methods, history and philosophy of science, interdisciplinary mental health, medical education, phase 1 medicine, public policy and health; BA(Hons), BA(Ed), BSc(Ed), BSc(Hons), Cert Leg Stud, DBA, EdD, LlB, LlM, MA, MBA, MBBS, MEd, MMus, MPhil, MProf, MSc, PGCert, PGCert/Dip, PGCE, PhD

Degrees validated by Durham University offered at:

CRAMNER HALL, ST JOHN'S COLLEGE
www.cranmerhall.com

theology and ministry; BA, MA, Theology & Ministry, Diploma certificate

NATIONAL TRAINING CENTRE FOR SCIENTIFIC SUPPORT TO CRIME INVESTIGATION
www.forensic-training.police.uk

Diplomas

NEW COLLEGE DURHAM
www.newdur.ac.uk

accounting, administration, business management, graphic design, information technology management, complementary healthcare, prescribing practice, community specialist practice, WESOL and modern languages, podiatry, social work; BA(Hons), BSc(Hons), Foundation degrees, HND, HNC

ROYAL ACADEMY OF DANCE
www.rad.org.uk

ballet education, ballet teaching studies, Benesh, dance education, movement notation; BA(Hons), Dip/CertHE, MTeach(Dance), licenciate

USHAW COLLEGE
www.ushaw.ac.uk

theology and ministry; BA, Certs, Dipls, MA, PGCerts/Dips

UNIVERSITY OF EAST ANGLIA
www.uea.ac.uk

Faculty of Arts and Humanities; www.uea.ac.uk/hum

American Studies; www.uea.ac.uk/ams
American studies, American literature, and American history/English history/politics, & creative writing,

School of World Art Studies; www.uea.ac.uk/art
archeology, anthrapology & art history, gallery & musem studies, north Africa, Oceanic, the Americas, creative enterprise, ancient art and African art, art history, contemporary art, cultural heritage and museology

School of Film & Television Studies; www.uea.ac.uk/ftv
film and television studies, film studies/English studies/American studies, film & televison archiving

School of History; www.uea.ac.uk/his
modern history, history, history and politics/languages, landscape archeology, medieval history

School of Literature and Creative Writing; www.uea.ac.uk/lit
creative writing/prose fiction, cultural studies, drama, scriptwriting and performance, English, English and American literature, culture & modernity, life writing, literature and history, poetry/prose fiction, popular culture, translation studies, women's writings, creative entrepreneurship

School of Language and Communication Studies; www.uea.ac.uk/lcs
cross-cultural communication with business & management, language studies, international development studies, film & TV, French, media, Spanish, applied translation studies, language & intercultural communication

School of Music; www.uea.ac.uk/mus
electroacoustic music and musicology, music, music and technology, music with mathematics, performance, conducting

School of Political, Social and International Studies; www.uea.ac.uk/psi
culture, literature /European studies with politics, international relations and European politics, international relations and politics, international studies, philosophy and politics, politics and economics, public policy & management, social and political theory, society, culture and media; BA(Hons), MA, MMus, MPhil, PGDip, PhD

Faculty of Health; www.uea.ac.uk/foh

School of Allied Health Professions; www.uea.ac.uk/ahp
occupational therapy, physiotherapy, speech and language therapy, clinical education, health services, advanced muscoskeletal research & practice

School of Medicine, Health Policy & Practice; www.uea.ac.uk/med
medicine, surgery, clinical education/psychology, cognitive behaviour therapy, health economics/sciences/research, cognitive behavourial therapy, medicine, primary care mental health

School of Nursing and Midwifery; www.uea.ac.uk/nam
acute, critical and emergency practice, community healthcare practice, midwifery practice, nursing practice, nurse practitioner (advanced practice), policy, planning and leadership for health professionals, pre-registration (midwifery, nursing, operating department practice, paramedic), neonatal/mental health nursing

Institute of Biomedical and Clinical Science; www.uea.ac.uk/foh/research/Institutes/biomed
infection and immunity, nutrition and healthy ageing

Health and Social Science Research Institute; www.uea.ac.uk/foh/research/Institutes/hss
economics, medical statistics, mental health and psychological sciences, public health and health services research, stroke and rehabilitation shared decision making

Education in Health Institute; www.uea.ac.uk/foh/research/Institutes/educationinhealth
medical education, interprofessional education, educational theory; BA(Hons), BSc(Hons), ClinPsyD, DipHE, Foundation degrees, MBBS, MClinEd, MD, MHeaRes, MPhil, MSc, PGDip, PhD

Faculty of Science; www.uea.ac.uk/sci

School of Biological Science; www.uea.ac.uk/bio
applied ecology, applied ecology and conservation, biochemistry and ecology, biological sciences, biomedicine, cell biology, microbiology, plant science, biotechnology for a sustainable future, computational biology, ecology, conservation and project administration, genetics and crop improvement

School of Chemical Science; www.uea.ac.uk/che
chemistry, adv organic chemistry, analytical science, biological and medicinal chemistry, chemical physics, environmental chemistry, forensic science, pharmaceutical chemistry

School of Computing Science; www.uea.ac.uk/cmp
actuarial sciences, applied computing science, information systems, business statistics, computational biology, computer graphics, computer systems engineering, computing for business, computing science, games development, geoinformatics, imaging and multimedia, knowledge discovery and data mining, software engineering, strategic information systems

School of Environmental Sciences; www.uea.ac.uk/env
applied ecology, environmental social science, climate atmospheric sciences, climate change/science,

environmental assessment and management, environmental chemistry/earth sciences, environmental geography and international development, environmental geophysics, environmental social sciences, geophysical sciences, meteorology & oceanography

School of Natural Science; www. uea.ac.uk/sci/natsci

natural science

School of Mathematics; www.uea.ac.uk/mth

mathematics, mathematics with economics/management studies/statistics/computing, business statistics

School of Pharmacy; www.uea.ac.uk/pha

general pharmacy practice, pharmacy; BSc(Hons), GradDip, MPhil, MSc, MSci, PGDip, PhD

Faculty of Social Sciences; www.uea.ac.uk/ssf

School of Economics; www.uea.ac.uk/eco

economics/ & accountancy, business economics, business finance and economics, economics with economic psychology, environmental/experimental economics, finance and economics, industrial economics, international business finance and economics, media economics, politics, philosophy and economics

School of Education and Lifelong Learning; www.uea.ac.uk/edu

adult literacy, advanced educational practice, counselling/ focusing-orientated psychotherapy, early childhood studies, education studiies, focusing and experiential psychotherapy, lifelong learning and development: international perspectives, mathematics education, PGCE primary /secondary teacher training, teacher education PE & sport, professional studies

School of International Development; www.uea.ac.uk/dev

climate change, conflict, governance and international development, cultural heritage and international development, development economics/studies, education and development, gender analysis of international development, globalization and international development/ and business, international development with social anthropology and politics/ economics/ environment and society, international relations and development studies, international social development, media and international development, rural development, theatre and development

Norwich Law School; www.uea.ac.uk/law

law, employment law, European legal systems, information, technology and intellectual property law, international commercial and business law, international competition law and policy, international trade law, law with American law/ French law and language, legal studies, media law, policy and practice

Norwich Business School; www.uea.ac.uk/nbs

accounting and finance/management, brand leadership, business management, international accounting and financial, international HRM, management, marketing, strategic information systems, strategic supply chain management, strategic carbon management

School of Social Work and Psychology; www.uea.ac.uk/swp

child and family research/ psychology, psychology, social work, social policy; BA(Hons), BSc(Hons), CPE/Dip, DEd, GradDip, LlBHons, LLM, MA, MA/DipSW, MBA, MPhil, MRes, MSc, MScEd, PGCert, PGDip, PhD

Degrees validated by University of East Anglia offered by:

CITY COLLEGE NORWICH
www.ccn.ac.uk

business computing, business management, child care and education, culinary arts, early childhood studies, engineering (civil, electrical, electronic, mechanical), English, financial services/retail: insurance/retail, health and exercise, health studies, hospitality management, hospitality tourism, interactive media, journalism, leisure and events management, licensed retail, psychology, public sector management, social work, teaching assistants, travel & tourism, music marketing; BA(Hons), BSc(Hons), FdA, FdSc, HNC, HND

OTLEY COLLEGE
www.otleycollege.ac.uk

foundation degrees in animal care, conservation, ecosystems, equine performance, landscape and garden design

UNIVERSITY OF EAST LONDON
www.uel.ac.uk

School of Architecture and the Visual Arts; www.uel.ac.uk/ava

animation, architecture, design, digital arts, graphic arts, illustration, fashion/design, photography, printmaking, textiles, landscape architecture; BA(Hons), BSc/BA, FdA, GradCert, MA, MArch, MPhil, MSc, PgC, PhD, ProfDoc

School of Combined Honours; www.uel.ac.uk/combined

range of subjects for which combined honours courses are conducted

School of Computing, Information Technology and Engineering; www.uel.ac.uk/cite

architecture, environmental & energy, bus inf systems, civil engineering, construction management, computer systems eng/ games/networks/technology, computing, digital media, electrical & electronics eng, GIS, information security systems, IT, mathematics, mobile computing/communications multimedia, nanotechnology, product design, software eng, surveying & mapping sci, sustainability; BA/BEng(Hons), BA/BSc, BSc(Hons), MPhil, MSc, PhD, ProfDoc

Royal Docks Business School; www.uel.ac.uk/business

accounting, investment and risk management, banks, business finance, project management, economics/ management, administration, international business, events management, finance, HRM, management studies, marketing, music industry, tourism management; BA(Hons), DBA, HND, LlB, MA, MBA, MPhil, MSc, PGDip, PhD

Cass School of Education; www.uel.ac.uk/education

early childhood, secondary/primary education, childcare, internation education, English language, playwork, teacher training, teaching, teaching assistants, youth studies and community work; BA(Hons), EdD, FdA, MA, PGCE, PGDip, ProfDoc, UnivCert

School of Health and Bioscience; www.uel.ac.uk/hal

bioscience, biochemistry, biomedical science, biotechnology, conservation and ecology, health studies/ science, medical/microbiology, paediatrics, toxology, public health, pharmacology, physiotherapy, podiatory, sports science; BA(Hons), BSc(Hons), FdSc, MPhil, MSc, PGCert, PhD, ProfDoc

School of Law; www.uel.ac.uk/law

law, criminal justice, criminology, human rights, international law and finance/world economy, Islamic & Middle East law, refugee studies, terrorism; BA(Hons), BSc(Hons), LlB, LlM, MSc, PostGDips

School of Psychology; www.uel.ac.uk/ psychology

counselling, mentoring, pysychology, critical/developmental/forensic/educational/child psychology, psychosocial studies; BA(Hons), BSc(Hons), ClinPSyD, FdA, GradDip/Cert, MA, MSc, ProfDoc, UnivCert

School of Humanities and Social Sciences; www.uel.ac.uk/hsocialsciences

advertising, anthroplogy, communication studies, computer games, cultural studies, dance, information technology film/video studies, Eng literature, history, refugee studies, international development/politics/ relations, journalism, media studies, music culture, social policy, social work/enterprise, sociology, theatre studies, voluntary sector studies; BA(Hons), BMus, BSc(Hons), FdA, GradDip/Cert, MA, ProfDoc, UnivCert

THE UNIVERSITY OF EDINBURGH
www.ed.ac.uk

College of Humanities and Social Sciences; www.hss.ed.ac.uk

School of Arts, Culture and the Environment; www.ed.ac.uk/schools-departments/arts-culture-environment

architecture, architectural facilities/project/conservation/ management, architectural history, architecture in composition, criticism, curating, fine art, history of art, landscape architecture, modern art, music, music informatics, musical acoustics, sound design, sustainable/urban design

The Business School; www.business-school.ed.ac.uk

analysis, accounting and finance, business studies, carbon energy markets economics, entrepreneurship and innovation, international business, management science, marketing, public management, work and employment

School of Divinity; www.div.ed.ac.uk

divinity, biblical studies, ethics, ministry, philosophy & theology, religious studies, theology, world Christianity

School of Economics; www.ed.ac.uk/schools-departments/economics

asset pricing, corporate finance, economics and accounting/economic history/law/mathematics/politics/sociology, international money and finance, macroeconomics, micreconomics

School of Health in Social Science; www.ed.ac.uk/schools-departments/health

advancing nursing practice, applied psychology for children and young people, clinical psychology, counselling, global health, medical sciences, nursing studies, psychotherapy, public policy, social science in health

School of History, Classics and Archaeology; www.shc.ed.ac.uk

American history, ancient philosophy, medieval studies/history, archaeology, architectural history/ & archaeology, Celtic, Scottish studies, classics, gender history European/forensic/Mediterranean/archaeology, economic & social history, environmental archaeology, Greek, the Hellenistic world, modern British & Irish history, osteoarcheology, cultural & social history, social anthropology, Scottish history, social history

School of Law; www.law.ed.ac.uk

law, English law, administrative/civil/commercial/company/competition/contract/criminal/environmental law, banking and finance law, contract law in Europe, criminology, data protection and information privacy, EC competition law, international law of the sea, international private law, international tax law, criminal & global crime

School of Literatures, Languages and Cultures; www.ed.ac.uk/schools-departments/literatures-languages-cultures

Asian studies, Celtic and Scottish studies, comparative literature, Euroculture, English literature, European theatre, film studies, Islamic and Middle Eastern studies, literature and transatlanticism, medieval /translation word and music studies

Moray House School of Education; www.education.ed.ac.uk

childhood practice, applied sport science, community education, dance science & education, design & technology, e-learning, headship, inclusive & special education, language – theory, practice & literacy, language teaching, management of training & development, outdoor education, performance psychology, PE, primary education, sport & recreation management, TESOL, university teaching

School of Philosophy, Psychology and Language Science; www.ppls.ed.ac.uk

ancient philosophy, artificial intelligence and philosophy/psychology, cognitive science, English language, epistemology, ethics, history & theory of psychology, human cognitive neuropsychology, linguistics, philosophy, psychology, psychology of individual differences, research ethics & political philosophy, mind & language/cognition; BA(Arch), BD, BEd(Hons), BMedSci, BMus, BN, BSc(Hons), DD, DLitt, DMus, DClinPyschol, EdD, LlM, MA, MA(Hons), MBA, MLA, MPhil/PhD, MSc, MTeach, MTh/Sc, PGDipCert, PGDE

College of Medicine and Veterinary Medicine; www.ed.ac.uk/schools-departments/medicine-vet-medicine

anaesthesia practice, applied animal behaviour and welfare, dental primary care, medical electives, medical sciences, medicine, oral health science, oral surgery, orthodontics, paediatric dentistry, prosthodontics, public health research, transfusion, transplantation and tissue banking, veterinary medicine and surgery

School of Clinical Sciences and Community Health; www.ed.ac.uk/schools-departments/clinical-sciences

clinical and surgical sciences, community health sciences, human anatomy, medical and radiological sciences, reproductive and developmental sciences

School of Biomedical Sciences; www.ed.ac.uk/schools-departments/biomedical-sciences

biomedical sciences, cognitive and neural systems, infectious diseases, integrative physiology, neurogeneration

School of Molecular and Clinical Medicine; www.mcm.ed.ac.uk

clinical brain services, clinical neurosciences, molecular medicine, pathology, pyschiatry, emerging & neglected diseases, translational medicine, international animal health, transfusion, transplantion, neuroimaging

The Royal (Dick) School of Veterinary Studies; www.ed.ac.uk/schools-departments/vet

veterinary medicine, clinical course, population medicine & veterinary public health; BSc(Hons), MBChB, MSC, BVMS, DipCert, MPhil, PhD

College of Science and Engineering; ww.w.scieng.ed.ac.uk

School of Biological Sciences; www.ed.ac.uk/schools-departments/biology

biochemistry, biodiversity and taxonomy of plants, bioinformatics, biological sciences, biotechnology, cell biology, developmental/evolutionary/ medical/ molecular/reproductive biology, drug discovery and translational biology, ecology science, plant science, pharmacology, zoology, quantitative genetics and genome analysis, immunology

School of Chemistry; www.chem.ed.ac.uk

chemical physics, chemistry/ with environmental & sustainable chemistry/materials chemistry, medicinal and biological chemistry

School of Engineering; www.see.ed.ac.uk

chemical engineering with environmental engineering/management

Civil and Environmental Engineering: civil engineering, civil and environmental engineering/construction management, NDT, silos and granular solids, structural engineering with architecture, structural and fire safety engineering, structures and fire safety

Electronics and Electrical Engineering: electrical engineering, electrical engineering with renewable energy, electronics, electronics and computer science/ bioelectronics, electronics and electrical engineering, communications/ electronics and software engineering, energy conversion and storage, energy delivery, integrated micro and nano systems, operation and control, power electronics, renewable energy, restructuring and regulation

Mechanical Engineering: advanced materials applications, electrical and mechanical engineering, fluid and particle dynamics, manufacturing and process optimization, materials and processes, mechanical engineering with management/ structural mechanics

Institute for Energy Systems: environmental mitigation, energy delivery, renewable energy, restructuring and regulation

General Engineering

School for Informatics; www.inf.ed.ac.uk

informatics, artificial intelligence, cognitive science, computational linguistics/physics, computer science, electronics and software engineering/computer science, informatics, mind and language music technology, software engineering,

Centre for Intelligent Systems and Their Applications; Institute for Adaptive and Neural Computation; Institute for Communicating and Collaborative Systems; Institute for Computing Systems Architecture; Institute of Perception, Action and Behaviour; e-Science Institute; Laboratory for Foundations of Computer Science; Informatics Life-Sciences Institute

School of Geosciences; www.geos.ed.ac.uk

Ecological Sciences, Geography, Earth Science: appraisal and development (petroleum, hydrocarbons), carbon capture & storage, carbon management, ecological economics, ecological science (conservation and ecological management/environmental science/management), ecological science (forestry), environment and development, protection and management, environmental sustainability, exploration geophysics, GIS, geoscience for subsurface exploration, integrated resource management, interactions of organisms with their physical and biological environment, principles and practice of managing ecological systems, environmental geoscience, geography/ and archaeology/economic & social history/economics/politics/social anthropology/social policy/sociology/environmental studies, geology, geophysics, meteorology, physical geography

School of Mathematics; www.maths.ed.ac.uk

pure & applied mathematics, computational/financial mathematics, mathematics & statistics/management/ physics/artificial intelligence/computer science/philosophy, operational research, pure mathematics, mathematical physics, geometry & topology, analysis

School of Physics and Astronomy; www.ph.ed.ac.uk

astrophysics, chemical physics, computational physics, distributed scientific computing, geophysics, physics and computer sci/mathematics/meteorology/ music, high performance computing, mathematical physics, physics; BEng, BSc, MChem, MChemPhys, MEarthSci, MEng, MInf, MPhil, MPhys, MS, MSc, MSci, PGDip, PhD

UNIVERSITY OF ESSEX
www.essex.ac.uk

Faculty of Humanities and Comparative Studies; www.essex.ac.uk/hcs

art and curatorial practices, art and film and contemporary art, art history and theory, critical management and curating, gallery studies and critical curating, history of art and modern languages/literature/film studies, Latin American art, theory and criticism; East 15: acting /and contemporary theatre/stage combat, acting for TV, film and radio, community theatre, filmmaking, physical theatre, technical theatre studies, theatre arts, theatre directing, world performance; History: American history, British and European history, contemporary history, digital history, historical studies, history, local, community and family history, modern history, researching history in Britain, social and cultural history

Department of Literature, Film, and Theatre Studies

comparative literature, creative writing, drama/and literature, English language and/with modern myth, English and United States literature, literature and film studies/history of art/sociology/philosophy/history, literature and myth, literature and the unconscious, wild writing: literature, science and the environment

Dept of Philosophy; www.essex.ac.uk/philosphy

continental philosophy, philosophy and literature/ politics/ sociology, with modern languages/law/ human rights, philosophy and psychoanalysis, philosophy, politics and economics, philosophy, politics and environmental issues,
International Academy: numerous cross-departmental courses; BA(Hons), CertHE, Dip/MA, FdA, MA, MFA, MPhil, PGCert, PhD

Faculty of Social Sciences; www.essex.ac.uk/ss

Dept of Economics; www.essex.ac.uk/economics

accounting and financial economics, applied economics and data analysis, business economics, econometrics, economics, economics with mathematics, financial economics, international economics, management economics

Dept of Government; www.essex.ac.uk/government

European integration/politics, global and comparative politics, government, ideology and discourse analysis, international development/relations, philosophy, politics and economics, political behaviour, political economy, political theory, politics, politics and law/ sociology/ human rights, public opinion and polling

Dept of Languages and Linguistics; www.essex.ac.uk/linguistics

applied linguistics, English, English language/ and literature/sociolinguistics, linguistics, teaching

English, language disorders, Portuguese, Spanish, TEFL, phonology, syntax

Dept of Sociology; www.essex.ac.uk/sociology

criminology, criminology and American studies/social psychology/the media, gender, culture and society media/society, migration and citizenship, humanities, psychology/history/literature/philosophy/human rights, social sciences, sociology, sociology with management/politics; BA(Hons), BSc(Hons), Diploma, GradDip, MA, MPhil, MRes, MSc, PGDip, PhD, ProcDoc

Faculty of Law and Management; www.essex.ac.uk/lm

Essex Business School; www.essex.ac.uk/ebs

Centre for Global Accountability; Centre for Entrepreneurship Research; Essex Finance Centre; Essex Management Centre

accounting, finance, banking, business, corporate governance, creative industry management, entrepreneurship and innovation, environmental governance, financial engineering and risk management, financial management/economics, international accounting/finance/ management/ small business management, investment, management/ psychology, management studies, marketing and society/innovation, new ventures, global projects organization studies, HRM

Human Rights Centre; www.essex.ac.uk/humanrightscentre

human rights and cultural diversity/research methods, human rights and public law, international human rights law, law/philosophy/sociology, politics with human rights

School of Law; www.essex.ac.uk/law

English and French laws, European business law, European Union law, EU & international law , health care law and human rights, information technology, media and e-commerce, international human rights/ and humanitarian law, international trade law, law, UK human rights and public law; BA(Hons), BSc(Hons), DocProg, LlM, LLB, MPhil, MSc, PhD

Faculty of Science and Engineering; www.essex.ac

Dept of Biological Sciences; www.essex.ac.uk/bs

biochemistry, biological sciences, biology, biodiversity and conservation, biomedical science, biotechnology, biotechnology: future crops for food and biofuels, cardiac rehabilitation, ecology, environmental governance: natural world, environmental resource management, genetics, marine and freshwater biology, mathematics and biology, molecular medicine, natural environment and society, science and society, sports and exercise science, sports science and biology, plant biotechnology

School of Computer Science and Electronic Engineering; www.essex.ac.uk/csee

computer games/networks/science/ systems engineering, computers and electronics, data communication, electronic/ software engineering, telecommunication engineering

School of Health and Human Sciences; www.essex.ac.uk /hss

adult nursing, health and human sciences, health studies/ and sociology, mental health nursing, occupational therapy, oral health sciences, physiotherapy, social psychology and sociology, speech and language therapy, healthcare practice

Department of Mathematical Sciences; www.essex.ac.uk/maths

accounting and mathematics, discrete mathematics and its applications, economics and mathematics, econometrics, finance and mathematics, mathematics and biomathematics, mathematics for secondary teaching, mathematics with computing, operational research and computer science, statistics, operational research/ data analysis/ econometrics/ computer science

Dept of Psychology; www.essex.ac.uk/psychology

cognitive psychology/ neuropsychology/ neuroscience, neuropsychology /and development perception and social and health psychology, psychology, research methods in psychology, social psychology and sociology; BA(Hons), BEng, BSc(Hons), GradDip, MA, MPhil, MRes, MSc, PGDip, PhD, ProfDoc

Degrees validated by the University of Essex offered at:

WRITTLE COLLEGE
www.writtle.ac.uk

agriculture, animals, business, conservation, countryside, design, engineering, equine, floristry, post-harvest technology, sport, vet nursing; BA(Hons), BSc(Hons), CertMS, Certs, DipMS, FDAs, Higher Certs, MA, MBA, MSc

UNIVERSITY OF EXETER
www.exeter.ac.uk

School of Arts, Languages and Literature; www.sall.exeter.ac.uk
arts, drama, English, film studies, medieval studies, modern languages, sexuality and gender; BA(Hons), MA, MPhil, PhD

School of Bioscience; www.bioscience.exeter.ac.uk
applied biochemistry, bioinformation, aquatic biology and resource management, biological and medicinal chemistry, medical informatics, biological sciences, biology, conservation biology and ecology, evolutionary biology/behavioural ecology, molecular biology, zoology, sports & health science; BSc(Hons), MPhil, MSc, PgDip/Cert, PhD

University of Exeter Business School; www.business-school.exeter.ac.uk
accounting, finance, business (economics, management studies), IT management, marketing, leadership, tourism; BA(Hons), MBA, MPhil, MSc, PGDip/Cert, PhD

Graduate School of Education; www.education.exeter.ac.uk
childhood and youth studies, early years, primary, secondary education, mentoring, special education, TESOL, educational psychology, educational studies, engineering and education, sports science and education, psychology and education; BA(Hons), EdD, MEd, MPhil, MSc, PGCE PhD

School of Engineering, Computing and Mathematics; www.secam.exeter.ac.uk & Physical Science www.emps.exeter.ac.uk
Computing: IT management for business, computer science, networking, electronics, applied artificial intelligence

Civil/ environmental/ectronic/computer/mechanical/materials engineering, engineering and management, mathematics, adv mathematics, financial mathematics

Geology; applied geotechnics, European minerals engineering, mining engineering/geology, surveying;

Medical Imaging, clinical research

Physics & Astronomy; astrophysics, medical imaging, biomedical physics, quantum science; BSc(Hons), BEng, MEng, MSc, MPhil, PhD

School of Geography, Archeology, and Earth Resources; www.geography.exeter.ac.uk
geography, archeology, earth resources, geology, mining engineering, renewable, sustainable development; BA(Hons), BSc(Hons), MA, MPhil, MRes, PGDip, PhD

School of Humanities and Social Sciences; www.huss.exeter.ac.uk
Arab and Islamic studies, archaeology, classics and ancient history, climate change, critical human geography, Cornish studies, earth system science, European studies/economics, history, politics, sociology and philosophy, theology; BA(Hons), MA, MPhil, MRes, PhD

School of Law; www.law.business law;
international law, comparative law, international human rights law, senior status studies, politics and law; BA(Hons), LlB, LlM, MA, MPhil, MRes, PhD

Peninsula College of Medicine and Dentistry; www.pms.exeter.ac.uk
biochemical and clinical sciences, infection prevention & control, diabetes, remote healthcare, obesity, clinical education, dentistry, health service resources, medicine, surgery; BClinM, BDS, BMMS, MPhil, MD/MS, PhD, MSc

School of Physics; www.newton.ex.ac.uk
astronomy, astrophysics, biomedical physics, quantum science, medical imaging, physics; BSc(Hons), MPhys, PhD

School of Psychology; www.psychology.exeter.ac.uk
animal behaviour, biology, psychology, social & organisational psychology, clinical & community psychology, psychological therapies, cognitive perception, sports exercise science; BA(Hons), BSc(Hons), DocCinicalPsychology, MSc, PhD, PGCert/Dip

School of Sport and Health Sciences; www.ssstsexeter.ac.uk
children's health, sport & health science, paediatric exercise, sport and exercise medicine, exercise, human biosciences, physiology, sports science; BSc(Hons), MPhil, MSc, PhD

Degrees validated by University of Exeter offered at:

UCP MARJON-UNIVERSITY COLLEGE PLYMOUTH ST MARK & ST JOHN
www.ucpmarjon.ac.uk

children, youth & community, drama & theatre arts, education & teacher training, English language, literature and writing, live music, media, outdoor, sociology, speech and language therapy, sport, health, coaching and PE; BA(Hons), BA/BSc, BEd, FdA church college certs; GTP, MA, MEd, MPhil, PGCE

UNIVERSITY COLLEGE FALMOUTH (INC DARTINGTON COLLEGE OF ARTS)
www.falmouth.ac.uk

3D design, advertising, art & performance/environment, choreography, contemporary crafts, creative events management, creative music technology, curatorial practice, dance, digital animation, English with creative writing/media, fashion design, film, fine art, garden design, graphic design, illustration, interior design, journalism, media studies, music performance/theatre/composition, photography, popular music, PR, professional writing, radio production, screen & media performance, spatial, sportswear design, television production, textile design, theatre (design and production, directing, performance, writing), writing; BA(Hons), FdA, MA, MPhil, PGDip, PhD

UNIVERSITY OF GLAMORGAN
www.glam.ac.uk

Cardiff School of Creative and Cultural Industries; www.ccc.glam.ac.uk
animation, art & design, computer music, drama and music/and sound, fashion & retail design, film studies, graphic communication, journalism, music engineerig, photography, media and communication/design, scripwriting, visual art; BA(Hons), FdA, MA, MPhil

Faculty of Health, Sport and Science; www.hesas.glam.ac.uk
biology, chemistry, child health & welfare, chiropractic, clinical physiology/practitioner, coaching, diagnostic clinical ultrasound, disaster relief healthcare, family therapy, forensic science and police studies, geology, geography, GIS, human/physical geography, environment, health science, human biology, international wildlife, midwifery, natural history, nursing, observational astronomy, forensic odontology, renewable energy, social work & social care, sports health and exercise; BA(Hons), BSc(Hons), BN, FoundCerts, HEDip, HNC, HND, MA, MPhil, MSC/PGD/, PGC, PhD

Faculty of Advanced Technology; www.fat.glam.ac.uk
built environment, building services, computing, engineering (aeronautical, aerospace, computer

forensics/systems), engineering/security/systems, electrical and electronic/ mechanical engineering, environmental management, electronics & infomation technology, energy systems engineering, GIS, intelligent computer games/systems, mathematics, mobile, sustainable power tech, total quality, business risk management computing/communications, real estate dev; BEng(Hons), BSc, BSc(Hons), CertHE, DipHE, HNC, HND, MEng

Glamorgan Business School; www.bus.glam.ac.uk

accounting, business, business management, economics, forensic audit & accounting, Islamic banking & finance, HRM, leisure and sport management, management, marketing, procurement, transport & logistics, tourism events management, supply chain management, transport; ACCA, BA(Hons), BSc(Hons), DBA, DocLC, FdA, MBA, MPhil, MSc

Faculty of Humanities and Social Sciences; www.hass.glam.ac.uk

adolescence, art practice, childhood, community regeneration, creative writing, criminology, early years, education and careers, English, gothic studies, health & public service management, health psychology, play therapy, history, humanities, languages, law (commercial, intellectual & ind property, international commercial), psychology, public services/leadership, sociology, TESOL; BA(Hons), BA/BSc, BSc(Hons), DocPublServ, FCert, FdA, GradDip Law, LlB(Hons), LlM/PhD/PgD, MA/PDip/Cert, MSc, PGD/PGC

The Centre for Lifelong Learning; www.cell.glam.ac.uk

astronomy, business courses, community courses/ regeneration, communication technology, craft and design, creative industries, environmental studies, information, languages, social sciences; BA(Hons), BSc(Hons), FdA, GCert/Dip/MA/MSc

UNIVERSITY OF GLASGOW
www.gla.ac.uk

Faculty of Arts; www.gla.ac.uk/faculties/arts

archaeology, arts & media informatics, Celtic civilization/studies, classics, comparative literature, Czech, English/English literature, history, film & television studies, French, German, Greek, history, history of art, Italian, Latin, literature, music, philosophy, Polish, Russian, Scottish literature, Slavonic studies, Spanish, theatre studies, theology & religious studies; BD(Min), BMus, DLitt, MA, MAHons, MLitt, MPhil, MTh, PhD

Faculty of Biomedical and Life Sciences; www.gla.ac.uk /faculties/fbls

anatomy, biochemistry, bioinformatics, biomedical sciences, biotechnology, ecological & environmental biology, evolutionary chemistry, exercise science, genetics, immunology, marine & freshwater biology, medical/and veterinary biochemistry, microbiology, molecular and cellular biology, neuroscience, parasitology, pharmacology, physiology, plant science, sports medicine, virology, zoology, animal biology, biology, biomolecular sciences, human biology, infection biology, sports science; BSc(Hons), MRes, MSc, MSci, PhD

Faculty of Education; www.gla.ac.uk/faculties/education

childhood practice, community development, music, primary education – with teaching qualifications, education in music, religious and philosophical education, English language teaching, inclusive education, organization leadership, psychological studies, teaching adults, technological education, technology and management; BA(Hons), BTechEd, BTechS, EdD, MA, MA(Hons), MEd, MLitt, MSc, MusicBEd, PhD

Faculty of Engineering; www.gla.ac.uk/faculties/engineering

aerospace engineering, architecture, audio & video engineering, automotive engineering, avionics, biomedical engineering, chemical engineering, civil engineering, computer/systems engineering, earthquake engineering, electrical & electronics engineering, electrical design, geotechnics, marine engineering, mechanical engineering/design engineering, microcircuits, nautical science, naval architecture, ocean engineering, offshore/subsea systems, structural engineering, telecommunications electronics, signal processing; BEng, BSc, EngD, MEng, MSc, PGDip, PhD

Faculty of Law, Business and Social Sciences; www.gla.ac.uk/faculties/lbss

law with European legal studies, common law, competition law, corporate & financial law, human rights, sociolegal/international law, central and east European studies, economics, economic and social history, management politics, sociology, urban studies; BAcc, BSc, LlB, MA, MAcc, MFin, MRes, MSc, PhD, MMedicalLaw

Glagow Business School; www.gla.ac.uk/faculties/business

accounting, economics, finance, financial accounting, banking, international finance, management, management with real estate, strategic marketing, international management & entrepreneurship, economic & social history; MAcc, MBA, MFin, MSc, PhD

Faculty of information & Mathematical Science; www.gla.ac.uk/faculties/fims

computer science, mobile software, electronic & software engineering, mathematics, applied mathematics, statistics, psychology, brain imaging

Faculty of Medicine; www.gla.ac.uk/medicine

Medical School; www.gla.ac.uk/departments/medicine

cardiovascular sci, clinical /human nutrition/pharmacology/physics, medical genetics, behavioural science, clinical psychology/practice, disability and rehabilitation, human disease, medical science, medicine, neuropsychology, paediatric science, surgical oncology, palliative medicine and the care of the dying, public health, sport & exercise science; B(MedSci), MBChB, MD, MML, MMLE, MPC, MPH, PhD

Dental School; www.gla.ac.uk/departments/dentalschool

clinical dental science, clinical medical science, dentistry, patient management and health, primary dental care, endodontics, orthodontics, paediatric dentistry, special care; BDS, BSc(Dent Sc), DDS, MSc, PhD

Nursing; www.gla.ac.uk/departments/nursing

clinical nursing practice, critical care nursing, health care, health studies in nursing, nursing & health studies/ integrated biomedical and life sciences, pathology and human diseases, specialist medical nursing, specialist surgical nursing; BN, BN(Hons), RegNurse, MSc(MedSci), PGC, PGDip, PhD

Faculty of Science; www.gla.ac.uk/science

anatomy, animal biology, astronomy, biochemistry, biomolecular science, biological sciences, biomedical sciences, biotechnology, chemical physics, chemistry, chemistry with forensic/medicinal chemistry, computing science, computing science & physiology (neuroinformatics), earth science, electronic & software engineering, environmental biogeochemistry/chemistry/geography, genetics, geography, immunology, marine & freshwater biology, mathematical sciences, pure mathematics applied mathematics, medical biochemistry, microbiology, mobile software engineering, molecular & cellular biology, neuroscience, parasitology, pharmacology, physics/theoretical physics, physics with astrophysics, physiology, sports science, nutrition, plant science, psychology, software engineering, sports medicine, statistics, virology, zoology; BSc(Hons), BSc(designated), MSc, MSci, PhD, MRes, PGDip

Faculty of Veterinary Medicine; www.gla.ac.uk/faculties/vet

anatomy, animal husbandry, biomolecular sciences and physiology; microbiology, pathology, parasitology and pharmacology, veterinary medicine/surgery/public health; BSc, BSc(Vet Sci), BVMS, MVPH, PhD

GLASGOW CALEDONIAN UNIVERSITY
www.caledonian.ac.uk

School of the Built & Natural Environment; www.caledonian.ac.uk/bne

building services engineering/ surveying, construction management, energy & environmental engineering, environmental civil engineering/management and planning, fire risk engineering, real estate & property management & valuation, quantity surveying, sustainable energy technology, waste management; BSc/BEng, BSc(Hons), MSc, MPhil, PhD

Caledonian School of Business; www.caledonian.ac.uk/cbs

accountancy, banking, business & management/studies, entertainment & events management, fashion, finance, innovation and enterprise marketing, investment, international trade, journalism, risk management, retailing, people management and leadership, public policy studies, retailing, risk; BA/BA(Hons), MRes, PhD

School of Engineering and Computing; www.caledonian.ac.uk/sec

3D computer animation, applied graphics technology, applied instumentation, audio technology with multimedia/electronics, computer engineering, computer games (design, software development), computing (information/networks, web systems development), digital security, electrical power, electronics/ forensics/engineering, graphic design for digital media, information technology management, manufacturing systems, mechanical & power plant systems/mechanical electronic systems engineering, mechatronics, multimedia visualization with product design, network security, telecommunications engineering, wireless communication; BA/BA(Hons), BEng/BEng(Hons), BSc/BSc(Hons), DipHE, MA/ PGD, MSc/PGD, PhD

School of Health and Social Care; www.caledonian.ac.uk/shsc

(now part of School of Health)

health & social care, cardiac rehabilitation, occupational therapy, physyiotherapy, podiatric medicine & surgery, radiography, social work; BSc(Hons), Grad-Cert, MPhil, MSc, PgC/D, PhD, ProfDoc,

School of Life Sciences; www.caledonian.ac.uk/sls

biochemistry, biological & biomedical sciences, cell & molecular biology, dietetics, food bioscience, forensics, human biology/biosciences, microbiology, nutrition, optometry, pharmacology, clinical physiology, psychology, vision sciences; BSc, BSc(Hons), DipHE, DPsych, MSc, OpthDisp, PGD/C, PhD

School of Law and Social Sciences; www.caledonian.ac.uk/sls

business law, criminology, law, legal studies, European /and international trade/business law, international contracts, international law, law and IT, Islamic and ME law, social sciences, women in the law; BA(Hons), LlB, LlM, MSc, PGD/C, PhD

School of Nursing, Midwifery, and Community Health; www.caledonian.ac.uk/nmch

adult, child, mental health or learning disabilities, community health, healthcare, midwifery, nursing studies, operating department practices, overseas nursing, public health, sexual health; BA/BA(Hons), BMidwifery, BN, BSc/BSc(Hons), DipN, MPhil, MSc, PGDip, PhD

THE GLASGOW SCHOOL OF ART
www.gsa.ac.uk

architecture, design, environmental art, fine art, photography, painting & printmaking, historical and critical studies, interior design, printmaking, product design/engineering, silversmithing and jewellery, fashion & textiles, visual communication; BA(Hons), BEng, BArch, DipArch, MA, MArch, MDes, MEng, MPhil, MRes, PhD

UNIVERSITY OF GLOUCESTERSHIRE
www.glos.ac.uk

The Business School; www.glos.ac.uk/faculties/bus

accounting, advertising, branding, business management(economics/enterprise/HRM/international business/and strategy), business information technology, financial management, forensic/IT/software/security systems, computing, information/communications technology, games design, events management, finance, hospitality management, HRM, international marketing, international business strategy, law, leisure & sports management, marketing, marketing management, multimedia web design, music and media management, tourism management

Faculty of Education, Humanities and Sciences; www.glos.ac.uk/ehs

animal biology, biology, bioscences, communications, creative writing, criminology, education leadership, educational admin & management, initial teacher education, primary education, early years, HE, inclusion/diversity, English language/literature, geography, landscape architecture, language, marketing, music and media management, philosophy and ethics, psychology, religion, return to teaching, sociology, teacher training; BA/BA(Hons), BEd, BSc/BSc(Hons), Cert HE, Foundation degrees, MA, MEd, MPhil, MSc, PGCE

Faculty of Media, Art, and Communication; www.glos.ac.uk/faculties/mac

advertising, animation, art & design, digital film production, drawing, editorial, fine art, film studies, graphics, illustration, interactive media, communications, painting, photography, photojournalism, popular music, PR, printmaking, sculpture, television production, textiles; BA/BA(Hons), BSc/BSc(Hons), MA, MPhil, MSc, PGCert, PGDip, PhD

Faculty of Sport, Health and Social Care; www.glos.ac.uk/faculties/shsc

applied health studies, applied sport and exercise studies, child care, community care with vulnerable adults, community health studies, exercise and health sciences, health and wellbeing, integrated youth practice, non-medical prescribing, performing arts, physical activity & public health, playwork, sports coaching, sports development/education/therapy/strength and conditioning, sport & Christian outreach theology, youth & community work, youth work; BA/BA(Hons), BSc/BSc(Hons), DipSW, Postgraduate; MA, MPhil, MRes, MSc, PGCert, PGDip, PhD

UNIVERSITY OF GREENWICH
www.gre.ac.uk

School of Architecture and Construction; www.gre.ac.uk/schools/arc

architecture, building design, building surveying, construction, design & construction management, digital design, real estate management, fine art, garden design, graphic design, health and environment, landscape architecture/ management, occupational safety, photography, quantity surveying, urban design, visual art and communication; BA(Hons), BSc(Hons), Certs, Dip, HNC, HND, MA, MSc, MPhil, PGDip, PhD

Business Information Technology and Enterprise (BITE); www.gre.ac.uk/schools/bite

information age education, information and communication technology, information technology, management for business, project management; BA(Hons), BSc(Hons), HND

Business School; www.gre.ac.uk/schools/business

accounting, audit & assurance services, banking, business administration/information systems, business entrepreneurship and innovation, business in Europe, business logistics & transport management, business management, business studies, China international business, economics, events management, finance, financial information systems, HRM, information technology, international business, marketing, public service management, marketing, multimedia, PR, public services, purchasing & supply chain management, leisure & tourism management; BA(Hons), BSc(Hons), Certs, DBA, Foundation degrees, HNC, HND, MA, MBA, MSc, PGDip, PhD

School of Computing & Mathematical Science; www.gre.ac.uk/schools/cms

business computing, business information systems, business information technology, computer science, computer security & forensics, computer systems & networking, computing (with games development, digital multimedia), digital animation & production/ film production/ television & interactive media, embedded computer systems, film & television production, financial mathematics, games, internet computing, mathematics & computing, mathematics for decision science, mathematics, statistics & computing, mobile computing & communications, networks, software engineering, web business systems, web technologies; BSc(Hons), FDSc, MA, MEng/ BEng, MPhil, MSc, PhD

School of Education and Training; www.gre.ac.uk/schools/education

childhood studies, community sport, design and technology with QTS, early years, education /and training, higher education, lifelong learning, physical education and sport, primary education with QTS, secondary education, teaching and training, youth and community studies; BA(Hons), BELT, Cert, DipHE, EdD, Foundation degree, MA, MPhil, MSc, PGCert/Dip, PhD

School of Engineering; www.gre.ac.uk/schools/engineering

civil engineering, communications systems engineering, computer networking, electrical and electronic engineering, engineering management, games and entertainment systems, information and communications technology/management, internet technology, manufacturing systems, marine engineering, mechanical engineering, project management, public health/water environment engineering, software engineering; BEng(Hons), BSc(Hons), HNC, HND, MEng, MSc

Greenwich Maritime Institute; www.gre.ac.uk/schools/gmi

maritime history, international maritime management, maritime policy; MA, MBA, MPhil, PhD

School of Health and Social Care; www.gre.ac.uk/schools/health

child development/protection, clinical practice, counselling, health, early years, learning disabilities management, mental health work, midwifery, nursing (adult, child/welfare, learning dissabilities, mental health), paramedic science, professional practice, psychology, public health, social work and social care, speech and language therapy, therapeutic counselling; BA(Hons), BSc(Hons), DipHE, Foundation degrees, GradDips, MA, MPhil, PGCert, PhD

School of Humanities and Social Sciences; www.gre.ac.uk/schools/humanities

creative industries, criminal psychology, criminology, drama, English, film studies, history, international studies, journalism and PR, justice and legal studies, language and culture, law, media and creative arts, media writing, modern languages (Chinese, English, French, German, Italian, Spanish), philosophy, politics, sociology, TESOL English language teaching; BSc(Hons), BA(Hons), FD, LlB, MA, MPhil, MSc, PGCert, PGDip, PhD

Medway School of Pharmacy; www.gre.ac.uk/schools/studying/index/html

medicine management, pharmacy practice, independant/supplementary prescribing; BSc(Hons), FdMM, FdPP, MPharm, MSc, PGCert/Dip

Natural Resources Institute; www.gre.ac.uk/schools/nri

development studies, ecology and global change management, food safety, natural resources; BSc(Hons), MPhil, MSc, PhD

School of Science; www.gre.ac.uk/schools/science

animal and equine studies, applied biology, biomedical, bioscience, biotechnology, chemistry, forensic science, environmental science, geography, GIS, human nutrition, international agriculture, life sciences, natural resources, pharmaceutical science, professional football coaching sport science, sustainability; BSc(Hons), HNC, HND, MPhil, MSc, PGDip, PhD

GRIMSBY INSTITUTE OF FURTHER AND HIGHER EDUCATION
www.grimsby.ac.uk

access, animal care, business admin & law, children's literature, computing, construction, creative arts, electrical/electronics engineering, hair & beauty, health & child care, humanities & science, leadership & management, manufacturing & logistics, mechanical engineering, international/media, professional/ writing, refrigeration, sports & fitness, teacher education, travel & tourism; BA(Hons), BSc(Hons), FdA, FdEd, FdSc, HEdDip, HNC, HND, MA, MBA, MSc, PGCE

HARPER ADAMS UNIVERSITY COLLEGE
www.harper-adams.ac.uk

agricultural/ engineering/law, animals, business, countryside management, engineering, environment, food/engineering/retail, food studies, rural land & estate management/resource management, management, marketing, leisure & tourism, veterinary/physiotherapy/pharmacy, sustainable agriculture; BSc(Hons), FdSc, MBA, MSc, PGDip/Cert

HERRIOT-WATT UNIVERSITY
www.hw.ac.uk

School of the Built Environment; www.hw.ac.uk/sbe

Architectural Engineering:
civil & environmental engineering, structural engineering with architectural design; building surveying, construction project management, planning and property development, quantity surveying, real estate management/investment and finance; environmental engineering, building conservation, housing and regeneration, urban and regional planning, planning & property development, urban & regional development, real estate management, water resources and catchment development
BSc(Hons, Ord), BEng, MEng, MRes, MSc, PGDip/Cert, PhD

School of Mathematical and Computer Sciences; www.macs.hw.ac.uk

actuarial mathematics/science, advanced internet applications, applied mathematical sciences, artificial intelligence, computer science, computer systems management, creative software systems, financial mathematics, human computer interaction, information systems, information technology (business/software systems), intelligent web technology, internet systems, mathematics, mathematical, statistical and actuarial sciences, mobile and handheld applications, multimedia systems, quantitative risk management, software engineering, statistical modelling, statistics, web entrepreneurship; BSc(Hons), MEng, MMath, MRes, MSc, PGDip/Cert, PhD

School of Engineering and Physical Sciences; www.eps.hw.ac.uk

biochemistry, chemistry/ with production chemistry, computational chemistry, forensic science, materials/ pharmaceutical chemistry, nanotechnology; chemical engineering, bioprocessing, chemical engineering with energy engineering/environmental management/pharmaceutical chemistry, nanotechnology and microsystems, oil & gas technology, sustainability engineering, sustainable process management, petroleum/pipeline engineering; physics, chemical/ computational/engineering physics, nano-science/ technology and microsystems, photonics, optoelectronic devices, physics with environmental, applied optics, lasers, plasmas, theoretical physics;
auromation, computer vision and robotics, computing and electronics, electrical and electronic engineering, information technology, information technology (embedded systems/mobile communications, applied systems), microsystems, photonics and optoelectronic devices, renewable energy and distributed generation), sustainability engineering, system level integration, vision, image and signal processing; automotive engineering, creative 3D digital

technologies, design and management, energy engineering, forensic materials, materials for sustainable and renewable energies, mechanical engineering, renewable energy engineering, robotics and cybertronics; BEng, BSc(Ord, Hons), EngD, MChem, MEng, MPhil, MPhys, PhD

School of Life Sciences; www.hw.ac.uk/sls
applied psychology (forensic science), psychology, psychology with human health, psychology with management; biology applied marine biology, biological sciences (cell and molecular biology/food science/human health/microbiology), bioprocesses, biotechnology, biology, microbiology; brewing and distilling; sport and exercise science with psychology; food science: food science, food science safety and health, technology and food science; marine science, applied marine biology, climate change: managing the marine environment, environmental analysis and assessment, marine biodiversity and biotechnology, marine resource development and protection; BSc(Hons), MSc/Cert/Dip, PGDip, PhD

School of Management and Languages; www.hw.ac.uk/sml
accountancy and business law/finance, business; business management with HRM/i marketing, entertainment, economics, international fashion marketing, international management, logistics and supply chain management, management with business law/enterprise/HRM/ marketing/operations management, maritime logistics and supply chain management, strategic project management
Languages and Intercultural Studies: Arabic–English translating and conference interpreting, applied languages and translating (French/German) (French/Spanish) (German/Spanish), Chinese–English translating and conference interpreting/computer-assisted translation tools, international management and languages, interpreting studies & skills, British sign language; BA(Hons, Ord), GradDip, MA(Hons), MSc

Heriot Watt Institute of Petroleum Engineering; www.pet.hw.ac.uk
geomechanics, geoscience for subsurface exploration appraisal and development, marine resonance methods, petroleum engineering, renewable energy development, reservoir evaluation and management; MPhil, MSc, PhD

School of Textiles and Design; www.tex.hw.ac.uk
design for textiles, fashion, fashion communication/marketing and retailing/menswear/technology/womenswear, fashion and textiles design/ textiles innovation and new applications, fashion and textiles management; BA, BSc(Hons, Ord), MA, MSc

Edinburgh Business School; www.ebs.hw.ac.uk
accounting, alliances and partnerships, competitive strategy, consumer behaviour, corporate governance, credit risk management, derivatives, developing effective managers and leaders, economics, employee relations, employee resourcing, finance, financial risk management/development leadership, HRM/dev and planning, int marketing, leadership, mergers & acquisitions, project management, project management, retailing, planning, strategic risk management; DBA, MBA, MSc

Degrees validated by Heriot-Watt University offered at:

EDINBURGH COLLEGE OF ART
www.eca.ac.uk

architecture/conservation, animation, art & design, contemporary art theory, fashion, film directing, film, fine art, glass, graphic design, illustration, jewellery & silversmithing, landscape architecture, painting, photography, sculpture, textiles, urban design, visual culture studies; BAArch, BA(Comb), BSc(Hons, Ord), MAHons, MPhil, MSc, PhD

UNIVERSITY OF HERTFORDSHIRE
www.herts.ac.uk

Business School; www.herts.ac.uk/courses/schools-of-study/business

accounting/ with mod languages/European studies, advertising, human resources, organizational change, bus adminstration/economics/studies, corporate governance, public services, economics, events management, fashion, finance, financial management, global business, hospitality, human resources, HRM, information technology, international business/management, investment management, marketing, tourism; BA/BSc, BA(Hons), BSc, DBA, DMan, MA, MBA, MPhil, MSc, PGC, PGD, PhD

School of Computer Science; www.herts.ac.uk/courses/schools-of-study/computer-science

artificial intelligence, business computing networks, computer science, distributed systems, entertainment systems, information technology, mobile computing, mutimedia technology, networks, robotics, secure computing systems, software eng, web-based systsems; BSc(Hons), MEng, MPhil, MSc, PGC, PGD, PhD

School of Creative Arts; www.herts.ac.uk/courses/schools-of-study/creative-arts

digital animation, games art, art & design, character creation, contemporay applied arts, engineering product design, fashion, film & television/directing/producing/screenwriting, fine art, graphic design, illustration, interactive media, software, contemporary textiles, design studies, art therapy, 3D modelling, interior/industrial/interactive/model/ multimedia/product design, music composition/technology, entertainment industry management, photography, screen cultures, sound design, special/visual effects; BA(Hons), MA, PgCert/Dip, MSc, MPhil, PhD

School of Education; www.herts.ac.uk/courses/schools-of-study/education

deaf children education, early years, education studies, leading learning, primary/ secondary education, work-related learning; BA(Hons), BEd, EdD, FdA, MA, MPhil, PGC, PGCE, PGD, PhD

School of Engineering & Technology; www.hearts.ac.uk/courses/schools-of-study/engineering-and-technology

aerospace engineering/systems engineering/technology, pilot studies, automotive engineering/with motorsport/management computer and network technology, digital communications and electronics/TV technology, digital film, digital forensic technology, digital rights technology/ systems, and computer engineering, games & graphics hardware, internet technology & e-commerce/engineering, mechanical engineering, motorsport technology, multimedia technology, biometrics & cycersecurity, telecomm networks, data communications & networks, embedded intelligent systems, manufacturing management, operations & supply chain management, radio & mobile communication systems; BSc(Hons), BEng, MEng MSc, PgDip/Cert, MPhil, PhD

School of Health and Emergency Professions; www.herts.ac.uk/courses/schools-of-study/health-and-emergency-professions

diagnostic imaging/radiography, dietetics, emergency management, medical imaging, oncology, paramedic science, physiotherapy, prehospital emergency care, radiation sciences, radiotherapy, sport and exercise rehabilitation, ultrasound; BSc(Hons), DHRes, Foundation degree, MPhil, MSc, PGC, PGD, PhD

School of Humanities; www.herts.ac.uk/courses/schools-of-study/humanities

acting & screen performance, American studies, creative writing, English language & communication/language teaching/ literature/teaching, film, French, history, journalism, media cultures, modern literature, new media publishing, philosophy, Spanish; BA(Hons), MA, MPhil, PGC, PGD, PhD

School of Law; www.herts.ac.uk/courses/schools-of-study/law

commercial law, criminal justice, e-commerce law, international law, legal practice, maritime law; BSc(Hons), Diploma, LlB(Hons), LlM, MPhil, PGD, PhD, univ cert

School of Life Sciences; www.herts.ac.uk/courses/schools-of-study/life.sciences
biochemistry, bioinformatics, biological science, biotechnology, biomedical science, environmental management, exercise science, genetics, geography, molecular biology, pharmaceutical science, pharmacology, physiology, sport, sports studies, sports therapy, water & environmental management; BSc/BSc(Hons), MSc, PgC/D

School of Nursing and Midwifery; www.herts.ac.uk/courses/schools-of-study/ nursing-and-midwifery/
child welfare and protection, clinical research, community public health, contemporary/ international nursing, infection prevention and control, midwifery and women's health, nursing (learning disability), social work, specialist community nursing, supportive immunology; BSc/BSc(Hons), DipHE, DipHE Nursing, MSc, NVQs, PGDip/PGCert

School of Pharmacy; www.herts.ac.uk/courses/schools-of-study/pharmacy
advancing pharmacy practice, medicinal chemistry, pharmacy; MPharm, MPhil, MSc, PGC, PGD, PhD

School of Physics, Astronomy and Mathematics; www.herts.ac.uk/courses/schools-of-study/physics-astronomy-and-mathematics
astrophysics, financial market analysis, financial maths, mathematics, physics; BSc(Hons), MPhil, MSc, PhD

School of Medicine; www.herts.ac.uk/courses/schools-of-study/postgraduate-medicine
child health, dermatology skills and treatment, health law and ethics, health and medical education, mental health practice, psychiatric practice, western medical acupuncture, skin integrity skills & practice; MD, MSc, PGC, PGD

School of Psychology; www.herts.ac.uk/courses/schools-of-study/psychology
business psychology, psychology, cognitive behavioral therapy/neuropsychology, psychotherapy & disability, clinical psychology, counselling, therapeutic counselling, health psychology, mental health studies/primary care, occupational/organizational psychology; BSc(Hons), DClinPsy, MSc, PGD

Degrees validated by the University of Hertfordshire offered at:

HERTFORDSHIRE REGIONAL COLLEGE
www.hrc. .ac.uk

3D dimensional design, computing, business, early years, engineering, fine art practice, graphic design, IT. performing arts, social and child care, teacher training; BA(Hons), BSc, C&G, Foundation degrees, national and higher diplomas, NVQs

---

NORTH HERTFORDSHIRE COLLEGE
www.nhc.ac.uk

art, design and creative studies, beauty, business, performing arts, music & dance, child care & education, teacher training, sport; BA, BSc, FD, National & Higher National Diplomas

---

OAKLANDS COLLEGE
www.oaklands.ac.uk

animal management, business, construction management, engineering, fine arts practice, health and social care, horticulture, IT, multimedia, equine performance & management, sports studies; C&G, Dips/Certs, FD Dips, HNC, HND, Nat Dips NVQs

WEST HERTS COLLEGE
www.westherts.ac.uk

accounting, advertising, art & design, beauty, business & management, care & early years, construction, counselling, crafts, electrical installation, ESOL, floristry, forensic science, hairdressing, holistic therapies, hospitality and catering, information technology, literacy and numeracy, marketing, media & photography, motor vehicle, performing arts and music, public services, retail, sign language, sport, teaching & training, travel; BA(Hons), BTEC, C&G, College Cert/Dips, Nat Dips, NVQs

THE UNIVERSITY OF HUDDERSFIELD
www2.hud.ac.uk.sas

School of Applied Sciences; www2.hud.ac.uk/sas

Chemical & Biological Sciences: analytical bioscience, chemistry, biochemistry, biology (molecular and cellular), chemical engineering, chemistry, food science/nutrition, forensic and analytical science, health, human biology, medical biochemistry, medical biology, medical genetics, microbiological sciences, pharmaceuticals, pharmacy, public health

Logistics & Hospitality Management: leisure management, air transport & logistics management, transport & supply chain management, global logistics, international hospitality management, events management, travel & tourism, transport; BA(Hons), BSc(Hons), HND, MA, MChem, MPharm, MSc, MSci, PhD

School of Art, Design and Architecture; www2.hud.ac.uk/ada

3D design, advertising, animation, architectural technology, architecture, art, communication design, construction, costume with textiles, craft design, arts & design, digital media, exhibition and retail design, fashion, fashion and textiles buying/management/retailing, fashion design with marketing/production, fine art and contemporary arts, graphic design, graphics, illustration, interior design, media and promotion, multimedia design/games, photography, product design, project management, property development, spatial design, sustainable architecture, surface/transport design, textile design and crafts, transport design; BA(Hons), BSc(Hons), CerHE, DipHE, FdA, FdSc, MA, MArch, MSc

University of Huddersfield Business School; www2.hud.ac.uk/uhbs

accountancy, advertising, brand management, business administration/information management/law & management/project management, business studies, corporate management, management, e-business. European business/legal studies, financial services, finance, global business, hospitality management, HRM, information systems, international business, marketing, journalism, law, law (commercial, international), leadership, legal practice, management studies, marketing communications, international/marketing, media relations, PR, retail, risk, disaster and environmental management, small businesses, sports marketing/ promotion, strategic change management; BA(Hons), FdA, GradDipLaw, HND, LlB(Hons), LlM, MBA, MSc, PGCE, PGDip, PGDip/Cert

School of Computing and Engineering; www2.hud.ac.uk/ce

audio systems, automotive design/engineering/systems design and analysis/technology, computer-aided design/engineering, computer control systems, computer-based system design, computer games, computer systems/aided design/engineerring/games, computing, digital media, electronic and communication engineering, electrical engineering, electronic design, energy engineering, engineering and technology management, engineering design: information systems, manufacturing engineering, automotive engineering, motorsport engineering/ music technology, product innovation, secure & forensic computing, software development, video, animation & music production, web technology; BEng(Hons), HNC, HND, MEng, MSc, PhD, UniFdCert

School of Education and Professional Development; www2.hud.ac.uk/edu

childhood studies, counselling, early childhood studies, early years, primary education, guidance, lifelong learning, post-compulsory education and training, religion and education, teacher training, youth and community work; BA(Hons), CertEd, FdA, MA, PGradDip/Cert, PSCE

Human and Health Sciences; www2.hud.ac.uk/hhs

applied psychotherapy, behavioural sciences, child welfare & safeguarding, children's public health, community nursing, criminology & politics, exercise, health care practitioner, physical activity and health, health and community studies, holistic therapies, mental health studies, midwifery, nursing(adult, child, mental health, occupational therapy, operating department practice, perioperative practice, physiotherapy, podiatry, police studies, primary health care, psychological studies, psychotherapy, public health, public management, social sciences, social work, sociology; DipHE, MA, MSc, PGDip, PhD

Music, Humanities and Media; www2.hud.ac.uk/mhm

British sign language, Chinese (Mandarin), French, German, Italian, Japanese, Spanish, Urdu, drama, English (mod language, creative writing, journalism), history, literary studies, gender studies, humanities, interpretation/translation, media and pop culture, modern languages, music, music technology, musicology, performance, politics, popular music, sociology, technical theatre; BA(Hons), FdA, MA, MPhil, PdF, PhD

UNIVERSITY OF HULL
www.hull.ac.uk

Faculty of Arts and Social Sciences; www.hull.ac.uk/fass

American studies, anthropology, archaeology, art & new media, British politics, criminal justice ethics, legislative studies, computer music, creative writing, criminology, digital media, drama, economics, English literature, English, film studies, forensic science, French, gender studies, geography, German, globalisation and governance, history (20th century, modern & contemporary, military, European, imperial, women's), history of art, human rights, Italian, jazz and pop music;
School of Law: law (common, international, business/ relations, French, European); internet computing, media studies, medieval/military European history, music/technology, performance, philosophy, politics, psychology, restorative justice, sonic art, social policy/work, sociology, Spanish law, theatre, theology, travel studies, war and security studies, web design; BA(Hons), BMus, BSc(Hons), LlB, LLM, MA, MEd, MMus, MPhil, MR/MRes, PGDip/Cert, PhD

The Hull University Business School; www.hull.ac.uk/hubs

accounting, business, business economics, business management, financial management, HRM, international business, logistics, marketing management, money, banking, finance, sport, leisure, tourism, supply chain management, transport; BA(Hons), BSc(Hons), MBA, MPhil, MRes, MSc, PhD

Faculty of Health and Social Care; www.hull.ac.uk/fhsc

community care, dental nursing practice, health professions, nursing (adult, children's, learning disabilities, mental health), midwifery, non-medical prescribing, operating department practice, primary care and social care, professional studies, public health; Adv Diploma, BSc(Hons), FD, MPhil, MRes, PhD

The Hull York Medical School; www.hyms.ac.uk

anatomy, cancer, cardiovascular medicine, child health, clinical sciences, clinical techniques and skills, dermatology, evidence-based decision making, gastrointestinal medicine, immunology, life sciences, managing resources, medicine, mental health, metabolic and renal medicine, pathology, person-centred care, population health and medicine, reproduction, respiration, surgery; BSc, MBBS, MPhil, MSc/Dip/ Cert, PGCert/Dip, PhD

The Institute for Learning; www.2.hull.ac.uk/ifl

applied digital media, early childhood studies, early years, educational studies, e-learning, HE, inclusive education, learning & support, primary teaching, special needs; BA, EdD, FD, GradCert, MA, MEd, MPhil, MSc, PGCE, PhD

Postgraduate Medical Institute; www2.hull.ac.uk/pgmi

cancer, cardiology, cardio-vascular-respiratory medicine, clinical psychology, community medicine and rehabilitation, diabetes, obstetrics and gynaecology, oncology, psychiatry, respiratory medicine, vascular surgery; MD, MPhil, PhD

Faculty of Science; www.hull.ac.uk/science

Biological Science: acquatic biology/zoology, biology, biomedical science, coastal marine biology, ecology, environmental biology, human biology, fisheries science, marine & freshwater biology, molecular medicine, pharmaceutical science, zoology
Chemistry: chemistry, forensic science, analytical chemistry, pharmaceutical science, molecular medicine, nanotechnology, toxology
Computer Science: computer & business informatics, computer science, games development, computer software, computer systems engineering, information technology, computer graphics/ games programming, distributed/financial systems development
Engineering: engineering, electronic engineering, mechanical engineering, medical engineering, medical product design, product innovation, wireless systems engineering, logistics technology, embedded systems, automatic control
Geography: human /physical geography, environmental management/technology, GIS & enviromental modelling
Physics: physics, astrophysics, chemical physics theory, lasers, nanotechnology/physics, organophotonics
Sports Science: coaching, sports & exercise science; BA, BEng, BSc, BSc/MEng, MPhil, MPhys, MPhysGeog, MRes, MSc, PhD

Degrees validated by the University of Hull offered at:

BISHOP BURTON COLLEGE
www.bishopburton.ac.uk

agriculture, animal management, art & design, countryside and environmental conservation, equine, floristry, food, garden design and horticulture management, planning and development, public services, sport, teacher training, ; BA(Hons), BSc(Hons), BSc(Ord), BTECExtel, FD, FdSc, HNC, MSc, PGCE

DONCASTER COLLEGE
www.don.ac.uk

airport travel & tourism, administration, business, retail, animal/horse care, animation and games, art & design, childcare, construction, counselling, dance, drama, engineering, fashion & textiles, forestry, & horticulture, hospitalty & catering, graphic design, ICT, languages, media, music/music technology, public services, sport & leisure; BA(Hons), BSc, BSc(Hons), FD, HNC, HND, MA, MSc, NVQs, PCE, PGCert

IMPERIAL COLLEGE, LONDON
www3.imperial.ac.uk

Faculty of Engineering; www3.engineering.imperial.ac.uk

aeronautics, aeronatical engineering, composites, flow, fluid-structure interaction; bioengineering, biochemical engineering, medical physics, neurotechnology; chemical technology, chemical engineeering, process systems eng, structured product, biotechnology; civil & environmental engineering, structural engineering, structured steel design, concrete & sustainable dev; computing, computer science, games, vision, artificial intelligence, software engineering; earth science & engineering, geology, geophysics, environmental/petroleum geopscience; electronic engineering, analog & digital circuit design, sustainable energy futures;material science, engineering, aerospace materials, biomaterials, tissue engineering, nuclear engineering, biomedical engineering, geology, geophysics, geoscience, materials; mechanical engineering, mechanical/nuclear engineering, innovation design engineering, mechanics, soil; BEng, MA, MEng, MSc, MSci, PhD

Faculty of Medicine; www1.medicine.imperial.ac.uk

medicine, cancer biology, drug discovery, epidemology, haematololgy, immunology, epidemiology, molecular medicine, molecular medicine, paediatrics, perioperative specialist, reventative cardiology, pharm & translational allergy, physiology & public health, reproductive biology, surgery/technology/ education, translational medicine, virology; BSc, CAS, MB BS, MEd, MPH, MRes, MSc, MSci, PhD

Imperial College Business School; www3.imperial.ac.uk/business-school

accounting, accounting management analysis, management, actuarial finance, business economics/strategy, entrepreneurship, financial management, finance, innovation management, international health management, management, managerial econpmics, marketing, metals-energy finance, organisational behaviour, project management, risk management and financial engineering, strategic management; BSc, MBA, MSc, PhD

Dept of Humanities; www3.imperial.ac.uk/ humanities

creative writing, European history 1870–1989, foreign languages (French, German, Italian, Mandarin Chinese and Spanish), history of medicine, global history of twentieth-century things, music and western civilization, music technology, philosophy/of science, politics, translation; MPhil, MSc, PhD

Faculty of Natural Sciences; www3.imperial.ac.uk/naturalsciences

catalysis and advanced materials, chemical biology, chemistry and management/medicinal chemistry/ molecular physics, chemistry with French/German/ Spanish for science, green chemistry, nanomaterials, plastic electronics

Life Sciences: biochemistry, biology, biology with French/German/Spanish for science, biology with management/microbiology, bioimaging sciences, biomedical physical, biomedical science, biotechnology, ecology and environmental biology, microbiology, plant biology, zoology

Mathematics: applied/pure mathematics, mathematical finance, mathematical physics, statistics

Physics: physics, optics and photonics, photonics, plastic electronics, quantum fields and fundamental forces, theoretical physics, theory and simulation of materials; BSc, MRes, MSci, PhD

KEELE UNIVERSITY
www.keele.ac.uk

Faculty of Health; www.keele.ac.uk/ facs/health

School of Medicine; www.keele.ac.uk/ depts/schoolofmedicine

biomedical engineering, cell and tissue engineering, clinical practice/pathology, primary care, parasitology, vector biology, foundation medical practice, geriatric medicine, medical education, medical science, medical ethics & law, medicine, surgery

School of Pharmacy; www.keele.ac.uk/ schools/pharm

clinical (hospital) pharmacy, community pharmacist, prescribing adviser, medical/non medical prescribing

Nursing and Midwifery; www.keele.ac.uk/ depts/ns

acute care, adult nursing, childrens nursing, clinical practice, critical care, end of life care, generic route, high dependency care, learning disability nursing, long term conditions, maternal and infant health, midwifery, operating dept practice, pre-registsration – mental health nursing, rheumatology nursing

School of Health and Rehabilitation; www.keele.ac.uk/depts/pt

anatomical science, health science, neurological rehabilitation, neuromusculoskeletal healthcare, osteopathy, pain science management physiotherapy; MBChB, BSc, MSc, MSci, MPharm, PGCert, MMedSci, MPhil, PhD, MD

Faculty of Humanities and Social Sciences; www.keele.ac.uk/facs/humass

Keele Management School; www.keele.ac.uk/schools/ems

accounting and finance, actuarial science, business administration, business economics, economics, finance, finance and IT/management, HRM, industrial relations, international business, leadership and management, management, management and IT, management science, marketing; MA, MBA, MSc, PGCert, PGDip, Univ Cert

School of Humanities; www.keele.ac.uk/schools/hums

American studies: American literature and culture, English and American literature, US history and politics; MPhil, MRes, PhD
English: creative writing, film studies, English and American literatures, humanities, Victorian studies, early modern history, history, local and public history, medieval cultural history, environment and cyberculture, film studies, globalization, media studies, moving and still image production
Modern Languages: French, German, Japanese, Russian, Spanish, TEFOL, TESOL; creative music technology, film music analysis, music, music technology, popular music, performance, composition

Keele Law School; www.keele.ac.uk/depts/law

child care law and practice, contract law, crime, equity and trusts, gender, sexuality and human rights, globalization and justice, land law, medical ethics and law, law, law with politics/criminology, law of the EU, social science research in law
Politics, International Relations and Philosophy: diplomatic studies, environmental politics, European politics and culture, global security, globalisation and justice, human rights, international relations, philosophy, politics

School of Public Policy and Professional Practice; www.keele.ac.uk/schools/pppp

Education: creative and critical practice, development, educational leadership, educational studies, management & learning, PGCE (English, geography, information and communication technology, mathematics, modern foreign languages, science, social sciences), teaching & learning, gerontology; health executive, health services management, communiity health; ageing, community and society, families, health, rehabilitation and well-being, psychology, clinical management, changing families/changing households, culture, family, community and society, family studies, health and society, risk and society, self, gender and consumption, social, cultural and post-colonial research, social inclusion and exclusion, sociology of the body, sociology of work, transnational communities, women, identity and global activism; specialist registrar, specialist doctors, consultants, coaching & mentorship; BA, BSc, DLitt, Diploma/GradDip Law, EdD, LlB, LLM, MA, MBA, MRes, MSc, PGCE, PGDip/Cert, PhD

Faculty of Natural Siences; www.keele.ac.uk/facs/sci/

School of Computing and Mathematics; www.scm.keele.ac.uk

actuarial science, computer science, creative computing, finance and IT, information systems, IT and management, IT management for business, mathematics (pure, applied, statistics), project management, smart systems, web technologies

School of Life Sciences; www. keele.ac.uk/depts/bi

biochemistry, biology, biomedical science, European scientific research training, human biology, molecular parasitology and vector biology, neuroscience

School of Physical and Geographical Sciences; www.keele.ac.uk/schools/dps/

analytical, materials & surface chemistry, analytical & spectroscopic research, bioinorganic chemistry of aluminium and silicon, chemical ecology group, chemistry, green chemistry and clean energy, integrated macromolecular structure, medicinal chemistry, organic and medicinal chemistry, photochemistry, porous materials, solid state and computational chemistry, zeolite research; applied environmental science, earth system science, environment and sustainability, environmental geology, forensic geophysics, geography, geology, geoscience, human geography, physical geography: forensic science; astrophysics, electromagnetism, nuclear physics, optics, quantum mechanics, statistical mechanics and solid state physics, thermodynamics

School of Psychology; www.keele.ac.uk/depts/ps

applied psychology, child social development, clinical psychology, counselling, counselling psychology, psychological research methods/(music), psychology/of health & wellbeing, supervision; BA, BSc, DClinPsy, DSc, MGeoscience, MRes, MSc, PGCert, PGDip, PhD

UNIVERSITY OF KENT
www.kent.ac.uk

Faculty of Humanities; www.kent.ac.uk/humanities

Kent School of Architecture; www.kent.ac.uk/architecture
architecture, architectural visualization, European architecture, urban design, interiors

School of Arts; www.kent.ac.uk/arts
creative events, drama & theatre studies, dramaturgy, European theatre, film studies, fine arts, history & philosophy of art/aesthetics, music technology, performance arts/practice

School of English; www.kent.ac.uk/english
English/American literature, post-colonial studies, creative writing, critical theory, gender, long 18th-century poetry, sexuality and writing, medieval studies

School of European Culture & Languages; www.kent.ac.uk/secl
classical and archaeological studies, comparative literature, English language, French, German, Hispanic studies, history of archeology, Italian, language and linguistic studies, modern European literature, philosophy, religious studies

School of History; www.kent.ac.uk/history
American studies, history of science, modern history, technology & medicine, medieval and modern studies, propaganda & war, war studies, war, media & modernity; BA(Hons), BSc(Hons), MA, MArch, MDram, MPhil, PhD

Faculty of Science, Technology and Medical Studies; www.kent.ac.uk/stms

Dept of Bioscience; www.kent.ac.uk/bio
biochemistry, biological/medical science, biology, biomedical imaging, forensic science, science, community & society

School of Computing; www.sc.kent.ac.uk/
artificial intelligence, computing & business accounting/business information, computer security, networks & security, computing science, business/IT, web computing, molecular computing, software development

School of Engineering and Digital Arts; www.eng.kent.ac.uk;
advanced electronic systems engineering, computer animation, digital visual effects, electronic & computer systems engineering/communications engineering, drama & multimedia, information security, multimedia technology, web computing, wireless communication & signal processing

School of Mathematics, Statistics & Actuarial Science; www.kent.ac.uk/IMS
actuarial science, business/financial mathematics, pure/applied maths, statistics, finance, investment

Medway School of Pharmacy; www.kent.ac.uk/msp
medicine management, pharmaceutical practice, pharmacy, independant & supplementary prescription

School of Physical Sciences; www.kent.ac.uk/physical-sciences
astrophysics, applied optics, astronomy, forensic chemistry/science, functional materials, imaging, physics, planetary/space science

Centre for Biomedical Informatics; Centre for Nueroscience and Cognitive Systems
BA(Hons), BEng, BSc(Hons), DClinPsych, MD, MRes, MPhil, MSc, Msurg, PCert, PDip, PhD,

Faculty of Social Sciences; www.kent.ac.uk/socsci

School of Anthropology and Conservation; www.kent.ac.uk/sac
anthropology (social/biological/medical), biodiversity conservation and management, conservation biology, environmental anthropology, ethnicity, ethnobotany, evolution and human behaviour, international trade and wildlife, nationalism and identity, rural development, tourism, visual anthropology, wildlife conservation; BA(Hons), BSc(Hons), MA, MSc, PhD

Kent Business School; www.kent.ac.uk/kbs
accounting, business administration, business/management studies, data modelling, employment relations, finance, financial services/management, HRM, international business, logistics, management science, marketing management, operational research, performance, sustainability management, tourism

management, value chain management; BA(Hons), BBA, BSc(Hons), MBA, MEBA, MPhil MSc

School of Economics; www.kent.ac.uk/economics
agricultural economics, applied environmental economics, econometrics, economics, finance, financial economics, economic development, international finance; BSc(Hons), MPhil, PhD, MSc

Kent Law School; www.kent.ac.uk/law
criminal justice, English, French, German, Spanish or Italian law, European legal studies/law, international environmental/commercial law, international criminal justice, medical law & ethics, public international law, senior status; BA(Hons), LlB, LlM, MPhil, PhD

Centre for Journalism; www.kent.ac.uk/journalism
journalism, multimedia journalism, journalism & the news industry; BA(Hons)

School of Politics and International Relations; www.kent.ac.uk/politics
comparative federalism, conflict, peace & security, European governance, international conflict analysis/law/relations/security, politics, security and terrorism; BA(Hons), MA, MPhil, PhD

Dept of Psychology; www.kent.ac.uk/psychology
applied psychology, cognitive psychology/neuropsychology, forensic psychology, group processes and intergroup relations, psychology, social psychology; BSc(Hons), MPhil, MSc, PhD

School of Social Policy, Sociology and Social Research; www.kent.ac.uk/sspssr
criminal justice studies, criminology, cultural studies, environmental social science, health & social care, health services, intellectual & development international social policies, disabilities, mental health and social care, migration studies, substance misuse management, urban studies; BA(Hons), BSc(Hons), Certificate and Diplomas, MA, MPhil, MSc, PhD

Centre for Sports Studies; www.kent.ac.uk/sports-studies
health & fitness, rehabilitation, sport science/therapy, sports, sports & exercise management; BA, BSc, BSc(Hons), MA

KINGSTON UNIVERSITY
www.kingston.ac.uk

Faculty of Art, Design and Architecture; www.kingston.ac.uk/faculties/#design
architecture, art and design/ history/ market, building surveying, design, contemporary design, curating, product space, fashion, film studies/making, fine art (painting, sculpture, intermedia, print), games development, garden design, graphic design, historic building conservation, illustration and animation, interior design, landscape architecture/planning/urbanism, museum and gallery studies, photography, planning and sustainability, product and furniture design, property planning and development, quantity surveying consultancy, real estate management, residential property, sustainable place making and urban design, user experience design, visual and material culture; BA(Hons), FdA, FDA, FdSc, MA, MSc, PGCert/Dip

Faculty of Arts and Social Sciences; www.fass.kingson.ac.uk
applied/business/financial economics, applied child psychology, applied econometrics, children's special educational needs, classical theatre, composing for film and television, creative writing, criminology, dance, development economics, developmental psychology, drama, early years: education and childcare/management and leadership/teaching, economics, electroacoustic composition, English language/teaching and communication, English literature, film studies, French, history(earlymodern/European/international/local/modern/modern British/early British), human rights, international economics/ politics/relations, journalism, making plays, media and cultural studies, media practice, music, music education/performance/ technology, performance and screen studies, poetry, politics, primary teaching, popular music, psychology, publishing, secondary teaching, sociology, Spanish, television and new broadcasting media, writing fiction/travel/children's literature; BA(Hons), MA, PgCert/Dip, EdD

Faculty of Law & Business; www.business.kingston.ac.uk

Kingston Business School: accounting, banking & finance, advertising, business/administration/management/ informatics/ information management technology/operations management/ studies/ systems management, business and finance/law administration/professional administration/professional administration/accounting/law, business with law, creative economy, entrepreneurship, HRM, international business/supply chain management & logistics/with law, marketing & entrepreneurship, strategy, strategic innovation, operations management

Kingston School of Law: law, business/commercial/ employment international law, law with criminology, legal studies, dispute resolution; BA(Hons), BSc(Hons), DBA, FdA, GradDip Law, HND, LlM, MA, MBA, MSC, PhD

Faculty of Computing, Information Systems and Mathematics; www.cism.kingston.ac.uk

biomedical informatics, computer science (graphics and digital imaging/games, network communications) computer-generated imager/vison, computing, cyber security and computer forensics, electronic commerce, embedded systems, health/informatics, information systems, IT business/multimedia/support/and strategic innovation, mathematical sciences, financial/actuarial mathematics, medical statistics/ technologies, mobile computing, networking and data communications/ information security, software engineering, statistics, strategic innovation, user experience design, web development, wireless communications; BSc(Hons), FdSc, HND, MComp, MPhil, MSc, PhD

Faculty of Engineering; www.engineering.kingston.ac.uk

advanced industrial and manufacturing systems, advanced product design engineering, aerospace/ aircraft engineering/maintenance, astronautics and space technology, automotive engineering, aviation studies for commercial pilots, civil engineering, construction engineering/management, engineering projects & systems management, historic building conservation, mechanical engineering, mechatronic systems, motorsport engineering, renewable energy engineering, structural design, sustainable concrete structures; BEng, BSc(Hons), FdSc, HND, MEng, MSc, PhD

Faculty of Health & Social Care Sciences; www.healthcare.kingston.ac.uk

advanced practice (health care), biomedical science/ information, clinical practice, exercise & nutrition, healthcare practice/information/education, long-term condition, maternal and child health, medical imaging, midwifery/registered midwife, nursing, oncology practice, paramedic science, physiotherapy, radiography, rehabilitation, social care, social work, specialist professional child and family studies/ community care/education and training in human services/education and training in human services; BSc(Hons), DipHE, FdSc, MREs, MPhil, MSc, MSw, PGCert/Dip, PhD

Faculty of Science; www.kingston.ac.uk/ science

acupuncture, applied chemistry, applied and environmental geology, biochemistry, biology, biomedical science, cancer biology, chemistry, cell and molecular biology, communication systems, computer graphics technology, computing, earth systems science, environmental management/science/studies, exercise, nutrition and health, forensic biology, forensic analysis/chemistry/science, gemmology and applied mineralogy, geography, geology/applied and environmental, geospatial investigation, GIS, hazards & disaster management, health and medical sciences, human biology, human geography media technology, medical biochemistry/chemistry, medicine, nutrition, paramedic sciences, pharmaceutical analysis/science/ services, pharmacology, pharmacy, sports analysis and coaching, sports science, TV & video technology, sustainable development; BSc(Hons), FdSc, MPharm, MPhil, MSc, PhD, PGCert/Dip

LANCASTER UNIVERSITY
www.lancs.ac.uk

Faculty of Arts and Social Sciences; www.lancs.ac.uk/fass/faculties

European Languages and Cultures; www.lancs.ac.uk/fass/eurolang

European languages, German, Italian, French, Spanish, modern languages, film studies, modern European history, European institutions & policy making/languages & cultures

Applied Social Science; www.lancs.ac.uk/fass/appsocsci

criminology, social work, child welfare practice

Educational Research; www.lancs.ac.uk/fass/edres

education, gender and women's studies and education, psychology in education, religious studies

English and Creative Writing; www.lancs.ac.uk/fass/english

English language/literature, theatre studies, creative writing, contemporary literature, literary & cultural studies, romantic & Victorian literature

History; www.lancs.ac.uk/fass/history

Medieval & renaissance/modern European/ social history

Institute for Cultural Research

cultural research, cultural studies and popular music, English literature, film studies, literary studies or media

Lancaster Institute for the Contemporary Arts; www.lancs.ac.uk/fass/licr

contemporary/creative arts, fine art, marketing & design, music, pop music, music technology, sustainability, theatre studies

School of Law; www.lancs.ac.uk/fass/law

law, bioethics, medical law, European legal studies, humanitarian /international business & corporate/ international human rights, international law, law and criminology, management & law, public administration

Philosophy; www.lancs.ac.uk/fass/philosophy

philosophy. anthropology of religion, ethics, combined philosophy, philosophy and religion. bioethics & medical law

Politics & International Relations; www.lancs.ac.uk/fass/politics

conflict, global politics, international law/relations, North America, peace studies, politics, security and war, strategic studies

Religious Studies; www.lancs.ac.uk/fass/relig

anthropology of religion, ethics, philosophy and religion, religious studies

Sociology; www.lancs.ac.uk/fass/sociology

sociology, society technology and nature, feminist culture theory, gender and women's studies, organisation studies, social history; BSc(Hons), LlB, LlM, MA, MPhil, MSc, PGD, PhD

School of Health and Medicine; www.lancs.ac.uk/shm/faculties

Biomedical & Health Sciences; www.lancs.ac.uk/shm/bls

biochemistry/with biomedicine or genetics, medical statistics, cell biology, clinical psychology, learning disabilities, life care, premedical studies, public mental health

Medicine; www.lancs.ac.uk/shm/med

basic biomedical research, medical education, medical statistics and epidemiology, medicine, sociology of medicine; BSc(Hons), CertHE, DClinPsych, MBChB, MBiomed, MD, MHospice leadership, MPhil, MRes, MSc, PgDip/Cert, PhD

Lancaster University Management School; www.lums.lancs.ac.uk

accounting, banking, business studies, consulting, economics, e-business, European management, finance, financial management, HR, information technology, international business kowledge management, logistics & supply chain management, management & law/ organizational change, management/ science & operations/analytics, marketing, market analytics, money, operational research, project management, quanitative finance; BA(Hons), BBA, BSc(Hons), LlM, MBA, MPhil, MRes, MSc, PhD

Faculty of Science and Technology; www.lancs.ac.uk/shm/sci-tech/faculties

Communication Systems; www.dcs.lancs.ac.uk
computer science, software engineering, digital signal processes, distributed systems engineering, electronic communication systems, human–computer interaction, information and communication systems, information technology and media, intelligent and robotic systems, mobile broadband engineering, multimedia networks, social network techniques, telecommunications

Engineering; www.engineering.lancs.ac.uk
computer systems/electronic/mechanical/mechatronic/nuclear/sustainable/safety engineering; decommissioning & environmental clean-up

Lancaster Environment Centre; www.lec.lancs.ac.uk
biology, biochemistry, biomedical sciences, cell biology, conservation biology, environmental biology & ecology;
environmental science, earth science, environment chemistry, plant sciences, resource and environmental management; geography, human/physical geography, volcanology and geological hazards, earth science, North America, environmental change

Mathematics and Statistics; www.maths.lancs.ac.uk
applied social statistics, computer science and mathematics, environmental/financial mathematics, mathematics, mathematics and philosophy/statistics/psychology, medical statistics, statistics

Natural Sciences; www.naturalsci.lancs.ac.uk
combined science, combined technology, natural sciences

Physics; www.lancs.ac.uk/depts/physics
astrophysics, cosmology, biomedical physics, physics, space science, theoretical physics/with mathematics, particle physics

Psychology; www.psych.lancs.ac.uk
development psychology/disorders, language, speech & learning, psychology, psychology of advertising, social psychology;
BEng(Hons), BSc(Hons), MChem, MEng(Hons), MPhil, MPhys(Hons), MRes, MSc, MSci(Hons), PGDip, PhD

Degrees validated by Lancaster University offered at:

BLACKPOOL AND THE FYLDE COLLEGE
www.blackpool.ac.uk

art, art, media and performance, business, management and IT, catering & food production, computing, construction, engineering (automotive, autosport, mechanical, production, electrical, electronic), catering, food production, beauty and related therapies, health, care and early years, hospitality, media and performance, sport and leisure, tourism, travel; FD, HNC, HND, BEng, BA(Hons), BSc/(Hons)

EDGEHILL UNIVERSITY
www.edgehill.ac.uk

Faculty of Education; www.edgehill.ac.uk/education

education with QTS (creative art, design & technology/ secondary education, early years, English, secondary education, mathematics, mod foreign langs, primary education, RE, science, PE; science key stage 2/3/secondary education/PE/secondary science, 14–19/11–16 education/PGCE(business education/creative media/design & technology/English/geography/history/info & communication technology/mathematics/mod langs/music/PE) psychology; BA(Hons), BSc(Hons), CertHE, Foundation degrees, PGCE, MA, MTL

Faculty of Health; www.edgehill.ac.uk/health

Nursing
cognitive behavioural therapies/psychotherapy, complementary therapies, counselling, health & social care practice, integrated practice (early years and children), management and supervision of offenders,

midwifery, nursing studies (adult, learning disabilities, mental health, children's), operating dept practice, paramedic science, person-centred support, playwork, positive behaviour support, public health, respiratory disease substance misuse interventions, support for families and communities, surgery, trauma, women's health, working with vulnerable adults; BSc(Hons), Dip/CertHE, FDA, FdSc, MCh, MPhil, MSc, PhD

Faculty of Arts and Science

Business School; www.edgehill.ac.uk/business

accountancy, business and management, communications, computing, control and embedded systems, information systems systems and software, information technology, international business marketing, leisure and tourism management, web systems development

Dept of English and History; www.edgehill.ac.uk/history

Chinese studies, creative writing, English language, English literature, film production, film studies, history, history and culture

Law & Criminology; www.edgehill.ac.uk/law

criminology and criminal justice/law, international sports regulation, law, law with management

Media; www.edgehill.ac.uk/media

animation, film and television production, journalism, media with advertising, film and television or music and sound, PR, television production management

Dept of Natural, Geographical and Applied Sciences; www.edgehill.ac.uk/ngas

biogeography, biology, conservation management, environmental science, geography, geology, geotourism, human/physical geography, laboratory operations management

Performing Arts; www.edgehill.ac.uk/performingart

theatre, applied drama and creativity, dance, design for performance, drama/ visual theatre/music & sound

Dept of Social & Psychological Sciences; www.edgehill.ac.uk/dsaps;

psychology, childhood & youth studies, social work & sociology, social research methods

Dept of Sport & Physical Activity; www.edgehill.ac.uk/sport

coach education, physical education & school sport, sport & exercise psychology/science, sports development/studies/therapy, football rehabilitation; BAHons), BSc(Hons), FDA, FDSc, LlB(Hons), MA, MSc, PhD

UNIVERSITY OF LEEDS
www.leeds.ac.uk

Faculty of Arts; www.leeds.ac.uk/arts

School of English; www.leeds.ac.uk/english

American literature and culture, English language/literature, modern & contemporary literature, Renaissance literature, post-colonial literary and cultural studies, romantic formations, theatre and global studies, theatre making/studies, Victorian literature

School of History; www.leeds.ac.uk/history

18th-century studies, history, international history and politics, medieval history, modern history, race & resistance, social & cultural history

School of Humanities; www.leeds.ac.uk/humanities

classical studies, development studies, health care ethics, history and philosophy of science, pastoral studies, philosophy, mind and knowledge, philosophy of physics, religion/theology and public life, religious studies, science communication, theology

Institute for Colonial and Post-colonial Studies; www.leeds.ac.uk/icps

post-colonial literary and cultural studies, race and resistance, world cinema, modern languages & cultures

School of Modern Languages and Cultures; www.leeds.ac.uk/smlc

Arabic & Middle Eastern studies, Chinese, Japanese, South/East Asian studies, French, German, Italian, linguistics and phonetics, modern languages and cultures, professional language & intercultural studies, Russian, Spanish, Portuguese and Latin

American studies, translation & interpreting, world cinema; BA(Hons), MA, MPhil, PGDip, PhD

Faculty of Biological Studies; www.fbs.leeds.ac.uk

biochemistry, biology, bioscience (biotechnology/bioinformatics and computer biology/human disease & therapy/infection & immunology/plant science), ecology & environmental biology, genetics, human/physiology, medical biochemistry/microbiology/sciences, microbiology, neuroscience, pharmacology, virology, molecular biology, sport & exercise sciences, zoology; BSc(Hons), MRes, MSc, PhD

Faculty of Business; www.fbs.leeds.ac.uk

Leeds University Business School; www.leeds.ac.uk/lbs

accounting, advertising and design/marketing, banking, business economics, computing and management, corporate communications and PR, diversity management, economics, finance, financial economics/ mathematics/risk, HRM, international business/finance/marketing management, management, textile innovation, manufacturing leadership, marketing, transport studies; BSc(Hons), ExecMBA, MA, MBA, MPhil, MSc, PhD

Faculty of Education, Social Sciences & Law; www.essl.leeds.ac.uk

School of Education; www.education.leeds.ac.uk

childhood studies, clinical education, deaf education, educational assessment, ICT, lifelong learning, mathematics education, PGCE biology/chemistry/English/mathematics/modern foreign languages/physics, children with learning difficulties/developmental disorders, science education, special educational needs, teaching, teaching English (TESOL) for young learners/studies/teacher education

School of Law; www.law.leeds.ac.uk

banking and finance law, criminal law and criminal justice, criminological research, criminology, European human rights law, European law/and society, international and comparative criminal justice, law, policing, European & international business law/corporatelaw/trade law, insolvency law, intellectual property law, European human rights law

School of Politics and International Studies; www.leeds.ac.uk/polis

global development, politics (parliamentary, political theory), international relations/development, conflict, development and security, conflict, security, terrorism and insurgency

School of Sociology and Social Policy; www.sociology.leeds.ac.uk

disability studies. gender studies/& culture, global genders, social research, international social transformation, racism and ethnicity studies, social science, sociology; BA(Hons), LLM, MA, MEd, MPhil, MSc, PGCert, PGCE, PhD

Faculty of Engineering; www.engineering.leeds.ac.uk

School of Civil Engineering; www.engineering.leeds.ac.uk/civil

architectural engineering, civil and environmental engineering/structural engineering/with construction management, international construction management engineering, environmental engineering, engineering project management, sustainable waste management

School of Computing; www.engineering.leeds.ac.uk/comp

artificial intelligence, cognitive science, computer science, computing/ for business/and management, information technology, electronic & computer engineering

School of Electronic and Electrical Engineering; www.engineering.leeds.ac.uk/elec

computational fluid mechanics, electrical engineering, electronic and communications engineering, computer engineering, mechatronics and robotics, music, multimedia and electronics, nanotechnology, computer music, nanomaterials

Mechanical Engineering; www.engineering.leeds.ac.uk/mech

aeronautical and aerospace engineering, automotive engineering, combustion and energy, mechanical engineering, mechatronics and robotics, medical engineering, oilfield corrosion engineering, product design

School of Process, Environmental and Materials Engineering; www.engineering.leeds.ac.uk/speme

aviation technology, chemical and energy/materials/minerals engineering/pharmaceutical engineering, chemical engineering, energy and environmental engineering, computational fluid mechanics, fire and explosion, materials, science, petroleum engineering; BEng, MEng, MSc, MSc(Eng), MPhil, PhD

Faculty of the Environment; www.leeds.ac.uk/foe

School of Earth & Environment; www.see.leeds.ac.uk

engineering geology, environment and business/management, climate science, environmental sustainability/management/science/conservation, exploration geophysics, geochemistry, geological/geophysical sciences, hydrogeology, physics of the earth & atmosphere, sustainability (transport/business environment and corporate responsibility/environmental consultancy and project management/environment & development/ environmental politics & policy), transport planning, meterology

School of Geography; www.geog.leeds.ac.uk

geography, activism & society, catchment dynamics, geography, geography with transport planning, geography–geology, GIS, global change and the biosphere, human geography, hydrology, social and cultural geography

Institute for Transport Studies; www.its.leeds.ac.uk

economics with transport studies, environment and transport planning, geography with transport planning, management with transport planning & environment, planning, transport economics, engineering/environment

Earth & Biosphere Institute; www.earth.leeds.ac.uk/ebi

global change and the biosphere; BA(Hons), BSc(Hons), MA, MGeol, MGeophys, MRes, MSc, DGCert/Dip, PhD

Faculty of Mathematics and Physical Science; www.maps.leeds.ac.uk

School of Chemistry; www.chemistry.leeds.ac.uk

chemistry, chemical process, colour and imaging science, chemistry/with analytical chemistry/colour science, medicinal chemistry, polymer and surface coatings science and technology

School of Food Science and Nutrition; www.food.leeds.ac.uk

food biotechnology/quality & innovation/science, nutrition, food studies

School of Physics and Astronomy; www.physics.leeds.ac.uk

astrophysics, nanotechnology, physics, medical physics, quantum technologies, theoretical physics

School of Mathematics; www.amsta.ac.uk

actuarial/applied/financial mathematics, mathematics, mathematics with finance, pure mathematics, statistics, statistics with applications to finance, atmosphere ocean dynamics

Self-organising Molecular Systems

nanotechnology; BSc(Hons), MChem, MMath, MNatSci, MPhil, MPhys, MSc, PhD

Faculty of Health and Medicine; www.leeds.ac.uk/medhealth

Leeds Dental Institute; www.leeds.ac.uk/dental

clinical dentistry, dental hygiene, dental nursing, dental surgery, dental technology, dental therapy

Leeds Institute of Medical Education; www.leeds.ac.uk/medicine/lime

medicine, surgery, child health, clinical embryology/psychology, health informatics/management, planning and policy, hospital management, medical physics/imaging, nutrition, obesity and health, patient safety and clinical risk management, primary care education/care, psychiatry, psychoanalytic observational studies, public health, statistical epidemiology, systematic family therapy, healthcare ethics

School of Healthcare; www.lhealthcare.leeds.ac.uk/

adult/child nursing, clinical physiology, counselling, diagnostic imaging, learning disability, audiology, health systems, symptoms management, medicines management, mental health, public health, complementary & alternative medicine

School of Medicine; www/leeds.ac.uk/ medicine
child health, clinical embrylology/psychology, clinical risk management, family therapy, health informatics/ management, hospital management, medical physics/imaging, medicine, nutrition, obesity and health, patient safety, primary health care, psychiatry, psychoanalytical observation, public health, statistical epidemiology, surgery

School of Psychological Sciences; www.psych.leeds.ac.uk
biological psychology, cognitive psychology, health and social psychology; BHSc, BSc(Hons), CPD, DClinPsych, GradDip, MA, MBChB, MD, MMedSci, MPH, MPsycObs, MSc, PGDip/Cert, PhD

Faculty of Performance, Visual Arts and Communication; www.leeds.ac.uk/pvac

Institute of Communication Sudies; www.ics.leeds.ac.uk
broadcast journalism, cinema and photography, communications studies, international/political communications, journalism, media industries, TV production

School of Design; www.design.leeds.ac.uk
textile and performance clothing, advertising & design, art and design, design and colour technology/technology management, fashion design, graphic and communication design, textile innovation and branding

School of Fine Art, History of Art and Cutural Studies; www.leeds.ac.uk/fine.art
art gallery and museum studies, art history with museum studies, cultural studies, fine art, history of art

School of Music; www.ics.leeds.ac.uk/ music
composition, English/German/Italian psychology of music, music, multimedia, music technology, musicology, performance

School of Performance & Cultural Industries; www.ics.leeds.ac.uk/paci
choreography, culture, creativity and entrepreneurship, dance, managing performance, performance culture, theatre and performance, writing for performance and publication; BA(Hons), GradDip, MFA, BMus, BSc(Hons), MA, MMus, MSc, PhD

Degrees validated by University of Leeds offered at:

ASKHAM BRYAN COLLEGE
www.askham-bryan.ac.uk

agriculture, animal management, business & IT, countryside & environment, engineering, plant and construction, equine, floristry, food, forestry & arboriculture, horticulture, landscape construction, sports & leisure, surface & greenkeeping, teacher education; BA(Hons), BSc(Hons), Nat Dips, FD

COLLEGE OF THE RESURRECTION
www.mirfield.org.uk

theology & pastoral studies; BA(Hons), DipHE, MA, MPhil, PGDip, PhD

LEEDS COLLEGE OF ART
www.leeds-art.ac.uk

art & design, creative advertising, digital film, games & animation, fashion, fine art, furniture making, graphic design, interior design, photography, printed textiles & surface pattern design, visual communication; BA(Hons), Foundation degrees, HNC, National Diploma

LEEDS COLLEGE OF MUSIC
www.lcm.ac.uk

music, composition, jazz, music production, music and sound production for the moving image, musicology, performance, popular music studies; BA (Hons), FD, MA, PGDip

LEEDS TRINITY & ALL SAINTS
www.leedstrinity.ac.uk

Faculty of Arts and Social Sciences; www.leedstrinity.ac.uk/departments/fass

English, history, psychology, sport, health, leisure and nutrition, theology & religious studies, Victorian studies; BA(Hons), BSc(Hons), MA, MSc, PGCE

Faculty of Education

Catholic education, children, young people & families, PGCE programmes, primary education, secondary education, teaching assistants; BA(Hons), FD, MA, PGCert, PGCE

Faculty of Media, Business & Marketing; www.leedstrinity.ac.uk/departments/FMBN

broadcast journalism, business and enterprise/finance/management, business studies, business with law/with marketing, film and television studies, journalism, management, marketing, media , film & culture, public communications, PR, sports journalism; BA(Hons), MA/PGDip, MB

NORTHERN SCHOOL OF CONTEMPORARY DANCE
www.nscd.ac.uk

contemporary dance, choreography; BPA(Hons), PgDip, MA

YORK ST JOHN UNIVERSITY
www.yorksj.ac.uk

Faculty of Arts

film & televison production, music production/composition/performance, American studies, creative writing, dance, English literature, fine arts, history, media, music, theatre; FD, BA(Hons), PgCert/Dip, MA

Faculty of Education & Theology

primary education, PGCE; primary/secondary education, religious studies, theology & ministry, teacher education; MFL, BA(Hons), GradDip, PgDip

Faculty of Health & Life Sciences

counselling, health studies, occupational therapy, physiotherapy, psychology, CPD & lifelong learning; BA(Hons), MA, PgDip/Cert

York St John Business School

international/business/management, HRM, finance, IT, web technologies, English language & linguistics, international/tourism management, marketing/management, tourism management, global marketing, languages, leadership & management, innovation & change, TESOL; BA(Hons), FD, MA, PGDip/Cert

LEEDS METROPOLITAN UNIVERSITY
www.leedsmet.ac.uk

Faculty of Arts & Society; www.leedsmet.ac.uk/as

The Leeds School of Architecture, Landscape & Design; www.lmu.ac.uk/as/ald

architecture/technology, urban/design, garden art, interior architecture & design, landscape architecture/planning

School of the Built Environment; www.lmu.ac.uk/as/benv

building surveying, civil engineering, construction commercial management, construction law, construction operations/project management, facilities management, heritage planning, housing studies, human geography, planning law & practice, project management, quantity surveying, town & regional/country planning

The Leeds School of Contemporary Art & Graphic Design; www.lmu.ac.uk/as/cagd

graphic/art & design, contemporary fine art practices, fine art

School of Cultural Studies; www.lmu.ac.uk/as/cs

contemporary literatures, English, English literature, history, media & popular culture, politics, screen media cultures

Film, Television, and Performing Arts; www.lmu.ac.uk/as/ftpa

animation, art, contemporary performance practice, creative enterprise, events, film and moving image production, film & TV production, filmmaking, playwork, performance/works, screenwriting (fiction)

School of Social Science; www.lmu.ac.uk/as/sss

criminology, politics, psychology & society, social sciences, sociology, working with young people, youth work & community development; BA(Hons), BSc(Hons), DipHE, FdAA, GradCert, MPhil, MRes, MSc, PGDip

Faculty of Business and Law; www.leedsmet.ac.uk/lbs

Leeds Business School; www.leedsmet.ac.uk/lbs/business

accounting, advertising, business, business studies, economics for business, finance, HRM, international business/communications, journalism, management, marketing, organisational behaviour, PR, public administration, purchasing and supply, strategy & business analysis

Leeds Law School; www.leedsmet.ac.uk/lbs/law

law, law with criminology, legal practice, commercial/employment/family law, personal injury

Leeds School of Accountancy and Financial Services; www.leedsmet.ac.uk/lbs/accfin

accounting & finance, international trade & finance; BA(Hons), HND, LlB(Hons), LlM, MA, MSc, PGDip/Cert

Faculty of Health; www.leedsmet.ac.uk/health

accupuncture, applied psychology/ social work, psychotherapy, biomedical sciences (human biology, microbiology, physiology), counselling, health, public health nursing, health sciences, mental health, nursing (adult health/mental health/district nursing, learning disabilities, practice nursing, community children's nursing, occupational therapy, physiotherapy, psychology and criminology, nutrition, safety, health & environmental management, social work, speech & language therapy, sport and exercise therapy/leisure & culture, therapeutic counselling; BA(Hons), BSc(Hons), CertHE, HNC, MA, MSc, PGDip/Cert, Prof Dip

Carnegie Faculty of Sport & Education; www.leedsmet.ac.uk/carnegie

childhood, early childhood education/years, physical education, primary education, secondary physical education, sport & exercise science, sport business, sport, law & society, management/coaching/development; BA(Hons), BSc(Hons), FdSc, MSc, PGCE, PGCert/Dip/MA, PhD

Faculty of Innovation & Technology; www.leedsmet.ac.uk/inn

broadcast media technologies, photographic/ journalism, games, multimedia & entertainment; computing, innovation & new technology, creative technology, business information systems, computer animation/ forensics/security & ethical hacking, creative technology, digital imaging & creative visualization, digital video & special effects, green computing, information management, information & technology, mobile & distributed computer networks, web applications, software development, mobile devices; music production/technology/for moving image, audio-post production, sound design; BSc(Hons), HND, MA, MSc, PGCert/Dip

Leslie Silver International Foundation; www.leedsmet.ac.uk/international

applied global ethics, English language teaching, hospitality/management, retailing, international/ retail business administration, tourism, international tourism management, events management (international/ sports), international festivals; Adv Dip, BA/ BA(Hons), HND, MA, MSc, PGCert/Dip, PhD

UNIVERSITY OF LEICESTER
www.le.ac.uk

College of the Humanities and Law, Centre forAmerican Studies; www.le.ac.uk/hi/centres/amstudies

American studies, English, English literarature, governance and democracy/world order, foreign policy, history, humanities, international relations, modern literature, new media, society

School of Archaeology & Ancient History; www.le.ac.uk/ar

ancient history, archaeology, classical Mediterranean, geography, historical archaeology, history, Rome & its neighbours

School of English; www.le.ac.uk/ee

American studies/history, English, English literary research, history of art, visual culture, modern literature and creative writing, Victorian studies

Dept of History of Art and Film Studies; www.le.ac.uk/arthistory

the country house in art, film studies and the visual arts, history of art, humanities

School of Historical Studies; www.le.ac.uk/hi

contemporary history, English local history, history, history and politics/international relations/ancient history, European urbanisation, archeology, urban history, social change & resistance

School of Law; www.le.ac.uk/law

law (European Union/ international/international/ commercial/public), law with French law, European law and integration, human rights, legal research

School of Modern Languages; www.le.ac.uk/ml

European studies, French, German, Italian, modern language studies, Spanish, humanities

Museum Studies; www.le.ac.uk /ms

art museum and gallery studies, digital heritage, interpretive studies, learning and visitor studies; BA(Hons), BSc(Hons), LlB, LlM, MA/GradDip, MPhil, PhD

College of Science and Engineering; www2.le.ac.uk/colleges/science

Dept of Chemistry; www.le.ac.uk/ch

biochemistry, chemical biology, chemistry, physical chemistry, forensic science, green chemistry, pharmaceutical chemistry

Dept of Computer Science; www.cs.le.ac.uk

advanced computational methods/distributed systems/software engineering, computer science, computers with management, computing, software engineering for financial services, agile software, geospatial informatics, web applications and services

Dept of Engineering; www2.le.ac.uk/ departments/engineering

advanced control and dynamics, advanced engineering, aerospace engineering, communications and electronic engineering, control and signal processing, electrical engineering, embedded systems and control engineering, general engineering, information and communication engineering, mechanical engineering, software and electronic engineering

Dept of Geography; www.le.ac.uk/geography

environmental informatics, geography, geology, GIS, global environmental change, human geography, physical geography, sustainable management of natural resources, archaeology

Dept of Geology; www2.le.ac.uk/departments/geology

applied and environmental geology, crustal processes, geology, borehole/geophysics, geophysics/borehole, palaeobiology

Centre for Interdisciplinary Science; www2.le.ac.uk/departments/interdisciplinary-science

communication science, complex systems, evolution, laboratory science, mathematics for science, nanoscale frontiers, sustainable livelihoods in Africa, virtual worlds

Dept of Mathematics; www2.le.ac.uk/departments/mathematics

actuarial science, computational mathematics, financial mathematics, mathematical modelling in biology

Dept of Physics and Astronomy; www2.le.ac.uk/departments/physics-and-astronomy

astronomy, astrophysics, condensed matter physics, earth observation, physics, radio & space plasma physics, physics with nanotechnology/astrophysics/space science and technology/planetary science, space projects & instrumentation; BA(Hons), BSc(Hons), BEng/MEng, MA, MChem, MComp, MGeol, MMath, MPhil, MPhys, MSc, MSci, PGDip, PhD

College of Medicine, Biological Sciences and Psychology; www2.le.ac.uk/colleges/medbiopsych

School of Biological Sciences; www.le.ac.uk/lbs

biochemistry, bioinformatics, biological science, biology, cell physiology & pharmacology, genetics, medical biochemistry/genetics/microbiology, microbiology, molecular biology/genetics/toxicology, pharmacology, zoology

School of Medicine, Leicester Medical School; www.le.ac.uk/sm/le

cancer studies and molecular medicine, cardiovascular sciences, health sciences, infection, medical and social care education, molecular pathology, molecular toxicology, operating dept practice, pain management, physiotherapy, primary care research, social science applied to health, child and adolescent mental health

School of Psychology; www.le.ac.uk/pc

clinical/forensic psychology, cognitive neuroscience, psychological research methods, psychology; DocClinPsych, BSc, MBChB, MBioSci, MD, MSc, PostgradDip/Cert, PhD

College of the Social Sciences www.le.ac.uk/colleges/socsci[

Dept of Criminology; www.le.ac.uk/criminology

applied/clinical/ criminology, terrorism, security and risk management

Dept of Economics; www.le.ac.uk/ec

banking and finance, business/financial economics, economics, business analysis and finance, money, public sector economics

Dept of Education; www.le.ac.uk/education

educational studies, education, learning and teaching, lifelong learning, dyslexia, education leadership, mentoring & coaching, teaching assistants, international education, teaching mathematics, PGCE primary/scondary education, TESOL and applied linguistics

The Centre for Labour Market Studies; www2.le.ac.uk/departments/clms

development management and globalization, high performance work practices, HRD and performance management, HRM, industrial relations and HR, international HR and globalization, organizational and employee development, people management, skills and performance, workplace learning

School of Management; www.le.ac.uk/ulsm

accounting, finance, management, management studies, marketing; MBA

Dept of Media & Communication; www.le.ac.uk/mc

communications, communications democracy, communication research, global systems &

communication, mass communications, new media & society/psychology, news & PR

Dept of Politics and International Relations; www.le.ac.uk/politics
American foreign policy/studies, contemporary history, diplomatic studies, economics, European studies, international relations/and world order, international security studies, management studies with politics, political research, politics

Dept of Sociology; www.le.ac.uk/sociology
contemporary/sociology, criminology/communications media and society, psychology social research; BA(Hons), DocSocSci, EdD, Foundation degrees, MA, MBA, MPhil, MSc, PGCE, PGDip/Cert, PhD

Degrees validated by the University of Leicester offered at:

NEWMAN UNIVERSITY COLLEGE
www.newman.ac.uk

art & design, contemporary Christian theology, counselling, creative arts, creative writing, drama, early years, education studies, English, English literature, history, information technology, management & business, media and communication, theology, religion and ethics, clinical applications of/psychology, religious education, science/biology, PE & sports studies, teaching and learning, youth and community work; BA/BSc(Hons), Foundation degrees, MA, MPhil, PGCE, PhD

UNIVERSITY OF LINCOLN
www.lincoln.ac.uk

Faculty of Agriculture, Food and Animal Science; www.lincoln.ac.uk/afas
agriculture and environment, bioveterinary science, clinical/animal behaviour and welfare, conservation biology, equine science/sports science, food manufacture, food science; BSc, FdSc, MPhil, MSc, PhD

Faculty of Art, Architecture & Design; www.lincoln.ac.uk/aad
animation, architecture, art & design, conservation of historic objects, conservation studies, creative advertising, restoration, construction project management, contemporary lens media, design/for exhibition & museums, development and regeneration planning, fashion studies, fine art graphic design, illustration, interactive design, interior design, product design, urban design; BA(Hons), BArch, GradDip, MA, March, MPhil, PhD

Faculty of Business & Law; www.lincoln.ac.uk /bl
accountancy, advertising, branding, business administration/management/studies, coastal & marine tourism, European business/marketing/law, finance, hospitality, HRM, HRD, international business/management studies/marketing strategy/tourism, law, law and business/criminology, marketing, PR, tourism/marketing/management, sports business management; BA(Hons), BSc(Hons), LlB(Hons), LlM, MA, MBA, MPhil, MRes, MSc, PhD

Faculty of Health, Life & Social Sciences; www.lincoln.ac.uk/hlsc
acupuncture, biomedical science, clinical psychology, contemporary culture & communication, criminology/and international relations/politics, employment-based social work, forensic investigation/conservation, globalising justice, golf science, health & social care, health science, herbal medicine, human nutrition, international relations politics/social policy, nursing (adult), psychology with criminology/marketing/social poloicy/child studies, social anthropology, social policy/ and management/work, social care/science, sport, coaching & exercise science, sport development and coaching; BA(Hons), BSc(Hons), CertHE, DClinPsy, MA, MClinRes, MPhil, PGCert, PhD

Faculty of Media, Humanities and Technology; www.lincoln.ac.uk/mht
advertising, audio production, American studies, community radio, computer games production/information systems/science, creative writing, criminology, dance, digital imaging, media and photography/

drama, documentary production, film & television, English, food science & technology, games, history, journalism/sports, cultural studies, culture & communications, web technology, media production/technology, politics, PR, public & community history, theatre and consciousness; BA(Hons), BS(Hons), FdA, MA, MComp, MPhil, MRes, MSc, PhD

Centre for Educational Research & Development; www.lincoln.ac.uk/cerd
EdD, PhD

School of Theology & Ministry Studies; www.lincoln.ac.uk/home/theology
theology; BA(Hons), Cert/Dip Theology, MA

Degrees validated by the University of Lincoln offered at:

EAST RIDING COLLEGE
www.eastridingcollege.ac.uk

access to higher education, applied digital media, art, design and media, business and administration, construction, early years & social care, education and training, hair and beauty, health and social care, hospitality and catering, information technology, motor vehicle and engineering, music, public services, sport and recreation, travel and tourism; BSc(Hons), DIDA, Foundation degrees, HNC, HND, Nat Award NVQs, Nat Dips/Certs, PGCE

HULL COLLEGE
www.hull-college.ac.uk

Hull School of Art & Design
animation, architecture, contemporary fine art practice, fashion and costume/textiles/design, games design, graphic design, interactive multimedia, jewellery and ceramics, lens-based photo media, television and film design, visual arts, web design; BA(Hons), Foundation degrees, HNC

Business, Computing and Professional Development
business and management, computing, education, IT & software design, retail; BA(Hons), Foundation degrees

Construction and Engineering
construction/management, electrical/electronic/ mechanical/ chemical engineering, engineering techn; BSc/BEng, FD, HNC, HND

Health and Science
biomedicine, chemistry, childcare and working with young people, counselling, criminology, health, social care; BSc(Hons), FD, HNC, HND

Performance Arts
acting, broadcast media, dance, music performance, production and community performance, musical theatre, stage management and technical theatre, touring and community theatre; BA, FD

Sport and Leisure
ICFT for travel and tourism, tourism planning and the environment, marketing and event management, travel and planning & the environment; HNC, HND

NORTH LINDSEY COLLEGE
www.northlindsey.ac.uk

art, design & performing arts, business, childcare, construction, education & counselling, ESOL, modern foreign languages, ETEC, hair & beauty, health & social care, IT & travel, motor vehicle, social sciences & humanities, sports, recreation & land-based industries, sustainability, teaching & learning; BA(Hons), Diplomas, FdA, FdSc, HNC, HND

UNIVERSITY OF LIVERPOOL
www.liv.ac.uk

Faculty of Humanities & Social Sciences; www.liv.ac.uk/humanities.and.social.sciences/hss

architecture, design studies; communication & business studies, English studies/ politics/ Italian studies, politics & mass media, cinema & mass politics; applied linguistics, ESOL, English/language and literature, 17th/18th century/ English Renaissance and romantic literature, contemporary literature, Victorian literature, science fiction; music, popular music, music industries studies; philosphy, art, aesthetics & culture, metaphysics, language & mind; history (social, economic, modern, political), Irish studies, historical research, international slavery studies, 20th/18th centuries, medieval & Renaissance studies, archive and records management; ancient history, archaeology, ancient civilizations, evolutionary anthroplogy, classics, classical studies, Egyptian archeology, Manx studies, palaeoanthropolgy; European film, French, German, Hispanic, Italian, Latin-American, Portugese, Corsican, Catalan comparative American studies; gender studies, medieval historiography studies, post-colonial studies, war & conflict studies, film studies

Liverpool Law School: law/and business. European/ international/international business/medical law, sociology & social policy; crime, sociology, social policy, criminal justice, citizenship, culture & regeneration

University of Liverpool Management School: accountancy, business economics/studies, international business, marketing, business finance & management, football industry, entrepreneurship, public administration, HRM, ebusiness strategy & systems, operational supply chain management BA(Hons), MA, MMus, MPhil, MBA, PhD

Faculty of Medicine; www.liv.ac.uk/medicine

School of Medical Education; www.liv.ac.uk/sme

medicine & surgery, anatomy and human biology, child health and paediatrics, dental surgery, health studies, life sciences applicable to medicine, nursing, occupational therapy, orthoptics, orthodontics, orthopaedic surgery, pharmacology, physiotherapy, physiology, psychiatry, public health, tropical medicine, tropical paediatrics, radiography; BDS, BSc(Hons), BN, BVSc, MBChB, MChOrth, MCommH, MClinPsychol, MDS, MPH, MRCPsych, MTCH&CP, MTropMed, MTropPaedMPhil, PhD, MD

Faculty of Science & Engineering; www.liv.ac.uk/science.and.engineering

avionics systems, civil engineering, computer science, electronics, electrical engineering and electronics, communications engineering, environmental engineering, maritime engineering, mechatronics & robotic systems, materials science, mechanical engineering/systems, mechatronics, engineering, structural engineering, medical electronics and instrumentation, microelectronic systems & tecommunications, information & intelligent systems, micro- and nanotechnology; mathematics, pure mathematics, applied mathematics, mathematical science, statisticals & probability, theoretical physics, computational mathematics, string theory; physics, astronomy, astrophysics, nuclear science, physics/medical applications/ocean & climate studies, mathematical physics, radioactive waste, advanced science, biochemistry, biological sciences, biosystems and informatics, computer information systems, ecology, environmental science, environment, genetics, geography, geology, geophysics, inorganic chemistry, investigative & forensic psychology, marine biology, medical chemistry, microbiology, molecular biology, nuclear technology, ocean and earth sciences, ; chemistry, analytical chemistry, pharmacology, physical chemistry, catalysis, biomedical chemistry, biomolecular chemistry, nanoscale with interfacial science/materials chemistry; psychology, pure mathematics, research methods in psychology, software development, statistics and probability, surface science, theoretical physics, zoology, civic design, town planning; BSc(Hons), MChem, BEnd, MEng, DEng, MPhil, MMath, MPhys, MESci, MRes, MSc, PhD

School of Veterinary Science; www.liv.ac.uk/vets

animal reproduction, bioveterinary science, medicine, parasitology, veterinary infection and disease control, veterinary, conservation, veterinary pathology, veterinary science; BSc(Hons), BVSc, DVSc, MSc, MPhil, PhD

Degrees validated at the University of Liverpool offered by:

LIVERPOOL HOPE UNIVERSITY
www.hope.ac.uk

accounting, applied social science, business management, childhood & youth studies, creative & performing arts, creative computing, criminology, dance, design, disability studies, drama & theatre studies, early childhood studies, education studies, English language/literature, environmental biology/management, film studies, fine art, footbal studies, geography, health, health sciences, history, human biology, information technology, international studies, law, leisure, marketing, mathematics, media, music, nutrition, philosophy & ethics/religion, politics, psychology, social policy/work, sport psychology/studies, teacher training, theology & religious studies, tourism; BA(Hons), BMin, BSc(Hons), BDes, FdA, FdSc, MA, MBA, MMin, MPhil, PGCE, PhD

LIVERPOOL JOHN MOORES UNIVERSITY
www.ljmu.ac.uk

Faculty of Business and Law; www.ljmu.ac.uk/BLW

accounting, business, business administration/management & information systems, commercial law, criminal justice, criminology, economics, finance, HRM, international business studies/law/banking & finance, law and commerce, legal practice, management, marketing, personnel & development, PR, retail management, risk and crisis management, social enterprise management, strategic HRM, TESOL; BA(Hons), BSc(Hons), DBA, HND, LlB, LlM, MA, MBA, MPhil, MRes, MSc, PgDip/Cert

Faculty of Education, Community and Leisure; www.ljmu.ac.uk/ECL

CPD, adv educational practice, coaching, dyslexia/ leadership and community nutrition, early years, dance studies, secondary & vocational education (information technology, leisure & tourism, mathematics, PE, science, design & technology, modern languages), early childhood studies (0–8 years), education studies and English/applied community studies/special and inclusive education, environmental educational tourism, events management, food & nutrition, outdoor education, physical education, primary & secondary education, mathematics, science education, primary early years (primary French (TS)), psychology and sport science, school sport management/development, sport & physical activity/ technology, teacher training courses (primary, secondary), work-related learning; BA(Hons), BSc(Hons), EdD, FD, MA, MPhil, MRes, PGCert, PgDip, PhD

Faculty of Media, Arts & Social Science; www.ljmu.ac.uk/MAS

architecture, art & desgn, cultural leadership. broadcast engineering, computer-aided design, creative writing, criminal justice, criminology, digital modelling, drama, English/literature, geography, imaginative writing/screen studies, fashion, film studies, fine art, graphic arts, history, history of art & museums, interactive media design, interior design, international/ journalism, media, literary & cultural history, mass communication, media handling training, television, popular music studies, product design & digital modelling, psychology, screenwriting, criminology, social sciences, social work, sociology, social work, textile design, urban design; BA, BA(Hons), BDes, DipArch, DipHE, MA, MPhil, MRes, PG, PGCE, PhD

Faculty of Science; www.ljmu.ac.uk/faculties/scs

sport, exercise & health, physical activity exercise & health, science & football, biomechanics of gait & posture, biomedical sciences, applied/industrial pharmaceutical science/analysis, nutrition, biochemistry, forensic science, molecular biology, genetics, medicinal & analytical chemistry, medicines management, industrial biotechnology, virology; natural sciences & psychology; biology, environmental sciences, geology, physical geography, wildlife conservation, animal behaviour, forensic anthropology, applied psychology, forensic psychology & criminal justice, applied sports psychology, health psychology, drug use and addiction; astronomy, astrophysics, physics, biological anthropology, forensic anthropology, geography, geology, health psychology, medical nutrition, physical geography, psychology, science & secondary education, zoology; BSc(Hons), MPhil, MPhys, MRes, MSc, PGCE, PhD

Faculty of Technology & the Environment; www.ljmu.ac.uk/faculties/TAE

computer animation & visualization/studies/forensics/games/ technology, computing information systems, IT, multimedia computing, software engineering, wireless & mobile computing; transport, logistics, nautical studies, maritime studies/business/operations, marine/offshore engineering; product innovation, sustainable design, sports technology, CAD, energy management, microelectronic systems, telecommunications engineering, manufacturing engineering, power & control engineering, architectural technology, building surveying, civil engineering, commercial property development/management, construction/project management, quantity surveying & commercial management, real estate management, environmental planning, bulidng maintenance management, quantity surveying, urban planning, water, energy & environment BA(Hons), BSc(Hons), FdSc, HND/C, MPhil, MSc, PgCert, PGCE, PgDip, PhD

Faculty of Health & Applied Social Services; www.ljmu.ac.uk/faculties/HEA

clinical case management, community public health nurse, psychological therapies, direct or general practice nursing, environmental health, health and social care, health sciences, health visiting or school nursing, midwifery, nursing (adult/child/mental health/paramedic practice), primary mental health care, public health, social work, specialist community practitioner, traumatic death and loss, working with young people, children; BA(Hons), BSc, DNurs, DMidw, DPH, DipHE, Foundation degrees, FdA MPhil, MRes, MSc, PGDip/Cert

UNIVERSITY OF THE ARTS LONDON
www.arts.ac.uk

Camberwell College of Art & Design; www.camberwell.arts.ac.uk

3D design, book arts, book conservation, conservation, designer–maker, design practice, digital arts, drawing, graphic design, fine art, visual art, illustration, painting, photography, printmaking, sculpture; BA(Hons), Dip, FdA, MA, MPhil, PGDip, PhD

Central Saint Martins College of Art & Design; www.csm.arts.ac.uk

acting, architecture: spaces and objects, art & design, criticism, curation & communication, communication & design, fashion, communication with promotion, creative practice for narrative environments, ceramics, furniture or jewellery, criticism, design for textile futures, design studies, European classical acting, fashion, fine art, graphic design, industrial design, innovation management, jewellery design, knitwear and print, performance design and practice, performance, photography, product design, screen: acting, directing, writing, textile design; BA(Hons), DipFndStudies FdA, FD, GradDip, MA, MPhil, PGCert/Dip, PhD

Chelsea College of Art & Design; www.chelsea.arts.ac.uk

art theory, curating, fine art, graphic design communication, graphic design, interior & spatial design, photography, print production (print media), spatial design, textile design; BA(Hons), FdA, Foundation Dip, GradDip, MA, MPhil, PGCert/Dip, PhD

London College of Communication; www.lcc.arts.ac.uk

3D design, animation, architecture, artefact & spatial design, book arts, curation & criticism, design, digital arts/media, drawing, enterprise management, events management, film, video & broadcast, floral design, games design, graphic design, illustration, industrial/interior design, interactive media, journalism, marketing, advertising, media & cultural studies, photography, print media & production, printmaking, product design PR, publishing, retail, screenwriting, sound arts, surface design, theatre design, travel & tourism, typography, visual display & design; BA(Hons), FdA, ABCDip, MA, MDes, MRes, MSc, PgDip

London College of Fashion; www.fashion.arts.ac.uk

beauty therapy, broadcasting, buying & merchandising, cosmetic science, costume, curation & criticism, design, digital arts/media, drawing, fashion, textiles, fashion journalism/ management/marketing/promotion/production, film, TV & video, footwear, graphic design, media & cultural studies, pattern cutting, photography, PR/, retail management, surface design, technical effects, theatre design & performing arts, visual design & display; BA(Hons), BSc(Hons), diplomas, FD MA, PgDip/Cert

Wimbledon College of Art; www.wimbledon.arts.ac.uk

acting & directing, animation, costume, design, digital arts/media, film video & broadcast, drawing, fine art, interactive media, painting, pattern cutting, printmaking, sculpture, sonic arts, theatre design/ & performing arts; BA(Hons), FdA, MA

LONDON CONTEMPORARY DANCE SCHOOL
www.theplace.org.uk

advanced dance training, choreography, contemporary dance, dance training and education, improvisation, performance; BA, PGDip

LONDON METROPOLITAN UNIVERSITY
www.londonmet.ac.uk

Dept of Applied Social Sciences; www.londonmet.ac.uk/depts/dass

community sector management, youth studies/work, organization & community development; community/district/occupational health/practice/school/public health nursing, health & social care management/ social policy, criminology; digital media, international jounalism, mass communications, media studies, information management; sustainable communities, city regeneration, urban policy, housing & inclusion sociology, social policy/research/statistics/ development practice, European social studies; social work, woman & child abuse, practice education; labour & TU studies; BA(Hons), BSc(Hons), MA, MPhil, MRes, MSc, PGCert/Dip, PhD

Dept of Architecture and Spacial Design; www.londonmet.ac.uk/architecture

architectural history, architecture, cities, design and urban cultures, energy and sustainability, interior design/digital design systems; BA(Hons), MA, MSc, PhD, ProfDip

Faculty of Computing; www.londonmet.ac.uk/depts/cctm

Communications Technology

communications systems, computer networking/systems engineering, digital communications networks, electronic & computer engineering, electronics, communications/ computer engineering, embedded systems, information and communications technology mobile & satellite communication, network management & security, telecommunications and networks

Computing

business computing, business information technology, computer forensics, computer science, computing, internet computing, IT security, mobile computing, mining/distributed systems/mobile computing/ advanced computing/software

Mathematics

computer science/engineering applications, computing, decision science, financial mathematics, mathematical sciences, mathematics, statistics

Multimedia

computer animation/games/e-learning/games/internet, creative technology (e-learning/games/multimedia), multimedia solutions (business/elearning/internet); BSc(Hons), FdSc, MEng, MRes, MSc, PhD

Faculty of Humanities, Arts, Language and Education; www.londonmet.ac.uk/depts/hale

School of Humanities, Arts and Language; www.londonmet.ac.uk/depts/hale

American studies, translation studies, Caribbean studies, creative writing, ELT & ALS, English language studies/literature, film studies, filmmaking, game studies, history, interpreting/public service, journalism, performing arts, philosophy, professional writing, screenwriting, French/Spanish/and Latin American studies, English teacher training, TESOL, theatre studies

School of Education; www.londonmet.ac.uk/education

early childhood studies, early years teaching, Jewish education, leading and managing school development, learning and teaching in HE, music education with QTS, therapy and education; BA(Hons), BEd, FdA, MA, PGCE, PGDip/Cert

Dept of Law, Governance and International Relations; www.londonmet.ac.uk/ depts/hale/lgr

advice work, law, business/international/European/human rights/ law, human rights and social justice, Asia Pacific studies, governance & international relations/law, international development, peace & conflict studies, politics, European studies, public service management, international relations and globalisation, public administration, international security; BA(Hons), BSc(Hons), FdG, LlB, LlM, MA, PGCE

Faculty of Life Sciences

School of Human Science; www.londonmet.ac.uk/depts/hhs

biochemistry, bioethics, biological and medicinal chemistry, biological sciences, biomedical sciences, chemistry, clinical nutrition, cosmetic science, food and consumer studies/medical microbiology, food science, forensic and bioanalytical science/industrial bioanalytical techniques/pharmaceutical sciences, genetics, health promotion, herbal medicinal science, home economics, human biology/nutrition, public health/sports/dietetics, medical bioscience, medical genetics, nutrition, osteopathic medicine, osteopathy, personal training and fitness consultancy, pharmaceutical science, pharmacology, sports and exercise science, sports psychology and performance, fitness evaluation, sports therapy, sustainability in the food industry

School of Psychology; www.londonmet.ac.uk/depts/dops

psychology, addiction/business/counselling/forensic/health/occupational/sport & performance psychology, cognitive behaviour therapy; BSc(Hons), DipHE, FdSc, GradDip/Cert, MOst, MOstMed, MSc, Prof Doc

London Metropolitan Business School; www.londonmet.ac.uk/lmb

accounting, advertising and marketing communication, arts management, finance, aviation management, banking, business, business economics/enterprise/information/ management/operations management/psychology, community sport coaching & management, computer systems, corporate finance and investment finance, corporate treasury management, economic studies, economics, events (marketing) management, fashion marketing, financial communications, financial economics, financial markets and derivatives/with information systems, financial regulation/and compliance management, HRM/development/strategy, insurance, international business and banking/finance/marketing, international business entrepreneurship/ business/business finance/economics and finance/hospitality management/hotel and restaurant management/sustainable tourism/tourism management, trade and transport, investment, investment fund management, law, leadership, marketing, media and music management, music and media marketing/management/PR, music industry management, purchase and supply chain management, retail management, sports management, strategic management accounting, technology; DPS, FdSc, GradConv, HND, MA, MBA, MSc, PGDip,

Sir John Cass Dept of Art Media and Design; www.londonmet.ac.uk/jcmd

communications management, conservation, curating the contemporary, design, digital film and animation, film production, fine art, furniture design, furniture and product design, graphic design, inclusive design, interior design/& technology, jewellery design, manufacture and design for polymer products, musical instruments, music, polymer science and engineering, product & management, research for disability, restoration & conservation, textile design; BA(Hons), BSc(Hons), FdA, MA, MPhil, MSc, PhD

THE LONDON SCHOOL OF OSTEOPATHY
www.lso.ac.uk

osteopathy; MOst

LONDON SCHOOL OF PUBLISHING
www.publishing-school.co.uk

editorial and proofreading, advanced editorial/feature and corporate writing, magazine sub-editing, picture research, QuarkXPress, InDesign, Photoshop, Illustrator, PageMaker, Dreamweaver, Flash, HTML, FrontPage, writing for web; Cert

LONDON SOUTH BANK UNIVERSITY
www.lsbu.ac.uk

Faculty of Arts and Human Sciences; www.lsbu.ac.uk/#ahs

Arts, Media & English; www.lsbu.ac.uk/ahs/departments/artsmediaen

critical/arts management, creative writing, digital film & video/media arts/photography, drama & performance studies, English, film studies, game cultures, media and cultural studies, media writing, new media, music & sonic media, jouralism, theatre practice; BA(Hons), MA, MPhil, PhD

Education; www.lsbu.ac.uk/#ahsedu

early years, education for sustainability, graduate teacher programme/PGCE with QTS (primary/secondary maths), HE, initial teacher training, learning and teaching (FE and HE), secondary mathematics (ages 11–16); BA(Hons), Cert, FdA, MA, PgDip/Cert

Law; www.lsbu.ac.uk/#ahslaw

common law, crime & litigation, international human rights and development, law, legal studies; GradDip, LlB(Hons), LLM

Psychology; www.lsbu.ac.uk/#ahspsycho

addiction psychology & counselling, investigative forensic psychology, psychology, psychology /with criminology, psychology (clinical psychology/child development), sexual and relationship studies/therapy; BSc(Hons), GradDip, MSc, PhD

Social and Policy Studies; www.lsbu.ac.uk/#ahssps

childhood and family studies, criminology, development studies, European policy studies, international politics, refugee studies, social policy, social research methods, sociology; BA(Hons), BSc(Hons), MSc, PhD

Urban, Environmental & Leisure Studies; www.lsbu.ac.uk/#ahsuel

built environment studies, cities & local development, housing studies, international business tourism and hospitality management, planning policy and practice, spatial urban planning, sustainable communities, urban and environmental planning, urban regeneration and community development; BA(Hons), FdA, HNC, MA, MSc, PGCert/Dip

Faculty of Business; www.bus.lsbu.ac.uk

accounting, banking, charity, marketing/fundraising/finance, corporate governance, information management, international finance, investment, quantitative finance & business analysis; BA(Hons), FdA, MSc, PgDip

accounting, business, business administration/information systems/& international studies/management/studies, economics/ of international business, enterprise/small business, finance, marketing; BA(Hons), BSc(Hons), FdA, HNC, HND, MSc, PgDip

Business Information Technology & Computing

business information systems/technology, computing, e-business IT, health information systems, information assurance, information systems management/technology, internet & database systems, managing wireless information systems, multimedia computing, social technology; BA(Hons), BSc(Hons), FdSc, HNC, HND, MSc

Management, Human Resources & Marketing

business administration, charity marketing & fundraising, management studies, health services & hospital management, international/HR, Eurasian business management, international business/management, management, personnel practice, marketing/communications/management, public administration, voluntary administration; Certs, Dips in Management Marketing, MA, MBA, various Masters degrees

Faculty of Engineering, Science & Built Environment; www.lsbu.ac.uk/esbe

Dept of Applied Science; www.lsbu.ac.uk/deparments/appsci

applied biology, applied science, bioscience, chemical & process engineering, biochemistry, culinary art, food and nutrition, food design and technology, food safety and control, food science, forensic science, human biology, integrated sciences, microbiology, petroleum engineering, sport and exercise science; BA(Hons), BEng(Hons), BSc(Hons), FdSc, MSc/PgCert/PgDip

Dept of Engineering & Design; www.lsbu.ac.uk/departments/engdes

computer-aided design/engineering, computer systems & networks(ing), electrical & electronic engineering, systems for environmental services, engineering product design, mechanical engineering/design, mechatronics/engineering, power distribution, product design/ computing, sports product design, telecommunications & computer networks engineering, design & manufacturing management, embedded & distributed systems, internet & multimedia engineering, manufacturing management, quality engineering management, structural design; BEng(Hons), BSc(Hons), FdEng, HNC, HND, MRes MSc, PgDip

Dept of the Built Environment; www.1lsbu.ac.uk/esbe/departments/builtenv

architecture, architectural technology, built environment, quantity surveying, construction/management/project management/health care, planning buildings for health, property development & planning, building/surveying, real estate; BA(Hons), FdSC, HNC, PgDip/Cert, MSc

Dept of Urban Engineering; www1.lsbu.ac.uk/departments/builtenv

architectural engineering, building services engineering, civil engineering, railway civil engineering, environmental & architectural acoustics, sustainable energy systems; BEng(Hons), BSc(Hons), FdEng, HNC, HND, MSc, PgDip

Dept of Surveying, Property & Construction

construction/management/project management, property development and planning, property management, quantity surveying, surveying; BSc(Hons), FdSc, HNC, MSc, PgDip

Faculty of Health & Social Care; www.lsbu.ac.uk/faculties/hsc

Adult and Mental Health and Learning Disabilities; Primary and Social Care; Traditional Chinese Medicine

acupuncture, acute and psychiatric intensive care, allied health science, Chinese medicine, continuous professional development, diagnostic radiography, health protection, health studies (family planning and women's health), learning disability, women's health, midwifery, non-medical prescribing, nursing (adult, mental health, children's, learning disability, public health), occupational therapy, operating department practice, palliative care, physiotherapy, primary and social care (nursing/public health/mental health), professional development for allied health professions, professional midwifery practice, social work, specialist community therapeutic/ radiography; FdSc, BSc, BSc(Hons), DipHE(Hons), MSc, PgDip/Cert, PhD, University AdvDip, ProfDoc, MCMAc

UNIVERSITY OF LONDON; BIRKBECK
www.bbk.ac.uk

School of Arts; www.bbk.ac.uk/arts

English and humanities, European cultures and languages, history of art and screen media, media and cultural studies, Iberian and Latin American studies

School of Business, Economics and Informatics; www.bbk.ac.uk/business

computer science and information systems, economics, mathematics and statistics, management, organizational psychology

School of Law; www.bbk.ac.uk/law

School of Science; www.bbk.ac.uk

biological sciences, earth and planetary sciences, psychological sciences

School of Social Sciences, History and Philosophy; www/bbk.ac.uk

applied linguistics and communication, geography, environment and development studies, history, classics and archaeology, philosophy, politics, psychosocial studies, social policy and education

UNIVERSITY OF LONDON; UNIVERSITY COLLEGE LONDON (UCL)
www.ucl.ac.uk

UCL School of Life and Medical Science (including UCL Medical School); www.ucl.ac.uk/slms

advanced paediatrics, ageing & mental health, anatomy and developmental biology, audiological science, biochemistry, biological sciences, biology of fertility and embryology development, biology of vision, biomedical sciences, brain and mind science, cancer, cardiorespiratory physiotherapy, clinical & applied paediatrics, clinical biochemistry, clinical dental, clinical neuroscience/experimental medicine, clinical ophthalmology, cognitive neuroscience/psychology, community child health, conservative dentistry, dental public health/sedation & pain management, drug design, endodontology, environmental biology, genetics/ human science, global health & development, haemaglobinopathy, health informatics, health psychology, healthcare, history of medicine, human genetics, human–computer interaction with ergonomics, immunology, implant dentistry, infection and immunity, international health, linguistics, medical mycology, medicine, molecular biology/medicine, musculoskeletal science, neuroimaging, neuroscience, oral medicine, oral surgery, orthodontics, paediatric dentistry, periodontology, pharmacology, phonetics, phonology, physiology, pragmatics, prenatal genetics & fetal medicine, prosthodontics, psychiatric research, psychology, psychoanalytic development psychology, public health nutrition, radiation biology, reproductive science and women's health, restorative dental practice, sexually transmitted infections and HIV, social epidemiology, special care dentistry, special needs dentistry, speech and language sciences, speech, language and cognition, sports & exercise medicine, surgical science, syntax, theoretical psychoanalytical studies, travel health & medicine, urology, voice pathology, zoology; BSc(Hons), DipCDSc, IbSc, MBBS, MClinDent, MD(Res), MPhil, MRes, MSc, MSci, PGCert/Dip, PhD

Faculty of the Built Environment

Built Environment; www.barlett.ucl.ac.uk

advanced architectural studies, architectural design, architectural history, architecture, building and urban design in development, environmental design and engineering/sustainable heritage, construction economics and management, development administration and planning, development planning, environment and sustainable development, facility and environment management, international planning, project and enterprise management, project management for construction, real estate & planning, sustainable heritage, urbanisation, social development practice, strategic management of projects, town and country planning, urban design/development planning/economic development/management/regeneration/studies; BSc(Hons), Diplomas, EngD, MA, MArch, MPhil, MSc, PhD, MArch, PGDip, MRes

Faculty of Engineering Sciences; www.ucl.ac.uk/engineering

Civil, Environmental & Geomatic Engineering; www.rege.ucl.ac.uk

civil engineering, earthquake engineering with disaster management, environmental engineering, environmental mapping, environmental systems engineering, GIS, hydrographic surveying, photogrammes, remote sensing, surveying, transport studies

Biochemical Engineering; www.ucl.ac.uk/biochemeng

biochemical engineering

Chemical Engineering; www.ucl.ac.uk/chemeng

chemical engineering/with biochemical engineering, chemical process engineering

Computer Science; www.cs.ucl.ac.uk/

computer science, computational analysis, computational statistics and machine learning, computer graphics, vision and imaging, financial systems engineering, human–computer interaction with ergonomics, information security, machine learning, mathematical computing, networked computer systems, software systems engineering

Electronic and Electrical Engineering; www.ee.ucl.ac.uk

communications engineering/computer science/nanotechnology, electrical & electronic engineering, internet engineering, nanotechnology, photonics systems, spacecraft technology and satellite communications, broadband communications, telecommunications/engineering

Management Science and Innovation; www.ucl.ac.uk/msi

information management for business, the business plan, management OR/decision analysis, project management, technology mastering entrepreneurship/enterprise

Mechanical Engineering; www.ucl.ac.uk/mecheng

engineering with business finance, marine engineering, mechanical engineering, naval architecture, power systems engineering, biomaterials & tissue engineering

Medical Physics & Bioengineering; www.ucl.ac.uk/medphys

biomedical engineering, medical imaging computing, medical physics/with physics, radiation physics, natural sciences

Jill Dando Institute of Crime Science; www.ucl.ac.uk/jdi

crime analysis, detection, crime prevention/science, community safety, detection of crime; BEng, BSc, Certs, MEng, MPhil, MRes, MSc, PgDip, PhD

Faculty of Mathematical and Physical Sciences; www.ucl.ac.uk/maps-faculty

Chemistry; www.chem.ucl.ac.uk

chemistry, chemical physics, materials for energy and the environment, medicinal chemistry, chemical research

Earth Sciences; www.es.ucl.ac.uk

earth science, environmental geoscience, geology, geophysical hazards, geophysics, geosciences, natural hazards for insurers, palaeobiology (with biology), planetary science

Mathematics; www.ucl.ac.uk/mathematics

mathematics with mathematical physics/economics/modern languages/management studies/physics/statistical science, mathematical modelling, pure/applied mathematics

Physics and Astronomy; www.phys.ucl.ac.uk

astronomy, astrophysics, nanotechnology, physics, theoretical physics, ultra precision, high energy physics, planetary science

Science and Technology Studies; www.ucl.ac.uk/sts

history, philosophy & social studies of science, science, communication & policy & technology studies

Space and Climate Physics; www.mssl.ucl.ac.uk

astrophysics, climate extremes, imaging, space plasma physics, plasma science, solar & stellar physics

Statistical Science; www.ucl.ac.uk/stats

economics, finance, mathematics, statistical science, statistics, statistics and management for business; BSc, BSc(Econ), EngD, MRes, MSc, MSci, PhD

Faculty of Arts & Humanities; www.ucl.ac.uk/ah

Dutch, modern languages, Dutch cultural studies/ golden age/langauge & culture, English language & literature, modern culture, Shakepeare in literature, medieval studies, film studies, French; modern languages, language & culture, French & francophone studies, adv translation, German, German studies, Greek & Latin, languages & literature, ancient world studies, reception of classical world, Hebrew & Jewish Studies, Jewish history, language & culture, Holocaust studies, modern Israeli studies, Information, information studies, electronic communication & publishing, archive & information studies, library studies, publishing, Italian, Italian and design/ history of art, contemporary Italian culture & history, gender studies, Philosophy, philosphical studies, philosophy, politics & economics of health; Scandinavian Studies, Icelandic, Viking studies; Spanish and Latin American Studies; Hispanic/ Latin-American studies, translation theory and practice; Slade School of Art: painting, fine art, media, history & theory of art; BA(Hons), BFA, MA, MPhil, MRes, PhD, MFA

Faculty of Law; www.ucl.ac.uk/laws

alternative dispute resolution, banking law, carriage of goods by sea, children and their rights, civil and public litigation, company law, comparative contract law, human rights law, competition law and intellectual property rights, constitutional and institutional law of the EU, corporate finance, corporate governance in the UK and US, corporate insolvency, liquidation, insolvent companies, criminal law doctrines, criminal procedure: economic analysis of law, environmental governance and regulation, environmental law of the EU, EU administrative law/internal market/law and policy on climate change/migration law, European competition laws/equality and employment law, family law and society: foreign relations law, insurance law, international and comparative competition law and policy insolvency law/ copyright and related rights/trade marks, international arbitration/criminal law/energy law/environmental law/human rights law/law of foreign investment/law andclimate change/trade law/law of the sea, Japanese commercial law, judges, courts, politics and democracy, judicial review, jurisprudence and legal theory, law and economics of regulated markets/governance/industries, law and policy of international courts & tribunals, law with advanced studies/another legal system regulated markets, technology & intellectual property law, copyright, trademarks and brands, war law, Western European legal history; LlB and Baccalaureus Legum, LlBHons, LlM, MPhil, PhD

Faculty of Historical and Social Sciences; www.ucl.ac.uk/shs

Anthropology; www.ucl.ac.uk/anthropology

archaeology, digital/social & cultural anthropology, human science, environment and development, human evolution and behaviour, medical anthropology, material and visual culture, paleoanthropology; BA(Hons), BSc(Hons), MA, MPhil, MRes, MSc, PhD

Archaeology; www.ucl.ac.uk/archeology

archeoloy & anthropology, African archaeology, archaeology of the eastern Mediterranean and the Middle East, artefact studies, classical archaeology and classical civilisation, comparative art and archaeology, conservation for archaeology and museums, cultural heritage studies, Egyptian archaeology, environmental archaeology, forensic archaeological science, GIS, managing archeological sites, maritime archaeology, museum studies, palaeoanthropology and palaeolithic archaeology, principles of conservation, public archaeology, skeletal and dental bioarchaeology, technology and analysis of archaeological materials; BA(Hons), BSc(Hons), MA, MPhil, MSc, PhD

Economics; www.ucl.ac.uk/economics

advanced macroeconomic theory, econometric theory and methods, economic policy, economics, economics of development/ migration, game theory, health economics, labour economics, macroeconomics, microeconometrics, money and finance, statistics economics and environmental ethics; BSc(Hons), MSc, PhD

Geography; www.geog.ucl.ac.uk/

aquatic science, conservation, environment, GIS, geography, glabal migration, globalisation, quaternary science, remote sensing, science and society, urban studies; BA(Hons), BSc(Hons), MSc, PhD

History; www.ucl.ac.uk/history

British history, Roman/Greek history, Tudor & Stuart Britain, industrial revolution, US since 1920, European history, Dutch golden age, medieval & renaiscance studies; BA(Hons), MA, MPhil, PhD

History of Art; www.ucl.ac.uk/art-history
history of art/with material studies, contemporary art & globalisation, popular imagery in 19th century, race/place/-exotic/erotic, the writing of art; BA(Hons), MA, MPhil, PhD

Political Science; www.ucl.ac.uk/ssp
political studies, international relations, European social & human rights, security studies, democracy & democratisation, European public policy, global government & ethics, international public policy, legal & political theory; MA, MPhil, MSc, PhD

School of Slavonic and Eastern European Studies; www.ssees.ucl.ac.uk
central and south-east European studies, politics, security & integration, social science, history 2008–2009, East European studies, identity, culture and power, politics and East European studies, institutions, development and globalisation, Russian and East European literature and culture, Russian studies; BA(Hons), Erasmus Mundus International Masters in Economy, State and Society, MA, MPhil, MRes, PhD

UNIVERSITY OF LONDON; COURTAULD INSTITUTE OF ART
www.courtald.ac.uk

conservation of easel paintings, curating the art museum, history of art, painting conservation (wall painting); BA(Hons), GradDip, MA, PGDip, MPhil, PhD

UNIVERSITY OF LONDON; GOLDSMITHS
www.goldsmiths.ac.uk

Dept of Anthropology; www.gold.ac.uk/anthroplogy
anthropology, media, development & rights, cultural politics, history, sociology, social anthropology, visual anthropology, community & youth work, development & rights, health with body in 21st century; BA(Hons), MPhil, PhD, MRes

Dept of Art; www.gold.ac.uk/art
fine art and history of art, art writing, curating; BA(Hons), MFA, MPhil, PhD

Centre for Cultural Studies; www.gold.ac.uk/cultural-studies
cultural studies/industry, interactive media: critical theory and practice, post-colonial culture and global policy; MA, MPhil, PhD

Dept of Computing, Computing & Interaction Design; www.gold.ac.uk/computing
arts & computational technology, cognitive computing, computational studio arts, computer games & entertainment, computer science/information systems, computing & interactive design, creative computing, creative & cultural entrepreneurship, information technology, internet computing; music computing; BMus, BA/BSc(Hons), MFA, MPhil, MSc, PhD

Dept of Design; www.gold.ac.uk/design
design, design & technology education, computing & interaction design, design & innovation/environment, design – critical practice/education/futures, innovation; BA(Hons), BA/BSc(Hons), BEng/MEng, MPhil, MRes, PhD

Dept of Drama; www.gold.ac.uk/drama
applied drama: theatre in educational, community & social contexts, arts administration & cultural policy, contemporary African theatre & performance, creative and cultural entrepreneurship, musical theatre, performance & culture, performance making, writing for performance, drama/& theatre culture; BA(Hons), MA, MPhil, PhD

Dept of Educational Studies; www.gold.ac.uk/educational-studies
artist teachers, education, language & identity/culture & society, public service professionals, teacher training (PGCE) – primary/secondary (art & design, design & technology, drama, English, geography, mathematics, modern languages, music, biology, chemistry, general science or physics); BA(Hons), DPS, MA, MPhil, PhD

Centre for Language, Culture & Learning; www.goldsmith.ac.uk/clcl; education, culture, language & identity

English and Comparative Literature; www.gold.ac.uk/ecl
American literature, applied linguistics, comparative literature, creative /and life writing, drama, English, history, media and modern literature/languages; BA(Hons), MA, MPhil, MRes, PhD

Dept of History; www.gold.ac.uk/history
history, history & anthropology/history of ideas/ politics/sociology; BA (Hons), MA, MPhil, MRes, PhD

Centre for the Arts and Learning; www.gold.ac.uk/cal
artist teachers & contemporary practice; culture, language & identity, education; MA, MPhil/PhD

Institute for Creative and Cultural Entrepreneurship; www.gold.ac.uk/ccl
creative and cultural entrepreneurship; MA, MPhil, PhD

Language Studies Centre; www.gold.ac.uk/ laguage-studies-centre
English language studies

Dept of Media and Communications; www.gold.ac.uk/media-communications
anthropology and media, media and communications/sociology/modern literature, brand development, creative & cultural entrepreneurship, digital media, filmmaking, gender & culture, photography, electronic graphics, television/ journalism, radio screen documentary, screen & film studies, script writing, media & communications; BA(Hons), MA, MPhil, PhD, MRes

Dept of Music; www.gold.ac.uk/music
arts administration & cultural policy, composition, contemporary & pop music, creative practice, ethnomusicology, historical musicology, music, music computing, popular music performance and related studies, studio composition; BMus(Hons), BMus/ BSc(Hons), MA, MMus, MPhil, PGCert, PhD

Dept of Politics; www.gold.ac.uk/politics
art & politics, economics, politics & public policy, history, international studies, politics, political science, public service professions, sociology; BA(Hons), DPS, MA, MPhil, MRes, PhD

Dept of Professional and Community Education; www.gold.ac.uk/pace
social work, HE work, social & cultural studies, performing arts; music/drama & theatre/Alexander technique; psychotherapeutic study, community & youth work; BA(Hons), DipHE, GradDip, PGCert

Dept of Psychology; www.gold.ac.uk/ psychology
cognitive and clinical neuroscience, music, mind & brain, occupational psychology, organisational behaviour, psychology, research methods in psychology; FoundationCert, BSc(Hons), MPhil, MSc, PhD

Dept of Sociology; www.gold.ac.uk/ sociology
critical & creative analysis, gender & culture, photography & urban cultures, social research, sociology and anthropology/history/media/cultural studies/ politics, visual sociology, world cities and urban life; BA(Hons), MA, MPhil, PhD

Dept of Visual Cultures; www.gold.ac.uk/ visual-cultures
aural and visual cultures, contemporary art theory, fine art, history of art, research architecture, curatorial knowledge; BA(Hons), MA, MPhil, PGDip, PhD

UNIVERSITY OF LONDON; HEYTHROP COLLEGE www.heythrop.ac.uk

Abrahamic religions, biblical studies, canon law, Christian spirituality/theology, Christianity and interreligious relations, contemporary ethics, divinity, pastoral liturgy/mission/theology, philosophy, religion and ethics/theology, psychology and theology, study of religions, theology; BA, Certs, FD, GradDip, MA

UNIVERSITY OF LONDON; INSTITUTE IN PARIS
www.ulip.ac.uk

French studies, Paris studies – history and culture; BA, MA, MPhil, PhD

UNIVERSITY OF LONDON; INSTITUTE OF EDUCATION
www.ioe.ac.uk

adult literacy, language & literature, advanced educational practice, art and design in education, bilingual learners in urban educational settings, business education, child development, citizenship, clinical education, comparative education, curriculum, development education, early years education, economics of education, education and citizenship/history/technology/psychology/international development, educational planning, effective learning, English education, gender and international/development/health promotion and international development, geography education, higher and professional education, history of education, inclusive education, information and communications technology, leadership, lifelong learning, literacy learning and literacy difficulties, mathematics education, media, culture and communication, museums and galleries in education, music education, pedagogy and assessment, Teacher Education: PGCE primary/secondary/post-comp, philosophy of education, policy studies in education, primary education(policy & practice), psychology of education, psychosocial studies & education, science education, social justice and education, social pedagogy, sociology of childhood and children's rights/education, special & inclusive education, teaching and learning in higher and professional education, TESOL, world English; BEd, Certs, DedPsy, EdD, GradDip, MA, MBA, MPhil, MRes, MSc, MTg, PGCE, PhD

UNIVERSITY OF LONDON; KING'S COLLEGE LONDON
www.kcl.ac.uk

The School of Arts & Humanities; www.kcl.ac.uk/humanities

American studies, Australian studies, Byzantine and modern Greek, classics, clinical methodologies, comparative literature, culture, media & creative industries, 18th-century studies, English, European studies, film studies, French, German, history, humanities and academic English, linguistics, medieval studies, Middle East & Mediterranean studies, modern languages, music, philosophy, Portuguese & Brazilian studies, Spanish & Spanish American studies, theology & religious studies; BA(Hons), MA, MMus, MRes, MSc

School of Biomedical & Health Sciences; www.kcl.ac.uk/biohealthbiochemistry

analytical science/toxicology, aviation science, biomedical science/& scientific English, drug discovery, human sciences, molecular genetics/science/biophysics, neuroscience, nutrition, dietetics, pain, pharmacology, pharmacy, primary care & community pharmacy, physiology, physiotherapy, space physiology & health; BS, BSc(Hons), DHC, MB, MPH, MPharm, MRes, MSc

Dental Institute; www.kcl.ac.uk/dentistry

dentistry, dental radiography, general dental practice, aesthetic dentistry, dental public health, endodontology, implant dentistry, orthodontics, paediatric dentistry, periodontology, prosthdontics, sedation & special care dentistry; BDS, MClinDent, MOrth, MScDL, PGDip

Institute of Psychiatry; www.iop.kcl.ac.uk

addiction, advanced psychosocial practice, applied clinical neuropsychology, child and adolescent mental health, clinical forensic psychiatry/psychology/neuroscience, cognitive behavioural therapies, family intervention in psychosis, therapy, forensic mental health, health psychology, science, mental health studies, neuroscience, neuropsychology, mental health/learning disabilities/population research/social work with children & adults, organizational psychiatry & psychology, psychiatric research, psychology, social, genetic & developmental psychiatry, law & psychiatry; BSc, DClinPsy, GradCert, MSc, PGDip

School of Law; www.kcl.ac.uk/law

Australian law, construction law & dispute resolution, criminology & criminal justice, English law & French law/German law/American law, law, European legal studies, medical ethics & law; LlB, LLM, MA, MPhil, MSc, PhD

School of Medicine; www.kcl.ac.uk/schools/medicine

clinical dermatology, immunology, medical immunology, medical engineering & physics, medical ultrasound, medicine, nuclear medicine, palliative care, primary health care, public health, rheumatology, translational cancer medicine, vascular ultrasound; MBBS, MPH, MSc, PDDip/Cert

Florence Nightingale School of Nursing & Midwifery; www.kcl.ac.uk/schools/nursing

advanced practice – cancer care/child care/critical care/education/leadership/midwifery/primary care, gastrointestinal nursing, nursing studies – adult nursing/child nursing/mental health nursing, midwifery studies, public health/women's health; BSc(Hons), DipHE, DHC, DPhil, MRes, MSc

School of Physical Sciences & Engineering; www.kcl.ac.uk /schools/pse

computational molecular biology, bioinformatics, biomolecular structure, genetics, molecular biology, protein structure predictions; MSc, PhD

computing, software engineering, computer science/with management/mathematics computing & internet systems/security, IT law and management, web intelligence; BSc(Hons), MSc, MSci

electronic engineering, engineering with business management, mechanical engineering, mechatronics, nanotechnology engineering, telecommunication engineering; BEng, MEng, MPhil, MSc, PhD

financial mathematics, information processing and neural networks, mathematics, mathematics & philosophy/computer science/management & finance/physics/physics with astrophysics, theoretical physics; BA(Hons), BSc(Hons)

biophysics, materials and molecular modelling, mathematics and physics/with astrophysics, nanotechnology, physics and philosophy, physics with medical applications/astrophysics/computer science/management, solid statephysics, theoretical and astroparticle physics, x-ray physics; BSc(Hons), MSci, PhD

School of Social Science and Public Policy; www.kcl.ac.uk/sspp

Defence Studies: defence studies, international relations. war/air power in the modern world

Education: assessment in education, child studies, creative arts in the classroom, education and professional studies, education management/policy & society, e-inclusion, ELT & applied linguistics, ICT education, English, English in education, Jewish education, language ethnicity & education, Latin American studies, mathematics, mathematics education, MFL with education, modern foreign languages education, PGCE in classics, RE, science education, education & social science, language, discourse & communication, theology & ministry, teaching & learning; BA, BSc, MA, MSc, PhD

Geography: geography, development geography with history/film studies/war studies, acquatic resource management, carbon science, society & change, cities, disasters, environment with development/politics/globalisation/health/management/geopolitics, global environmental change, Latin American studies, risk analysis, sustainable cities, tourism, water, science & governance; BA, Bsc, MA, MSc, MPhil, PhD

Gerontology: ageing, public policy and ageing; MSc, MA, MRes, PGDip/Cert, PhD

business management, HRM, international management/marketing, management/and social science, public services policy & management; BSc(Hons), MRes, MSc

War Studies: applied social science, approaches to war, security & development, history of warfare, international relations, violence, the state & global politics, intelligence in war & peace; BA(Hons), MA, MPhil, MRes, PhD

UNIVERSITY OF LONDON; LONDON SCHOOL OF ECONOMICS & POLITICAL SCIENCE
www.lse.ac.uk

Departments at LSE: Accounting, Anthropology, Economics, Finance, Geography and Environment, Government, International History, International Relations, Law, Management, Mathematics, Media and Communications, Philosophy, Logic and Scientific Method, Social Policy, Sociology, Statistics

accounting/organizations & institutions, anthropology, applicable mathematics, biomedicine, bioscience & society, business, management, city design, communications, criminal justice, policy, culture & society, decision science, development studies, economic history, econometrics, economics, economic history, employment relations, environment, European political economy/public & economic policy/ social policy, finance, financial mathematics, gender, geography, global history/media/politics, health economics, human geography, HRM, human rights, information systems, international development/political economy/ relations, law, local economic development, logic and scientific method, management, managerial economics, mathematics, media, methodology, operational research, organizational behaviour, philosophy, political science/economy/sociology/theory, logic and scientific method, politics, public policy, race & ethnicity, real estate economics, regulation, risk and stochastics, social anthroplogy/ policy, social psychology, social research methodology, sociology/contemporary social thought/crime, statistics, urbanisation & development; BA(Hons), BSc(Hons), Dips, EMBA, Ll, M, MBA, MPA, MPhil, MRes, MSc, PhD

UNIVERSITY OF LONDON; LONDON SCHOOL OF JEWISH STUDIES
www.lsjs.ac.uk

ethics, Jewish ethics, Jewish studies; MA

UNIVERSITY OF LONDON; QUEEN MARY
www.qmul.ac.uk

Humanities, Social Sciences and Law

School of Business & Management; www.busman.qmul.ac.uk

management with/business computing, business management with /computer science/accounting/ engineering/science/geography/mathematics/finance/ politics/French/German/Hispanic studies/Russian, international financial management, international HRM and employment relations, management and organisational innovation, marketing; BA(Hons), BSc(Hons), MSc

Dept of Economics; www.econ.qmul.ac.uk

banking, business economics, econometrics, economics, finance, investment law, management, mathematics, mathematics, statistics and financial economics, statistics; BA(Hons), BSc(Econ), MPhil, MSc(Econ), PhD

Centre for Editing Lives and Letters; www.livesandletters.qmul.ac.uk

Renaissance and early modern studies; MRes, PhD

Centre for the Study of Migration; www.politics.qmul.ac.uk/migration

migration, migration and law; MA, MRes, MSc

School of English and Drama; www.sed.qmul.ac.uk

Dept of Drama

drama, drama and English/French/German/Hispanic studies/Russian/film studies, historiography and archives, performance research, theatre and performance theory

Dept of English

English/ and drama/film studies, history/modern language/French/German/Hispanic studies/Russian/ linguistics, English literature, in Renaissance and early modern studies, writing and society 1700–1820, writing in the modern age; BA(Hons), MA, MRes, PhD

School of Languages, Linguistics & Film; www.sllf.qmul.ac.uk

French/German/Hispanic studies/Russian, language with business management/film studies/linguistics, European studies, Anglo-German cultural relations, comparative literature; BA(Hons), MA, PhD

Dept of Geography; www.geog.qmul.ac.uk

cities, economies and social change, cities and cultures, community organising, environmental geography/science, business management, geography, global change: environment, economy and development, globalisation and development, human geography, London studies, physical geography; BA(Hons), BSc(Econ), BSc(Hons), MA, MSc, PhD

Dept of History; www.history.qmul.ac.uk

contemporary/history, journalism, history and politics/film studies/English/French, German language, crusader studies, Islam & the West, European Jewish history, medieval history, Paris studies and twentieth-century history; BA(Hons), MA, PhD

School of Law; www.law.qmul.ac.uk law

banking and finance law, commercial and corporate law, comparative and international dispute resolution, competition law, computer and communications law, economic regulation, English and European law, environmental law, human rights law, intellectual property law, international business law, law and development/politics, legal theory and history, medical law, public international law, public law, tax law, media law; Dips, LlB, LlM, MPhil, MSc, PGDip, PhD

Dept of Philosophy; www.philosophy.qmul.ac.uk

philosophy; BA(Hons), MPhil, PhD

Dept of Politics; www.politics.qmul.ac.uk

politics, global and comparative politics, international relations, migration/and law, public policy, law with management/economics geography/modern languages; BA(Hons), MA, MPhil, MRes, PhD

School of Medicine & Dentistry; www.smd.qmul.ac.uk

Barts and The London School of Medicine and Dentistry; www.smd-edu.qmul.ac.uk/medicine/

biomedical engineering, community health sciences, experimental pathology, infection medicine, integrated clinical studies, medicine, molecular medicine, molecular therapeutics, neuroscience, preparation for clinical practice, psychology, psychiatry, surgery, systems in disease, systems in health, dentistry, oral biology, dental science, dental hygiene, immunity & inflammatory disease, oral cancer

Institute of Cancer

experimental cancer medicine, medical oncology, molecular oncology & imaging, tumour biology

Institute of Cell and Molecular Science

aesthetic surgery, burn care, clinical dermatology, clinical microbiology, gastroenterology

Institute of Dentistry

dental surgery, dentistry, caries, hard tissue and materials research, oral cancer research

Institute of Health Science and Education

primary care, public health, sports & exercise medicine

William Harvey Research Institute

clinical drug development, forensic human identification, healthcare research methods, mechanisms of vascular disease

Wolfson Institute of Preventative Medicine

mental health pathways: transcultural mental healthcare, psychological therapies, screening for Down's Syndrome; BDS, BMedSci, MBBS, MClinDent, MD, MRes, MPhil, MSc, NVQ, PGDip, PhD

Department of Science & Engineering

School of Biological and Chemical Sciences; www.sbcs.qmul.ac.uk

aquatic biology, biochemistry, biology, biomedical sciences, chemistry, freshwater and coastal sciences, genetics, marine ecology and environmental management, medical genetics, microbiology, pharmaceutical chemistry, psychology, zoology; BSc(Hons), Foundation degree, MPhil, MSci, PhD

School of Electronic Engineering & Computer Science; www.eecs.qmul.ac.uk

audio & music systems engineering, bioinformatics, business computing, communication engineering, computer engineering/science, digital music processing, digital signal processing, electrical engineering, electronic engineering, information/systems/management and communication technologies, interactive media design, internet, language & linguistics, multimedia computing, networks, security & surveillence, software engineering, telecommunications, web technologies, wireless networks; BEng, BSc(Eng), MEng, MSc, PhD

School of Engineering and Materials Science; www.sems.qmul.ac.uk

aerospace engineering, avionics, biomedical engineering, engineering science, materials; biomedical materials science/and engineering/design, materials science and engineering/research, dental materials, biomaterials, mechanical engineering, medical materials, medical electronics and physics, medical engineering, sports engineering, sustainable energy engineering/systems; BEng, BSc, MEng, MPhil, MRes, PhD

Interdisciplinary Research Centre in Biomedical Materials; www.materials.qmul.ac.uk

forming and processing technology, hard tissue replacement and biology, interfaces and sensors, orthopaedic cell and tissue engineering; PhD

School of Mathematical Sciences; www.maths.qmul.ac.uk

mathematics, pure mathematics, statistics & financial economics, maths with business management, computing, physics, accountancy; BSc(Hons), MPhil, MSc, MSci, PGDip/Cert, PhD

Dept of Physics; www.phy.qmul.ac.uk

astrophysics, physics, theoretical physics and nanoscience, particle physics, Euromasters degrees; BSc(Hons), MSc, MSci, PGDip, PhD

Research Centre in Psychology; www.psychology.sbcs.qmul.ac.uk

applied psychology, biological and experimental psychology, biology with psychology, computational psychology, language and communication, psychology; BSc(Hons), MPhil, PhD

UNIVERSITY OF LONDON; ROYAL HOLLOWAY www.rhul.ac.uk

Faculty of Arts; www.rhul.ac.uk/departments/arts

Dept of Drama & Theatre; www.rhul.ac.uk/drama

British theatre culture, classics/French/German/Italian/creative writing/music/philosophy, drama/and English, Greek theatre performance, theatre; BA(Hons), MPhil, PhD

Dept of Media Arts; www.rhul.ac.uk/media-arts

documentary by practice, feature film screenwriting, media arts, film & television studies, screenwriting for TV & film; BA(Hons), MA, MPhil, PhD

Dept of Music; www.rhul.ac.uk/Music

advanced musical studies, music, composition, ethnomusicology, historical musicology, performance, music with performance studies; BA(Hons), BMus, MMus, MPhil, PhD

Faculty of History & Social Sciences; www.rhul.ac.uk/departments/hss

Dept of Classics; www.rhul.ac.uk/classics

ancient history, classical art/and archeology classical studies, Greek and Latin languages, literature & philosophy, Hellenic studies, late antique & Byzantine studies; BA(Hons), MPhil, PhD

Dept of Economics; www.rhul.ac.uk/economics

applied microeconomics & political economy, economic history, economics, econometrics, experimental economics, financial & business economics, industrial economics, financial labour market, labour economics, economics of education, microeconomic theory and game theory, macroeconomics, development and finance; BA(Hons), BSc(Econ)Hons, MPhil, MSc, PGDip, PhD

Dept of European Studies; www.rhul.ac.uk/European-Studies

French/Spanish/Italian/German; management/history/ politics/international relations, economics, geography; classics/ computing/music, European integration, global security and international affairs; BA(Hons), MA, MPhil, PhD

Dept of Health and Social Care; www.rhul.ac.uk/health-and-socialcare

criminology (youth justice, risk and violence), health (medical sociology, health, clinical and lifespan psychology), social care (social policy and social work), children & families, BA(Hons), MA, MSc, Grad Dip, PGdip, PhD, MPhil

Dept of History; www.rhul.ac.uk/history

history, public history, history/and French/German/ Spanish/international relations, history of political thought and intellectual history late antique and Byzantine studies, modern history and politics; BA(Hons), MA, MPhil, PhD

School of Management; www.rhul.ac.uk/management

accounting, finance, entrepreneurship, European business, HR, business information systems, marketing, international accounting/business/HRM management/management, leadership and management in health, Asia Pacific business, production & operations, strategy, sustainability and management; BA(Hons), BSc(Hons), MA, MSc, PhD

Dept of Politics & International Relations; www.rhul.ac.uk/politics-and-IR

politics/with international relations/philosophy, economics, European studies/history/politics, politics and international geography, political theory, global politics; BA(Hons), MA, MBA, MSc

Faculty of Science; www.rhul.ac.uk/departments/science

School of Biological Sciences; www.rhul.ac.uk/biological-sciences

biochemistry, biology, biosciences, biotechnology, global health, molecular neuroscience, molecular biology and genetics, biomedical sciences; BA(Hons), BSc(Hons), MSc, PhD

Dept of Computer Science; www.cs.rhul.ac.uk

computer science (information security, AI), bioinformatics, machine learning, constraints, discrete optimisation (langs and architectures), computing & business; BSc(Hons), MPhil, MSc, PhD

Dept of Earth Sciences; www.gl.rhul.ac.uk

environmental geology, environmental geoscience, geology and geography/biology, geoscience, petroleum geology, environmental diagnosis & management; BSc, MSC, MSci, PhD

Dept of Geography; www.gg.rhul.ac.uk

cultural geography, geography, geology, human geography, physical geography, politics and international relations, practising sustainable development, sustainability & management, cultural geography, quarternary science; BA, BSc, MA, MSc, PhD

Dept of Mathematics; www.ma.rhul.ac.uk

information science, mathematics, mathematics for applications, maths of cryptology & communication, statistics; BSc(Hons), MSc, MSci, PhD

Dept of Physics; www.rhul.ac.uk/physics

physics, applied physics, astrophysics, low temperature physics, nanotechnology, particle physics, physics, theoretical physics; BSc(Hons), MPhil, MPhys, MSc, PhD

Dept of Psychology; www.pc.rhul.ac.uk

applied social psychology, human neuroscience, psychology; BSc(Hons), DClinPsych, MSc, PhD

UNIVERSITY OF LONDON; ROYAL VETERINARY COLLEGE
www.rvc.ac.uk

bioveterinary sciences, control of infectious diseases in animals, livestock health and production, veterinary epidemiology, veterinary nursing/medicine, wild animal health, veterinary pathology/ physiotherapy/education, wild animal biology; BSc(Hons), BVetMed, FdSc, MPhil, PhD, MVMed, MRes, MSc, PGDip/Cert

UNIVERSITY OF LONDON; SCHOOL OF ORIENTAL AND AFRICAN STUDIES
www.soas.ac.uk

African language and culture/literature/ politics/ studies, ancient Near Eastern languages/studies, anthropological research methods, anthropology of food/media, applied Japanese linguistics, applied linguistics and language pedagogy, Arabic cultural studies/ literature, Arabic/and Islamic studies, Asian politics, banking law, Chinese (modern and classical), Chinese law/ literature/studies, comparative literature (Africa/Asia), critical media and cultural studies, development and globalisation, development economics/studies, development studies/central Asia, dispute and conflict resolution, economics: Africa/ south Asia/Asia Pacific region/Middle East, economics, environmental law, ethnomusicology, finance and development/financial law, gender studies, geography, Georgian, Bengal, Burmese (Myanmar), global cinemas and the transcultural, global media and postnational communication, Hausa, Hebrew and Israeli studies, Hindi, history of art/archaeology/ Asia/Africa & Europe, history, history: Asia/Africa, human rights, conflict and justice, Indonesian, international and comparative legal studies, international and comparative/commercial law, international economic law, international management (China/Japan/ Middle East and north Africa), international politics, Islamic law, Japanese literature/studies, Japanese, Korean, Korean literature/studies, languages and cultures of south Asia, languages and literatures of south east Asia, law in the Middle East and north Africa, law, culture and society, development and governance, linguistics, medical anthropology, Middle East politics/ studies, migration and diaspora studies, migration mobility and development, music studies, Nepali, Pacific Asian studies, religions, performance, Persian, political economy of development, Sanskrit, Sinology, social anthropology, south Asian area studies/law/studies, state, society and development, study of religions, sustainable development, Taiwan studies, Thai, translation (Asian and African languages); BA(Hons), LlB, LlM, MMus, MPhil, MSc, PGDip, PhD

UNIVERSITY OF LONDON; THE SCHOOL OF PHARMACY
www.pharmacy.ac.uk

clinical pharmacy, drug delivery, drug discovery, medicine management, pharmacognosy, pharmacy, pharmacy practice; Certs, MPharm, MSc, PGDip, PhD

UNIVERSITY OF LOUGHBOROUGH
www.lboro.ac.uk

Faculty of Engineering; www.lboro.ac.uk/eng

Aeronautical and Automotive Engineering; www.lboro.ac.uk/departments/tt/

advanced methods/aeronautical engineering, automotive engineering, automotive systems engineering

Chemical Engineering; www.lboro.ac.uk/departments/cg

advanced chemical engineering, advanced process engineering, chemical engineering/with environmental protection/management, /IT pharmaceutical engineering

Civil and Building Engineering; www.lboro.ac.uk/departments/cv

air transport management, architectural engineering and design management, civil engineering, commercial management and quantity surveying, building surveying, construction management/ project management/construction business management, transport and business management, building surveying, low carbon builiding design, sustainable transport & travel building, infrastructure in emergencies, water and waste engineering/environmental management

Electronic and Electrical Engineering; www.lboro.ac.uk/departments/el

advanced systems engineering, digital communication systems, electronic and electrical engineering, electronics and computer systems engineering/software engineering, media communications, networked communications, renewable energy systems technology, signal processing in communication systems, systems engineering

Mechanical and Manufacturing; www.lboro.ac.uk/departments/mm

advanced manufacturing engineering and management, engineering design, manufacture, innovative manufacturing engineering, mechanical engineering, mechatronics, product design engineering, sports technology

Water Engineering and Development Centre (WEDC)

infrastructure in emergencies, sustainable infrastructure services management, sustainability in the built environment, water and environmental management, water and waste engineering; BEng, BSc(Hons), MDes, MRes, MSc, PhD

Faculty of Science; www.lboro.ac.uk/sci

Faculty of Chemistry; www.lboro.ac.uk/departments/cm

analytical and pharmaceutical science, analytical chemistry, environmental science, chemistry, forensic analysis, sports science, chemistry and information technology, medicinal and pharmaceutical chemistry, medicinal chemistry

Dept of Computer Science; www.lboro.ac.uk/departments/co

applied computing/and maths, computer science/and artificial intelligence/e-business/maths, computing and management, digital imaging computer graphics and vision, information management and computing, information technology management for business, computing and network security, network multimedia and internet computing

Dept of Ergonomics (Human Sciences); www.lboro.ac.uk/departments/hu

ergonomics (human factors), ergonomics for health professionals, human factors in transport/inclusive design; BSc(Hons), MSc, PhD, Dip

Dept of Information Sciences; www.lboro.ac.uk/departments/is

information management & business studies/computing/ business technology, information and knowledge management, library management, publishing with English/e-business, web development and design; BSc(Hons), MPhil, PhD

Dept of Materials; www.lboro.ac.uk/departments/materials

automotive materials, design with engineering materials, materials engineering, materials for industry, packaging technology, polymer technology; BEng/MEng, BSc(Hons), Diploma in Industrial Studies, MSc, PG Dip/Cert, PhD

Dept of Mathematics; www.lboro.ac.uk/departments/ma

financial mathematical finance, industrial mathematical modelling, IT and mathematics, mathematical processes in finance, mathematics, mathematics and accounting & financial management/management/sports science/computing, mathematics with economics/physics; BSc(Hons), MSc, PhD

Dept of Physics; www.lboro.ac.uk/departments/ph

astrophysics and cosmology, engineering physics, materials physics and applications, nanoscience, physics, physics & maths/management/sports science, physics with cosmology, psychophysics, quantum information and computing, science of the internet, surface physics, theoretical condensed matter physics; BSc(Hons), MSc, PhD

Faculty of Social Sciences and Humanities; www.lboro.ac.uk/ssh

Loughborough University Business School; www.lboro.ac.uk/departments/bs

accounting and financial management, banking, finance and management, international business/management, management business analysis and management, management sciences, marketing and management, retailing; BSc(Hons), MBA, MPhil, MRes, MSc, PhD

Dept of Economics; www.lboro.ac.uk/departments/ec

banking and finance, business economics and finance, economics, economics with accounting, economics and finance, financial markets, international banking, international economics, money, banking and finance; BSc(Hons), MSc, PhD

Dept of English & Drama; www.lboro.ac.uk/departments/ea

creative writing, drama, English, film, history, North American literature, performance and multi-media, sports science; BA(Hons), MA, PhD

Dept of Politics, International Relations & European Studies; www.lboro.ac.uk/departments/eu

history and geography/English, international relations, politics, research methods (European and international); BSc(Hons), MPhil, MSc, PhD

Dept of Geography; www.lboro.ac.uk/departments/gy
environmental monitoring, geography, geography and management/economics, global transformations, globalization, human geography research, international financial & political relations, space & sport; BSc, MPhil, MSc, PhD

Dept of Sport, Exercise and Health Sciences; www.lboro.ac.uk/departments/ssehs
human biology, physical activity and health, physical education/and sport pedagogy, psychology, sociology of sport, sport biomechanics, sport coaching, sport and exercise nutrition/psychology, exercise science/physiology, sport management/science; BSc(Hons), MPhil, MSc, PhD

School of Art & Design; www.lboro.ac.uk/departments/ac
2D and 3D visualisation, 3D design, fine art, studio ceramics, textiles, visual communication, art & design, art design & performance by practice, art in the public sphere; BA(Hons), MA, MPhil, MSc, PhD

Dept of Social Sciences; www.lboro.ac.uk/departments/ss
communications and media studies, criminology and criminal justice/social policy, cultural sociology/cultural analysis, media and cultural analysis, social science research, social psychology, sociology; BSc(Hons), MPhil, MSc, PhD

Teacher Education Unit; www.lboro.ac.uk/departments/teu
design and technology, physical education, science; MSc, PGCE

UNIVERSITY OF MANCHESTER
www.manchester.ac.uk

Faculty of Engineering and Physical Sciences; www.eps.manchester.ac.uk

School of Chemical Engineering and Analytical Science; www.ceas.manchester.ac.uk
biotechnology, chemical engineering with /biotechnology/chemistry/environmental technology/industrial experience/business management, chemical process design, chemical engineering with design, environmental & sustainable technology, process design for energy & the environment, refinery design and operation; BEng, MEng, MSc, PhD

School of Chemistry; www.chemistry.manchester.ac.uk
biological, inorganic, materials, chemistry, forensic & analytical/medicinal chemistry, organic, physical & theoretical chemistry, patent law; BSc(Hons), EngD, MChem, MEnt, MPhil, MSc, PhD

School of Computer Science; www.cs.manchester.ac.uk
artificial intelligence, applications of NLP, computer science, computer security, computer systems engineering, computing for business applications, data and knowledge modelling, digital technology, distributed computing, internet computer technology, multicore computing, semantic web technology, software engineering BSc(Hons), MEng, MEnt, MPhil, MSc, PhD

School of Earth, Atmospheric & Environmental Sciences; www.seas.manchester.ac.uk
earth sciences, environmental sciences/studies, geochemistry, geography, geology, planetary science, experimental & resource geology, petroleum geoscience/engineering, pollution and environmental control, policy and management; BSc(Hons), MEarthSci, MEng, MSc, PhD

School of Electrical and Electronic Engineering; www.eee.manchester.ac.uk
communication engineering, advanced control & systems engineering, digital image & signal processing, electrical & electronic engineering, electronic systems engineering, electrical energy conversion systems, electrical power systems engineering, mechatronic engineering, nanoelectronics, sensors and electronic instrumentation; BEng(Hons), Dip, BSc(Hons), EngD, MEng(Hons), MPhil, MSc, PhD

School of Materials; www.materials.manchester.ac.uk
advanced /engineering materials, biomedical materials science, corrosion control engineering, design manufacture for fashion retailing, materials science &

engineering, metallic materials, nanostructured materials, paper science, polymer materials, textile science & technology, textile design, marketing & management of fashion textiles; BSc, MEng, MPhil, PhD

School of Mathematics; www.maths.manchester.ac.uk

applied maths, biostatistics, computational science, financial mathematics, mathematical finance, mathematics, mathematical logic, numerical analysis, pure maths, probability and statistics, quantitative finance and financial engineering, statistics, theoretical and applied fluid dynamics; BSc, MMath, MPhil, MSc, PhD

School of Mechanical, Aerospace and Civil Engineering; www.mace.manchester.ac.uk

advanced manufacturing technology & systems management, aerospace engineering, civil engineering, maintenance engineering & asset management, management of projects, mechanical engineering, structural engineering, thermal power & fluid engineering, theoretical & applied fluid dynamics; BEng, EngD, MEng, MEnt, MPhil, MSc, PhD

School of Physics & Astronomy; www.physics.manchester.ac.uk

physics & astrophysics, biological physics, mathematics and physics, nuclear science & technology, particle physics, photon science (laser photonics), physics, technical physics, theoretical physics; BSc, EngD, MMath & Phys, MPhys, MSc, PhD

Faculty of Humanities; www.humanities.manchester.ac.uk

School of Arts, Histories and Cultures; www.arts.manchester.ac.uk

American studies, ancient history, applied theatre, art gallery and museum studies, archeology/(identity, complex soceties, neolithic), art history, arts management, policy and practice, biblical studies, classical studies, classics, comparative religion, composition, the holy and the supernatural, contemporary literature and culture, creative writing, cultural history, drama, early modern history, economic and social history, economics, electroacoustic music composition, English literature, gender, sexuality and culture, Greek, history, humanitarianism & conflict response, Latin, medieval studies, modern British/European history, music, musicology, performance, screen & visual cultures, politics, post-1900 literatures, postcolonial literatures and cultures, religion and social history/sociology/theology, screen studies, social anthropology, south Asian studies, Jewish studies, theatre studies, theology, culture and society, Victorian times, war, culture and history, world history; BA(Hons), MA, MMus, PhD

School of Education; www.education.manchester.ac.uk

community and youth work studies, counselling, digital technology, communication & education, education, educational leadership and improvement/research/technology & TESOL, HE, inclusive education, language, literacy & communication, leadership and school improvement, learning disability studies, management & leisure, PGCE primary/secondary business education/secondary/design technology/secondary English/secondary mathematics/secondary modern languages/secondary science, profound & complex learning disability, psychology of education, supervision of counselling and the helping professions, TESOL; BA(Hons), DCons, DEd, EdD, MA, MEd, MPhil, MSc, PGCE, PGCert/Dip, PhD, UGCert/Dip

School of Environment and Development; www.sed.manchester.ac.uk

architecture, city & regional development, conflict and reconstruction, development economics/ finance/ management/ projects/informatics/policy, environment & development, HRM/HRD/environmental / governance/impact/management/monitoring, geography, geology, GIS, global urban development and planning, globalisation and development, industry, trade and development, international development, planning and landscape, politics & governance, poverty, rural development, social policy and social development, town & country planning, urban regeneration development, urbanism; BSc, MA, MPlan, MSc, MTCP, PGDip, PhD

School of Languages, Linguistics and Cultures; www.llc.manchester.ac.uk

Chinese studies, contemporary China, East Asian studies, English language, European languages and cultures, E.European studies, French, Italian, German, Hebrew studies, history, history of art, Islamic studies and Arabic, Italian studies, Italian, Japanese studies, Jewish studies, Latin American cultural/ studies, linguistics, Middle Eastern languages, Middle Eastern studies, modern languages, Persian, Portuguese, Russian, Russian and east European studies, screen studies, social anthropology, sociology, Spanish, translation & interpreting studies, Turkish; BA(Hons), MA, MML, MPhil, PhD

School of Law; www.law.manchester.ac.uk

law, bioethics and medical jurisprudence, corporate governance, crime/law & society, criminology/law with French law, European law & governance, health care ethics, intellectual property law, international business & commercial law, international financial law, international trade transactions, law & economics/development/society/criminology/politics, law, socio-legal studies; BA, LlB, LlM, MA, MPhil, MRes, PGDip, PhD

Manchester Business School; www.mbs.manchester.ac.uk

accounting, American business studies, analytics/OR & risk analysis, business economics, Chinese business, commercial management, corporate communications, decision science, e-business technology, economics, e-government, finance, financial markets and management, global business analysis, healthcare management, HR, industrial relations, information systems, information technology management, innovation management and entrepreneurship, international business, finance, management and economics/studies/marketing/operations and technology, information systems/organisation & management, IT management for business, managerial psychology, management (accounting & finance/decision science/ HR/international studies/marketing/information systems), management accounting, management of science, marketing, mathematical finance, operations, project and supply chain management, organisational psychology, public administration, quantitative finance: financial reputation management, risk analysis; BA, BSc, MBA, MBus, MDA, MEnt, MPA, MRes, MSc, PhD

School of Social Sciences; www.socialsciences.manchester.ac.uk

accounting, anthropology, archaeology, business studies, criminology, development studies, economic & social history, economics, human rights, international development: international business/finance/economics/politics/relations, political economy/science/ theory, philosophy, politics, social anthropology, social change, social history, statistics, sociological research, sociology; BAEcon, BSc, MA, MRes, MSc, PGDip, PhD

Centre for Continuing Education, Centre for Educational Leadership; www.cel.manchester.ac.uk

educational leadership, process consultancy; MEd, PGCert

Faculty of Life Sciences; www.lf.manchester.ac.uk

anatomical sciences, biochemistry, bioinformatics, biological sciences, biology, biomechanics, biomedical and forensic studies in Egyptology, biomedical sciences, biotechnology, cell biology, cancer biology, cognitive neuroscience and psychology, computational neuroscience, developmental biology, genetics, history of science, technology and medicine, immunology and immunogenetics, integrative biology. life sciences, medical biochemistry, microbiology, molecular parasitology & vector biology, neuroscience, optometry, pharmacology, physiology, plant science, post-genomic biology, structural biology and biophysics, zoology; BSc, MNeuroSci, MRes, MSc, PhD

Faculty of Medical & Human Sciences; www.mhs.manchester.ac.uk

School of Dentistry; www.dentistry.manchester.ac.uk

dental implantology, dental public health, dentistry, endodontics, fixed and removable prosthodontics, oral and maxillofacial surgery, oral health sciences, orthodontics, periodontology, restorative & aesthetic dentistry; BDS, BSc, MDen, MDPH, MSc, MSc(Clin), PGDip/Cert, PhD

School of Medicine; www.medicine.manchester.ac.uk

cardiovascular sciences, maternal and fetal health, medical sciences, medicine, oncology, pathology, primary care, public health, tissue engineering for regenerative medicine, translational medicine: inter molecular medicine/pharmaceutical cancer; ChB, MB, MD/ChM, MPH, MPhil, MRes, MSc, PGCert, PGDip, PhD

School of Nursing and Midwifery & Social Work; www.nursing.manchester.ac.uk

advanced nursing/midwifery studies, adv audiology studies, health and social care, midwifery, adult nursing/child nursing/mental health nursing, professional health studies, cancer & palliative care, critical/ surgical care, clinical care, maternal & child care, psychosocial interventions for psychosis, dementia, social work; BMidwif, BNurs, MA, MClinRes, MPhil, MRes, MSc, PgCert, PgD, PGDip, PhD

School of Pharmacy & Pharmaceutical Sciences; www.pharmacy.manchester.ac.uk

clinical & health services pharmacy, pharmaceutical industrial/engineering advanced training, pharmacy; MPharm, MPhil, MSc, PGCert/Dip, PhD

School of Psychological Sciences; www.psych-ci.manchester.ac.uk
audiology, clinical and health psychology, cognitive brain imaging, cognitive neuroscience and psychology, deaf education, pyschology, speech & language therapy; BSc, MPhil, MRes, MSc, PGDip, PhD

MANCHESTER METROPOLITAN UNIVERSITY
www.mmu.ac.uk

Faculty of Art & Design; www.artdes.mmu.ac.uk
acting, architecture, art and design, art direction, contemporary film and video, professional practice for artists and designers, creative practice, design/ and art direction, embroidery, fashion, fashion design and technology, film and media studies, filmmaking, fine art, history of art and design, illustration, animation, interactive arts, interior design, international creative advertising, landscape architecture, media arts, photography, visual culture; BA(Hons), BArch, BL and Arch, MA, MEnterprise, MPhil, PGDip/Cert, PhD

Faculty of Health, Psychology & Social Care; www.hpsc.mmu.ac.uk

Health Professions
clinical counselling, health & social care, manual therapy, musculoskeletal physiotherapy, physiotherapy, psychology & speech, speech pathology and therapy, teaching speech reading; BSc(Hons), CertHE, FdA, MPhil, MSc, PhD

Nursing
community health, contemporary health practice, nursing/adult branch, practice development, health visiting, school nursing; BSc, BSc(Hons), MSc, PGDipPsychology, postgrad modular

Social Work and Social Change
social change/communication studies/community and society/health and social care/policy and management, social work; MA, MPhil, Msc, PGDip, PhD

Faculty of Humanities, Law & Social Science; www.hlss.mmu.ac.uk

Criminology
criminology; BA(Hons)

Economics; www.hlss.mmu.ac.uk/economics
BA(Hons), BSc(Hons), MA/MPhil/PhD

English; www.hlss.mmu.ac.uk/english
creative writing, American literature/creative writing/film, English studies: contemporary literature and film/critical theory/the Gothic, TEFL; BA(Hons), MA, MPhil, PGDip, PhD

European Studies
European urban cultures, globalisation, societies and cultures; MA

History & Economic History; www.hlss.mmu.ac.uk/history
medieval and early modern/ modern/social history; BA(Hons), MA, MPhil, PhD

Information & Communications
communications, digital media, information, information management, librarianship, library management, web development; BA(Hons), BSc(Hons), MA/MSc/MPhil/PhD

Islamic
Islamic and Middle Eastern studies; BA(Hons), CertHE

Languages
Arabic, Chinese or Japanese, EFL, French, French studies, German, Italian, linguistics, Spanish, BA(Hons), MA, MPhil, PhD

Law; www.hlss.mmu.ac.uk/law
law, legal practice (LPC), legal practice at the bar; PGDip, LLB(Hons), LLM, MPhil, PhD

Politics and philosophy; www.hlss.mmu.ac.uk/polphil
politics, public policy, public services, philosophy, European philosophy; BA(Hons), BSc(Hons), MA, MPhil, PhD

Sociology; www.hlss.soc.mmu.ac.uk/
criminology, European urban cultures, globalisation, societies and cultures, sociology; BA(Hons), MA, MPhil, PhD

Institute of education

childhood studies, design and technology, early childhood studies, primary education, professional studies (early years education/careers education and guidance/education/special educational needs), school administration/business management, secondary education, specific learning difficulties, supporting teaching and learning, teaching, youth & community work; BA(Hons), BA/BSc, Certs, EdD, FD, MA, MPhil, MSc, PGDip/Cert, PhD

Faculty of Science & Engineering; www.sci-eng.mmu.ac.uk

School of Biology, Chemistry and Health Science Division of Biology; www.sci-eng.mmu.ac.uk/bchs/biology

animal behaviour, biology, cell and molecular biology, conservation biology, human behaviour ecology, microbiology, ornithology, tropical ecology, wildlife biology, zoo conservation biology, zoo studies; BSc(Hons), HNC, MPhil, MSc, PGDip/Cert, PhD

Division of Chemistry & Materials; www.sci-eng.mmu.ac.uk/chemistry

applied/chemistry, pharmaceutical chemistry, chemical & pharmaceutical science, forensic chemistry, medicinal & biological chemistry; BSc(Hons), HNC, MChem(Hons), MSc, PGCert/Dip

Divison of Health Science; www.sci-eng.mmu.ac.uk/bchs/healthscience

biomedical science, cellular pathology, clinical/applied chemistry, clinical physiology, dental technology, haematology, human biology, medical microbiology, transfusion science, medicinal and biological chemistry, pharmaceutical chemistry, pharmaceutical science, biological and biomedical psychology physiology with pharmacology; BSc(Hons), MPhil, MSc/PGDip/PgCert, PhD

Dept of Computing and Mathematics; www.sci-eng.docm.mmu.ac

applied/adv/computing, computer games technology, computer science, digital media computing, enterprise computing, forensic computing, information systems, internet computing, mobile computing, multimedia computing, software engineering, mathematics; financial mathematics; BSc, FdSc, MPhil, MSc, PhD

Department of Engineering & Technology; www.sci-eng.mmu.ac.uk/engtech

aircraft maintenance technology, automation & control, automotive engineering, computer-aided engineering, computer and communication engineering/network technology, electrical, electronic engineering, electronic systems design, engineering, manufacture & management, mechanical design & technology, mechanical engineering, mechatronics, media technology, post-production technology for film, TV & CGI, product design & technology, sports tech; BEng(Hons), BSc(Hons), HND, MSc, PhD

Dept of Environmental and Geographical Sciences; www.sci-eng.egs.mmu.ac.uk

climate change, countryside management, ecological monitoring, ecology and conservation, environment & enterprise, environmental and climate change/management and sustainability/development/business, environmental science, geography, GIS & spatial analysis, human geography, physical geography, sustainable aviation; BSc(Hons), MPhil, MSc, PhD

Hollings Faculty; www.hollings.mmu.ac.uk

Department of Clothing Design & Technology

clothing, clothing technology, fashion buying/materials, fashion design, fashion marketing

Department of Food and Tourism Management

clothing/ product development, consumer marketing, environmental health, events management, food management/marketing, hospitality/and licensed retail management/business management/culinary arts/tourism, food and nutrition, food technology, human nutrition, international hospitality management, tourism management/and e-business, trading standards; BA(Hons), BSc(Hons), FdA, FdSc, HND, MA, MPhil, PhD

Business School; www.business.mmu.ac.uk

accounting, advertising management, brand management, business, business administration/enterprise/management, finance, business, digital marketing communications/marketing communication/publishing, economics, finance, financial planning & wealth management, financial services, health & social care, HRM, international business/ management/creative advertising/HRM/PR, leadership, logistics and supply chain management, marketing/communications, place management, PR, practising management, professional accounting, project management, strategic financial mgt, business information technology management, sustainable business; BA(Hons), MA, MBA, MPhil, MRes, MSc, PGDip/Cert, PhD

MMU Cheshire; www.cheshire.mmu.ac.uk

Dept of Business & Management Studies

Dept of Contemporary Arts

Dept of Exercise & Sports Science

abuse studies, applied social studies, art media performance, business, business management (financial management/HRM/ legal studies/marketing, childhood /& youth studies, coaching /& sports studies, community arts, contemporary theatre & performance, creative music production/, crime studies, dance, drama, early years, education, English, film, TV /& cultural studies, financial mgt, HRM, legal studies, leisure mgt, music, marketing/ management, organisational change and development management, outdoor studies, philosophy, PE & pedagogy, pop, primary education, psychology/of sport & exercise science, sports/leisure event management, sport development/managegment/science, strategic leadership and change; BA/BSc, BA(Hons), FD, HNC, HND, MBA, MSc, MPhil, PhD

Dept of Contemporary Arts; www.cheshire.mmu.ac.uk/dcu

abuse studies, art media performance, community arts, contemporary arts, contemporary theatre & performance, creative music production, creative writing, dance, drama, music, popular music; BA(Hons), MA, MPhil, PhD

Dept of Exercise and Sports Science; www.cheshire.mmu.ac.uk/exspsci

coaching and sport development, coaching studies, sport development, exercise and physical activitiy, exercise & sport (biomechanics/coaching studies/ physiology/psychology/sport development/sports injury), leisure management, sport & exercise science, psychology of sport and exercise; BA, BSc, Foundation degree, MA, MSc

MIDDLESEX UNIVERSITY
www.mdx.ac.uk

School of Arts and Education; www.mdx.ac.uk/schools/arts

Art & Design

animation, 3D animation & games, art /& design, interior & applied arts, digital arts, fashion/design/ textiles, fine art/& critical theory, interior architecture, jewellery & accessories, photography, product design, robotics, sonic arts; BA(Hons), FdA, MA, MSc

Dance, Music and the Theatre

choreography, dance performance/studies, education(drama), music and arts management, jazz, music omposition/performance, popular music, technical theatre design/performance/solo performance, theatre arts/ directing; BA(Hons), BMus, MA, MMus

English Literature and Language

English/English literature /& media, TEFL, English language

Film, Television & Media Arts

digital arts, film & creative writing, media & cultural studies, film studies, film, video and interactive arts, sonics, television journalism, television production/ technical arts; BA(Hons)

Media, Culture and Communication

advertising, PR and media, communications management, creative and media writing, English literature/ journalism studies, journalism and communication studies/media and cultural studies/magazine publishing/and media/journalism and media/cultural studies, design for interactive media, moving image; BA(Hons), MA

Language and Translation Studies

international business & Arabic/Mandarin/Russian/ Spanish, TEFL, translation theory and practice of translation; BA(Hons), MA

Philosophy

aesthetics and art theory, contemporary critical theory, fine art & critical theory, modern European philosophy, philosophy; MA

Teaching and Education

early childhood studies, early years, education studies/and religious studies/English language/English literature, learning & teaching studies, professional studies; PGCE qualifications in range of subjects, supported education, TESOL/with applied linguistics; BA(Hons), FdA, MA, PGCE, PGCert

Middlesex University Business School; www.mdx.ac.uk/schools/bs

Accounting and Finance

accounting, business accounting, business economics, corporate accountability, finance, financial management, investment, statistics; BA(Hons), BSc(Hons), MSc

Business and Management

business administration, business and business economics/HRM/marketing, business studies international business and Arabic/Mandarin/Russian/ Spanish, business & statistics, business management, engineering management, engineering projects management, international business management/for China, management, strategic management & marketing; BA(Hons), BSc(Hons), MSc, MBA

Economics & Statistics

banking, business & business economics, economics, finance, international business economics, international finance, money, business & statistics; BSc(Hons), MA, MBA, MSc

Human Resource Management

business & HRM, personal and professional development, employment law, hospitality management, HRM/and marketing, HRD, international HRM and employment relations/law, recruitment practice; AdvDip, BA(Hons), FdA, PGCert, PGDip

Marketing and Enterprise

health and social marketing, international and cross-cultural marketing, marketing, marketing communications/management, psychology with marketing, strategic management and marketing; BA(Hons), BSc(Hons), MA, MSc

Law

business/HR & employment law/business, human rights & business, international business law, business, minorities, rights & the law; BA(Hons), GradDip, LlBHons, LlM, MA, PGDip

The School of Engineering and Information Sciences; www.mdx.ac.uk/schools/eis

Business Information Systems

business information systems/management/technology, computing, data and knowledge, engineering, digital forensics, electronic security, enterprise management technologies, forensic computing, information technology & business, information systems; BSc(Hons), MSc

Computer Communications

computer communication/networks, computing, digital inclusion, mobile computing, network programming, network management and security, networks, professional network engineering, telecommunication engineering; BEng, BSc(Hons), MSc

Computing and Multimedia Technology

biomedical modelling and informatics, computer science, computing, graphics and games, information technology, interactive systems design, internet application development, multimedia computing, networking, software engineering; BSc, MSc

Product Design and Engineering

design engineering, engineering management, engineering project management, interaction design, manufacturing management, product design, robotics; BA(Hons), BSc(Hons), MSc

School of Health & Social Sciences; www.mdx.ac.uk/schools/hssc

Biomedical and Biological Sciences

biomedical modelling and informatics, biomedical science, bioscience, clinical physiology, obstestrics & gynaecological science, medical microbiology, molecular pathology, sports biomedicine; BSc(Hons), MSc

Complementary Health Sciences

Ayurvedic medicine, Chinese acupuncture, Chinese herbal formulae, traditional Chinese medicine; AdvDip, BSc(Hons), MSc

Criminology & Sociology

community safety, criminal justice, criminology/psychology/sociology, crime, conflict and control, drugs & alcohol, forensic computing, forensic psychology, policing, criminology, public protection, sociology with crime/psychology, youth justice; BA(Hons), BSc(Hons), MA, MSc

Environment & Public Health
environmental health, public health, health promotion, occupational safety & health, food premises, risk management, environmental pollution control, social policy, sustainable development, sustainable environmental management, complementary health; BSc(Hons), MA, MSc

Nursing, Midwifery & Health
child, adolescent, nursing (child, adult, mental health), acute & critical care, children, dual diagnosis, drugs & alcohol, families & public health, health promotion, midwifery, nursing studies; specialist practitioner, AdvDip, BSc, BSc(Hons), Dip, MSc, PGCert

Social Science, Politics & Development
criminology, global social science, housing studies, international political studies, international relations/development, psychoanalysis, social science, sociology, politics, youth work; BA, BSc, CertHE, FdA, FdSc, MA

Social Work
social work; BA(Hons), MA

Psychology
applied psychology, criminology with forensic psychology, health psychology, psychology, psychology with criminology/sociology/counselling skills/marketing HRM; BA(Hons), BSc(Hons), GradDip; MSc

Sport & Exercise Science
coaching and sports development, sport and exercise science, sport rehabilitation and injury prevention, strength and conditioning; BSc(Hons), FdSc, MSc

NAPIER UNIVERSITY
www.napier.ac.uk

The Business School; www.napier.ac.uk/business-school

Accounting, Economics and Statistics
accounting, corporate strategy, economics, entrepreneurship, finance, financial services, HRM, international finance, investment promotion and economic development, management, marketing management, professional banking, wealth management; BA(Hons), DBA, MPhil, MSc, PhD

Management & Law
business & enterprise, business management, business studies, finance, criminal justice, entrepreneurship, health & social welfare law, HRM, international business management – international business studies, managerial leadership, marketing; BA/BA(Hons), BMA, LlB, LlM, MBA, MSc

Marketing Tourism and Languages
festival and event and hospitality/marketing/ management, hospitality management/festival & event management, with entrepreneurship/language/HRM, heritage and cultural tourism management, intercultural business communication/communication with TESOL, international business languages/event & festival management/marketing, languages and intercultural communication, marketing management, tourism and airline management; BA, BA(Hons), MSc

Faculty of Engineering, Computing and Creative Industries; www.napier.ac.uk/fecci

School of Computing
advanced networking, applied informatics, business information systems/technology, computer networks & distributed systems, computing security & forensics, computing, digital media/networking, embedded computer systems, information systems for financial services, interactive media design/systems/entertainment & games development, internet computing, network computing, web-based systems, security & digital forensics, software engineering/web; BEng, BSc, MPhil, MSc, PhD

Creative Industries
adv film practice, advertising, PR, communication, creative writing, design and digital arts, English, film, graphic design, interaction design, interactive entertainment, interior architecture, journalism, music (pop), music industries, photography, product design, publishing, screen project development, screenwriting, sound production, television; BA/BA(Hons), BDes, BDes(Hons), BMus, BMus(Hons), MDes, MFA, MSc, PGCert/Dip

Engineering & the Built Environment
architectural technology & building performance, building surveying, built environment, timber

engineering, civil engineering, communication engineering, computer engineering, construction engineering /and project management, electronic/computer/electrical engineering, electronic & communication engineering, energy and environmental engineering, engineering design, environmental sustainability, information technology, materials engineering, mechanical engineering, mechatronics, polymer engineering, product design engineering, product manufacture, project management, property and construction management, property development and valuation, investment, quantity surveying, safety and environmental management, sports technology, structural engineering, timber industry management, transport management, transport planning and engineering, transportation engineering; BSc/BSs(Hons), BEng, BEng/Hons, MEng, MSc, MSci, PGCert/Dip

Faculty of Health, Life & Social Science; www.napier.ac.uk/fhlss

Health & Social Sciences

career guidance & development, complementary healthcare (aromatherapy / reflexology), complementary therapies practitioner, criminology, psychology, with sport & exercise science/sociology, social science, reflexology, social research; BA(Hons), MSc, PGCert/Dip

Life Sciences

aquatic ecosystem management, biological science, biotechnology, animal biology, biomedical science, conservation, drug design, ecotourism, environmental biology, forensic biology, herbal medicine, immunology & toxicology, marine & freshwater biology, microbiology & biotechnology, pharmaceutical design, sport science, wildlife biology & conservation; BSc(Hons), MSc

School of Nursing, Midwifery and Social Care

adult nursing, child health, intellectual disability, mental health, midwifery, social care, veterinary nursing, advanced practice; BMid, BN, Diploma HE, MSc

UNIVERSITY OF NEWCASTLE UPON TYNE
www.ncl.ac.uk

Faculty of Humanities and Social Sciences; www.ncl.ac.uk/hass

School of Architectural Planning and Landscape; www.ncl.ac.uk/apl

architecture/and planning, architectural practice/studies/management, digital architecture, geography planning, planning & and environmental, research, planning in deve;oping countries, planning studies, planning for sustainable & climate change, town planning, transportation planning & policy, urban design; BA, BArch, Cert, Dip, MA, MPhil, MSc, PGCert, PhD

School of Arts and Cultures/music; www.ncl.ac.uk/sacs

folk and traditional music, music, music and education, popular and contemporary music, theoretical & cultural musical origins, ethnomusicology, early & medieval music; BA, BMus, Diploma, MA, MLitt, MMus, MPhil, PhD

Fine Art

fine art, history of art; BA(Hons), MFA, MPhil, PhD

Digital Media

digital media/theoretical foundations/techn; Dip, MA, MRes

Museum, Gallery and Heritage Studies

art museum & gallery education/gallery studies, art as enterprise, heritage education & interpretation/management, museum studies; MA, MPhil, MPrac, PGCert, PGDip, PhD

Media & Cultural Studies

media & jounalism, international multimedia journalism, mass media, community culture; BA(Hons), MA, PhD

Business School; www.ncl.ac.uk/nubs

accounting, arts, banking, business accounting, business management, e-business and information systems, economics, finance, e-marketing, financial & business economics, financial regulation, innovation, creativity and entrepreneurship, HRM, international business management/economics and finance/financial analysisi/HR/ marketing, Islamic finance, law, management, marketing, operations management and logistics, strategic planning and investment, quantitative finance & marketing; BA, BSc, DBA, MA, MBA, MSc, PhD

School of Education, Communication and Language Sciences; www.ncl.ac.uk/ecls

applied linguistics and TESOL, cross-cultural communication and applied linguistics/education/international management/marketing/international relations/media studies, education media & journalism, PR, PGCE primary/secondary, educational psychology, practictioner enquiry, education, speech & language science, languge pathology, international development/multimedia, journalism, language and linguistics, media, communication and cultural studies, PR; BA(Hons), BSc(Hons), DedPsych, EdD, MA, MEd, MSc, PGCE, PhD

Combined Studies Centre

combined studies; BS(Hons)

School of English Literature, Language, Linguistics; www.ncl.ac.uk/elll

English language, literature, literary studies: writing, memory, culture, linguistics, creative writing, language acquisition, modern and contemporary studies; BA(Hons), MA, MLitt, MPhil, PGCert, PhD

Geography, Politics and Sociology; www.ncl.ac.uk/gps

applied policy research, critical geopolitics/global justice and ethics/globalisation, economics, European union studies, gender research, geography, government, health research, human geography, international political economy/studies, regional development, physical geography, planning, politics, poverty and development, social research, social science, sociology; BA(Hons), BSc(Hons), MA, MSc, PhD

Global Urban Research Unit; www.ncl.ac.uk/guru

cities and international development, place and social cohesion, unit spatial planning and environment; MPhil, PhD

Institute of Health and Society

public health & health service; MSc, PGDip/Cert

School of Historical Studies; www.ncl.ac.uk/historical

ancient history, archaeology, archaeology of historic periods, British history, Byzantine archaeology/studies, classical studies, classics, east Asian history, European history, Greek and Roman archaeology, history /& politics, history of medicine, history of the Americas, neolithic and bronze age Europe, politics, Roman frontier studies; BA(Hons), MA, MLitt, MPhil, PhD

Centre for History of Medicine; www.ncl.ac.uk/historical

history of medicine, medical history; BA(Hons), MLitt, MPhil, PhD

Centre for Knowledge, Innovation, Technology and Enterprise

economic development, older enterprise, enterprise education, innovation and economic development; DBA, MSc, PhD

Newcastle Law School; www.ncl.ac.uk/nuls

environmental law and policy, international legal studies, international commercial law, law (complete range of legal areas taught at undergrad level); LlB, LlM, MPhil, PhD

Centre for Learning and Teaching; www.ncl.ac.uk/cflat

PGCE primary & secondary education, educational leadership and management, educational research, information, communication and entertainment technology, inclusive education, international development and education, pedagogy and learning, practitioner enquiries; EdD, MA, MEd, PGCE

School of Modern Languages; www.ncl.ac.uk/sml

Chinese, French, German, international film, language acquisition, Latin American interdisciplinary studies, linguistics, Portuguese, professional translating for European languages, Spanish, translating and interpreting – Chinese strand, Catalan, Dutch, Ouecha; BA(Hons), MA, MLitt, PhD

Newcastle Institute for the Arts, Social Sciences and Humanities

Policy, Ethics and Life Sciences Research Centre; www.ncl.ac.uk/peals

ageing, biosecurity, bioinformation and security studies, clinical ethics, disability, fertility, genetics, human stem cell research, public participation; PhD

Centre for Research in Linguistics and Language Science; www.ncl.ac.uk/linguistics

applied lingustics & TESOL, cross-cultural communication, education (TESOL), English language, human communication sciences, language acquisition, language pathology, linguistics/ of European languages, speech & language science; MA, MEd, MSc, PhD

Centre for Urban and Regional Development Studies; www.ncl.ac.uk/curds

local and regional development; MA

Faculty of Medical Sciences; www.ncl.ac.uk/aboutpeoplestudies academic/ biosciences

Biomedical and Biomolecular Sciences & Medicine; www.ncl.ac.uk/biomed

ageing and health, biochemistry, biological sciences, biomedical sciences, biomolecular science, biotechnology, clinical education, clinical psychology, clinical research, experimental medicine and therapeutics, genetics, human genetics, immunobiology, immunology, infection prevention & control, medical and molecular biosciences, medical biotechnology, medical genetics, medical microbiology, medicine and surgery, nanomedicine, neuroscience, oncology and palliative care, pharmacology, physiological sciences, public health & health services, stem cells and regenerative medicine, systems biology, therapeutics, toxicology; BSc(Hons), DClinPsychol, MB, MClinEd, MClinRes, MD, MRes, MSc, MSci, PGCert, PGDip

Dental Sciences; www.ncl.ac.uk/dental

clinical dental implants, conscious sedation in dentistry, dental surgery, endodontics, orthodontics, restorative dentistry; BDS, DDS, MSc, PGDip, PhD

Faculty of Agriculture, Food and Rural Development; www.ncl.ac.uk/aboutpeoplestudies/academic/sage

School of Agriculture, Food and Rural Development; www.ncl.ac.uk/afrd

advanced food marketing, agri-business management, agricultural and environmental science, agriculture, animal science, countryside management, ecological farming and food production systems, environmental resource assessment/science, food and human nutrition, livestock technology, medicinal plants and functional foods, rural social science, rural studies, wildlife conservation & management; BSc(Hons), MPhil, MSc, PhD

School of Biology; www.ncl.ac.uk/biology

applied biology, biodiversity, conservation and eco-tourism, biology, environmental consultancy, industrial and commercial biotechnology, zoology; BSc(Hons), MSC, PhD

School of Chemical Engineering and Advanced Materials

Biopharmaceutical Biprocess Technology Centre; www.ncl.ac.uk/ceam

applied process control, materials, design & engineering, chemical engineering, processing engineering, bioprocess automation, biopharmacological technology, clean technology, drug development, industrial quality technology, materials and process engineering, materials, design & engineering, process automation/ control, sustainable chemical engineering; BEng(Hons), MEng(Hons), MSc, PGDip

School of Chemistry; www.ncl.ac.uk/chemistry

chemistry, drug /medicinal chemistry, chemical nanoscience, molecular physics; BSc(Hons), MChem, MPhil, MSc, PhD

Civil Engineering and Geosciences; www.cegsncl.ac.uk

civil engineering, environmental engineering, geochemistry, geotechnical engineering, structural engineering, surveying & mapping science, physical geography, resources engineering, transport engineering, water environment; BEng, BSc(Hons), MEng, MPhil, MSc, PhD

Computing Science; www.cs.ncl.ac.uk/

computer game engineering, computer security and resilience, bioinformatics and computational systems biology, computing science, distributed systems/ games and virtual environments/software engineering, e-business and information systems, information systems, software engineering, internet technologies and enterprise computing; network systems & internet technology, BSc(Hons), MPhil, MSc, PhD

Electrical, Electronic and Computer Engineering; www.ncl.ac.uk/eece

adv sensor technology, automation and control, communications and signal processing, electrical & electronics engineering, electrical power, electronic communications, computer engineering, microelectronics, mobile and pervasive computing, power distribution; BEng, EngD, MEng, MPhil, PhD

Institute for Research on Environment and Sustainability; www.ncl.ac.uk/environment

agriculture, food and environment, biological sciences, biosciences, medicine & dentistry, engineering and science in the marine environment, environmental engineering, geography, rural development, rural social science, water resources engineering; MPhil, MRes, PhD

Informatics Research Institute; www.ncl.ac.uk/iri

research projects; PhD

Institute for Nanoscience and Technology; www.ncl.ac.uk/irisat

cellular medicine, chemical nanoscience, chemical energy systems, MEMS and smart materials, nano materials and electronics, nanoscience and nanotechnology, policy, ethics and life sciences, products and processes

Newcastle Centre for Railway Research; www.ncl.ac.uk/newrail

rail freight and logistics, rail infrastructure, rail systems, rail vehicles

School of Marine Science and Technology; www.ncl.ac.uk/marine

aquaculture enterprise and technology, international marine environmental consultancy, marine & offshore power systems/technology, marine biology, marine engineering/structures & integrity/transport & management, marine zoology, marine electrical power technology, naval architecture, oceanography, offshore engineering, pipeline engineering, small craft technology/design, subsea engineering & management, tropical coastal management; BEng, BSc(Hons), MEng, MRes MSc

Mathematics and Statistics; www.ncl.ac.uk/math

applied/ financial mathematics, mathematics, pure mathematics, statistics; BSc(Hons), MMath, MMathStat, MPhil, PhD

School of Mechanical & Systems Engineering; www.ncl.ac.uk/mech

automotive engineering, design engineering, manufacturing engineering, materials engineering, mechanical engineering, mechanical engineering with mathematical modelling, mechatronics, microsystems engineering, BEng, MEng, MSc

Centre for Rural Economy; www.ncl.ac.uk/cre

rural social science research; MPhil, MSc, PhD

Sir Joseph Swan Institute for Energy Research; www.ncl.ac.uk/energy

bioinformatics, environmental consultancy, industrial & commercial biotechnology, medical and molecular biosciences, medicinal plants & functional foods, renewable energy, rural science, wild life conservation; MRes, MSc, PhD

Centre for Software Reliability; www.csr.ncl.ac.uk

dependability of computer-based systems, dependable computing systems centre

UNIVERSITY OF NORTHAMPTON
www.northampton.ac.uk

School of Applied Sciences; www.northampton.ac.uk/departments/applied science

Division of Computing; w.w.w2.northampton.ac.uk/appliedsciences/appliedscience/computing

computing, internet technology/computer networks engineering/ security/software engineering/mobile technology, computer systems engineering/graphics & visualisation; BA/BSc, BSc(Hons), HND, MSc, PhD

Division of Engineering; w.ww2.northampton.ac.uk/appliedsciences/appliedscience/engineering

electrical and electronic engineering, engineering, lift and escalator technology/engineering, mechanical/production engineering, non-destructive testing; BSc(Hons), BTEC, FdSc, HNC, HND, MSc, Prof Cert

Environmental Science; w.ww2.northampton.ac.uk/ appliedsciences/appliedscience/geoenvsci
applied conservation biology, biology, biological conservation, environmental management/science, geography, international environmental conservation, physical geography; BA/B/Sc, BSc(Hons), FdSc, HNS, MBA, MSc, Univ Certs

British School of Leather Technology; www2.northampton.ac.uk/ appliedsciences/appliedscience/bslt
leather studies, leather technology, materials technology (leather); BSc(Hons), BTEC National Certificate, Leathersellers Certificate, MSc, PhD/MPhil

The School of The Arts; www.northampton.ac.uk/departments/ arts

Division of Design; www2.northampton.ac.uk/arts/home/ Design
architectural technology, advertising with design, creative advertising, graphic communication, horticutural & garden design, illustration, interior design, surface design & printed textiles, product design; BA(Hons), BSc(Hons)

Division of Fine Art; www2.northampton.ac.uk/arts/home/Fine Art
art and design, drawing, fine art, painting, photographic practice; BA(Hons), FD, MA

Division of Media, English and Culture; www2.northampton.ac.uk/arts/home/ Media English Culture
creative writing, English, film and television studies, English language, gender studies, journalism, media production, modern English studies, popular music; BA(Hons), MA

Division of Performance Studies; www2.northampton.ac.uk/arts/home/ Performance Studies
acting, dance, drama, music production/practice, performance arts, popular music, theatre studies; BA(Hons), HND, MA, PhD

Division of Fashion; www2.northampton.ac.uk/arts/home/ Division of Fashion
fashion; BA(Hons)

School of Education; www.northampton.ac.uk/departments/ education

Teacher Education Division; www2.northampton.ac.uk/education/ home1/teacher-education
education (early years & primary), graduate teacher programme (GTP), primary education, initial teacher training; BA(Hons), GTP, PGCE

Profession Development & Training Division; www2.northampton.ac.uk/ education/home1/teaching-assistants
learning and teaching, supporting learners higher level teaching assistant status; BA, CertHE, Foundation degree

Early Years & Educational Studies Division; www2.northampton.ac.uk/education/ home1/early-years
early childhood studies, early years education, GTP: early years primary and secondary routes; BA/BSc, FD

Special Needs and Inclusion Division;
boy-friendly teaching, behaiour learning, making sense of mental health, dyslexia in primary schoolchildren, teacher training use of classroom support; PhD

School of Health; www.northampton.ac.uk/departments/ health

adult/children's/ dental nursing, health studies, learning disability, mental health, human bioscience, midwifery, occupational therapy, paramedic science, podiatry, primary care & child health, social work, sport and exercise, work-based learning; BSc(Hons), MPhil, PGCert, PhD

Northampton Business School; www.northampton.ac.uk/departments/ business

accounting, advertising/with design or PR, applied management, business, business computing/systems/ entrepreneurship/studies, economics, EFL, events management, fashion marketing, finance, financial services, French, German, HRM, international accounting/HRM/international logistics and trade finance, IT service management, management, marketing, office administration, retailing, social enterprise development, sports marketing, tourism marketing, tourism, travel & tourism management, web design; BA(Hons), BA/BscHons, CMS, DBA, DMS, FdA, HND, MA, MBA, MSc, PGDip (marketing), ProfDip

School of Social Sciences; www.northampton.ac.uk/departments/ social sciences

History

history, social and cultural history; BA(Hons), PhD

Law; www2.northampton.ac.uk/ socialsciences/sshome/law-2

international business law/ criminal law and security, law, appl criminal justice, offender management, police & criminal justice; LlB, LlM, PhD, FdA

Psychology

child & adolescent mental health, development and educational psychology/counselling, psychology, transpersonal psychology and consciousness; BA/ BSc, BSc(Hons), PhD

Sociology

criminology, geography (human, physical), media, philosophy, politics, international relations, offender management, sociology; BA(Hons), MA

UNIVERSITY OF NORTHUMBRIA AT NEWCASTLE www.northumbria.ac.uk

Newcastle Business School; www.newcastlebusinessschool.ac.uk

accounting, advertising management, business administration, business creation/management/studies, corporate management, economics, finance, global financial management, global logistics and supply chain management, hospitality and tourism management, HRM, legal management, international business administration/business management/hospitality & tourism management/HRM/management, investment management, logistics and supply chain management, marketing management, multidisciplinary design innovation, tourism, travel and tourism management; BA, DBA, MA, MBA, MSc, PhD

School of Applied Sciences; www.northumbria.ac.uk/sd/academic/ sac

Biosciences

applied biology, applied biomedical sciences, biology with forensic biology, biomedical, biotechnology, human biosciences, medical biosciences, medical sciences, microbiology, molecular biology; BSc(Hons), MSc, PhD

Chemistry

analytical/applied chemistry, biomedical sciences, forensic/ pharmaceutical chemistry; BSc, BSc(Hons), MChem, MRes, MSc

Food and Nutritional Sciences

food science, human nutrition, nutritional science, nutrition & psychological science; BS(Hons), MSc

Forensic and Crime Sciences

biology, crime science, criminology, forensic biology/ chemistry/science; BA(Hons), BSc(Hons), MSc, MSci

Geography and Environment

community wellbeing, environmental health/management, geography, human geography, physical geography

School of Arts & Social Sciences; www.northumbria.ac.uj./sd/academic/ sass

English & CreativeWriting

creative writing, English language/literature, film studies, history, journalism, applied linguistics for TESOL

English Language Centre

media & communication, modern foreign languages, performing arts

Politics & History Division

sociology & criminology, TESOL, visual arts; BA(Hons), MA, MRes

Media & Communication

advertising & media, journalism, media production/ culture; BA(Hons), MA

Modern Foreign Languages
area studies, British Sign Language, French, German, Italian, Japanese, Mandarin Chinese, modern languages, Polish; BA(Hons), Dip

Performing Arts
choreograpy, dance, drama, performance, scriptwriting; BA(Hons)

Politics & History
media culture and society, politics, public administration, regeneration, urban policy and renewal; BA(Hons), MA, MRes, MSc, PGDip/Cert

Sociology & Criminology
criminal justice, criminology, forensic science, international policing, psychology sociology; BSc(Hons), BSc(Hons), MA, PGDip/Cert

Visual Arts
art & design, contemporary photographic practice, film and televison studies, fine art/and education, practice/conservation; cultural management, event & conference management, museum & heritage management, music management & promotion; BA(Hons), FdA, MA

School of Built Environment; www.northumbria.ac.uj./sd/academic/sobe

architectural technology, architecture, building design management/project management/services engineering/surveying, commercial/quantity surveying, construction, construction management/ project management/for construction, estate management, housing policy and management, international real estate management, planning & development surveying, surveying (minerals), sustainable communities, sustainable development in the built environment; BA(Hons), BSc(Hons), FdSc, MA, MSc, PGDip/Cert, PhD, ProfDip

Business Information Systems

business information management/systems/technology, business IT with entrepreneurship, IT management for business, technology, innovation & entrepreneurship; BSc(Hons), FdSc, MSc

School of Computing, Engineering & Information Science: northumbria.ac.uj./sd/academic/ceis

Computing
applied/ business computing, computer design & production, computer forensics/games software engineering/network/technology/science, computing and IT, computing studies, embedded computer systems engineering, informatics, IT, technical innovation & entrepreneurship

Engineering & Technology
communication & electronic engineering, computer aided production design, computer and network technology, electrical engineering, electrical power engineering, embedded computer systems engineering, mechanical design techniques, mechanical engineering, microelectronics and communication engineering, product design technology, technical innovation & entrepreneurship; BEng, BSc(Hons), MSc

Information and Communications Management
communication & PR, computing and IT, information & library management, librarianship, records management; BSc(Hons), MA, MSc

Mathematics & Statistics
mathematics, mathematics with business; BSc(Hons)

School of Design; www.northumbria.ac.uk/sd/academic/scd

3D design, design for industry/management, design/for industry, professional practice, fashion, fashion communication/management /marketing, graphic design, interactive media design, interior design, motion graphics & animation, transportation design; BA(Hons), Des, Doc, BSc(Hons), MA, MSc, Pract

School of Health, Community & Education Studies; www.northumbria.ac.uj./sd/academic/shes

health, midwifery studies, nursing studies/registered nurse/child/mental health/adult/learning disabilities, occupational therapy, operating dept practice, physiotherapy; AdvDip, BSc, MSc, PGDip

Northumbria Law School: northumbria.ac.uj./sd/academic/law

business law, child law, commercial property law, bar vocational course, commercial law, employment law, information rights law and practice, international commercial/trade law, legal practice, medical law, mental health law/mental health law policy and practice; BVC, GDL, GradCert, LlM, LLb, LPC, PGCert

School of Psychology and Sport Science; www.northumbria.ac.uj./sd/academic/psychsport

applied sport and exercise science, business psychology, coaching, criminology, exercise & nutrition, international sport management, nutrition & psychological sciences, occupational psychology, psychology/of sport & exercise behaviour, sport development/management; BSc(Hons), MSc

UNIVERSITY OF NOTTINGHAM
www.nottingham.ac.uk

Faculty of Arts; www.nottingham.ac.uk/arts

School of American and Canadian Studies (including the Institute of Film and Television Studies); www.nottingham.ac.uk/american

American & Canadian Studies (literature, history, culture), American studies (history, literature, visual art) with European studies/English, international study, film and television, Hollywood studies; BA(Hons), MA, MRes, PhD

School of English Studies; www.nottingham.ac.uk/english

Anglo Saxon studies, applied linguistics, communication and entrepreneurship, drama & performance, early modern literature, English language teaching, old/English studies/creative writing/literature, literary linguistics, the 20th century and contemporary literature, Viking studies, world Englishes; BA(Hons), MA, MPhil, MSc, PGDip, PhD

School of History; www.nottingham.ac.uk/history

ancient history, archaeology, British history, gender history, contemporary Chinese studies/ancient history/archaeology/art history/politics, medieval history, modern history, warrior societies; BA(Hons), MA, MPhil, PhD

Centre for English Language Education; www.cele.nottingham.ac.uk

teacher training, languages & applied linguistics, arts & social sciences, business, teaching English for academic purposes; BA(Hons)

School of Humanities; www.nottingham.ac.uk/humanities

Archeology

archaeological materials, archaeology, ancient history, classical civilisation, bioarchaeology, medieval archaeology, Mediterranean archaeology, Roman archaeology, underwater archaeology; BA(Hons), BSc(Hons), MA, MPhil

Art History; www.nottingham.ac.uk/art-history

art history, painting, sculpture, graphic arts, museum studies, high art & popular culture, Renaissance to the modern day modern art, art, photography & film; BA(Hons), MA

Dept of Classics; www.nottingham.ac.uk/classics

classical civilisation, visual culture; BA(Hons), MA ancient drama/history & archeology, classical literature, Greek, Greek and Roman studies, Latin, philosophy, visual culture of classical antiquity, warrior societies; BA(Hons), MPhil/PhD

Music; www.nottingham.ac.uk/music

music, early music, film music & music on stage & screen, music theory & analysis; BA(Hons), MPhil, PhD

Philosophy; www.nottingham.ac.uk/philosophy

philosophy, joint honours degrees; BA(Hons), MA, MPhil/PhD

Theology and Religious Studies; www.nottingham.ac.uk/theology

biblical interpretation, church studies, philosophical theology, philosophy, philosophy and literature, systemic & philosophical theory, religious studies, theology; BA(Hons), MA, MPhil/PhD

School of Modern Languages & Cultures; www.nottingham.ac.uk/modern-languages

20th & 21st century French thought, critical theory, Chinese/English translation, German, modern & contemporary German studies, contemporary Chinese studies, early modern French studies, post-conflict cultures, modern languages & critical theory, contemporary Middle East studies, francophone and post-colonial studies, French culture and politics, international media communications studies; BA(Hons), MA, MPhil, PhD

German Studies; www.nottingham.ac.uk/german

German, modern and contemporary German studies, modern languages & critical theory, contemporary literature, English translation; BA(Hons), MA, MPhil, PhD

Spanish, Portuguese and Latin American Studies; www.nottingham.ac.uk/splas

Hispanic studies, Portuguese (beginners), Spanish (beginners), Spanish and Latin American studies or Portuguese and Lusophone studies; BA(Hons), MA, MPhil, PhD

Russian & Slavonic Studies; www.nottingham.ac.uk/slavonic

East European civilisations, Russian and East European civilisations, Russian studies, Slavonic studies; BA(Hons), MA, MPhil

Cultural Studies; www.nottingham.ac.uk/cultural-studies

cultural studies, entrepreneurship, international media communications studies, critical theory, post-conflict, cultures, contemporary Middle East studies; BA(Hons), MA, MPhil

Faculty of Science; www.nottingham.ac.uk/science

School of Biosciences; www.nottingham.ac.uk/biosciences

Agricultural and Environmental Sciences

agriculture, integrative systems biology, adv genomic & proteonomic science, environmental science; BSc(Hons), MSc, PhD

Plant and Crop Sciences

agriculture and biotechnology, applied biology, crop improvement/biotechnology technology & entrepreneurship, environmental biology, genomic and proeonomic science, integrative biology, plant genetic manipulation, plant science; BSc(Hons), MSc, PhD

Animal Sciences

animal science, integrative systems biology, preveterinary science; BSc(Hons), Cert, MRes, MSc, PhD

Food Sciences

applied biomolecular technology, brewing science and food production management, food microbiology/science, industrial biochemistry, microbiology, nutrition and food science; BSc(Hons), MPhil, MRes, MSc, PGDip, PhD

Nutritional Sciences

advanced dietetic practice, food science, nutrition, nutritional biochemistry; BSc(Hons), MPhil, MRes, MSc, PGDip, PhD, MNutrition

School of Chemistry; www.nottingham.ac.uk/chemistry

biochemistry, biological chemistry, nanoscience chemistry/& entrepreneurship, molecular physics, medicinal chemistry; BSc(Hons), MChem, MPhil, MSc, MSci, PhD

School of Computer Science; www.nottingham.ac.uk/computerscience

advanced computing sci, artificial intelligence, computer science, computing and information systems, information technology, interactive systems design, management of/ information technology, scientific computation, software systems, technology; BSc(Hons), MPhil, MSc

School of Mathematical Sciences; www.maths.nottingham.ac.uk/

mathematical physics, mathematics, numerical techniques for finance, statistics, scientific computation/ with industrial mathematics/mathematical medicine and biology, statistics with biomedical applications/ applied probability; BSc(Hons), MSc, PhD

School of Physics & Astronomy; www.nottingham.ac.uk/physics

astronomy, mathematical physics, medical physics, nanoscience, particle theory, physics, physics and philosophy, theoretical astrophysics, theoretical physics, chemistry and molecular physics; BSc(Hons), MSc, MSci, PhD

School of Psychology; www.nottingham.ac.uk/psychology

cognitive neuroscience & neuroimaging, psychology /& cognitive neuroscience/philosophy; BSc(Hons), MSc, PhD

Faculty of Engineering; www.nottingham.ac.uk/engineering

Dept of Built Environment; www.nottingham.ac.uk/sbe

architectural environment engineering, architecture, architecture & critical theory, design, energy conversion and management, environmental design, renewable energy, sustainable built environment/energy & entrepreneurship, sustainable tall buildings/building technology, technology, theory & design, urban design; BA(Hons), BArch (Hons), BEng (Hons), Dip Arch, MEng, MPhil, PhD

Dept of Chemical and Environmental Engineering; www.nottingham.ac.uk/scheme

chemical engineering, environmental engineering, petroleum and environmental process engineering, environmental & resource engineering; BEng(Hons), MEng(Hons), MPhil, MRes, MSc, PhD

Dept of Electrical & Electronic Engineering; www.nottingham.ac.uk/eee

biophotonics, computer engineering/communications engineering, electrical engineering, electrical technology for sustainable and renewable energy systems, electromagnetics design, electronic communications and computer engineering, electronic engineering, electronic and ultrasonic instrumentation, optical engineering techniques, photonic communications, power electronics, machines and drives, renewable energy systems; BEng, MEng, MPhil, MRes, MSc, PGDip, PhD

Dept of Civil Engineering; www.nottingham.ac.uk/civil

civil engineering/mechanics, environmental engineering, environmental fluid mechanics, geotechnical engineering, infrastructure, pavement engineering, structural engineering, transportation, engineering surveying, survey & geodosy, positioning & navigation technology; BEng(Hons), MEng(Hons), MPhil, MSc, PhD

Dept of Mechanical, Materials and Manufacturing Engineering; www.nottingham.ac.uk/schoolm3

advanced materials/manufacture, bioengineering, biomedical materials science, design engineering, engineering materials failure and analysis, healthcare, human factors, manufacturing engineering, materials, mechanical engineering, product design and manufacture; BEng, MEng, MSc, PGCert, PhD

Faculty of Medicine & Health Science; www.nottingham.ac.uk

School of Biology; www.nottingham.ac.uk/biology

biochemical genetics, biological photography and imaging, biology, human genetics; BSc, MSc, MSci, PhD

School of Biomedical Sciences; www.nottingham.ac.uk/biomedsci

biochemistry, biological chemistry, genetics, molecular medicine, surgery, anatomy, pharmacy, physiology, neuroscience, sports medicine, integrated physiology in health & disease; BSc(Hons), MPhil, MRes, MSc, PhD, BMBS, BMedSci

School for Clinical Sciences; www.nottingham.ac.uk/scs

assisted reproduction/stem cell technology, sports and exercise medicine; translational neuroimaging; DM, MSc, PhD

School of Community Health Sciences; www.nottingham.ac.uk/chs

epidemiology, medical education, mental health studies, primary care, psychiatry, psychopharmacology, public health, rehabilitation and ageing; MBBS, BMedSci, MMedSci, MPH, MSc, PGDip/Cert, PhD

School of Molecular Medical Sciences; www.mol1.nottingham.ac.uk

human genetics, immunology, molecular and cellular bacteriology, translational cancer, virology; MSc, PhD

School of Nursing, Midwifery and Physiotherapy; www.nottingham.ac.uk/nursing

adult /critical care, advanced clinical practice/skills, advanced nursing, child health, cognitive behaviour therapy, care of neonates, health and social care, health communication, health care sciences, infants & children, long-term conditions, mental health & social care, midwifery, neurorehabilitation, operating dept practice, physiotherapy, nursing – adult/mental health/learning disabilities, physiotherapy, manual therapy, psychological therapies, trauma & orthopaedics; BMid(Hons), BSc(Hons), DHSci, MA, MNursSci, MPhil, MSc, PGDip/Cert, PhD

School of Pharmacy; www.nottingham.ac.uk/pharmacy

medicinal and biological chemistry, pharmacy, nanoscience, stem cell technology; MPharm, MRes, MSc, MSci, PhD

School of Veterinary Medicine & Science; www.nottingham.ac.uk/vet

laboratory animal medicine, veterinary medicine & surgery; BVMBVS, BVMedSci, MPhil, MRes, PhD, DVM, DVS

Faculty of Social Sciences, Law, & Education; www.nottingham.ac.uk

Nottingham University Business School; www.nottingham.ac.uk/business

corporate social responsibility/strategy and governance, entrepreneurship, finance accounting and management, finance and investment, global supply chain management, industrial economics/with insurance, industrial engineering, international business, logistics and supply chain management, management studies, management with Asian studies/ Chinese studies/French/German/Spanish, manufacturing systems, marketing, operations management, risk management, supply chain and operations management, tourism and travel management and marketing; BA(Hons), ExecMBA, MA, MBA, MSc

School of Contemporary Chinese Studies; www.nottingham.ac.uk/chinese

Chinese/English translation and interpreting, contemporary Chinese studies, management/business & economics of contemporary China, global issues; BA, MSc, MSci, PhD

Economics; www.nottingham.ac.uk/ economics

applied economics, behavioural economics, economic development and policy analysis, economics, economics with modern languages/international economics/development economics/ financial economics, econometrics, international economics, philosophy; BA(Hons), BSc(Hons), MPhil, PGDip, PhD

School of Education; www.nottingham.ac.uk/education

counselling/children & young people, HE, initial teacher education – secondary (English, geography, history, mathematics, mentoring & coaching, modern languages, science, society, health), learning, primary education, QTC, technology and education, special needs, TESOL; BA(Hons), MA, MPhil, MRes, PGCE, PGCert/Dip, PhD, SCITT

School of Geography; www.nottingham.ac.uk/geography

geography, environmental management/history, GIS, human geography, landscape and culture, contaminated land management, economy, space, society; BA(Hons), PhD

School of Law; www.nottingham.ac.uk/law

environmental law, European law, human rights law, international commercial law/ criminal justice and armed conflict, international law/and development, law and environmental science, law with French/ German law/American law/Australian law/Chinese law/European law/New Zealand law, law, maritime law, senior status; BA(Hons), LlB, LlM, MA, MSc, PhD

Politics & International Relations; www.nottingham.ac.uk/politics

diplomacy, European /and global politics, international relations & global issues, international security and terrorism, politics, politics and contemporary history/American studies/German/French, social and global justice; BA(Hons), MA, MPhil, MRes, PhD

School of Sociology and Social Policy; www.nottingham.ac.uk/sociology

administration, citizenship, identities and human rights, health communication, cultural sociology, public administration/policy, social and cultural studies, international/social policy, social work, sociology, trauma studies; BA(Hons), MA, MPA, MPhil, MSWS, PhD

NOTTINGHAM TRENT UNIVERSITY
www.ntu.ac.uk

School of Animal, Rural and Environmental Sciences; www.ntu.ac.uk/ares

animal biology, biodiversity surveying, environmental conservation and countryside management/ design and management/science, equine sports science (equestrian psychology/health & welfare), geography/wildlife conservation, zoo biology; BSc(Hons), MSc/MRes/PGCert/PGDip, FdSc

School of Architecture, Design and Built Environment; www.ntu.ac.uk/adbe

art & design, civil engineering, product design, property construction & surveying/development investment, project management, real estate; BSc(Hons), MA, MSc, PGDip/Cert

School of Art & Design; www.ntu.ac.uk/art

art direction, computer aided product design, decorative arts, design for film and television, fashion/ and textile management/design/communication and promotion/knitwear design and knitted textiles/marketing and branding, fashion, knitwear and textiles, film, fine art, graphic design, innovation management, interaction design, international fashion business and textile design/illustration, knitwear business/marketing and communication, motion graphic design, multimedia, photography product design, product design, puppetry and digital animation, textile design and innovation, theatre design, visual communication; BA(Hons), GradDip, MA, MPhil, PhD

School of Arts & Humanities; www.ntu.ac.uk/hum

childhood, communication, English, the environment, geography, history, horticulture, international studies, journalism, language, linguistics, media, philosophy, politics, teacher training education, youth studies; BA(Hons), MA, PGDip, PhD

Nottingham Business School; www.ntu.ac.uk/nbs

accounting and finance, business and management, economics, HRM, information management and systems, marketing, strategic management and international business; BA(Hons), DBA, MBA, MSc

School of Education; www.ntu.ac.uk/edu

business and education development, childhood studies, design and technology education, early years, educational support, ICT and education, primary education, psychology and education/educational development/business and education, special and inclusive education, sport and leisure, teaching adult literacy, teaching adult numeracy/ literacy, TESOL, undergraduate teacher training; BA(Hons), MA, PGCE, PGCert, ProfCert, ProfDoc

Nottingham Law School; www.ntu.ac.uk/nls

competition law, corporate law, criminal justice, employment law, Europe and the law, health law, human rights, insolvency law, intellectual property, international trade law, law /and professional practice/business/criminology/psychology, sports law; GDL, GradDip, LlB, LlM, LPC, PhD

School of Science & Technology; www.ntu.ac.uk/sat

astrophysics, biological sciences, biomedical science, biosciences, biotechnology, chemical, forensics, coaching, computer science/systems (networks, forensics and security), computing and technology, digital media, environmental management, financial mathematics, forensic science, games technology, geonomic and proteonomic science, healthcare science, information and communication techn, information systems, materials science, mathematics, molecular cell biology, multimedia engineering, neuroscience, nutrition and health, pharmaceutical and medicinal chemistry, pharmacology, physics and mathematics, software engineering, sport sciences/ and management/exercise science, technological physics; BSc, FdSc, MChem, MRes, MSc, MSci, PhD

School of Social Sciences; www.ntu.ac.uk/soc

applied child psychology, career education/guidance, child care practice, children's services (education welfare,), corporate responsibility, counselling skills, criminology, cyberpsychology, forensic mental health/psychology, health and environment/social care, health and safety risk management, politics, psychological well-being and mental health, psychology with criminology/sociology/sports science/philosophy, public health, safety and environment, safety, health and environmental management, social work, sociology, youth studies /work; BA(Hons), MA, MRes, MSC, Pfdip/Cert, PGDip/Cert, PhD, ProfDoc

Degrees validated by Nottingham Trent University offered at:

SOUTHAMPTON SOLENT UNIVERSITY
www.solent.ac.uk

Arts, Design and Media; www.solent.ac.uk/courses/artsandmedia

advertising, animation, PR with communication/media, promotional media, computer & video games, media writing/(English, creative writing), fashion graphics/management & media, fashion marketing management, film/& TV studies, graphic design, interior design, journalism, media studies performing arts, (comedy, performance,) production design, TV & video production, fine art, illustration; industrial design, BA(Hons), HND, MA

Business and Law; www.solent.ac.uk/courses/BusinessandLaw

accountancy, business, business IT, business management, business administration, business studies, commercial law, entrepreneurship, finance, HRM, international business, international business management & English, law/& practice, management, marketing/management, advertising management, entrepreneurship, event management, public service management, personnel & development, tourism studies; BA(Hons), Cert, CIM, FdA, GradDip, HND/C, LLM, MA, MBA, MProf, PGDip, ProfCert/Dip

Education

learner support and administration, learning and teaching (higher education), professional development; MProf, PGC

Human Resources/Personnel

HRM, personnel and development, personnel practice

Languages

English for business and cross-cultural communication, international business management and English, international language programme; BA(Hons), DipHE, FD, MPhil, PGDip/Cert, PhD

Maritime and Environmental Science; www.solent.ac.uk/courses/MaritimeandEnvScience

Geography

geography with environmental studies/marine studies

Maritime Industry

international maritime studies (management/shipping and commercial law/shipping and logistics/shipping ports and environment,) ship and port management, ships & shipping management, yacht and boat design/powercraft design, yacht production and surveying; BEng, BSc(Hons), MPhil, MSc, PhD

Social Sciences; www.solent.ac.uk/courses/SocialSciences

criminology; criminal investigation with psychology, psychology (counselling/criminal behaviour/education/health), social work/adults; BA(Hons), BSc(Hons), DipHE, MPhil, PhD

Sports & Tourism; www.solent.ac.uk/courses

event management, fitness, coaching & sports development, fitness & personal training, exercise & physical activity, health promotion and fitness, outdoor and watersports, extreme sports management, outdoor adventure management, watersports studies, sport, football studies, sport and the media/recreation management, applied sport science, football, tourism, cruise and travel operations, tourism management; BA(Hons), BSc(Hons), HND, MPhil, MSc, PhD

Technology; www.solent.ac.uk/courses/Technology.aspx

Architecture

architectural technology, architecture

Business IT

business information systems/technology, business information technology, information and communication technology

Civil Engineering
building surveying, civil engineering, construction/management, property development, quantity surveying, surveying

Computer Networking/Computing
cisco network, computer games development, computer network management, web design, computer systems and networks, computing (including internet), software engineering, web design – and internet technology

Construction
construction management

Engineering
electrical engineering, electronic engineering, engineering (general), engineering with business (manufacture/service)

Mechanical Engineering;
mechanical engineering, manufacturiing engineering, mechanical design

Media Technology
audio technology, live and studio sound, media technology, music studio technology

Music and Music Technology
sound engineering, sound for film, television and games

Outside Broadcast
outside broadcast/technology; BA(Hons), BEng(Hons), BSc(Hons), FdSc, HNC, HND, MPhil, MSc, PhD

UNIVERSITY FOR THE CREATIVE ARTS www.ucreative.ac.uk (at Canterbury, Epsom, Farnham, Maidstone and Rochester)

advertising & branding, animation, architecture, computer games & digital arts, jewellery, ceramics & glass, design for teatre, management, fashion, & textiles, film and video, fine art, graphic design, illustration, interior design, journalism broadcasting & management, marketing, performance & events, photography, media arts, 3D & product design; BA(Hons), FD, Grad Dip, MA, MPhil, PGCert, PhD

THE OPEN UNIVERSITY www.open.ac.uk

Undergraduate subjects

Arts and Humanities Studies; www3.open.ac.uk/study/undergraduate/arts-and-humanities/index.htm
art history, classical studies, English language & literature, history, humanities, literature, music, politics, philosophy, economics, psychological studies, religious studies; BA(Hons), MA, PGDip

Business and Management; www3.open.ac.uk/study/undergraduate/business_and_management/index.htm
accounting, business, business studies, delivering public services, financial services, leadership and management, management of software projects, management of information systems, HRM, international finance; BA/BSc, Diplomas, DipHE, FD, MA, MSc, PGDip

Childhood and Youth; www3.open.ac.uk/study/undergraduate/childhood-and-youth/index.htm
social care, working with young people, childhood and youth studies, early years, primary teaching and learning, youth justice, effective practice (youth justice), youth work, youth: perspectives and practice; BA(Hons), Diplomas, DipHE, Certificates

Computing and ICT; www3.open.ac.uk/study/undergraduate/computing-and-ICT/index.htm
advanced networking, business information technology, computing, computing and design/commerce and industry/business, information and communication technologies, information systems, management of software, software development; BSc(Hons), Certs, Diplomas, DipHE, FD, MSc, PgD

Education; www3.open.ac.uk/study/undergraduate/education/index.htm
academic practice, applied linguistics, child development, equality and diversity, childhood and youth studies, early years, language and literacy, education, mathematics & its learning, online and distance education, primary teaching and learning, professional practice, secondary education in physics, supporting learning in primary schools, understanding children, working together for children, working with young people, youth work; BA/BSc, Certs, DipHE, FD, MA, PGCert

Engineering and Technology; www3.open.ac.uk/study/undergraduate/erngineering_and-technology/index.htm
advanced networking, computing and design/systems practice, design & innovation, ECT practice, engineering, information systems/technology, pollution control, materials fabrication and engineering, technology management; BEng, FD, MBA, MEng, MSc, PGDip

Environment, Development and International Studies; www3.open.ac.uk/study/undergraduate/environment-development-and-international-studies/index.htm
environment and development, conflict & development, development management and international studies, human rights, international development and business innovation, pollution control; BSc(Hons), MSc, PGDip/Cert

Health and Social Care; www3.open.ac.uk/study/undergraduate/health-and-social-care/index.htm
adult nursing, childhood and youth studies, counselling, CPD courses, early years, health studies/science, health & social care, managing care, mental health nursing, paramedic sciences, promoting public health, social work studies, sport and fitness, working with young people, youth justice, youth work; BA(Hons), BA/BSc, CertHE, DipHE, FD

Language Sudies; www3.open.ac.uk/study/undergraduate/language-studies/index.htm
French, German, modern language studies, Spanish, English language & literature, humanities; BA(Hons), UGDip/Cert

Law; www3.open.ac.uk/study/undergraduate/law/index.htm
agreements, ownership & trusts, legal system, rights & responsibilities, criminal justice, businesss & consumer, company law, employment law, English law; Certs, Dips, LlB(Hons), PGDip

Mathematics and Statistics; www3.open.ac.uk/study/undergraduate/mathematics_and_statistics/index.htm
computing/economics and mathematical sciences, statistics, mathematics /and its learning/education; BA/BSc, BSc(Hons), MMath, MSc, UGCert

Psychology; www3.open.ac.uk/study/undergraduate/psychology/index.htm
counselling, forensic psychology and criminology, forensic psychological studies, investigating the psychological world/social world, psychological studies & computers/criminology/psychology; BA/BSc, MSc, PgDip, UGDip

Science; www3.open.ac.uk/study/undergraduate/science/index.htm
analytical sciences, astronomy, planetary science/studies, contemporary science, earth science, environmental studies, geosciences, health sciences, life sciences, medical physics, molecular science, natural sciences, operating department practice, paramedic sciences, physical science, physics, secondary education in physics; BSc(Hons), DipHE, FD, MSc

Social Sciences; www3.open.ac.uk/study/undergraduate/social_sciencess/index.htm
counselling, economics, financial services, forensic psychology, criminology, psychological studies, social policy/research methods, social sciences; BA(Hons), BA/BSc, FD, MA, PGDip

Postgraduate subjects

arts and humanities, business and management, childhood and youth, computing and ICT, education, engineering and technology, environment, development and international studies, health and social care, languages, law, mathematics and statistics, psychology, science, social sciences

UNIVERSITY OF OXFORD
www.ox.ac.uk

Division of Humanities; www.ox.ac.uk/divisions/humanities

Rothermere American Institute; www.rai.ox.ac.uk/
English and American studies; MSt

Faculty of Classics; www.classics.ox.ac.uk
ancient and modern history, classical archaeology and ancient history, classical languages & literature, modern languages, Greek and/or Latin language and literature; BA(Hons), MPhil, MSt

Ruskin School of Drawing and Fine Art; www.ruskin-sc.ox.ac.uk
art history and theory, drawing, fine art, theoretical and practice-led research; BFA, MLitt, DPhil

Faculty of English; www.english.ox.ac.uk
classics and English, English and modern languages, English language and literature (650 to present), English and American studies, film aesthetics, history and English, medieval studies, women's studies, Shakespeare; BA(Hons), DPhil, MLitt, MPhil, MSt

History of Art Department; www.hoa.ox.ac.uk
history of art, authenticity and replication in art and visual culture, media and modernity: art and mass culture, 1880–2000; BA(Hons), DPhil, MLitt, MSt

Faculty of History; www.history.ox.ac.uk
ancient and modern history, economic and social history, international global and imperial history, Gothic, history of science, medicine, and technology, media & modernity: art & mass culture, medieval history/studies, modern British and European history, US history, women, art & culture in early modern Europe; BA(Hons), DPhil, MPhil, MSc, MSt

Faculty of Linguistics, Philology and Phonetics; www.ling-phil.ox.ac.uk
comparative philology and comparative linguistics, philology and phonetics, modern languages and linguistics

Faculty of Medieval and Modern Languages; www.mod-langs.ox.uk
Celtic, comparative literature or medieval literature, cultural studies, Czech, French, German, linguistics, literature, modern Greek, Italian, medieval literature, language history, medieval & modern languages, European enlightenment, Polish, Portuguese, Russian, Russian, Spanish, Slavonic languages, Yiddish; BA(Hons), DPhil, MPhil, MSt

Faculty of Music; www.music.ox.ac.uk
aesthetics & criticism, chamber music, choral studies/conducting performance, composition, analysis and criticism, dance music, ethnomusicology, historical musicology, jazz, musical history, orchestration, psychology of music, theory & analysis; BMus, DPhil, MA(Hons), MPhil, MSt

Faculty of Oriental Studies; www.orinst.ox.ac.uk
Buddhist studies, Chinese studies, eastern Christianity, Egyptology and ancient Near East, south and inner Asia and East Asian studies, Hebrew and Jewish studies, Islamic world, Japanese studies, Korean studies; BA(Hons), DPhil, MPhil, MSt

Faculty of Philosophy; www.philosophy.ox.ac.uk
aesthetics, Aquinas, Aristotle, ethics, formal logic, Frege, history of philosophy Descarte to Kant, knowledge & reality, post-Kant, logic and language, medieval philosophy, philosophy of mind/ physics/ religion/language & linguistics, Plato, post-Kantian philosophy, Russell, Wittgenstein; BA(Hons), BPhil, MPhil, PhD

Faculty of Theology; www.theology.ox.ac.uk
theology, oriental studies, pastoral studies, literature and theology of the old testament, the New Testament, development of early church doctrine/ from a contemporary perspective, history & doctrine, biblical studies, religious studies, philosophical , eastern Christian studies, study of religion, Judaism in Graeco-Roman world, applied theology; BA(Hons), BTh, MTh, MSt, MLitt, MPhil, DPhil, PGDip/Cert

Division of Mathematical, Physical and Life Sciences; www.ox.ac.uk/divisions/mpls

Dept of Chemistry; www.chemistry.ox.ac.uk
chemical biology, inorganic chemistry, mathematical techniques, medical chemistry, organic and chemical biology, organic reactions/synthesis, organometallic

chemistry, physical and theoretical chemistry, quantum mechanics, reaction mechanisms, solid state chemistry, spectroscopy, theoretical chemistry, thermodynamics; DPhil, MChem, MSc

Oxford University Computing Laboratory; www.comlab.ox.ac.uk

computer science/ and mathematics, mathematics & scientific computation, systems security, object technology, languages, software engineering; BA(Hons), MSc, DPhil

Dept of Engineering Science; www.eng.ox.ac.uk

biomedical engineering, chemical engineering, computer engineering, process engineering, civil and offshore engineering, electrical and opto-electronic engineering, electronic engineering, information/control and vision engineering, materials engineering, mechanical/civil/structural engineering; DPhil, MEng, MSc

Doctoral Training Centre

biological physics, computational biology, medical imaging and signals, bioinformatics, evolution & genetics; DPhil

Division of Materials; www.materials.ox.ac.uk

materials science, materials structures and mechanical properties of metals, electrical/mechanical properties, nanoelectronics, non-metallic materials; composites, polymers, packaging materials, superconducting materials, semiconducting materials, etc; DPhil, MEng, MSc, MS, MEm

Mathematical Institute; www.maths.ox.ac.uk

algebra, analysis, applied maths, statistics, geometry, pure maths, differential equations, probability; BA(Hons), DPhil, MCF, MFoCS, MS, MSc, MMath

Dept of Physics; www.physics.ox.ac.uk

atmospheric oceanic and planetary physics, astrophysics, condensed matter physics, particle physics, physics, atomic & laser/ theoretical physics; BA(Hons), DPhil, MPhys, MPhysPhil

Dept of Plant Science; www.lps.plants.ox.ac.uk/plants

biochemistry and cell biology/physiology, biological science, biology, comparative developmental genetics, evolution, ecology and systematics, plant science; BA(Hons), DPhil, MRes, MSc

Dept of Statistics; www.stats.ox.ac.uk

applied statistics, bioinformatics, mathematics & statistics, probability; BA(Hons), DPhil, MMath, MSc, PGDip

Dept of Zoology; www.zoo.ox.ac.uk

animal behaviour, biological science, biology, molecular biology and bioinformatics, ornithology, integrative bioscience, wildlife conservation; BA(Hons), DPhil, MRes, MSc

Division of Medical Science; www.oc.ac.uk/divisions/ medical_science

Dept of Biochemistry; www.bioch.ox.ac.uk

biochemistry, bioenergetics, cell biology, chromosome & developmental biology, genetics and molecular biology, infection, immunity and translational medicine, macromolecular structure, medical sciences, molecular biochemistry & chemical biology, structural biology; DPhil, MBiochem, MSc, PhD

Dept of Cardiovascular Medicine; www.cardiov.ox.ac.uk

cardiovascular science; DPhil

Nuffield Dept of Clinical Laboratory Services; www.ndcls.ox.ac.uk

cellular genetics, clinical laboratory services, radiation oncology, radiobiology; DPhil, MSc

Nuffield Dept of Clinical Medicine; www.ndm.ac.uk

imunology, biochemistry, structural biolgy, genetics, bioinformatic, infectious disease, developmental biology, cancer. endocrinology, metabolic medicine, epidemiology; integrated immunology, global health science; DPhil, MSc

Dept of Clinical Neurology; www.clneuro.ox.ac.uk

neurology, multiple sclerosis, neuropathology, neurosurgery, nuerointensive care, neurophysiology, neuropsychology, neuroradiology stroke; PhD

Dept of Clinical Pharmacology; www.clinpharm.ox.ac.uk

clinical pharmacology, experimental theraapeutics, practical drug therapy; DPhil

Dept of Experimental Psychology; www.psy.ox.ac.uk

clinical/ experimental psychology, philosophy & psychology, psychological research; BA(Hons), DPhil, MSc

Wellcome Trust Centre for Human Genetics; www.well.ox.ac.uk
human/statistical genetics, functional genomics, bioinformatics, structural biology; PhD

Wetherall Institute of Molecular Medicine; www.imw.ox.ac.uk
cancer, haematology and single gene disorders, immunology and infection; DPhil

Nuffield Dept of Obstetrics & Gynaecology; www.obs-gyn.ox.ac.uk
clinical embryology, human reproduction, obstetrics and gynaecology, womens' health; MSc

Nuffield Laboratory of Ophthalmology; www.eye.ox.ac.uk
retinal genetics, artificial vision, ocular biology, vision & disease, gene theory, circadian biology, sleep; DPhil, MSc

Nuffield Department of Orthopaedics, Rheumatology and Musculoskeletal Sciences; www.ndorms.ox.ac.uk
orthopaedics, rheumatology; MSc

Dept of Paediatrics Sir William Dunn School of Pathology; www.paediatrics.ox.ac.uk
paediatric molecular medicine/endocrinological disease, infection & immunity/gastroenterological & nutrition/neurology; PhD, MSc

Dept of Pharmacology; www.pharm.ox.ac.uk
drug discovery/medicinal chemistry, molecular neuroscience and disease, medicinal chemistry for cancer; DPhil, MSc

Dept of Physiology, Anatomy, and Genetics; www.dpag.ox.ac.uk
cardiac science, metabolic control, functional genomics, neuroscience, molecular neuroscience and disease, metabolism & endocrinology, development and reproduction; MPhil, MSc, Dphil

Dept of Psychiatry; www.pschiatry.ox.ac.uk
child & adolescent psychiatry, eating disorders, experimental psychopathology and cognitive therapy, developmental/forensic psychiatry, molecular neuropathology, old age psychiatry, psychiatric treatment, psychopharmacology, suicide research; DPhil, MRCPsych

Division of Public Health & Primary Health Care; www.dphpc.ox.ac.uk
cardiovascular disease, cancer, infectious disease, diebetes, global health science; DPhil, MSc

Nuffield Dept of Surgery; www.surgery.ox.ac.uk
cardiothoracic surgery, diagnostic imaging, integrated immunology, ENT/paediatric/vascular/neurological surgery, neuroradiology, transplants, urology; DPhil, MCh, MSc

Divison of Social Sciences; www.socsci.ox.ac.uk

Oxford Institute of Ageing; www.ageing.ox.ac.uk
economic security, work & retirement, health, longevity and bio-demography, intergenerational relationships, families and communities, education, lifelong learning & technology; DPhil, MPhil

School of Anthropology and Museum Ethnography, Institute of Social and Cultural Anthroplogy; www.anthro.ox.ac.uk
material anthropology and museum ethnography, medical/ social/visual anthropology, migration studies; DPhil, MSc

Institute of Cognitive & Evolutionary Anthropology; www.iceq.ox.ac.uk
anthropology, cognitive evolutionary anthropology; DPhil, MSc

Institute of Human Sciences; www.ihs.ox.ac.uk
human sciences; BA(Hons)

Centre for Anthropology and Mind, Centre on Migration, Policy & Society
civil society & everyday life, dynamics of migration, migrants /& labour markets, migration; DPhil, MPhil

PittRivers Museum; www.prm.ox.ac.uk
material anthropology, museum ethnography; DPhil, MPhil, MSc

School of Archaeology; www.arch.ox.ac.uk
archeological science, archaeology & anthropology, classical archaeology & ancient history, European/ landscape archaeology, visual cultures, world/environmental/ archaeology; BA(Hons), DPhil, MLitt, MSc, MSt

SAID Business School; www.sbs.ox.ac.uk

economics and management/ in materials/financial economics, financial strategy, law and finance, management, management research, organisational leadership, public policy, strategy & innovation; BA(Hons), DPhil, MBA, MEng, MSc, Oxford Dip

Dept of Economics; www.economics.ox.ac.uk

economics/development, economics & management, history & economics engineering, financial economics, philosophy, politics & economics; BA(Hons), DPhil, MEng, MSc

Dept of Education; www.education.ox.ac.uk

applied linguistics and second language, child development and education, comparative & international education, e-learning, educational research methodology, HE, learning and teaching, PGCE, teaching English in University setting; DPhil, MSc, PGCE, PGDip

School of Geography & the Environment; www.geog.ox.ac.uk

biodiversity systems, conservation & management, environmental change & management, nature, and practice of geography, nature, society & environmental policy, water science, policy & management; BA(Hons), DPhil, MSc

Dept of International Development; www.qeh.ox.ac.uk

development studies, diplomatic studies, economics for development, forced migration, refugee & forced migration studies, global governance, diplomacy; Cert/Dip, DPhil, MPhil, MSc

Oxford Internet Institute; www.oil.ox.ac.uk

social science of the internet; DPhil, MSc

Faculty of Law; www.law.ox.ac.uk

common law, company law, competition law, constitutional & administration, criminal law, criminlogy, environmental law, EU/ family, human rights, intellectual property, law, judicial process, jurisprudence, media, law, property & trusts, public interest, Roman law, social legal studies, tax, justice, intellectual property law and practice law, law and finance, law studies in Europe; BA(Hons), BCL, Dip, DPhil, MJur, MLitt, MPhil, MSc, MSt, PGDip

Dept of Politics & International Relations; www.politics.ox.ac.uk

comparative government, history and politics, international relations, philosophy, political theory, politics and economics, politics (comparative government/European politics and society/political theory); BA(Hons), DPhil, MLitt, MPhil, MSc

Dept of Social Policy & Social Work; www.spsw.ox.ac.uk

comparative social policy, evidence-based social intervention, family policy; MPhil, MSc

Dept of Sociology; www.sociology.ox.ac.uk

political sociology, quantitative methods in politics and sociology, sociological theory, sociology, sociology of industrial societies; BA(Hons), DPhil, MPhil, MSc

OXFORD BROOKES UNIVERSITY
www.brookes.ac.uk

School of Arts & Humanities; www.ah.brookes.ac.uk

English and Drama; www.ah.brookes.ac.uk/english

English, contemporary literature, creative writing, drama, post-colonial literatures, Victorian popular theatre; BA(Hons), MA, PhD

Film Studies; www.ah.brookes.ac.uk/filmstudies

film studies; BA (Hons), MA

Fine Art; www.ah.brookes.ac.uk/art

fine art, composition & sonic art, contemporary art, & music, social sculpture; BA(Hons), MA

History; www.ah.brookes.ac.uk/history

history, history of art, history of medicine; theory & practice (number of subject modules) BA(Hons), MA

Dept of Modern Languages; www.ah.brookes.ac.uk/languages

European business, culture and language, French studies, Japanese studies, Italian, Mandarin, Spanish; BA(Hons), MA

Dept of Music; www.ah.brookes.ac.uk/music

composition & sonic arts, music, music and interdisciplinary arts; BA(Hons), BSc(Hons), MA

Oxford International Centre for Publishing Studies; www.ah.brookes.ac.uk/publishing

digital publishing, publishing – magazines, journals, books, language, publishing media, book history & publishing culture; BA(Hons), European Master in Publishing; MA

School of Built Environment; www.brookes.ac.uk/schools/be

advanced architectural design, architecture, cities – environment, design and development, city and regional planning, climate change & built environment, construction project management, development & emergency planning, environmental assessment and management/technology, environmental impact assessment, historic conservation, interior architecture, international architectural regeneration, leisure planning, planning, project management, real estate, spatial planning, surveying and commercial management, tourism: development, shelter after disaster, sustainable building, transport planning, urban design/planning, urban and regional regeneration; BA(Hons)/BSc(Hons), Cert, FBE, FdSc, MArch, MPhil, MPlan, MRes, MSc, PGCert, PGDip, PhD

Business School; www.business.brookes.ac.uk

accounting, advanced marketing strategy, biotechnology with business, business analysis/ information systems, business management, business and marketing, e-business, e-marketing, economics/finance & international business, finance, information technology, HRM, international business, international hospitality and tourism management/hotel and resort management, international hospitality management, tourism management, management economics, management for business; BA(Hons), BSc(Hons), Certs, DCaM, DBA, Dips, MA, MBA, MRes, MSc, PhD

School of Health and Social Care; http://shsc.brookes.ac.uk

adult nursing, cancer care, children & families, children's nursing, emergency care, health and social care, group pychotherapy, learning disability nursing, mental health nursing, midwifery, occupational therapy, operating department practice, osteopathy, physiotherapy palliative care, rehabilitation, public health, social work; BScHons, DipHE, FD, MPhil, PhD

School of Life Sciences; www.brookes.ac.uk/lifesci

animal biology & the environment, applied human bio, applied sport & exercise nutrition, bioimaging with molecular technology, biological sciences, biomedical science, biotechnology, cell and molecular biology, conservation ecology, environmental management & technology/science, human biology, science, exercise, nutrition and health, human biology, nutrition, sport and exercise science, health, safety & environmental management; BA(Hons)/BSc(Hons), MSc, PGDip, PhD, BMedSci

School of Technology; http://tech.brookes.ac.uk

advanced engineering design, automotive engineering, broadband networks, business informatics/information systems/statistics, communication and network engineering, communication networks, computer-aided mechanical engineering, computer networks and multimedia systems, computer science, computing, digital media production/music, ebusiness, electrical and electronic engineering, information systems, information technology management for business, mathematical sciences, mathematics and statistics, mechanical engineering, media technology, medical statistics, high speed networks, mobile computing, network computing, motorsport – technology/engineering, multimedia production, racing engine design, software engineering, software engineering, sound technology, statistics, web technologies, wireless computing; BEng/MEng, FdSc, HNC, MPhil, MSc, PhD

Westminster Institute of Education; www.brookes.ac.uk/wie

advanced educational practice, communication, media and culture, early childhood studies, early years, education and human development, English language & communication, ethics, hearing aid technology, ministry, philosophy, post-compulsory education, PGCE primary/secondary, primary teacher education, practice framework, religion, & theology, culture and ethics, secondary teacher training, sport and coaching studies, support for learning, theology; BA(Hons), BA/BSSc(Hons), CertEd, FdA, MA, MPhil, PGCE, PGDip, PhD

UNIVERSITY OF PAISLEY
www.paisley.ac.uk

Faculty of Business & Creative Industries; www.paisley.ac.uk/schools/depts/business

Business School; www.uws.ac.uk/schoolsdepts/business

accounting, business analysis/economics/studies, corporate real estate management, enterprise, event management, HRM, information management, international business, tourism, economics/financial management/marketing, law, management

School of Creative and Cultural Industries; www.uws.ac.uk/schoolsdepts/mlm

broadcast journalism/production, commercial music, creative media practice, digital art, film-making & screen writing, journalism, languages, music technology, performance, sports journalism; BA, BA(Hons), BAcc, ExecMBA, MA, MSc, PGDip, PhD

Faculty of Science & Technology; www.paisley.ac.uk/schools/depts/es

Biological Science; www.paisley.ac.uk/schools/depts/es/biol

applied bioscience and psychology/zoology/forensic investigation/immunology/microbiology/multimedia, biology, biomedical science, earth science, environment, environmental biology, forensic science, general science, health and lifestyle, health science; BSc(Hons), CertHE, DipHE, MSc, PhD

Centre for Environment & Waste Management; www.paisley.ac.uk/schools/depts/es/cewm

managing environmental responsibilities, occupational safety and health, waste management, environmental management, working with environmental responsibilities; BSc, IOSHCert, MSc, PGDip

Chemistry & Chemical Engineering; www.paisley.ac.uk/schools/depts/es/chemistry

chemical engineering, chemistry, forensic science, health science, medicinal chemistry, occupational safety and health, pharmaceutical science; BEng(Hons), BSc(Hons), MSc, PhD

Design & Engineering; www.paisley.ac.uk/schools/dept/es/eng

civil engineering, computer-aided design/engineering, design/with manufacturing systems/product development, engineering management, mechanical engineering, motorsport design engineering, product design & development, quality; BEng(Hons), GradDip, MSc

Earth Science; www.paisley.ac.uk/schools/dept/es/geology

earth science with applied bioscience/chemistry/physics/geology; BSc(Hons)

Mathematics & Statistics; www.paisley.ac.uk/schools/depts/es/maths

business analysis, computational methods/number theory, mathematical science/ education, simulation, statistics; BA(Hons), BSc(Hons), MSc, PhD

Physics; www.paisley.ac.uk/schools/depts/es/physics

medical technology, microscale sensors, physics, sensor design; BSc(Hons), Cert, MSc, PgD, PhD

Sports, Exercise & Therapy; www.paisley.ac.uk/schools/depts/es/sports-studies

sports therapy

School of Computing; www.paisley.ac.uk/schools/depts/computing

advanced computer systems development, business technology, computer animation, games development tecchnology/networking, computing, information technology, management of ebusiness, multimedia and web authoring, multimedia technology; BA(Hons), BSc(Hons), MSc, PGDip

Faculty of Education, Health & Social Science; www.paisley.ac.uk/schools/depts

School of Education; www.paisley.ac.uk/schools/depts/education

chartered teacher & CPD for school teachers, childhood studies, education (secondary), inclusive education, primary education; BA, BEd MEd, PGCert/Dip

School of Health, Nursing & Midwifery; www.paisley.ac.uk/schools/depts/hnm

child protection, community mental health nursing, community nursing, gerontologics, health studies, independent and supplementary non-medical prescribing, midwifery, nursing studies, occupational health/orthopaedic/ perioperative/ public health nursing, unscheduled practice, palliative care; BSc(Hons), MSc, PGCert

School of Social Sciences; www.paisley.ac.uk/schools/depts/socialsciences

alcohol and drug studies, careers guidance and development, criminal justice, economics, politics, psychology, race equality, social policy, social sciences, social work, sociology; BA(Hons), MSc, PGDip/Cert

UNIVERSITY OF PLYMOUTH
www.plymouth.ac.uk

Faculty of Arts; www.plymouth.ac.uk/arts

School of Architecture, Design, Environment

architecture, architectural technology & the environment, architectural conservation/ professional practice, design; 3D design, contemporary/designer maker, product design, furniture and interiors, spatial practice, service design, sustainable future, design thinking; environment; building surveying & the environment, sustainable construction, construction management (project management/cost management)

School of Art & Media

graphic communication with typography, illustration, publishing, design ecologies, design for visual art & technology, multimedia production & technology, fine art, media arts, contemporary film practice, design; photography; BA(Hons, MA, MArch, BA(Hons), GradDip, MA, MRes, PhD, MSc, BSc

School of Humanities & Performing Arts

art history, dance/ theatre, digital performance arts, 18th century: art, literature, identity, English/ and creative writing/history/media arts/art history, history/with English/international relations/media arts/ politics, music, sound & music production, computer music, performance practice, social history, theatre & performance; BA(Hons), MA, PGDip, MRes, PhD

Faculty of Health; www.plymouth.ac.uk/faculties/health

School of Applied Psychosocial Sciences

health & social care studies, mental health, social work, sociology/with criminology/social research, cognitive behavioural therapy, social & educational research, social & market/educational research, social research /& evaluation

School of Nursing & Midwifery

midwifery, adult/child health nursing, adv practice in education for health professionals/healthcare/service improvement, genetic healthcare, health & social care education, surgical care practitioner; BSc(Hons), DipHE, MSc, PgDip

School of Health Professions

dietetics, mental health, neurological rehabilitation, occupational therapy, physiotherapy, podiatry, women's health; BSc(Hons), DipHE, MSc, PGCert, PGDip

Plymouth Business School; www.plymouth.ac.uk/faculties/pbs

Plymouth Law School

criminology & criminal justice studies with international relations/law/politics/psychology/social research/sociology, law, law with business studies, legal practice, maritime & marine law; BA(Hons), BSc(Hons), LlM, PgDip

School of Management

accounting, finance, business economics, marketing, business enterprise/ management/English/studies, economics, financial economics, international business/economics/finance, international financial services/logistics/relations, international supply chain & shipping management, international trade & operations management, maritime business & logistics/ law, politics with criminology & criminal justice studies, politics, public services, shipping & logistics, applied strategy & international security, business administration, international logistics, global security & development, international shipping, leadership &

management, management studies, marketing management & strategy, organisational leadership, personnel & development, port management, public administration, public management; BA(Hons), BSc(Hons), MA, DBA, MSc, PgCert/Dip, DMS, DPA

School of Tourism & Hospitality

business & tourism, cruise management, event management, international/hospitality management, marketing, tourism & hospitality management; BSc(Hons), BA(Hons), MSc, DgDip

Faculty of Education; www.plymouth.ac.uk/education

School of Early Years and Primary Education Studies

early childhood studies, humanities, primary art & design/English/information & communication/maths/science; BA(Hons), BEd, PGCE

School of Secondary & Further Education Studies

secondary art and design/citizenship/ drama/English/geography/mathematics/music, teaching in the lifelong learning sector, children's workforce; CertEd, BA(Hons), FdA, PGCE

School of Partnership, Enterprise and Professional Studies

early childhood studies, education, learning for sustainability, learning & teaching; EdD, MA, MSc PGCert, PGDip

Faculty of Science & Technology; www.plymouth.ac.uk/faculties/scitech

School of Biomedical & Biological Sciences

animal science, biomedicine, bioscience, environmental biology & conservation, marine biology, ecology & environmental biology; BSc(Hons), MRes, PGDip

School of Computing & Mathematics

computing, computer science/systems & networks, computing for business application/commerce & business computing & games development/software/web technologies, information technology/systems, multimedia computing, information security, network systems engineering, web applications dev; BSc, MSc, MRes

School of Electronics & Communication

electrical and electronic engineering, electronic communication engineering, communications engineering & signals processing, network systems engineering; BSc(Hons), BEng, MEng, MRes, MSc

School of Mathematics & Statistics

mathematics, mathematics with statistics/education finance, applied statistics, statistics; BSc(Hons), MMath, MStat

Robotics; robotics;BSc(Hons), BEng, MSc, MEng, MRes

School of Geography, Earth, & Environmental Science

analytical chemistry, applied geology, environmental science, biodiversity & conservation/climate change/ marine conservation/resource sustainability), extended science, geography/with geology, geology (with geography/ocean science/physical geography), geosciences, environmental consultancy, global environmental change, holistic science, marine geosciences, sustainable environmental management; BA(Hons), BSc(Hons), MGeol, MSc, MRes, MSc, PGDip

School of Marine Science & Engineering

applied marine sports science/technology, architecture, design & structures, civil & coastal engineering, civil engineering/and CAD, construction design & technology, marine & composites technology, marine biology/& coastal ecology/oceanography, marine studies, (merchant shipping/navigation/ocean yachting), marine technology, mechanical design & manufacture, mechanical engineering/& CAD/composites, ocean exploration, ocean science, surf science & technology, coastal engineering, flood risk, geomatics, hydrography, marine policy & planning, marine renewable energy, water & coastal management; BSc(Hons), BA(Hons), MEng, MRes, MSc, Euro Masters

School of Psychology

applied psychology, psychology/with law, human biology/sociology, criminology & criminal justice studies, psychology research methods; BSc(Hons), MSc, PGDip

Peninsula College of Medicine and Dentistry; www.pcmd.ac.uk

Peninsula Dental School; www.pcmd.ac.uk/dentistry

dental surgery; BDS

Pensinsula School of Medicine; www.pcmd.ac.uk/pms

medicine, surgery; BM, BS

Peninsula Graduate School; www.pcmd.ac.uk/gradschool
MB, BS, BDS, MD, MS, MPhil, PhD

Degrees validated by the University of Plymouth offered at:

SOUTH DEVON COLLEGE
www.southdevon.ac.uk

animal science, automotive master technician diploma, biosciences, building services engineering, business, computing, construction and building services, creative digital media, teaching in the lifelong learning sector, law, early years care and education, electrical & electronics engineering, events and conference management, healthcare practice, hospitality management, mechanical, electrical and electronic engineering, outdoor education, performance practice and events management, 3D design, tourism and hospitality management, visual studies, yacht operations, young people and community services; BA/BSc, BSc(Hons), FD, HNC, HND, PGCE

TRURO COLLEGE
www.trurocollege.ac.uk

action photography, applied literary studies, archaeology, children & young people's workforce, commercial fashion, contemporary world jazz, community studies, complementary body therapies, counselling, dance, digital visualization, early childhood education, education/and training, environmental & public health, hairdressing & salon management, history heritage, HRM, information, advice & guidance, interior design, law, libraries, museums & archives, media advertising, post-compulsory education & training, music performance, outdoor education, personal trainer, photography & digital imaging, popular music, biology, biomedical studies, public admininistration/services, silversmithing & jewellery, sound engineering, sports coaching & therapy, sports science & injury management, web technology; BA(Hons), BSc, FdA, FdSc, HNC, HND, PCET, PGCE, UnivCert/Dip

UNIVERSITY OF PORTSMOUTH
www.port.ac.uk

Portsmouth Business School; www.port.ac.uk/departments/faculties/portsmouthbusinessschool

Department of Accounting and Finance; www.port.ac.uk/departments/academic/accountingandfinance
accountancy, business, business English, finance, financial decision analysis, financial management, forensic accounting, international finance and trade; BA(Hons), BSc(Hons), MSc

Department of Economics; www.port.ac.uk/departments/academic/economics
applied economics/with business law, banking, business economics, e-banking, cultural and tourism management, economics, finance, marine resource economics; BA(Hons), BScEcon(Hons), MA, MSc, PgDip

Department of Human Resource and Marketing Management; www.port.ac.uk/departments/academic/hrmm
business administration/studies, coaching and development, hospitality management/with tourism, HRD, international/HRM, marketing, marketing with digital media/business English/psychology, sales management, training management and consultancy; BA(Hons), MA, MPhil, PGCet/Dip, PhD

School of Law; www.port.ac.uk/departments/academic/law

law with European studies, international relations/business English, corporate governance, criminology, employment law, forensic accounting, international business law; BA(Hons), LlB, LlM

Department of Strategy and Business Systems; www.port.ac.uk/academic/sbs

business/administration/enterprise systems, European business, international business studies, leadership & management, leadership in health and wellbeing, management, project management & leadership, risk management, strategic quality management; BA(Hons), FdA, HND, MBA, MSc, PGDip/Cert

Faculty of Creative and Cultural Industries; www.port.ac.uk/departments/faculties/facultyofcreativeartsandindustries

Portsmouth School of Architecture; www.port.ac.uk/departments/academic/architecture/

architecture, interior design, professional practice, sustainable architecture, urban design; BA(Hons), MA, MArch

School of Art, Design and Media; www.port.ac.uk/departments/academic/adm

design for digital media, art, contemporary fine art fashion and textile design with enterprise, fine art, graphic design, illustration, photography; BA(Hons), MA

School of Creative Arts, Film and Media; www.port.ac.uk/departments/academic/scafm

creative and performing arts, creative writing drama, drama, English, entertainment technology, film studies, media studies, television studies; BA(Hons), MA

School of Creative Technologies; www.port.ac.uk/departments/academic/ct

animation, computational sound, computer animation/games enterprise/technology, creative computing technologies/technologies and enterprise, digital media, entertainment technology, music and sound technology, TV and film production, video and broadcasting; BA(Hons), BSc(Hons), FdSc, MSc

Institute for Industrial Research; www.port.ac.uk/departments/academic/iir

data analysis, image processing, monitoring systems & ambient, intelligent robotics, traffic analysis & resource management

Faculty of Humanities and Social Science; www.port.ac.uk/departments/faculties/facultyofhumanities

Institute of Criminal Justice Studies; www.port.ac.uk/departments/academic/icjs

counter fraud & corruption studies, crime & criminology, criminology & community safety/criminal justice/criminal psychology/crime culture, digital forensics, forensic studies/accounting/IT, criminal psychology, international criminal justice, investigation & evidence, law/sociology & criminality, police studies, policing, policy and leadership, risk & security management; BSc(Hons), FdA, LlB, MSc

School of Education and Continuing Studies; www.port.ac.uk/departments/academic/iecs

childhood and youth studies, early child studies, early years care and education, education administration, education and training/management, English, geography, learning support, mathematics, modern foreign languages, PGCE, numerous subject courses/post-compulsory education, practice and pedagogy in education, learning and teaching/ in HE; BA(Hons), CertEd, FdA, MA, MSc, PGCE, PGCert

School of Languages and Area Studies; www.port.ac.uk/departments/academic/slas

American studies & history, applied languages/linguistics & TESOL, area studies, combined modern languages, communication & English studies/language skills, English language, European studies, francophone Africa, French studies, German studies, international business English/development studies/& languages/property development and languages/relations and languages/trade, languages & international trade, American studies, European studies/law, linguistics and business English, Spanish and Latin American studies, technical communication, translation; BA(Hons), MA

School of Social, Historical and Literary Studies; www.port.ac.uk/departments/academic/sshls

criminology/media studies/psychology, English & history/media studies/literature, English literature, psychology, European law & policy, European studies, government, history/& politics, history & heritage, history of war, culture & society, international relations/ & history/politics, journalism, media studies, local government, politics, psychology, sociology /& crime, literature, culture & identity, memory cultures, public administration; BA(Hons), BSc(Hons), FdA, MPA, MSc

Faculty of Science; www.port.ac.uk/departments/faculties/faculty of science

School of Biological Sciences; www.port.ac.uk/departments/academic/biology

applied aquatic biology, biochemistry, biology, forensic biology, genome science, marine sciences, genome science; BSc(Hons), MSc, MPhil, PhD

School of Earth and Environmental Sciences; www.port.ac.uk/departments/academic/isees

applied physics, contaminated land, crisis & disaster management, earth sciences, engineering geology & geotechnics, environmental forensics/hazards/health, environmental science, geological and environmental hazards, geology, marine environmental science, palaeobiology and evolution; BSc(Hons), MEng(Hons), MSc

Department of Geography; www.port.ac.uk/departments/academic/geography

environmental geography, geography, GIS, human geography, physical geography; BA(Hons), BSc(Hons), MSc

School of Professionals Complementary to Dentistry; www.port.ac.uk/departments/academic/dentistry

dental hygiene and dental therapy, dental nursing, science and dental therapy; BSc (Hons), CertHE, FdSc

School of Health Sciences and Social Work; www.port.ac.uk/departments/academic/shssw

applied clinical healthcare, child care social work, clinical health science, diagnostic radiography, medical imaging, operating department practice, paramedic science, social work, speech, language and communication science, therapeutic radiography; BSc(Hons), DipHE, FdSc, GradDip, MSc, PGDip

Pharmacy & Biomedical sciences

applied/biomedical science, pharmacy, medicines management, pharmacology, biomedicine; FdSc, BSc(Hons), MSc

Psychology

forensic/psychology, applied psychology of intellectual disabilities, child forensic studies; BSc(Hons), MSc, PgCert, MPhil, PhD

Sport & Exercise Science

sport & exercise science, sports development/business developmemt/performance, clinical exercise science; BSc(Hons), MSc

Faculty of Technology www.port.ac.uk/departments/faculties/facultyoftechnology

Civil Engineering; www.port.ac.uk/departments/academic/civils

civil engineering, construction engineering management, property development, environmental engineering, geotechnical engineering, structural engineering, construction project management; BSc(Hons), BEng(Hons), MEng, MSc

Computing; www.port.ac.uk/departments/academic/comp

business/information systems, computer science, computing/& digital sound/information systems/society/digital image, digital forensics, ecommerce & internet systems, software engineering, web technologies, forensic/IT; BSc(Hons), MSc

Electronic & Computer Engineering; www.port.ac.uk/departments/academic/ece

commmunication systems/engineering, computer engineering, computer network management & design, electronic engineering/systems engineering, communication network planning & management/administration, internet engineering/technology; BSc(Hons), BEng(Hons), MEng, MSc

Environmental Design & Management; www.port.ac.uk/departments/academic/edam

environmental management, heritage & museum studies, historic building conservation, occupational & environmental health & safety management, occupational hygiene, property development, quantity surveying; PGCert, MSc

Mathematics; www.port.ac.uk/departments/academic/maths
mathematics for finance & management/with statistics, logistics & transportation, supportability engineering; BSc(Hons) MSc, PgCert/Dip, MPhil, PhD

Mechanical & Design Engineering; www.port.ac.uk/departments/academic/mde
computer-aided product design, engineering & technology, engineering, marine sports/mechanical & manufacturing engineering, petroleum engineering, product design innovation, advance manufacturing technology, logistics & organisation, technology management; BSc(Hons), BEng(Hons), MEng, MSc, PgCert

QUEEN MARGARET UNIVERSITY COLLEGE
www.qmuc.ac.uk

School of Business, Enterprise and Management; www.qmuc.ac.uk/be
business management, consumer studies, cultural management, entrepreneurship, events management, golf and country club management, international hospitality, hospitality and tourism management, marketing, public services, retail business; BA/BA(Hons), MBA, PhD

The School of Drama and Creative Industries; www.qmuc.ac.u/facultiesschool/drama
arts/production and cultural management, costume, drama and performance, festival management, theatre management; BA/BA(Hons), MA, MBA

The School of Health Sciences; www.qmuc.ac.uk/healthscience
applied pharmacology, dietetics, human biology, nursing, nutrition, occupational and arts therapies, palliative/primary nusing, physiotherapy, podiatry, public health nutrition, radiography, continuing prof development; BSc(Hons), MSc

Institute for International Health and Development; www.qmuc.ac.uk/iild
health economics, health systems, human resources for health, sexual and reproductive health, social justice, development and health; PgDip, MSc

The School of Social Sciences, Media and Communication; www.qmuc.ac.uk/schools/socialsciences
audiology, culture politics and economy, film, health psychology, marketing, media, PR, public health practice, psychology, screen studies; DocHealth Psych, PhD

UNIVERSITY OF READING
www.reading.ac.uk

Faculty of Arts and Humanities; www.reading.ac.uk/fah

School of Arts, English and Communication, Design; www.reading.ac.uk/saed
children's literature, early modern literature and drama, English, English literature and classical studies/French studies, German studies/history/Italian studies/international relations/history of art & architecture, typography, modern and contemporary writing, 19th-century literature; BA(Hons), MA, PhD

Film, Theatre and Television; www.reading.ac.uk/ftt
film & theatre/TV/English literature/art/German/history of art/ Italian, film studies, TV /theatre studies; BA(Hons), MA, MPhil, PhD

Fine Art; www.reading.ac.uk/fineart
art, art and philosophy/psychology/history of art/film & theatre, fine art; BA(Hons), MFA, MPhil, PhD

Typography & Graphic Communication; www.reading.ac.uk/typography

book design, information design, typeface design, typography & graphic communication; BA(Hons), MA, MA(Res), MPhil, PhD

School of Continuing Education; www.reading.ac.uk/conted

archaeology and combined studies, English literature, history, history of art and architecture; Cert HE

School of Humanities; www.reading.ac.uk/humanities

School of Classics; www.reading.ac.uk/classics

ancient art, ancient history, history of art, the city of Rome, classical and medieval studies, classical studies, the classical tradition, classics; BA(Hons), MA, MPhil, PhD

History of Art; www.reading.ac.uk/arthistory

history of art and architecture/art, English/history/ ancient history/ history of art/classics; BA(Hons), MA, MPhil, PhD

Department of History; www.reading.ac.uk/history

early modern history, Franco-British history, history/ history of art/numerous jt subjects, medieval studies, modern history; BA(Hons), MARes, MPhil, PhD

Philosophy; www.reading.ac.uk/Phil

ethics, ethics & political theory, value and philosophy, philosophy; BA(Hons), MA, MPhil, PhD

School of Linguistics & Applied Languages; www.reading.ac.uk/slas

applied English language studies, English language teaching, applied linguistics, ELT, linguistic research; BA(Hons), MA, PhD

French Studies; www.reading.ac.uk/languages/about/les-aboutfrench.aspx

French, French and Franco-British history, French studies; BA(Hons), MA, MPhil, PhD

Italian; www.reading.ac.uk/languages/about/les-aboutitalian

Italian, Italian and classical studies, Italian studies, modern Italian history; BA(Hons), MA, MPhil, PhD

Faculty of Social Sciences; www.reading.ac.uk/internal/fss

Institute of Education; www.reading.ac.uk/education

children's development and learning, creative , education (art/English/music specialism), theatre studies, education & deaf studies, PGCE (secondary, primary, graduate teacher practice, subject knowledge enhancement), music teaching, teaching and learning, BA(Hons), FdA, PGCE, PhD

School of Law; www.reading.ac.uk/law

law, advanced legal studies, European union law, international law & world order, law & society, law with legal studies in Europe, legal history; DPhil, LLM, MARes, PhD

School of Politics & International Relations; www.reading.ac.uk/spirs

politics/peace/economics/history & international relations, politics & economics/history/philosophy, war, peace and international relations, diplomacy, international law & world order, security, studies, strategic studies); BA(Hons), MA, MPhil, PhD

School of Health & Social Care; www.reading.ac.uk/hsc

advanced professional practice, children & young people, counselling, leadership & management, primary care nursing, public health nursing, social work (bursary/employment)/with children and young people, their families and carers/adults, social work practice education; BSc(Hons), MA, PgDip, MSc/PG, PhD

The School of Economics; www.reading.ac.uk/economics

banking and finance/business & management in emerging economies, business analysis, business economics, econometrics; accounting, economic development in emerging markets, economics, international banking and financial services/ business and economic development/finance/economic development/relations; BA(Hons), BSc(Hons), MSc, PhD

Henley Business School; www.henley.ac.uk as at School of Economics

Faculty of Life Sciences; www.reading.ac.uk/internal/lifesci

School of Agriculture, Policy & Development; www.reading.ac.uk/apd

agricultural business management/development economics, applied development studies, development agriculture, animal science, applied development studies, consumer behaviour and marketing, development finance/policy, environment and development, environmental and countryside management, food economics, food marketing and business economics, research agricultural and food economics, social development and sustainable livelihoods; BA(Hons), BSc(Hons), MPhil, PhD

School of Biological Sciences; www.reading.ac.uk/biologicalsciences

applied ecology and conservation, biochemistry, biological sciences, biomedical sciences, biometry, environmental biology, horticulture, medical microbiology, plant diversity, wildlife management & conservation, zoology; BSc(Hons), MPhil, MSc, PhD

School of Chemistry, Food & Pharmacy; www.reading.ac.uk/fcfp

chemistry, food science, food technology, nutrition, pharmacy, nutritional studies; BSc(Hons), MPharm, MSc, PhD

School of Psychology & Clinical Language Science; www.reading.ac.uk/pcls

childhood and ageing, mental and physical health, neuroscience/of language, psychology/& mathematics/biology/philosophy/art, speech & language therapy; BSc(Hons), MSc, PhD

Faculty of Science; www.reading.ac.uk/internal/facsci

School of Systems Engineering; www.reading.ac.uk/sse

computer science and informatics, cybernetics, digital signal processing & communications, electronic engineering, network & e-business-centered computing, systems engineering; BEng, BSc(Hons), FdSc, MEng, MPhil, MRes, MSc, PhD

School of Construction Management and Engineering; www.reading.ac.uk/CME

building construction and management, building surveying, construction management and surveying, construction cost inclusive environments, intelligent buildings, project management, quantity surveying, renewable energy: technology and sustainability; BSc(Hons), MPhil, MSc, PGD, PhD

School of Mathematics, Metereology, & Physics; www.smmp.reading.ac.uk

applied meteorology, atmosphere, oceans & climate, computational mathematics, mathematics, mathematics and economics/meterology/psychology/statistics/applied statistics, mathematics of scientific and industrial computation, meteorology, physics, modelling; BSc(Hons), MMath, MPhil, MSc, PhD

ROBERT GORDON UNIVERSITY
www.rgu.ac.uk

Faculty of Health and Social Care

School of Applied Social Studies; www.rgu.ac.uk/social

applied social sciences, mental health, practice learning psychology, social care/work, sociology; BA(Hons), HNC, MSc, PGDip PhD

School of Health Sciences; www.rgu.ac.uk/health

diagnostic radiography, health improvement and health promotion, occupational therapy, physiotherapy, radiography, sport and exercise science, sports nutrition; BSc(Hons), CertHE, MPhil, MSc, PhD

School of Nursing & Midwifery; www.rgu.ac.uk/nursing

acute/adult/children's mental health, occupational health, community nursing, midwifery, nurse education; BN, DipHE, MPhil, MSc, PhD, MMid, MNurs

School of Pharmacy & Life Sciences; www.rgu.ac.uk/pharmacy-life

applied /biomedical science, applied chemistry, bioscience, nutrition, dietetics, pharmacy, prescribing science; MPharm, MSc, PGDip, PhD

Aberdeen Business School; www.rgu.ac.uk/abs

Accounting, Finance & Law; Communication, Marketing, Media; Information management; Management; Law,

information studies, management studies, project management, accounting & finance, international business management, management/with finance/HRM/marketing, health safety & risk management, HRM, international business, international marketing management with retailing/tourism & hospitality management, management, purchasing & supply chain management, quality management, communication with PR, journalism, media studies, publishing, corporate communication & public affairs, business administration, oil & gas management/ accounting, accounting & finance, financial management, events management, fashion management, hospitality, international hospitality management/ tourism management, retail management, law, law & management, construction law & arbitration, employment law, international commercial/IT law, international trade, oil & gas law, information science, information management, information & llibrary studies, public administration, politics & research methods; BA/BA(Hons), DBA, DInfSc, LlB, LlM, MBA, MPA, MPhil, MSc, PGDip/Cert, PhD

Faculty of Design & Technology

School of Computing/ www.rgu.ac.uk/ computing

business information systems, computer science, computing for graphics and animation/internet and multimedia, computing: information engineering/ with network management/software technology, information systems technology, information technology management, multimedia development

School of Engineering; www.rgu.ac.uk/eng

asset integrity management, oil & gas /drilling & well/ petroleum production engineering, subsea engineering, communications engineering, intelligent biometric security systems, offshore engineering; BSc, BSc(Hons), MPhil, MSc, PhD

Gray's School of Art, Design & Craft; www.rgu.ac.uk/grays

art & design, commercial photography, design for digital media, fashion design, fine art, graphic design, painting, photographic & electronic media, printmaking, product design, textiles & surface design; BA/BA(Hons), BDes/BDes(Hons), MDes, MRes, PGDip/MA

The Scott Sunderland School of Architecture and Built Environment; www.rgu.ac.uk/sss

advanced architecture studies, design management, construction project management, property development, surveying; Grad Dip, MArch, MSc, PhD

ROEHAMPTON UNIVERSITY
www.roehampton.ac.uk

School of Arts; www.roehampton.ac.uk/ arts

art history, ballet studies, children's literature, classical civilisation, creative writing, dance anthropology/ choreography/ studies, documentary practices, drama, theatre & performance studies, early modern literature & culture (1500–1700), English language & linguistics/ literature, film studies/& screen practice, historical research, history, journalism & news media, material culture 1750 on, media & culture, modern languages, translation, music, philosophy, photography, religious studies, Spanish, sociolinguistics, South Asian dance studies, theology/and religious studies; BA(Hons), MA, MFA, MPhil, PGDip/Cert, PhD, PsychD

School of Business and Social Sciences; www.roehampton.ac.uk/bss

Business; www.roehampton.ac.uk/bss/ business

business management/HRM/retail management, international business, international management information systems/finance, marketing; BSc(Hons), MBA, MSc, PGDip, PhD

Computing; www.roehampton.ac.uk/bss/ computing

computing with database systems/web and multimedia/computing with information management, computing studies, international management of / information systems, information system; BA/BSc, BSc(Hons), MSc/PGDip, PhD

Social Sciences; www.roehampton.ac.uk/ bss/socialsciences

childhood & society, criminology, human rights/and society/international relations, social anthropology, sociology; BA/BSc, MA/PGDip/PGCert

School of Education; www.roehampton.ac.uk/education

applied music education, art, craft and design education, education leadership and management, early child studies, education, English education, primary education, secondary education, social research methods, special education needs (special and inclusive education); BA(Hons), BA/BSc, EdD, FdA, Froebel Certificates and Graduate Certificate, MA, MPhil, PGCEPrimary, PGCESecondary, PhD

School of Human and Life Sciences; www.roehampton.ac.uk/hals

Biological Sciences; www.roehampton.ac.uk/hals/subjectareas/biologicalsciences

animal ecology, anthropology, biodiversity and conservation, biological anthropology/sciences, biology, biomedical sciences, conservation biology, ecology, environmental sciences, human biosciences, life sciences, neurobiology, primatology, zoology

Health Sciences; www.roehampton.ac.uk/hals/subjectareas/healthsciences

clinical neuroscience, clinical nutrition, health & the community, health & social care/human sciences, health sciences, health studies, nutrition, nutrition & health, stress & health

Psychology; www.roehampton.ac.uk/hals/subjectareas/psychology

applied music psychology, counselling, counselling psychology, health, integrative counselling, psychology, psychotherapy

Sport Sciences; www.roehampton.ac.uk/hals/subjectareas/psychotherapy

coaching, exercise, nutrition and health, sport & exercise biomechanics/physiology, sport psychology/science/ studies; BA/BSc, BSc(Hons), MA, MPhil, MRes, MSc, PGDip/PGCert, PhD, PsychD

Arts and Play Therapies; www.roehampton.ac.uk/hals/subjectareas/artsandplaytherapies

art therapy, arts & play therapies, dance movement psychotherapy, drama therapy, music therapy, play therapy; MA, MPhil, PGDip, PhD

THE ROYAL ACADEMY OF DANCE
www.rad.org.uk

ballet education, dance education, professional dancer's teaching diploma; BA, PGCert

ROYAL ACADEMY OF DRAMATIC ART
www.rada.org

acting, technical theatre and stage management, property making, scenic art, scenic construction, stage electrics and lighting design, theatre costume, theatre design, theatre directing; BA, MA, PGDip

ROYAL BALLET SCHOOL
www.royalballetschool.co.uk

character, classical ballet training, contemporary gymnastics, Irish, Morris and Scottish dancing; BTEC

ROYAL COLLEGE OF ART
www.rca.ac.uk

Departments
animation, architecture, communication art & design, ceramics & glass, conservation, critical writing in art & design, curating contemporary art, critical and historical studies, curating, design interactions, design products, drawing studio, fashion menswear, fashion womenswear, goldsmithing, history of design, innovation design engineering, metalwork & jewellery, painting, photography, printmaking, sculpture, silversmithing, textiles, vehicle design; MA, MPhil, PGCert, PhD

ROYAL COLLEGE OF MUSIC
www.rcm.ac.uk

advanced vocal performance, composition and composition for screen, creative leadership, opera, performance/advanced performance, physics with studies in musical performance, vocal studies; DipRCM, BMus, BSc, PGDip, MMus, GradDip,

THE ROYAL COLLEGE OF ORGANISTS
www.rco.org.uk

CertRCO, DipCHD, ARCO, FRCO, LTRCO

ROYAL NORTHERN COLLEGE OF MUSIC
www.rncm.ac.uk

chamber music, composition, music psychologym, musicology, opera studies, orchestral studies, performing arts education, instrumental teaching, performing arts leadership, popular music practice, solo performance; PGCert, PGCE, PGDip, MMus, PhD

ROYAL SCOTTISH ACADEMY OF MUSIC & DRAMA
www.rsmad.ac.uk

acting, arts in social contexts, classical and contemporary text, composition, conducting, contemporary performance practice, digital film and television, modern ballet, musical theatre, opera, technical and production, performance, Scottish music; BA (Hons), BEd(Hons), BMus(Hons), MA, MA(Musical Theatre), MMus, MOpera, MPhil, PGDip, PhD

UNIVERSITY OF ST ANDREWS
www.st-andrews.ac.uk

Faculty of Arts

School of Art History; www-ah.st-andrews.ac.uk

art history, history of photography, mediaeval studies, museum & gallery studies; GradCert, GradDip, MA, MLitt, MPhil, PhD

School of Classics; www.st-andrews.ac.uk/classics

ancient history & archeology, classical studies, Greek, Latin; MA, MLitt, MPhil, PGDip, PhD

School of Economics & Finance; www.st-andrews.ac.uk/economics

analytical finance, applied economics, applied quantitative finance, economics, international finance/strategy & economics, money, banking & finance, microeconomics, macroeconomics, sustainable development; BSc, MA, MSc, MPhil, PhD

School of English; www.st-andrews.ac.uk/english

creative writing, English, mediaeval English, Romantic/Victorian studies, Shakespeare studies, women, writing & gender; GradDip, MA, MLitt, MPhil, PhD

School of History; www.st-andrews.ac.uk/history

Arabic, book history, central & Eastern European studies, environmental history, history, international political theory/relations/security studies, Iranian studies, mediaeval history & archaeology, Middle East studies, modern historiography/history/studies, peace & conflict studies, Reformation studies, Scottish historical studies/history; GradDip, MA, DLitt, MPhil, PhD

School of International Relations; www.st-andrews.ac.uk/intrel

international relations/politics, Middle East & Central Asian security studies, peace & conflict, sustainable development; MA, MLitt, MPhil, MRes, PhD

School of Management; www.st-andrews.ac.uk/management

corporate social responsibility/finance, finance & accounting/management, dynamic strageic management, entrepreneurship, global business management, HRM, information technology, dynamic strategic management, international business/marketing/banking, management, managing in the creative industries, marketing, organisational studies, sustainable development; BSc, DipRes, MA, MLitt, MSc, MRes, PhD

School of Modern Languages; www.st-andrews.ac.uk/modlang

advanced language studies, Arabic & comparative literature, European/cultural identity studies, French/German/ Italian studies, language /& linguistics, modern Hispanic literature & film, Russian, Central & Eastern European studies, Spanish, Spanish & Latin American studies, medieval studies; DLang, MA, MLitt, MPhil, PGDip, PhD

School of Philosophical, Anthropological & Film Studies; www.st-andrews.ac.uk/philosophy

analytical/ classical philosophy, film studies, logic & philosophy of science, philosophy, moral & political philosophy of 18th cent, Scottish enlightenment, social anthropology; BSc, MA, MLitt, MPhil, MRes, PhD

Faculty of Divinity

School of Divinity; www.st-andrews.ac.uk/divinity

bible & the contemporary world, biblical studies, divinity, theological studies/interpretaion of scripture, theological image & the arts, theology; BD, MA, MLitt, MPhil, MTheol, PGDip, PhD

Faculty of Medicine

Bute Medical School; www.medicine.st-andrews.ac.uk

health psychology, medicine, surgery; BSc, MD, MPhil, MSc, PhD, MRes

Faculty of Science

School of Biology; www.biology.st-andrews.ac.uk

behavioural/cell/environmental/evolutionary/marine/molecular biology, biochemistry, biology, ecology & conservation, marine mammal sci/systems sci, behavioural & neural sci, neuroscience, zoology; BSc, MPhil, MRes, PhD

School of Chemistry; www.ch.st-andrews.ac.uk

biomolecular/chemical sciences, chemistry, materials science; BSc, MChem, MSci, PGDip, PhD

School of Computer Science; www.cs.st-andrews.ac.uk

advanced/computer science, artificial intelligence, computer information technology/coding/graphics/architecture/security, databases, data communications & networks, distributed systems, human computer interaction, programming language design, operating systems, multimedia, component technology, internet programming, computer, management & IT, networks & distributed systems, software engineering; BSc, MPhil, MSc, PhD

School of Geography & Geosciences; www.st-andrews.ac.uk/gg

environmental geoscience/history, geography, geoscience, health geology, managing environmental change, physical geography & geosciences, sustainable development; BSc, MA, MLitt, MPhil, MRes, MSc, PGCert, PGDip, PhD

School of Mathematics & Statistics; www-maths.mcs.st-andrews.ac.uk

applied mathematics, applied statistics & data mining, mathematics, pure mathematics, statistics; BSc, GradDip, MA, MLitt, MMath, MPhil, MSc, PhD

School of Physics & Astronomy; www.st-andrews.ac.uk/physics

astrophysics, physics, theoretical physics, photonics & optoelectronic devices; BSc, EngDoc, MPhys, MSc, PhD

School of Psychology; www.psy.st-andrews.ac.uk

behavioural & neural sciences, evolutionary & comparative psychology, learning disabilities, neuroscience, psychology; BSc, MA, MPhil, MRes, MSc, PhD

UNIVERSITY OF SALFORD
www.salford.ac.uk

Faculty of Arts, Media & Social Sciences; www.famss.salford.ac.uk

School of Art & Design; www.artdes.salford.ac.uk

advertising design, animation, art & design, arts and museum management, communication design, computer and video games, contemporary fine art, creative games/technology, design for digital media, design management/for the creative industries, design futures, fashion, graphic design, heritage studies, interior design, journalism and design studies, museum & heritage exhibition design, product design, visual arts; BA(Hons), BSc(Hons), HND, MA, PGDip, PhD

School of English, Politics & Contemporary History; www.espach.salford.ac.uk

Creative Writing: innovation and experiment, drama and performance studies film studies/creative writing/linguistics/cultural studies/journalism, English, English language/literature, literature, culture & modernity

Sociology & Criminology

crime and criminal justice, criminology, cultural studies, human rights & ethics, journalism, law, politics, psychology, social sciences, sociology

Contemporary History

contemporary history, contemporary military & international history, East and West European political studies, intelligence & security studies, international relations and globalization/politics, journalism, politics, terrorism & security, war studies

School of Languages; www.languages.salford.ac.uk

Arabic/English translation & interpreting/security/politics, Chinese/English, interpreting, French, German, Italian, Portugese, Spanish, linguistics, modern language studies/with TESOL, translating and interpreting, translating for international business

School of Media, Music & Performance; www.smmp.salford.ac.uk

animation, broacasting, computer & video games, comedy writing, contemporary theatre practice, critical musicology, English, fiction film production, film screenwriting/ studies, journalism, media & performance, media production/technology, mobile

& internet television, music, performance, physical & dance theatre, popular music & production/ & recording, popular musicology, radio production, social media, television & radio, television and radio scriptwriting, television documentary production, war studies, wildlife documentary production; BA(Hons), BSc(Hons), HND, MA, MPhil, MSc, PgCert, PgDip, PhD

Faculty of Business, Law & the Built Environment; www.flbe.salford.ac.uk

Salford Business School; www.business.salford.ac.uk

accounting, business and management studies/with law, business information technology/management/ studies with financial management/HRM/analysis, corporate finance, economics, events management, finance, financial services management, hospitality management, information security/technology, international banking and finance/business management/ marketing marketing, operational research and applied statistics, logistics & supply chain management, project management, sport and leisure/exercise management, tourism management; BA(Hons), BSc(Hons), CertHE, DipHE, Foundation degrees, GradCert, HNC, HND, MA, MBA, MPhil, ProfDip, ProfPGDip, PhD

School of the Built Environment; www.sobe.salford.ac.uk

accessibilty & inclusive design, adv manufacturing in construction, architectural design and technology, building surveying, construction & property, construction law & practice/ management/project management, corporate real estate, digital architectural design, disaster mitigation & reconstruction, facilities management, low carbon building design, project management in construction, property management and investment, quantity surveying, real estate development/management, regeneration and urban renewal; BSc(Hons), DBEnv, DConstMangt, DReal-Est, MSc, PGDip/Cert, PhD

Salford Law School; www.law.salford.ac.uk

construction law & practice, environmentall/ health care law, health law, health and safety law, international business law and regulation, law, law & criminology; LlB, LLM, MA, MSc, PgCert, PgDip

Faculty of Health & Social Care; www.fhsc.salford.ac.uk

School of Social Work, Psychology & Public Health; www.swpph.salford.ac.uk

adult care, attachment trauma, applied psychology (therapies), applied psychiatric trg, child care, cognitive behavioural therapy, comparative safeguard strategy, complementary medicine/ therapy, counselling & psychotherapy, counselling, learning disabilities, psychology/criminology, public health, social policy: protecting adults and children, social work; nursing, sociology; BA, MA, MPhil, MSc, PgCert, PgDip, PhD

School of Health, Sport & Rehabilitation Sciences; www.healthcare.salford.ac.uk

, prosthetics & orthotics, physiotherapy, podiatry, occupational therapy, radiography, advanced medical imaging, nuclear medicine, diagnostic radiography, sport and exercise; applied sports science, sports development/injury rehabilitation/ strength & conditioning rehabilitation, trauma & orthopaedics; BSc(Hons), MSc, PGDip/Cert

School of Nursing & Midwifery; www.nursing.salford.ac.uk

adult/children's/mental health/child & family nursing, advanced nursing, advanced practice (health and social care/neonatal), ageing, child and adolescent mental health, social care, leadership and management for health care practice, midwifery, non-medical prescribing, nursing and social work (learning disabilities), public health, therapeutic intervention; BSc, BSc(Hons), DipHE, DProfMed & Social Care, MSc, PGDip/Cert

Faculty of Science, Engineering & Environment; www.fsee.salford.ac.uk

School of Computing, Science & Engineering; www.cse.salford.ac.uk

acoustics, advanced control systems, aeronautical engineering, aerospace design and manufacture/ engineering, aircraft engineering, animation, architectural engineering, audio acoustics, audio and video systems, audio production/technology, aviation technology, civil engineering, computer networks/science, computing, creative games, data telecommunications and networks, databases and web-based systems, digital broadcast technology, gas engineering and management, industrial and commercial combustion engineering, information security, internet computing, mathematics, manufacturing systems and management, materials physics, mechanical engineering, multimedia and internet technology, petroleum and gas engineering, pure & applied physics, pilot studies, professional sound and video technology, space technology, sound & video technology, structural engineering, sustainable energy, management & development, transport engineering and planning, vacuum engineering and applications, water, energy, waste; BEng, BSc(Hons), HND, MEng, MEnt(Tech), MPhys, MSc, PGDip, PG(Tech)

School of Environmental & Life Sciences; www.els.salford.ac.uk

Biosciences

analytical biosciences & drug design, biochemistry, biology, biomedical science, pharmaceutical science, molecular parasitology & vector biology

Geography

applied GIS & remote sensing, GIS, biogeography aquatic environments, environmental geography, geography,

Environmental Studies

environmental assessment & management, environmental management, environmental studies

Environmental Health management

environmental & public health, occupational safety & health, safety, health & environment, environment management

Housing & Regeneration

housing practice, housing, regeneration & sustainability(neighbourhood renewal), sustainable communities

Wildlife & Zoo Biology

biotechnology, molecular parasitology & vector biology, wildlife documentary production, drug design, wildlife & practical conservation, wildlife conservation with zoo biology, zoology; BSc(Hons), FD, MA, MSc, PhD

Degrees validated by University of Salford offered at:

RIVERSIDE COLLEGE, HALTON
www.riversidecollege..ac.uk

applied drama and creativity, business & management, laboratory operations and management, manufacturing technology, mechanical technology, sports coaching, teaching in the lifelong learning sector, theatre; Dip, FD, FdSc, PGDip

UNIVERSITY OF SHEFFIELD
www.sheffield.ac.uk

Faculty of Arts & Humanities; www.sheffield.ac.uk/faculties/arts-and-humanities

Dept of Archaeology

Aegean archaeology, archaeological materials/science, archaeology, bible and ancient cultures, classical and historical archaeology, cognitive studies, environmental archaeology and palaeoeconomy, European historical archaeology, European prehistory, experimental archaeology, geoarchaeology, human osteology and funerary archaeology, landscape archaeology, material culture studies, palaeoanthropology; BA(Hons), BSc(Hons), MA, MPhil, MSc, PhD

School of English Literature, Language and Linguistics

19th-century studies, American literature, applied linguistics with TESOL, biblical studies and English, English literature, English language linguistics, international cinema, language acquisition, language, history and society, theatre and performance studies; BA(Hons), MA, MPhil, PhD

Dept of History

18th-century studies, 19th-century studies, 20th-century history, American early modern history, historical research, history, international history, medieval history, modern European history; BA(Hons), MA, MPhil, PhD

School of Modern Languages and Linguistics

Catalan, Chinese studies, Czech, Dutch, East Asian studies, French, German, Hispanic studies, intercultural communication, interpreting, Italian, Korean studies, linguistics, multilingual information management, Polish, Portuguese, Russian, Russian and Slavonic studies, screen translation, Spanish, Swedish, translation studies; BA(Hons), MA, MPhil, PhD

Department of Music

ethnomusicology, music, music management/performance, music psychology in education, psychology of music, sonic arts, traditional musics with folklore studies, world music; BA(Hons), BMus(Hons), DPhil, MA, MMus, PhD

Dept of Philosophy

philosophy, metaphysics and epistemology, language and the mind, politics and value; BA(Hons), MA, MPhil, PhD

Faculty of Engineering; www.sheffield.ac.uk/faculties/engineering

Dept of Aerospace Engineering

aerospace, aerospace engineering, aerospace engineering with private pilot instruction; BEng, MEng, MPhil, MSc, PhD

Dept of Materials

aerodynamics and aerostructures, aerospace materials, avionic systems; BEng, MEng, MPhil, MRes, MSc(Eng), PhD

Dept of Automatic Control & Systems Engineering

business skills & management, control systems, gas turbine control, computer systems engineering, electronic, mechanical systems engineering, mechatronics, medical systems engineering, systems & control engineering; BEng, MEng, MPhil, MSc, PhD

Dept of Chemical & Process Engineering

biological and bioprocess engineering, chemical & process engineering, environmental and energy engineering, fuel technology, process safety and loss prevention; BEng, MEng, MPhil, MSc, MSc(Eng), PhD

Dept of Civil & Structural Engineering

architectural engineering design, civil and structural engineering, civil structures, contaminant hydrogeology, earthquake and civil engineering dynamics, mechanical engineering, environmental management of urban land and water, groundwater and water engineering, steel construction, structural and concrete engineering, structural engineering and architecture/architectural studies, urban water engineering and management; BEng, MEng, MPhil, MSc, PGDip/Cert, PhD

Dept of Computer Science

advanced computer science, advanced software engineering, computer science, computer science with maths/software engineering/artificial intelligence/speech and language processing, data communications information systems, information technology management for business, software systems and internet technology; BEng, BSc, MComp, MEng, MPhil, MSc, MSc(Eng), PhD

Dept of Electrical & Electronic Engineering

avionic systems, data communications, digital electronics, electrical engineering, electronic and communications engineering/ with management, electronic engineering, microelectronics; Eng, MEng, MPhil, MSc, PhD

Dept of Engineering Materials

aerospace materials, biomaterial science and tissue engineering, biomedical engineering, materials science and engineering/modern language/industrial management, metallurgy; BEng, EngD, MEng, MPhil, MSc, PhD

Dept of Mechanical Engineering

advanced mechanical engineering, aerodynamics and aerostructures, automotive engineering, computational biomechanics, mechanical engineering/with Spanish/industrial management/foundation year, motor sports engineering management, sports engineering, structural integrity; BEng, MEng, MPhil, MSc, MSc(Res), PhD

Faculty of Medicine, Dentistry & Health; www.sheffield.ac.uk/faculties/medicine-dentistry-health

Dept Cardiovascular Science

cell biology, coronary artery disease, haemostasis, medical physics, non-mammalian models, vascular biology; MPhil, PhD

School of Clinical Dentistry

adult dental care, dental hygiene and therapy, dental implantology, dental public health, dentistry, oral & maxillofacial surgery and oral pathology, oral health and development, oral pathology, orthodontics, periodontics, restorative dentistry; BDS, ClinDent, Diploma, MDPH, MMedSci, MPhil, PhD

Dept of Human Communication Sciences

cleft palate studies, clinical communication studies, human communication sciences, language and communication impairment in children, speech, speech difficulties; AdvCert, BMedSci(Hons), BSc(Hons), MMedSci, MPhil, MSc, PGCert/Dip, PhD

The Medical School

cardiovascular science, endocrinology & reproduction, human metabolism, human nutrition, infection & immunity, medicine, molecular and genetic medicine, molecular medicine, musculoskeletal science, nephrology, neuroscience, orthoptics, surgery; BMedSci, ChB, MB, MD, PhD

School of Nursing & Midwifery

advanced nursing studies, advancing practice, health & social care studies (various topics), developmental disorders, infection control, maternity care, midwifery/ nursing studies, occupational health nursing, orthoptics, palliative care, public health, speech & cleft; BMedSci, MMedSci, MMid, MPhil, PGCert, PhD

The Faculty of Science; www.sheffield.ac.uk/faculties/science

Dept of Animal and Plant Science

animal behaviour, biology, conservation and biodiversity, ecology, plant sciences; evolution and behaviour, global change biology, plant molecular science, population and community ecology, zoology; MBiolSci, PhD, Phil, Sc

Dept of Biomedical Science

biomedical science, molecular and cellular basis of human disease, neuroscience, integrative physiology & pharmacology, stem cell and regenerative medicine; BSc(Hons), MSc, PhD

Dept of Chemistry

biological chemistry, chemistry, chemical physics, polymers for advanced technologies; BSc, MChem, MPhil, MPhys, PhD

Dept of Molecular Biology & Biotechnology

biochemistry, genetics, medical biochemistry, medical genetics, medical microbiology, microbiology, molecular cell biology, biology; genomics, cell biology, molecular microbiology, structural biology; BSc(Hons), MBiolSci, PhD

Dept of Physics & Astronomy

astronomy, astrophysics, medical physics, nanoscale science and technology, nanoelectronics & nanomechanics, physics, theoretical physics; BS(Hons), MPhys, MSc, PhD

Dept of Psychology

cognitive studies, cognitive and computational neuroscience, psychology, psychological research; BA(Hons), BSc(Hons), DClinPsych, MA, MPhil, MSc, PhD

Faculty of Social Science; www.sheffield.ac.uk/faculty/social-science

School of Architecture

architectural design, architecture/and landscape, computer-aided environmental design, conservation & regeneration, designing learning environments, structural engineering, sustainable architectural studies, urban design; BA(Hons), MArch, MPhil, MSc, PhD

School of East Asian Studies

Chinese studies, East Asian studies, Japanese studies, Korean studies; BA(Hons), MA, PhD

Dept of Economics

development economics and policy, economics, economics and mathematics/politics/economics/sociology/social policy/business management, finance, financial economics, health economics, international finance and economics, money, banking and finance; Adv Cert, BA(Hons), BSc(Hons), MSc, PhD

Sheffield Law School

biotechnological law and ethics, commercial law, conflict and security law, European law/politics & governace, global politics and law, international criminology, international legal studies/law, law, law (European and international), politics and governance, socio-legal research; LlB, LlM, MAPhil, PhD

Sheffield Management School

HRM, information management systems, international management/business, management (creative & cultural industries/health service), international management & marketing, marketing, ocuoational therapy, work psychology, strategic management; MSc, MPhil, PhD, SheffieldMBA, ExecMBA

Dept of Politics

economics, European governance and politics, European law, governance and politics, geography, global politics and law/ security, globalisation and development, governance and public policy, history, international history/east Asian studies, international political economy/international relations, philosophy, political theory, politics, sociology; BA, MA, MPhil, PhD

Dept of Sociological Studies

international childhood studies, children and their families, economics, global/social policy, international aid, social work, sociology; BA(Hons), MA, MPhil, PhD

Dept of Town & Regional Planning

commercial property, European development and planning, geography, international development and planning, landscape architecture, planning /& development, planning research, town and regional planning, urban studies; BA(Hons), MA, MPlan, PhD

The School of Education

applied professional studies in education, early childhood education, education policy and practice, educational research, PGCE; English, geography, history, mathematics, modern languages and science; education culture & literacy, initial teracher education, education & child psychology, new literacies, teaching and learning in higher education, working with communities: identities, regeneration and change; EdD, MA, MEd, MPhil, PhD

Dept of Geography

arid land studies, environmental mathematics/ science/change, geography & archaeology, human geography, international development, social & spatial inequalities, environmental analysis of terrestial systems, physical geography, polar & alpine change, social & cultural geographies; BA(Hons), BSc(Hons), MEnvSci, PhD

Dept of Information Studies

accounting, business management, electronic and digital library management, health informatics, informatics, information literacy, information management, information systems, information systems management, librarianship, multilingual information management; MA, MChem, MSc, MSc(Res), PhD/ MPhil

Dept of Journalism Studies

broadcast journalism, journalism studies, global/ magazine journalism studies/with a modern language, political communication, print journalism, web journalism; BA, MPhil, PhD

Dept of Landscape

landscape architecture with ecology/planning, landscape management, architecture & landscape, landscape studies; BA(Hons), BSc(Hons), MA, PGDip, PhD

SHEFFIELD HALLAM UNIVERSITY
www.shu.ac.uk

Faculty of Arts, Computing, Engineering & Science; www.shu.ac.uk/art/ faculties.aces

Business Systems and ICT; www.shu.ac.uk/ systems

business information systems, computing, grid-based computing, internet and business technologies, IT management/ & business/business studies; BSc(Hons), FdSc

Communication, Media & Journalism; www.shu.ac.uk/media

corporate communication, communication & international broadcast/PR, computing media production, film & mediavisual effects, media, PR/and communication/media, online communication, professional communication, sports journalism, technical communication; BA(Hons), MA, MPhil, PhD

Computing, Computer and Electronic Systems; www.shu.ac.uk/computing

animation for computer games, business information systems/technology, busines & ICT, computer and information security/network engineering, computer aided design technology, computer networks/studies, computing & IT/information systems/network eng/ information systems security, databases, enterprise systems, forensic and security technologies, games design/software development, information technology networks/software, interactive media with animation, internet and business technologies, multimedia technologies, network management technologies, software engineering, web & cloud technology; BEng, BSc(Hons), FdSc, GradDip, HND, MComp, MSc

Engineering & Technology; www.shu.ac.uk/engineering

advanced/design/ engineering, aeronautical engineering, aerospace electonic systems/ technology, automotive design technology, computer and network engineering, computer-aided engineering and design/technology, electrical & electronic engineering, design engineering /technology, electronics and information technology, forensic engineering, industrial management, logistics and supply chain management, mechanica/ & computer aided engineering, manufacturing engineering materials and product design, software engineering, sport technology/engineering, telecommunication and electronic engineering; BSc(Hons), FdSc, MBA, MSc, PhD

Mathematics & Statistics; www.shu.ac.uk/mathematics

applied statistics, mathematical modelling, mathematics; BSc(Hons), MSc, PhD

Sheffield Institute of the Arts; www.shu.ac.uk/art

arts and cultural management, creative media practice, design, fine art; BA(Hons), MA, MArt, PhD

Faculty of Development & Society; www.shu.ac.uk/faculties/ds

Built Environment; www.shu.ac.uk/built

architectural technology, architecture, environmental design, building surveying/studies, built environment, construction and real estate, construction management, estate agency, planning and property development/appraisal, project management, quantity surveying, real estate investment and management, technical architecture, sustainable communities & environment; BSc(Hons), HNC, HND, MPhil, MSc, PGDip/Cert, PhD

Counselling; www.shu.ac.uk/counselling

educational studies & psychiatry & counselling, foundations of counselling, integrative counselling and psychotherapy; BA(Hons), Cert, DipHE, MA, PGDip/Cert

Criminology & Community Justice; www.shu.ac.uk/justice

criminology and psychology/sociology/politics, forensic biosciences, international criminal justice; BEng, BSc(Hons), FdSc, MA/PgDip/PgCert, MSc

Education; www.shu.ac.uk/education

Asperger's syndrome, autism, early/childhood studies, early years/education with QTS, design & technology, education and disability studies/specialist learning, education for international students, support/sociology/TESOL/psychology & counselling/education studies, learning & skills, education & trainng, primary ed with QTS, design & technology/science with education & QTS; PGCE; early years education, learning & skills, primary education, secondary (broad range of taught subjects), inclusion, integrated working, teaching & learning in HE, mentoring, TESOL, TESOL or numeracy learning and skills, inclusion, business education/citizenship/design and technology/English/information and communication technology/mathematics/modern foreign languages/physical education/religious education/science, integrated working, learning and skills, young people's services, youth work; BA(Hons), CertE, EdD, FdA, MA, MPhil, MSc, PGCert/Dip, PhD

Environment; www.shu.ac.uk/environment

environmental management (business/international resource & climate management/wildlife and landscape conservation, sustainable communities and environment, environmental conservation/science/studies; BA(Hons), BSc(Hons), MPlan, MSc/PGDip/PGCert

English; www.shu.ac www.shu.ac.uk/english

creative writing, history, English language/literature/teaching, screen studies, Shakespeare & Renaissance literature, writing; BA(Hons), MA, PgDip, MPhil, PhD

History; www.shu.ac.uk/history

history and criminology/politics, history, local & global, history, imperialism & cultureBA(Hons), MA, PGDip, MPhil, PhD

Film, Theatre, & Performance; www.shu.ac.uk/performance

animation & special effects, film studies, film and media, drama, dance and music, performance and professional practice, screen studies/with scenewriting/English, visual effects; BA(Hons), FdA, MA, MA/PGDip/PGCert

Geography; www.shu.ac.uk/geography

geography/with planning, GIS, human geography, international relations; BA(Hons), BSc(Hons), MSc, PGDip/Cert

Forensic; www.shu.ac.uk/forensic

forensic accounting, & analytical science/biosciences/criminology/engineering/ psychology, intelligence and forensics management, forensic and security technologies; BSc(Hons), FdSc, MSc

Law; www.shu.ac.uk/law

business law, corporate law and strategy, forensic accounting/criminology/psychology/science, law, law and criminology, măîtrise en droit Frañcais; LlB, LLM, MSc, PGCert/Dip

Planning Regeneration & Housing; www.shu.ac.uk/planning

geography & planning, GIS, housing for environmental health, housing policy and practice, human geography, int real estate, sustainable communities/ and environments, transport/planning and management, urban land economics, urban and regional/ environmental planning, urban regeneration; BA(Hons), BSc(Hons), MPlanning and Transport, MSc/PGDip

Psychology; www.shu.ac.uk/psychology

pyschology & law/sociology/criminology, applied cognitive neuroscience, cognitive analytical psychology, developmental/forensic/organisational/sport & exercise/health psychology; BSc(Hons), MRes/ PGDip/PGCert, MSc

Sociology & Politics; www.shu.ac.uk/social

applied social science, business, cuilture, criminology, sociology, education, health & society, history, human geography, international relations, politics, psychology, public health, social sciences, social work, planning and policy, youth & community work, working with children, young people & families; BA(Hons), GradDip, MA, MPhil/PhD, MRes/PgDip/ PgCert

Faculty of Health & Wellbeing; www.shu.ac.uk/faculties/hwb

Sport and Active Lifestyles; www.shu.ac.uk/active

sport business/event management/culture & society, PE, youth sport, sport development, coaching, sport science for performance coaching, physical activity for health, sport & exercise science/psychology, sport injury management and therapy, sport business management, sports engineering; physical ed & youth sport, sport culture & community, sport & active lifestyles; BA(Hons), BSc(Hons), MA, MSc, PgDip/Cert, PRofDoc

Biosciences; www.shu.ac.uk/bio

biochemistry, biology, biomedical sci/basis for disease, biosciences, biotechnology, cardiovascular medicine, forensic and analytical science, forensic biosciences, genes & proteins, human biology, international and travel health, medical sci, pathological sciences, pharmaceutical analysis/sciences, pharmacology and biotechnology; BSc(Hons), MSc/PGDip/ PGCert, ProfDocBiomedSci

Diagnostic Radiography; www.shu.ac.uk/ radiography

breast imaging and diagnosis, diagnostic radiography, medical imaging programme, medical ultrasound programme; DocProf Studies (Health and Social Care), BA(Hons), BSc(Hons), MSc/PGDip/ PGCert

Management and Leadership; www.shu.ac.uk/faculties/hwb/cpod

health and social care leadership/management/services management; BA(Hons), DipHE, MSc, PhD

Nursing & Midwifery; www.shu.ac.uk/ midwifery/nursing

acute and critical care, advancing paediatric practice, clinical education, health and social care, international nursing, learning disabilty, maternal health care, midwifery, adult, child or mental health nursing, supportive and palliative care, primary care nursing/district nursing, public health, health visiting and school nursing, social work; AdvDip, AdvProfDev Framework, BA(Hons), BSc(Hons), DocProfStud, Foundation degree, MSc/PGDip/ PGCert

Occupational Therapy; www.shu.ac.uk/ occupational

occupational therapy, paediatric practice, vocational rehabilitation, occupational social care practice; BSc(Hons), DocProf, MSc/PGDip/PGCert

Operating Department Practice; www.shu.ac.uk/opd

advanced communcation skills, operating dept practice; BA(Hons), BSc(Hons), DipHE, DocProfStud, MSc/PGDip/Cert

Paramedic Studies; www.shu.ac.uk/ paramedic

paramedic practice, health & social care; BSc(Hons), DipHE

Physiotherapy; www.shu.ac.uk/physio

advancing/applying paediatric practice, physiotherapy, sport injury management and therapy, physical activity for health; BA(Hons), BSc(Hons), MSc, PGCert, PGDip

Radiotherapy and Oncology; www.shu.ac.uk/radiotherapy
psychological aspects, radiotherapy and oncology practice, supportive and palliative care; BA(Hons), BSc(Hons), DipHE, MSc/PGDip/PGCert

Social Work; www.shu.ac.uk/socialwork
applied nursing and social work (learning disability), safeguarding and caring for children and young people, social work, specialist mental health practice/practitioner, working with children, young people and families, youth and community work; BA(Hons), GradDip, MScPgDip, MSW, PGCert, Doc SocWork

Sheffield Business School; www.shu.ac.uk/faculties/sbs

Accounting, Banking & Finance
accounting and finance, audit management and consultancy, banking, business accounting/economics/financial management, forensic accounting, risk management, international finance/banking/economics/stockbroking; BA(Hons), MA, MSc, PGDip/Cert

Business & Management
business and management, business admin/economics/studies, enterprise management, finance, financial management, ICT, international businees studies, global marketing/business/strategic marketing, HRM/HR development, leadership, industrial management, international business and management/HRM/marketing/business studies, marketing, tourism; BSc(Hons), DBA, FD, GradDip, HNC, HND, MBA, MPhil, MSc, PGCert, PGDip, PhD

Facilities Management
food management, events management (arts & entertainment), tourism, hospitality and facilities management; BA(Hons), BSc(Hons), Cert, FD, MA, MPhil, MSc, PGCert, PGDip, PhD

Languages
business and English, English language teaching, educational studies & TESOL, int business studies & languages, teaching English for academic purposes; GradDip/Cert, MPhil, PGCert, PhD

Tourism, Hospitality & Events Management
events & leisure management, international events and conference management, international hospitality and tourism management, hospitality business management; BSc(Hons), FdSc, HND, MA, MPhil, MSc, PGCert, PGDip, PhD

UNIVERSITY OF SOUTHAMPTON
www.soton.ac.uk

The Faculty of Engineering, Science and Mathematics; www.soton.ac.uk/about/academicschools/esm

School of Chemistry; www.soton.ac.uk/chemistry
chemical biology, chemistry, electrochemistry, interfaces & materials, structural & materials chemistry, synthesis; BSc(Hons), MChem, MPhil, PhD

School of Civil Engineering and the Environment; www.civil.soton.ac.uk
civil engineering, environmental engineering, environmental sciences; BEng, BSc(Hons), EngD, MEng, MenvSci, MRes, MSc, PhD

School of Electronics & Computer Science; www.ecs.soton.ac.uk
computer science, electrical engineering, electromechanical engineering, electronic engineering, software engineering, artificial intelligence, bionanotechnology, microelectronic systems design, microelectromechanical systems, nanoelectronics, nanotechnology, radio frequency communications systems, system-on-chip, web science/technology; BSc, BEng, MComp, MEng EngD, MEng, MSc, PhD

School of Engineering Sciences; www.soton.ac.uk/ses
adv mechanical engineering science, aerodynamics & computation, aerospace, aeronatics, astronautics, air vehicles, space craft engineering, space systems, mechanical engineering/automotive, adv materials, aerospace, bioengineering, engineering management, mechatronics, naval engineering, sustainable energy systems, ship science (advanced materials, naval architecture/eng), yacht & small craft, marine engineering/ technology; EngD, European Master, MPhil, MSc, PhD

School of Geography; www.soton.ac.uk/geography
archaeology, creative cities, geography, geology, oceanography, physical geography, applied remote sensing & GIS, health cities, city & regional

development, paleogeology, river science & management; BA(Hons), BSc(Hons), MA, MSc, PhD

School of Mathematics; www.soton.ac.uk/maths

mathematical studies, mathematics, statistics, operational research/with finance, statistics in medicine, actuarial studies joint degree subjects; BSc(Hons), MMath, MPhil, MSc PgDip, PhD

School of Ocean & Earth Sciences; www.soton.ac.uk/soes

engineering in the coastal environment, geology, biological geophysics, marine biology/environment and resources/geology/ resource management/ science, policy and law, ocean and earth system science, oceanography; BSc(Hons), MRes, MSc, PhD

Dept of Physics and Astronomy; www.phys.soton.ac.uk/

astronomy, theoretical particle physics, physics with astronomy/nanotechnology/space science/photonics/ astronomy/mathematics, quantum, light & matter; BSc(Hons), MPhys, MSc, PhD

Institute of Sound and Vibration Research; www.isvr.soton.ac.uk

acoustical engineering, acoustics/ & music, applied digital signal processing, audiology, biomedical signal processing, engineering acoustics, sound and vibration studies, structural dynamics; DClinPract, European Doctorate, MSc, PhD

Optioelectronic Research Centre; www.soton.ac.uk/orc

biophotonic microsystems, fundamental photonics, high-power, high energy laser, nanophotonics and meta-materials, optical fibres and materials, optical networks and systems, planar lightwave integration, ultrafast lasers and applications; MPhil, PhD

Faculty of Law, Arts and Social Sciences; www.lass.soton.ac.ak/academicschools/lass

Centre for Contemporary China; www.soton.ac.uk/ccc

international comparative studies; MSc

School of Art (Winchester School of Art); www.wsa.soton.ac.uk

advertising design, design management, fashion management, fashion & textile management, graphic design, illustration, photography, motion graphics, luxury illustration & digital animation, photography & digital media, fine art; fashion & fibre, fashion design, fashion promotion & marketing, new media, painting, printmaking, sculpture, textile, textile design, time-based media; BA(Hons), MA, MPhil, PhD

School of Education; www.education.soton.ac.uk

computer-based learning and training, education, education and training (primary) with QTS/PCET training, educational practice and innovation, institutional management and leadership in mathematics education/professional development, management, leadership and innovation, mathematics education, social justice and inclusive education, specific learning difficulties (dyslexia), sport studies, teacher training, PGCE English/geography/mod languages/ music/primary/RE/Science; BA, BA(Hons), EdD, MA, MA(Ed), MPhil, MSc, PhD

School of Humanities; www.soton.ac.uk/humanities

archaeology, English, film studies, history, medieval & Renaissance studies, modern languages/contemporary Europe/English language studies/French studies/German studies/linguistic studies, music, philosophy, Spanish, Portugese & Latin American Studies; BA(Hons), BSc(Hons), CertHE, GradDip, MA, MSc, MPhil, PhD

School of Law; www.soton.ac.uk/law

commercial and corporate law, European and comparative property law, European law, European legal studies, information technology and commerce/telecommunications, international business law, international law, international legal studies, law, maritime law; LlB, LlM, MPhil, PhD

School of Management; www.management.soton.ac.uk/

accounting, business administration, business analytics & management studies, corporate risk & security management, economics, entrepreneurship, finance, global supply chain management, HE management / and policy, HRM, human resource strategies, international banking & financial studies/financial markets/marketing, management of research & enterprise in HE, knowledge and information systems management, management, marketing analytics, marketing management, mathematics, risk management, strategic entrepreneurship; BSc(Hons), DBA, MBA, MSc, PhD

School of Social Sciences; www.soton.ac.uk/socsci
gerontology, applied social sciences, citizenship & democracy, demography, official/social statistics, finance /& economics, econometrics, international comparative studies, global politics/security & international relations, population & geography, social statistics, social work criminology, contemporary Europe, sociology & social policy, international relations, sustainable development; MA, MLitt, MPhil, MRes, PhD, GradDip

School of Health Sciences; www.soton.ac.uk/healthsciences
health and social care, midwifery, nursing (adult, children's, mental health), mental health practioner, clinical practice, public health practice, occupational therapy, physiotherapy, podiatry

Statistical Science Research Institute; www.soton.ac.uk/ssri

Faculty of Medicine, Health & Life Sciences; www.soton.ac.uk/academicschools/mhls

School of Biological Sciences; www.sbs.soton.ac.uk
biochemistry, biology, biomedical sciences, molecular biosciences, neuroscience, pharmacology, zoology, ecology & the environment; BSc(Hons), CertHE, DipHE, MPhil, PhD

School of Psychology; www.psychology.soton.ac.uk
clinical psychology, cognitive therapy for severe mental health problems, anxiety & distress, long-term physical problems), companion animal counselling, educational/ health psychology, psychology; BSc(Hons), DocClinPsych, MPhil, MSc, PgDip, PhD

School of Medicine; www.som.soton.ac.uk
advanced clinical practice, allergy, cancer sciences, developmental origins of health and disease, health and rehabilitation, human genetics, leaders and management, medicine, mental health practitioner/ studies, nursing, podiatry, public health, public health nutrition; BM, MSc, PgDip/Cert, PhD

STAFFORDSHIRE UNIVERSITY
www.staffs.ac.uk

Staffordshire University Business School; www.staffs.ac.uk/business
accounting, business, business analysis/economics/ information systems/ management/start-ups/studies, e-business, event management, economics/for business analysis/of international trade & European/ international marketing, educational leadership, international supply chain management, Chinese management, entrepreneurship, events management, finance, forensic accounting, strategic/HRM, international business/management marketing/supply chain /management, multimedia marketing, personnel practice, tourism management; BA, BSc, HNC, HND, MA, MBA, MPhil, MSc, PGCert, PGDip, PhD

Faculty of Arts, Media & Design; www.staffs.ac.uk/faculties/art.and.design
advertising/brand design management, animation, 3D design (ceramics, jewellery, interior products), arts media & design, community & participatory arts, design management, design product innovation, publication design, surface pattern/product/transport design, comic arts, fine art (digital media, photography, video, theory), illustration, interior design, visual effects, journalism, product innovation/publication/transport design, international history/policy & diplomacy/relations, regeneration, media management, transnational organised crime
film, television & radio studies/documentary , film production/practice & theory/visual cultures, media studies, leisure industries, scriptwriting, sports PR, children & family work, creative writing, crime, deviance & society/security,

drama, performance & theatre arts, English/literature, history, i international history/relations/diplomacy, literature & contemporary culture, philiosophy, school, youth & community work, practical theology, sociology, theatre studies & tech stage production/design, digital media production, drama, performance & theatre arts; BA, FdA, MA, MFA, MPhil, MSc, PhD

Faculty of Computing, Engineering & Technology; www.staffs.ac.uk/faculties/comp_eng_tech

3D games modelling, computing/technology, aeronautical technology, applied computing/information technology/internet commerce/multimedia systems/network management, automotive electronics/engineering, autosport engineering, bioinformatics, health & geoinformatics, broadcast technology, business computing/information technology, computer game design & programming/development/networks & security/science systems, computing science, creative music technology, database technology, digital feature film production/3D animation technology, educational software development, electrical/electronic/electronic & broadcast engineering, embedded games tech, environmental engineering, music technology, forensic computing/engineering, mathematics & applied statistics, mechanical engineering, mechatronics, medical engineering, mobile computer systems, motorsport technology, multimedia computing/systems/design/programming, music production/technology, network computing/engineering/systems management, product design engineering/technology, robotics/software engineering, sports technology, technology for teaching & learning, telecommunications engineering, web computing/multimedia/development; BA, BEng, BSc, FdSc, HND, MEng, MSc, MPhil, MRes, PGCE, PGCert, PGDip, PhD

Faculty of Health; www.staffs.ac.uk/faculties/health

ageing/dementia, counselling, social studies, sport & exercise psychology/science, mental health, clinical biomechanics/diabetes/pain management/ coaching science, exercise & lifestyle management, health management & policy/social care, hypnosis & stress, medical education, midwifery practice, nursing practice: adult /children's /district nursing/mental health/specialist /clinical practice (public health – health visiting) nursing, leadership, palliative & end of life care, PE & youth sport coaching, paramedic science, peri-operative care, physical activity, public health, social care/work, sport & exercise nutrition/psychology/science, sport studies/ therapy; BSc, MA, MPhil, MSc, PGCE, PGCert, PGDip, PhD

Faculty of Sciences; www.staffs.ac.uk/faculties/sciences

animal biology & conservation, applied sport & exercise psychology, biochemistry & microbiology, biology, biomedical science, clinical psychology, counselling, child development, criminology, early childhood studies, environment & sustainability, environmental conservation/forensics/management & protection, forensic biology/investigation/psychology/science, geography, governanace, habitat creation & management, health psychology, human biology, molecular biology, policing & criminal investigation, psychology, psychotherapeutic counselling, sociology, sport & exercise psychology, sustainable communities dev, teaching psychology, water & environment; BA, BSc, DClinPsy, DHealthPsy, FdSc, MA, MSc, MPhil, PGCert, PGDip, PhD

Law School; www.staffs.ac.u/faculties/law

business law, criminology, environmental/family/employment/international trade & commerce law, HRM, human rights law, law, legal practice, international/sports law; LLB, LLM, MPhil, PhD

UNIVERSITY OF STIRLING
www.external.stir.ac.uk

Dept of Applied Social Science; www.dass.stir.ac.uk

applied social research, child welfare & protection, criminology, dementia studies, European /social policy, social work, adult services support & protection, managers in social services, sociology; BA, GradCert, MSc, PGCert, PGDip, PhD

Dept of Computing Science & Mathematics; www.cs.stir.ac.uk

advanced computing, business computing, computing, computing for financial markets, variant/information /technology, mathematics; BSc, MSc, PhD, MBA

Dept of English Studies; www.english.stir.ac.uk

English studies, creative writing, the Gothic imagination, humanities, modern Scottish writing, postcolonial studies, international publishing management, publishing studies; BA, MLitt, MPhil, MRes, MSc, PhD

Dept of Film, Media & Journalism; www.fmj.stir.ac.uk

film & media studies, financial journalism, global cinema, journalism studies, media & culture/management, public communications management, PR; BA, MLitt, MPhil, MSc, PGDip, PhD

Dept of Nursing & Midwifery; www.nm.stir.ac.uk

advanced practice, health research, midwifery studies, nursing (adult, learning disabilities, mental health), HE (nursing); BM, BN, BSc, DAHP, DM, DN, MPhil, MRes, MSc, PGDip, PhDDipHE

Dept of Philosophy; www.philosophy.stir.ac.uk

philosophy, logic & language, legal, moral; BA, MLitt, MPhil, PhD

Dept of Psychology; www.psychology.stir.ac.uk

child development: early years, evolution & behaviour, health psychology, psychology, psychological research methods/therapy & primary care, measuring perception; BA, BSc, MSc, PGDip, PhD

Dept of Sports Studies; www.sports.stir.ac.uk

sport & exercise science, sports coaching/management/studies, physical education & professional education; BA, BSc, MPhil, MSc, PGDip, PhD

Institute of Aquaculture; www.aqua.stir.ac.uk

aquaculture/& the environment/development/business management/nutrition/systems, aquatic veterinary studies/pathobiology, marine biology, sustainable aquaculture; BSc, MPhil, MSc, PGCert, PGDip, PhD

School of Biological & Environmental Sciences; www.sbes.stir.ac.uk

animal biology, biology, cell biology, conservation biology & management, ecology, environmental geography/ history, management/science & outdoor education, river basin management, psychology, sports & exercise science; BSc, MPhil, MRes, MSc, PGCert, PGDip, PhD

School of History & Politics; www.historyandpolitics.stir.ac.uk

environmental history, history, international conflict & cooperation, politics, revolution & counter-revolution; BA, MLitt, MPhil, MRes, MSc, PhD

School of Languages, Culture and Regions; www.slcr.stir.ac.uk

hermeneutics, humanities, French/ Spanish & Latin American/ translation studies, TESOL, film studies; BA, MLitt, MRes, PhD

School of Law; www.law.stir.ac.uk

business/commercial law, law; BA, LLB, LLM, PhD

Stirling Institute of Education; www.ioe.stir.ac.uk

academic practice, EFL, English language teaching, international policing, professional enquiry, TESOL; BA, BSc, EdD, MEd, MPhil, MRes, MSc, PGCert, PGDip, PhD

Stirling Management School; www.management.stir.ac.uk

Accounting & Finance Division

accountancy, finance, international accounting & finance, investment analysis; BA, BAcc, MPhil, MSc, PhD

Business & Organization Division

business & management, business studies, HRM, international business, management science, public management & administration, public service management; BA, BSc, MBA, MPhil, MRes, MSc, PhD

Division of Economics

banking & finance, economics, energy management, environmental finance, money, politics, philosophy & economics; BA, MSc, PhD

Division of Marketing

international tourism management, marketing, retail marketing, retailing; BA, MBA, MSc, PhD

STOCKPORT COLLEGE
www.stockport.ac.uk

access to HE, art, design, media, building/ services/ constructions & civil eng, business & IT technology/ management/marketing, childcare, early childhood studies, photography, computing, illustration, surface design, graphic design/illustration/moving image/ surface design, engineering, forensic science, graphic communication, photography, social work /counselling, health & social care; BA, FdA, FDSc

UNIVERSITY OF STRATHCLYDE
www.strath.ac.uk

Faculty of Education; www.strath.ac.uk/ education

Dept of Childhood & Primary Studies; www.strath.co.uk/cps

autism, childhood practice, early childhood studies, education & social services, maths recovery; BA, BEd, MSc, PGCE, PGCert, PGDip

Dept of Creative & Aesthetic Studies; www.strath.ac.uk/caasl

applied music, creative & aesthetic studies; BA, MPhil, PhD

Dept of Curricular Studies; www.strath.ac.uk/curricularstudies

business & computer education, design & technology education, education (secondary), language, mathematics, science & technology/social studies education; DBA, MPhil, MSc, PGDE, PGCert, PGDip, PhD

Dept of Educational & Professional Studies; www.strath.ac.uk/eps

adult guidance/literacies, advanced academic studies/professional studies, applied educational research, community education, counselling/psychology, educational support, management & leadership in education, philosophy with children, safety & risk management, school leadership & management, speech & language pathology; BA, BSc, EdD, MEd, MPhil, MSc, PGCert, PGDE, PGDip, PhD

Dept of Sport, Culture & the Arts; www.strath.ac.uk/scu

community arts, sport & physical activity, secondary art & education/drama/PE; BA, BSc, MPhil, PGDE, PhD

Glasgow School of Social Work; www.strath.ac.uk/gssw

residential childcare, community care, social work/ management; BA, MPhil, MSc, MSW, PGCert, PhD

Faculty of Engineering; www.strath.ac.uk/engineering

Bioengineering Unit; www.strath.ac.uk/ bioeng

bioengineering, medical devices, biomedical engineering, medical technology; EngD, MPhil, MRes, MSc, PGCert, PGDip, PhD

Dept of Architecture; www.strath.ac.uk/ architecture

adv architectural design/s, building design & management for sustainability, lean design & practice management, urban design; MArch, MRes, MSc, PGCert, PGDip

Dept of Chemical & Process Engineering; www.strath.ac.uk/chemeng

applied chemistry & chemical engineering, chemical engineering/technology & management, process technology & management, product dvelopment, chemical processing; BEng, MEng, MSc, PGCert, PGDip

Dept of Civil Engineering; www.strath.ac.uk/civeng

architectural/civil/environmental engineering, forensics/health/science/studies, environmental management/health forensics, geotechnics, global water sustainability, hydrogeology, science, technology & sustainability; BEng, BSc, MEng, MPhil, MRes, MSc, PhD

Dept of Design, Manufacture & Engineering Management; www.strath.ac.uk/dmen

computer aided engineering design, digital creativity, engineering design, global innovation, integrated product development, management of competitive manufacturing, mechatronics & automation, operations management in engineering, product design engineering/design & innovation, production engineering & management, sports engineering, supply chain & ops management, management, technology management; BEng, BSc, MEng, MSc, PGCert, PGDip

Dept of Electronic & Electrical Engineering; www.strath.ac.uk/eee

communications, computer & electronic systems, control & digital processing systems, digital multimedia & communication systems, electrical energy systems, electrical & mechanical engineering, electrical power engineering, electronic & digital systems, electronic engineering; BEng, MEng, MSc, PGCert, PGDip

Dept of Mechanical Engineering; www.strath.ac.uk/mecheng

aeronautics, aero-mechanical/enviro-mechanical/ mechanical engineering, power plant engineering/ technologies, sustainable engineering: energy systems & the environment, materials engineering; BEng, MEng, MPhil, PGCert, PGDip, PhD

Dept of Naval Architectural & Marine Engineering; www.strath.ac.uk/na-me

marine engineering/technology, naval architecture, with marine engineering/ocean engineering/small craft engineering, subsea engineering, sustainable energy, offshore renewable energy/floating systems, technical management of ship operations; BEng, MEng, MPhil, MSc, PGCert, PGDip, PhD

National Centre for Prosthetics & Orthotics; www.strath.ac.uk/prosthetics

prosthetics & orthotics, rehabilitation studies; BSc, MPhil, MSc, PGCert, PGDip, PhD

Faculty of Law, Arts & Social Sciences; www.strath.ac.uk/arts

Dept of English Studies; www.strath.ac.uk/english

English, journalism, literature, creative writing, culture & place, Renaissance studies; BA, MLitt, MPhil, MRes, MSc, PGDip, PhD

Dept of Geography & Sociology; www.gs.strath.ac.uk

geography, human ecology, investigative journalism, media & communication research, refugee & migration studies, social research, sociology; BA, MRes, MSc, PGCert, PGDip, PhD

Dept of Government; www.strath.ac.uk/goverment

European/international public policy, political research, politics, public policy; BA, MSc, PhD

Dept of History; www.strath.ac.uk/history

historical studies, history, social history, health history, oral history; BA, MPhil, MRes, MSc, PGCert, PGDip, PhD

Dept of Modern Languages; www.strath.ac.uk/modlang

French, Italian, Spanish; BA, MPhil, MRes, PhD

Dept of Psychology; www.strath.ac.uk/psychology

educational psychology, psychology; BA, MRes, MSc, PhD

The Law School; www.law.strath.ac.uk

law, construction law, criminology & criminal justice, human rights law, international economic law, international law & sustainable development, IT & telecommunications law, legal practice, mediation & conflict resolution; BA, LLB, LLM, PGCert, PGDip

Faculty of Science; www.strath.ac.uk/science

Centre for Forensic Science

forensic & analytical chemistry, forensic biology/ informatics/science; BSc, MSc, PGDip

Dept of Pure & Applied Chemistry; www.chem.strath.ac.uk

applied chemistry, analytical/organic/inorganic/physical/bioorganic chemistry, chemical engineering, chemistry, drug discovery, forensic chemistry/science; BSc, MChem, MSc, PGDip, PhD

Dept of Computer & Information Sciences; www.strath.ac.uk/cis

automated planning for autonomous systems, business information systems/technology systems, computer & electronic systems, internet technologies, computer science, forensic informatics, information management, software engineering; BEng, BSc, MEng, MPhil, MRes, MSc, PGCert, PGDip

Dept of Mathematics & Statistics; www.mathstat.strath.ac.uk

mathematics (business/science/engineering based), mathematics & computer science/physics/statistics, acccounting/economics/finance/management science/ teaching; BSc, MSc, PhD

Dept of Physics; www.strath.ac.uk/physics
nano science, optics, plasma, physics, physics with teaching; BSc, MPhys, MSc, PhD

Strathclyde Institute of Pharmacy & Biomedical Sciences; www.strath.ac.uk/sibs
biochemistry & immunology/microbiology, biological/biomedical sciences, clinical/ pharmacy, food biotechnology/science & microbiology, forensic biology, immunology & microbiology/pharmacology, pharmaceutical analysis, sport, exercise science; BSc, MPharm, MPhil, MSc, PGCert, PGDip, PhD

Strathclyde Business School; www.strath.ac.uk/business

Dept of Accounting & Finance; www.strath.ac.uk/accfin
accounting, business enterprise/law/technology, economics, finance, hospitality & tourism, HRM, international accounting & finance/banking & finance, investment & finance, management, management science, marketing; BA, MSc

Dept of Economics; www.strath.ac.uk/economics
economics economic management & policy, BA, BSc, DBA, MPhil, MRes, MSc, PhD

Dept of Human Resource Management; www.strath.ac.ukhrm
HRM; BA, DBA, MRes, MSc, PGCert, PGDip, PhD; HRM, executive coaching, equality in pay & reward

Dept of Management; www.strath.ac.uk/management
business IT systems, hospitality & tourism management, international business management, management; BA, MBA, MBM, MSc

Dept of Management Science; www.strath.ac.uk/mansci
business analysis & consulting, operational research, international business; DBA, MSc, DPhil, PhD

Dept of Marketing; www.strath.ac.uk/marketing
international marketing, marketing & French/German/Spanish/psychology/tourism; DBA, MPhil, MRes, MSc, PhD

UNIVERSITY CAMPUS SUFFOLK
www.ucs.ac.uk

School of Arts & Humanities; www.ucs.ac.uk/study/SchoolsAndCentres/SchoolOfArtsAndHumanities
computer games design, creative music, dance, design, graphic & typographic design, English, history, family, local & community history, fashion & textiles, film, fine art, football development & coaching, graphic communication/design, graphic illustration/motion graphics, history, interior architectural design, landscape & garden design, music production, photographic & digital media, photography, visual media production; BA, FdA, MA, PGCert, PGDip

School of Health, Science & Social Care; www.ucs.ac.uk/study/SchoolsAndCentres/SchoolOfHealthScienceAndSocialCare
animal science & welfare, applied computing, architectural technology, building control/services engineering/surveying, civil engineering, clinical practice, computing, construction management, counselling, English, event management, electrical/electronic/mechanical/operations engineering, holistic therapies, hospitality, leadership & innovation in health & social care, nutrition & human health, photography, operating department practice, person-centred counselling, personal training with sports massage therapy, social care practice, social work, specialist community public health nursing, society; FdA, FdSc, MA, PGCert, PGDip

School of Nursing & Midwifery; www.ucs.ac.uk/study/SchoolsAndCentres/SchoolOfArtsAndHumanities/events/events
adult/child health/mental health nursing, health administration, health & wellbeing, health care practice, health sciences (diagnostic imaging)/(radiotherapy & oncology), public health practice; BSc, DipHE, FdA, FdSc

School of Social Science & Business; www.ucs.ac.uk/study/SchoolsAndCentres/SchoolOfSocialScienceAndBusiness
business administration/management, children's care, criminology, youth studies, employment law, event management, HR strategy, leadership &

development/management, leisure/tourism management, network & communication technologies, pers-management, psychology & business management/criminology/sociology/youth studies; BA, BSc, CertEd, FdA, FdSc, GradCert, MA, MBA, PGCert, PGDip

UNIVERSITY OF SUNDERLAND
www.sunderland.ac.uk

Faculty of Applied Sciences; www.sunderland.ac.uk/faculties/apsc

Dept of Computing, Engineering & Technology; www.sunderland.ac.uk/faculties/apsc/ourfaculty/ourdepartments/cet

applied business/forensic/network computing, mechanical/manufacturing eng, automotive/electronic & electrical / manufacturing/mechanical engineering, business computing, software/telecommunications engineering, business computing, computer applications/science/systems engineering, health information management, information & communications technologies, IT applications, network systems, performance improvement/management, project management, software engineering, sound & music technology; BA, BEng, BSc, FdSc, MSc

Dept of Pharmacy, Health & Well-being; www.sunderland.ac.uk/faculties/apsc/ourfaculty/ourdepartments/phw

advanced clinical practice, biomedical sciences, biotechnology, chemical & pharmaceutical science, clinical pharmacy/prescribing sciences, clinical physiology, community health, drug discovery & development, environment/health/management, drug & alcohol, public health, geography, health & safety/social care, nursing, pharmacotherapy & medicines management, pharmacy; BA, BSc, FdA, MPharm, MSc, PGCE, Univ Dip

Dept of Psychology; www.sunderland.ac.uk/faculties/apsc/ourfaculty/ourdepartments/psychology

counselling, psychology, sport & exercise psychology; BA, FdA, MA, MSc

Dept of Sport & Exercise Sciences; www.sunderland.ac.uk/faculties/apsc/ourfaculty/ourdepartments/sport

exercise, health & fitness, outdoor & adventure education, sport & exercise development/psychology/sciences, sport studies, sports coaching/development; BA, BSc, FdA MSc

Faculty of Arts, Design & Media; www.sunderland.ac.uk/faculties/adm/

Dept of Arts & Design; www.sunderland.ac.uk/faculties/adm/ourfaculty/ourdepartments/departmentofartsdesign

advertising/animation & design, applied art, art & design, performance arts, dance, design: graphics, design studies, drama, fashion, textiles & promotion, film, TV & culture/ media, media studies, radio, 3D design, fine art, glass, graphic communication/illustration, interior design, jewellery & silversmithing, performing arts, photography; BA, BSc, FdA, MA

Dept of Media; www.sunderland.ac.uk/faculties/adm/ourfaculty/ourdepartments/departmentofmedia

film & cultural studies/media, writing (film, TV & radio, broadcast/fashion/international/news journalism, media & cultural studies/production (TV radio, video, new media), PR, radio (production & management), screenwriting, scriptwriting, video, television studies; BA, BSc, FdA, MA

Faculty of Business & Law; www.sunderland.ac.uk/faculties/bl

accountancy, business & enterprise/financial management, criminology, HRM, marketing, business education/computing/studies, law, leadership & management, legal studies, leisure management, marketing, retail management, hospitality & tourism, tourism & events/hospitality, travel & tourism; BA, CertHE, FdA, GradDip, LLB, LLM, MA, MBS, MSc, PGDip

Faculty of Education & Society

Dept of Education; www.sunderland.ac.uk/faculties/es/ourfaculty/ourdepartments/departmentofeducation

advanced professional practice (primary)/(primary/secondary)/(secondary), advancing pedagogy, primary education, professional learning & guidance, secondary education (various subjects), special needs

& inclusive education, teaching & learning in HE/ with ICT, TESOL; BA, BSc, MA, PGCE

Dept of Culture; www.sunderland.ac.uk/faculties/es/ourfaculty/ourdepartments/departmentofculture
American studies, Buddhist studies, contemporary history & politics, English/creative writing/drama/film/ education (11–18 years)/language & linguistics/secondary education, French, German, history, politics, Spanish, world literatures; BA, BSc, MA, PGCE

Dept of Social Sciences; www.sunderland.ac.uk/faculties/es/ourfaculty/ourdepartments/departmentofsocialsciences/
applied family studies, career guidance, childhood studies, community & youth work studies, criminology, education & care/curriculum studies, health & social care, interprofessional practice education, social work, sociology, working with young people; BA, FdA, MA, BA(Hons), BEng(Hons), BSc(Hons), EdEng, FdA, FdSc, LLM, MA, MBA, MSc, PGCE, PGCert

Degrees validated by University of Sunderland offered at:

CITY OF SUNDERLAND COLLEGE
www.citysun.ac.uk

accountancy, art and design, beauty therapy, business administration, business and management, care, catering and hairdressing, childcare, construction, planning and the built environment, counselling and health, education, training and teaching assistants, engineering and motor vehicle, English courses, horticulture, ICT and computing, media and performing arts, science and mathematics

UNIVERSITY OF SURREY
www.surrey.ac.uk

Faculty of Arts & Human Sciences; www2.surrey.ac.uk/fahs/

Dept of Dance, Film & Theatre; www.surrey.ac.uk/dance
dance, dance cultures, film studies, theatre studies; BA, MA, MPhil, PGDip, PhD

Dept of Economics; www.econ, surrey.ac.uk
finance, economics, energy economics & policy, business/international economics, finance & development; BSc, MSc, PhD

Dept of English; wwwr.english.surrey.ac.uk
communication & international marketing, cultural studies, English literature, creative writing, intercultural communication with international business; BA, MA, MPhil, PGDip, PhD

Dept of Languages & Translation Studies; www.surrey.ac.uk/languages
audiovisual translation, French/German/Spanish, languages & contemporary cultures, business/translation, international communication, public service/service translation; BA, BSc, MA, MSc, PGDip

Dept of Music & Sound Recording; www.surrey.ac.uk/music
creative music technology, music, music & sound recording, musicology; BMus, BSc, MMus, MPhil, MRes, PGDip, PhD

Dept of Political, International & Policy Studies; www2.surrey.ac.uk/politics
European politics/ business & law, law /with international politics, politics/ & languages; BA, LLB, MA, MPhil, PhD

Dept of Psychology; www.psy.surrey.ac.uk
applied psychology & sociology, clinical/environmental/forensic/health/occupational & organizational/psychotherapeutic & counselling/social psychology, psychology, social research; BSc, MSc, PhD, PsychD

Dept of Sociology; www.soc.surrey.ac.uk
criminology, criminal justice & criminal research, media studies, social research methods, sociology, culture & media; BSc, MSc, PhD

Faculty of Engineering & Physical Sciences; www.surrey.ac.uk/feps

Dept of Computing; www2, surrey.ac.uk/computing

computer science/ & engineering, computing & information technology, information systems, internet computing, security technologies & applications; BSc, MSc, PhD

Dept of Electronic Engineering; www.ee.surrey.ac.uk

audio & digital media/communications/satellite communications engineering/networks & software, electronics engineering, satellite engineering, media imaging, microwave engineering, & wireless subsystems, mobile & satellite communication, communication systems, multimedia technology & systems, nanotechnology & nanoelectronic devices, signal processing & machine intelligence, space technology & planetary exploration; BEng, MEng, MPhil, MSc, PhD

Dept of Mathematics; www2.maths.surrey.ac.uk

financial mathematics, statistics, mathematics; BSc, MMath, MSc, PhD

Dept of Physics; www2.surrey.ac.uk/physics

medical physics/imaging, physics, nuclear astronomy, satellite technology, radiation detection & instrumentation, radiation & environmental protection; BSc, MSc, MPhys

Division of Civil, Chemical & Environmental Engineering; www.surrey.ac.uk/cce

chemical & bio-systems, civil/information & business systems, information & process systems, environmental systems, structural/water & environmental engineering, corporate environmental management/strategy, sustainable development, technology management, transport planning & practice, water regulation & management; BEng, MEng, MSc, PGCert, PGDip

Division of Mechanical, Medical, & Aerospace Engineering; www.surrey.ac.uk/mma

advanced materials/aerospace/biomedical/mechanical/medical engineering, entrepreneurship in technology, IT & business; BEng, MEng, MSc, PGCert, PGDip

Faculty of Health & Medical Sciences; www2.surrey.ac.uk/fhms

Division of Biochemical Sciences; www2.surrey.ac.uk/biochem

applied/genetic toxicology, biochemistry, clinical biochemistry/pharmacology, toxicology; BSc, MSc

Division of Chemical Sciences; www2.surrey.ac.uk/chemistry

chemistry/ with forensic investigation, medicinal chemistry, natural drug discovery/design; BSc, MChem, MRes, MSc, PGDip, PhD

Division of Health & Social Care; www2.surrey.ac.uk/healthandsocialcare

advanced/clinical practice, health ergonomics, health & social care, learning & teaching for professional practice, mental health (primary care), midwifery studies, nursing studies: adult/child/mental health, occupational health & safety, operating department practice, paramedic practice, public health practice, safety & ergonomics; BSc, DipHE, MSc, PGCert, PGDip

Division of Microbial Sciences; www2.surrey.ac.uk/microbial

biotechnology, food science & microbiology, microbial genetics, microbiology, veterinary biosciences; BSc, MSc

Division of Nutritional Sciences; www.surrey.ac.uk/nutrition

nutrition, food science, dietetics, nutritional medicine; BSc, MSc, PGCert, PGDip

Faculty of Management & Law; www.surrey.ac.uk/fml

School of Management; www.som.surrey.ac.uk

accounting & financial management, business management, entrepreneurship, financial services, finance, food /health care management, HRM, management information systems, international business/event/financial/tourism/hotel marketing/retail marketing management, marketing/operations & logistics management, retail management, tourism development/management/marketing; BSc, DBA, MBA, MSc, PhD

School of Law; www2.surrey.ac.uk/law

employment/environmental law, health/European/international/international commercial law, justice, law with criminology, French law, German law,

Spanish law, international studies; LLB, LLM, MA, PhD

Degrees validated by the University of Surrey offered at:

FARNBOROUGH COLLEGE OF TECHNOLOGY
www.farn-ct.ac.uk

accounting, aeronautical engineering, business management, childcare, complementary medicine, computing, education early childhood, early years, holistic therapies, hospitality management, learning support, media, motorsport, multimedia, performing arts, photography, public service (uniformed), salon & spa management, social care, sports performance, tourism & event management; BA, BSc, FdA, FdSc

NESCOT(NORTH EAST SURREY COLLEGE OF TECHNOLOGY)
www.nescot.ac.uk

acoustics & noise control, applied biological science, biomedical science, healthcare science, business, computing & IT/systems dev, omplementary therapies, counselling, early years, health & social care, media (moving image), music production, osteopathy, performing arts, photo imaging, perfusion sci, sports therapy, teaching in the lifelong learning sector, travel & tourism management; BA(Hons), BSc(Hons), DipHE, FdA, FdSc, HNC, HND, MSc, PGDip

ST MARY'S COLLEGE
www.smuc.ac.uk

applied linguistics, ELT, sport & exercise physiology, sport psychology, bioethics, business law, Catholic school leadership, charity management, clinical hypnosis, creative & professional writing, drama, applied theatre, drama & physical theatre leading innovation & change/pedagogy & professional values & practice, education & social science, English, employment & corporate law, film, geography, health & exercise, history, culture & belief, international business practice, Irish studies, management studies, media arts, mentoring & coaching, nutrition, physical activity for public health, pastoral theology, philosophy, physical education, sport education, physical theatre, PGCE (primary, secondary), psychology, sociology, sport & exercise rehabilitation, sport science/ coaching science/ journalism, strength & conditioning science, theatre directing, theology & religious studies, tourism; BA, BSc, FdA, LLM, MA, MPhil, MSc, PGCE, PGCert, PGDip, PhD

UNIVERSITY OF SUSSEX
www.sussex.ac.uk

Brighton & Sussex Medical School; www.bsms.sussex.ac.uk

cardiology, clinical education, global health, health or social care, diabetes, leadership & management in health care, medical education, medicine, nephrology, professional development in health & social care, psychopharmacology, public health, surgery, trauma & orthopaedics; MA, MD, MPhil, PGCert, PGDip, PhD

School of Business, Management & Economics; www.sussex.ac.uk/aboutus/schoolsdepartments/bmec

Dept of Business & Management; www.sussex.ac.uk/Units/spru/bams

business (finance/international business/marketing, HR), business & management studies, economics, finance, corporate & financial risk management, economics & management studies, financial mathematics, international accounting, finance & strategy, international finance/management, management & entrepreneurship/finance, managing knowledge & intellectual property, technology & innovation management; BA, BSc, MSc, PGDip

Dept of Economics; www.sussex.ac.uk/economics
economics/and development studies/international relations/politics, development economics, international finance; BA, BSc, GradDip, MSc

Dept of Science & Technology Policy Research (SPRU); www.sussex.ac.uk/spru
public policies for science, technology & innovation, science & technology policy/for sustainability, technology & innovation management; BA, BSc, DPhil, MPhil, MSc

School of Education & Social Work; www.sussex.ac.uk/aboutus/schoolsdepartments/esw

Dept of Education; www.sussex.ac.uk/education
education, professional educational studies, PGCE 11-18 (in seven subjects), PGCE 7-14 (maths, modern foreign languages, graduate teaching programme); BA, PGCE, PGCert, PGDip, MA

Dept of Social Work; www.sussex.ac.uk/socialwork
leadership & management with children, childhood & youth studies, young people, their families & carers, practice education, practice with children, young people, social research methods, social work/with children & young people, their families & carers; BA, DPhil, MA, MPhil, MSc, PGCert

School of Engineering & Design; www.sussex.ac.uk/aboutus/schoolsdepartments/engdes

advanced mechanical engineering, aerospace technology, automotive engineering, biomedical instrumentation, computer engineering, digital communications & embedded systems, electrical engineering, communication engineering, electronic engineering, mechanical engineering, product design, robotics, satellite communications & space systems, security technologies & systems; BEng, BSc, DPhil, MEng, MPhil, MSc

School of English; www.sussex.ac.uk/aboutus/schoolsdepartments/english

English, English literature, early modern literature & culture, literature, film & visual culture, sexual dissidence & culture, creative & criitical writing, colonial & post-colonial culture, critical thought, literature & philosophy, applied/linguistics; BA, DPhil, MA, MPhil

School of Global Studies; www.sussex.ac.uk/aboutus/schoolsdepartments/global

Dept of Anthropology; www.sussex.ac.uk/anthroplogy
anthropology/(Africa/Europe/South Asia), anthropology of conflict, violence & conciliation/development & social transformation, comparative & cross-cultural research methods (anthropology), medical/social anthropology; BA, DPhil, MA, MSc

Dept of Geography; www.sussex.ac.uk/geography
geography and international relations/development, climate change & policy/development, human geography, migration studies, rural development, comparitive & cross-culture; BA, BSc, DPhil, MA, MPhil, MSc

Dept of International Relations; www.sussex.ac.uk/ir
conflict, security & development, geopolitics & grand strategy, global political economy, international relations & security/law/politics/sociology; BA, DPhil, MA

School of History, Art History & Philosophy; www.sussex.ac.uk/aboutus/schoolsdepartments/hahp

Dept of American Studies; www.sussex.ac.uk/americanstudies
American literature: critical reading, American studies (number of joint degrees); BA, MA, MPhil, DPhil

Dept of Art History; www.sussex.ac.uk/arthistory
art history & archeology, cultural studies, film studies; BA, MA, MPhil, DPhil

Dept of History; www.sussex.ac.uk/history
contemporary history/& politics, early modern history, history, intellectual history, modern European history; BA, MPhil, DPhil, MA

Dept of Philosophy; www.sussex.ac.uk/philosophy:

philosophy, philosophy & cognitive science, aesthetics, analytical philosophy, continental philosophy; BA, MA, MPhil, DPhil

School of Informatics; www.sussex.ac.uk/aboutus/schoolsdepartments/informatics

computer science, computing & artificial intelligence, creative systems, e-learning systems, evolutionary & adaptive systems, games & multimedia environments, human-centred computer systems/interaction design, information technology for e-commerce, intelligent systems, multimedia & digital systems, music informatics; BA, BSc, DPhil, MA, MComp, MPhil, MSc, PGCert

School of Law, Politics & Sociology; www.sussex.ac.uk/aboutus/schoolsdepartments/lps

Dept of Politics & Contemporary European Studies; www.sussex.ac.uk/polces

contemporary European studies, European politics, politics & international relations/languages/dev studies; BA, DPhil, MPhil

Sussex Law School; www.sussex.ac.uk/law

law, European law, family & child law, international criminal law, international law/trade law, rights & responsibilities, law & international security; DPhil, GradDip, LLB, LLM, MPhil, MSc

Dept of Sociology; www.sussex.ac.uk/sociology

comparative & cross-cultural research methods, gender studies, social & political thought, social research in health & medicine, sociology & cultural/dev studies; BA, DPhil, MA, MPhil, MSc

School of Mathematical & Physical Sciences; www.sussex.ac.uk/aboutus/schoolsdepartments/mps

Dept of Mathematics; www.sussex.ac.uk/maths

corporate & financial risk management, financial mathematics with computer science/economics, scientific computation; BSc, DPhil, MMath, MPhil, MSc

School of Physics & Astronomy; www.sussex.ac.uk/physics

astronomy, astrophysics, cosmology, physics, astrophysics, theoretical physics, particle physics; BSc, DPhil, MPhil, MPhys

School of Life Sciences; www.sussex.ac.uk/aboutus/schoolsdepartments/lifesci

Dept of Biology & Environmental Science; www.sussex.ac.uk/biology

biology, biosciences, cellular & molecular neuroscience, cognitive neuroscience, developmental cell biology, ecology & conservation, environmental science, human sciences, medical/ neuroscience, plant conservation; BSc, DPhil, MPhil, MSc, PGDip

Dept of Biochemistry & Biomedical Science; www.sussex.ac.uk/biochemistry

biochemistry, bioinformatics, biological sciences, biomedical science, genetic manipulation & molecular cell biology, molecular genetics, molecular medicine; BSc, DPhil, MPhil, MSc

Dept of Chemistry; www.sussex.ac.uk/chemistry

chemistry, inorganic & bioorganic chemistry, physical & computational chemistry; BSc, DPhil, MPhil, MChem, MSc

School of Media, Film & Music; www.sussex.ac.uk/aboutus/schoolsdepartments/mfm

creative media practice, digital documentary/media, film studies, gender & media, media & cultural studies, media practice, journalism, media studies, music, music informatics, opera & music theatre, professional musicianship; BA, BSc, DPhil, MA, MPhil, PGDip

School of Psychology; www.sussex.ac.uk/aboutus/schoolsdepartments/psychology

applied social psychology, experimental psychology, clinical psychology & mental health, health psychology, psychological methods, psychology, substance misuse; BSc, MRes, MSc, PGDip

SWANSEA UNIVERSITY
www.swansea.ac.uk

School of Arts & Humanities; www.swansea.ac.uk/artsandhumanities

applied linguistics, classics, English language studies, English literature, finance, French, German, Italian, Spanish, language & communication, Latin, media studies, public & media relations, screen studies, TEFL, translation, Welsh, American studies, ancient Egyptian culture/history, ancient & medieval history, child welfare, childhood studies, classical archaeology/civilization, classics, ancient/economic/social / European history, global politics & intercultural studies, Greek, international communication/relations/security, early modern history, maritime & imperial medieval studies, modern Celtic studies/history, philosophy, politics & economics (PPE), political communications/theory, politics, social history & social policy, social research, war & society; BA, MA, MPhil, MSC, MScEcon, PhD

School of Business & Economics; www.swansea.ac.uk/business

accounting and finance, actuarial studies, business economics/management, business management with law, economics, finance, financial economics, international business management, international management science, management theory & practice/finance/marketing/international management, marketing/management, strategic management; BA, BSc, MBA, MPhil, MSc, MScEcon, PhD

School of Engineering; www.swansea.ac.uk/engineering

aerospace engineering/with propulsion, chemical engineering, biochemical engineering/bioprocess engineering, computational engineering/modelling/mechanics, civil engineering, communication systems, computer modelling in engineering, electronic & electrical engineering, electronic systems design engineering, electronics with computer science/for sustainable energy, environmental engineering/management, materials engineering/science/mechanical engineering, medical engineering, telecommunication engineering, physics, nanomedicine/technology/science, product design, engineering/technology, sports science, structural materials for gas turbines; BEng, EngD, MEng, MPhil, MRes, MSc

School of the Environment & Society; www.swansea.ac.uk/environmentsociety

aquaculture & the environment, aquatic ecology & conservation, biochemistry, environmental/biology: conservation & resource management, development & human rights, earth science & geoinformatics, environmental dynamics & climate change, human / geography, marine biology, medical biochemistry, migration & international development, social development & communication/conflict, social research, sustainable aquaculture & fisheries, zoology; BA, BSc, MA, MPhil, MSc, PhD

School of Health Science; www.swansea.ac.uk/healthscience

adult nursing, audiology, advanced clinical practice/(infection control/nurse practitioner), chronic condition management, clinical physiology with cardiology/respiratory physiology, clinical nursing(cardio), clinical technology (medical physics), community health studies, ethics of health care/law/management, health informatics/science, infection prevention & control, medical humanities/sciences & humanities, medical physics, mental health nursing, midwifery, nursing (adult/child/mental health), paramedic science, professional practice, public health & health promotion/partnerships in care/specialist community public health nursing; BMid, BN, BSc, DipHE, MA, MPhil, MSc, PGCert, PGDip, PhD

School of Human Sciences; www.swansea.ac.uk/human-sciences

abnormal & clinical psychology, ageing studies, applied criminal justice & criminology, child welfare, childhood studies, psychology/social policy, developmental & therapeutic play, law & criminology, applied social studies, social policy, social work; BA, BSc, HND, LLB, MA, MPhil, MSc, MScEcon, PhD

School of Law; www.swansea.ac.uk/law

global legal orders & law, international commercial law/commercial & maritime law/maritime law/trade law, law, law & globalization; GradDip, LLB, LLM, MA, MPhil, PGDip, PhD

School of Medicine; www.swansea.ac.uk/medicine

genetics, medical/biochemistry, medical genetics, medicine, trauma surgery; BSc, MBBCh, MD, MPhil, MSc, PhD

School of Physical Sciences; www.swansea.ac.uk/physical.sciences

applied mathematics, computer science, computing, computing & communications/future interaction technologies/software technology, computing with finance, geoinformatics, logic & computation, pure/ mathematics/(information & communications technology), modelling, uncertainty & data, physics, physics with nanotechnology/particle physics & cosmology, stochastic processes, theoretical physics, visual computation; BSc, MEng, MMath, MPhil, MPhys, MRes, MSc, PhD

UNIVERSITY OF TEESSIDE
www.tees.ac.uk

School of Arts & Media; www.tees.ac.uk/schools/sam

broadcast media production, creative writing, dance, design, digital arts, creating theatre, English & cultural studies European history, fine art, future design, graphic arts/advertising/illustration/multimedia & web publishing), graphical image, history, interior architecture/design, journalism, local & regional /social & cultural history, mass communication, media studies, modern & contemporary European history, motion graphics, multimedia PA/ journalism/PR, music creation, performance & events production, product design (contemporary lifestyle & furniture, industrial & transportation/marketing, social & cultural history, television & film production; BA, FdA, MA, MPhil, MSc, PhD

School of Computing; www.tees.ac.uk/schools/scm

applied computing, business computing/systems design, computer networks/science, digital forensics/animation, IT/management, computing/IT/networking, ICT, software development, networks & communication, applied/creative digital media, computer /character animation/, games, creative digital media, graphic arts (motion graphics), graphic design (multimedia & web publishing), music technology, creative digital media, business IT, web multimedia design, web design/development; BA, BSc, DProf, FdSc, HNC, HND, MA, MPhil, MProf, MSc, PGDip, PhD

School of Health & Social Care; www.tees.ac.uk/schools/soh

advanced clinical practice, neurological rehabilitation/manipulative therapy, muscoskeletal studies, cardiac care, clinical psychology, dental hygiene/ therapy/nurse practice, diagnostic radiography, evidence-based medicine/practice, forensic radiography, leadership in/managing/ health & social care, midwifery, public health, nursing studies (adult, child, learning disabilities, mental health), manipulative therapy, medical ultrasound, occupational therapy, operating dept practice, orthopaedics, physiotherapy, primary care, surgical care, social work; BA, BSc, DipHE, FdSc, HND, MA, MPhil, MSc, PGCert

Engineering; www.tees.ac.uk/schools/sse

advanced manufacturing systems, analytical chemistry, chemistry, biological sciences, biotechnology, chemical engineering, civil engineering, computer & digital forensics, disaster management, computer-aided design engineering, control & electronics, crime & investigation, crime scene science, death investigation, digital forensics, disaster management, electrical & electronic engineering, electronics & communications, engineering, environmental science/sustainability/technology, fabrication & welding, food & consumer safety/nutrition & health science, forensic biology/science, instrumentation & control engineering, mechanical engineering, petroleum technology, process manufacturing management, project management; BEng, BSc, FdEng, HNC, HND, MPhil, MRes, MSc, PGDip, PhD

School of Social Sciences & Law; www.tees.ac.uk/schools/ss

counselling & psychology, criminal investigation/law, criminology, digital technologies for learning, drug use, early childhood studies, education, forensic / psychology, global development, health psychology, human rights, international law, law, criminology, outdoor leadership, psychology & counselling/criminology/education studies, social research methods, social sciences, sociology, sociology & politics/with psychology/youth studies, sport & exercise, sport science/coaching science/psychology, teaching in lifelong learning, youth & childhood studies, youth work, youth studies with criminology/psychology; BA, BSc, DProf, FdA, FdSc, FdSocSc, GradCert, HNC, HND, LLB, LLM, MA, MPhil, MProf, MSc, PhD

Teeside Business School; www.tees.ac.uk/schools/tubs/

accounting & finance, advertising, audit management, business administration/finance/management, business management (international business/tourism), business with law, financial crime, fraud management, HRM, international management, management, marketing, public services, sport management, transport & logistics, tourism, leadership & change; BA, BSc, DBA, FdA, FdSc, HND, MA, MBA, MSc, PGDip

THAMES VALLEY UNIVERSITY
www.tvu.ac.uk

Faculty of the Arts; www.tvu.ac.uk/the_university/faculties_and_schools/Faculty_of_the_Arts

London College of Music; www.tvu.ac.uk/music/london college of music

applied sound engineering, audio technology, music (performance & composition management & artist development/performance/technology, pop music, Naad yoga, personal health & personal development, record production; BA, BMus, BSc, DipHE, FdA, FdMus, MA, MMus, PGCert, PGDip

School of Art Design, & Media; www.tvu.ac.uk/artdesign/school_of_art_and_design

digital animation/media production, fashion & textiles, games development (games art/games design), graphic design (visual communication & interaction design), illustration, interaction design, new media art & design, photography, digital imaging, web design, advertising, broadcast journalism, broadcasting, community radio, event management, media studies, music & media, practical filmmaking, PR, video production & film studies; BA, FdA, MA, DipHE

Faculty of Health & Human Studies; www.tvu.ac.uk/the_university/faculties_and_schools/Faculty_of_Health_and_Human_Sciences

School of Psychology, Social Casre & Human Sciences

substance use & misuse studies, advanced nutritional practice, clinical hypnotherapy, counselling & psychotherapy, food & consumer health, complementary medicine, criminology with psychology, forensic sciences, health promotion & public health, health psychology, homeopathy, human sciences, nutritional therapy, performance, health & personal development, primary health care, psychology, social care/work, personal & professional development, operating department practice, sport, health & exercise science; BSc, CertHE, DipHE, FdSc, MA, MPhil, MSc, PGCert, PGDip, PhD

School of Nursing & Midwifery

learning disability/adult/child nursing, midwifery; BSc, DipHE, MA, MM, MPhil, PGDip, PhD

Faculty of Professional Studies

Business School; www.tvu.ac.uk/businessschool/Business_School.jsp

accounting & finance, business studies/HRM/marketing/management, English, HRM, HR, international business management/marketing/culinary arts management, corporate management, logistics management, management studies (health & social care), marketing, music management, personnel practice, project management, PR, public service management, purchasing & supply, tourism management; DMS, FdA, GradCert, GradDip, HND, MA, MBA, MPhil, MSc, PGDip, PhD

Ealing Law School; www.tvu.ac.uk/law/Ealing_Law_School.jsp

applied law, criminology, criminology & law/ forensic science/psychology/substance use & misuse, international business & commercial law/finance law, law, legal practice; GradDip, LLB, LLM

London School of Hospitality & Tourism; www.tvu.ac.uk/hospitality/ London_School_of_Hospitality_and tourism.jsp

airline & airport management, business travel & tourism, cruise ship management, culinary arts/ management, event design/management, food & professional cookery/control, hospitality/ management, international culinary arts/hotel management, tourism, licensed hospitality, travel & tourism/management; BA, DipHE, FdA, GradCert, HND, MA, MPhil, PGDip, PhD

School of Computing & Technology; www.tvu.ac.uk/computing/ School_of_Computing_and_Technology.jsp

applied sound engineering, civil & environmental engineering, power & control, communications technology, mechanical engineering, electronics with communication/control, mechatronics, microelectronics, business /information systems, computer network management, computing science/interaction design, information management, construction management, architectural technology, quantity surveying, sustainable design; BSc, FdSc, HND, MSc

School of Education; www.tvu.ac.uk/ higher-education

teaching in lifelong learning sector

TRINITY COLLEGE LONDON
www.trinitycollege.co.uk

dance, drama and speech, music, performing arts; PGDip, SfL, TESOL

UNIVERSITY OF ULSTER
www.ulster.ac.uk

Faculty of Art, Design & the Built Environment; www.adbe.ulster.ac.uk

School of Architecture & Design; www.adbe.ulster.ac.uk/schools/ archi_design

3D design (interior, product & furniture design), architectural studies/technology & management, architecture, interior design, landscape architecture; BA, BDes, BSc, CertHE, MArch, MLA, MSc

School of Art & Design; www.adbe.ulster.ac.uk/schools/art_design

art & design, design for visual communication, fine & applied arts, fine art, interactive multimedia design, photography, textile material product, textiles & fashion design; BA, BDes, BSc, MA, MDes, MFA, PGDip

School of the Built Environment; www.adbe.ulster.ac.uk/schools/ built_environment

building engineering & materials, building services & energy engineering, building surveying, civil engineering, construction engineering, construction & project management, energy & building services engineering, environmental health, fire safety engineering, housing management/studies, infrastructure engineering, occupational therapy, property investment & development/ planning, quantity surveying, renewable engineering & energy management, transportation; BEng, BSc, MEng, MPhil, MSc, PGCert, PGDip, PhD

Faculty of Arts; www.arts.ulster.ac.uk

School of Creative Arts

dance, design & communication, drama, music; BA, BDes, BMus, BSc, MDes, MMus, MPhil, MRes, MSc, PGDip, PhD

School of History, English and Politics

American studies, English, cultural heritage, history, Irish/history & politics, international politics, Irish literature in English; BA, MA, MRes, PGDip, PhD

School of Languages, Literatures & Cultures;

Celtic studies, English, European studies, film studies, French, German, Spanish, Irish; BA, CertHE, MA, MPhil, PGDip, PhD

School of Media, Film & Journalism; www.adbe.ulster.ac.uk/schools/mediafilm

documentary practice, film studies (with options), film & TV management & policy, interactive media arts, international journalism (with options), media studies/& production, photo-imaging; BA, MA, MPhil, PGDip, PhD

Faculty of Computing & Engineering; www.compeng.ulster.ac.uk

School of Computing & Information Engineering; www.compeng.ulster.ac.uk/cie

computing, computing (artificial intelligence/digital games development/internet systems), financial engineering, telecommunications & internet systems; BSc, MSc, PGDip, PhD

School of Computing & Intelligent Systems; www.scis.ulster.ac.uk

computer games development, computer science, computing & creative technologies/e-business/intelligent systems/ financial services, electronics & computer systems, mobile robotics, multimedia computing & design, multimedia computer games; BEng, BSc, MSc, PGDip, PhD

School of Computing & Mathematics; www.infj.ulst.ac.uk/cm/

computing & information systems, computing science/ & mathematics, computing/(web technology/health informatics/communication/artificial intelligence), information & communication technologies, industrial practice, interactive multimedia design, interactive teaching technologies, software engineering; BSc, MSc, PGCert, PGDip, PhD

Faculty of Engineering; www.seng.ulster.ac.uk/eme

biomedical engineering, electronics, communications & software, engineering (electrical/electronic)/management, mechanical engineering, sports technology, technology with design, adv composites & polymers, medical electronics, manufacturing management, nanotechnology, industrial practice; BSc, BEng, MEng, MSc, PGDip, PhD

Faculty of Life & Health Sciences; www.science.ulster.ac.uk

School of Biomedical Sciences; www.biomed.science.ulster.ac.uk

biology, biomedical science, biotechnology, dietetics, European food regulatory affairs, food & nutrition, forensic & legal medicine, food biotechnology, forensic studies, human nutrition, medical science, optometry, pharmaceutical sciences, pharmacology, pharmacy, veterinary public health; BSc, DMedSc, GradCert, MPharm, MSc, PGCert, PGDip

School of Environmental Sciences; www.science.uster.ac.uk/envsci

coastal zone management, environmental management/science/studies/toxicology & pollution monitoring, geographic information systems, geography, marine science; AB, BSc, DEnvSci, MPhil, MRes, MSc, PGCert, PGDip, PhD

School of Health Sciences; www.science.uster.ac.uk/health

advanced practice clinical physiology/research, health science, occupational therapy, physiotherapy, podiatry, radiography (diagnostic/therapeutic), speech & language therapy; BSc, MClinRes, MSc

School of Nursing; www.science.ulster.ac.uk/nursing

community & public health nursing, dementia studies, education for nurses, health promotion & population health, health & social care, independent & supplementary nurse prescribing, midwifery, nursing (adult/mental health), primary care & general practice, palliative care & cancer healthcare, specialist midwifery/nursing practice; BSc, CertHE, MSc, PGCert, PGDip

School of Psychology; www.science.ulster.ac.uk/psychology

applied behaviour analysis, applied psychology (mental health), health psychology, psychology/ (social); BSc, MSc, PGDip

School of Sports Studies; www.science.ulsportsster.ac.uk

physical activity & population health, sport & exercise sciences, sports management/coaching/studies/technology/development, sports-related studies; BSc, FdSc, MPhil, MSc, DPhil, PGDip, PhD

Faculty of Social Sciences; www.socsci.ulster.ac.uk

School of Communication; www.comms.ulster.ac.uk

communication, advertising & marketing, PR, counselling, therapeutic political lobbying, public affairs, language & linguistics, linguistics; BSc, MPhil, MSc, PGCert, PGDip, PhD

School of Economics; www.socsci.ulster.ac.uk/ecompolitics

applied/ business economics, economics, economics with accounting/marketing/politics; BSc, MSc, PGDip

School of Education; www.socsci.ulster.ac.uk/education

PGCE (post-primary, primary, in numerous school subjects), Certificate in Teaching, educational leadership & management, ICT, inclusive & special education, teaching & learning, library & information management (TESOL); MA, MEd, PGCE, PGCert, PGDip

School of Law; www.socsci.ulster.ac.uk/law

law, human rights law, criminology, human rights & transitional justice; LLB, LLM

School of Criminology, Politics & Social Policy; www.socsci.ulster.ac.uk/policy

criminology & criminal justice, health & social care policy, politics, public administration, social policy, executive development, international studies, procurement; BSc, MPA, PGCert, PGDip

School of Sociology & Applied Social Studies; www.socsci.ulster.ac.uk/sociology

cognitive therapy, community development/youth work, restorative practices, profession development in social work, sociology, international politics; BSc, MSc, PGCert, PGDip

Graduate School of Professional Legal Education; www.socsci.ulster.ac.uk/gsple

legal practice; PGDip

Ulster Business School; www.business.ulster.ac.uk

accounting, advertising, agrifood business development, computing, business & management, business administration/development & innovation/improvement/studies, consumer studies, cultural management, executive leadership, financial services, HRM, international business/hospitality management/hotel & tourism management/travel & tourism management, leisure & events management, management & corporate governance/leadership, marketing, sport management, social enterprise; BSc, CertHE, HND, MBA, MBS, MSc, PGDip

UNIVERSITY OF WALES INSTITUTE, CARDIFF
www.uwic.ac.uk

Cardiff School of Art & Design; www.csad.uwic.ac.uk

advanced/ product design, architectural design technology, building maintenance & management, art & design, ceramics, contemporary textile practice, fine art, graphic communication, illustration, interior architecture, media studies with visual cultures, product design, web & game design, music production & technology, photographic practice; BA, BSc, HNC, HND, MA, MFA, MPhil, MSc, PGCert, PhD

Cardiff School of Education; www3.uwic.ac.uk/English/education

Dept of Humanities; www3.uwic.ac.uk/English/education/humanities

educational studies, early childhood studies, English, psychology, sport & physical activity, Welsh, creative writing, drama, modern history, politics, contemporary media; BA, MA, PGCert, PGDip

Dept of Professional Development; www3.uwic.ac.uk/English/education/profdevelopment

education, management in the community professions, youth & community education; BA, MA, MPhil, MSc, PhD

Dept of Teacher Education & Training; www3.uwic.ac.uk/English/education/teachedu

Initial teacher training, PGCE (primary, secondary): teacher training, music, Welsh, French; BA, PGCE

Cardiff School of Health Sciences; www3.uwic.ac.uk/English/health

Centre for Applied Social Sciences; www3.uwic.ac.uk/English/health/ass

health & social care, housing: policy & practice/ supported housing, youth & communities, management in the community professions, health & social science res, social work; BA, BSc, FdSc, GradCert, GradDip, HNC, HND, MRes, MSc PGCert, PGDip

Centre for Biomedical Science; www3.uwic.ac.uk/English/health/cbs

biomedical science, applied biomedical sciences, sports biomedicine & nutrition; BSc, FdSc, HNC, HND, MSc, PGCert, PGDip

Centre for Complementary Therapies; www3.uwic.ac.uk/English/health/cct

complementary therapies, aromatherapy, reflexology, holistic massage; BSc, Dip/Cert

Centre for Dental Technology; www3.uwic.ac.uk/English/health/cdt

dental technology; BSc, FdSc, MSc, PGCert, PGDip

Centre for Nutrition, Dietetics & Food Sciences; www3.uwic.ac.uk/English/health/cnfc

applied public health, dietetics, food science & technology, human nutrition, public health nutrition, sorts biomedicine & management, adv dietetic practice, sports & exercise nutrition/ biomedicine; BSc, FdSc, HNC, MSc, PGDip

Centre for Psychology; www3.uwic.ac.uk/English/health/cp

forensic psychology, health psychology, lifestyle psychology, psychology, psychology & human biology; BSc, FdSc, MSc

Centre for Public Protection; www3.uwic.ac.uk/English/health/cpp

applied public health, environmental health/risk management, health science, consumer & trading standards, occupational health & safety, waste management; BSc, FdSc, HNC, MSc, PGDip

Centre for Speech & Language Therapy; www3.uwic.ac.uk/English/health/cslt

speech & language therapy; BSc

Wales Centre for Podiatric Studies; www3.uwic.ac.uk/English/health/wcps

musculoskeletal studies, podiatry, therapeutic footware; BSc, MSc, PGCert, PGDip

Cardiff School of Management; www3.uwic.ac.uk/English/management

Business & Management Department; www3.uwic.ac.uk/English/management/dbm

business administration/studies, business & management, management studies, health sector management, international business management/ management/administration, management consultancy, marketing, product design, project management, social entrepreneurship; BA, HND, MBA, MSc

Dept of Accounting, Economics & Finance; www3.uwic.ac.uk/English/management/dafe

accounting, finance, economics, financial management, information management; BA, BSc, FdA, MSc

Information Systems Department; www3.uwic.ac.uk/English/management/dis

business information systems/ technology, computer studies, information systems management, software development; BSc, HNC, HND, MSc

Dept for International Studies & Learning Support; www3.uwic.ac.uk/English/management/disls

international business administration/management; BA, MSc

Tourism, Hospitality & Events Management Dept; www3.uwic.ac.uk/English/management/dthem

events management, hospitality management, international tourism & hospitality management, tourism management; BA, FdA, HNC, HND, MSc, PGCert, PGDip

Cardiff School of Sport; www3.uwic.ac.uk/English/sport

dance, sports coaching/development, sport & exercise science, PE, sport management/conditioning, rehabilitation & massage; BA(Hons), BSc(Hons), MA, MSc, PGDip/Cert

UNIVERSITY OF WALES: GLYNDWR UNIVERSITY
www.newi.ac.uk

North Wales School of Art & Design; www.newi.ac.uk/en/Academicschools/ArtandDesign

animation, applied arts, computer-generated imagery, graphic design: animation/creative lens media/digital art for computer games/fashion & textiles/graphic design/illustration/illustration for children's publishing/ for graphic novels, interactive multimedia design, design for decorative arts, digital media design & production, fine art; BA, FdA, MA, MPhil, PhD

School of Business; www.newi.ac.uk/en/Academicschools/ArtandDesign/

accounting & financial management, business & management, business accounting/management, business management with accounting/marketing, festival & events management, HRM, legal/logistics operations management, management, public sector management, marketing/tourism management; BA, FdA, HNC, MBA, MSc, MPhil, PhD

School of Computing & Communications Technology; www.newi.ac.uk/en/Academicschools/Computingand CommunicationsTechnology/

applied computing, communications technology, computer game development/network management & security/science/networking, computing, creative industries/media computing, creative audio/media technology, information management, IT support, mobile computing, music technology, radio production & communication, studio technology, television; BA, BSc, FdEng, FdSc, HNC, HND, MPhil, MSc, PhD

School of Education & Community; www.newi.ac.uk/en/Academicschools/EducationandCommunity

community studies, families/education & childhood studies, e-learning, theory & practice, learning & development of babies & young children, learning & teaching support, play & playwork, post-compulsory education & training, primary education with QTS, professional development in HE, youth & community studies; PGCert, PGDip, PhD

School of Health, Social Care, Sport & Exercise Studies; www.newi.ac.uk/en/Academicschools/EducationandCommunity

advanced clinical /nursing practice, community/specialist practice (community children's nursing/district nursing/general practice/adult/mental health nursing), equestrian psychology, health & care studies, interdisciplinary palliative care, leadership in health & social care, occupational health, safety & environmental management, occupational therapy, public health, professional education, psychology, specialist community public health nursing; BA, BN, BSc, CertHE, DipHE, FdA, FdSc, MA, MPH, MPhil, MSc, PGCert, PhD

School of Humanities; www.newi.ac.uk/en/Academicschools/Humanities

broadcasting, journalism & creative writing, creative writing, history, English, broadcasting & journalism, media communications/screen studies, history & screen studies/Welsh language studies, library & information practice local history, media communications, print journalism, theatre, television & performance, Welsh translation; BA, CertHE, FdA, MA, MPhil, PhD

School of Science & Technology; www.newi.ac.uk/en/Academicschools/ScienceandTechnology

advanced electronic techniques, aeronautical & electronic engineering (avionics)/mechanical engineering/mechanical manufacturing, animal studies, architectural design technology, automation, instrumentation & control, building studies (construction management/maintenance management), digital sound & vision processing, electrical engineering/technology, electrical & electronic systems & digital technologies, electrical & electronic technologies, environmental science, estate agency/management, forensic science, horticulture production management, housing studies, landscape design & management, mechanical technology, medical electronics, organic horticulture management, performance car electronics & technology, motorsport design, polymer science & technology, renewable energy & sustainable technologies, renewable energy systems, sound & broadcast engineering, sports surface management, sustainable development, supported housing; BEng, BSc, FdEng, FdSc, HNC, HND, MPhil, MRes, PhD

UNIVERSITY OF WALES: LAMPETER
www.lamp.ac.uk

Dept of Archaeology & Anthropology; www.lamp.ac.uk/archanth

anthropology, anthrozoology, archaeology, archaeology (environmental/practice), theology, ancient history, civilizations of Mediterranean, cultural astronomy & astrology/heritage, death studies, environmental anthropology, social anthropology/archaeology; BA, DipHE, MA, PgCert, PGDip, MPhil, PhD

Centre for Chinese Studies; www.lamp.ac.uk/chinese/

Chinese studies, culture & society: East & West from 2010 onwards; BA, MA, MPhil, PhD

Dept of Classics; www.lamp.ac.uk/classics

ancient history, classical studies, medieval history, ancient myth & society/narrative literature, classical language & literature, classics, Greek, Latin; BA, MA, MPhil, PhD

Dept of English; www.lamp.ac.uk/english

creative & script writing, English, English literature, modern literatures, medieval studies, creative writing/TEFL; BA, MA

Dept of Film & Media; www.lamp.ac.uk/fm

film & media, film studies, media production/studies, screen studies; BA, MA, MPhil, PhD

Dept of History; www.lamp.ac.uk/history

ancient & medieval history, historical studies, history, medieval studies; BA, MA, MBA, PGDip, MPhil, PhD

Dept of Management & Information Technology; www.lamp.ac.uk/mit

business information technology/management/administration, e-commerce, entrepreneurial management, leadership; BA, MA, MSc, MPhil, PhD

Dept of Philosophy; www.lamp.ac.uk/philosophy

applied philosophy, philosophical studies, ethics of life & death, European philosophy, medical ethics, nature, philosophy, religion, ethics; BA, MA, MPhil, PhD

Dept of Theology & Religious Studies; www.lamp.ac.uk/trs

Arthurian studies, Biblical interpretation, Celtic christianity, church history, death & immortality, divinity, Indian religions, Islamic studies, medical ethics, monastic studies, orthodox studies, religion, ethics & society, religious history/studies, systematic & philosophical theology, theology, the world's religions; BA, DMin, DPT, LTh, MA, MMin, MTh

Dept of Welsh; www.welsh.lamp.ac.uk/Department/English

Welsh studies, Celtic studies; BA(Hons), MPhil, PhD

Dept of Voluntary Sector Studies; www.volstudy.ac.uk

voluntary sector studies, interpersonal skills for volunteers, intergeneration practice; BA(Hons), MA, PgCert/Dip

UNIVERSITY OF WALES: NEWPORT
www.newport.ac.uk

Centre for Community & Lifelong Learning; www.ccll.newport.ac.uk
combined open studies; CertHE

Newport Business School; www.nbs.newport.ac.uk
accounting & economics/finance/financial management/law/business, building studies, e-marketing, energy management, HRM, law, management, marketing, business information studies business leadership/enterprise development/studies, construction engineering, civil engineering, computing, electrical engineering, electronic & communication engineering, engineering, fire safety engineering, forensic computing, games development & artificial intelligence, information security, IT management, mechanical & manufacturing engineering, networks & web development, project management, robotic & intelligent systems engineering, public sector management, strategic management, technology management, telecommunications with management; BA, BSc, BEng, FdSc, HNC, HND, MBA, MSc

School of Art, Media & Design; www.amd.newport.ac.uk
advertising design, animation, computer games design, creative music practice/sound & music, design by practice, development disorders, documentary film & television/photography, fashion design, film, video, fine art, graphic design, interactive media, performing arts, photographic art, photography for fashion & advertising, printmaking, smart clothes & wearable technology; BA, MA, MFA

School of Education; www.education.newport.ac.uk
adult literacy/numeracy, applied drama, art therapy, attention deficit, autism, child & adolescent mental health, childhood studies, creative therapies in education, creative writing, critical & creative thinking, early years, education & ICT, education leadership & management, education studies, English/literature: health promotion & education, history, learning support (secondary & further education), inclusive practice health & education, learning & teaching dev & support, mobilty & orientation, post-compulsory education/& training, primary studies, regional history, rehabilitation (visual impairment), religious education/studies, secondary design & technology, secondary teaching mathematics & science with ICT, SEN specific learning difficulties/teaching English as an additional language, TESOL, TAEL; BA, BSc, FdA, MA, PGCE, PGCert, PGDip, CertHE

School of Health & Social Sciences; www.hss.newport.ac.uk
community health & social care/studies, consultative support, counselling/children & young people, criminology & criminal justice, evaluation studies, health, exercise & nutrition, interprofessional practice, psychology, social ethics & public advocacy, social work, social studies, sports coaching, sports studies, working with young people, youth & community studies, youth justice; BA, BSc, MA, PGCert, PGDip

UNIVERSITY OF WALES: SWANSEA METROPOLITAN UNIVERSITY
www.smu.ac.uk

Faculty of Applied Design & Engineering; www.smu.ac.uk/index.php/potential-students/faculty-of-applied-design-and-engineering

School of Applied Computing; www.smu.ac.uk/index.php/potential-students/faculty-of-applied-design-and-engineering/school-ofapplied-computing
business information technology, computer games development, computer networks/systems & electronics, computing & information systems/technology, e-commerce, electronic engineering, software engineering, web development; BEng, BSc, HND, MSc

School of Automotive Engineering; www.smu.ac.uk/index.php/potential-students/faculty-of-applied-design-and-engineering/school of automotive engineering
automotive engineering, motorcycle engineering, motorsport engineering & design/technology; BEng, BSc, HND

School of Built & Natural Environment; www.smu.ac.uk/index.php/potential-students/faculty-of-applied-design-and-engineering/school- of-natural-environment
building conservation, building studies, civil engineering & environmental management, environmental conservation/& management, facilities management, project & construction management, quantity surveying; BSc, HNC, HND, MSc

School of Digital Media; www.smu.ac.uk/index.php/potential-students/faculty-of-applied-design-and-engineering/school-of digital-media
3D/computer animation, creative computer games design, interactive digital media, multimedia, music technology; BA, BSc, HND, MA, MSc

School of Industrial Design; www.smu.ac.uk/index.php/potential-students/faculty-of-applied-design-and-engineering/school-of-industrial-design
automotive design, industrial design, product design /& innovation; BA, BSc, MA, MSc

School of Logistics & Manufacturing Engineering; www.smu.ac.uk/index.php/potential-students/faculty-of-applied-design-and-engineering/school-of-logistics-a-manufacturing
logistics & supply chain management, lean & agile manufacturing, manufacturing systems engineering, mechanical & manufacturing engineering, food lofgistics, motorsport management/manufacturing engineering, transport management, non-destructive testing & evaluation; BSc, BEng, HND, MA, MSc

Welsh School of Architectural Glass; www.smu.ac.uk/index.php/faculty-of-applied-design-a-engineering/welsh-school-of-architectural-glass
architectural glass, stained glass; BA, MA

Faculty of Art & Design; www.smu.ac.uk/index.php/potential-students/faculty-of-art-and-design

School of Contextual Studies & Visual Communication; www.smu.ac.uk/index.php/potential-students/faculty-of-art-and-design/csvc
graphic/design for advertising, general illustration; BA, HND

School of Fine & Applied Arts; www.smu.ac.uk/index.php/potential-students/faculty-of-art-and-design/school-of-fine-a-applied-arts
fine arts (ceramics/combined media/painting & drawing), art & design, surface pattern design (contemporary applied arts practice/textiles for fashion/textiles for interiors), fine art contemporary dialogs, art & design; BA, FdA

School of Photography & Video; www.smu.ac.uk/index.php/potential-students/faculty-of-art-and-design/school-of-photography-video
documentary video, photography in the arts, photojournalism, video arts, photography contemporary dialogues; BA

School of Research & Postgraduate Studies; www.smu.ac.uk/index.php/potential-students/faculty-of-art-and-design/rps-art
fine art/contemporay dialogues, photography, textiles, visual communication; MA

Faculty of Humanities

Centre for Leisure, Tourism & Sport; www.smu.ac.uk/index.php/faculty-of-humanities/clts
events management, international tourism/travel & tourism /leisure/ sports/facilties management, water-sports & adventure activities management; BA, HND, MBA, MSc

Swansea Business School; www.smu.ac.uk/index.php/faculty-of-humanities/swansea-business-schools
accounting, business & finance, business studies /& psychology, HRM, management, marketing; BA, FdA, GradDip, HND, MA, MA(Ed), MRes, PGCE, MBA

Swansea School of Education; www.smu.ac.uk/index.php/faculty-of-humanities/swansea-school-of-education
counselling, educational studies, English studies, post compulsory education & training, primary education, professional development (education), learning support, intro to learning & teaching, maths education, PGCE primary/secondary (in numerous subjects), secondary education, youth & community studies; BA, PGCE, PGCert, PGDip

School of Performance & Literature; www.smu.ac.uk/index.php/faculty-of-humanities/school-of-performance-a-literatuture
art history & English studies, counselling/education studies/psychology, performing arts, technical theatre; BA, HNC, HND

School of Psychology & Counselling; www.smu.ac.uk/index.php/faculty-of-humanities/school-of-psychology-a-counselling
business studies & psychology, counselling & educational studies/psychology, educational studies & psychology, English studies & counselling/psychology counselling studies/practice; BA, MPhil, PhDHE-Cert, MA

School of Public Service Leadership; www.smu.ac.uk/index.php/faculty-of-humanities/school-of-public-service-leadership
health & social care, public administration/services; BA, MPhil, PhD

UNIVERSITY OF WALES: TRINITY COLLEGE, CARMARTHEN www.trinity-cm.ac.uk

Faculty of Arts & Social Sciences; www.trinity-cm.ac.uk/en/facarts

School of Computing, Business & Tourism; www.trinity-cm.ac.uk/en/facarts/schcbt
business information technology, business & management, community development, computing, heritage tourism, information systems management, local history, management (heritage), management /& sustainability, tourism management; BA, BSc, FdA, FdSc, MA, MBA

School of Creative Arts & Humanities; www.trinity-cm.ac.uk/en/facarts/schcah
arts management, creative writing, educational studies, English, film studies, fine art, media studies; BA, MBA

School of Sport, Health & Outdoor Education; www.trinity-cm.ac.uk/en/facarts/schshoe
health & exercise, sports studies, health, nutrition & lifestyle, outdoor/physical education, adventure & outdoor education; BA, MA

School of Theatre & Performance; www.trinity-cm.ac.uk/en/facarts/schtp
acting, drama & education, educational drama, theatre design & production, context & practice, theatre & society; BA, MA

Faculty of Education & Training; www.trinity-cm.ac.uk/en/fac.edu

School of Education Studies & Social Inclusion; www.trinity-cm.ac.uk/en/fac.edu/essi

adolscent psychology, additional learning needs, health & social care, social justice, youth, teaching assts, community support, early years education & social inclusion, education studies & English/religious studies/social inclusion, inclusive studies, primary education studies, psychology, religious studies & social inclusion; BA, BSc, CertHE, DipHE, FdA, GradCert, MA

School of Initial Teacher Education Training; www.trinity-cm.ac.uk/en/fac.edu/tet

education, primary education, professional development; BA, GradCert, GradDip, MA, PGCEBA

School of Early Years Education; www.trinity-cm.ac.uk/en/fac.edu/eye

early years education, nursery management, Welsh & bilingual practice, foundation practice; BA, CertHE, MA, PGDip

School of Theology and Religious Studies; www.trinity-cm.ac.uk/en/fac.edu/trs

religious studies, religion in society, religious education, Christianity & community studies; education studies/social inclusion; BA

UNIVERSITY OF WARWICK
www.warwick.ac.uk

Faculty of Arts; www2.warwick.ac.uk/fac/arts

Dept of Classics & Ancient History; www2.warwick.ac.uk/fac/arts/classics

ancient history & classical archaeology, ancient visual & material culture, visual & material culture in ancient Rome, classical civilization/with philosophy, classics, English & Latin literature; BA, MA, MPhil, PhD

Dept of English & Comparative Literary Studies; www2.warwick.ac.uk/fac/arts/english

English literature, creative writing, English & theatre studies, pan-romanticisms, philosophy & literature; BA, MA, MPhil, PhD

Dept of Film & TV Studies; www2.warwick.ac.uk/fac/arts/film

film & literature/TV studies; BA, MA, MPhil, PhD

Dept of French Studies; www2.warwick.ac.uk/fac/arts/french

English & French, French studies with German/history/international studies/Italian/politics/film/sociology, film, French culture & thought, French & francophone studies; BA, MA, MPhil, PGDip, PhD

Dept of German Studies; www2.warwick.ac.uk/fac/arts/german

English & German literature, German cultural studies, German/German studies with business studies/French/international studies/Italian/Spanish, pan-romanticism; BA, MA, MPhil, PGDip, PhD

Dept of History; www2.warwick.ac.uk/fac/arts/history

18th-century studies, global history, history, history & culture/politics/sociology, history of race in the Americas, modern history, religious & social history, 1500-1700; BA, MA, MPhil, PhD

Dept of History of Art; www2.warwick.ac.uk/fac/arts/arthistory

art history with Italian, history of art, history of art & French, history & business of art & collecting; BA, MA, MPhil, PGDip, PhD

Dept of Italian; www2.warwick.ac.uk/fac/arts/italian

English & Italian literature, Italian/& theatre studies/film studies/international studies Italian culture & communication, translation, writing & cultural difference; BA, MA, MPhil, PGDip, PhD

School of Comparative American Studies; www2.warwick.ac.uk/fac/arts/cas

history, literature & culture of the Americas, history of race in the Americas; BA, MA, PhD

School of Theatre, Performance & Cultural Policy Studies; www2.warwick.ac.uk/fac/arts/Theatre_s

European cultural policy & administration, theatre & performance studies; BA, MA, MPhil, PhD

Faculty of Medicine; www2.warwick.ac.uk/fac/med

Warwick Medical School

child health, clinical systems improvement, diabetes, emergency care, health sciences, health services management, kidney disease, medical education/leadership, medicine & surgery, occupational health, orthopaedics & trauma, orthodontics, palliative care, philosophy & ethics of /mental health, pre-hospital critical care, primary care, public health, & epidemiology, sexual & reproductive health care, dentistry, implant dentistry, otho/endodontics, resorative dentistry; MBChB, MD, MMedSci, MPhil, MSc, PhD

Faculty of Science; www2.warwick.ac.uk/fac/sci

Dept of Biological Sciences; www2.warwick.ac.uk/fac/sci/bio

biochemistry, biomedical science, biological sciences, ecology & epidemiology, environmental biology, microbiology & virology, neuroscience, molecular cellular biology, physiology, virology & structural biology; BSc, MD, MPhil, MSc, PhD

Dept of Chemistry; www2.warwick.ac.uk/fac/sci/chemistry

chemical biology, chemistry, molecular /physical chemistry, chemical physics, materials chemistry, synthetic chemistry, theoritical & computational chemistry; BSc, MChem, MSc, PhD

Dept of Computer Science; www2.warwick.ac.uk/fac/sci/dcs

computer & business studies/management sciences, computer science, computing systems, discrete mathematics, large number of taught Master modules; BSc, MEng, MPhil, MSc, PhD

School of Engineering; www2.warwick.ac.uk/fac/sci/eng

automotive engineering, biomedical engineering, civil engineering, computer & information engineering, electronic engineering/systems, electronic systems with communications/sensor technology, energy & power electronic systems, engineering/ & business, engineering business management, manufacturing & mechanical engineering/systems, systems engineering; BEng, BSc, EngD, MPhil, MSc, PhD

Dept of Mathematics/Warwick Mathematics Institute; www2.warwick.ac.uk/fac/sci/maths

financial/interdisciplinary mathematics, mathematics, mathematics & business studies/economics/philosophy/physics/statistics; BSc, MMath, MSc, PhD

Dept of Physics; www2.warwick.ac.uk/fac/sci/physics

mathematics & physics, physics/& business studies; BSc, MPhys, MSc, PhD

Dept of Psychology; www2.warwick.ac.uk/fac/sci/psych

philosophy with psychology, economics with clinical applications of psychology, psychology; BSc, MPhil, MSc, PhD

Dept of Statistics; www2.warwick.ac.uk/fac/sci/statistics

statistics, mathematics, operational research, financial mathematics; MMathStat, MPhil, MSc, PgDip, PhD

Warwick HRI; www2.warwick.ac.uk/fac/sci/whri

enterprise in horticulture, environmental biology/bioscience in a changing climate, plant bioscience for crop production, sustainable crop production; BSc, MSc, MPhil, PhD

Faculty of Social Studies; www2.warwick.ac.uk/fac/soc

Centre for Applied Linguistics; www2.warwick.ac.uk/fac/soc/al

English language teaching/for young learners, / studies & methods, ICT & multimedia, testing & assessment; EdD, MA, MPhil, PGCert, PGDip, PhD

Dept of Economics; www2.warwick.ac.uk/fac/soc/economics

economics & industrial organization, economic history, international financial economics, economics, politics & international studies; BA, BSc, MSc, PGDip, PhD

Dept of Philosophy; www2.warwick.ac.uk/fac/soc/philosophy

continental philosophy, philosophy, philosophy & literature/maths, philosophy of mind, philosophy, politics & economics; BA, BSc, MA, MPhil, PGDip, PhD

Dept of Politics & International Studies; www2.warwick.ac.uk/fac/soc/pais
economics, politics & international studies, French/German/Italian with international studies, globalization & development, history & politics, international political economy, international politics & East Asia/Europe, international relations/ security, politics, philosophy & economics politics/ & sociology/international studies; BA, MA, MPhil, PhD

Dept of Sociology; www2.warwick.ac.uk/fac/soc/sociology
gender, imperialism, & international development, politics & social theory, sociology & postcolonialism, contemporary feminism, racism & global order, social research, gender analysis & international development, sociology; BA, MA, MPhil, PGDip, PhD

School of Health & Social Sciences; www2.warwick.ac.uk/fac/soc/shss
applied social research with health studies, Islam in contemporary societies, social work; MA, MPhil, PGDip, PhD

Warwick Business School; www2.wbs.warwick.ac.uk/fac/soc/
accounting & finance, business & consulting, finance & economics, financial mathematics, global energy, industrial relations & managing human resources, information systems & management, international business, international & European employment relations, international management, management, management & organizational analysis, management science & operational research, marketing & strategy, public sector; BA, BSc, MA, MBA, MPA, MPhil, MSc, PGDip, PhD

Warwick Institute of Education; www2.warwick.ac.uk/fac/soc/wie
applied education & training, business & enterprise education, early childhood studies, drama & theatre education, educational assessment/leadership & innovation research methods/studies, learning & teaching, mathematics education/subject leadership, religious education, multiagency leadership, teaching advanced mathematics; BA, EdD, FdA, MA, MPhil, MSc, PGCE, PhD

Warwick School of Law; www2.warwick.ac.uk/fac/soc/law
advanced legal studies, European law, international corporate governance & financial regulation, international economic/ development law & human rights, law & business/sociology, socio-legal studies; BA, LLB, LLM, MPhil, PhD, PGCert, PGDip

THE UNIVERSITY OF WESTMINSTER
www.wmin.ac.uk

School of Architecture & the Built Environment; www.westminster.ac.uk/schools/architecture
architectural technology, architecture/cultural identity & globalisation, antisocial behaviour, building engineering/surveying, business management & urban development, business with property, project management, construction & surveying/management, domestic violence studies, environmental design, facilities & property management, housing law & policy/practice, interior design, international planning & sustainability, leisure property, logistics & supply chain management, property with business/urban development, quantity surveying, real estate development, tourism & planning, transport planning & management, travel & tourism, urban design, urban estate management, urban regeneration, urban & regional planning; BA, BSc, MA, MPhil, MSc, PGCert, PGDip, PhD

School of Electronics & Computer Science; www.westminster.ac.uk/schools/computing
business & information systems, computer games development/science/& software/systems engineering, computer network security/networks & communications, media technology, multimedia computing & animation, network & computer engineering, human intraction & multimedia, data mining, database systems, decision sciences, multimedia communications, e-commerce with online databases, electronic engineering, embedded systems, enterprise information systems, information & knowledge management/quality/systems, interactive multimedia, IT security, media technology, mobile & web computing, software engineering; BEng, BSc, MEng, MPhil, MSc, PhD

School of Law;www.westminster.ac.uk/schools/law

commercial law, corporate finance law, dispute prevention & resolution, entertainment law, EU law, European legal studies, international & commercial dispute resolution, international commercial law/banking law, international law, law, legal practice; GradDip, LLB, LLM, LPC

School of Life Sciences; www.westminster.ac.uk/schools/science

applied biomedical science/microbiology & biotechnology, biochemistry, biochemical engineering, biological sciences, biomedical sciences, biotechnology, cellular pathology, Chinese medicine/acupuncture, clinical chemistry, complementary therapies, drug discovery & development, environmental biotechnology, forensic biology, health sciences, herbal medicine/naturopathy/nutritional therapy, haematology, human nutrition/medical science, micobiology, medical biotechnology/microbiology/molecular biology, genetics, nutrition & exercise science, physiology & pharmacology, psychology with neuroscience, governance in healthcare communities; BSc, FdSc, MA, MPhil, MSc, PGCert, PhD

School of Media, Arts & Design; www.westminster.ac.uk/schools/media

animation, art & media practice, audio production, ceramics, clinical photography, commercial music, communication/policy, contemporary media practice, digital & photographic imaging, fashion /buying/business management/design/merchandise management, film & TV directing/production/theory, global media, graphic information design, illustration, journalism, media management, mixed media fine art, music business management/informatics, photographic arts/studies, photography & digital imaging, photojournalism, popular musician, PR, radio production, TV, screenwriting/producing; BA, BMus, BSc, FdA, GradDip, MA, PGDip

School of Social Sciences, Humanities & Languages; www.westminster.ac.uk/schools/humanities

creative writing, cultural & critical studies, English language/literature, linguistics, international relations, London studies, TESOL, visual culture; modern & applied languages, journalism, Arabic/studies, bilingual translation, Chinese, conference interpreting, French, German, Russian, Spanish, Asian studies, technical & specialized translation, translation & linguistics, visual culture, politics, global culture, contemporary political theory, psychology. neuroscience, cognitive science, business/health psychology, applied market & social research, history, economic & government reform, European studies, globalisation, criminal justice, sociology; BA, MA, MPhil, PhD

Westminster Business School; www.westminster.ac.uk/schools/business

accounting, business, business administration, economics/management/studies, coaching & mentoring at work, diversity & equality inemployment, digital enterprise management, economics. entrepreneurship, European management, finance financial management/ services, global marketing, HRM/D, information management & finance, international business/marketing/management, international development management/finance, investment & quantitative finance, management, managing health & social care, marketing communications/management/strategy, purchasing & supply chain management, social work; BA, MA, MBA, MPhil, MSc, PGCert, PhD

THE UNIVERSITY OF WINCHESTER
www.winchester.ac.uk

Faculty of Arts; www.winchester.ac.uk/aboutus/university structure/art

arts management, choreography & dance, contemporary literature, creative industries/writing, critical writing, cultural & arts management/studies digital media, drama, English/contemporary/literature & language, film & cinema technologies, film studies, global radio, journalism, media studies, performance management/arts, rhetoric, stage management, street arts, theatre & media for development, vocal & choral studies; BA, FdA, MA, PGCert, PGDip, PhD

Faculty of Humanities and Social Sciences; www.winchester.ac.uk/aboutus/universitystructure/hss

Dept of Archaeology

archaeology, archaeological practics, ancient and medieval archaeology & art, cultural & heritage & resource management regional and local archaeology

Dept of Theology and Religious Studies

ethics & spirituality, theology & religious studies, Christian theology & ministry, practical theology, rhetoric & rituals of death

Dept of History

history, regional and local history &/or archaeology, modern, medieval, world history, historical studies

Dept of Psychology

psychological research methods, psychology; BA, BSc, MA, MPhil, MRes, MSc, PGCert, PGDip, PhD

Faculty of Education, Health and Social Care; www.winchester.ac.uk/?page=2989

educational studies, childhood studies, childhood, youth & community studies, education: education studies, primary education practice; community development, health and wellbeing, health and social care, PGCE secondary (RE), primary ed, primary health care, social care studies, social work; BA, FdA, MA(Ed), MPhil, PGCE, PhD

Faculty of Business, Law & Sport; www.winchester.ac.uk/?page=9734

Winchester Business School

accounting, finance, enterprise & innovation, management IT, health & social care, logistics, voluntary sector, cultural events, retail), business administration/management, event management, HRM, management, managing contemporary global issues, marketing, politics & global studies, sport, sustainable business; BA, FdA, MBA, MSc, PGCert, PGDip

Dept of Law

law; BA/LLB, LLB

Dept of Sports Studies

sports coaching & development, sports management, sports science, sports studies; BA, BSc, FdA

UNIVERSITY OF WOLVERHAMPTON
www.wlv.ac.uk

School of Applied Sciences; www.wlv.ac.uk/default.aspx?page=6878

animal behaviour & wildlife conservation, animal management, biochemistry, biological science, biomedical sciences, biotechnology, clinical physiology, cognitive behaviour therapy, counselling psychology, environmental fieldwork practice/health/management/science & management/technology, equine sports science, forensic science/molecular biology, genetics, geography, human biology/physiology, life sciences, microbiology, molecular biology, pharmaceutical science, pharmacology, pharmacy, occupational/psychology; BA, BSc, DBMS, FdSc, GradDip, HND, MPharm, MSc, PGDip

School of Art & Design; www.wlv.ac.uk/default.aspx?page=6963

animation, applied arts, art & design, computer games design, commercial video production, design for advertising, fashion & textiles/accessories, film studies, fine art, graphic communication, illustration, interactive media, interior design, photography, product design, video & film production; BA, FdA, HND, MA

School of Computing & IT; www.wlv.ac.uk/default.aspx?page=6964

business information systems/technology, computer science (digital media/internet engineering/software/networks/games development), information systems, IT management, computing, interdisciplinary mathematics; BSc, FdSc, HNC, HND, MSc, PGCert

School of Education; www.wlv.ac.uk/default.aspx?page=6965

childhood & family studies, conductive education, early years services, education studies, TESOL, post-compulsory education, RE, society, childhood & family studies, PGCE (numerous taught secondary subject, early/ primary education, special needs & inclusion studies; BA, EdD, FdA, MA, PGCert, PGDip, PhD

School of Engineering & Built Environment; www.wlv.ac.uk/default.aspx?page=6966

advanced technology management, architectural studies, auctioneering & valuation, automotive systems engineering, building surveying, civil engineering, environmental engineering, commercial management & quantity surveying, computer-aided design & construction, construction, construction law/management/project management, design technology, electronics & communications engineering, engineering design management, interior architecture & property development, mechanical engineering, mechatronics, polymer engineering, product design & innovation, property management, quantity surveying, rapid production, advanced development & manufacture, real estate, transport & environmental management, transport & infrastructure management; BDes, BEng, BSc, FdSc, HNC, MEng, MSc, PGCert

School of Health & Wellbeing; www.wlv.ac.uk/default.aspx?page=6067

advancing clinical practice, case management, complementary therapies, health studies, learning disabilities, mental health/adult/child/public health/district/practice/public health/school nursing, long-term conditions, mental health & psychosocial care, palliative care, physician assistant, primary healthcare practice, social care, social studies (mental health), specialist/social work, specialist community nursing (health visiting), district nursing, specialist social work (adults/children, young people, their families & carers/mental health); BA, BSc, DipHE, FdA, GradDip, MA, MPH, MSc, PGCert, PGDip

School of Law, Social Sciences & Communications

broadcasting & journalism, conflict studies, consumer protection, contemporary media, corporate & financial law, creative & professional writing, criminology & criminal justice, deaf studies, English/language, film studies, French, German, history, international corporate & financial law, HR, interpreting, law, linguistics, media & communication/cultural studies, philosophy, policing, politics, popular culture, practice management, PR, public sector, religious studies, social policy, sociology, Spanish, ESOL, TESOL, voluntary & public sectors: policy & practice, uniform public services, war studies; BA, FdA, LLB, LLM, MA

School of Sport, Performing Arts & Leisure; www.wlv.ac.uk/default.aspx?page=6970

applied sport & exercise science, creative music production/writing, dance practice & performance/science, drama & performance, English, event & venue management, hospitality management, music/theatre, musicology, exercise & health/education, performing arts management, popular music/technology, sound production, sport & exercise science, sports, tourism management, travel operations management; BA, BSc, FdA, FdSc, MA, MSc

University of Wolverhampton Business School; www.wlv.ac.uk/default.aspx?page=6971

accounting, business/management/accounting/administration, business economics, coaching & mentoring, e-business management, enterprise, finance, healthcare leadership, HRD/M, information systems & networking, integrated children's services, international/small business management; BA, FdA, HND, MA, MBA, PGDip/Cert, MSC

UNIVERSITY COLLEGE WORCESTER
www.worc.ac.uk

Institute of Education; www.worc.ac.uk/departments/661.html

early childhood studies, education (early years/children/in service), educational management & leadership, HE, improving practice in education, integrated children's service, ICT in education, ITT for teachers in lifelong learning, learning support, teaching & learning English/PGCE (primary, secondary, graduate teacher) retraining to teach, special needs & inclusive education, teaching & learning in HE, teaching primary languages; BA, CertHE, FdA, MA, MSc, PGCE, PGCert, PGDip

Institute of Health & Safety; www.worc.ac.uk/departments/659.html

advanced social & health care studies/practice, applied health sciences, business psychology, changing health behaviours, child & adolescent mental health, counselling, counselling psychology, dance, drama therapy, forensic psychology, health & complementary therapies/social care/well-being, health management/ psychology/sciences, learning disabilities, midwifery, nursing studies, nutritional therapy, pre-hospital, psycho therapies, unscheduled & emergency care, applied/psychology, social welfare/work, sports therapy, substance misuse, young people services, youth & community services; BSc, DipHE, FdA, FdSc, GradDip, MA, MSc, PGCert, PGDip

Institute of Humanities & Creative Arts; www.worc.ac.uk/departments/663.html

American studies, animation, art & design/professional practice, creative digital media, dance, digital film production, drama & performance, English language studies/literary studies/literature: politics & identity, film making/studies, fine art practice, graphic design & multimedia, history, illustration, journalism, media & cultural studies, performance (costume & make-up), politics, screenwriting, sociology, theatre studies, urban & electronic music production, visual arts; BA, HND, MA, MSc

Science & the Environment; www.worc.ac.uk/departments/652.html

animal biology/care science/welfare & management, applied nutrition for professional practice, arboriculture, archaeology & heritage studies, landscape studies/construction, biology, medical communication, conservation/ecology, environmental conservation/ management/science, food safety & quality assurance, garden design, human/physical/geography, organic/horticulture, human nutrition, professional gardening, sustainable woodland management, water & environmental management; BSc, FdSc, HNC, HND, MSc, PGCert, PGDip

Institute of Sport & Exercise Science; www.worc.ac.uk/departments/652.html

applied sport science, outdoor adventure leadership & management/education, physical education, sport & exercise psychology/science, sports coaching/management/performance & coaching/therapy/business management; BSc, HND, MSc

Worcester Business School; www.worc.ac.uk/departments/655.html

accountancy, accounting, advertising, business IT/ management, computing, computer game design, economics, entrepreneurship, finance, financial management, hospitality, HRM, innovation, international business, IT for education , leadership, management/ studies, marketing, networks & information security, retail, travel & tourism, service sector management, PR, public services, web design/development; BA, BSc, DMS, GradCert, MBA, MSc

UNIVERSITY OF YORK
www.york.ac.uk

Dept of Archaeology; www.york.ac.uk/depts/arch

archaeology/of buildings, archaeological information systems, coastal & marine/field /medieval archaeology, bioarchaeology, conservation studies, cultural heritage management, early prehistory, historic landscape studies, historical archaeology, mesolithic studies, zooarcheology; BA, BSc, MA, MPhil, MSc, PhD

Dept of Biology; www.york.ac.uk/depts/biol

biology, bioscience technology, biotechnology & microbiology, computational biology, ecology & environmental management, conservation & environment, functional genomics, genetics, molecular cell biology; BSc, MPhil, MRes, MSc, PhD

Dept of Chemistry; www.york.ac.uk/depts/chemistry

chemistry, chemistry with biological & medicinal chemistry/management & industry/resources & the environment, chemoinformatics, green chemistry; BSc, MChem, MPhil, MSc, PhD

Dept of Computer Science & Engineering; www.cs.york.ac.uk/depts

computer science/with artificial intelligence/business enterprise systems/embedded systems/software engineering, natural/computing, gas turbine control, human-centred interactive technologies, information technology, safety critical systems engineering; BEng, BSc, MEng, MMath, MPhil, MSc, PGCert, PGDip

Dept of Economics & Related Studies; www.york.ac.uk/depts/econ

economics, econometrics & finance/economic history/ sociology/philosophy/politics, project analysis, health economics, economic & social policy analysis, finance & investment; BA, BSc, MSc, PGCert, PGDip, PhD

Dept of Educational Studies; www.york.ac.uk/depts/educ
educational studies, language & literature in education, TESOL, PGCE (English, history, maths, foreign languages), global & international citizenship, education for sustainable development, equity issues, language learning, science education & learning; BA, MA, MPhil, PhD

Dept of Electronics; www.york.ac.uk/depts/elec
avionics, digital systems engineering/signal processing, electronic engineering, internet & wireless technology, music technology systems, nanotechnology, communication engineering, computer engineering; BEng, MEng, MSc, MPhil, PhD

Dept of English & Related Literature; www.york.ac.uk/depts/engl
English, English & history/history of art/linguistics/philosophy/politics, English literary studies, film & literature; BA, MA, MPhil, PhD

Dept of Environment; www.york.ac.uk/depts/eeem
environmental economics & marine/environmental management, environmental geography/science, ecology, corporate social responsibilty; BSc, MPhil, MSc, PGDip, PhD

Dept of Health Sciences; www.york.ac.uk/depts/healthsciences
haematopathology, health sciences, health & social care, public health, midwifery practice, nursing studies (adult/child/learning disability/mental health); BA, BSc, DipHE, MPhil, MSc, PGCert, PGDip, PhD

Dept of History; www.york.ac.uk/depts/hist
history, history with archaeology/economics/English, medieval history, railway studies & transport history, early modern history; BA, GradCert, MA, MPhil, PhD

Dept of History of Art; www.york.ac.uk/depts/histart
history of art/with English/history, stained glass conservation & heritage management; BA, MA, MPhil, PhD

Dept of Language & Linguistic Science; www.york.ac.uk/depts/lang
modern languages, linguistics, phonetics & phonology, psycholinguistics, sociolinguistics, French, German, Spanish, syntax & semantics, phonological development; BA, MA, MPhil, MSc, PhD

York Law School; www.york.ac.uk/depts/law
law, law & society, international corporate & commercial law, international HR & practice; LLB, LLM. MPhil, PhD

Dept of Mathematics; www.york.ac.uk/depts/maths
mathematics, chemoinformatics, mathematics with computer science/economics/physics/statistics, maths with modern applications, mathematics in living world, environmental mathematics, mathematical finance; BA, BSc, MMath, MPhil, MRes. MSc, PGCert, PGDip, PhD

Dept of Music; www.york.ac.uk/depts/music
music, music with education/ technology; BA, MA, MPhil, PhD

Dept of Philosophy; www.york.ac.uk/depts/phil
philosophy, philosophy of art & literature, practical ethics, PPE, theology & ethics; BA, BSc, GradDip, MA, MPhil, PGCert, PGDip, PhD

Dept of Physics; www.york.ac.uk/depts/physics
physics, physics with astrophysics, theoretical physics, fusion energy; BA, BSc, MMath, MPhil, MPhys, MSc, PhD

Dept of Politics; www.york.ac.uk/depts/poli
conflict, governance & development, history & politics, international political economy, political philosophy, public administration & public policy, PPE, politics/with English/history/international relations/social policy/sociology, postwar recovery; BA, MA, PGDip, PhD

Dept of Psychology; www.york.ac.uk/depts/psych
cognitive neuroscience, applied/forensic psychology, reading, language & cognition, psychology; BSc, MPhil, MRes, MSc, PhD

Dept of Social Policy & Social Work; www.york.ac.uk/depts/spsw
applied social science (children & young people/crime/health), social policy, social work, comparative & international social policy; BA, MA, MPhil, MRes, PGCert, PhD

Dept of Sociology; www.york.ac.uk/depts/soci
communication studies, sociology /with criminology/economics/education/history/philosophy/politics/social psychology, social research, social informatics interactive technology, ; BA, MA, MPhil, MSc, PhD

Dept of Theatre, Film & Television; www.york.ac.uk/depts/tft
cinema, television & society, post-production with visual effects/sound design, theatre, film & television production, theatre writing, directing & performance; BA, MA, MPhil, MSc, PhD

Hull York Medical School; www.hyma.york.ac.uk
medicine, medical education; BMBS, MD, MPhil, MSc, PGCert, PhD

School of Politics, Economics & Philosophy; www.york.ac.uk/depts/pep
economics, philosophy, politics, development, political economy, public affairs; BA, MA, MRes, PGCert, PhD

York Management School; www.york.ac.uk/depts/management
accounting, business finance & management, management, international & strategic management, financial management, corporate social responsibilty & environmental management; HRM, BA, BSc, MA, MPhil, MRes, MSc, PhD

YORKSHIRE COAST COLLEGE
www.yorkshirecoastcollege.ac.uk

Higher education
applied digital media (design), business & management, costume, fine art, sport & leisure management, teacher education; BA, FdA

Part 5

Qualifications Awarded by Professional and Trade Associations

Qualifications

Some associations qualify individuals to act in a certain professional capacity. They also try to safeguard high standards of professional conduct. Few associations have complete control over the profession with which they are concerned. Some professions are regulated by the law, and their associations act as the central registration authority. Entry to others is directly controlled by associations which alone award the requisite qualifications. If a profession is required to be registered by the law and is controlled by the representative council, a practitioner found guilty by his or her council of misconduct may be suspended from practice or completely debarred by the removal of his or her name from the register of qualified practitioners. In other professions the consequence of misdemeanour may not be so serious, because the profession does not exercise the same degree of control. The professions registered by statute, and therefore subject to restrictions on entry and loss of either privileges or the right to practise on erasure, are listed in Table 5.1. Certain other professions are closed.

Table 5.1 Professions registered by statute

Profession	Statutory committee controlling professional conduct
Architects	Architects Registration Board
Dentists	General Dental Council
Doctors	General Medical Council
Professions supplementary to medicine: chiropodists; dieticians; medical laboratory technicians; occupational therapists; orthoptists, physiotherapists; radiographers	Health Professions Council
Nurses and midwives	Nursing and Midwifery Council
Opticians	General Optical Council
Patent agents	Chartered Institute of Patent Attorneys
Social workers	General Social Care Council
Teachers	General Teaching Councils for England, Wales, Scotland and Northern Ireland

Study

Some associations give their members an opportunity to keep abreast of a particular discipline or to undertake further study in it. Such associations are especially numerous in medicine, science and applied science. Many qualifying associations also provide an information and study service for their members. Some of the more famous learned societies confer added status upon distinguished practitioners by electing them to membership or honorary membership.

Protection of Members' Interests

Some associations exist mainly to look after the interests of individual practitioners and the group. A small number are directly concerned with negotiations over salary and working conditions.

Qualifying Associations

The principal function of qualifying associations is to examine and qualify persons who wish to become practitioners in the field with which they are concerned. As already indicated, some regulate professional conduct and many offer opportunities for further study. Membership is divided into grades, usually classified as corporate and non-corporate. Non-corporate members are those not yet admitted to full membership, mainly students; they are divided from corporate membership by barriers of age and levels of responsibility and experience. The principal requirement for admission to membership is the knowledge and ability to pass the association's exams; candidates may be exempted from the association's exams if they have acceptable alternative qualifications.

Non-Corporate or Affiliated Members

Non-corporate members are those who are as yet unqualified or only partly qualified. They are accorded limited rights and privileges, but may not vote at meetings of the corporate body. Most associations have a student membership grade. Students are those who are preparing for the exams which qualify them for admission to corporate membership. Some associations have licentiate and graduate membership grades, which are senior to the student grade. Graduates are those who have passed the qualifying exams but lack other requirements, such as age and experience, for admission to corporate membership.

Corporate or Full Members

Corporate members are the fully qualified, constituent members of incorporated associations. They are accorded full rights and privileges and may vote at meetings of the corporate body. Corporate membership is often divided into 2 grades, a senior grade of members or fellows and a general grade of associate members or associates.

Honorary Members

Some associations have a special class of honorary members or fellows for distinguished members or individuals who have made an outstanding contribution to the profession in question.

Examinations and Requirements

Professionals normally become corporate members by exam or exemption, with or without additional requirements. Many final professional exams are of degree standard, and a number of professional qualifications are accepted as evidence of competence at operational level by employers. Ongoing professional development is encouraged by most associations to ensure members' skills and knowledge are up to date and relevant.

The transition from the general grade of membership to the senior can be automatic in some associations (for instance, on reaching a prescribed age), but in others the higher grade is reached only after the submission of evidence of research or progress in the profession.

Qualifying exams are usually conducted in two or more stages. The first stage leads to an Intermediate or Part I qualification. The second stage leads to a Final or Part II or Part III qualification, which is about the standard of a degree.

Gaining Professional Qualifications

Prospective students can study by any of the following means:

- correspondence courses (distance learning and/or online support);
- personal attendance at the schools maintained by some associations (eg the Architectural Association School of Architecture);
- further and higher education institutions.

ACCOUNTANCY

Membership of Professional Institutions and Associations

ASSOCIATION OF ACCOUNTING TECHNICIANS

140 Aldersgate Street
London EC1A 4HY
Tel: 0845 863 0802
Fax: 020 7397 3009
E-mail: aat@aat.org.uk
Website: www.aat.org.uk

AAT is the UK's leading qualification and membership body for accounting professionals. We have over 120,000 members, including students, people working in accountancy, and self-employed business owners, in more than 90 countries worldwide. Established in 1980 to ensure consistent training and regulation for accounting support staff, our qualifications provide a vocation progression route to the UK's senior accountancy qualifications: ACCA, CIMA, CIPFA, ICAS, ICAEW.

MEMBERSHIP
Student Member
Affiliate Member
Full Member (MAAT)
Fellow Member (FMAAT)

QUALIFICATION/EXAMINATIONS
AAT Accounting Qualification (QCF)
Certificate in Payroll Administration (QCF)
AAT Level 2 Award in Bookkeeping (QCF)

DESIGNATORY LETTERS
MAAT

ASSOCIATION OF CHARITY INDEPENDENT EXAMINERS

The Gatehouse
White Cross
South Road
Lancaster
Lancashire LA1 4XQ
Tel: 01524 348920
Fax: 01524 348920
E-mail: info@acie.org.uk
Website: www.acie.org.uk

ACIE provides support, training and qualifications for anyone acting as an independent examiner of charity accounts in the UK (subscriptions apply). For details, and news of conferences focusing on independent examination in both England & Wales and Scotland, visit the website; www.acie.org.uk (registered charity in E&W 1077154 & SC039066).

MEMBERSHIP
Associate

Full Member (with category of Licentiate, Member or Fellow)

QUALIFICATION/EXAMINATIONS
Licentiate (Receipts & Payments Accounts only): LCIE
Licentiate (All Accounts): LCIE
Member: MCIE
Fellow: FCIE

DESIGNATORY LETTERS
LCIE, MCIE, FCIE

CHARTERED INSTITUTE OF INTERNAL AUDITORS

13 Abbeville Mews
88 Clapham Park Road
London SW4 7BX
Tel: 020 7498 0101
Fax: 020 7978 2492
E-mail: info@iia.org.uk
Website: www.iia.org.uk

The Chartered Institute of Internal Auditors (IIA) is the only professional body in the UK and Ireland focused exclusively on internal auditing and we are passionate about supporting, promoting and training the professionals who work in it. Every year we help internal auditors at every stage of their career with training, qualifications and technical resources.

MEMBERSHIP
Student Member
Affiliate Member
Voting Member (PIIA, CMIIA)
Head of Internal Audit Service Member
Fellow (FIIA, CFIIA)

QUALIFICATION/EXAMINATIONS
IIA Certificate in Internal Audit and Business Risk (IA Cert)
IIA Diploma in Internal Audit Practice (PIIA)
IIA Advanced Diploma in Internal Auditing and Management (CMIIA)
IT Auditing Certificate

DESIGNATORY LETTERS
IA Cert, PIIA, CMIIA, FIIA, CFIIA

CIMA – THE CHARTERED INSTITUTE OF MANAGEMENT ACCOUNTANTS

26 Chapter Street
London SW1P 4NP
Tel: 020 8849 2251
Fax: 020 8849 2450
E-mail: cima.contact@cimaglobal.com
Website: www.cimaglobal.com

CIMA is a global professional institute that specializes in the training, qualification and support of management accountants. Our Professional Qualification is highly regarded by businesses around the world. Our members work in business analysis, management consulting, operations management, project management, etc and many top finance directors and chief executives are CIMA members.

MEMBERSHIP
Member
Associate (ACMA)
Fellow (FCMA)

QUALIFICATION/EXAMINATIONS
Certificate in Business Accounting
Chartered Management Accounting Qualification
Certificate in Islamic FInance
Diploma in Islamic Finance

DESIGNATORY LETTERS
ACMA, FCMA

ICAEW (THE INSTITUTE OF CHARTERED ACCOUNTANTS IN ENGLAND AND WALES)

Metropolitan House
321 Avebury Boulevard
Milton Keynes MK9 2FZ
Tel: 01908 248 040
Fax: 01908 248 260
E-mail: careers@icaew.com
Website: www.icaew.com/careers

ICAEW is a world leader of the accountancy profession, with more than 134,000 members in over 160 countries. Our members work at the highest levels of business, across all industry sectors around the world. Our professional qualification, the ACA, delivers essential knowledge, skills and technical expertise in accountancy and business.

MEMBERSHIP
Associate Chartered Accountant (ACA)
Fellow Chartered Accountant (FCA)

QUALIFICATION/EXAMINATIONS
Please see the ICAEW website.

DESIGNATORY LETTERS
ACA, FCA

INSTITUTE OF FINANCIAL ACCOUNTANTS

Burford House
44 London Road
Sevenoaks
Kent TN13 1AS
Tel: 01732 458080
Fax: 01732 455848
E-mail: mail@ifa.org.uk
Website: www.ifa.org.uk

The IFA was established in 1916 and is the oldest body of non-Chartered Accountants in the world. We represent members and students in more than 80 countries, providing qualifications for those wishing to work in financial management and accountancy, and CPD for qualified Financial Accountants, particularly in SMEs.

MEMBERSHIP
Affiliate
Financial Accounting Executive
Associate (AFA)
Fellow (FFA)

QUALIFICATION/EXAMINATIONS
Financial Accounting Diploma
Professional Financial Accountant

DESIGNATORY LETTERS
AFA, FFA

INTERNATIONAL ASSOCIATION OF BOOK-KEEPERS

Suite 30
40 Churchill Square
Kings Hill
West Malling
Kent ME19 4YU
Tel: 01732 897750
Fax: 01732 897751
E-mail: mail@iab.org.uk
Website: www.iab.org.uk

The IAB specializes in providing high-quality, accredited and regulated financial and business qualifications for financial professionals and owners or managers of small businesses. We continue to be the leading international membership body for professional book-keepers. Established in 1973, we now have many thousands of students and members worldwide.

MEMBERSHIP
Associate (AIAB)
Member (MIAB)
Fellow (FIAB)
IAB FinAdm
IAB FinMgr

QUALIFICATION/EXAMINATIONS
Certificate in Book-keeping (Level 1)
Certificate in Book-keeping (Level 2)
Diploma in Accounting and Advanced Book-keeping (Level 3)
Diploma in Accounting to International Standards (Level 4)
Certificate in Cost and Management Accounting (Level 3)
Diploma in Financial Information for Managers (Level 4)
Certificate in Finance for Non-Financial Managers (Level 3)

DESIGNATORY LETTERS
AIAB, MIAB, FIAB, IAB FinAdm, IAB FinMgr

THE ASSOCIATION OF CHARTERED CERTIFIED ACCOUNTANTS

London WC2A 3EE
Tel: 020 7059 5000
Fax: 020 7059 5050
E-mail: info@accaglobal.com
Website: www.accaglobal.com

The ACCA is the global body for professional accountants, with 131,500 members and 362,000 students in 170 countries. Our aim is to support our members throughout their career in accounting, business or finance so that they achieve the highest professional, ethical and governance standards.

MEMBERSHIP
Associate (ACCA)
Fellow (FCCA)

QUALIFICATION/EXAMINATIONS
Diploma in Financial Management (DipFM)
Certified Accounting Technician (CAT) qualification
ACCA Qualification
BSc in Applied Accounting (awarded by Oxford Brookes University)
MBA (awarded by Oxford Brookes University; accredited by the Association of MBAs)

DESIGNATORY LETTERS
ACCA, FCCA

THE ASSOCIATION OF CORPORATE TREASURERS

51 Moorgate
London EC2R 6BH
Tel: 020 7847 2540
Fax: 020 7374 8744
E-mail: enquiries@treasurers.co.uk
Website: www.treasurers.org

The ACT is the international body for professionals working in treasury, risk and corporate finance. We are the leading examining body for international treasury, providing the widest scope of benchmark qualifications and continuing development through training, conferences and publications – including *The Treasurer* magazine.

MEMBERSHIP
Student Member
Faculty Member
Associate Member (AMCT)
Member (MCT)
Fellow (FCT)
Corporate Member
International Affiliate

QUALIFICATION/EXAMINATIONS
Advanced Diploma in Treasury, Risk and Corporate Finance (MCT)
Diploma in Treasury (AMCT)
Certificate in Financial Fundamentals for Business (CertFin)
Certificate in International Treasury Management (CertITM)
Certificate in International Treasury Management – Public Finance (CertITM-PF)
Certificate in Corporate Finance and Funding (CertCFF)
Certificate in Financial Maths and Modelling (CertFMM)
Certificate in International Cash Management (CertICM)
Certificate in Risk Management (CertRM)

DESIGNATORY LETTERS
AMCT, MCT, FCT

THE ASSOCIATION OF INTERNATIONAL ACCOUNTANTS

Staithes 3
The Watermark
Metro Riverside
Newcastle upon Tyne
Tyne & Wear NE11 9SN
Tel: 0191 493 0277
Fax: 0191 493 0278
E-mail: aia@aiaworldwide.com
Website: www.aiaworldwide.com

The AIA was founded in the UK in 1928 as a professional accountancy body and from conception has promoted the concept of 'international accounting' to create a global network of accountants in over 85 countries worldwide. We are recognized by the UK government as a Recognized Qualifying Body (RQB) for statutory auditors.

MEMBERSHIP
Student Member
Graduate Member
Affiliate Member (AMIA)
Academic Member
Associate (AAIA)
Fellow (FAIA)
Honorary Member
Retired Member

QUALIFICATION/EXAMINATIONS
Professional Accountancy Qualification
Statutory Audit Qualification
Audit Diploma
Corporate Finance Diploma
IFRS Diploma
Management Accounting & Costing Diploma

DESIGNATORY LETTERS
AMIA, AAIA, FAIA

THE CHARTERED INSTITUTE OF PUBLIC FINANCE AND ACCOUNTANCY

3 Robert Street
London WC2N 6RL
Tel: 020 7543 5656
Fax: 020 7543 5700
E-mail: students@cipfa.org.uk
Website: www.cipfa.org.uk

The CIPFA is the professional body for people in public finance. Our 14,000 members work throughout the public services and as the only UK professional accountancy body to specialize in public services, CIPFA's qualifications are the foundation for a career in public finance.

MEMBERSHIP
Student Member
Affiliate
Associate
Full Member

QUALIFICATION/EXAMINATIONS
CIPFA Professional Qualification
Certificate in Charity Finance and Accountancy
Certificate in International Treasury Management – Public Finance

THE INSTITUTE OF CERTIFIED BOOKKEEPERS

1 Northumberland Avenue
Trafalgar Square
London WC2N 5BW
Tel: 0845 060 2345
Fax: 01635 298960
E-mail: info@bookkeepers.org.uk
Website: www.bookkeepers.org.uk

The ICB is the largest bookkeeping institute in the world. Our aims are to promote bookkeeping as a profession, to improve training in the principles of bookkeeping, and to establish qualifications and the award of grades of membership that recognize academic attainment, work experience and professional competence, and thereby enable qualified bookkeepers to gain recognition as an integral part of the financial world.

MEMBERSHIP
Registered Student
Affiliate
Associate Member (AICB)
Member (MICB)
Fellow (FICB)

QUALIFICATION/EXAMINATIONS
Level 1: Certificate in Basic Bookkeeping
Level 2: (Intermediate): Certificate in Computerized Bookkeeping
Level 2: (Intermediate): Certificate in Manual Bookkeeping
Level 3: (Advanced): Diploma in Computerized Bookkeeping
Level 3: (Advanced): Diploma in Manual Bookkeeping
Level 3: (Advanced): Diploma in Payroll Management
Level 3: (Advanced): Diploma in Self-Assessment Tax Returns

Level 4: (Advanced) Diploma in Drafting Financial Statements, Management Accounts, Personal and Business Taxation.

DESIGNATORY LETTERS
AICB, MICB, FICB

THE INSTITUTE OF CHARTERED ACCOUNTANTS OF SCOTLAND

CA House
Edinburgh EH12 5BH
Tel: 01313 470161
Fax: 01313 470112
E-mail: catraining@icas.org.uk
Website: www.icas.org.uk

The Institute of Chartered Accountants of Scotland (ICAS) was the world's first professional body of accountants, receiving its Royal Charter in 1854. It was also the first to adopt the designation 'Chartered Accountant' and the designatory letters CA.

MEMBERSHIP
To qualify as a Chartered Accountant (CA) students must secure a training contract with an organization authorized to train CA students. The three-year training programme comprises supervised work experience in the training office, completion of a competency-based Achievement Log, and participation in the ICAS education programme in preparation for the professional examinations. For further information please see the ICAS website.

QUALIFICATION/EXAMINATIONS
Test of Competence: Financial Accounting, Principles of Auditing and Reporting, Finance, Business Management, Business Law.
Test of Professional Skills: Taxation, Advanced Finance, Financial Reporting, Assurance and Business Systems.
Test of Professional Expertise: One multidisciplinary case study designed to test candidates' ability to apply their theoretical knowledge and practical skills to problems likely to be encountered by the newly qualified accountant. Additional material includes Corporate Planning, Corporate Strategies and Management, Business Improvement, Management of Financial Structures, and Ethics.

DESIGNATORY LETTERS
CA

ACOUSTICS

Membership of Professional Institutions and Associations

INSTITUTE OF ACOUSTICS

77A St Peter's Street
St Albans
Hertfordshire AL1 3BN
Tel: 01727 848195
Fax: 01727 850553
E-mail: ioa@ioa.org.uk
Website: www.ioa.org.uk

The IOA is the UK's professional body for those working in acoustics, noise and vibration, and has more than 3,000 members in research, educational, environmental, government and industrial organizations. We offer a range of professionally recognized courses and are licensed by the Engineering Research Council to offer registration at Chartered and Incorporated Engineer levels.

MEMBERSHIP
Student
Affiliate
Technician Member (TechIOA)
Associate Member (AMIOA)
Member (MIOA)
Fellow (FIOA)
Honorary Fellow (HonFIOA)
Incorporated Engineer (IEng)
Chartered Engineer (CEng)
Sponsor

QUALIFICATION/EXAMINATIONS
Certificate of Competence in Environmental Noise Measurement
Certificate of Competence in Workplace Noise Risk Assessment
Certificate Course in the Management of Occupational Exposure to Hand–Arm Vibration
Diploma in Acoustics and Noise Control

DESIGNATORY LETTERS
TechIOA, AMIOA, MIOA, FIOA, HonFIOA, IEng, CEng

ADVERTISING AND PUBLIC RELATIONS

Membership of Professional Institutions and Associations

CHARTERED INSTITUTE OF PUBLIC RELATIONS

52–53 Russell Square
London WC1B 4HP
Tel: 020 7631 6900
Fax: 020 7631 6944
E-mail: info@cipr.co.uk
Website: www.cipr.co.uk

The CIPR, founded in 1948, is the professional body for PR practitioners and has more than 9,000 members, to whom it offers information, advice, support and training. Our aim is to raise standards within the profession through the promotion of best practice and our members abide by our strict code of professional conduct.

MEMBERSHIP
Student
Affiliate
Associate (ACIPR)
Member (MCIPR)
Fellow (FCIPR)
Honorary Fellow (Hon FCIPR)

QUALIFICATION/EXAMINATIONS
Foundation Award in Public Relations
Advanced Certificate
Diploma

DESIGNATORY LETTERS
ACIPR, MCIPR, FCIPR

INSTITUTE OF PRACTITIONERS IN ADVERTISING

44 Belgrave Square
London SW1X 8QS
Tel: 020 7235 7020
Fax: 020 7245 9904
E-mail: training@ipa.co.uk
Website: www.ipa.co.uk

The IPA is the UK's leading professional body for advertising, media and marketing communications agencies. We promote the services of our member agencies, which have access to a range of services and benefits, including a Legal Department, Information

Centre and training courses provided by our Professional Development Department.

MEMBERSHIP
Personal Member (MIPA)
Fellow/Honorary Fellow (FIPA)
Member Agency

QUALIFICATION/EXAMINATIONS
Foundation Certificate
Advanced Certificate
LegRes Certificate
Excellence Diploma

DESIGNATORY LETTERS
MIPA, FIPA

INSTITUTE OF PROMOTIONAL MARKETING

70 Margaret Street
London W1W 8SS
Tel: 020 7291 7733
E-mail: enquiries@theipm.co.uk
Website: www.theipm.org.uk

The Institute of Promotional Marketing represents promoters, agencies and service partners engaged in promotional marketing in the UK by protecting, promoting and progressing effective sales promotion across all media channels through its education, legal advice, awards, and other products and services.

MEMBERSHIP
Personal Member (MISP)
Corporate Member

QUALIFICATION/EXAMINATIONS
Certificate in Digital Promotions
Certificate in Experiential Marketing
Diploma in Motivation
Certificate in Promotional & Interactive Marketing
Diploma in Promotional & Interactive Marketing

DESIGNATORY LETTERS
MISP

LONDON SCHOOL OF PUBLIC RELATIONS

David Game House
69 Notting Hill Gate
London W11 3JS
Tel: 020 7221 3399
Fax: 020 7243 1730
E-mail: info@lspr-education.com
Website: www.pr-school-london.com

The LSPR provides up-to-date training for those wishing to enter public relations as a career or for those already in PR or an information/communications job who require some formal training. Our Diploma, *An Integrated Approach to Public Relations for the 21st Century*, is awarded to students upon successful completion of a 2-week full-time intensive course or 3-month part-time evening course.

QUALIFICATION/EXAMINATIONS
Diploma

AGRICULTURE AND HORTICULTURE

Membership of Professional Institutions and Associations

INSTITUTE OF HORTICULTURE

Capel Manor College
Bullsmoor Lane
Enfield
Middlesex EN1 4RQ
Tel: 01992 707025
Website: www.horticulture.org.uk

The IoH represents all those professionally engaged in horticulture in the UK and the Republic of Ireland. Our main aim is to promote the profession and its importance in food and ornamental plant production, improving the environment, providing employment and as the leisure pursuit of gardening. We are also developing CPD and mentoring schemes for our members and liaise with government and other bodies on matters of interest or concern.

MEMBERSHIP
Student Member
Affiliate
Associate (AI Hort)
Member (MI Hort)
Fellow (FI Hort)
Group Membership

DESIGNATORY LETTERS
AI Hort, MI Hort, FI Hort

ROYAL HORTICULTURAL SOCIETY

RHS Qualifications
RHS Garden Wisley
Woking
Surrey GU23 6QB
Tel: 0845 260 9000
E-mail: qualifications@rhs.org.uk
Website: www.rhs.org.uk

RHS Qualifications is a nationally recognized awarding body offering a range of qualifications to provide recognition of horticultural knowledge and skills. Part-time courses leading to RHS qualifications are offered by approved centres throughout the UK and Ireland, and by distance-learning providers.

QUALIFICATION/EXAMINATIONS
RHS Level 1 Award in Practical Horticulture
RHS Level 2 Certificate in the Principles of Plant Growth, Propagation and Development
RHS Level 2 Certificate in the Principles of Garden Planning, Establishment and Maintenance
RHS Level 2 Certificate in the Principles of Horticulture
RHS Level 2 Certificate in Practical Horticulture
RHS Level 2 Diploma in the Principles and Practices of Horticulture
RHS Level 3 Certificate in the Principles of Plant Growth, Health and Applied Propagation
RHS Level 3 Certificate in the Principles of Garden Planning, Construction and Planting
RHS Level 3 Certificate in Practical Horticulture
RHS Level 3 Diploma in the Principles and Practices of Horticulture
Master of Horticulture

THE ROYAL BOTANIC GARDEN EDINBURGH

20A Inverleith Row
Edinburgh EH3 5LR
Tel: 01312 482825
Fax: 01312 482901
E-mail: education@rbge.org.uk
Website: www.rbge.org.uk

The RBGE was founded in the 17th century as a physic garden, growing medicinal plants. Now it extends over four Gardens boasting a rich living collection of plants, and is a world-renowned centre for plant science and education.

QUALIFICATION/EXAMINATIONS
Certificate in Practical Field Botany
Certificate in Practical Horticulture
Diploma in Botanical Illustration
Diploma in Garden Design
Diploma in Herbology
HND/BSc in Horticulture with Plantsmanship
MSc in The Biodiversity and Taxonomy of Plants

AMBULANCE SERVICE

Membership of Professional Institutions and Associations

AMBULANCE SERVICE INSTITUTE

Suite 183
Maddison House
226 High Street
Croydon CR9 1DF
E-mail: enquiries@asi-international.com
Website: www.asi-international.com

The ASI is a non-union, non-political, independent institute whose membership is dedicated to raising the standards and quality of ambulance provision and thereby improving the professionalism and quality of care available to patients. Membership is open to non-NHS personnel as well as to employees of NHS Ambulance Services.

MEMBERSHIP
Student
Member (MASI)
Licentiate (LASI)
Associate (AASI)
Graduate (GASI)
Fellow (FASI)

QUALIFICATION/EXAMINATIONS
The Institute offers professional examinations and qualifications in the areas of Pre-Hospital Care, Control and Communications, and Management, for those who desire a career in the ambulance service.

DESIGNATORY LETTERS
MASI, LASI, AASI, GASI, FASI

ARBITRATION

Membership of Professional Institutions and Associations

THE CHARTERED INSTITUTE OF ARBITRATORS

12 Bloomsbury Square
London WC1A 2LP
Tel: 020 7421 7444
Fax: 020 7404 4023
E-mail: info@ciarb.org
Website: www.ciarb.org

The CIArb is a not-for-profit, UK-registered charity with 12,000 members worldwide that exists to promote and facilitate the settlement of private disputes by arbitration and alternative dispute resolution. We provide training for arbitrators, mediators and adjudicators and act as an international centre for practitioners, policy-makers, academics and those in business concerned with the cost-effective and early settlement of disputes.

MEMBERSHIP
Associate (ACIArb)
Member (MCIArb)
Fellow (FCIArb)

QUALIFICATION/EXAMINATIONS
Introductory Certificate
Advanced Certificate
Diploma

DESIGNATORY LETTERS
ACIArb, MCIArb, FCIArb

ARCHAEOLOGY

Membership of Professional Institutions and Associations

THE INSTITUTE FOR ARCHAEOLOGISTS

SHES
University of Reading
Whiteknights
PO Box 227
Reading RG6 6AB
Tel: 0118 378 6446
Fax: 0118 378 6448
E-mail: admin@archaeologists.net
Website: www.archaeologists.net

The IfA is a professional organization for all archaeologists and others involved in protecting and understanding the historic environment, with more than 2,700 members. We advance the practice of archaeology and allied disciplines by promoting professional standards and ethics for conserving, managing, understanding and enjoying our heritage.

MEMBERSHIP
Student
Affiliate
Practitioner (PIfA)
Associate (AIfA)
Member (MIfA)
Registered Organization

ARCHITECTURE

Membership of Professional Institutions and Associations

ARCHITECTS REGISTRATION BOARD

8 Weymouth Street
London W1W 5BU
Tel: 020 7580 5861
Fax: 020 7436 5269
E-mail: info@arb.org.uk
Website: www.arb.org.uk

The ARB is the regulatory body for architects in the UK. Only individuals registered with the Board can use the title 'architect'. Applicants must have passed the recognized exams at a school of architecture in the UK (or have an equivalent non-UK professional qualification) and have at least 2 years' practical experience working under the supervision of an architect.

CHARTERED INSTITUTE OF ARCHITECTURAL TECHNOLOGISTS (CIAT)

397 City Road
London EC1V 1NH
Tel: 020 7278 2206
Fax: 020 7837 3194
E-mail: info@ciat.org.uk
Website: www.ciat.org.uk

CIAT represents over 9,500 professionals working and studying in the field of Architectural Technology. We are internationally recognized as the qualifying body for Chartered Architectural Technologists (MCIAT) and Architectural Technicians (TCIAT).

MEMBERSHIP
Student member
Profile candidate
Associate (ACIAT)
Architectural Technician (TCIAT)
Chartered Architectural Technologist (MCIAT)
Honorary Member (HonMCIAT)

DESIGNATORY LETTERS
ACIAT, TCIAT, MCIAT

ROYAL INSTITUTE OF BRITISH ARCHITECTS

60 Portland Place
London W1B 1AD
Tel: 020 7580 5533
Fax: 020 7255 1541
E-mail: info@inst.riba.org
Website: www.architecture.com

The Royal Institute of British Architects is the UK body for architecture and the architectural profession. We provide support for our 40,500 members worldwide in the form of training, technical services, publications and events, and set standards for the education of architects, both in the UK and overseas. We also work with government to improve the design quality of public buildings, new homes and new communities.

MEMBERSHIP
Student Member

Affiliate Member
Associate Member
Chartered Member
Chartered Practice

ART AND DESIGN

Membership of Professional Institutions and Associations

BRITISH ASSOCIATION OF ART THERAPISTS

Claremont
24–27 White Lion Street
London N1 9PD
Tel: 020 7686 4216
E-mail: info@baat.org
Website: www.baat.org

The BAAT is the professional organization for art therapists in the UK and has its own Code of Ethics of Professional Practice. We maintain a comprehensive directory of qualified art therapists and work to promote art therapy in the UK through 20 regional groups. We also have a European section and an international section.

MEMBERSHIP
Trainee Member
Associate Member
Full Member
Honorary Member
Fellow
Corporate Member

QUALIFICATION/EXAMINATIONS
The BAAT organizes a programme of CPD courses for Art Therapists. For details see the website.

BRITISH ASSOCIATION OF PAINTINGS CONSERVATOR-RESTORERS

PO Box 258
Norwich NR13 4WY
Tel: 01603 516237
Fax: 01603 510985
E-mail: office@bapcr.org.uk
Website: www.bapcr.org.uk

The BAPCR (founded in 1943 as the Association of British Picture Restorers) is the professional association for conservator-restorers of paintings and has more than 400 members worldwide. Our aims are to advance the profession by providing means for CPD to our members and thereby a service to the public.

MEMBERSHIP
Associate (Student)
Associate
Fellow

D&AD (BRITISH DESIGN & ART DIRECTION)

9 Graphite Square
Vauxhall Walk
London SE11 5EE
Tel: 020 7840 1111
Fax: 020 7840 0840
E-mail: info@dandad.co.uk
Website: www.dandad.org

Founded in 1962, D&AD is a professional association and educational charity with a membership of more than 2,000, working on behalf of the design and advertising communities. Our mission is to set creative standards, educate and inspire the next creative generation, and promote the importance of good design and advertising to business as a whole.

MEMBERSHIP
Student
New Creative
Elected Associate
Associate
Member

SOCIETY OF DESIGNER CRAFTSMEN

24 Rivington Street
London EC2A 3DU
Tel: 020 7739 3663
E-mail: info@societyofdesignercrafstmen.org.uk
Website: www.societyofdesignercraftsmen.org.uk

The Society, which was founded in 1887 as the Arts and Crafts Exhibition Society, is the largest and oldest multi-craft society in the UK. Our aim is to emphasize designer-making where innovation, originality and quality are important, and we provide promotional services and exhibiting opportunities to members.

MEMBERSHIP
Associate
Licentiate (LSDC)
Member (MSDC)
Fellow (FSDC)

DESIGNATORY LETTERS
LSDC, MSDC, FSDC

THE CHARTERED SOCIETY OF DESIGNERS

1 Cedar Court
Royal Oak Yard
Bermondsey Street
London SE1 3GA
Tel: 020 7357 8088
Fax: 020 7407 9878
E-mail: info@csd.org.uk
Website: www.csd.org.uk

The CSD, which was founded in 1930, is the professional body for designers and has more than 3,000 members. We promote sound principles of design in all areas in which design considerations apply, further design practice and encourage the study of design techniques for the benefit of the community.

MEMBERSHIP
Student Member

Graduate Member
Member (MCSD)
Fellow (FCSD)

DESIGNATORY LETTERS
MCSD, FCSD

THE INDEX OF PROFESSIONAL MASTER DESIGNERS

Kensington House
33 Imperial Square
Cheltenham Spa
Gloucestershire GL50 1QZ
Tel: 08701 161823
Fax: 08702 626146
E-mail: masterdesigners@kensington-house.com

The Index was formed to provide a register of designers practising in all areas of design. Our objectives are to enable designers to achieve recognition and attain qualifications and also to accredit schools and training organizations offering suitable courses.

MEMBERSHIP
Student
Professional Designer (IPMD (DIP))
Master Designer (IPMD (MAS))

QUALIFICATION/EXAMINATIONS
Certificate of Excellence – Interior Design Students

DESIGNATORY LETTERS
IPMD (DIP), IPMD (MAS)

ASTRONOMY AND SPACE SCIENCE

Membership of Professional Institutions and Associations

THE BRITISH INTERPLANETARY SOCIETY

27/29 South Lambeth Road
London SW8 1SZ
Tel: 020 7735 3160
Fax: 020 7587 5118
E-mail: mail@bis-spaceflight.com
Website: www.bis-spaceflight.com

The BIS was formed in 1933 and has been at the forefront of actively promoting new ideas on space exploration at technical, educational and popular levels for almost 70 years. We serve the interests of those professionally involved with space, promote fundamental space research, technology and applications, encourage technical and scientific space studies, and undertake educational activities on space topics.

MEMBERSHIP
Member
Fellow (FBIS)

DESIGNATORY LETTERS
FBIS

AVIATION

Membership of Professional Institutions and Associations

THE GUILD OF AIR PILOTS AND AIR NAVIGATORS

Cobham House
9 Warwick Court
London WC1R 5DJ
Tel: 020 7404 4032
Fax: 020 7404 4035
E-mail: gapan@gapan.org
Website: www.gapan.org

The Guild, an active Livery Company of the City of London, represents pilot and navigator interests within all areas of aviation. Most of our members are, or have been, professional licence holders, or hold a private licence. Our aims include promoting the highest standards of air safety, liaising with all authorities connected with licensing, training and legislation, providing advice and facilitating exchange of information.

MEMBERSHIP
Associate
Freeman
Upper Freeman

QUALIFICATION/EXAMINATIONS
Master Air Pilot Certificate
Master Air Navigator Certificate

THE GUILD OF AIR TRAFFIC CONTROL OFFICERS

4 St Mary's Road
Bingham
Nottingham
Nottinghamshire NG13 8DW
Tel: 01949 876405
Fax: 01949 876405
E-mail: caf@gatco.org
Website: www.gatco.org

Founded in 1954, GATCO is an independent professional organization that exists to promote honourable practice and the highest standards in all aspects of aviation. It is dedicated to the safety of all who seek their livelihood or pleasure in the air.

MEMBERSHIP
Student Member
Associate Non-Operational Member
Associate Operational Member
Full Member
Corporate Member

QUALIFICATION/EXAMINATIONS
Qualifying criteria apply to all memberships categories. Further information should be sought from GATCO Ltd, Central Administrative Facility (CAF).

BANKING

Membership of Professional Institutions and Associations

IFS SCHOOL OF FINANCE

8th Floor
Peninsular House
36 Monument Street
London EC3R 8LJ
Tel: 01227 818609
Fax: 01227 784331/786030
E-mail: customerservices@ifslearning.ac.uk
Website: www.ifslearning.ac.uk

The ifs School of Finance is a world-class provider of financial learning, and has more than 50,000 students in over 90 countries. Having built a reputation for excellence in learning, all the qualifications it provides combine innovation and quality, and draw from over 130 years of educational experience.

MEMBERSHIP
Member
Affiliate
Associate
Fellow
Chartered Associate
Adviser Membership (for financial and mortgage advisers)

QUALIFICATION/EXAMINATIONS
The ifs offer a wide range of qualifications for those employed or aspiring to a career in the financial services industry, and for consumers. For details see; www.ifslearning.ac.uk

THE CHARTERED INSTITUTE OF BANKERS IN SCOTLAND

Drumsheugh House
38B Drumsheugh Gardens
Edinburgh EH3 7SW
Tel: 0131 473 7777
Fax: 0131 473 7788
E-mail: info@charteredbanker.com
Website: www.charteredbanker.com

The Chartered Institute of Bankers in Scotland provides world-class professional qualifications for both the UK and international markets. Our vision for the financial services industry is one of professionalism. We are the only organization in the world entitled to award the designation 'Chartered Banker' to its members.

MEMBERSHIP
Student
Affiliate
Associate (ACIBS)
Member (MCIBS)
Fellow (FCIBS)

QUALIFICATION/EXAMINATIONS
Certificate
Diploma
Advanced Diploma
Chartered Banker

DESIGNATORY LETTERS
ACIBS, MCIBS, FCIBS

BEAUTY THERAPY AND BEAUTY CULTURE

Membership of Professional Institutions and Associations

ASSOCIATION OF THERAPY LECTURERS

18 Shakespeare Business Centre
Hathaway Close
Eastleigh
Hampshire SO50 4SR
Tel: 0844 875 2022
Fax: 023 8062 4399
E-mail: info@fht.org.uk
Website: www.fht.org.uk

(Part of the Federation of Holistic Therapists)

The ATL began in 1963 as the Society of Beauty Teachers, when Beauty Therapy teaching was still in its infancy. In the 1990s it amalgamated with the National Beauty Teachers and Lecturers Association (NBTLA) and today it represents Lecturers in a wide range of therapies.

MEMBERSHIP

Student
Associate
Member
Ireland Member

QUALIFICATION/EXAMINATIONS

Please see www.fht.org.uk for details.

BRITISH ASSOCIATION OF BEAUTY THERAPY AND COSMETOLOGY LTD

BABTAC Limited
Ambrose House, Meteor Court
Barnett Way
Barnwood
Gloucester GL4 3GG
Tel: 0845 065 9000
Fax: 0845 065 9001
E-mail: enquiries@babtac.com
Website: www.babtac.com

BABTAC was formed in 1977 and is a non-profit-making organization for beauticians and therapists in the UK. Members work to a rigorous code of ethics and good practice, both in terms of the treatments and therapies they offer and the way they conduct their relationships with their clients. CIBTAC, an international, educational awarding body that works closely with BABTAC, offers over 30 internationally recognized diplomas in beauty and complementary therapies to accredited colleges and students in the UK and abroad.

MEMBERSHIP

Student Member
Associate Member
Nail Technician
Full Member
Overseas Member
Salon Plan Member

QUALIFICATION/EXAMINATIONS

BABTAC offers a programme of short courses. For details see the BABTAC website. For CIBTAC diplomas see www.cibtac.com/courses_home.htm

BRITISH INSTITUTE AND ASSOCIATION OF ELECTROLYSIS LTD

40 Parkfield Road
Ickenham
Middlesex UB10 BLW
Tel: 08445 441373
E-mail: sec@electrolysis.co.uk
Website: www.electrolysis.co.uk

The BIAE is a non-profit-making organization that demands a high standard of skill and ethical conduct from its members, who are spread throughout the UK and overseas. Candidate Electrolysists must complete the rigorous assessments, both theoretical and practical, of the BIAE Examining Board before being accepted onto the Register.

MEMBERSHIP
Member

QUALIFICATION/EXAMINATIONS
Certificate in Remedial Electrolysis (CRE)

FEDERATION OF HOLISTIC THERAPISTS

18 Shakespeare Business Centre
Hathaway Close
Eastleigh
Hampshire SO50 4SR
Tel: 0844 875 2022
Fax: 023 8062 4396
E-mail: info@fht.org.uk
Website: www.fht.org.uk

The FHT is the leading and largest professional beauty, sports and complementary therapist association in the UK, which has been representing the interests of holistic therapists since 1962. The FHT leads the industry by offering its members a Code of Ethics, public liability insurance, access to regulation, a robust CPD programme with auditing, class leading journal, local therapist network, and comprehensive business and public affairs updates.

MEMBERSHIP
Student
Associate
Member
Ireland Member

QUALIFICATION/EXAMINATIONS
Please see the FHT's website.

ITEC

2nd Floor, Chiswick Gate
598–608 Chiswick High Road
London W4 5RT
Tel: 020 8994 4141
Fax: 020 8994 7880
E-mail: info@itecworld.co.uk
Website: www.itecworld.co.uk

ITEC is an international examination board offering a variety of qualifications in the beauty therapy, complementary therapy and sports therapy sectors worldwide. We also offer teacher training courses in:

Skincare; Make-up; Manicure and Pedicure; Waxing; Holistic Massage; Aromatherapy; Reflexology; Body Treatments; and other areas as required.

QUALIFICATION/EXAMINATIONS
Please see the ITEC website.

BIOLOGICAL SCIENCES

Membership of Professional Institutions and Associations

INSTITUTE OF BIOMEDICAL SCIENCE

12 Coldbath Square
London EC1R 5HL
Tel: 020 7713 0214
Fax: 020 7837 9658
E-mail: mail@ibms.org
Website: www.ibms.org

The IBMS is the professional body for biomedical scientists in the UK. We aim to promote and develop the role of biomedical science within healthcare to deliver the best possible service for patient care and safety.

MEMBERSHIP
Associate
Licentiate (LIBMS)
Member (MIBMS)
Fellow (FIBMS)
Company member

QUALIFICATION/EXAMINATIONS
Certificate of Competence (also required for registration with the Health Professions Council (HPC))
Specialist Diploma in:
Cellular Pathology, Clinical Biochemistry, Clinical Immunology, Cytopathology, Haematology & Transfusion Science, Histocompatibility & Immunogenetics (developed in conjunction with BSHI), Medical Microbiology, Transfusion Science, Virology.
Diploma of Specialist Practice
Higher Specialist Diploma in:
Cellular Pathology, Clinical Chemistry, Cytopathology, Haematology, Immunology, Histocompatibility & Immunogenetics (developed in conjunction with BSHI), Medical Microbiology, Transfusion Science, Virology.
Diploma of Higher Specialist Practice
Complementary qualifications/examinations related to areas of scientific expertise (available to Members and/or Fellows)
Certificates and Diplomas of Expert Practice
Advanced Specialist Diplomas

DESIGNATORY LETTERS
LIBMS, MIBMS, FIBMS

SOCIETY OF BIOLOGY

9 Red Lion Court
London EC4A 3EF
Tel: 020 7936 5900
Fax: 020 7936 5901
E-mail: info@societyofbiology.org
Website: www.societyofbiology.org

The Society of Biology aims to be a single unified voice for biology: advising government and influencing policy; advancing education and professional development; supporting members, and engaging and encouraging public interest in the life sciences.

MEMBERSHIP
Associate Member (AMSB)
Member (MSB)
Fellow (FSB)
Chartered Biologist (CBiol)

DESIGNATORY LETTERS
AMSB, MSB, FSB, CBiol

BREWING

Membership of Professional Institutions and Associations

INSTITUTE OF BREWING & DISTILLING

33 Clarges Street
Mayfair
London W1J 7EE
Tel: 020 7499 8144
Fax: 020 7499 1156
E-mail: enquiries@ibd.org.uk
Website: www.ibd.org.uk

The IBD is a members' organization dedicated to the education and training needs of brewers and distillers and those in related industries. We do this by offering a range of internationally recognized qualifications and the training to support them, through either direct instruction or distance learning.

MEMBERSHIP
Member
Honorary Member
Senior Member
Fellow (FIBD)
Honorary Fellow
Corporate Member

QUALIFICATION/EXAMINATIONS
Certificate in the Fundamentals of Brewing and Packaging of Beer (FBPB)
General Certificate in Brewing (GCB) (Level 3)
General Certificate in Distilling (GCD) (Level 3)
General Certificate in Packaging (GCP) (Level 3)
Diploma in Beverage Packaging (Beer) (Dipl Pack) (Level 4)
Diploma in Brewing (DiplBrew) (Level 4)
Diploma in Distilling (DiplDistill) (Level 4)
Master Brewer (MBrew)

DESIGNATORY LETTERS
FIBD, Hon FIBD

BUILDING

Membership of Professional Institutions and Associations

INSTITUTE OF ASPHALT TECHNOLOGY

Paper Mews Place
280 High Street
Dorking
Surrey RH4 1QT
Tel: 01306 742792
Fax: 01306 888902
E-mail: secretary@instofasphalt.org
Website: www.instofasphalt.org

The IAT is the UK's professional body for persons working in asphalt technology and those interested in aspects of the manufacture, placing, technology and uses of materials containing asphalt or bitumen.

A fully audited CPD system for members has been available since 1994 and is now also offered in computerized format for ease of data entry and auditing, via members' own PCs.

MEMBERSHIP
Student
Technician (Tech IAT)
Affiliate (AIAT)
Member (MIAT)
Fellow (FIAT)

DESIGNATORY LETTERS
Tech IAT, AIAT, MIAT, FIAT

THE CHARTERED INSTITUTE OF BUILDING

Englemere
Kings Ride
Ascot
Berkshire SL5 7TB
Tel: 01344 630808
Fax: 01344 630777
E-mail: educationadmin@ciob.org.uk
Website: www.ciob.org

The CIOB represents for the public benefit the most diverse set of professionals in the construction industry. Our mission is to contribute to the creation of a modern, progressive, and responsible construction industry, able to meet the economic, environmental and social challenges faced in the 21st century.

MEMBERSHIP
Student Member
Associate (ACIOB)
Incorporated (ICIOB)
Member (MCIOB)
Fellow (FCIOB)
Chartered Environmentalist (CENV)

QUALIFICATION/EXAMINATIONS
Chartered Member status is recognized internationally as the mark of a true, skilled professional in the construction industry and CIOB members have a common commitment to achieving and maintaining the highest possible standards within the built environment. To find out more about our qualifications and joining the CIOB just visit our website www.ciob.org.
CIOB courses:
Level 3 Diploma in Site Supervisory Studies
Level 4 Certificate in Site Management
Level 4 Diploma in Site Management
The CIOB qualifications give you the skills and confidence to manage and co-ordinate all types of construction projects; a nationally recognized qualification; ability to progress to a higher level of study and professional qualification; increased promotional prospects and progression to S/NVQs and then CSCS registration.

DESIGNATORY LETTERS
ACIOB, ICIOB, MCIOB, FCIOB, CENV

THE INSTITUTE OF CARPENTERS

3rd Floor D
Carpenters' Hall
1 Throgmorton Avenue
London EC2N 2BY
Tel: 020 7256 2700
Fax: 020 7256 2701
E-mail: info@instituteofcarpenters.com
Website: www.instituteofcarpenters.com

The IOC was founded in 1890 to oversee training for carpenters and joiners and maintain high professional standards at a time when many feared that traditional skills were being lost. Today, while remaining committed to our original aims, we embrace many other wood craftsmen, such as shopfitters, furniture and cabinetmakers, boat builders (woodworking skills), structural post & beam carpenters (heavy structural timber framers), wheelwrights, wood carvers and wood turners, and offer professional status to those holding recognized qualifications.

MEMBERSHIP
Student
Mature Student
Affiliate
Licentiate (LIOC)
Member (MIOC)
Fellow (FIOC)
College Member
Corporate Member
Corporate Associate

QUALIFICATION/EXAMINATIONS
Certificate of Competence in Joinery & Shopfitting Setting-Out
Foundation Certificate in Carpentry and Joinery
Intermediate Examination
Advanced Craft Examination
Fellowship Examination

DESIGNATORY LETTERS
LIOC, MIOC, FIOC

THE INSTITUTE OF CLERKS OF WORKS AND CONSTRUCTION INSPECTORATE OF GREAT BRITAIN INC

28 Commerce Road
Lynch Wood
Peterborough PE2 6LR
Tel: 01733 405160
Fax: 01733 405161
E-mail: info@icwgb.co.uk
Website: www.icwgb.org

The ICWCI is the professional body that supports quality construction through inspection. As a membership organization, we provide a support network of meeting centres, technical advice, publications and events to help keep our members up to date with the ever-changing construction industry.

MEMBERSHIP
Student
Licentiate (LICWCI)
Member (MICWCI)
Fellow (FICWCI)

DESIGNATORY LETTERS
LICWCI, MICWCI, FICWCI

BUSINESS STUDIES

Membership of Professional Institutions and Associations

ASSOCIATION OF BUSINESS RECOVERY PROFESSIONALS (R3)

8th Floor
120 Aldersgate Street
London EC1A 4JQ
Tel: 020 7566 4200
Fax: 020 7566 4224
E-mail: association@r3.org.uk
Website: www.r3.org.uk

The Association of Business Recovery Professionals (known by its brand name 'R3') is the leading professional association for insolvency, business recovery and turnaround specialists in the UK. A not-for-profit organization, it promotes best practice for professionals working with financially troubled individuals and businesses, and provides a forum for debate on key issues facing the profession.

MEMBERSHIP
Student Member
Networking Member
Associate Member (AABRP)
Full Member (MABRP)
Fellow (FABRP)

QUALIFICATION/EXAMINATIONS
R3 provides comprehensive Continuing Professional Education in the field of Insolvency and Restructuring. For details of courses see R3's website.

DESIGNATORY LETTERS
AABRP, MABRP, FABRP

INSTITUTE OF ASSESSORS AND INTERNAL VERIFIERS

PO Box 148
Wirral CH62 7WB
Tel: 01925 485 786
E-mail: office@iavltd.co.uk

The IAV is the professional organization representing assessors and internal verifiers in the UK in vocational training and assessment.

MEMBERSHIP
Affiliate Member
Associate Member
Licentiate Member

THE ACADEMY OF EXECUTIVES & ADMINISTRATORS

Head Office
Warwick Corner
42 Warwick Road
Kenilworth
Warwickshire CV8 1HE
Tel: 01926 866623
E-mail: info@group-ims.com
Website: www.academyofexecutivesandadministrators.org.uk

The Academy of Executives & Administrators was founded in 2002 to give professional status and recognition to the knowledge and skills of executives and administrators. We encourage excellence and flexibility in the changing environment of executive and administrative roles, and support lifelong learning to help members fulfil their career ambitions.

MEMBERSHIP
Student Member (StudAEA)
Member (MAEA)
Fellow (FAEA)
Companion (CAEA)

QUALIFICATION/EXAMINATIONS
Please see the Academy of Executives & Administrators' website.

THE ACADEMY OF MULTI-SKILLS

Head Office
Warwick Corner
42 Warwick Road
Kenilworth
Warwickshire CV8 1HE
Tel: 01926 866623
E-mail: info@group-ims.com
Website: www.academyofmultiskills.org.uk

The Academy of Multi-Skills was founded in 1995 to give professional recognition to multi-skilled personnel, skilled trades, crafts and professions. The Academy encourages a positive and energetic attitude to the challenges of careers that require diversity, creativity and intellect, and recognizes the valuable contribution that these skills provide to society.

MEMBERSHIP
Student Member (StudAMS)
Affiliate Member (AffAMS)
Associate Member (AMAMS)
Member (MAMS)
Fellow (FAMS)
Companion (CAMS)

QUALIFICATION/EXAMINATIONS
Diploma of Merit

THE FACULTY OF SECRETARIES AND ADMINISTRATORS (1930) WITH THE ASSOCIATION OF CORPORATE SECRETARIES

Brightstowe
Catteshall Lane
Godalming
Surrey GU7 1LL
Tel: 01483 427323

The Faculty and Association is a professional body for company and corporate secretaries whose prime qualified designation is that of Certified Public or Corporate Secretary.

MEMBERSHIP
Membership Fellows (FFCS)
Associates (AFCS)
Member (MACS)
Ordinary Member
Student Member

QUALIFICATION/EXAMINATIONS
Part 1 The Generic Business Assessment to ONC/D Level
Part 2 Professional Papers in Company Secretarial Practice, Company Law and Management, Secretarial and Administrative Practice, Commercial Law
Part 3 Professional Meetings Law and Procedure, Company Taxation, Accountancy and Finance, Company Law

DESIGNATORY LETTERS
FFCS, AFCS, MACS

THE INSTITUTE OF CHARTERED SECRETARIES AND ADMINISTRATORS

16 Park Crescent
London W1B 1AH
Tel: 020 7580 4741
Fax: 020 7323 1132
E-mail: studentsupport@icsa.co.uk
Website: www.icsa.org.uk

The Institute of Chartered Secretaries and Administrators is the international qualifying and membership body for Chartered Secretaries. ICSA offers a professional qualifying scheme which covers areas such as corporate governance, corporate law, corporate administration and accountancy and can be studied on a full-time basis or part-time while working.

MEMBERSHIP
Affiliate
Graduate (GradICSA)
Associate (ACIS)
Fellow (FCIS)

QUALIFICATION/EXAMINATIONS
Chartered Secretaries Qualifying Scheme (CSQS)
Certificate in Offshore Finance and Administration
Diploma in Offshore Finance and Administration
Certificate in Company Secretarial Practice and Share Registration Practice
Certificate in Irish Company Secretarial Practice and Share Registration Practice
Certificate in Employee Share Plans
Postgraduate Certificate in Charity Management

DESIGNATORY LETTERS
GradICSA, ACIS, FCIS

CATERING AND INSTITUTIONAL MANAGEMENT

Membership of Professional Institutions and Associations

BII

Wessex House
80 Park Street
Camberley
Surrey GU15 3PT
Tel: 01276 684449
E-mail: info@bii.org
Website: www.bii.org

Founded in 1981, BII is the professional body for the licensed retail sector with a remit to raise standards throughout the industry. BIIAB, the wholly owned awarding body of BII, does this through offering qualifications specifically tailored to, and designed in conjunction with, the industry.

MEMBERSHIP
There is a wide range of membership grades available, from those who have just started their careers in licensed retailing to those who have been in the industry for many years. The grade of membership awarded depends on both experience and qualifications and is determined by a points system. Member of the Hotel Catering and Management Association, HCIMA.

QUALIFICATION/EXAMINATIONS
Qualifications for licensing
National Certificate for Personal Licence Holders (Level 2)
Scottish Certificate for Personal Licence Holders
Scottish Certificate for Licensed Premises Staff
National Certificate for Door Supervisors (Level 2)
National Certificate for Door Supervisors (Scotland)
National Certificate for Door Supervisors (Northern Ireland) (Level 2)
Certificate in Physical Interventions (in conjunction with Maybo)
National Certificate for CCTV Operators (Public Space Surveillance) (Level 2)
National Certificate for Security Guards (Level 2)
National Certificate for Security Guards (Scotland)
National Certificate for Licensees (Drugs Awareness) (Level 2)
Scottish Licensee's Certificate in Drug Awareness
National Certificate for Designated Premises Supervisors (Level 2)

Qualifications for new licensed retail managers
National Certificate in Licensed Retailing (Level 2)
Award in Beer and Cellar Quality

Qualifications for staff development
Award in Responsible Alcohol Retailing (Level 1)
Award in Conflict Management
Award in Essentials of Catering (Level 1)
Award in Cooking Theory and Practice (Level 2)
Certificate in Kitchen Management (Level 3)
Award in Customer and Drinks Service (Licensed Hospitality) (Level 1)
Scottish Award in Customer and Drinks Service (Licensed Hospitality)
Qualifications for management development
Profitable Business Portfolio (professional development programme)
Advanced Certificate in Licensed Hospitality (Level 3)
Diploma in Licensed Hospitality (Level 3)
Qualifications for personal and social responsibility
Certificate in Alcohol Awareness (Level 1)
Scottish Certificate in Alcohol Awareness
Award for Music Promoters (Level 2)

CONFEDERATION OF TOURISM AND HOSPITALITY

13–16 Manchester Street
London W1U 4DJ
Tel: 020 7258 9850
Fax: 020 7258 9869
E-mail: info@cthawards.com
Website: www.cthawards.com

The CTH was established in 1982 to provide recognized standards of management and vocational training appropriate to the needs of the hotel and travel industries, via its syllabuses, examinations and awards. We work with approved centres worldwide and are acknowledged by leading hotel and travel industry organizations.

MEMBERSHIP
Student Member
Associate Member (AMCTH)
Member (MCTH)
Fellow (FCTH)

QUALIFICATION/EXAMINATIONS
Diploma in Hotel Management
Advanced Diploma in Hotel Management
Diploma in Hotel and Casino Management
Diploma in Tourism Management
Advanced Diploma in Tourism Management
Diploma in Travel Agency Management

DESIGNATORY LETTERS
AMCTH, MCTH, FCTH

GUILD OF INTERNATIONAL PROFESSIONAL TOASTMASTERS

Life President: Ivor Spencer
12 Little Bornes
Alleyn Park
London SE21 8SE
Tel: 020 8670 5585
Fax: 020 8670 0055
Website: www.guildoftoastmasters.co.uk

The Guild of Professional Toastmasters was established over 30 years ago to improve standards in the profession and support its members. A 5-day course is offered to prospective members, who may apply for membership upon successful completion of the course. Applications are considered by the Fellows of the Guild.

MEMBERSHIP
Fellow (FGIntPT)

DESIGNATORY LETTERS
FGIntPT

INSTITUTE OF HOSPITALITY

Trinity Court
34 West Street
Sutton
Surrey SM1 1SH
Tel: 020 8661 4900
Fax: 020 8661 4901
E-mail: awardingbody@instituteofhospitality.org
Website: www.instituteofhospitality.org

The Institute of Hospitality is the professional body for managers and aspiring managers in the hospitality, leisure and tourism industries. We are an accredited awarding body in the UK and have more than 10,000 members worldwide, whose professional and career development we promote to ensure the highest standards.

MEMBERSHIP
Student Member
Affiliate
Associate (AIH)
Member (MIH)
Fellow (FIH)

DESIGNATORY LETTERS
AIH, MIH, FIH

CHEMISTRY

Membership of Professional Institutions and Associations

SOCIETY OF COSMETIC SCIENTISTS

Suite 6
Langham House East
Mill Street
Luton
Bedfordshire LU1 2NA
Tel: 01582 726661
Fax: 01582 405217
E-mail: ifscc.scs@btinternet.com
Website: www.scs.org.uk

The main object of the Society, which was formed in 1948, is to advance the science of cosmetics. We endeavour to do this by attracting highly qualified scientists with both academic and industrial experience in cosmetics or a related science to our membership of around 900 members, and by means of our publications, educational programmes and scientific meetings.

MEMBERSHIP
Student
Affiliate
Associate Member
Member – B Grade
Member – A Grade
Honorary Member

QUALIFICATION/EXAMINATIONS
Diploma in Cosmetic Science (validated by De Montfort University)

THE OIL AND COLOUR CHEMISTS' ASSOCIATION

1st Floor
3 Eden Court
Eden Way
Leighton Buzzard
Bedfordshire LU7 4FY
Tel: 01525 372530
Fax: 01525 372600
E-mail: membership@occa.org.uk
Website: www.occa.org.uk

OCCA, founded in 1918, is a learned society comprising individual qualified persons employed in, or associated with, the worldwide surface coatings industries. Most of our members work in a technical capacity, but there are senior personnel from throughout the surface coating industries. The word 'oil' in our title refers to vegetable oils, which once formed a major part of surface coatings' formulations.

MEMBERSHIP
Student Member
Ordinary Member
Honorary Member
Licentiate (LTSC)
Associate (ATSC)
Fellow (FTSC)

DESIGNATORY LETTERS
LTSC, ATSC, FTSC

THE ROYAL SOCIETY OF CHEMISTRY

Thomas Graham House
Science Park
Milton Road
Cambridge CB4 0WF
Tel: 01223 420066
Fax: 01223 423623
E-mail: membership@rsc.org
Website: www.rsc.org

The RSC is the UK professional body for chemical scientists and an international learned society for advancing the chemical sciences. With over 46,000 members worldwide and an internationally acclaimed publishing business, our activities span education and training, conferences, science policy and the promotion of the chemical sciences to the public.

MEMBERSHIP
Affiliate
Associate Member (AMRSC)
Member (MRSC)
Fellow (FRSC)

QUALIFICATION/EXAMINATIONS
NVQ Analytical Chemistry (Level 5)
Qualified Person (QP) for the Pharmaceutical Industry
Mastership in Chemical Analysis (MChemA)
Chartered Chemist (CChem)
Chartered Scientist (CSci)

DESIGNATORY LETTERS
AMRSC, MRSC, FRSC, CChem

CHIROPODY

Membership of Professional Institutions and Associations

BRITISH CHIROPODY AND PODIATRY ASSOCIATION

New Hall
149 Bath Road
Maidenhead
Berkshire SL6 4LA
Tel: 01628 632440
Fax: 01628 674483
E-mail: membership@bcha-uk.org
Website: www.bcha-uk.org

The BCPA, formed in 1959, is the largest professional organization in the UK representing the interests of independent private chiropodists / podiatrists. Since 2005 we have added foothealth practitioners to include our 7,000 members, most of whom work mainly in private practice. Those who are registered with the Health Professions Council may work in the NHS or in education.

MEMBERSHIP
Member (MSSCh & MBChA) – Podiatrists
Fellow (FSSCh) – Podiatrist
Associate members are foothealth practitioners trained by The SMAE Institute.

QUALIFICATION/EXAMINATIONS
Diploma in Podiatric Medicine (DipPodMed)
Foothealth practitoners carry the qualification – MAFHP

DESIGNATORY LETTERS
MSSCh, MBChA, FSSCh and MAFHP

THE INSTITUTE OF CHIROPODISTS AND PODIATRISTS

27 Wright Street
Southport
Merseyside PR9 0TL
Tel: 01704 546141
Fax: 01704 500477
E-mail: secretary@iocp.org.uk
Website: www.inst-chiropodist.org.uk

The IOCP represents all levels of the profession and our CPD is open to both members and non-members, as by elevating professional standards we aim to improve public safety. We have branches throughout the UK and the Republic of Ireland, and members overseas, and hold lectures, seminars and workshops to enable members to keep up to date.

MEMBERSHIP
Full Member
Fellow

THE SOCIETY OF CHIROPODISTS AND PODIATRISTS

1 Fellmongers Path
Tower Bridge Road
London SE1 3LY
Tel: 020 7234 8620
Fax: 0845 450 3721
E-mail: enq@scpod.org
Website: www.feetforlife.org

The SCP is the professional body and trade union for registered podiatrists. Membership is restricted to those qualified for registration and the Society represents around 10,000 NHS podiatrists, private practitioners and students. We monitor standards of undergraduate education and provide opportunities for CPD for our members.

MEMBERSHIP
Member (MChS)
Fellow (FChS)

DESIGNATORY LETTERS
MChS, FChS

CHIROPRACTIC

Membership of Professional Institutions and Associations

MCTIMONEY CHIROPRACTIC ASSOCIATION

Crowmarsh Gifford
Wallingford
Oxfordshire OX10 8DJ
Tel: 01491 829211
Fax: 01491 829494
E-mail: admin@mctimoney-chiropractic.org
Website: www.mctimoneychiropractic.org

The McTimoney Chiropractic Association is the professional association for McTimoney chiropractors, who in the UK are registered with the General Chiropractic Council.

MEMBERSHIP
Provisional Member
Full Member
Fellow

SCOTTISH CHIROPRACTIC ASSOCIATION

1 Chisholm Avenue
Bishopton
Renfrewshire PA7 5JH
Tel: 0141 404 0260
Fax: 0)141 404 0260
E-mail: admin@sca-chiropractic.org
Website: www.sca-chiropractic.org

The SCA was formed in 1979 and now has more than 60 members practising in Scotland and over 120 associated members elsewhere in the UK and abroad. Our aims are to enhance the chiropractic profession in the UK, maintain high standards of professional practice, and provide advice and support to our members.

MEMBERSHIP
Member

UNITED CHIROPRACTIC ASSOCIATION

1st Floor
45 North Hill
Plymouth
Devon PL4 8EZ
Tel: 01752 658785
Fax: 01752 658786
E-mail: admin@united-chiropractic.org
Website: www.united-chiropractic.org

The UCA is a UK-based organization for qualified, professional, principal-based chiropractors, associates and students. Full membership is open to qualified, GCC-registered chiropractors from any recognized school of chiropractic.

MEMBERSHIP
Student
Associate
Affiliate
1st Year Graduate
2nd Year Graduate
Full Member
Overseas Member

THE CHURCHES

Membership of Professional Institutions and Associations

BAPTIST UNION OF SCOTLAND

Baptist House
14 Aytoun Road
Glasgow G41 5RT
Tel: 0141 423 6169
Fax: 0141 424 1422
E-mail: admin@scottishbaptist.org.uk
Website: www.scottishbaptist.org.uk

The Baptist Union of Scotland was formed in 1869, when 51 churches with a total congregation of about 3,500 united. Today, with 142 churches and about 14,000 members, the Union strives for simplicity in organizational structure and promotes increasing contact between the local churches and Council-appointed Core Leaders, who function under the overall direction of the General Director.

QUALIFICATION/EXAMINATIONS
Certificate/Diploma of Higher Learning in Theology
BD in Theology & Pastoral Studies
Graduate Diploma in Applied Theology through Work Based Learning
Graduate Diploma in Pastoral Studies
(awarded by the Scottish Baptist College, Paisley, and validated by the University of Paisley)

BRISTOL BAPTIST COLLEGE

The Promenade
Clifton Down
Clifton
Bristol BS8 3NJ
Tel: 0117 946 7050
Fax: 0117 946 7787
E-mail: admin@bristol-baptist.ac.uk
Website: www.bristol-baptist.ac.uk

The central aim of the College is to train men and women for ministry in the Church and in the world. We do this by enabling critical reflection upon the Bible and Christian theological tradition and on the contexts from which we come and within which we are placed.

QUALIFICATION/EXAMINATIONS
Certificate in Theological Studies
Diploma in Theological Studies
BA in Theological Studies
MA in Biblical Studies
MA in Mission Studies
(all validated by the University of Bristol)

METHODIST CHURCH IN IRELAND

Board of Examiners
Secretary: Rev Peter D Murray, BA, BD
28 Windermere Drive
Bangor
Co Down BT20 4QF

MEMBERSHIP
Candidates for training must normally have the standard of general education for university entrance. They must be accredited Local Preachers of the Methodist Church, and are examined by written papers in Biblical Studies and Theology and by oral aptitude and personality tests. After admission to training, candidates normally spend 3 years at Edgehill Theological College, Belfast, studying for a diploma or degree of Queen's University, Belfast, in New Testament Greek, Hebrew, the English Bible, Theology, Church History, Pastoral Psychology, or Homiletics. This is followed by 3 years as a probationer Minister working under a superintendent Minister. During probation the candidate continues study within a tutorial system and is examined by continuous assessment.

THE CHURCH OF ENGLAND

Ministry Division of The Archbishops' Council
Church House
Great Smith Street
London SW1P 3AZ
Tel: 020 7898 1404
Fax: 020 7898 1421
E-mail: david.way@c-of-e.org.uk (ordination training) susan.hart@c-or-e.org.uk (Reader training)
Website: www.cofe.anglican.org www.archbishopofcanterbury.org/1027

The Church of England's Ministry Division oversees training for ordination and issues certificates for successful completion for Reader ministry. Enquiries about entry into training should be directed to the candidate's own diocese. In addition, The Archbishop's Examination in Theology offers means of study at three postgraduate levels.

QUALIFICATION/EXAMINATIONS
Archbishop's Examination:
PG Diploma of Student of Theology
Master of Philosophy
Doctor of Philosophy

THE CHURCH OF SCOTLAND

Church of Scotland Offices
121 George Street
Edinburgh EH2 4YN
Tel: 0131 225 5722
Fax: 0131 220 3113
Website: www.churchofscotland.org.uk

The Ministries Council runs an enquiry process to help those who sense a call to any of the ministries within the Church of Scotland to consider it in a supportive environment. Attendance at one of our enquirers' conferences, which are held twice each year, is the first stage of the enquiry process. For more information see; www.churchofscotland.org.uk/councils/ministries/mintraining.htm

THE METHODIST CHURCH

Formation in Ministry Office (Initial Development of Ministries)
25 Marylebone Road
London NW1 5JR
Tel: 020 7486 5502

Candidates for Diaconal or Presbyteral Ministry in the Methodist Church must have been members of the Methodist Church at least 2 years and are expected to offer at least 10 yrs of ministerial service. The first stage of preparation is Foundation Training, which requires 1 year (FT) or 2 years (PT) to complete, during which a person may apply to become a candidate for ordained ministry. The process of selection takes 6 months. To enter into training for Presbyteral Ministry, a candidate must be a trained Local Preacher, which involves taking the Methodist Local Preachers' Training Course, Faith & Worship. Deacons become members of the Methodist Diaconal and are not required to be preachers. Accepted candidates for either order receive 1 or 2 years of further theological training, which in most cases leads to a degree or diploma in Theology or Ministry. Upon completion of training, a candidate serves as a Methodist Minister for 2 years on probation before ordination. For Presbyters, the appointment may be to an itinerant appointment (stipendiary) or to a local appointment (usually non-stipendiary) or as licensed to minister in secular employment. Deacons are always itinerant.

THE MORAVIAN CHURCH IN GREAT BRITAIN AND IRELAND

Moravian Church House
5–7 Muswell Hill
London N10 3TJ
Tel: 020 8883 3409
Fax: 020 8365 3371
E-mail: moravianchurchhouse@btinternet.com
Website: www.moravian.org.uk

Candidates for Moravian Church Service must be members of the Moravian Church and would normally have completed the Lay Training Course and have the support of their local church committee. They should make an initial application to the Provincial Board of the Moravian Church. Their qualifications are examined by the Church Service Advisory Board, which reports on them to the Provincial Board, with whom the final decision rests. Normally the standard of education required for the work of the Ministry is a university Divinity degree or Certificate together with a thorough acquaintance with the history, principles and methods of the Moravian Church. Candidates receive guidance for the Ministry during a period of supervised service under the direction of experienced Ministers. A class of non-stipendiary Ministers has been established for those who wish to serve on a non-maintained basis. Training varies according to candidates' needs. In all cases applications should be made to the address given above.

THE PRESBYTERIAN CHURCH IN IRELAND

The Director of Ministerial Studies
Union Theological College
108 Botanic Avenue
Belfast BT7 1JT
Tel: 02890 205088
Fax: 02890 205099

Qualifications required: Under 30 – a non-theological degree; over 30 but under 40 (as reckoned on 1 October following application) – either a non-theological degree or 2 years, non-graduating Arts or 4 modules of PT BD study or 6 modules of PT study in Humanities acceptable to the Board of Studies; over 40 – not normally accepted, except in exceptional circumstances, where candidate is already possessed of good educational background and/or professional experience.

THE PRESBYTERIAN CHURCH OF WALES

Tabernacle Chapel
81 Merthyr Road
Whitchurch
Cardiff CF14 1DD
Tel: 02920 627465
Fax: 02920 616188
E-mail: swyddfa.office@ebcpcw.org.uk
Website: www.ebcpw.org.uk

The Presbyterian Church of Wales (PCW) is a Protestant non-conformist denomination. Ordination is dependent on successful application through the local church and Presbytery to the Candidates and Training Department.

MEMBERSHIP

Ministers are ordained to the full-time, part-time or non-stipendary ministry.

QUALIFICATION/EXAMINATIONS

Pastoral Studies course

THE ROMAN CATHOLIC CHURCH

Candidates for the priesthood in the RC Church attend a residential seminary course of at least 6 years. Among subjects studied are Philosophy, Psychology, Dogmatic and Moral Theology, Scripture, Church History, Canon Law, Liturgy, Catechetics, Communications and Pastoral Theology. Each College/Seminary has its own arrangements for the university education of its students. Those who do not attend university take a final internal exam.

THE SALVATION ARMY

UK Headquarters
101 Newington Causeway
London SE1 6BN
Tel: 020 7367 4500
E-mail: thq@salvationarmy.org.uk
Website: www.salvationarmy.org.uk

Salvation Army officers engaged in FT service are ordained ministers of religion, and are commissioned following a 2-year period of residential training at the William Booth College, Denmark Hill, London SE5 8BQ. This course – an HE Diploma in Salvation Army Officer Training – may now be undertaken by distance learning, and a mixture of residential and distance learning. Officers may be appointed to corps (church) work, to social services centres (for which additional professional qualifications are required) or to administrative posts.

THE SCOTTISH EPISCOPAL CHURCH

Theological Institute of the Scottish Episcopal Church
Forbes House
21 Grosvenor Crescent
Edinburgh EH12 5EE
Tel: 0131 225 6357
Fax: 0131 346 7247
E-mail: tisec@scotland.anglican.org
Website: www.scotland.anglican.org

Candidates are trained for lay and ordained, stipendiary and non-stipendiary ministries in the Scottish Episcopal Church, Methodist Church and the United Reformed Church.

The curriculum is delivered centrally through residential sessions and regionally through diocesan groups. The Diploma in Theology for Ministry course run by the Institute is validated by York St John's University. Some students undertake further studies through universities, leading to degree qualifications.

THE SCOTTISH UNITED REFORMED AND CONGREGATIONAL COLLEGE

The Principal
Glasgow G1 2BQ
Tel: 0141 332 7667
E-mail: Scottishcollege@urcscotland.org.uk
Website: www.scotland.urc.org.uk

The College is recognized as a resource centre for learning by the General Assembly of the United Reformed Church and is one of the institutions charged with responsibility for initial ministerial education.

QUALIFICATION/EXAMINATIONS
The College awards only its own certificate, which is part of the process of accreditation of ordinands as ministers of the United Reformed Church. Students, however, are normally concurrently matriculated for a degree, normally in Theology or Religious Studies, at a university.

THE UNITARIAN AND FREE CHRISTIAN CHURCHES

Essex Hall
London WC2R 3HY
Tel: 020 7240 2384
Fax: 020 7240 3089
E-mail: info@unitarian.org.uk
Website: www.unitarian.org.uk

Candidates accepted for training for the ministry in the Unitarian and Free Christian Churches take courses of training either at Manchester Academy & Harris College, Oxford (2 to 4 years study for an Oxford degree in Theology/or Theology & Philosophy or an Oxford Certificate in Theology/Religious Studies), or at the Unitarian College (Luther King House, Brighton Grove, Rusholme, Manchester; an individually designed contextual theology course of the Partnership for Theological Education which may lead to a degree or other academic qualification validated by Chester or Manchester University). Alternative arrangements can be made for candidates wishing to study through the Welsh language. Placement work and Unitarian studies are also integral to ministerial preparation. Training normally takes 2 or more years.

THE UNITED REFORMED CHURCH

Church House
86 Tavistock Place
London WC1H 9RT
Tel: 020 7916 2020
Fax: 020 7916 2021
E-mail: training@urc.org.uk
Website: www.urc.org.uk

Stipendiary Ministry: URC Ministers are usually trained in the Church's theological colleges. All training is ecumenical. Candidates must been a member of the URC for at least 2 years and go through a candidating process in the other Councils of the Church to decide whether they should be sponsored for training. Most then take a 3- or 4-year degree in Theology or a diploma of the university to which their college is attached. In certain cases it is possible to train PT on an ecumenical course. The

minimum requirement on training completion is a Theology diploma and 800 hrs placement in a church.
Non-Stipendiary: A training programme of PT study usually over 4 years is open to committed members of the URC. Candidates must be recommended by their local church and go though the process indicated above. A Director of Training guides the student. Most students study PT on a recognized ecumenical course, with an additional programme to study Reformed History Ethics and Worship, but some train FT in a college. A Leaving Certificate for a call to the ordained ministry is granted. Training is arranged by the Board of Studies of the Training Committee.

Church-related Community Workers: They help lead and strengthen the local church's mission through community development in an area where specialist help is required to meet unusual needs. Candidates must be members of the URC and show capabilities for leadership. They are required to obtain at least a Diploma in Theology and a Diploma in Community Work before being commissioned.
Lay Preacher's Certificate: Training for Learning & Serving is the qualifying course for this. The course takes 3 years. Work is done in local groups and there are five residential weekend courses each year. Candidates are also expected to undertake some practical work in churches.

THE WESLEYAN REFORM UNION

Wesleyan Reform Church House
123 Queen Street
Sheffield S1 2DU
Tel: 0114 272 1938
E-mail: admin@thewru.co.uk
Website: www.thewru.com

The Wesleyan Reform Union has no training college of its own and encourages candidates for its Ministry to enter a Bible College for 2 or 3 years. All candidates are, however, under the personal supervision of a Union Tutor, who directs a Biblical Studies & Training Department offering fairly extensive courses. Candidates attend Headquarters once a year for an oral exam in Theology conducted by the Tutor in the presence of the Union Examination Committee; they also take written exams.

UNITED FREE CHURCH OF SCOTLAND

11 Newton Place
Glasgow G3 7PR
Tel: 01413 323435
Fax: 01413 331973
E-mail: office@ufcos.org.uk
Website: www.ufcos.org.uk

The United Free Church of Scotland is a small presbyterian denomination which came into being in 1929. Those seeking to become candidates for the ministry should normally have been members of the denomination for at least a year. They will require to undertake a degree course in theology.

THE CHURCH IN WALES

St Michael's College
Llandaff
Cardiff CF5 2YJ
Tel: 029 205 63379
Fax: 029 208 38088

The Church in Wales expects candidates for ordination to satisfy the requirements of recognized theological courses. University graduates usually spend at least 2 years at a theological college, and if they are non-theological graduates, they are encouraged to study for a university degree or diploma in Theology. Non-graduate candidates must have at least 5 passes at GCSE and normally study for a university diploma in Theology or a degree in Theology if they have obtained the necessary grades at A level. These requirements may be modified in the case of older candidates.

CINEMA, FILM AND TELEVISION

Membership of Professional Institutions and Associations

BRITISH KINEMATOGRAPH SOUND AND TELEVISION SOCIETY (BKSTS)

Pinewood Studios
Pinewood Road
Iver Heath
Buckinghamshire SL0 0NH
Tel: 01753 656656
E-mail: info@bksts.com
Website: www.bksts.com

The BKSTS was founded in 1931 to serve the growing film industry and today arranges meetings, presentations, seminars, international exhibitions and conferences, as well as organizing an extensive programme of training courses, lectures, workshops and special events. We ensure that our members remain up to date with the latest techniques through master classes and our print and electronic publications.

MEMBERSHIP
Student Member
Intermediate Member
Associate Member
Full Member (MBKS)
Retired Member
Fellow (FBKS)

DESIGNATORY LETTERS
MBKS, FBKS

THE LONDON FILM SCHOOL

24 Shelton Street
Covent Garden
London WC2H 9UB
Tel: 020 7836 9642
Fax: 020 7497 3718
E-mail: info@lfs.org.uk
Website: www.lfs.org.uk

The LFS is one of the foremost independent film schools in Europe and is recognized by Skillset as a Centre of Excellence. It is a registered charity and a non-profit-making company, limited by guarantee. Since 1956 we have trained thousands of directors, cinematographers, editors and other film professionals from around the world.

QUALIFICATION/EXAMINATIONS

MA in Filmmaking (validated by London Metropolitan University)
MA in Screenwriting (validated by London Metropolitan University)

THE NATIONAL FILM AND TELEVISION SCHOOL

Beaconsfield Studios
Station Road
Beaconsfield
Buckinghamshire HP9 1LG
Tel: 01494 671234
Fax: 01494 674042
E-mail: info@nfts.co.uk
Website: www.nfts.co.uk

A Skillset Screen & Media Academy, the UK's leading film and television school offers full-time MA and Diploma courses in all the key film and television disciplines, from Animation to VFX. Purpose-built studios include two film stages, a large television studio, and post-production facilities rivalling those of many professional companies.

QUALIFICATION/EXAMINATIONS

Diploma (in 1 of 3 disciplines)
MA in Film and Television (specializing in 1 of 13 disciplines)

CLEANING, LAUNDRY AND DRY CLEANING

Membership of Professional Institutions and Associations

BRITISH INSTITUTE OF CLEANING SCIENCE

9 Premier Court
Boarden Close
Moulton Park
Northampton NN3 6LF
Tel: 01604 678710
Fax: 01604 645988
E-mail: info@bics.org.uk
Website: www.bics.org.uk

The BICSc is the largest independent professional and educational body within the cleaning industry. Our aim is to raise the status and standards of the cleaning industry through training and education. We offer our 5,000 members a range of assessment schemes and training courses, together with a telephone and e-mail helpline.

MEMBERSHIP
Practitioner
Associate
Member
Corporate Member

THE GUILD OF CLEANERS AND LAUNDERERS

5 Portland Place
London W1B 1PW
Tel: 0845 600 1838
E-mail: enquiries@gcl.org.uk
Website: www.gcl.org.uk

The Guild, formed in 1949, is a technical and professional society whose aim is to further knowledge and skill in all branches of the industry. We keep out members up to date through lectures, seminars and written reports, exchange information of mutual benefit with other organizations in the industry, and voice our opinion in relevant forums.

MEMBERSHIP
Young Guilder
Member
Associate (AGCL)
Advanced Member (AdGCL)
Licentiate (LGCL)
Fellow (FGCL)

DESIGNATORY LETTERS
AGCL, AdGCL, LGCL, FGCL

COLOUR TECHNOLOGY

Membership of Professional Institutions and Associations

PAINTING AND DECORATING ASSOCIATION

32 Coton Road
Nuneaton
Warwickshire CV11 5TW
Tel: 024 7635 3776
Fax: 024 7635 4513
E-mail: info@paintingdecoratingassociation.co.uk
Website: www.paintingdecoratingassociation.co.uk

The PDA is a registered trade and employers' organization, catering exclusively for the needs of professional painting and decorating trade employers. The Association conducts no examinations, but all membership applications are scrutinized at branch level to ensure that only bona fide firms who agree to abide by our code of conduct are admitted.

MEMBERSHIP
Full Member
Associate

THE SOCIETY OF DYERS AND COLOURISTS

Perkin House
82 Grattan Road
Bradford BD1 2JB
Tel: 01274 761792
Fax: 01274 392888
E-mail: members@sdc.org.uk
Website: www.sdc.org.uk

The SDC is recognized globally as the authority for colour science and technology, delivering high-quality, international qualifications and training programmes. An educational charity, professional body and chartered society, it serves the global textile supply chain through the knowledgeable and enthusiastic involvement of its professional members and industry partners.

MEMBERSHIP
Individual Member
Professional Member
Corporate Member
College Member
Licentiate (LSDC)
Associate (CCol ASDC)
Fellow (CCol FSDC)

QUALIFICATION/EXAMINATIONS
Colour Management Diploma
Certificate of Licentiateship
Diploma of Associateship
Diploma of Fellowship

DESIGNATORY LETTERS
LSDC, CCol ASDC, CCol FSDC

COMMUNICATIONS AND MEDIA

Membership of Professional Institutions and Associations

THE PICTURE RESEARCH ASSOCIATION

Box 105 Hampstead House
176 Finchley Road
London NW3 6BP
Tel: 07771 982308
Website: www.picture-research.org.uk

The PRA, founded in 1977, is a professional organization for picture researchers, picture editors and anyone specifically involved in the research, management and supply of visual material to the media industry. Our aims are to provide information and give support to our members, and to promote their interests and specific skills to potential employers.

MEMBERSHIP
Introductory Member
Associate Member
Full Member

COMPUTING AND INFORMATION TECHNOLOGY

Membership of Professional Institutions and Associations

ASSOCIATION OF COMPUTER PROFESSIONALS

ACP
Chilverbridge House
Arlington
East Sussex BN26 6SB
Tel: 01323 871874
Fax: 01323 871875
E-mail: admin@acpexamboard.com
Website: www.acpexamboard.com

The ACP is an independent professional examining body, founded in 1984 to set and maintain standards of education that reflect the constantly changing requirements of the computer industry, both in the UK and overseas. We do so through the provision of course syllabuses and examinations to our carefully vetted training centres around the world.

MEMBERSHIP
Student
Practitioner
Graduate (GradACP)
Licentiate (LACP)
Associate (AACP)
Member (MACP)
Fellow (FACP)

QUALIFICATION/EXAMINATIONS
Please see the ACP's website for details of certificates and diplomas.

DESIGNATORY LETTERS
GradACP, LACP, AACP, MACP, FACP

BRITISH COMPUTER SOCIETY

1st Floor, Block D
North Star House
North Star Avenue
Swindon
Wiltshire SN2 1FA
Tel: 01793 417417
Fax: 01793 417444
E-mail: customerservices@hq.bcs.org.uk
Website: www.bcs.org.uk

The BCS is the professional membership and accreditation body for IT and has more than 70,000 members, including practitioners, businesses, academics and students, in the UK and internationally. Our aim is to promote the academic study and professional practice of computing and to show the public that IT is about far more than simply using a PC.

MEMBERSHIP
Student
Affiliate
Associate Member (AMBCS)
Professional Fellow (FBCS)
Honorary Fellow
Distinguished Fellow
Incorporated Engineer (IEng)
Chartered Engineer (CEng)
Chartered IT Professional (MBCS CITP)
Chartered Fellow (FBCS CITP)
Chartered Scientist (CSci)
Education Affiliate (institutional member)

QUALIFICATION/EXAMINATIONS
Certificate in IT
Certificate in IT for Insurance Professionals (developed jointly with The Chartered Insurance Institute)
Diploma in IT
Professional GradDip in IT

See the BCS website for details of other qualifications.

INSTITUTE FOR THE MANAGEMENT OF INFORMATION SYSTEMS

5 Kingfisher House
New Mill Road
Orpington
Kent BR5 3QG
Tel: 07000 023456
Fax: 07000 023023
E-mail: central@imis.org.uk
Website: www.imis.org.uk

IMIS is one of the leading professional associations in the IT sector. A registered charity, it plays a prominent role in fostering greater understanding of IS management, in working to enhance the status of those engaged in the profession, and in promoting higher standards through better education and training worldwide.

MEMBERSHIP
Student Member
Practitioner Member
Licentiate Member (LIMIS)
Associate Member (AIMIS)
Full Member (MIMIS)
Fellow (FIMIS)

QUALIFICATION/EXAMINATIONS
Foundation
Diploma
Higher Diploma

DESIGNATORY LETTERS
LIMIS, AIMIS, MIMIS, FIMIS

INSTITUTION OF ANALYSTS AND PROGRAMMERS

Charles House
36 Culmington Road
London W13 9NH
Tel: 020 8567 2118
Fax: 020 8567 4379
E-mail: dg@iap.org.uk
Website: www.iap.org.uk

The IAP is a professional organization for people who work in the development, installation and testing of business systems and computer software. Our aim is to promote high standards of competence and conduct among our members, to encourage them to develop their skills and progress their career, and to facilitate the advancement and spreading of knowledge within the profession.

MEMBERSHIP
Licentiate
Graduate (GradIAP)
Associate Member (AIAP)
Member (MIAP)
Fellow (FIAP)

DESIGNATORY LETTERS
GradIAP, AIAP, MIAP, FIAP

COUNSELLING

Membership of Professional Institutions and Associations

COUNSELLING LTD

Registered Office
5 Pear Tree Walk
Wakefield
West Yorkshire WF2 0HW
E-mail: E-mail via the website
Website: www.counselling.ltd.uk

Counselling, a registered charity founded in 1998, is a membership organization for counsellors and psychotherapists in the UK that has established a network of about 2,700 affiliated CCC-registered counsellors, many of whom are able to provide occasional free or discounted face-to-face counselling with clients on low incomes.

MEMBERSHIP
Affiliate

COUNSELLORS AND PSYCHOTHERAPISTS IN PRIMARY CARE

Queensway House
Queensway
Bognor Regis
West Sussex PO21 1QT
Tel: 01243 870701
Fax: 01243 870702
E-mail: cpc@cpc-online.co.uk
Website: www.cpc-online.co.uk

CPC is a professional membership association for individual practitioners, whose names are entered in a Register of Members. The aims of the Association are to represent counsellors and psychotherapists working in an NHS setting and to lead the way in establishing national standards and guidelines for further development of professional and effective counselling throughout the NHS.

MEMBERSHIP
Student
Subscriber
Intermediate Member
Registered Member
Supervisor
Organizational Member

QUALIFICATION/EXAMINATIONS
PGDip in Supervision for the Primary Care Setting

CSCT COUNSELLING TRAINING

13 Coleshill Street
Sutton Coldfield
West Midlands B72 1SD
Tel: 0121 321 1396/0870 1
Fax: 0121 355 5581
E-mail: info@counsellingtraining.com
Website: www.counsellingtraining.com

CSCT has been producing counselling training courses for over 25 years, during which time we have trained over 50,000 students. Our courses are offered PT via a network of colleges and private providers throughout the UK. Our training materials are written to the specifications of the appropriate awarding body and we provide 24-hour e-mail and telephone support from Client Services and the Academic Team.

QUALIFICATION/EXAMINATIONS
Please see the CSCT's website.

CREDIT MANAGEMENT

Membership of Professional Institutions and Associations

INSTITUTE OF CREDIT MANAGEMENT

The Water Mill
Station Road
South Luffenham
Oakham
Leicestershire LE15 8NB
Tel: 01780 722900
Fax: 01780 721333
E-mail: info@icm.org.uk
Website: www.icm.org.uk

The ICM is the largest professional credit management organization in Europe and the only one accredited by Ofqual as an awarding body. We represent the credit profession across trade, consumer and export credit, as well as in related activities such as collections, credit reporting, credit insurance and insolvency, promote excellence in credit management and raise awareness of its vital role in business and the community.

MEMBERSHIP
Affiliate
Asociate Member (AICM)
Graduate Member (MICM(Grad))
Member (MICM)
Fellow (FICM)

QUALIFICATION/EXAMINATIONS
Diploma in Credit Management (Level 2)
Diploma in Credit Management (Level 3)
Diploma in Credit Management (Level 5)

DESIGNATORY LETTERS
AICM, MICM (Grad), MICM, FICM

DANCING

Membership of Professional Institutions and Associations

BRITISH BALLET ORGANIZATION

Woolborough House
39 Lonsdale Road
Barnes
London SW13 9JP
Tel: 020 8748 1241
Fax: 020 8748 1301
E-mail: info@bbo.org.uk
Website: www.bbo.org.uk

The BBO, founded in 1930, is an awarding body offering teacher training and examinations in classical ballet, tap, modern dance and jazz. We have schools throughout the UK and in several other countries.

MEMBERSHIP
Student Member
Senior Student Member
Affiliated Member
Student Teacher Member
Teacher Member

QUALIFICATION/EXAMINATIONS
Please see the BBO website for details.

IMPERIAL SOCIETY OF TEACHERS OF DANCING

Imperial House
22/26 Paul Street
London EC2A 4QE
Tel: +44 (0)20 7377 1577
Fax: +44 (0)20 7247 8309
E-mail: education@istd.org
Website: www.istd.org

The ISTD is a registered educational charity and examinations board. We aim to promote knowledge of dance, to maintain and improve teaching standards, and to qualify (by examination) teachers of dancing. Our dance techniques cover more than 12 different genres and are taught by more than 7,500 members in our Approved Dance Centres worldwide.

MEMBERSHIP
A range of 9 categories from Student to Life Membership.

QUALIFICATION/EXAMINATIONS
Please see our website www.istd.org.

DESIGNATORY LETTERS
ISTD

INTERNATIONAL DANCE TEACHERS' ASSOCIATION LIMITED

International House
76 Bennett Road
Brighton BN2 5JL
Tel: 01273 685652
Fax: 01273 674388
E-mail: info@idta.co.uk
Website: www.idta.co.uk

The IDTA is one of the world's largest dance examination boards, with more than 7,000 members in 55 countries. Our aims are to promote knowledge and foster the art of dance in all its forms, to maintain and improve dancing standards, and to offer a comprehensive range of professional qualifications in all dance genres.

MEMBERSHIP
Associate (AIDTA)
Licentiate (LIDTA)
Fellow (FIDTA)

DESIGNATORY LETTERS
AIDTA, LIDTA, FIDTA

THE BENESH INSTITUTE

36 Battersea Square
London SW11 3RA
Tel: 020 7326 8031
Fax: 020 7924 3129
E-mail: beneshinstitute@rad.org.uk
Website: www.benesh.org

The Benesh Institute is the international centre for Benesh Movement Notation (BMN) founded in 1962 to promote, develop and offer education in BMN. We also function as an examining body and professional centre, and are responsible for coordinating technical developments. Since 1997 The Benesh Institute has been incorporated within the Royal Academy of Dance.

MEMBERSHIP
Fellow (FI Chor)

QUALIFICATION/EXAMINATIONS
Certificate in Benesh Movement Notation (CBMN) (validated by the Royal Academy of Dance)
Diploma for Professional Benesh Movement Notators (DPBMN) (validated by the Royal Academy of Dance)

DESIGNATORY LETTERS
FI Chor

DENTISTRY

Membership of Professional Institutions and Associations

GENERAL DENTAL COUNCIL

37 Wimpole Street
London W1G 8DQ
Tel: 0845 222 4141
Fax: 020 7224 3294
E-mail: information@gdc-uk.org
Website: www.gdc-uk.org

The GDC regulates dental professionals in the UK. All dentists, clinical dental technicians, dental hygienists, dental nurses, dental technicians, dental therapists and orthodontic therapists must be registered with the GDC in order to work in the UK.

THE BRITISH DENTAL ASSOCIATION

64 Wimpole Street
London W1G 8YS
Tel: 020 7935 0875
Fax: 020 7487 5232
E-mail: enquiries@bda.org
Website: www.bda.org

The BDA, which was founded in 1880, is the professional association and trade union for dentists in the UK. Our aims are to advance the science, arts and ethics of dentistry, improve in UK's oral health, and promote the interests of our members. Membership, which is voluntary, stands at around 23,000, mostly in general practice.

MEMBERSHIP
Student Member
(Recently) Qualified Member
Ordinary Member
Retired Member
Overseas Member

BRITISH SOCIETY OF DENTAL HYGIENE AND THERAPY

3 Kestrel Court
Waterwells Business Park
Gloucester GL2 2AT
Tel: 01452 886365
Fax: 01452 886468
E-mail: enquiries@bsdht.org.uk
Website: www.bsdht.org.uk

The BSDHT is the only nationally recognized body that represents dental hygienists, dental hygienist-therapists and students of dental hygiene. We have a membership of more than 3,500 in the UK and beyond, and look after their interests through liaising with the Department of Health, General Dental Council, British Dental Association and other organizations.

MEMBERSHIP
Member

BRITISH ASSOCIATION OF DENTAL NURSES

PO Box 4, Room 200
Hillhouse International Business Centre
Thornton-Cleveleys
Lancashire FY5 4QD
Tel: 01253 338360
Fax: 01253 773266
E-mail: admin@badn.org.uk
Website: www.badn.org.uk

The BADN represents dental nurses, whether qualified or unqualified, working in general practice, hospital, the community, the armed forces, industry, practice management or reception, and has representation on the National Examining Board, the Dental Nurses Standards and Training Advisory Board and its Registration Committee, the Joint Consultative Committee, and other bodies.

MEMBERSHIP
Associate Member
Full Member

CLINICAL DENTAL TECHNICIANS ASSOCIATION

Room 3b, Ground Floor
Tower House Business Centre
Fishergate
York YO10 4UA
Tel: 01904 625130
Fax: 01904 658361
Website: www.cdta.org.uk

The CDTA provides political and educational representation for its members, who are registered with the General Dental Council and trained in designing, creating, constructing, repairing and rebasing removable appliances to ensure optimal fit, maximum comfort and general well-being of patients. We are committed to team dentistry and ensure that our members work to the highest professional standards.

MEMBERSHIP
Member

DENTAL TECHNOLOGISTS ASSOCIATION

3 Kestral Court
Waterwells Drive
Waterwells Business Park
Gloucester GL2 2AT
Tel: 0870 243 0753
E-mail: sueadams@dta-uk.org
Website: www.dta-uk.org/

The DTA is an organization that supports the development of the dental technology profession by encouraging and promoting education, including CPD, and for the exchange of views between dental technicians. We advise, develop and support dental technicians and maintain links with the government, other dental organizations, service providers and the public.

MEMBERSHIP
Member

DIETETICS

Membership of Professional Institutions and Associations

THE BRITISH DIETETIC ASSOCIATION

5th Floor
Charles House
Queensway
Birmingham B3 3HT
Tel: 0121 200 8080
Fax: 0121 200 8081
E-mail: info@bda.uk.com
Website: www.bda.uk.com

The BDA, established in 1936, is the professional association and trade union for dietitians. Our aims are to advance the science and practice of dietetics and associated subjects, to promote education and training in the science and practice of dietetics and associated subjects, and to regulate relations betweens our more than 6,500 members and their employers.

MEMBERSHIP
Student Member
Associate Member
Affiliate Member
Full Member

DISTRIBUTION

Membership of Professional Institutions and Associations

THE CHARTERED INSTITUTE OF LOGISTICS AND TRANSPORT (UK)

Earlstrees Court
Earlstrees Road
Corby
Northamptonshire NN17 4AX
Tel: 01536 740104
Fax: 01536 740101
E-mail: membership@ciltuk.org.uk
Website: www.ciltuk.org.uk

The CILT(UK) is the professional body for transport, logistics and integrated supply chain management and has more than 20,000 members in manufacturing, distribution, passenger transport, retail, import and export, national and local government, purchase and supply, warehousing, education, research and the armed forces. Our aim is to promote professional excellence and the development of modern techniques, and to encourage the adoption of efficient and sustainable policies.

MEMBERSHIP
Part-time Student
Full-time Student
Affiliate
Member (MILT)
Chartered Member (CMILT)
Chartered Fellow (CFILT)

QUALIFICATION/EXAMINATIONS
Certificate (Level 2)
Certificate (Level 3)
Professional Diploma (Level 5)
Advanced Diploma in Logistics and Transport (Level 6)
MSc in International Transport and Logistics *or* International Logistics and Supply Chain Management

DESIGNATORY LETTERS
MILT, CMILT, CFILT

DIVING

Membership of Professional Institutions and Associations

DIVING CERTIFICATES

Health & Safety Executive, Diving Operations Strategy Team
Wren House, Hedgerows Business Park
Colchester Road, Springfield
Chelmsford
Essex CM2 5PF
Tel: 01245 706256
Fax: 01245 706222
E-mail: cathy.uprichard@hse.gsi.gov.uk
Website: www.hse.gov.uk/diving

The Health and Safety Executive (HSE) issues diver competence certificates to divers who have been assessed as competent by an HSE-recognized diver-training organization (a list of which can be obtained from the HSE) for the following competencies: SCUBA, Surface Supplied, Surface Supplied (top-up) and Closed Bell.

DRAMATIC AND PERFORMING ARTS

Membership of Professional Institutions and Associations

EQUITY

Guild House
Upper St Martins Lane
London WC2H 9EG
Tel: 020 7379 6000
Fax: 020 7379 7001
E-mail: info@equity.org.uk
Website: www.equity.org.uk

Equity is the UK trade union representing professional performers and other creative workers from across the entertainment, creative and cultural industries. The main function of Equity is to negotiate minimum terms and conditions of employment for its members and to represent its members interests to the government and other bodies.

MEMBERSHIP
Youth Member
Student Member
Graduate Member
Full Member

NATIONAL COUNCIL FOR DRAMA TRAINING

249 Tooley Street
London SE1 2JX
Tel: 020 7407 3686
Fax: 020 7387 3860
E-mail: info@ncdt.co.uk
Website: www.ncdt.co.uk

The NCDT is a partnership of employers in the theatre, broadcast and media industries, employee representatives and training providers. We accredit vocational courses, act as a champion for the sector and work to optimize support for professional drama training and education in acting, stage management and technical theatre, embracing change and development.

THE BRITISH (THEATRICAL) ARTS

12 Deveron Way
Rise Park
Romford
Essex RM1 4UL
Tel: 01708 756263
Website: www.britisharts.org

The British Arts is a non-profit-making organization dedicated to maintaining and where necessary raising the standard of the teaching of Performing Arts subjects. We work to encourage a strong technical foundation combined with an understanding of professional theatrical presentation and conduct exams in Dramatic Art, Classical, Stage Ballet, Mime, Tap, Musical Theatre and Modern Dance.

MEMBERSHIP
Student Member
Companion
Associate (Teaching and Non-teaching)
Member (Teaching and Non-teaching)
Advanced Teacher Member
Fellow

QUALIFICATION/EXAMINATIONS
Please see the British Arts website.

DRIVING INSTRUCTORS

Membership of Professional Institutions and Associations

REGISTER OF APPROVED DRIVING INSTRUCTORS

The Axis Building
112 Upper Parliament Street
Nottingham NG1 6LP
Tel: 0300 200 1122
E-mail: ADIReg@dsa.gsi.gov.uk

The Register of Approved Driving Instructors (ADI) and the licensing scheme for trainee instructors (PDI) are administered under the provisions of the Road Traffic Act 1988 by the Department for Transport (DfT). It is an offence for anyone to give professional instruction (that is instruction paid for by or in respect of the pupil) in driving a motor car unless: (a) his or her name is on the Register of Approved Driving Instructors; or (b) he or she holds a 'trainee's licence to give instruction' issued by the Registrar.

QUALIFICATION/EXAMINATIONS
Please see the Transport Office's website (www.transportoffice.gov.uk) for details of the qualifying exam.

EMBALMING

Membership of Professional Institutions and Associations

INTERNATIONAL EXAMINATIONS BOARD OF EMBALMERS

39 Poplar Grove
Kennington
Oxford OX1 5QN
Tel: 01865 735788
Fax: 01865 730941

The Board examines candidates who wish to become qualified members of the British Institute of Embalmers (qv), which is not itself an examining body but can provide information packs (also available from the above address) that contain lists of approved schools and accredited tutors.

THE BRITISH INSTITUTE OF EMBALMERS

Anubis House
21c Station Road
Knowle
Solihull
West Midlands B93 0HL
Tel: 01564 778991
Fax: 01564 770812
E-mail: enquiries@bioe.co.uk
Website: www.bioe.co.uk

The BIE, founded in 1927, is an organization for professional embalmers. Its objectives include supporting and protecting the status, character and interests of embalmers, promoting the efficient tuition of persons seeking to become embalmers, and encouraging the study and practice of improved methods of embalming.

MEMBERSHIP
Member (MBIE)
Fellow (FBIE)

DESIGNATORY LETTERS
MBIE, FBIE

EMPLOYMENT AND CAREERS SERVICES

Membership of Professional Institutions and Associations

RECRUITMENT AND EMPLOYMENT CONFEDERATION

4th Floor
Albion House
Chertsey Road
Woking
Surrey GU21 6BT
Tel: 020 7009 2100
Fax: 01483 714979
E-mail: info@rec.uk.com
Website: www.rec.uk.com

The REC is the representative body for the UK's £27 billion private recruitment and staffing industry, with a membership of more than 8,000 Corporate Members comprising agencies and businesses from all sectors, and 6,000 members of the Institute of Recruitment Professionals (IRP) made up of recruitment consultants and other industry professionals.

MEMBERSHIP
Affiliate (AIRP)
Member (MIRP)
Fellow (FIRP)

QUALIFICATION/EXAMINATIONS
Certificate in Recruitment Practice (CertRP)
Diploma in Recruitment Practice (DipRP)
BA in Recruitment Practice (run jointly with Middlesex University Business School)
MA in Recruitment Practice (run jointly with Middlesex University Business School)

DESIGNATORY LETTERS
AIRP, MIRP, FIRP

THE INSTITUTE OF CAREER GUIDANCE

Ground Floor
Copthall House
1 New Road
Stourbridge
West Midlands DY8 1PH
Tel: 01384 376464
Fax: 01384 440830
E-mail: hq@icg-uk.org
Website: www.icg-uk.org

The ICG is the oldest and largest professional association for career guidance practitioners in the UK. Our aim is to promote access to high-quality guidance services, delivered by professionally qualified staff working within an appropriate ethical framework, and to underpin this our members adhere to a strict code of ethics.

MEMBERSHIP
Student Member
Full Member
Fellow
Honorary Fellow
School Member
Organizational Member

QUALIFICATION/EXAMINATIONS
Qualification in Career Guidance (QCG)

ENGINEERING, AERONAUTICAL

Membership of Professional Institutions and Associations

ROYAL AERONAUTICAL SOCIETY

4 Hamilton Place
Hyde Park Corner
London W1J 7BQ
Tel: 020 7670 4300
Fax: 020 7670 4309
E-mail: raes@aerosociety.com
Website: www.aerosociety.com

The RAeS, founded in 1866 to further the science of aeronautics, is a multidisciplinary professional institution dedicated to the global aerospace community. We work on our members' behalf to promote the highest professional standards in all aerospace disciplines, to provide specialist information and act as a central forum for the exchange of ideas, and to play a leading role in influencing opinion on aviation matters.

MEMBERSHIP
Student Affiliate
Affiliate
Associate (ARAeS)
Associate Member (AMRAeS)
Member (MRAeS)
Companion (CRAeS)
Fellow (FRAeS)
Engineering Technician (EngTech)
Incorporated Engineer (IEng)
Chartered Engineer (CEng)

ENGINEERING, AGRICULTURAL

Membership of Professional Institutions and Associations

BRITISH AGRICULTURAL AND GARDEN MACHINERY ASSOCIATION

Middleton House
2 Main Road
Middleton Cheney
Oxfordshire OX17 2TN
Tel: 01295 713344
Fax: 01295 711665
E-mail: info@bagma.com
Website: www.bagma.com

BAGMA is the trade association representing agricultural and garden machinery dealers in the UK. We have some 850 dealer members and 75 affiliated suppliers and allied industry companies. We offer a range of training and assessment courses through our online learning package and at approved Training and Assessment Centres.

QUALIFICATION/EXAMINATIONS
Please see the BAGMA website.

THE INSTITUTION OF AGRICULTURAL ENGINEERS

The Bullock Building
University Way
Cranfield
Bedford MK43 0GH
Tel: 01234 750876
Fax: 01234 751319
E-mail: secretary@iagre.org
Website: www.iagre.org

The IAgrE is the professional body for engineers, scientists, technologists and managers in agricultural and allied land-based industries, including forestry, food engineering and technology, amenity, renewable energy, horticulture and the environment.

MEMBERSHIP
Student
Associate (AIAgrE)
Associate Member (AMIAgrE)
Member (MIAgrE)
Fellow (FIAgrE)
Honorary Fellow

DESIGNATORY LETTERS
AIAgrE, AMIAgrE, MIAgrE, FIAgrE

ENGINEERING, AUTOMOBILE

Membership of Professional Institutions and Associations

INSTITUTE OF AUTOMOTIVE ENGINEER ASSESSORS

Brooke House
24 Dam Street
Lichfield
Staffordshire WS13 6AA
Tel: 01543 266906
Fax: 01543 257848
E-mail: secretary@iaea-online.co.uk
Website: www.iaea-online.org

The IAEA, a Professional Affiliate of the Engineering Council, was founded in 1932 and now represents more than 1,500 automotive engineer assessors responsible for activities such as vehicle damage assessment, accident reconstruction, investigation of mechanical failures, electrical failures and vehicle fires, providing expert witness testimony, repair assessment, car fleet surveys, and conciliation and arbitration.

MEMBERSHIP
Student
Graduate
Associate
Licensed Estimator
Incorporated Member (IMInstAEA)
Member (MInstAEA)
Fellow (FInstAEA)

QUALIFICATION/EXAMINATIONS
Basic Principles of Maths & Physics Application to Accident Reconstruction
Motor Vehicle Legislation as related to Insurance Principles
Principles and Practice of Vehicle Damage Assessment
Motor Insurance

DESIGNATORY LETTERS
IMInstAEA, MInstAEA, FInstAEA

SOCIETY OF AUTOMOTIVE ENGINEERS

PO Box 13312
Birmingham B28 1BG
E-mail: info@sae-uk.org
Website: www.sae-uk.org

SAE-UK is the only professional society dedicated solely to the vehicle and component manufacturing industries and has more than 2,000 members. Our aims are to improve the standards of design, use of materials, methods of manufacturing and safety, to encourage the development and continuous updating of automotive technology, and to improve the status of our members.

MEMBERSHIP
Personal Member
Corporate Member

THE INSTITUTE OF THE MOTOR INDUSTRY

Fanshaws
Brickendon
Hertford SG13 8PQ
Tel: 01992 511521
Fax: 01992 511548
E-mail: imi@motor.org.uk
Website: www.motor.org.uk and www.automotivetechnician.org.uk

The IMI is the professional association for individuals working in the motor industry and exists to help individuals and employers improve professional standards and performance by qualifying, recognizing and developing people. We are the Sector Skills Council for the automotive retail industry, a Licensed Member of the Engineering Council and the governing body for Automotive Technician Accreditation (ATA) – the UK's first national voluntary assessment system for vehicle technicians.

MEMBERSHIP
Affiliate (AffIMI)
Licentiate (LIMI)
Associate (AMIMI)
Member (MIMI)
Fellow (FIMI)
For technicians only, there are two special IMI awards recognizing technical qualifications and experience:
AAE (Advanced Automotive Engineer)
CAE (Certificated Automotive Engineer)

DESIGNATORY LETTERS
AffIMI, LIMI, AMIMI, MIMI, FIMI, AAE, CAE

ENGINEERING, BUILDING SERVICES

Membership of Professional Institutions and Associations

THE CHARTERED INSTITUTION OF BUILDING SERVICES ENGINEERS

222 Balham High Road
London SW12 9BS
Tel: 020 8675 5211
Fax: 020 8675 5449
Website: www.cibse.org

CIBSE is the professional body for people involved in the design, construction, operation and maintenance of the engineering elements of a building other than its structure and emables it to operate efficently by saving energy and contributing to a low carbon built environment. This includes heating, ventilation, air conditioning, electrical services, lighting etc.

MEMBERSHIP
Student Affiliate
Affiliate
Graduate
Companion
Licentiate (LCIBSE)
Associate (ACIBSE)
Member (MCIBSE)
Fellow (FCIBSE)

QUALIFICATION/EXAMINATIONS
Please see the CIBSE website.

DESIGNATORY LETTERS
LCIBSE, ACIBSE, MCIBSE, FCIBSE

ENGINEERING, CHEMICAL

Membership of Professional Institutions and Associations

THE INSTITUTION OF CHEMICAL ENGINEERS

Davis Building
Railway Terrace
Rugby
Warwickshire CV21 3HQ
Tel: 01788 578214
Fax: 01788 560833
E-mail: onlineassistance@icheme.org
Website: www.icheme.org

The IChemE, founded in 1922, is an international professional membership organization for chemical, biochemical and process engineers, and we have some 30,000 members in more than 113 countries. We promote competence and a commitment to sustainable development, advance the discipline for the benefit of society, and support the professional development of our members.

MEMBERSHIP
Student
Affiliate
Associate Member (AMIChemE)
Member (MIChemE)
Fellow {FIChemE)
Chartered Chemical Engineer (CEng MIChemE)
Chartered Engineer (CEng)
Chartered Scientist (CSci)
Chartered Environmentalist (CEnv)

DESIGNATORY LETTERS
AMIChemE, MIChemE, FIChemE, CEng MIChemE, CEng, CSci, CEnv

ENGINEERING, CIVIL

Membership of Professional Institutions and Associations

INSTITUTION OF CIVIL ENGINEERS

1 Great George Street
Westminster
London SW1P 3AA
Tel: 020 7222 7722
Fax: 020 7233 0515
E-mail: membership@ice.org.uk
Website: www.ice.org.uk

The ICE is a UK-based international organization with 80,000 members that strives to promote and progress civil engineering around the world. Our purpose is to quality professionals engaged in civil engineering, exchange knowledge and best practice, and support our members, and in the UK we liaise with government and publish reports on civil engineering issues.

MEMBERSHIP
Student
Graduate
Affiliate
Technician Member
Associate Member (AMICE)
Member (MICE)
Companion
Fellow (FICE)

ENGINEERING, ELECTRICAL, ELECTRONIC AND MANUFACTURING

Membership of Professional Institutions and Associations

INSTITUTION OF LIGHTING PROFESSIONALS

Regent House
Regent Place
Rugby
Warwickshire CV21 2PN
Tel: 01788 576492
Fax: 01788 540145
E-mail: info@ile.org.uk
Website: www.ile.co.uk

The ILP is a professional lighting association with about 2,200 members, including lighting designers, consultants and engineers. We are dedicated to excellence in lighting and to raising awareness about the important contribution of lighting in road safety, crime prevention and the environment. We support members by providing technical advice and encourage their CPD through our bimonthly journal and by holding a wide range of conferences, regional meetings, seminars and courses.

MEMBERSHIP
Student
Affiliate
Associate Member (AMILP)
Member (MILP)
Fellow (FILP)
Siver Group Member
Gold Group Member
Engineering Technician (EngTech)
Incorporated Engineer (IEng)
Chartered Engineer (CEng)

QUALIFICATION/EXAMINATIONS
Exterior Lighting Diploma

DESIGNATORY LETTERS
AMILP, MILP, FILP, EngTech, IEng, CEng

THE INSTITUTION OF ENGINEERING AND TECHNOLOGY

Michael Faraday House
Stevenage
Hertfordshire SG1 2AY
Tel: 01438 313311
Fax: 01438 765526
E-mail: postmaster@theiet.org
Website: www.theiet.org

The IET was formed in 2006 by the amalgamation of the Institution of Electrical Engineers and the Institution of Incorporated Engineers and has more than 150,000 members in 127 countries worldwide. We provide a global knowledge network to facilitate the exchange of ideas and promote the positive role of science, engineering and technology in the world.

MEMBERSHIP
Student
Associate
Member (MIET)
Fellow (FIET)
Honorary Fellow
ICT Technician (ICTTech)
Engineering Technician (EngTech)
Incorporated Engineer (IEng)
Chartered Engineer (CEng)

DESIGNATORY LETTERS
FIET, ICTech, EngTech, IEng, CEng, MIET

ENGINEERING, ENERGY

Membership of Professional Institutions and Associations

ENERGY INSTITUTE

61 New Cavendish Street
London W1G 7AR
Tel: 020 7467 7100
Fax: 020 7255 1472
E-mail: info@energyinst.org.uk
Website: www.energyinst.org.uk

The EI is the leading professional body for the energy industries, supporting almost 13,500 professionals internationally. A Royal Charter membership organization, we are licensed to offer Chartered, Incorporated and Engineering Technician status to engineers, and to award Chartered Scientist and Chartered Environmentalist status.

MEMBERSHIP
Student Member
Affiliate
Graduate Member (Grad EI)
Member (MEI)
Fellow (FEI)
Engineering Technician (EngTech)
Incorporated Engineer (IEng)
Chartered Engineer (CEng)
Chartered Scientist (CSci)
Chartered Environmentalist (CEnv)

DESIGNATORY LETTERS
GradEI, MEI, FEI, EngTech, IEng, CEng

ENGINEERING, ENVIRONMENTAL

Membership of Professional Institutions and Associations

INSTITUTE OF ENVIRONMENTAL MANAGEMENT AND ASSESSMENT

St Nicholas House
Lincoln LN1 3DP
Tel: 01522 540069
Fax: 01522 540090
E-mail: info@iema.net
Website: www.iema.net

The IEMA is a not-for-profit membership organization that provides recognition and support to environmental professionals and promotes sustainable development through improved environmental practice and performance. We have about 15,000 individual and corporate members in 87 countries, in the public, private and non-governmental sectors.

MEMBERSHIP
Student Member
Affiliate Member
Graduate Member
Associate (AIEMA)
Full Member (MIEMA)
Fellow (FIEMA)
Chartered Environmentalist (CEnv)
Corporate Member

QUALIFICATION/EXAMINATIONS
Foundation Certificate in Environmental Management
Associate Certificate in Environmental Management
Diploma

DESIGNATORY LETTERS
AIEMA, MIEMA, FIEMA, CEnv

THE CHARTERED INSTITUTION OF WATER AND ENVIRONMENTAL MANAGEMENT

15 John Street
London WC1N 2EB
Tel: 020 7831 3110
Fax: 020 7405 4967
E-mail: admin@ciwem.org
Website: www.ciwem.org

Founded in 1895, CIWEM is an independent professional body and registered charity with 12,000 members that advances the science and practice of water and environmental management for a clean, green and sustainable world by promoting environmental excellence and professional development and training, supplying independent advice and evidence-based opinion, and providing a forum for debate through conferences, technical meetings and its publications.

MEMBERSHIP
Student
Associate ACIWEM
Graduate
Member MCIWEM C.WEM
Fellow FCIWEM C.WEM
Environmental Partner
Chartered Engineer (CEng)
Chartered Environmentalist (CEnv)
Chartered Scientist (CSci)

QUALIFICATION/EXAMINATIONS
Online training courses in partnership with Staffordshire University, accredited university courses at 12 leading institutions, CPD modules and Rural Environmental Management Programme

DESIGNATORY LETTERS
CEng, CEnv, CSi. C.WEM

THE SOCIETY OF ENVIRONMENTAL ENGINEERS

The Manor House
High Street
Buntingford
Buntingford
Hertfordshire SG9 9AB
Tel: 01763 271209
Fax: 01763 273255
E-mail: office@environmental.org.uk
Website: www.environmental.org.uk

The SEE, founded in 1959, is a professional society that promotes awareness of the discipline of environmental engineering (the measurement, modelling, control and simulation of all types of environment). We provide members with information, training and representation within this field and encourage communication and good practice in quality, reliability, and cost-effective product development and manufacture.

MEMBERSHIP
Student
Member
Corporate Member
Engineering Technician (EngTech)
Incorporated Engineer (IEng)
Chartered Engineer (CEng)

DESIGNATORY LETTERS
EngTech, IEng, CEng

ENGINEERING, FIRE

Membership of Professional Institutions and Associations

ASSOCIATION OF PRINCIPAL FIRE OFFICERS

10/11 Pebble Close
Amington
Tamworth
Staffordshire B77 4RD
Tel: 01827 302300
Fax: 01827 302399
E-mail: enquiries@apfo.org.uk
Website: www.apfo.org.uk

The APFO is the staff association of the most senior Fire Officers in the UK. Our objectives are: to represent and promote the interests of members in conditions of service and legal and employment matters; to negotiate and promote the settlement of disputes involving members; to provide assistance to members and their dependants in exceptional circumstances; and to provide support to members in matters concerning employment or a work-related injury.

MEMBERSHIP
Associate Member
Lifetime Past Member

CHIEF FIRE OFFICERS' ASSOCIATION

9–11 Pebble Close
Amington
Tamworth
Staffordshire B77 4RD
Tel: 01827 302300
Fax: 01827 302399
Website: www.cfoa.org.uk

The CFOA is a professional membership association of the most senior fire officers in the UK. We provide independent advice to the government, local authorities and others. Our aim is to reduce loss of life, personal injury and damage to property by improving the quality of fire fighting, rescue, fire protection and fire prevention in the UK.

MEMBERSHIP
Member

THE INSTITUTION OF FIRE ENGINEERS

London Road
Moreton-in-March
Gloucestershire GL56 0RH
Tel: 01608 812580
Fax: 01608 812581
E-mail: info@ife.org.uk
Website: www.ife.org.uk

The IFE, founded in 1918, is a non-profit-making professional body for fire professionals and has more than 12,000 members worldwide. Our aim is to encourage and improve the science and practice of fire extinction, fire prevention and fire engineering, to enhance technical networks, and to give advice and support to our members for the benefit of the community at large.

MEMBERSHIP
Student
Affiliate Member
Technician (TIFireE)
Graduate (GIFireE)
Associate (AIFireE)
Member (MIFireE)
Fellow (FIFireE)
Engineering Technician (EngTech)
Incorporated Engineer (IEng)
Chartered Engineer (CEng) Affiliate Organization

QUALIFICATION/EXAMINATIONS
Level 2 Certificate Level 3 Certificate
Level 3 Diploma Level 4 Certificate

DESIGNATORY LETTERS
TIFireE, GIFireE, AIFireE, MIFireE, FIFireE, EngTech, IEng, CEng

ENGINEERING, GAS

Membership of Professional Institutions and Associations

THE INSTITUTION OF GAS ENGINEERS AND MANAGERS

IGEM House
High Street
Kegworth
Derbyshire DE74 2DA
Tel: 0844 375 4436
Fax: 01509 678198
Website: www.igem.org.uk

IGEM is licensed by EC(UK) and serves a wide range of professionals in the UK and international gas industry through membership and technical standards, having a diverse membership ranging from university students to qualified professionals. Anyone working or interested in the gas industry can form positive connections to enhance their career through IGEM.

MEMBERSHIP
Student Member
Associate (AIGEM)
Associate Member (AMIGEM)
Graduate Member (GradIGEM)
Member Manager (MIGEM)
Technician Member (Eng Tech (MIGEM))
Incorporated Member (I Eng (MIGEM))
Chartered Member (C Eng (MIGEM))
Fellow (C Eng (FIGEM))
Industrial Affiliate (company membership)

DESIGNATORY LETTERS
MIGEM, Eng Tech (MIGEM), I Eng (MIGEM), C ENG (MIGEM), C Eng (FIGEM)

ENGINEERING, GENERAL

Membership of Professional Institutions and Associations

ASSOCIATION OF COST ENGINEERS

Lea House
Sandbach
Cheshire CW11 1XL
Tel: 01270 764798
Fax: 01270 766180
E-mail: enquiries@acoste.org.uk
Website: www.acoste.org.uk

The ACostE represents the professional interests of those with responsibility for the prediction, planning and control of resources for engineering, manufacturing and construction. As a Professional Affiliate of The Engineering Council, we can propose suitably qualified members for the award of the titles of Chartered Engineer (CEng) and Incorporated Engineer (IEng).

MEMBERSHIP
Student
Associate (AA Cost E)
Companion (Companion A Cost E)
Graduate (Grad A Cost E)
Member (MA Cost E)
Fellow (FA Cost E)
Honorary Fellow (Hon FA Cost E)
Certified Cost Engineer (CCE)
Engineering Technician (EngTech)
Incorporated Engineer (IEng)
Chartered Engineer (CEng)

DESIGNATORY LETTERS
AA Cost E, Companion A Cost E, Grad A Cost E, MA Cost E, FA Cost E, CCE, EngTech, IEng, CEng

INSTITUTE OF MEASUREMENT AND CONTROL

87 Gower Street
London WC1E 6AF
Tel: 020 7387 4949
Fax: 020 7388 8431
E-mail: membership@instmc.org.uk
Website: www.instmc.org.uk

The IMC is a multidisciplinary body that brings together thinkers and practitioners from the many disciplines that have a common interest in measurement and control. Our object is to promote for the public benefit, by all available means, the general advancement of the science and practice of measurement and control technology and its application.

MEMBERSHIP
Student Member
Affiliate Member
Associate Member
Member (MemInstMC)
Fellow (FInstMC)
Honorary Fellow (HonFInstMC)

SEMTA – THE SECTOR SKILLS COUNCIL FOR SCIENCE, ENGINEERING AND MANUFACTURING TECHNOLOGIES

14 Upton Road
Watford
Hertfordshire WD18 0JT
Tel: 01923 238441
Fax: 01923 256086
E-mail: customerservices@semta.org.uk
Website: www.semta.org.uk

Semta is part of the Skills for Business network of 25 employer-led Sector Skills Councils in the UK and works with employers in the aerospace, automotive, electrical, electronics, marine, mechanical, metals and science & bioscience sectors to ascertain their current and future skills needs and provide short- and long-term solutions to meet those needs.

THE ENGINEERING COUNCIL

2nd Floor
246 High Holborn
London WC1V 7EX
Tel: 020 3206 0500
Fax: 020 3206 0501
Website: www.engc.org.uk

The Engineering Council holds the national registers of Chartered Engineers (CEng), Incorporated Engineers (IEng), Engineering Technicians (EngTech) and Information and Communications Technology Technicians (ICTTech). We set and maintain internationally recognized standards of competence and ethics, ensuring that employers, government and society can have confidence in registrants' skills and commitment.

DESIGNATORY LETTERS
ICTTech, EngTech, IEng, CEng

THE INSTITUTION OF BRITISH ENGINEERS

Clifford Hill Court
Clifford Chambers
Stratford upon Avon
Warwickshire CV37 8AA
Tel: 01789 298739
Fax: 01789 294442
E-mail: info@britishengineers.com
Website: www.britishengineers.com

MEMBERSHIP
Vice President
Fellow (FIBE)
Member (MIBE)
Associate Member (AMIBE)
Graduate Member (GradIBE)
Qualified Sales Engineer (SEng)
Bi-Lingual Engineer (BLEng)
Diploma in Business Engineering (DBE)
Certificate of Competence in Engineering

DESIGNATORY LETTERS
FIBE, MIBE, AMIBE, GradIBE, SEng, BLEng, DBE

WOMEN'S ENGINEERING SOCIETY

Michael Faraday House
Six Hills Way
Stevenage
Herts SG1 2AY
Tel: 01438 765506
E-mail: info@wes.org.uk
Website: www.wes.org.uk

The WES, founded in 1919, is a professional, not-for-profit network of women engineers, scientists and technologists, who offer inspiration, support and professional development. Working in partnership, we campaign to encourage women to participate and achieve as engineers, scientists and as leaders.

MEMBERSHIP
Student Member
Associate
Member (MWES)
Group Member
Corporate Member

DESIGNATORY LETTERS
MWES

ENGINEERING, MARINE

Membership of Professional Institutions and Associations

THE INSTITUTE OF MARINE ENGINEERING, SCIENCE AND TECHNOLOGY

80 Coleman Street
London EC2R 5BJ
Tel: +44 (0)20 7382 2600
Fax: +44 (0)20 7382 2670
E-mail: membership@imarest.org
Website: www.imarest.org

The IMarEST, established in 1889, is the leading international membership body and learned society for marine professionals and has more than 15,000 members worldwide. We have a strong international presence, with a network of 50 international branches, affiliations with major marine societies around the world, representation on the key marine technical committees and non-governmental status at the International Maritime Organization.

MEMBERSHIP

Membership Categories

IMarEST Membership is open to everyone with an interest in the marine world across scientific, engineering and technological disciplines and applications.

Categories of membership are available to those who are seeking professional recognition, those who are currently studying or just starting out in their careers, or those who simply have a general interest in the IMarEST and its activities. There are no academic requirements for Non-corporate Membership of the IMarEST. However, professionals seeking Corporate Membership will require certain academic qualifications according to the type of membership being sought.

Corporate Membership Categories

Fellow (FIMarEST)

Fellows are those who qualify for the category of Member and have demonstrated to the satisfaction of Council a level of knowledge and understanding, competence and commitment involving superior responsibility for the conceptual design, management or the execution of important work in a marine related profession, and have given a commitment to abide by the Institute's Code of Professional Conduct.

Member (MIMarEST)

Members are those who qualify for the category of Associate Member and have demonstrated to the satisfaction of Council that they have achieved a position of professional standing having normally been professionally engaged in the marine sector for a period of 5 years that includes significant responsibility and have given a commitment to abide by the Institute's Code of Professional Conduct.

Associate Member (AMIMarEST)

Associate Members are those demonstrating to the satisfaction of Council that they have achieved a position as a technician, or are professionally engaged in Initial Professional Development or occupy an occupational role in the marine sector, and have given a commitment to abide by the Institute's Code of Professional Conduct.

Non-corporate Membership Categories

Affiliate

Affiliates may either be those with an interest in, or who may contribute to, the activities of the Institute or; persons who, in the opinion of Council, can contribute to, or wish to have access to, the technical services of the Institute, being resident in a recognised overseas territory and also members of a professional society with which the Institute has a reciprocal arrangement.

Student (SIMarEST)

Student members are those enrolled on a programme of further or higher education accredited or recognised by the IMarEST.

Professional Registration

In addition to Membership, the IMarEST is licensed to provide a range of registers covering the fields of engineering, science and technology. In addition, the IMarEST's Royal Charter empowers the Institute to offer registers designed to meet the specific needs of the marine profession. Corporate members can become registered (chartered) as follows:

Engineers

Chartered Engineer (CEng)

Chartered Marine Engineer (CMarEng)

Incorporated Engineer (IEng)
Incorporated Marine Engineer (IMarEng)
Engineering Technician (EngTech)
Marine Engineering Technician (MarEngTech)
Scientists
Chartered Scientist (CSci)
Chartered Marine Scientist (CMarSci)
Registered Marine Scientist (RMarSci)
Marine Technician (MarTech)
Technologists
Chartered Marine Technologist (CMarTech)
Registered Marine Technologist (RMarTech)
Marine Technician (MarTech)

DESIGNATORY LETTERS
SIMarEST, AMIMarEST, MIMarEST, FIMarEST

ENGINEERING, MECHANICAL

Membership of Professional Institutions and Associations

INSTITUTION OF MECHANICAL ENGINEERS

1 Birdcage Walk
Westminster
London SW1H 9JJ
Tel: 020 7304 6999
E-mail: membership@imeche.org
Website: www.imeche.org

The IMechE is a professional engineering body with about 80,000 members. Our aims are to promote sustainable energy and engineering sustainable supply, economic growth while mitigating and adapting to climate change and the depletion of natural resources, and safe, efficient transport systems to ensure less congestion and emissions, and to inspire, prepare and support tomorrow's engineers so we can respond to society's changes.

MEMBERSHIP
Affiliate
Associate Member (AMIMechE)
Member (MIMechE)
Fellow (FIMechE)
Engineering Technician (EngTech)
Incorporated Engineer (IEng)
Chartered Engineer (CEng)

DESIGNATORY LETTERS
AMIMechE, MIMechE, FIMechE, EngTech, IEng, CEng

ENGINEERING, MINING

Membership of Professional Institutions and Associations

INSTITUTE OF EXPLOSIVES ENGINEERS

Wellington Hall 289
Cranfield University
Defence Academy of the UK
Shrivenham, Swindon
Wiltshire SN6 8LA
Tel: 01793 785322
Fax: 01793 785772
E-mail: iexpe@cranfield.ac.uk
Website: www.iexpe.org

The Insitute of Explosives Engineers promotes the occupational competency, education and professional standing of those who work with explosives and provides consultative facilities for organizations and government departments within the explosives field.

MEMBERSHIP
Student
Associate (AIExpE)
Member (MIExpE)
Fellow (FIExpE)
Company

DESIGNATORY LETTERS
AIExpE, MIExpE, FIExpE

THE INSTITUTE OF MATERIALS, MINERALS AND MINING (IOM^3)

1 Carlton House Terrace
London SW1Y 5DB
Tel: 020 7451 7300
Fax: 020 7839 1702
Website: www.iom3.org

IOM^3 is a major UK engineering institution whose activities encompass the whole materials cycle, from exploration and extraction, through characterization, processing, forming, finishing and application, to product recycling and land reuse. We promote and develop all aspects of materials science and engineering, geology, mining and associated technologies, mineral and petroleum engineering and extraction metallurgy, as a leading authority in the worldwide materials and mining community.

MEMBERSHIP
Student
Graduate
Affiliate
Member (MIMMM)
Fellow (FIMMM)

DESIGNATORY LETTERS
MIMMM, FIMMM

THE INSTITUTE OF QUARRYING

7 Regent Street
Nottingham NG1 5BS
Tel: 0115 945 3880
Fax: 0115 948 4035
E-mail: mail@quarrying.org
Website: www.quarrying.org

The Institute of Quarrying, which dates from 1917, is the international professional body for quarrying, construction materials and related extractive and processing industries, and has 6,000 members in some 50 countries. Our aim is to improve all aspects of operational performance through education and training at supervisory and management level.

MEMBERSHIP
Student
Associate
Member (MIQ)
Fellow (FIQ)

QUALIFICATION/EXAMINATIONS
Professional Examination

DESIGNATORY LETTERS
MIQ, FIQ

ENGINEERING, NUCLEAR

Membership of Professional Institutions and Associations

THE NUCLEAR INSTITUTE

Allan House
1 Penerley Road
London SE6 2LQ
Tel: 020 8695 8220
Fax: 020 8695 8229
E-mail: admin@nuclearinst.com
Website: www.nuclearinst.com

The NI (a Nominated Body of the Engineering Council) is a registered charity established to support the nuclear sector. We organize lectures, seminars and events at a regional and national level, and can award EngTech, IEng and CEng to suitably qualified individuals.

MEMBERSHIP
Student Member
Learned Member
Graduate Member
Technician Member (TNucI)
Associate Member (AMNucI)
Member (MNucI)
Fellow (FNucI)
Honorary Fellow

DESIGNATORY LETTERS
TNucI, AMNucI, MNucI, FNucI

ENGINEERING, PRODUCTION

Membership of Professional Institutions and Associations

THE INSTITUTE OF OPERATIONS MANAGEMENT

CILT(UK)
Earlstrees Court
Earlstrees Road
Corby
Northamptonshire NN17 4AX
Tel: 01536 740105
E-mail: info@iomnet.org.uk
Website: www.iomnet.org.uk

The IOM is the professional body for persons involved in operations and production management in the manufacturing and service industries and in the public sector in the UK. Our object is to equip operations professionals with the skills and resources they need to maximize individual potential and organizational success.

MEMBERSHIP
Student
Associate
Member (MIOM)
Fellow (FIOM)
Group Member
Corporate Member

QUALIFICATION/EXAMINATIONS
Certificate in Operations Management (COM)
Diploma in Operations Management (DOM)
Advanced Diploma in Operations Management
IOM now offer APICS certifications

DESIGNATORY LETTERS
MION, FIOM

ENGINEERING, REFRACTORIES

Membership of Professional Institutions and Associations

INSTITUTE OF REFRACTORIES ENGINEERING

25 Woodland Way
Long Newton
Stockton-on-Tees
Co Durham TS21 1DJ
Tel: 01642 583840
Fax: 01642 589397
E-mail: secretary@ireng.org
Website: www.ireng.org

The IRE is a non-profit-making organization dedicated to fostering the science, technology and skills of refractories engineering and to serving the needs of refractories engineers worldwide. Our members have a background in R&D, design, engineering, manufacturing and installation contracting in the iron & steel, cement, non-ferrous, glass, chemical/petrochemical incineration, power generation, ceramics/bricks and similar industries.

MEMBERSHIP
Student
Associate Member (AMI Ref Eng)
Member (MI Ref Eng)
Fellow (FI Ref Eng)

DESIGNATORY LETTERS
AMI Ref Eng, MI Ref Eng, FI Ref Eng

ENGINEERING, REFRIGERATION

Membership of Professional Institutions and Associations

THE INSTITUTE OF REFRIGERATION

Kelvin House
76 Mill Lane
76 Mill Lane
Carshalton
Surrey SM5 2JR
Tel: 020 8647 7033
Fax: 020 8773 0165
E-mail: ior@ior.org.uk
Website: www.ior.org.uk

The IOR is the professional body for the refrigeration and air conditioning industries. We promote the technical advancement and perfection of refrigeration, and the minimization of its effects on the environment, encourage the extension of refrigeration, air conditioning and heat pump services for the benefit of the community, and provide advice, CPD and support to our members.

MEMBERSHIP
Student
Affiliate
Associate Member (AMInstR)
Member (MInstR)
Fellow (FInstR)
Engineering Technician (EngTech)
Incorporated Engineer (IEng)
Chartered Engineer (CEng)

DESIGNATORY LETTERS
AMInstR, MInstR, FInstR

ENGINEERING, ROAD, RAIL AND TRANSPORT

Membership of Professional Institutions and Associations

INSTITUTE OF HIGHWAY ENGINEERS

De Morgan House
58 Russell Square
London WC1B 4HS
Tel: 020 7436 7487
Fax: 020 7436 7488
E-mail: secretary@theihe.org
Website: www.theihe.org

The IHE is the professional body for highway and traffic professionals. We are run by engineers for engineers and technicians, and work to keep the standards of the profession high, to safeguard the interests of our members, and to ensure that their contribution is recognized.

MEMBERSHIP
Student Member
Graduate Member
Associate Member (AMIHE)
Member (MIHE)
Fellow (FIHE)
Engineering Technician (EngTech)
Incorporated Engineer (IEng)
Chartered Engineer (CEng)

QUALIFICATION/EXAMINATIONS
Prof Cert in Traffic Sign Design
Prof Cert in Traffic Signal Control

Prof Cert in Transport Development Management

DESIGNATORY LETTERS
AMIHE, MIHE, FIHE, EngTech, IEng, CEng

INSTITUTION OF RAILWAY SIGNAL ENGINEERS

4th Floor
1 Birdcage Walk
Westminster
London SW1H 9JJ
Tel: 020 7808 1180
Fax: 020 7808 1196
E-mail: hq@irse.org
Website: www.irse.org

The Institution of Railway Signal Engineers, known more usually as the IRSE, is an international organization, active throughout the world. It is the professional institution for all those engaged or interested in railway signalling and telecommunications and allied disciplines. Membership is open to anyone engaged or interested in the management, planning, design, installation, telecommunications or associated equipment.

MEMBERSHIP
Student
Associate
Accredited Technician
Associate Member
Member
Fellow
Companion

QUALIFICATION/EXAMINATIONS
Professional Examination

DESIGNATORY LETTERS
AMIRSE, MIRSE, FIRSE, CompIRSE

SOCIETY OF OPERATIONS ENGINEERS

22 Greencoat Place
London SW1P 1PR
Tel: 020 7630 1111
Fax: 020 7630 6677
E-mail: soe@soe.org.uk
Website: www.soe.org.uk

The SOE is a professional membership organization that represents more than 18,000 individuals and companies in the engineering industry. It was formed in 2000 by the merger of the Institute of Road Transport Engineers (IRTE) and the Institution of Plant Engineers (IPlantE). The Society's third professional sector, the Bureau of Engineer Surveyors (BES), joined us in 2004.

MEMBERSHIP
Associate Member (AMSOE)
Member (MSOE)
Fellow (FSOE)
Honorary Fellow (HonFSOE)
Companion (CompanionSOE)
Engineering Technician (EngTech)
Incorporated Engineer (IEng)
Chartered Engineer (CEng)

THE CHARTERED INSTITUTION OF HIGHWAYS AND TRANSPORTATION

119 Britannia Walk
London N1 7JE
Tel: 020 7336 1555
Fax: 020 7336 1556
E-mail: info@ciht.org.uk
Website: www.ciht.org.uk

The CIHT is a learned society concerned with the planning, design, construction, maintenance and operation of land-based transport systems and infrastructure. We provide professional development and networking opportunities to members, with routes to qualifications, cutting-edge technical conferences and exciting social events

MEMBERSHIP
Student
Associate Member (AMCIHT)
Member (MCIHT)
Fellow (FCIHT)
Incorporated Engineer (IEng)
Chartered Engineer (CEng)

QUALIFICATION/EXAMINATIONS
Transport Planning Professional (TPP) status (awarded jointly with the Transport Planning Society (TPS))

DESIGNATORY LETTERS
AMCIHT, MCIHT, FCIHT, IEng, CEng

ENGINEERING, SHEET METAL

Membership of Professional Institutions and Associations

INSTITUTE OF SHEET METAL ENGINEERING

102 Richmond Drive
Perton
Wolverhampton
West Midlands WV6 7UQ
Tel: 07891499146
E-mail: ismesec@googlemail.com
Website: www.isme.org.uk

The ISME is a learned body with individual membership open to those employed in the sheet metal and associated industries and corporate membership open to relevant companies. Our aims are to promote the science of working and using sheet metal by providing opportunities for the exchange of ideas and information, and to encourage the professional development of our members.

MEMBERSHIP
Student Member
Member (MISME)
Fellow (FISME)
Corporate Member

DESIGNATORY LETTERS
MISME, FISME

ENGINEERING, STRUCTURAL

Membership of Professional Institutions and Associations

THE INSTITUTION OF STRUCTURAL ENGINEERS

11 Upper Belgrave Street
London SW1X 8BH
Tel: 020 7235 4535
Fax: 020 7235 4294
E-mail: membership@istructe.org
Website: www.istructe.org

The Institution of Structural Engineers, founded in 1908, is the world's largest membership organization dedicated to the art and science of structural engineering. Our aims include: maintaining professional standards for structural engineering; ensuring continued technical excellence; advancing safety, creativity and innovation; and promoting a sustainable approach to both the structural engineering profession and the built environment.

MEMBERSHIP
Student
Affiliate
Graduate
Technician (TIStructE)
Associate Member (AMIStructE)
Associate (AIStructE)
Chartered Member (MIStructE)
Fellow (FIStructE)
Engineering Technician (EngTech)
Incorporated Engineer (IEng)
Chartered Engineer (CEng)

DESIGNATORY LETTERS
TIStructE, AMIStructE, AIStructE. MIStructE, FIStructE, EngTech, IEng, CEng

ENGINEERING, WATER

Membership of Professional Institutions and Associations

INSTITUTE OF WATER

4 Carlton Court
Team Valley
Gateshead
Tyne and Wear NE11 0AZ
Tel: 0191 422 0088
Fax: 0191 422 0087
E-mail: info@instituteofwater.org.uk
Website: www.instituteofwater.org.uk

The IW is the only institute concerned with the UK water industry. Our aim is to promote high standards of integrity, conduct and ethics, and to provide our members with an opportunity for CPD and growth through sharing knowledge, experience and networking opportunities.

MEMBERSHIP
Student Member
Associate Member
Full Member
Fellow
Honorary Member
Engineering Technician (EngTech)
Incorporated Engineer (IEng)
Chartered Engineer (CEng)
Chartered Environmentalist (CEnv)
Company Member

DESIGNATORY LETTERS
EngTech, IEng, CEng, CEnv

ENGINEERING DESIGN

Membership of Professional Institutions and Associations

THE INSTITUTION OF ENGINEERING DESIGNERS

Courtleigh
Westbury Leigh
Westbury
Wiltshire BA13 3TA
Tel: 01373 822801
Fax: 01373 858085
E-mail: ied@ied.org.uk
Website: www.ied.org.uk

Established in 1945, the IED represents 4,000 members worldwide working in engineering design, product design and CAD. Benefits include a bimonthly journal, access to an extensive library, legal advice helpline, local branch activities, and guidance and support to registration with the EC(UK) for suitably qualified members.

MEMBERSHIP
IED membership has two divisions: Engineering Design, and Product Design and Technology.

Each division has a range of membership grades: Student Member (StudIED), Graduate/Diplomate Member (GradIED/DipIED), Competent Draughting Associate (CDAIED), Associate (AIED), Member (MIED), Fellow (FIED).

QUALIFICATION/EXAMINATIONS
Registration with EC(UK) for suitably qualified members

DESIGNATORY LETTERS
AIED, MIED, FIED

ENVIRONMENTAL SCIENCES

Membership of Professional Institutions and Associations

INSTITUTE OF ECOLOGY AND ENVIRONMENTAL MANAGEMENT

43 Southgate Street
Winchester
Hampshire SO23 9EH
Tel: 01962 868626
Fax: 01962 868625
E-mail: enquiries@ieem.net
Website: www.ieem.net

The IEEM was founded in 1991 to advance the science, technology and practice of ecology, environmental management and sustainable development to further conservation and the enhancement of biodiversity through education, training, study and research. We now have more than 4,000 members drawn from local authorities, government agencies, industry, environmental consultancy, teaching/research and NGOs.

MEMBERSHIP
Student Member
Affiliate Member

Graduate Member
Associate Member (AIEEM)
Full Member (MIEEM)
Fellow (FIEEM)

DESIGNATORY LETTERS
AIEEM, MIEEM, FIEEM

EXPORT

Membership of Professional Institutions and Associations

THE INSTITUTE OF EXPORT

Export House
Minerva Business Park
Lynch Wood
Peterborough PE2 6FT
Tel: 01733 404400
E-mail: info@export.org.uk
Website: www.export.org.uk

Established since 1935 offering training and professional qualifications to those working within international trade. We are the only professional institute in the UK offering qualifications ranging from the new 14–19 Diploma up to a level 5 Diploma as well as standard and bespoke training courses for individuals and companies.

MEMBERSHIP
Affiliate
Student
Associate
Member MIEx (Grad)
Member MIEx
Fellow
Business
Corporate

QUALIFICATION/EXAMINATIONS
Diploma in International Trade (DIT)
Certified International Trade Advisor (CIT)
Advanced Certificate in International Trade (ACIT)

FISHERIES MANAGEMENT

Membership of Professional Institutions and Associations

INSTITUTE OF FISHERIES MANAGEMENT

22 Rushworth Avenue
West Bridgford
Nottingham NG2 7LF
Tel: 01159 822317
Fax: 01159 826150
E-mail: info@ifm.org.uk
Website: www.ifm.org.uk

The Institute of Fisheries Management is an international organization of persons sharing a common interest in the modern and sustainable management of recreational and commercial fisheries. It is a non-profit-making body and is a constituent body of the Society for the Environment.

MEMBERSHIP
Subscriber
Student Member
Associate Member (AMIFM)
Registered Member (MIFM)

Fellow (FIFM)
Honorary Fellow (Hon FIFM)
Corporate Member

QUALIFICATION/EXAMINATIONS
Certificate
Diploma (accredited by The Open University)

DESIGNATORY LETTERS
AMIRM, MIFM, FIFM, Hon FIFM

FLORISTRY

Membership of Professional Institutions and Associations

SOCIETY OF FLORISTRY LTD

Tel: 07896 639520
E-mail: info@societyoffloristry.org
Website: www.societyoffloristry.org

The SOF, founded in 1951, is an awarding body that promotes the highest standards in professional floristry. We are responsible for preparing and setting the highest floristry qualifications and for designing programmes for the training of SOF judges and examiners. We provide help, advice and information to our more than 1,000 members, who include business owners, florists, training providers, and students.

MEMBERSHIP
Member
Corporate Member

QUALIFICATION/EXAMINATIONS
Level 4 Higher Diploma in Floristry (ICSF)
Level 5 Master Diploma in Professional Floristry (NDSF)

FOOD SCIENCE AND NUTRITION

Membership of Professional Institutions and Associations

INSTITUTE OF FOOD SCIENCE AND TECHNOLOGY

5 Cambridge Court
210 Shepherd's Bush Road
London W6 7NJ
Tel: 020 7603 6316
Fax: 020 7602 9936
E-mail: info@ifst.org
Website: www.ifst.org

IFST is the leading independent qualifying body for food professionals in Europe and the only professional body in the UK concerned with all aspects of food science and technology. As a registered charity we are independent of government, industry, lobby or special interest groups.

MEMBERSHIP
Associate
Member (MIFST)
Fellow (FIFST)
Chartered Scientist (CSci)

DESIGNATORY LETTERS
MIFST, FIFST, CSci

FORESTRY AND ARBORICULTURE

Membership of Professional Institutions and Associations

INSTITUTE OF CHARTERED FORESTERS

59 George Street
Edinburgh EH2 2JG
Tel: 0131 240 1425
Fax: 0131 240 1424
E-mail: icf@charteredforesters.org
Website: www.charteredforesters.org

The ICF is the Royal Chartered body for foresters and arboriculturists in the UK. We have over 1,000 members, to whom we offer advice, guidance and support. We also strive to foster a greater public understanding and awareness of the profession, as the environment and its management become more relevant to everyone.

MEMBERSHIP
Student Member
Supporter
Associate Member
Professional Member (MICFor)
Fellow (FICFor)

QUALIFICATION/EXAMINATIONS
Professional Membership Entry (PME) exam

DESIGNATORY LETTERS
MICFor, FICFor

THE ARBORICULTURAL ASSOCIATION

Ullenwood Court
Ullenwood
Cheltenham
Gloucestershire GL53 9QS
Tel: 01242 522152
Fax: 01242 577766
E-mail: admin@trees.org.uk
Website: www.trees.org.uk

The Arboricultural Association, founded in 1964, is the leading body in the UK for the amenity tree care professional in either civic or commercial employment at craft, technical, supervisory, managerial or consultancy level. There are currently over 2,000 members of The Arboricultural Association in a variety of membership classes.

MEMBERSHIP
Individual Membership
Student Member
Ordinary Member
Associate Member
Technician Member
Professional Member
Fellow
Corporate Membership
Corporate Member
Corporate Gold Member

THE ROYAL FORESTRY SOCIETY

102 High Street
Tring
Hertfordshire HP23 4AF
Tel: 01442 822028
Fax: 01442 890395
E-mail: rfshq@rfs.org.uk
Website: www.rfs.org.uk

The RFS was founded in 1882 and now has over 4,000 members. We are dedicated to promoting the wise management of trees and woodlands, and to increasing people's understanding of forestry. We publish a popular magazine, the *Quarterly Journal of Forestry*, arrange outdoor meetings, organize woodland study tours in the UK and overseas, run exams in arboriculture and manage model woodlands.

MEMBERSHIP
Member

QUALIFICATION/EXAMINATIONS
Certificate in Arboriculture (Level 2)
Professional Diploma in Arboriculture (DipArb(RFS) (Level 6)

FOUNDRY TECHNOLOGY AND PATTERN MAKING

Membership of Professional Institutions and Associations

THE INSTITUTE OF CAST METALS ENGINEERS

National Metalforming Centre
47 Birmingham Road
West Bromwich
West Midlands B70 6PY
Tel: 01216 016979
Fax: 01216 016981
E-mail: info@icme.org.uk
Website: www.icme.org.uk

The ICME is the professional body for those in the castings and associated industry. It was formed in 1904, granted its first Royal Charter in 1921, a Third Supplemental Charter in 1994 and changed its name in 2001. The granting of the Third Supplemental Charter aligned its membership requirements with those of the ECUK.

MEMBERSHIP
Student
Member (MICME)
Professional Member (Prof MICME)
Fellow (FICME)
Engineering Technician (EngTech)
Incorporated Engineer (IEng)
Chartered Engineer (CEng)
European Engineer (EurIng)

DESIGNATORY LETTERS
MICME, Prof MICME, FICME, EngTech, IEng, CEng, EurIng

FREIGHT FORWARDING

Membership of Professional Institutions and Associations

BRITISH INTERNATIONAL FREIGHT ASSOCIATION

Redfern House
Browells Lane
Feltham
Middlesex TW13 7EP
Tel: 020 8844 2266
Fax: 020 8890 5546
E-mail: bifa@bifa.org
Website: www.bifa.org

BIFA is the principal trade association providing representation and support to British companies engaged in the international movement of freight to and from the UK by air, rail, road and sea. It is a not-for-profit organization. Members are encouraged to contribute to the running of the Association.

MEMBERSHIP
Associate Member
Trade Member

FUNDRAISING

Membership of Professional Institutions and Associations

INSTITUTE OF FUNDRAISING

Park Place
12 Lawn Lane
London SW8 1UD
Tel: 020 7840 1000
Fax: 020 7840 1001
E-mail: training@institute-of-fundraising.org.uk
Website: www.institute-of-fundraising.org.uk

The Institute of Fundraising is the professional body for fundraisers in the UK. We offer professional support, act as a voice for fundraisers and promote best practice. We run a number of training courses and our annual National Convention is the largest fundraising conference of its type in the UK.

MEMBERSHIP
Associate
Full Member (MInstF)
Full Certificated Member (MInstF(Cert))
Fellow (FInstF)
Organizational Member
Corporate Member

QUALIFICATION/EXAMINATIONS
Certificate in Fundraising Management

DESIGNATORY LETTERS
MInstF, MInstF(Cert), FInstF

FUNERAL DIRECTING, BURIAL AND CREMATION ADMINISTRATION

Membership of Professional Institutions and Associations

NATIONAL ASSOCIATION OF FUNERAL DIRECTORS

618 Warwick Road
Solihull
West Midlands B91 1AA
Tel: 0845 230 1343
Fax: 0121 711 1351
E-mail: info@nafd.org.uk
Website: www.nafd.org.uk

The NAFD, founded in 1905, is an independent trade association whose members include more than 3,200 funeral homes throughout the UK, suppliers to the profession, and overseas funeral directing businesses. We provide support to our members and offer informed opinion to government.

MEMBERSHIP
Funeral Director (Category A) Member
Supplier (Category B) Member
Overseas Member

QUALIFICATION/EXAMINATIONS
Foundation Certificate in Funeral Service
Advanced Certificate in Funeral Services
Diploma in Funeral Directing (DipFD)
Diploma in Funeral Service Management (DipFSM)
Advanced Diploma in Funeral Arranging and Administration

NATIONAL ASSOCIATION OF MEMORIAL MASONS

1 Castle Mews
Rugby
Warwickshire CV21 2AL
Tel: 01788 542264
Fax: 01788 542276
E-mail: enquiries@namm.org.uk
Website: www.namm.org.uk

The NAMM was formed in 1907 to promote excellence and craftsmanship within the memorial masonry trade. Our services to members include training, business advice, technical advice, promotion, a legal helpline, a conciliation and arbitration service, trade exhibitions and a conference. We protect members' interests through representation to the British Standards Institution (BSI) and the Burial & Cemeteries Advisory Group (BCAG).

MEMBERSHIP
Individual Associate Member
Affiliate Retail Member
Full Retail and Wholesale Members
Company Associate Member
Corporate Associate Member

THE INSTITUTE OF BURIAL AND CREMATION ADMINISTRATION

Kelham Hall
Newark
Nottinghamshire NG23 5QX
Tel: 01636 708311
Fax: 01636 706311

MEMBERSHIP
Student
Registered Licentiate (LInstBCA)
Associate Member (AInstBCA)
Member (MInstBCA)
Fellow (FInstBCA)

QUALIFICATION/EXAMINATIONS
Diploma
Final Diploma

DESIGNATORY LETTERS
LInstBCA, AInstBCA, MInstBCA, FInstBCA

FURNISHING AND FURNITURE

Membership of Professional Institutions and Associations

FLOORING INDUSTRY TRAINING ASSOCIATION

4c St Marys Place
The Lace Market
Nottingham NG1 1PH
Tel: 0115 9506836
E-mail: info@fita.co.uk
Website: www.fita.co.uk

The FITA was set up and is fully supported by the CFA and NICF to provide training for the floor-covering industry. We have a fully equipped training centre at Loughborough, where the majority of courses are run, and the use of a training facility in Manchester. We also offer tailor-made courses to suit individual specifications and requirements.

QUALIFICATION/EXAMINATIONS
FITA standard courses are:
Basic carpet – 5 days
Intermediate carpet – 5 days
Advanced carpet – 4 days
Essential (basic) wood – 3 days
Intermediate wood – 3 days
Solid wood sanding and finishing – 2 days
Laminate and floating wood – 2 days
Domestic vinyl – 2 days
Safety and smooth vinyl (commercial) – 4 days
Luxury vinyl tile – 4 days
Estimating and planning – 2 days
Damp testing floors – 1 day
Sub-floor preparation – 2 days

NATIONAL INSTITUTE OF CARPET AND FLOORLAYERS

4c St Marys Place
The Lace Market
Nottingham NG1 1PH
Tel: 0115 9583077
Fax: 0115 9412238
E-mail: info@nicfltd.org.uk
Website: www.nicfltd.org.uk

The NICF furthers the interests of its members by promoting excellence in the field of carpet and floorlaying and providing a range of benefits, products and services.

MEMBERSHIP
Master Fitter
Approved Fitter
Trainee Fitter
Retailer Member
Associate Member
Patron Member

QUALIFICATION/EXAMINATIONS
Master Fitter qualification assessment

GEMMOLOGY AND JEWELLERY

Membership of Professional Institutions and Associations

THE GEMMOLOGICAL ASSOCIATION OF GREAT BRITAIN

27 Greville Street
London EC1N 8TN
Tel: 020 7404 3334
Fax: 020 7404 8843
E-mail: edu@gem-a.com
Website: www.gem-a.com

The Gemmological Association of Great Britain (Gem-A), a UK-registered charity, is the world's longest established provider of gem and jewellery education, our first diploma having been awarded in 1913. We are committed to promoting the study of gemmology and to providing CPD to our members – an international community of gem professionals and enthusiasts.

MEMBERSHIP
Member
Fellow (FGA)
Diamond Member (DGA)
Corporate Member

QUALIFICATION/EXAMINATIONS
Foundation Certificate in Gemmology
Diploma in Gemmology
Gem Diamond Diploma

DESIGNATORY LETTERS
FGA, DGA

THE NATIONAL ASSOCIATION OF GOLDSMITHS

78A Luke Street
London EC2A 4XG
Tel: 020 7613 4445
Fax: 020 7613 4450
E-mail: nag@jewellers-online.org
Website: www.jewellers-online.org

The NAG, established in 1894, serves and supports the jewellery industry of Great Britain and Ireland. We promote high professional standards among our members, who must adhere to a code of professional practice. In return, we offer them advice, support and CPD in the form of distance learning courses, seminars and tutorials.

MEMBERSHIP
Alumni Member
Allied Member
Affiliate Member
Ordinary Member

QUALIFICATION/EXAMINATIONS
Professional Jewellers' Diploma
Professional Jewellers' Gemstone Diploma
Professional Jewellers' Management Diploma
Professional Jewellers' Valuation Diploma

GENEALOGY

Membership of Professional Institutions and Associations

SOCIETY OF GENEALOGISTS

14 Charterhouse Buildings
Goswell Road
London EC1M 7BA
Tel: 020 7251 8799
Fax: 020 7250 1800
E-mail: info@sog.org.uk
Website: www.sog.org.uk

The Society (founded 1911) is the National Library and Education Centre for Family History. A registered educational charity, it was founded to encourage and foster the study, science and knowledge of genealogy. This it does chiefly through its library, publications and extensive education programme of courses and events. It currently does not hold exams.

MEMBERSHIP
Member
Fellow (FSG)
Honorary Fellow (FSG Hon)

DESIGNATORY LETTERS
FSG, FSG Hon

THE HERALDRY SOCIETY

PO Box 772
Guildford GU3 3ZX
Tel: 01438 237373
Fax: 01483 237375
Website: www.theheraldrysociety.com

The Heraldry Society is a registered charity that aims to encourage interest in heraldry through publications, lectures, visits and related activities. Members receive *The Heraldry Gazette*, which contains heraldic news and comment, and Society information quarterly. We maintain contact with heraldic societies in many parts of the UK and abroad.

MEMBERSHIP
Associate Member
Ordinary Member
Fellow (FHS)
Honorary Fellow (Hon FHS)
Institutional Member

QUALIFICATION/EXAMINATIONS
Elementary Certificate
Intermediate Certificate
Advanced Certificate
Diploma (DipHS)

DESIGNATORY LETTERS
FHS, Hon FHS

THE INSTITUTE OF HERALDIC AND GENEALOGICAL STUDIES

79–82 Northgate
Canterbury
Kent CT1 1BA
Tel: 01227 768664
Fax: 01227 765617
E-mail: registrar@ihgs.ac.uk
Website: www.ihgs.ac.uk

The IHGS, founded in 1961, is an independent educational charitable trust that offers a wide range of courses on family history, heraldry and related historical subjects, and has an extensive library, archive and research facilities. We also publish a monthly e-mail newsletter and a quarterly journal, *Family History*.

MEMBERSHIP
Associate Member
Graduate Member
Licentiate (LHG)
Fellow (FHG)

QUALIFICATION/EXAMINATIONS
Correspondence Course in Genealogy
Higher Certificate in Genealogy
Diploma in Genealogy

DESIGNATORY LETTERS
LHG, FHG

GEOGRAPHY

Membership of Professional Institutions and Associations

ROYAL GEOGRAPHICAL SOCIETY (WITH THE INSTITUTE OF BRITISH GEOGRAPHERS)

1 Kensington Gore
London SW7 2AR
Tel: 020 7591 3000
Fax: 020 7591 3001
E-mail: info@rgs.org
Website: www.rgs.org

The RGS-IBG is the learned society and professional body for geography. We aim to foster an understanding and informed enjoyment of our world: developing, supporting and promoting geographical research, expeditions and fieldwork, education, public engagement, and providing geography input to policy.

MEMBERSHIP
Young Geographer
Member
Postgraduate Fellow
Fellow
Chartered Geographer (CGeog)
Corporate Member

DESIGNATORY LETTERS
FRGS, CGeog

GEOLOGY

Membership of Professional Institutions and Associations

THE GEOLOGICAL SOCIETY

Burlington House
Piccadilly
London W1J 0BG
Tel: 020 7434 9944
Fax: 020 7439 8975
E-mail: enquiries@geolsoc.org.uk
Website: www.geolsoc.org.uk

The Geological Society, founded in 1807, is the UK's national organization for professional Earth scientists. The normal grade of membership is Fellow. Students may become Candidate Fellows. Members of the public not eligible for any other status may join as Friends.

MEMBERSHIP
Friend
Candidate Fellow
Fellow
Chartered Geologist

DESIGNATORY LETTERS
FGS, CGeol

GLASS TECHNOLOGY

Membership of Professional Institutions and Associations

BRITISH SOCIETY OF SCIENTIFIC GLASSBLOWERS

Unit W1, MK2 Business Centre
Barton Road
Bletchley
Milton Keynes
Buckinghamshire MK2 3HU
Tel: 01908 821191
Fax: 01908 821195
E-mail: bssg@biochemglass.co.uk
Website: www.bssg.co.uk

The Society was founded in 1960 for the benefit of those engaged in Scientific Glassblowing and its associated professions, and to uphold and further the status of Scientific Glassblowers. We welcome written submissions to our quarterly journal, which is circulated to members.

MEMBERSHIP
Associate
Student Member
Craft Member
Full Member
Master
Honorary Member
Retired Member
Overseas Member

SOCIETY OF GLASS TECHNOLOGY

Unit 9
Twelve O'clock Court
21 Attercliffe Road
Sheffield
South Yorkshire S4 7WW
Tel: 01142 634455
Fax: 01142 634411
E-mail: info@sgt.org
Website: www.sgt.org

The objects of the Society of Glass Technology are to encourage and advance the study of the history, art, science, design, manufacture, after treatment, distribution and end use of glass of any and every kind.

MEMBERSHIP
Personal Member
Fellow (FSGT)
Fellow Emeritus
Honorary Fellow (HonFSGT)
Corporate Member

QUALIFICATION/EXAMINATIONS
Peer review by the Board of Fellows

DESIGNATORY LETTERS
FSGT, HonFSGT

HAIRDRESSING

Membership of Professional Institutions and Associations

HABIA

Oxford House
Sixth Avenue
Sky Business Park, Robin Hood Airport
Doncaster
South Yorkshire DN9 3GG
Tel: 0845 2 306080
Fax: 01302 774949
E-mail: info@habia.org
Website: www.habia.org

Habia is the government-appointed standards-setting body for hair, beauty, nails, spa therapy, barbering and African type hair, and creates the standards that form the basis of all qualifications, including NVQs, SVQs, apprenticeships, diplomas and foundation degrees, as well as industry codes of practice.

THE GUILD OF HAIRDRESSERS

Archway House
Barnsley S71 1AQ
Tel: 01226 786555
Fax: 01226 786555

The Guild of Hairdressers dates back to 1340, when it was part of the Guild of Barbers and Surgeons. Then in the late 16th century, when the surgeons split off, it became the Guild of Hairdressers, Wigmakers and Perfumers. Today it still exists for the benefit of its members, who adhere to a code of ethics and to whom it provides help and advice.

HEALTH AND HEALTH SERVICES

Membership of Professional Institutions and Associations

BRITISH OCCUPATIONAL HYGIENE SOCIETY – FACULTY OF OCCUPATIONAL HYGIENE

5/6 Melbourne Business Court
Millennium Way
Pride Park
Derby DE24 8LZ
Tel: 01332 298101
Fax: 01332 298099
E-mail: admin@bohs.org
Website: www.bohs.org

The BOHS promotes public and professional awareness, good practice and high standards to help reduce work-related ill-health. The Faculty is our professional arm and examining board, and administers examinations and awards qualifications in Occupational Hygiene and allied subjects.

MEMBERSHIP
Individual
Student
Affiliate
Retired
Licentiate (LFOH)
Member (MFOH)
Specialist Member (MFOH(S))
Fellow (FFOH)

QUALIFICATION/EXAMINATIONS
A range of UK and international qualifications in occupational hygiene and related subjects, which include stand-alone modules covering general principles and practical applications at the technician level, through to BOHS's own professional level Certificate and Diploma qualifications.
The Occupational Hygiene Modules are aimed at those who want to gain a qualification in a particular topic of occupational hygiene to demonstrate technical expertise in that area or, grouped together, to gain exemption from the Faculty's professional level Certificate Core examination.
The International Occupational Hygiene Modules are based on the Occupational Hygiene Modules, without specific reference to UK or other legislation.
The Proficiency Modules cover both theory and practical training in a specific subject, and are aimed at those needing to demonstrate a level of proficiency to carry out the area of work covered by the Module.
Our professional qualifications are as follows: The Certificate of Competence in an individual subject is for candidates wanting to establish their competence in a specific field, and follows on from successful completion of one of the Occupational Hygiene Modules. This is an oral examination, supported by submission of a written report. The Certificate of Operational Competence in Occupational Hygiene is the entry level qualification required to join the Faculty of Occupational Hygiene as a Licentiate, and demonstrates knowledge and competence in the broad principles and practice of occupational hygiene. This is a two-part written and oral examination. The Diploma of Professional Competence in Occupational Hygiene is the highest professional occupational hygiene qualification. Candidates must already hold the Certificate of Operational Competence, and be able to demonstrate five years' experience in the field of occupational hygiene. Award of the Diploma qualifies the holder to become a Member of the Faculty, and demonstrates knowledge of, and competence in, assessment of health hazards and the extent of risk in various workplace circumstances, and an ability to advise on suitable control procedures. This is also a two-part, written and oral, examination.
For further information see; www.bohs.org/education/examinations/

DESIGNATORY LETTERS
LFOH, MFOH, FFOH, MFOH(S)

CHARTERED INSTITUTE OF ENVIRONMENTAL HEALTH

Chadwick Court
15 Hatfields
London SE1 8DJ
Tel: 020 7827 5800
Fax: 020 7827 5832
E-mail: customerservices@cieh.org
Website: www.cieh.org

The CIEH is a professional, awarding and campaigning body at the forefront of environmental and public health and safety.

MEMBERSHIP
Student member
Associate
Accredited Associate
Graduate Member
Fellow

QUALIFICATION/EXAMINATIONS

The CIEH offers a range of QCA-accredited qualifications at four levels in health and safety, food safety and environmental protection.

ERGONOMICS SOCIETY

Elms Court
Elms Grove
Loughborough
Leicestershire LE11 1RG
Tel: 01509 234904
Fax: 01509 235666
E-mail: ergsoc@ergonomics.org.uk
Website: www.ergonomics.org.uk

The Ergonomics Society, founded in 1949, is a UK-based professional society for ergonomists worldwide. We encourage and maintain high standards of professional practice through education, accreditation and development, promote the interests of our members across government, academia, business and industry, and raise awareness of ergonomics in general.

MEMBERSHIP

Student Member
Associate Member
Graduate Member
Registered Member (MErgS)
Fellow (FErgS)

INSTITUTE OF HEALTH PROMOTION AND EDUCATION

c/o Helen Draper
School of Dentistry, University of Manchester
Coupland 3, Oxford Road
Manchester M13 9PL
Tel: 01612 756610
Fax: 01612 756299
E-mail: honsec@ihpe.org.uk
Website: www.ihpe.org.uk

The IHPE was established 40 years ago to bring together professionals with a common interest in health education and promotion to share their experience, ideas and information. Our members come from a diverse range of backgrounds, including nursing, midwifery, health visiting, medicine, dentistry, public health, stress management, psychology and teaching.

MEMBERSHIP

Student Member
Associate Member (AIHPE)
Full Member (MIHPE)
Fellow (FIHPE)
Corporate Member

DESIGNATORY LETTERS

MIHPE, AIHPE, FIHPE

INSTITUTE OF HEALTH RECORDS AND INFORMATION MANAGEMENT

744a Manchester Road
Rochdale
Lancashire OL11 3AQ
Tel: 01706 868481
Fax: 01706 868481
E-mail: ihrim@zen.co.uk
Website: www.ihrim.co.uk

IHRIM was founded in 1948, primarily as an educational body, to provide qualifications as well as career and professional assistance to members. We encourage professionalism and high standards among our members who work in the fields of health records, information management, clinical coding and information governance.

MEMBERSHIP
Student
Affiliate
Licentiate
Certificated Member (CHRIM)
Accredited Clinical Coder (ACC)
Associate (AHRIM)
Fellow (FHRIM)
Corporate Affiliate

QUALIFICATION/EXAMINATIONS
Certificate of Technical Competence
Foundation exam
Certificate
Diploma
National Clinical Coding Qualification

DESIGNATORY LETTERS
CHRIM, ACC, AHRIM, FHRIM

INSTITUTE OF HEALTHCARE ENGINEERING AND ESTATE MANAGEMENT

2 Abingdon House
Cumberland Business Centre
Northumberland Road
Portsmouth PO5 1DS
Tel: 023 92 823186
Fax: 023 92 815927
E-mail: office@iheem.org.uk
Website: www.iheem.org.uk

IHEEM is the learned society and professional body for those working in the Healthcare Estates sector. Our members are architects, builders, engineers, estate managers, surveyors, medical engineers and other related professionals. We provide benefits to members to keep them up to date with developing technology and changing regulations.

MEMBERSHIP
Graduate (GIHEEM)
Associate Member (AMIHEEM)
Member (MIHEEM)
Fellow (FIHEEM)

DESIGNATORY LETTERS
GIHEEM, AMIHEEM, MIHEEM, FIHEEM

INSTITUTE OF HEALTHCARE MANAGEMENT

18–21 Morely Street
London SE1 7QZ
Tel: 020 7620 1030
Fax: 020 7620 1040
E-mail: enquiries@ihm.org.uk
Website: www.ihm.org.uk

The IHM is the professional organization for managers throughout healthcare, including the NHS, independent providers, healthcare consultants and the armed forces. Our focus is on improving patient/user care by publishing standards of management practice, promoting the IHM Code (which covers behavioural and ethical aspects of management practice) and establishing a CPD framework for our members.

MEMBERSHIP
Associate Member
Full Member (MIHM)
Fellow (FIHM)
Companion (CIHM)

QUALIFICATION/EXAMINATIONS
Certificate in Health Management Studies (CertHMS)
Certificate in Health Services Management (CertHSM)
Certificate in Managing Health Services (CertMHS)
Certificate in Managing Health & Social Care (CertMHSC)
Diploma in Health Services Management (DipHSM)

DESIGNATORY LETTERS
MIHM, FIHM, CIHM

THE ROYAL SOCIETY FOR PUBLIC HEALTH

3rd Floor
Market Towers
1 Nine Elms Lane
London SW8 5NQ
Tel: 020 3177 1600
Fax: 020 3177 1601
E-mail: info@rsph.org.uk
Website: www.rsph.org.uk

The RSPH was formed in October 2008 by the merger of the Royal Society for the Promotion of Health (RSPH/RSH) and the Royal Institute of Public Health (RIPH). We offer a wide range of vocationally related qualifications in the fields of food safety and nutrition, hygiene, health and safety, pest control, health promotion and the built environment.

MEMBERSHIP
Associate (ARSPH)
Licentiate (LRSPH)
Member (MRSPH)
Fellow (FRSPH)

QUALIFICATION/EXAMINATIONS
Please see the RSPH's website.

DESIGNATORY LETTERS
ARSPH, LRSPH, MRSPH, FRSPH

HORSES AND HORSE RIDING

Membership of Professional Institutions and Associations

THE BRITISH HORSE SOCIETY

Contact: Equestrian Qualifications GB Limited
c/o The British Horse Society
Abbey Park
Kenilworth
Warwickshir CV8 2XZ
Tel: 01926 707700
E-mail: exams@bhs.org.uk
Website: www.bhs.org.uk

The British Horse Society offers vocational and work-based examinations for grooms, stable managers, riding instructors and coaches. Founded in 1947, the BHS exams system is world renowned as credible and rigorous, producing competent, practical people who follow safe practices. We also offer competency certificates for the recreational rider.

MEMBERSHIP
Individual Member
Trade Member
Corporate Member

QUALIFICATION/EXAMINATIONS
Equestrian Qualifications GB Limited awards examinations and qualifications for grooms, stable managers, riding instructors and coaches on behalf of The British Horse Society and British Equestrian Federation. Please see the BHS's website, www.bhs.org.uk, for details.

HOUSING

Membership of Professional Institutions and Associations

THE CHARTERED INSTITUTE OF HOUSING

Octavia House
Westwood Way
Coventry CV4 8JP
Tel: 02476 851700
Fax: 02476 695110
E-mail: customer.services@cih.org
Website: www.cih.org

The CIH is the professional body for people involved in housing and communities. We are a registered charity and not-for-profit organisation. We have a diverse and growing membership of over 22,000 people – both in the public and private sectors – living and working in over 20 countries on five continents across the world.

MEMBERSHIP
Student
Affiliate
Housing Practitioner (Cert. CIH)
Associate Member (ACIH)
Corporate Member (MCIH)
Fellow Member (FCIH)

CIH has recently undertaken a fundamental review of membership. Proposals include reducing the number of grades to two – CIH Member and CIH Chartered Member. It is hoped that the changes will be introduced in 2011. Visit www.cih.org to find out about changes to CIH membership.

QUALIFICATION/EXAMINATIONS

Certificate Courses

The CIH offers a range of Certificated courses at Levels 2, 3 and 4 delivered at various centres across the UK. They are also available by distance learning. We also offer, jointly with the Chartered Institute of Building (CIOB), a suite of Certificated courses in repairs and maintenance, also at Levels 2, 3 and 4.

Professional Qualifications

The CIH Professional Qualification can be achieved at either undergraduate or postgraduate level, FT or PT.

Please see the CIH's website for details.

DESIGNATORY LETTERS

Currently: Cert. CIH, ACIH, MCIH, FCIH (The membership changes mentioned above will also affect the designatory letters for all grades of membership)

INDEXING

Membership of Professional Institutions and Associations

SOCIETY OF INDEXERS

Woodbourn Business Centre
10 Jessell Street
Sheffield S9 3HY
Tel: 01142 449561
E-mail: admin@indexers.org.uk
Website: www.indexers.org.uk

The Society of Indexers is the professional body for indexing in the UK and Ireland, and exists to promote indexing, the quality of indexes and the profession of indexing. We offer information to publishers and other organizations on commissioning indexes and our online directory 'Indexers Available' provides an up-to-date guide to indexers currently working in a wide range of fields.

MEMBERSHIP

Student Member
Member
Professional Member (MSocInd)
Advanced Professional Member (MSocInd(Adv))
Fellow (FSocInd)
Corporate Member

QUALIFICATION/EXAMINATIONS

Training in Indexing course
Advanced Test
Fellowship index submission

DESIGNATORY LETTERS

MSocInd, MSocInd(Adv), FSocInd

INDUSTRIAL SAFETY

Membership of Professional Institutions and Associations

BRITISH SAFETY COUNCIL

70 Chancellors Road
London W6 9RS
Tel: 020 8741 1231
Fax: 020 8741 4555
E-mail: mail@britsafe.org
Website: www.britsafe.org

The BSC is one of the world's leading health and safety organizations. Our mission is to keep people healthy and safe at work. Our range of charitable initiatives, such as free health and safety qualifications for school children, is supported by a broad mix of commercial activities centred on membership, training, auditing and qualifications.

MEMBERSHIP
UK Member
International Member

QUALIFICATION/EXAMINATIONS
Certificate in Process Safety
Certificate in COSHH Risk Assessment (Level 2)
Certificate in DSE Risk Assessment (Level 2)
Certificate in Fire Risk Assessment (Level 2)
Certificate in Manual Handling Risk Assessment (Level 2)
Certificate in Risk Assessment (Level 2)
Certificate in Supervising Staff Safely (Level 2)
Certificate in Occupational Health and Safety (Level 3)
Diploma in Occupational Health and Safety (Level 6)
Diploma in Environmental Management (DipEM)
International Certificate in Occupational Health and Safety
International Diploma in Environmental Management
International Diploma in Occupational Health and Safety

HEALTH & SAFETY EXECUTIVE APPROVED MINING QUALIFICATIONS

Mining Qualifications, The Health & Safety Executive
3rd Floor, Edgar Allen House
241 Glossop Road
Sheffield
South Yorkshire S10 2GW
Tel: 0114 291 2394
Fax: 0114 291 2399
E-mail: sarah.johnson@hse.gsi.gov.uk
Website: www.hse.gov.uk/mining

The HSE issues First and Second Class Qualification of Competency certificates as required under the Management and Administration of Safety and Health at Mines Regulations (MASHAM) 1993 for the appointment of a manager and undermanager, respectively, in mines of coal, shale and fireclay in the UK. It also issues certificates to Mining Mechanical and Mining Electrical Engineers and Mechanics, Electricians Class I and Class II, and the Mines Surveyor and Deputy Mines Surveyor. For details see; www.hse.gov.uk/mining

INTERNATIONAL INSTITUTE OF RISK AND SAFETY MANAGEMENT

Suite 7a
77 Fulham Palace Road
London W6 8JA
Tel: 020 8741 9100
Fax: 020 8741 1349
E-mail: info@iirsm.org
Website: www.iirsm.org

The IIRSM is a professional body for health & safety practitioners and specialists in associated professions. Our aim is to advance professional standards in accident prevention and occupational health throughout the world. We have more than 8,100 members, in the UK and over 70 other countries, to whom we provide support and offer advice via a technical helpline.

MEMBERSHIP
Student
Affiliate
Associate (AIIRSM)
Member (MIIRSM)
Specialist Member (SIIRSM)
Fellow (FIIRSM)

DESIGNATORY LETTERS
AIIRSM, MIIRSM, SIIRSM, FIIRSM

NEBOSH (THE NATIONAL EXAMINATION BOARD IN OCCUPATIONAL SAFETY AND HEALTH)

Dominus Way
Meridian Business Park
Leicester LE19 1QW
Tel: 0116 263 4700
Fax: 0116 282 4000
E-mail: info@nebosh.org.uk
Website: www.nebosh.org.uk

NEBOSH offers globally recognized qualifications designed to meet the health, safety, environmental and risk management needs of all places of work. Courses leading to NEBOSH qualifications attract over 30,000 candidates annually in nearly 80 countries around the world. NEBOSH also offers qualifications in Oil and Gas, and Health and Well-being.

MEMBERSHIP
NEBOSH's National General Certificate, National Certificate in Fire Safety and Risk Management, National Certificate in Construction Health and Safety, and the International General Certificate are all accepted as meeting the academic requirements to apply for Technician Membership (Tech IOSH) of the Institution of Occupational Safety and Health (IOSH), and Associate Membership (AIIRSM) of the International Institute of Risk and Safety Management (IIRSM).

NEBOSH's National Diploma and International Diploma are accepted as meeting the requirements to apply for Graduate Membership (Grad IOSH) of the Institution of Occupational Safety and Health (IOSH). Diplomates may also apply to become full Members (MIIRSM) of the International Institute of Risk and Safety Management (IIRSM). The National Diploma provides a sound basis for progression to MSc level: a number of UK universities offer MSc programmes that accept the National Diploma as a full or partial entry requirement.

The NEBOSH Environmental Diploma fulfils the academic requirements for both Associate Membership (AIEMA) of the Institute of Environmental Management and Assessment (IEMA) and Associate Membership (AIIRSM) of the International Institute of Risk and Safety Management (IIRSM).

QUALIFICATION/EXAMINATIONS

Award in Health and Safety at Work

National Certificate in Construction Health and Safety (Level 3)

National Certificate in Environmental Management

National Certificate in Fire Safety and Risk Management (Level 3)

NEBOSH National General Certificate in Occupational Health and Safety (Level 3)

International General Certificate in Occupational Health and Safety

NEBOSH International Technical Certificate in Oil and Gas Operational Safety

NEBOSH National Certificate in the Management of Health and Well-being at Work

NEBOSH International Certificate in Construction Health and Safety

NEBOSH National Diploma in Environmental Management (Level 6) (EnvDipNEBOSH)

NEBOSH National Diploma in Occupational Health and Safety (Level 6) (DipNEBOSH)

International Diploma in Occupational Health and Safety (IDipNEBOSH)

THE INSTITUTION OF OCCUPATIONAL SAFETY AND HEALTH

The Grange
Highfield Drive
Wigston
Leicestershire LE18 1NN
Tel: 0116 257 3100
Fax: 0116 257 3101
E-mail: membership@iosh.co.uk
Website: www.iosh.co.uk

IOSH is the world's largest organization for health and safety professionals, with more than 36,000 members worldwide, including 13,000 Chartered Safety and Health Practitioners. The Institution was founded in 1945 and is an independent, not-for-profit organization that sets professional standards, supports and develops members, and provides authoritative advice and guidance on health and safety issues.

MEMBERSHIP

Affiliate Member

Technician Member (Tech IOSH)

Graduate Member (Grad IOSH)

Chartered Member (CMIOSH)

Chartered Fellow (CFIOSH)

DESIGNATORY LETTERS

Tech IOSH, Grad IOSH, CMIOSH, CFIOSH

INSURANCE AND ACTUARIAL WORK

Membership of Professional Institutions and Associations

ASSOCIATION OF AVERAGE ADJUSTERS

Secretariat: The Baltic Exchange
St Mary Axe
London EC3A 8BH
Tel: 020 7623 5501
Fax: 020 7369 1623
E-mail: aaa@balticexchange.com
Website: www.average-adjusters.com

The AAA was founded in 1869 to promote correct principles in the adjustment of marine insurance claims and general average, uniformity of practice among average adjusters and the maintenance of good professional conduct. It ensures the independence and impartiality of its members by imposing a strict code of conduct and has close links with other international associations and insurance markets.

MEMBERSHIP
Subscriber
Associate
Fellow

QUALIFICATION/EXAMINATIONS
The Association's examination consists of 6 modules. Passes in Modules 1 & 2 are required for Associateship, passes in Modules 3–6 for Fellowship. For details see the Association's website.

THE CHARTERED INSTITUTE OF LOSS ADJUSTERS

Warwick House
65/66 Queen Street
London EC4R 1EB
Tel: 020 7337 9960
Fax: 020 7929 3082
E-mail: info@cila.co.uk
Website: www.cila.co.uk

The CILA, which was founded in 1941, is the professional body representing the claims specialists who investigate, negotiate and agree the conclusion of insurance and other claims on behalf of insurers and policyholders. We safeguard the interests of our members and maintain the high standards of the profession by requiring them to abide by our code of professional conduct.

MEMBERSHIP
Student Member
Ordinary Member
Associate (ACILA)
Fellow (FCILA)
Honorary Member

QUALIFICATION/EXAMINATIONS
CILA examination

DESIGNATORY LETTERS
ACILA, FCILA

THE CHARTERED INSURANCE INSTITUTE

42–48 High Road
South Woodford
London E18 2JP
Tel: 020 8989 8464
Fax: 020 8530 3052
E-mail: customer.serv@cii.co.uk
Website: www.cii.co.uk

The CII is the premier professional body for those working in the insurance and financial services industry. We are dedicated to promoting higher standards of competence and integrity through the provision of relevant qualifications for employees at all levels across all sectors of the industry.

MEMBERSHIP
Ordinary Member
Qualified Member
Associate Member (ACII)
Fellow (FCII)

QUALIFICATION/EXAMINATIONS
Award in Financial Planning
Award in Insurance
Certificate in Equity Release
Certificate in Financial Administration
Certificate in Financial Planning
Certificate in Insurance

Certificate in Life and Pensions
Certificate in Mortgage Advice
Diploma in Financial Planning
Diploma in Insurance
Advanced Diploma in Financial Planning
Advanced Diploma in Insurance
MSc in Insurance and Risk Planning (in association with Cass Business School)

DESIGNATORY LETTERS
ACII, FCII

THE FACULTY AND INSTITUTE OF ACTUARIES

Faculty of Actuaries
Maclaurin House
18 Dublin Street
Edinburgh EH1 3PP
Tel: 0131 240 1313
E-mail: faculty@actuaries.org.uk
Website: www.actuaries.org.uk

Napier House
4 Worcester Street
Oxford OX1 2AW
Tel: 01865 268211
E-mail: institute@actuaries.org.uk

Institute of Actuaries
Staple Inn Hall
High Holborn
London WC1V 7QJ
Tel: 020 7632 2111
E-mail: institute@actuaries.org.uk

Actuaries are experts in assessing the financial impact of tomorrow's uncertain events. They enable financial decisions to be made with more confidence by analysing the past, modelling the future, assessing the risks involved, and communicating what the results mean in financial terms.

MEMBERSHIP
Student Member
Affiliate Member
Associate (AFA or AIA)
Fellow (FFA or FIA)
Honorary Fellow

QUALIFICATION/EXAMINATIONS
Certificate in Financial Mathematics

DESIGNATORY LETTERS
AFA, AIA, FFA, FIA

JOURNALISM

Membership of Professional Institutions and Associations

NATIONAL COUNCIL FOR THE TRAINING OF JOURNALISTS

NCTJ Training Ltd
The New Granary
Newport
Saffron Walden
Essex CB11 3PL
Tel: 01799 544014
Fax: 01799 544015
E-mail: info@nctj.com
Website: www.nctj.com

The NCTJ provides a range of journalism training products and services in the UK, including: accredited courses; qualifications and examinations; awards; careers information; distance learning; short courses and CPD; information and research; publications and events. We play an influential role in all areas of journalism education and training.

QUALIFICATION/EXAMINATIONS
Certificate in Journalism
National Certificate Examination (NCE) for Press photographers and photo-journalists
National Certificate Examination (NCE) for Reporters
National Certificate Examination (NCE) for Sub-editors
National Certificate Examination (NCE) for Sports Reporters

THE CHARTERED INSTITUTE OF JOURNALISTS

2 Dock Offices
Surrey Quays Road
London SE16 2XU
Tel: 020 7252 1187
Fax: 020 7232 2302
E-mail: memberservices@cioj.co.uk
Website: www.cioj.co.uk

The CIoJ, which dates back to 1884, is a professional body and trade union for journalists. We expect our members to uphold high standards in the way they work and to adhere to a strict code of conduct, and in return we champion journalistic freedom, protect their interests in the workplace and campaign for better working conditions.

MEMBERSHIP
Student Member
Affiliate Member
Trainee Member
Full Member
International Member

LAND AND PROPERTY

Membership of Professional Institutions and Associations

RICS (ROYAL INSTITUTION OF CHARTERED SURVEYORS)

Parliament Square
London SW1P 3AD
Tel: 0870 333 1600
Fax: 020 7334 3811
E-mail: contactrics@rics.org
Website: www.rics.org/careers

RICS, an independent, not-for-profit organization, has around 100,000 qualified members and more than 50,000 students and trainees in some 140 countries, and provides the world's leading professional qualification in land, property, construction and associated environmental issues. We accredit over 600 courses at leading universities worldwide and provide impartial, authoritative advice on key issues for business, society and governments.

MEMBERSHIP
Student
Associate (AssocRICS)
Member (MRICS)
Fellow (FRICS)

DESIGNATORY LETTERS
AssocRICS, MRICS, FRICS

THE COLLEGE OF ESTATE MANAGEMENT

Whiteknights
Reading
Berkshire RG6 6AW
Tel: 0118 921 4696
Fax: 01189 921 4620
E-mail: courses@cem.ac.uk
Website: www.cem.ac.uk

CEM is dedicated to helping professionals working in the property and construction industries achieve career success through supported distance learning. We cover almost every conceivable aspect of real estate and the built environment at diploma, undergraduate and postgraduate level. Courses are accredited by a range of professional bodies.

QUALIFICATION/EXAMINATIONS
Diploma in Construction Practice
Diploma in Shopping Centre Management
Diploma in Surveying Practice
BSC in Building Services Quantity Surveying
BSc in Building Surveying
BSc in Construction Management
BSC in Estate Management
BSc in Property Management
BSc in Quantity Surveying
Graduate Development Programme
Graduate Development Programme (Construction Management Route)
MBA in Construction and Real Estate
MSc in Real Estate
Postgraduate Diploma in Adjudication
Postgraduate Dipoma in Arbitration
Postgraduate Diploma in Project Management
Postgraduate Diploma/MSc in Conservation of the Historic Environment
Postgraduate Diploma/MSc in Facilities Management
Postgraduate Diploma/MSc in Property Investment
RICS Professional Membership Graduate Route – Adaptation 1

THE INSTITUTE OF REVENUES, RATING AND VALUATION

41 Doughty Street
London WC1N 2LF
Tel: 020 7831 3505
Fax: 020 7831 2048
Website: www.irrv.org.uk

The Institute offers professional and technical qualifications for all those whose professional work is concerned with local authority revenues and benefits, valuation for rating, property taxation and the appeals procedure. Our qualifications are widely recognized throughout the profession.

MEMBERSHIP
Student Member
Affiliate Member
Graduate Member
Technician Member (Tech IRRV)
Diploma Member (Dip IRRV)
Honours Member (IRRV Hons)
Honorary Member
Fellow (FIRRV)

QUALIFICATION/EXAMINATIONS
Level 3 Certificate
NVQ Level 3/SVQ Level 3
Diploma
Honours

DESIGNATORY LETTERS
Tech IRRV, IRRV (Dip), IRRV (Hons), FIRRV

THE NATIONAL FEDERATION OF PROPERTY PROFESSIONALS

Arbon House
6 Tournament Court
Edgehill Drive
Warwick CV34 6LG
Tel: 01926 417794
Fax: 01926 417789
E-mail: quals@nfopp.co.uk
Website: www.nfopp.co.uk

The NFOPP Awarding Body is committed to raising standards within agency through the provision of accredited, nationally recognized qualifications. We are recognized by the Qualifications and Examinations Regulator (Ofqual) and have to follow strict guidelines and maintain quality standards in the provision of all our qualifications.

MEMBERSHIP
For membership details of the following organizations please refer to the relevant website:
APIP; www.apip.co.uk
ARLA; www.arla.co.uk
ICBA; www.icba.uk.com
NAEA; www.naea.co.uk
NAVA; www.nava.org.uk

QUALIFICATION/EXAMINATIONS
Technical Award in Commercial Property Agency (Level 3)
Technical Award in Real Property Auctioneering (Level 3)
Technical Award in Residential Letting and Property Management (Level 3)
Technical Award in Sale of Residential Property (Level 3)
Diploma in Commercial Property Agency (DipCPA) (Level 5)
Diploma in Commercial Property Agency (DipREA) (Level 5)
Diploma in Residential Letting and Management (DipRLM) (Level 5)

THE PROPERTY CONSULTANTS SOCIETY

Basement Office
Surrey Court
1 Surrey Street
Arundel
West Sussex BN18 9DT
Tel: 01903 883787
E-mail: info@propertyconsultantssociety.org
Website: www.propertyconsultantssociety.org

The Property Consultants Society is a non-profit-making organization that offers advice to qualified surveyors, architects, valuers, auctioneers, land and estate agents, master builders, construction engineers, accountants and members of the legal profession to help them to undertake their property consultancy in a competent, legitimate and publicly acceptable way.

MEMBERSHIP
Student (SPCS)
Licentiate (LPCS)
Associate (APCS)
Fellow (FPCS)
Honorary Member

DESIGNATORY LETTERS
SPCS, LPCS, APCS, FPCS

LANDSCAPE ARCHITECTURE

Membership of Professional Institutions and Associations

LANDSCAPE INSTITUTE

33 Great Portland Street
London W1W 8QG
Tel: 020 7299 4500
Fax: 020 7299 4501
E-mail: membership@landscapeinstitute.org
Website: www.landscapeinstitute.org

The LI is an educational charity and chartered body responsible for protecting, conserving and enhancing the natural and built environment for the benefit of the public. We champion well-designed and well-managed urban and rural landscape. Our 6,000 members include chartered landscape architects, academics and scientists working for local authorities, government agencies and in private practice, and students.

MEMBERSHIP
Student Member
Affiliate Member
Licentiate Member
Chartered Member (CMLI)
Fellow (FLI)
Academic Fellow (FLI)

QUALIFICATION/EXAMINATIONS
Pathway to Chartership oral examination conferring chartered professional status (CMLI).

DESIGNATORY LETTERS
CMLI, FLI

LANGUAGES, LINGUISTICS AND TRANSLATION

Membership of Professional Institutions and Associations

INSTITUTE OF TRANSLATION & INTERPRETING

Fortuna House
South Fifth Street
Milton Keynes MK9 2PQ
Tel: 01908 325250
Fax: 01908 325259
E-mail: info@iti.org.uk
Website: www.iti.org.uk

The Institute of Translation & Interpreting is one of the primary sources of information on these services to government, industry, the media and the general public. We promote the highest standards, providing guidance to those entering the profession and advice to those who offer language services and to their customers.

MEMBERSHIP
Student Associate
Associate
Academic
Qualified Member (MITI)
Corporate Member

QUALIFICATION/EXAMINATIONS
Applicants for qualified membership must take an exam (translators) or attend an interview (interpreters).

THE CHARTERED INSTITUTE OF LINGUISTS

Saxon House
48 Southwark Street
London SE1 1UN
Tel: 020 7940 3100
Fax: 020 7940 3101
E-mail: info@iol.org.uk
Website: www.iol.org.uk

The Chartered Institute of Linguistics, founded in 1910, is a respected language assessment and accredited awarding body, with about 6,500 members. Our aims include promoting the learning and use of modern languages, improving the status of all professional linguistics, and ensuring the maintenance of high professional standards through adherence to our code of conduct.

MEMBERSHIP
Registered Student
Associate Member (ACIL)
Member (MCIL)
Fellow (FCIL)
Chartered Linguist (CL)

QUALIFICATION/EXAMINATIONS
Certificate in Bilingual Skills (CBS)
Diploma in Public Service Interpreting (DPSI)
International Diploma in Bilingual Translation (IDBT)
Diploma in Translation (DipTrans)

DESIGNATORY LETTERS
ACIL, MCIL, FCIL, CL

THE GREEK INSTITUTE

34 Bush Hill Road
London N21 2DS
Tel: 020 8360 7968
Fax: 020 8360 7968
E-mail: info@greekinstitute.co.uk
Website: www.greekinstitute.co.uk

The Greek Institute, which was founded in 1969, is a non-profit-making cultural organization that promotes Modern Greek studies and culture through lectures, publications, literary competitions, Greek cultural evenings and the award of Certificates and a Diploma which are recognized by many UK universities as equivalent to GCSE and GCE A level Modern Greek.

MEMBERSHIP
Member
Associate (AGI)
Fellow (FGI)

QUALIFICATION/EXAMINATIONS
Certificate in Greek Conversation – Basic Stage: Levels 1 and 2
Certificate in Greek Conversation – Intermediate Stage: Levels 3 and 4
Certificate in Greek Conversation – Higher Stage: Levels 5 and 6
Preliminary Certificate
Intermediate Certificate
Advanced Certificate
Diploma in Greek Translation (DipGrTrans)

DESIGNATORY LETTERS
AGI, FGI

LAW

ENGLAND AND WALES

MAGISTRATES

Following the Constitutional Reform Act 2005, which came into force in April 2006, the Lord Chief Justice has become head of the Judiciary. He is responsible for the welfare, training and deployment of magistrates, for approving the names of the candidates recommended for appointment and for disciplinary action, short of removal. The Lord Chancellor also has responsibility for the protection for judicial independence and for working to endure that the magistracy reflects the diversity of society as a whole.

There are six key qualities that a magistrate must possess: good character, social awareness, maturity and sound temperament, sound judgement, commitment and reliability. Political views are no longer sought and considered.

Before sitting in court, magistrates must undertake some basic training which includes structured observations in court. This covers practice and procedure in court, structured decision making, sentencing etc. New magistrates are assigned a mentor for their first two years. Consolidation training takes place about 18 months to two years after appointment, followed by appraisals. Magistrates only sit in adult courts when first appointed. Having got that experience they may apply to sit in youth courts and family courts and have to undertake more training before they can sit.

JUDGES

All judicial office holders are Her Majesty's Judges, as such all appointments are made by the Queen or her Ministers. Since 2006 all candidates for judicial appointment in England and Wales have been selected by the independent Judicial Appointments Commission (JAC), which passes its recommendations to the Lord Chancellor for approval; Once the JAC's selections have been received, the actual appointments are made in slightly different ways depending on the type of post. The Lord Chancellor himself appoints Deputy District Judges and most members of tribunals. He also appoints the 30,000 unpaid magistrates (who are selected by local Advisory Committees, not by the JAC). The Queen appoints High Court and Circuit Judges, Masters, Registrars and District Judges, District Judges (Magistrates' Courts) and Recorders on the advice of the Lord Chancellor. The most senior appointments – the Lord Chief Justice and other Heads of Division, and the Lords Justices who are the judges of the Court of Appeal – are approved by the Lord Chancellor and then passed to the Queen via the Prime Minister. Scotland and Northern Ireland have their own separate court systems, with their own arrangements for appointing members of the judiciary. The Supreme Court has jurisdiction over the whole of the UK, so its Justices are not selected by the JAC, which is an England and Wales body. Rather, a special committee is set up, which is made up of the three judicial appointments bodies from around the UK (England and Wales, Scotland and Northern Ireland), who recommend a name to Ministers. The Queen appoints the Justices on the basis of advice from the Prime Minister.

Appointments to salaried or fee-paid judicial posts are made from among judges or practising lawyers. In general the requirement for appointment is that the candidate must have been a practising barrister or solicitor for 7 years (for appointment to the Circuit Bench or above) or for 5 years (appointments to the District Bench and to most tribunal posts). Certain posts are also open to legal executives, patent agents and trade mark agents of the required seniority. Candidates for appointment as Justices of the Supreme Court must be existing holders of high judicial office or must have been practising barristers or solicitors for 15 years.

OFFICERS OF THE COURT

Officers of the Court include judicial and administrative staff; the former include Masters and Registrars, the latter secretaries and clerks to the judges and the staff who administer the court service. Details are given in 'The English Legal System 2009–2010' (Routledge Cavendish). Qualifications for the judicial offices vary somewhat, but most appointments are limited to established barristers and solicitors.

THE LEGAL PROFESSION

The legal profession consists of two branches. Each performs distinct duties, although there is a degree of overlap in some aspects of their work.

Solicitors undertake all ordinary legal business for their clients (with whom they are in direct contact). They may also appear on behalf of a client in the magistrates' and county courts and in some circumstances in the Crown Court.

Barristers (known collectively as the 'Bar' and collectively and individually as 'Counsel') advise on legal problems submitted by solicitors and conduct cases in court; in the High Court advocacy may be practised only by barristers.

CORONERS

Coroners must be barristers, solicitors or legally qualified medical practitioners of not less than 5 years' standing. They are appointed by local authorities. There are approximately 110 coroners' jurisdictions in England and Wales. Coroners are independent judicial officers. When not engaged in coronal duties, coroners (apart from 'whole-time' coroners) continue in their legal or medical practices. Further information from the Coroners' Society of England and Wales, website; www.coronersociety.org.uk.

Qualification as a Barrister at the Bar of England and Wales

There are three stages that must be completed in order to qualify as a barrister. The Academic Stage consists of an undergraduate degree in law or an undergraduate degree in any other subject with a minimum of a 2ii. For those with an undergraduate degree in a subject other than law a one year conversion course (CPE/GDL) must be completed. Before commencing the Vocational Stage candidates must join one of the four Inns and then undertake the Bar Professional Training which is either one year full-time or two years part-time as well as undertaking twelve qualifying sessions. Once these have been successfully completed candidates are 'Called to the Bar' by their Inn. The Pupillage Stage consists of one year spent in an authorised pupillage training organisation.

To find out more about all three stages of qualification as a barrister visit www.barcouncil.org.uk.

Qualification as a Solicitor in England and Wales

To practise as a solicitor in England and Wales a person must have been admitted as a solicitor, his or her name having been entered on the Roll of Solicitors, and must hold a practising certificate issued by **The Solicitors Regulation Authority (SRA)**, Ipsley Court, Berrington Close, Redditch, Worcestershire B98 0TD, Tel: 0870 666 2555. The SRA is the independent regulatory body of the Law Society of England and Wales. Persons will be admitted as solicitors only if they have passed the appropriate academic and vocational course and have completed a training contract and Professional Skills Course, or have transferred from another jurisdiction or the Bar. The SRA controls the training of solicitors. Most solicitors become members of the Law Society, but membership is not compulsory. Intending solicitors other than Fellows of the Institute of Legal Executives and Justices' Clerk's Assistants, and qualified lawyers from other jurisdictions, are required to serve a period of training with a practising solicitor after they have completed the Legal Practice Course.

All new entrants to the profession are required to complete a Criminal Records Bureau standard disclosure prior to admission. A candidate who wishes to start training must enrol as a student with the SRA and satisfy them that they have successfully completed the academic stage of training and have no issues which may call their character and suitability into question.

THE COMMON PROFESSIONAL EXAM/ POSTGRADUATE DIPLOMA IN LAW

Subjects: the foundations of legal knowledge: Public Law, including Constitutional Law, Administrative Law and Human Rights, Law of the European Union, Criminal Law, Obligations including Contract, Restitution and Tort, Property Law, and Equity and the Law of Trusts.

For an up-to-date list of course providers for the CPE, visit the SRA website at www.sra.org.uk/students/conversion-courses.

THE LEGAL PRACTICE COURSE

Compulsory subjects: Litigation & Advocacy, Business Law & Practice.

Three elective subjects: from a range of Corporate Client or Private Client topics (the range of elective available can differ from institution to institution).

Pervasive subjects: Accounts, Professional Conduct and Client Care, Land Accounts, Human Rights, European Union Law, Revenue Law. These areas pervade the compulsory and elective subjects of the course.

Legal Skills: Practical legal research, writing and drafting, interviewing and advising, advocacy. These skills form an integral part of the compulsory and elective subjects.

New courses were phased in from September 2009 to September 2010. Since 2010, all courses comply with new underpinning outcomes and structural requirements, as follows: *Compulsory subjects* (called 'Stage 1'): Professional Conduct and Regulation, Wills and Administration of Estates, and Taxation; *Core Practice areas:* Business Law and Practice, Property Law and Practice, and Litigation; *Course Skills:* Practical Legal Research, Writing, Drafting, Interviewing and Advising, and Advocacy;

Three Elective subjects (called 'Stage 2'): from a range of Corporate Client or Private Client topics (the range of elective available differs from institution to institution). An up-to-date list of course providers for the LPC, in its current and new forms, is available from the SRA website at www.sra.org.uk/students/lpc.page.

TRAINING CONTRACT

The training contract to be served by all intending solicitors, other than Fellows of the Institute of Legal Executives and Justices' Clerk's Assistants is 2 years. The training contract can also be delivered on a PT basis, lasting 4 years.

The training contract can be taken following the LPC or at the same time as a PT LPC. The law graduate who holds a qualifying law degree must complete the Legal Practice Course at a recognized institution, and then serve under the training contract for 2 years. The non-law graduate must first pass the Common Professional Exam (CPE) or the Postgraduate Diploma in Law, having attended either a 1-yr FT or 2-yr PT preparatory course. He or she may then serve under the training contract for 2 years after completion of a Legal Practice Course. A Professional Skills Course must be taken prior to application for admission.

FILEX/JUSTICES' CLERKS' ASSISTANTS

Fellows of the Institute of Legal Executives and Justices' Clerk's Assistants may obtain up to 8 exemptions from the CPE by virtue of similar subjects passed in their Fellowship exams. After passing or being exempted from the CPE, the Fellow/Justices' Clerk's Assistant may be exempt from serving under a training contract following successful completion of an LPC. A Professional Skills Course must be taken prior to application for admission.

THE PROFESSIONAL SKILLS COURSE

The aim of the Professional Skills Course is to build on the foundations laid in the LPC so as to develop a trainee's professional skills. Providers of the course, trainees and their employers are encouraged to regard the course as the first stage of a trainee's lifetime professional development.

Built upon the LPC, the course provides training in three subject areas, *viz:* Financial and Business Skills; Advocacy and Communication Skills; Client Care and Professional Standards. Elective topics will also be chosen which fall within one or more of these three core areas.

All trainees have to complete all sections of the course satisfactorily before being admitted. The course consists of a minimum of 48 hours' face-to-face instruction on the core subjects and 24 hours on the elective subjects, and must be taken during the training contract. Subject to the SRA being satisfied that the syllabuses will be properly covered and that appropriate tutors and teaching material will be used, it should be possible for the course to be provided by firms in-house, or by local law societies as well as by approved teaching institutions and commercial organizations.

QUALIFIED LAWYERS FROM OTHER JURISDICTIONS

UK lawyers together with lawyers from certain foreign jurisdictions and EU lawyers can apply for admission under the Qualified Lawyers Transfer Regulations 2009.

Under the European Communities Directive No 2005/36/EC, lawyers from EU jurisdictions may apply for admission following successful completion of an aptitude test – the Qualified Lawyers Transfer Test. The test covers Property, Litigation, Professional Conduct and Accounts, and Principles of Common Law. Lawyers from other jurisdictions are required to pass such aptitude tests as well as completing at least 2 years experience in common law jurisdiction with at least 12 months practising in English and Welsh law. All transferees are required to prove their character and suitability to be a solicitor.

European lawyers can apply to be a Registered European Lawyer (REL) under the Establishment of Lawyers Directive 98/5/EC. RELs can apply for admission as a solicitor after 3 years, with an expected minimum of 2 years practice in UK law. Applications under the QLTR system will cease on 31 August 2010 as this will be superseded by the Qualified Lawyer Transfer Scheme (QLTS) on 1 September 2010 following approval by the Legal Services Board in March this year. Prospective candidates wanting more information on QLTR or QLTS can consult the website http://www.sra.org.uk/

solicitors/QLTT/qlts-faq.page for guidance, or contact the SRA on 0870 606 2555.

SCOTLAND

The Court of Session, High Courts, Sherriff Courts and Justice of the Peace Courts are administered by the Scottish Court service, an Executive Agency of the Scottish Government. For further information on Scottish Courts go to www.scotcourts.gov.uk.

THE LEGAL PROFESSION

The profession consists of **Solicitors** and **Advocates.**

Qualification as a Solicitor in Scotland

Solicitors in Scotland have their names inserted in a Roll of Solicitors and are granted annual **Certificates** entitling them to practise by **The Law Society of Scotland**, 26 Drumsheugh Gardens, Edinburgh EH3 7YR, Tel: 01312 267411 Fax: 01312 252934 E-mail: lawscot@lawscot.org.uk Website: www.lawscot.org.uk. A Certificate is granted to candidates who have passed approved exams, completed a term of practical training and been admitted as solicitors. (The Law Society will be happy to provide copies of its 'Careers Information' leaflet on request.).

THE QUALIFYING EXAMINATIONS

Scots Law (the LLB) can be studied as a first degree in ten higher education institutions in Scotland. Admission requirements to the LLB degree are high, typically four A grades and one B at Higher. The only preferred subject is English. Students with a background in science and those who have studied modern languages and/or history, geography and modern studies are equally acceptable.

At each university there are compulsory professional subjects for anybody who wishes to enter the legal profession. These subjects reflect the requirements of the syllabus for the Society's professional exams, which are detailed on the Law Society website.

An alternate route to qualifying as a solicitor in Scotland is by a combination of the Law Society's own examinations and three years pre-Diploma training. In order to be eligible to sit the Law Society's examinations, non-law graduates must find full time employment as a pre-Diploma trainee with a qualified solicitor practising in Scotland. A pre- Diploma training contract lasts for three years and during that time training must be given in the three prescribed areas of conveyancing, litigation, and either trusts and executries or the legal work of a public authority. To be eligible to enter into a pre-Diploma training contract, non-law graduates must fulfil certain educational requirements as outlined in Appendix 1 of the leaflet 'pre-Diploma training' found on the Law Society of Scotland website http://www.lawscot.org.uk/training/default.aspx. During the period of the training contract, a pre-Diploma trainee will study for the Law Society's examinations (having four years from commencement of the first examination) in which to complete eight core subjects (Public Law & the Legal System, Conveyancing, Scots Private Law I and II, Evidence, Scots Criminal Law, Taxation, European Community Law and Scots Commercial Law I and II). The two routes to qualification (degree and law society exams) merge at this point as all intending solicitors are required to complete the Diploma in Legal Practice. Upon successful completion of the Diploma the graduate will enter into a two year post-Diploma training contract with a qualified solicitor practicing in Scotland.

Please note, legal education and training in Scotland has undergone a major review, and the changes resulting from this will be implemented from 2011. The LLB will be replaced with a new 'Foundation programme', which will be offered at the same level as the LLB with the benefits of more flexibility in the programme to deliver subjects outside the professional subjects. The Diploma will be replaced by PEAT 1; that is Professional Education and Training Stage 1, incorporating a Diploma with increased choice and flexibility around electives. The introduction of PEAT 1 to replace the Diploma means that entry selection criteria and process for entry onto the PEAT 1 stage will be reviewed in due course. The Law Society of Scotland's website will continue to detail these changes as they are updated. The final stage of qualification – the 'Traineeship' will be replaced with Professional Education and Training Stage 2 from 2011, which will follow on from PEAT 1. The alternative route to qualification has also been reviewed and there is a commitment to retain it until a replacement can be found. However, it is likely that within the next few years details will emerge on how this route is to be phased out, with other flexible options for qualifying being phased in.

Qualification as an Advocate in Scotland

Barristers in Scotland are called Advocates. Scottish Advocates are not only members of the **Faculty of Advocates**, but also members of the College of Justice and officers of the Court. The procedure for the admission of Intrants is subject in part to the control of the Court and in part to the control of the Faculty; the Court is responsible for most of the formal procedures and the Faculty for the exams and periods of professional training. In order to become an Intrant, applicants must produce evidence that they hold one of the following standard of degree, a degree with Honours, Second Class (Division 2) or above, in Scottish Law at a Scottish university, or a degree in Scottish Law at a Scottish university together with a degree with Honours, Second Class (Division 2) or above, in another subject at a United Kingdom university or an ordinary degree with distinction in Scottish Law at a Scottish university. A Diploma in Legal Practice from a Scottish University is also required, although in exceptional cases this requirement may be waived. Once this evidence is provided and the relevant references obtained, a notice is posted outside Parliament House for a period of 21 days declaring the candidate's intention to present a Petition. At the end of this period the Petition is presented to the Court. After the Petition has been remitted by the Court to the Faculty, and it is signed off by the Clerk of Faculty and Dean of Faculty the candidate is considered to have **Matriculated** as an Intrant. An Intrant must also comply with the professional training required by the Faculty, wihch consists of a period of 21 months' training in a Solicitors office (in some cases 12 months). The Faculty **Exams in Legal Scholarship** are conducted on the standard known as the 'LLB standard' at the Scottish universities. Subject-for-subject exemptions are granted to Intrants who have passed exams at this standard in the course of a curriculum for a law degree at a Scottish university. Every Intrant must pass or be exempted from exams in 9 compulsory subjects and 2 optional subjects. The compulsory subjects include Roman Law of Property and Obligations, Jurisprudence, Constitutional and Administrative Law, Scottish Criminal Law, Scottish Private Law, Commercial Law and Business Institutions, Evidence, International Private Law and European Law and Institutions. In addition, and prior to the commencement of pupillage (also known as devilling) every Intrant must sit the Faculty's entrant examination in Evidence, Practice and Procedure. If successfully passed the Intrant can then commence their pupillage.

During the first 5 or 6 weeks of pupillage pupils undertake the Foundation Course. Intrants who have passed all the necessary exams and undergone the necessary professional training as well as successfully completing their pupillage may apply to be admitted to membership of the Faculty and are admitted at a public meeting of the Faculty. Once admitted to the Faculty, Intrants are introduced to the Court by the Dean of Faculty, make a Declaration of Allegiance to the Sovereign in open Court and are then admitted by the Court to the public office of Advocate. For further information on becoming an advocate contact Scott Brownidge, Secretariat Administrator, Faculty of Advocates, Parliament House, Edinburgh, EH1 1RF, Tel: 0131 260 5765.

NORTHERN IRELAND

As in England and Wales, the **superior courts** are the Court of Appeal, the High Court and the Crown Court. The latter is an exclusively criminal court. The Court of Appeal hears appeals in civil cases from the High Court and in criminal cases from the Crown Court and cases stated on a point of law from, *inter alia,* the County Court and the Magistrates' Courts. Appeals lie from the Court of Appeal to the House of Lords.

Inferior Courts: As in England and Wales, the **county courts** are principally civil courts, but in Northern Ireland they also hear appeals from conviction in the Magistrates' Courts for summary offences.

Magistrates' Courts: Magistrates' Courts deal principally with minor criminal offences (summary offences) and are presided over by Resident Magistrates (stipendiaries). Resident Magistrates are appointed by the Crown on the advice of the Lord Chancellor.

Coroners: Coroners must be barristers or solicitors of not less than 5 years standing practising in Northern Ireland.

THE LEGAL PROFESSION
The legal profession in Northern Ireland consists of barristers and solicitors belonging to professional bodies organized on similar lines to those in England and Wales.

Qualification as a Barrister in Northern Ireland

To qualify for practice as a barrister in Northern Ireland a candidate must be admitted to the degree of Barrister-at-Law by the **Honorable Society of the Inn of Court of Northern Ireland**, enquiries to Under Treasurer, Bar Council Office, Bar Library, 91 Chichester Street, Belfast BT1 3JQ, Tel: Belfast 028 9056 2349.

A candidate must be at least 21, hold a recognized law degree (the list of recognized law degrees can be found at www.qub.ac.uk/ilps) of not lower than 2nd class honours and have obtained their Certificate of Professional Legal Studies or otherwise be qualified to Call to the Bar of Northern Ireland.

Qualification as a Solicitor in Northern Ireland

The solicitors' professional body in Northern Ireland is the **Law Society of Northern Ireland**, Law Society House, 96 Victoria Street, Belfast BT1 3GN, Tel 028 9023 1614. It has overall responsibility for education and admission to the profession.

Admission to training is generally dependent upon possession of a recognised law degree from a university. Details of the recognised law degrees are available on the website of the Institute of Professional Legal Studies; www.qub.ac.uk/ips, see the Admissions section. Details are also available on the Graduate School website (see Information Booklet for Applicants; www.soc.sci.ulster.ac.uk/qsplc/info-booklet.pdf). Law graduates must attend a 2-year vocational apprenticeship course at the Institute of Professional Legal Studies, The Queen's University of Belfast, or the Graduate School of Professional Legal Education at the University of Ulster's Magee Campus after which they may be admitted as solicitors, but they are restricted from practising on their own account until they have served for 3 years as the qualified assistant of a practising solicitor.

Non-law graduates must complete a 2-year FT academic course in law at the Law Faculty at Queen's University, followed by the 2-year vocational apprenticeship course, and may then be admitted on the same conditions as indicated above.

Membership of Professional Institutions and Associations

COUNCIL FOR LICENSED CONVEYANCERS

16 Glebe Road
Chelmsford
Chelmsford
Essex CM1 1QG
Tel: 01245 349599
Fax: 01245 341300
E-mail: clc@clc-uk.org
Website: www.conveyancer.org.uk/

The CLC was established under the provisions of the Administration of Justice Act 1985 as the Regulatory Body for Licensed Conveyancers. Our purpose is to set entry standards and regulate the profession of Licensed Conveyancers effectively.

MEMBERSHIP
Student
Licensed Conveyancer
Probate Practitioner

QUALIFICATION/EXAMINATIONS
Foundation
Finals
Practical Training

THE LAW SOCIETY OF SCOTLAND

26 Drumsheugh Gardens
Edinburgh EH3 7YR
Tel: 0131 226 7411
Fax: 0131 225 2934
E-mail: lawscot@lawscot.org.uk
Website: www.lawscot.org.uk

The Law Society of Scotland is the membership organization of Scottish solicitors. We promote the interests of the profession and of the public in relation to the profession. Our services include providing initial career advice, overseeing legal education in Scotland, handling admissions to the profession, monitoring trainees, providing post-qualifying legal education, and administering courses and examinations for the Society of Law Accountants in Scotland.

MEMBERSHIP
All practising solicitors in Scotland must be members of the Society and must hold a current Practising Certificate which is issued by the Society.

QUALIFICATION/EXAMINATIONS
Please see the Law Society of Scotland's website.

INSTITUTE OF LEGAL EXECUTIVES

Kempston Manor
Kempston
Bedford MK42 7AB
Tel: 01234 841000
E-mail: info@ilex.org.uk
Website: www.ilex.org.uk

ILEX, founded in 1892, is a professional body representing around 22,000 practising and trainee legal executives (qualified lawyers who specialize in a particular area of law). Our objectives are to provide for the education, training and development of our Fellows, to advance and protect their interests, and to promote cooperation among everyone engaged in legal work.

MEMBERSHIP
Student Member
Affiliate Member
Associate Member (AInstLEX)
Graduate Member (GInstLEX)
Fellow (FInstLEX)

QUALIFICATION/EXAMINATIONS
Level 3 Certificate in Law and Practice
Level 3 Professional Diploma in Law and Practice
Level 6 Certificate in Law
Level 6 Professional Higher Diploma in Law and Practice
Graduate Fast Track Diploma (Level 6)

DESIGNATORY LETTERS
AInstLEX, GInstLEX, FInstLEX

THE ACADEMY OF EXPERTS

3 Gray's Inn Square
Gray's Inn
London WC1R 5AH
Tel: 020 7430 0333
Fax: 020 7430 0666
E-mail: admin@academy-experts.org
Website: www.academy-experts.org

The Academy of Experts is a multidisciplinary body established in 1987 to establish and promote high objective standards for those acting as expert witnesses. We act as an accrediting and professional body, offering training, technical guidance and representation. In addition we promote cost-efficient dispute resolution, maintaining a register of qualified dispute resolvers.

MEMBERSHIP
Non-Practising Subscriber
Associate Member
Associate Member (AMAE)
Full Member (MAE)
Fellow (FAE)
Practising Corporate Member
Dispute Resolver Member

QUALIFICATION/EXAMINATIONS
There are examinations for upgrade.

DESIGNATORY LETTERS
AMAE, MAE, FAE, QDR

THE INSTITUTE OF LEGAL CASHIERS AND ADMINISTRATORS (ILCA)

2nd Floor
Marlowe House
109 Station Road
Sidcup
Kent DA15 7ET
Tel: 020 8302 2867
Fax: 020 8302 7481
E-mail: info@ilca.org.uk
Website: www.ilca.org.uk

The ILCA, which was founded in 1978, is a non-profit-making professional body dedicated to the education and support of specialist financial and administrative personnel working within the legal community. We encourage the development of our members' skills through educational courses, training workshops, seminars, conferences and our bimonthly magazine, *Legal Abacus*.

MEMBERSHIP
Ordinary Member
Diploma Member (ILCA (Dip))
Associate Member (AILCA)
Fellow Member (FILCA)
Affiliated Professional Member

QUALIFICATION/EXAMINATIONS
Diploma
Associateship examination

DESIGNATORY LETTERS
ILCA (Dip), AILCA, FILCA

LEISURE AND RECREATION MANAGEMENT

Membership of Professional Institutions and Associations

INSTITUTE FOR SPORT, PARKS AND LEISURE

Abbey Business Centre
1650 Arlington Business Park
Theale
Reading RG7 4SA
Tel: 0844 418 0077
Fax: 0118 929 8001
E-mail: infocentre@ispal.org.uk
Website: www.ispal.org.uk

ISPAL is the membership body for sport, parks and leisure industry professionals. We promote high standards and provide CPD as well as a wide range of training courses to our members in-house and at venues across the UK. We also work hard to influence government policy on behalf of our members.

MEMBERSHIP
Student
Studying Member
Full Member
Retiree
Local Authority Member
Corporate Member

INSTITUTE OF GROUNDSMANSHIP

28 Stratford Office Village
Walker Avenue
Wolverton Mill East
Milton Keynes MK12 5TW
Tel: 01908 312511
Fax: 01908 311140
E-mail: iog@iog.org
Website: www.iog.org

The Institute of Groundsmanship is the only membership organization supporting the whole of the grounds care industry. Serving the industry for 75 years, we provide a range of quality products, services and events including education, training and membership services, exhibitions, local information days, an annual conference and awards programme.

MEMBERSHIP
Junior Member
Student Member
Amateur Associate
Professional Associate
Full Individual Member
Affiliate Member
Corporate Member

QUALIFICATION/EXAMINATIONS
For details see; www.iog.org/training-training-courses.asp

INSTITUTE OF SPORT AND RECREATION MANAGEMENT (ISRM)

Sir John Beckwith Centre for Sport
Loughborough University
Loughborough
Leicestershire LE11 3TU
Tel: 01509 226474
Fax: 01509 226475
E-mail: info@isrm.co.uk
Website: www.isrm.co.uk

ISRM is the only national professional body for those involved exclusively in providing, managing, operating and developing sport and recreation services in the UK. Our aim is to ensure that the benefits of sport and physical activity are delivered effectively through the professional, safe and efficient management and development of facilities and services.

MEMBERSHIP
Associate Member
Member
Diploma Member
Companion (CInstSRM)
Fellow (FInstSRM/FInstSRM(Hons))
Corporate Affiliate
Further & Higher Education Corporate Affiliate
Commercial Affiliate

QUALIFICATION/EXAMINATIONS
National Pool Plant Operators Foundation Certificate
National Spa Pool Foundation Certificate
National Spa Pool Operators Certificate
National Pool Carers Certificate (Level 2)
Operations Certificate (Level 2)
Events Management Certificate (Level 3)
Fitness Management Certificate (Level 3)
Food and Beverage Management Certificate (Level 3)
Health & Safety Management Certificate (Level 3)
National Pool Plant Operators Certificate (Level 3)
Supervisory Management Certificate (Level 3)
National Pool Lifeguard Qualification (NPLQ)
Pool Technical Management Diploma

DESIGNATORY LETTERS
CInstSRM, FInstSRM, FInstSRM(Hons)

LIBRARIANSHIP AND INFORMATION WORK

Membership of Professional Institutions and Associations

CHARTERED INSTITUTE OF LIBRARY AND INFORMATION PROFESSIONALS

7 Ridgmount Street
London WC1E 7AE
Tel: 020 7255 0500
Fax: 020 7255 0501
E-mail: quals@cilip.org.uk
Website: www.cilip.org.uk

CILIP is the professional body representing those working within libraries and the information profession in the UK.

MEMBERSHIP
Certified Affiliate (ACLIP)
Chartered Member (MCLIP)
Chartered Fellow (FCLIP)
Revalidated Chartered Member or Fellow

QUALIFICATION/EXAMINATIONS
Application for membership qualifications is through the submission of a portfolio of evidence meeting published criteria. Please contact the Institute for further information.

DESIGNATORY LETTERS
ACLIP, MCLIP, FCLIP

MANAGEMENT

Membership of Professional Institutions and Associations

ASSOCIATION FOR PROJECT MANAGEMENT

Ibis House, Regent Park
Summerleys Road
Princes Risborough
Buckinghamshire HP27 9LE
Tel: 0845 458 1944
Fax: 0845 458 8807
E-mail: info@apm.org.uk
Website: www.apm.org.uk

APM is the largest independent professional body of its kind in Europe. We have over 18,000 individual and 500 corporate members throughout the UK and abroad. Our aim is to develop and promote project management across all sectors of industry and beyond.

MEMBERSHIP
Student Member
Associate Member
Full Member (MAPM)
Fellow (FAPM)
Corporate Member

QUALIFICATION/EXAMINATIONS
Introductory Certificate in Project Management
APMP
APM Practitioner
Certified Project Manager

DESIGNATORY LETTERS
MAPM, FAPM

ASSOCIATION OF CERTIFIED COMMERCIAL DIPLOMATS

ACCD Global Headquarters
Central Administration Office
PO Box 50561
Docklands, London E16 3WY
Tel: 08445 864249
Fax: 08445 864252
E-mail: enquiries@commercialdiplomats.eu
Website: www.commercialdiplomats.eu

Association of Certified Commercial Diplomats is the first independent global professional awarding body for commercial diplomats (ie trade negotiators, policy advisers, commercial counsellors and commercial diplomacy practitioners, negotiators of investment agreements, policy-makers and government officials involved in investment issues, international investment policy experts, academia, NGO/IGO representatives and senior officials in government ministries, parastatals, corporations, public and private institutions worldwide). Its principal objectives are to provide accreditation and regulation and to advance the interests of its members as qualified, certified and competent commercial diplomats. As the global voice, ACCD has overall responsibility, including the setting of policy and guidelines, as well as the qualification and accreditation procedures for the commercial diplomacy profession. It is non-partisan, not-for-profit, independent of government and uniquely the professional regulatory body for commercial diplomats and institutions of higher learning, providing advanced postgraduate courses on commercial diplomacy.

MEMBERSHIP
Associate
Fellow

Institutional Member

QUALIFICATION/EXAMINATIONS
Advanced Certificate in Commercial Diplomacy Level 5 (ACDipl)
Advanced Certificate in Commercial Diplomacy Level 6 (ACDipl)
Master of Commercial Diplomacy (M.CDipl or M. CD)
Doctor of Commercial Diplomacy (D.CDipl or D.CD)
Qualified Certified Diplomat (QCD)
Chartered Diplomat (C. Dipl)

DESIGNATORY LETTERS
ACDipl, FCDipl, M.CDipl, M.CD, D.CDipl, D.CD, QCD, C. Dipl

AUA

AUA National Office
University of Manchester
Oxford Road
Manchester M13 9PL
Tel: 0161 275 2063
Fax: 0161 275 2036
E-mail: aua@aua.ac.uk
Website: www.aua.ac.uk

As a member-led organization with over 4,000 members, AUA promotes best practice in higher education management and exists to advance and promote professional recognition and development of those who work in higher and further education by encouraging and fostering sound methods of leadership, management and administration, through a range of professional development initiatives.

AUA members are individually and collectively committed to:

- the continuous development of their own and others' professional knowledge, skills and practices
- actively championing equality of educational and professional opportunity
- the advancement of higher education through the robust application of professional knowledge, skills and practices
- the highest standards of fair, ethical and transparent professional behaviors

AUA is at the forefront of professional development in higher education and has developed a sector-wide Framework to support the development of professional services colleagues. Through continuing professional development, individuals, teams and institutions can foster skills and behaviours associated with the profession. AUA also holds the largest professional development annual conference in the UK higher education calendar.

MEMBERSHIP
Member (MAUA)
Associate Member (AUA (A))
International Associate Member (AUA (A))
Fellow (FAUA)

QUALIFICATION/EXAMINATIONS
Postgraduate Certificate in Professional Practice (PG Cert)
This programme is validated by The Open University and credits from the course can be used on a number of MA courses.

BRITISH INSTITUTE OF FACILITIES MANAGEMENT

Number One Building
The Causeway
Bishop's Stortford
Hertfordshire CM23 2ER
Tel: 0845 058 1356
Fax: 01279 712669
E-mail: info@bifm.org.uk
Website: www.bifm.org.uk

The BIFM is the 'natural home' of facilities management (FM) in the UK. Founded in 1993, the Institute provides information, education, training and networking services for nearly 13,000 members – both individual professionals and organizations. The BIFM's mission is to advance the profession – to consolidate FM as a vital management discipline.

MEMBERSHIP
Associate
Member (MBIFM)
Certified Member (CBIFM)
Fellow (FBIFM)
Corporate Member

QUALIFICATION/EXAMINATIONS
Award in Facilities Mangement (Level 4)
Certificate in Facilities Management (Level 4)
Diploma in Facilities Management (Level 4)
Certificate in Facilities Management (Level 5)
Diploma in Facilities Management (Level 5)
Diploma in Facilities Management (Level 6)

DESIGNATORY LETTERS
MBIFM, CBIFM, FBIFM

BUSINESS MANAGEMENT ASSOCIATION

Coborn House
3 Coborn Road
Docklands
London E3 2DA
Tel: 0871 231 1689
Fax: 01920 823261
E-mail: enquiries@businessmanagement.org.uk
Website: www.businessmanagement.org.uk

The Business Management Association is a professional body for businesses owners and managers. We promote the aims and interests of the small business sector internationally, provide information and advice to our members, encourage networking between members, and seek to provide members with advanced knowledge, skill and qualifications in several aspects of management.

MEMBERSHIP
Affiliate (AffBMA)
Associate (ABMA)
Member (MBMA)
Fellow (FBMA)
Companion (CBMA)
Certified Manager (CertMgr)
Certified Master of Management (CMMgt)
Certified Master of Business Administration (CMBA)
Certified Doctor of Business Administration (CDBA)
Member Certified Business Management Accountant (MCBMA)
Fellow Certified Business Management Accountant (FCBMA)

QUALIFICATION/EXAMINATIONS
Entrepreneurs Award (EA)
Diploma In Business Management (DipBMA)

DESIGNATORY LETTERS
AffBMA, ABMA, MBMA, FBMA, CBMA, CertMgr, CMMgt, CMBA, CDBA, MCBMA, FCBMA

DIPLOMATIC ACADEMY OF EUROPE AND THE ATLANTIC

Research, Development and Training Division
ACCD Global Headquarters
Docklands
Greater London E16 3WY
Tel: 08445 857027
Fax: 08445 857077
E-mail: enquiries@eatcd.org
Website: www.commercialdiplomacy.org.uk

The Diplomatic Academy of Europe is a key professional diplomatic organisation that enjoys global reputation for excellence in advanced specialized diplomatic training. A Member of the Global Community (UN Global Compact), DAE offers complete portfolio of commercial diplomacy training, including the Commercial Diplomat Mandatory Qualifying Course and the Post-qualification Continuing Professional Development. Its advanced projects offer commercial diplomacy practitioners the opportunity to excel in their diplomatic careers as qualified commercial diplomats. The renowned diplomatic academy is a professional diplomatic body and the world's leading provider of advanced specialized courses on commercial diplomacy and anti-corruption.

MEMBERSHIP
Associate of the Diplomatic Academy
Fellow of the Diplomatic Academy (FDA)

QUALIFICATION/EXAMINATIONS
Advanced Certificate in Commercial Diplomacy Level 5
Advanced Certificate in Commercial Diplomacy Level 6
Master of Commercial Diplomacy
Doctor of Commercial Diplomacy

DESIGNATORY LETTERS
FDA, ACDipl, MCDipl (MCD), DCDipl (DCD)

INSTITUTE OF ADMINISTRATIVE MANAGEMENT

6 Graphite Square
Vauxhall Walk
London SE11 5EE
Tel: 020 7091 9620
Fax: 020 7091 7340
E-mail: info@instam.org
Website: www.instam.org

The IAM is the leading professional body and UK government recognized awarding body for those involved in the administration and management of business. We offer a range of qualifications, from an introduction to the subject up to a full BA Hons degree.

MEMBERSHIP
Student Member
Associate (AInstAM)
Member (MInstAM)
Fellow (FInstAM)

QUALIFICATION/EXAMINATIONS
Introductory Award in Administrative Management (Level 2)
Certificate in Administrative Management (Level 3)
Diploma in Administrative Management (Level 4)
Advanced Diploma in Administrative Management (Level 5)
BA Hons degree in Business Management, from The Open University, Sheffield Hallam University or The University of Teeside

DESIGNATORY LETTERS
AInstAM, MInstAM, FInstAM

INSTITUTE OF BUSINESS CONSULTING

4th Floor
2 Savoy Court
Strand
London WC2R 0EZ
Tel: 020 7497 0580
Fax: 020 7497 0463
E-mail: ibc@ibconsulting.org.uk
Website: www.ibconsulting.org.uk

The Institute of Business Consulting was formed in 2007 by the merger of the Institute of Business Advisers and the Institute of Management Consultancy, and we are the professional body for business consultants and advisers. Our aim is to raise the standards of professional practice in support of better business performance.

MEMBERSHIP
Student
Affiliate
Associate (AIBC)
Member (MIBC)
Fellow (FIBC)
Certified Business Advisor (CBA)
Certified Management Consultant (CMC)
Practice Member (corporate membership)

QUALIFICATION/EXAMINATIONS
Certificate in Business Support
Certificate in Management Consulting Essentials
Diploma in Business Support
Diploma in Management Consultancy (in conjunction with the Chartered Management Institute)

DESIGNATORY LETTERS
AIBC, MIBC, FIBC

INSTITUTE OF DIRECTORS

116 Pall Mall
London SW1Y 5ED
Tel: 020 7766 2601
Fax: 020 7930 1949
E-mail: professionaldev@iod.com
Website: www.iod.com/development

The IoD is the UK's largest organization representing professional leaders, with individual members ranging from entrepreneurs of start-up companies to CEOs of multinational organizations. The Institute's principal objectives are to advance the interests of its members as company directors, and to provide them with business facilities and a variety of services.

MEMBERSHIP
Associate Member
Member (MIoD)
Fellow (FIoD)
Chartered Director (C Dir)

QUALIFICATION/EXAMINATIONS
Certificate in Company Direction (CertIoD)
Diploma in Company Direction (DipIoD)

DESIGNATORY LETTERS
MIoD, FIoD, C Dir

INSTITUTE OF LEADERSHIP & MANAGEMENT

Stowe House
Netherstowe
Lichfield
Staffordshire WS13 6TJ
Tel: 01543 266867
Fax: 01543 266893
E-mail: customer@i-l-m.com
Website: www.i-l-m.com

The ILM supports, develops and informs leaders and managers at every stage of their career. With our broad range of industry-leading qualifications, membership services and learning resources, the ILM provides flexible development solutions that can be blended to meet the specific needs of employers and learners.

MEMBERSHIP
Studying Member
Professional Member

QUALIFICATION/EXAMINATIONS
Management
Award in Effective Team Skills (Level 2)
Award and Certificate in Team Leading (Level 2)
Award, Certificate and Diploma in First Line Management (Level 3)
Award, Certificate and Diploma in Management (Level 4)
Award, Certificate and Diploma in Management (Level 5)
Award in Management (Level 6)
Award, Certificate and Diploma in Executive Management (Level 7)
Leadership
Award and Certificate in Leadership (Level 3)
Award in Leadership (Level 4)
Award and Certificate in Leadership (Level 5)
Award, Certificate and Diploma in Strategic Leadership (Level 7)
Leadership and management
Award, Certificate and Diploma in Leadership and Management (Level 3)
Award, Certificate and Diploma in Leadership and Management (Level 5)
Award, Certificate and Diploma in Strategic Leadership and Executive Management (Level 7)
Coaching and mentoring
Award and Certificate in Workplace Coaching for Team Leaders and First Line Managers (Level 3)
Certificate in Workplace Coaching and Mentoring (Level 3)
Certificate in Coaching and Mentoring in Management (Level 5)
Diploma for Professional Management Coaches and Mentors (Level 5)
Certificate in Executive Coaching and Leadership Mentoring (Level 7)
Diploma for Professional Executive Coaches and Leadership Mentors (Level 7)
Specialist management qualifications
Environmental Management
Facilities Management
Managing Equality and Diversity
Managing Volunteers
Sales Management
Site Waste Management

INSTITUTE OF MANAGEMENT SERVICES

Brooke House
Lichfield
Staffordshire WS13 6AA
Tel: 01543 266909
Fax: 01543 257848
E-mail: admin@ims-stowe.fsnet.co.uk
Website: www.ims-productivity.com

The IMS is the primary body in the UK concerned with the promotion, practice and development of methods and techniques for the improvement of productivity and quality. We act as the qualifying body for the management services profession in the UK, focusing developments in practice and knowledge and acting as a forum for information exchange.

MEMBERSHIP
Affiliate
Associate (AMS)
Member (MMS)
Fellow (FMS)

QUALIFICATION/EXAMINATIONS
Management Services Certificate
Management Services Diploma

DESIGNATORY LETTERS
AMS, MMS, FMS

INSTITUTE OF VALUE MANAGEMENT

Westminster
London SW1H 9JJ
Tel: 08709 020905
E-mail: secretary@irm.org.uk
Website: www.ivm.org.uk

The Institute aims to establish Value Management as a process for achieving value in every sector of the economy and to provide support in the innovative use of value management techniques.

MEMBERSHIP
Corporate Membership: Open to any company or organization practising or promoting value techniques. Each corporate member may nominate up to 10 members of their organization as representatives to the Institute. A member nominated by a corporate body can hold executive office and has full voting rights.
Ordinary Membership: Open to any professional person who has an interest in and can demonstrate an involvement in practising value techniques.
Student Membership: Open to students who have an interest in value management and who are registered FT students possessing a valid student card.
Fellow: Awarded to a member as a special honour for outstanding contribution to the field of value management.

QUALIFICATION/EXAMINATIONS
Certificate and Training: The Institute has worked closely with the Commission of the European Communities to establish a European Training System and Certification Procedure.
Roll of Practitioners: The Institute maintains an authorized list of value practitioners who are members of the Institute.
It launched its European Training and Certification System in 1998. This European Commission funded initiative offers, through the IVM's Certification Board, certification in the following categories: Certificated Value Analyst (CVA); Professional in Value Management (PVM); Certificated Value Manager (CVM); Trainer in Value Management (TVM). The Certification Board also approves basic and advanced courses in value management that have been designed by trainers in value management. The Institute provides a list of trainers.

INTERNATIONAL PROFESSIONAL MANAGERS ASSOCIATION

5 Starnes Court
Union Street
Maidstone
Kent ME14 1EB
Tel: 01622 672867
Fax: 01622 755149
E-mail: admin@ipma.co.uk
Website: www.ipma.co.uk

The IPMA is an international examining, licensing and regulatory professional body, which, through its qualifying examinations, enables practising managers to participate in and be part of the process of improving managerial performance and effectiveness in all areas of business, industry and public administration.

MEMBERSHIP
Student member
Graduate Member (GRD PMA)
Licentiate Member (LMPMA)
Certified Associate (AMPMA)
Certified Member (MPMA)
Certified Fellow (FPMA)
Honorary Member (MPMA)
Honorary Fellow (FPMA)

QUALIFICATION/EXAMINATIONS
Certified International Professional Manager (CIPM) examinations

DESIGNATORY LETTERS
GRD PMA, LMPMA, AMPMA, MPMA, FPMA, CIPM

PROFESSIONAL BUSINESS & TECHNICAL MANAGEMENT

Head Office
Warwick Corner
42 Warwick Road
Kenilworth
Warwickshire CV8 1HE
Tel: 01926 866623
E-mail: info@group-ims.com
Website: www.pbtm.org.uk

PBTM was founded in 1983 to forge the link between business and technology. We give professional recognition to the knowledge and skills of managers in business and technology, supporting lifelong learning to help members fulfil their career ambitions and develop their potential.

MEMBERSHIP
Student Member (StudProfBTM)
Associate Member (AMProfBTM)
Member (MProfBTM)
Fellow (FProfBTM)
Companion (CProfBTM)

QUALIFICATION/EXAMINATIONS
Diploma of Merit

THE ASSOCIATION OF BUSINESS EXECUTIVES

President: Edward de Bono
5th Floor, CI Tower
St Georges Square
New Malden
Surrey KT3 4TE
Tel: 020 8329 2930
Fax: 020 8329 2945
E-mail: info@abeuk.com
Website: www.abeuk.com

The ABE is a professional membership body and examination board. We develop business and management qualifications at Certificate, Diploma, Advanced Diploma and Postgraduate Diploma levels. ABE qualifications provide progression routes to degree and Master's programmes worldwide.

MEMBERSHIP
Student Member
Associate Member (AMABE)
Member (MABE)
Fellow (FABE)

QUALIFICATION/EXAMINATIONS
Certificate, Diploma and Advanced Diploma (Levels 3, 5 and 6) in:
Business Information Systems
Business Management
Financial Management
Human Resource Management
Marketing
Travel, Tourism and Hospitality Management
and Postgraduate Diploma (Level 7) in Business Management

DESIGNATORY LETTERS
AMABE, MABE, FABE

THE CAMBRIDGE ACADEMY OF MANAGEMENT

Wellington House
Cambridge CB1 1BH
E-mail: info@cambridge-uk.org
Website: www.businessmanagement.org.uk

The Cambridge Academy of Management (CAM) is a professional, autonomous, not-for-profit institution established in to foster the concept of UK management education made available to all internationally. CAM is built on the foundation of promoting state-of-the-art knowledge and expertise in all facets of management education, training and development for the global educational arena.

MEMBERSHIP
Associate Category (ACAM)
Member Category (MCAM)
Fellowship Category (FCAM)

QUALIFICATION/EXAMINATIONS
All programmes offered by Cambridge Academy of Management are accredited by Quality Assurance Commission UK. Programmes offered:

CAM International Foundation Diploma CAM International Certificate in Restaurant & Catering Management
CAM International Diploma in Business Management CAM International
Diploma in Business (Restaurant & Catering Management)
CAM International Diploma in Business (Tourism Management)
CAM International Advanced Diploma in Business Management
CAM International Advanced Diploma in Business (Restaurant & Catering Management)
CAM International Advanced Diploma in Business (Tourism Management)
CAM International Postgraduate Diploma in Hospitality Management

CAM International Postgraduate Diploma in Business

CAM International Postgraduate Diploma in Business with Specialization in: Marketing Finance Human Resource

THE CHARTERED MANAGEMENT INSTITUTE

Membership Department
Management House
Cottingham Road
Corby
Northants NN17 1TT
Tel: 01536 207307
Fax: 01536 400388
E-mail: membership@managers.org.uk
Website: www.managers.org.uk

The CMI is the only chartered professional body dedicated to managers and leaders, and to the organizations they work in. As founders of the National Occupational Standards for Management and Leadership excellence, we set the standards that others follow. As a membership organization we give our members the tools they need to make a genuine impact on business in the UK.

MEMBERSHIP
Associate (ACMI)
Member (MCMI)
Fellow (FCMI)
Chartered Manager (CMgr)

DESIGNATORY LETTERS
ACMI, MCMI, FCMI, CMgr

THE INSTITUTE OF COMMERCIAL MANAGEMENT

ICM House
Castleman Way
Ringwood
Hampshire BH24 3BA
Tel: 01202 490555
Fax: 01202 490666
E-mail: info@icm.ac.uk
Website: www.icm.ac.uk

The Institute is the leading professional body for Commercial and Business Development Managers. A fully accredited QCA/ofqual UK Examining and Awarding Board for those undertaking business and management studies, ICM offers in excess of 200 programmes at HND, first degree, and Master's levels. It works with education and training providers and government agencies in more than 100 countries.

MEMBERSHIP
Student
Associate Member (AMInstCM)
Graduate Member (GradDipCM)
Member (MInstCM)
Fellow (FInstCM)

QUALIFICATION/EXAMINATIONS
ICM Awards cover the following areas: Accounting & Finance; Business Studies; Commercial Management; Hospitality Management; Human Resource Development; Journalism; Legal Studies; Management Studies; Maritime Management; Marketing Management; Sales Management; Travel & Tourism.

DESIGNATORY LETTERS
AMInstCM, MInstCM, FInstCM

THE INSTITUTE OF MANAGEMENT SPECIALISTS

Head Office
Warwick Corner
42 Warwick Road
Kenilworth
Warwickshire CV8 1HE
Tel: 01926 866623
E-mail: info@group-ims.com
Website: www.instituteofmanagementspecialists.org.uk

The Institute of Management Specialists was founded in 1971 to give professional recognition to the knowledge and skills of managers and specialists. The Institute encourages management excellence and specialist expertise, and supports lifelong learning to help members fulfil their career ambitions.

MEMBERSHIP
Student Member (StudIMS)
Associate Member (AMIMS)
Member (MIMS)
Fellow (FIMS)
Companion (CompIMS)

QUALIFICATION/EXAMINATIONS
Diploma of Frontline Management

THE SOCIETY OF BUSINESS PRACTITIONERS

PO Box 11
Sandbach
Cheshire CW11 3GE
Tel: 01270 526339
Fax: 01270 526339
E-mail: info@mamsasbp.org.uk
Website: www.mamsasbp.org.uk

The SBP is an international organization formed by experienced educationalists and executives to fulfil a need to set standards in business practice to be achieved by examinations/assessments. Both inexperienced and mature students should be able to follow careers in further education and/or be proficient in employment and receive the benefits of Membership.

MEMBERSHIP
Student (StuSBP)
Member (MSBP)
Certified Professional Manager (CPMSBP)
Professional Memberships *(Senior Professional Qualifications)*
Associateship (ASBP)
Licentiateship (LSBP)
Graduateship (GSBP)
Fellowship (FSBP)
These are certified competency-based Membership Awards open to persons occupied in business practice who are considered suitable by the Membership Committee.
CPD programmes are also offered for the Asia region.

QUALIFICATION/EXAMINATIONS
Diploma in Business Administration
Advanced Diploma in Business Administration
PGDip in Business Administration
PGDip in International Marketing
Diploma in Computer Studies
Advanced Diploma in Computer Studies
GradDip in IT & E-Commerce
GradDip in Entrepreneurship
Advanced Diploma in Accounting
Diploma & Advanced Diploma in Marketing Management (Joint Award with the Managing & Marketing Sales Association)

DESIGNATORY LETTERS
StuSBP, MSBP, CPMSBP, ASBP. LSBP. GSBP. FSBP

MANUFACTURING

Membership of Professional Institutions and Associations

THE INSTITUTE OF MANUFACTURING

Head Office
Warwick Corner
42 Warwick Road
Kenilworth
Warwickshire CV8 1HE
Tel: 01926 866623
E-mail: info@group-ims.com
Website: www.instituteofmanufacturing.org.uk

The Institute of Manufacturing was founded in 1978 to give professional recognition to the knowledge and skills of people in all aspects of manufacturing. The Institute supports lifelong learning to help members fulfil their career ambitions and develop their potential.

MEMBERSHIP
Student Member (StudIManf)
Associate Member (AMIManf)
Member (MIManf)
Fellow (FIManf)
Companion (CompIManf)

QUALIFICATION/EXAMINATIONS
Diploma of Merit

MARKETING AND SALES

Membership of Professional Institutions and Associations

LONDON CENTRE OF MARKETING

Buckingham House East
Stanmore
London HA7 4EB
Tel: 020 8385 7766
Fax: 020 8385 7755
E-mail: info@lcmuk.com
Website: www.lcmuk.com

The London Centre of Marketing is an accredited, non-political, non-profit-making institution based in London, which exists with the sole aim of providing internationally recognized professional qualifications in marketing and marketing management.

QUALIFICATION/EXAMINATIONS
Diploma, Higher Diploma, Professional Diploma, Graduate Diploma and Postgraduate Dipolma in:
Business Management & Marketing
Human Resource Development & Marketing
Sales & Marketing Management
Travel & Tourism Marketing
Public Relations & Marketing
Entrepreneurship & Marketing

MANAGING AND MARKETING SALES ASSOCIATION EXAMINATION BOARD

PO Box 11
Sandbach
Cheshire CW11 3GE
Tel: 01270 526339
Fax: 01270 526339
E-mail: info@mamsasbp.org.uk
Website: www.mamsasbp.org.uk

MAMSA is an international organization offering qualifications in Sales, Marketing and Management and its senior specialist Stategic Marketing Diploma. The importance of 'Customer Service' is emphasized throughout all the programmes.

MEMBERSHIP
Graduate (GradMAMSA)
Graduate Affiliate (GradAfMAMSA)
Professional (MMAMSA)
Fellow (FMAMSA)

QUALIFICATION/EXAMINATIONS
Standard Diploma in Salesmanship
Certificate in Sales Marketing
Higher Diploma in Marketing
Advanced Diploma in Sales Management
Certificate in Marketing Strategy
Diploma in Marketing Strategy & Management (Hypothesis/Thesis)
Diploma in Sales and Marketing Practices (Joint Award with the Society of Business Practitioners)
A CPD programme is also offered.

DESIGNATORY LETTERS
GradMAMSA, GradAfMAMSA, MMAMSA, FMAMSA

MRS (THE MARKET RESEARCH SOCIETY)

15 Northburgh Street
London EC1V 0JR
Tel: 020 7490 4911
Fax: 020 7490 0608
E-mail: profdevelopment@mrs.org.uk
Website: www.mrs.org.uk

With members in more than 70 countries, MRS is the world's largest association serving those with professional equity in the provision or use of market, social and opinion research. We offer various qualifications and membership grades, and are an awarding body for vocationally related qualifications in market and social research.

MEMBERSHIP
Affiliate
Studying Affiliate
Associate Member (AMRS)
Full Member (MMRS)
Fellow (FMRS)
Honorary Member

QUALIFICATION/EXAMINATIONS
Certificate in Market and Social Reseach
Certificate in Interviewing Skills in Market and Social Research
Advanced Certificate in Market and Social Research Practice
Diploma in Market and Social Research Practice

DESIGNATORY LETTERS
AMRS, MMRS, FMRS

THE CHARTERED INSTITUTE OF MARKETING

Moor Hall
Maidenhead
Berkshire SL6 9QH
Tel: 01628 427120
Fax: 01628 427158
E-mail: qualifications@cim.co.uk
Website: www.cim.co.uk/learningzone

The Chartered Institute of Marketing is the leading international professional marketing body, with 47,000 members worldwide. We aim to improve the skills of marketing practitioners, enabling them to deliver exceptional results for their organization. Qualifications from Introductory to Chartered postgraduate level are offered to anyone wanting to develop their career in marketing.

MEMBERSHIP
Affiliate (Studying/Professional)
Associate (ACIM)
Member (MCIM)
Fellow (FCIM)
Chartered Marketer

QUALIFICATION/EXAMINATIONS
Introductory Certificate in Marketing
Professional Certificate in Marketing
Professional Diploma in Marketing
Chartered Postgraduate Diploma in Marketing
Diploma in Marketing Communications
Diploma in Managing Digital Media
Diploma in Digital Marketing
Diploma in Hospitality and Tourism Marketing

DESIGNATORY LETTERS
ACIM, MCIM, FCIM

THE INSTITUTE OF DIRECT MARKETING

1 Park Road
Teddington
Middlesex TW11 0AR
Tel: 020 8977 5705
Fax: 020 8943 2535
E-mail: enquiries@theidm.com
Website: www.theidm.com

The IDM is Europe's leading professional development body for direct, data and digital marketing. Founded in 1987, we are an educational trust and registered charity. We advocate lifelong learning and maintain an up-to-date education portfolio designed to meet the needs of marketing practitioners throughout their career.

MEMBERSHIP
Affiliate Member
Associate Member
Member
Fellow
Corporate Member

QUALIFICATION/EXAMINATIONS
Certificate in B2B Marketing (Cert BusM)
Certificate in Digital Marketing (Cert DigM)
Certificate in Direct and Interactive Marketing (Cert IDM)
Diploma in B2B Marketing (Dip BusM)
Diploma in Digital Marketing (Dip DigM)
Diploma in Direct and Interactive Marketing (Dip IDM)
Diploma in Integrated Marketing Communications (Dip IMC)

THE INSTITUTE OF SALES AND MARKETING MANAGEMENT

Harrier Court
Woodside Road
Lower Woodside
Bedfordshire LU1 4DQ
Tel: 01582 843260
Fax: 01582 849142
E-mail: education@ismm.co.uk
Website: www.ismm.co.uk

The ISMM offers professional qualifications in sales and marketing. The qualifications are accredited by the Qualification and Curriculum Authority, the body set up by the government to regulate qualifications. The programmes are available through ISMM-accredited centres.

MEMBERSHIP
Student
Associate (AInstSMM)
Member
Fellow

QUALIFICATION/EXAMINATIONS
Award in Basic Sales Skills (Level 1)
Award and Certificate in Sales and Marketing (Level 2)
Award, Certificate and Diploma in Advanced Sales and Marketing (Level 3)
Award, Certificate and Diploma in Operational Sales and Marketing (Level 4)
Award, Certificate and Diploma in Account Management/Sales Management (Level 5)
Diploma in Sales and Account Management (Level 5)
Executive Award, Executive Certificate and Executive Diploma in Strategic Sales and Account Management (Level 6)

DESIGNATORY LETTERS
AInstSMM, MInstSMM, FInstSMM

THE SOCIETY OF SALES & MARKETING

40 Archdale Road
East Dulwich
London SE22 9HJ
Tel: 0845 643 6832
Fax: 0845 643 6834
E-mail: info@ssm.org.uk
Website: www.ssm.org.uk

The Society is the only professional examining body that awards Certificates and Diplomas in all the four areas of selling, namely selling and sales management, marketing, retail management, and international trade and services. The Society celebrated its Silver Jubilee in style in 2005 at Imperial College London.

MEMBERSHIP
Graduate (GSSM)
Associate (ASSM)
Fellow (FSSM)

QUALIFICATION/EXAMINATIONS
Candidates for the Certificate, Advanced Certificate or Diploma choose any one of the following: (A) Selling & Sales Management, (B) Marketing, (C) Retail Management and (D) International Trade & Services.
(A) Selling & Sales Management subjects:
Certificate: (1) Business Communication, (2) Book-keeping & Accounts, (3) Selling & Sales Management, (4) Fundamentals of Marketing
Advanced Certificate: (5) Marketing Research Management, (6) Consumer Behaviour, (7) Principles of Selling, (8) Consumer Law

Diploma: (9) Management Information Systems, (10) Consumerism, Ethics & Social Responsibility, (11) Marketing Planning & Control, (12) Marketing Communication
(B) Marketing subjects:
Certificate: (1) Business Communication (2) Book-keeping & Accounts, (3) Selling & Sales Management, (4) Fundamentals of Marketing
Advanced Certificate: (5) Marketing Research Management, (6) Consumer Behaviour, (7) Principles of Selling, (8) Consumer Law
Diploma: (9) Management Information Systems, (10) Consumerism, Ethics & Social Responsibility, (11) Marketing Planning & Control, (12) Marketing Communication
(C) Retail Management subjects:
Certificate: (1) Business Communication, (2) Book-keeping & Accounts, (3) Selling & Sales Management, (4) Retail Management
Advanced Certificate: (5) Marketing Research Management, (6) Consumer Behaviour, (7) Principles of Selling, (8) Consumer Law
Diploma: (9) Management Information Systems, (10) Consumerism, Ethics & Social Responsibility, (11) Fundamentals of Marketing, (12) Marketing Communication
(D) International Trade & Services:
Certificate: (1) Business Communication, (2) Book-keeping & Accounts, (3) International Trade & Services, (4) Fundamentals of Marketing
Advanced Certificate: (5) Marketing Research Management, (6) Import & Export Management, (7) Finance for Export, (8) Consumer Law
Diploma: (9) Management Information Systems, (10) Consumerism, Ethics & Social Responsibility, (11) Marketing Planning & Control, (12) Marketing Communication

DESIGNATORY LETTERS
GSSM, ASSM, FSSM

MARTIAL ARTS

Membership of Professional Institutions and Associations

INSTITUTE OF MARTIAL ARTS AND SCIENCES

1 Henrietta Street
Bolton
Lancashire BL3 4HL
Tel: 01942 212378
Fax: 01942 211650
E-mail: admin@institute-of-martialarts-and-sciences.com
Website: www.institute-of-martialarts-and-sciences.com

The IMAS was formed by a group of high-ranking martial arts instructors, educators, researchers and academics to encourage education and research in martial arts, promote professionalism among martial arts instructors, afford martial artists the opportunity of obtaining recognized and accredited qualifications, and to act as a platform to encourage academic debate.

MEMBERSHIP
Associate (AIMAS)
Member (MIMAS)
Fellow (FIMAS)

QUALIFICATION/EXAMINATIONS
Bachelors, Masters and Doctoral in Martial arts and Sciences

DESIGNATORY LETTERS
Grad.IMAS, MSc, PhD

MASSAGE AND ALLIED THERAPIES

Membership of Professional Institutions and Associations

BRITISH MEDICAL ACUPUNCTURE SOCIETY

BMAS House
3 Winnington Court
Winnington Street
Northwich
Cheshire CW8 1AQ
Tel: 01606 786782
Fax: 01606 786783
E-mail: admin@medical-acupuncture.co.uk
Website: www.medical-acupuncture.co.uk

The BMAS was formed in 1980 as an association of medical practitioners interested in acupuncture and we now have a membership of more than 2,700 registered doctors and allied health professionals who practise acupuncture alongside more conventional techniques. We believe that acupuncture has an important role to play in healthcare and promote its use as a therapy following orthodox medical diagnosis by suitably trained practitioners. We run training programmes in the UK for doctors, dentists and other healthcare professionals.

MEMBERSHIP
Affiliated Member
Member
Accredited Member
Dental/Veterinary Member
Retired Member
Honorary Member
Overseas Member

QUALIFICATION/EXAMINATIONS
Certificate of Basic Competence (CoBC)
Diploma of Medical Acupuncture (DipMedAc)

INTERNATIONAL COUNCIL OF HOLISTIC THERAPISTS

18 Shakespeare Business Centre
Hathaway Close
Eastleigh
Hampshire SO50 4SR
Tel: 0844 875 2022
Fax: 023 8062 4399
Website: www.fht.org.uk

(Part of the Federation of Holistic Therapists)

This professional association supports therapists in holistic therapies, including aromatherapy, reflexology, Indian head massage, body massage, and many more. Membership is open only to those qualified through awarding bodies such as the IIHHT, VTCT, NVQ/SVQ, BTEC and C&G. Exemptions from these requirements are granted only for those who have other acceptable qualifications and experience.

INTERNATIONAL REGISTER OF MASSAGE THERAPISTS

PO Box 5537
Hatfield Peverel
Essex CM3 2QN
Tel: 06626 713867
Fax: 01323 440282
E-mail: irmt-eb@yahoo.co.uk
Website: www.irmt.co.uk

The IRMT is a professional trade association that provides courses, through external tutors, for anyone serious about a career in the complementary or physical therapy professions. We offer courses in: Massage/Anatomy & Physiology; Remedial Back Therapy; Sports Therapy; Aromatherapy; Reflexology; Reiki; Skin Care; Head Massage; and On-site Massage.

MEMBERSHIP
Associate (AIRMT)
Member (MIRMT)
Fellow (FIRMT)

QUALIFICATION/EXAMINATIONS
Diploma

DESIGNATORY LETTERS
AIRMT, MIRMT, FIRMT

LCSP REGISTER OF REMEDIAL MASSEURS AND MANIPULATIVE THERAPISTS

38A High Street
Lowestoft
Suffolk NR32 1HY
Tel: 01502 563344
Fax: 01502 582220
E-mail: lcsp@btconnect.com
Website: www.lcsp.uk.com

The Register accepts practitioners who currently work in Massage, Remedial Massage or Manipulative Therapy. Applicants must have completed a course of education at an establishment whose training meets or exceeds the National Occupational Standards. The Register offers heavily discounted comprehensive medical malpractice insurance, business support, regular communications and CPD opportunities.

MEMBERSHIP
Student Member
Associate Member (LCSP (Assoc))
Full Member (LSCP (Phys))
Affiliate
Fellow (FLCSP)
Honorary Member

DESIGNATORY LETTERS
LCSP (Assoc), LCSP (Phys), FLCSP

NORTHERN INSTITUTE OF MASSAGE LTD

14–16 St Mary's Place
Bury
Greater Manchester BL9 0DZ
Tel: 0161 797 1800
E-mail: information@nim.co.uk
Website: www.nim.co.uk

The NIM was founded in 1924 and offers professional training in Remedial Massage, Advanced Remedial Massage, and Manipulative Therapy. We also offer a number of CPD seminars and short courses to supplement our main training programme. Research is carried out mostly by therapists on patients from their own clinics or by students completing university courses.

QUALIFICATION/EXAMINATIONS

Diploma in Remedial Massage
Advanced Remedial Massage Diploma
Manipulative Therapy Diploma

SOCIETY OF HOMEOPATHS

11 Brookfield Duncan Close
Moulton Park
Northampton NN3 6WL
Tel: 08454 506611
Fax: 08454 506622
E-mail: info@homeopathy-soh.org
Website: www.homeopathy-soh.org

The Society of Homeopaths was established in 1978 and is now the largest organization registering professional homeopaths in Europe. Our vision is 'homeopathy for all' and we aim to achieve this both by supporting our members and by raising the profile of homeopathy in general.

MEMBERSHIP

Subscriber
Student Member
Student Clinical Member
Registered Member (RSHom)

DESIGNATORY LETTERS

RSHom

MATHEMATICS

Membership of Professional Institutions and Associations

EDINBURGH MATHEMATICAL SOCIETY

School of Mathematics, Edinburgh University
James Clerk Maxwell Building
Mayfield Road
Edinburgh EH9 3JZ
Tel: 01316 505040
Fax: 01316 506553
E-mail: edmathsoc@maths.ed.ac.uk
Website: www.maths.ed.ac.uk

The EMS, founded in 1883, is the principal mathematical society for the academic community in Scotland as well as mathematicians in industry and commerce. We organize meetings, publish a journal and support mathematical activities through various funds.

MEMBERSHIP
Ordinary Member
Reciprocal Member
Honorary Member

THE INSTITUTE OF MATHEMATICS AND ITS APPLICATIONS

Catherine Richards House
16 Nelson Street
Southend-on-Sea
Essex SS1 1EF
Tel: 01702 354020
Fax: 01702 354111
E-mail: post@ima.org.uk
Website: www.ima.org.uk

The IMA, founded in 1964, is the UK's learned society for mathematics and its applications. We promote mathematical research, education and careers, and the use of mathematics in business, industry and commerce. In 1990 the Institute was incorporated by Royal Charter and subsequently granted the right to award the status of Chartered Mathematician, Chartered Scientist and Chartered Mathematics Teacher.

MEMBERSHIP
Student
Affiliate
Associate Member (AMIMA)
Member (MIMA)
Fellow (FIMA)
Chartered Mathematician (CMath)
Chartered Mathematics Teacher (CMathTeach)
Chartered Scientist (CSci)

DESIGNATORY LETTERS
AMIMA, MIMA, FIMA, CMath, CMathTeach, CSci

THE MATHEMATICAL ASSOCIATION

259 London Road
Leicester LE2 3BE
Tel: 01162 210013
Fax: 01162 122835
E-mail: office@m-a.org.uk
Website: www.m-a.org.uk

The MA dates from 1871 and supports and improves the teaching and learning of mathematics and its applications, and provides opportunities for communication and collaboration between teachers and students of mathematics. We publish a number of books, journals and magazines, hold an annual conference and regional meetings, and organize CPD events for our members. We also confer with government re the curriculum and assessment.

MEMBERSHIP
Student Member
Personal Member
Institutional Member

MEDICAL HERBALISM

Membership of Professional Institutions and Associations

THE NATIONAL INSTITUTE OF MEDICAL HERBALISTS

Elm House
54 Mary Arches Street
Exeter
Devon EX4 3BA
Tel: 01392 426022
Fax: 01392 498963
E-mail: info@nimh.org.uk
Website: www.nimh.org.uk

The NIMH is the UK's leading professional organization of qualified medical herbal practitioners. We maintain high standards of practice and patient care, and work to promote the benefits of western herbal medicine. We provide codes of conduct, ethics and practice, and represent the profession, patients and the public through participation in external processes.

MEMBERSHIP
Member (MNIMH) Membership is open to graduates holding a BSc(Hons) degree in Herbal Medicine from: the Scottish School of Herbal Medicine, Edinburgh Napier University, University of Central Lancashire, Middlesex University, University of East London, University of Lincoln or University of Westminster. There is also a student affiliate membership scheme for those who are undergraduates of any of the above schools.
Fellow (FNIMH)

QUALIFICATION/EXAMINATIONS
Universities that currently offer the accredited BSc(Hons) degree in Herbal Medicine are: Middlesex University, University of Lincoln, University of Westminster and University of East London. The programme at the University of East London is delivered by blended learning.

DESIGNATORY LETTERS
MNIMH, FNIMH

MEDICAL SECRETARIES

Membership of Professional Institutions and Associations

ASSOCIATION OF MEDICAL SECRETARIES, PRACTICE MANAGERS, ADMINISTRATORS AND RECEPTIONISTS

Tavistock House North
Tavistock Square
London WC1H 9LN
Tel: 020 7387 6005
Fax: 020 7388 2648
E-mail: info@amspar.co.uk
Website: www.amspar.com

AMSPAR is a professional membership and educational organization. We work with City & Guilds to provide non-clinical qualifications for health administration within the UK qualification frameworks. We aim to promote quality and coherence in the delivery of qualifications, and encourage and support standards of excellence in the pursuit of continuous professional development and lifelong learning.

MEMBERSHIP
Associate Member (AAMS)
Member (MAMS)
Fellow (FAMS)

QUALIFICATION/EXAMINATIONS
The Level 5 Diploma in Primary Care & Health Management
The Level 5 Certificate in Primary Care & Health Management
The Level 3 Diploma for Medical Secretaries
The Level 3 Certificate in Medical Administration
The Level 3 Certificate in Medical Terminology
Diploma in Medical Administration
The Level 2 Certificate in Medical Administration
The Level 2 Award in Medical Terminology

DESIGNATORY LETTERS
AAMS, MAMS, FAMS

MEDICINE

Membership of Professional Institutions and Associations

COLLEGE OF OPERATING DEPARTMENT PRACTITIONERS

197–199 City Road
London EC1V 1JN
Tel: 0870 746 0984
Fax: 0870 746 0985
E-mail: office@codp.org
Website: www.codp.org

The CODP is the professional body for Operating Department Practitioners. It is a membership, not-for-profit organization that sets standards of education for the pre-registration aspect of the profession and promotes the enhancement of knowledge and skills, in the context of the multidisciplinary team, through regional, national and international networks.

MEMBERSHIP
Student Member
Association Member
Full College Member

ROYAL COLLEGE OF GENERAL PRACTITIONERS

1 Bow Churchyard
London EC4M 9DQ
E-mail: info@rcgp.org.uk
Website: www.rcgp.org.uk

The aims of the College are to encourage, foster and maintain the highest possible standards in general medical practice. Full entry to the College is by exam undertaken whilst in training for General Practice, or assessment as a qualified GP.

MEMBERSHIP
Associate in Training
Associate
Member (MRCGP)
Fellow (FRCGP)

Undergraduate medical students and Foundation programme students may register with the College's Student Forum, which exposes the students to life in general practice.

QUALIFICATION/EXAMINATIONS
Assessment for Membership of the RCGP (MRGGP)

DESIGNATORY LETTERS
MRCGP, FRCGP

ROYAL COLLEGE OF OBSTETRICIANS AND GYNAECOLOGISTS

27 Sussex Place
London NW1 4RG
Tel: 020 7772 6200
Fax: 020 7723 0575
E-mail: library@rcog.org.uk
Website: www.rcog.org.uk

The RCOG encourages the study and advancement of the science and practice of obstetrics and gynaecology. We do this through postgraduate medical education and training development, and the publication of clinical guidelines and reports on aspects of the specialty and service provision. The RCOG International Office works with other international organizations to help lower maternal morbidity and mortality in under-resourced countries.

MEMBERSHIP
Junior Affiliate
Affiliate
Associate
Diplomate
Trainee – pre-membership
Member without Examination (MRCOG)
Member (MRCOG)
Fellow (FRCOG)
Fellow *honoris causa*
Fellow *ad eumdem* (FRCOG)
Honorary Fellow (FRCOG)

QUALIFICATION/EXAMINATIONS
MRCOG
DRCOG

DESIGNATORY LETTERS
MRCOG, FRCOG

ROYAL SOCIETY OF MEDICINE

1 Wimpole Street
London W1G 0AE
Tel: 020 7290 2900
Fax: 020 7290 2989
E-mail: membership@rsm.ac.uk
Website: www.rsm.ac.uk

The RSM, founded in 1805, is a medical charity that promotes the exchange of information and ideas in medical science. We provide a broad range of educational activities and opportunities for doctors, dentists, veterinary surgeons, students of these disciplines and allied healthcare professionals, organize conferences, and publish books and journals through our publishing division, RSM Press.

MEMBERSHIP
Student
Associate
Fellow

THE FEDERATION OF THE ROYAL COLLEGES OF PHYSICIANS OF THE UNITED KINGDOM

MRCP(UK) Central Office
11 St Andrews Place
Regent's Park
London NW1 4LE
Tel: +44 (0)20 7935 1174
Fax: +44 (0)20 7935 4143
E-mail: part1@mrcpuk.org
Website: www.mrcpuk.org

The Federation is a partnership between the Royal College of Physicians of Edinburgh, the Royal College of Physicians and Surgeons of Glasgow and the Royal College of Physicians of London. Working together, the colleges develop and deliver membership and specialty examinations that are recognized around the world as quality benchmarks.

MEMBERSHIP
Membership of the Royal Colleges of Physicians (MRCP(UK)): Once a candidate has successfully completed their final Part of the examination they must then submit and complete the Form of Faith and a testimonial for election to membership. The testimonial must be completed by a Fellow or Member of the Royal Colleges of Physicians of the United Kingdom. The latter should have worked with the candidate within the previous 3 years and must be a holder of MRCP(UK) for at least 8 years.

QUALIFICATION/EXAMINATIONS
The Federation is responsible for a portfolio of examinations: **MRCP(UK) Diploma (Membership of the Royal Colleges of Physicians of the United Kingdom):** Candidates for the MRCP(UK) Diploma may enter through the Royal College of Physicians of Edinburgh, the Royal College of Physicians and Surgeons of Glasgow, the Royal College of Physicians of London, or through the online application system. There are three components to the MRCP(UK) Diploma. The **part 1 examination** has a two-paper format. Each paper is 3 hours in duration and contains 100 multiple choice questions in one from five (best of five) format, where a candidate chooses the best answer from five possible answers. The **part 2 written examination** has a three-paper format. All papers in the MRCP(UK) part 2 written examination are 3 hours in duration and contain 70 multiple choice questions. The questions will usually have a clinical scenario, may include the results of investigations and may be illustrated. The **Part 2 clinical examination (PACES)** consists of five clinical stations, each assessed by two independent examiners. Candidates will start at any one of the five stations, and then move round the carousel of stations at 20

minute intervals until they have completed the cycle. There is a five-minute period between each station. Candidates may apply to sit the MRCP(UK) part 1 examination provided they graduated at least 12 months in advance of the examinations date (and have had at least 12 months' experience in medical employment). Candidates who have passed the part 1 examination can proceed to complete the remaining components. **The Specialty Certificate Examinations (SCEs):**The Federation of Royal Colleges of Physicians of the UK, in association with the Specialist Societies, has developed a programme to deliver Specialty Certificate Examinations within the new specialist training structure. The aim of these national assessments is to ensure that trainees have sufficient knowledge of their specialty to practice safely and competently as consultants. The Specialty Certificate Examination comprises two three-hour multiple choice tests of 100 items each and is delivered in computer-based format (referred to as CBT) at a Pearson VUE test centre. Each paper is based on the MRCP(UK) written paper format and contains 100 multiple choice questions in 'best of five' format.

THE INSTITUTE OF CLINICAL RESEARCH

Institute House
Boston Drive
Bourne End
Buckinghamshire SL8 5YS
Tel: 0845 521 0056/01628
Fax: 01628 530641
E-mail: info@icr-global.org
Website: www.icr-global.org

The ICR was founded in 1978 and is now the largest professional clinical research body in Europe and India. Our aim is to promote knowledge and understanding by engaging with the healthcare community and the general public, to support and facilitate communication between our members, and to provide opportunities for learning and development to enhance professional competence.

MEMBERSHIP
Affiliate
Registered Member (RICR)
Professional Member (MICR)
Fellow (FICR)
Honorary Fellow (Hon FICR)

QUALIFICATION/EXAMINATIONS
Please see the ICR's website.

DESIGNATORY LETTERS
RICR, MICR, FICR, HonFICR

THE ROYAL COLLEGE OF ANAESTHETISTS

Churchill House
35 Red Lion Square
London WC1R 4SG
Tel: 020 7092 1500
Fax: 020 7092 1730
E-mail: info@rcoa.ac.uk
Website: www.rcoa.ac.uk

The RCA, which dates from 1948, is the professional body responsible for the specialty of anaesthesia throughout the UK. Our principal responsibility is to ensure the quality of patient care through the maintenance of standards in anaesthesia, pain management and intensive care. We set and run examinations, and provide CPD for all practising anaesthetists.

MEMBERSHIP
Trainee
Affiliate
Associate Member
Member (MRCA)
Associate Fellow
Fellow *ad eundem* (FRCA)
Fellow (FRCA)
Honorary Fellow (FRCA)

QUALIFICATION/EXAMINATIONS
FRCA Examinations

DESIGNATORY LETTERS
MRCA, FRCA

THE ROYAL COLLEGE OF PATHOLOGISTS

2 Carlton House Terrace
London SW1Y 5AF
Tel: 020 7451 6700
Fax: 020 7451 6701
E-mail: info@rcpath.org
Website: www.rcpath.org

The College aims to advance the science and practice of pathology, to provide public education, to promote research in pathology and to disseminate the results.

MEMBERSHIP
Affiliate Member
Associate
Diplomate Member (DipRCPath)
Fellow (FRCPath)

QUALIFICATION/EXAMINATIONS
Training programmes are approved for all pathology specialities and sub-specialities. The exact examination arrangements vary for each speciality but they will all involve a Part 1 and a Part 2 which include, inter alia, written, practical and oral components. In addition the College offers a Diploma in Cytopathology, a Diploma in Dermatopathology and a Diploma in Forensic Pathology. Further details may be obtained from the Examinations Department or the College's website.

DESIGNATORY LETTERS
DipRCPath, FRCPath

THE ROYAL COLLEGE OF PHYSICIANS AND SURGEONS OF GLASGOW

232–242 St Vincent Street
Glasgow G2 5RJ
Tel: 0141 2216072
Fax: 0141 2211804
Website: www.rcpsg.ac.uk

Granted a Charter from James V1 in 1599 and the honorific 'Royal' in 1910, the College welcomes professionals from a diverse range of disciplines. Our collegiate body includes physicians, surgeons, and professionals in dentistry and travel medicine, as well as professions allied to medicine.

MEMBERSHIP
Introductory Member
Associate Member
Member (MRCPS(Glasg)/MFDS RCPS(Glasg)/ MRCS(Glasg))
Fellow (FRCP(Glasg)/FRCS(Glasg)/FDS RCPS(Glasg))

QUALIFICATION/EXAMINATIONS
Diploma in Child Health (DCH)
Diploma in Dermatology (Dip Derm)
Diploma in Geriatric Medicine (DGM)
Diploma in Travel Medicine (DTM)

Diploma of Membership of the Royal College of Physicians of the United Kingdom (MRCP(UK)) (see RCP(UK) website)
Diploma of Membership of the Royal College of Surgeons (MRCS (Glasg))
Diploma of Membership of the Faculty of Dental Surgery (MFDS RCPS(Glasg))
Diploma of Membership of the Faculty of Travel Medicine (MFTM RCPS(Glasg))
Diploma of Fellowship of the Royal College of Physicians and Surgeons of Glasgow in Ophthalmology (FRCS (Glasg))
Diploma of Fellowship of the Royal College of Physicians and Surgeons of Glasgow (FDS (dental speciality))
Diploma of Fellowship of the Royal College of Physicians and Surgeons of Glasgow (FRCS (surgical specialty))
MSc in Clinical Leadership (offered jointly with the University of Glasgow Business School (UGBS))

DESIGNATORY LETTERS
MFDS RCPS(Glasg), MFTM RCPS(Glasg), MRCP(UK), MRCPS(Glasg), FRCP(Glasg)/FRCS(Glasg)/FDS RCPS(Glasg)/FRCS(Urol)(Glasg)

THE ROYAL COLLEGE OF PHYSICIANS OF EDINBURGH

9 Queen Street
Edinburgh EH2 1JQ
Tel: 01312 257324
Fax: 01312 266124
E-mail: l.tedford@rcpe.ac.uk
Website: www.rcpe.ac.uk

The RCPE promotes the highest standards in internal medicine internationally. Along with our sister Colleges in Glasgow and London we oversee the Member of the Royal College of Physicians (MRCP(UK)) examination enabling doctors to enter higher specialist training, leading eventually to a Certificate of Completion of Specialist Training (CCST).

MEMBERSHIP
e-Associate
Associate
Collegiate Member (MRCPE)
Fellow (FRCPE)

QUALIFICATION/EXAMINATIONS
MRCP(UK)
Specialty Certificate Examinations

DESIGNATORY LETTERS
MRCPE, FRCPE

THE ROYAL COLLEGE OF PHYSICIANS OF LONDON

11 St Andrews Place
Regent's Park
London NW1 4LE
Tel: +44 (0)20 7935 1174
Fax: +44 (0)20 7935 4143
E-mail: DGM@rcplondon.ac.uk; DTMH@rcplondon.ac.uk
Website: www.rcplondon.ac.uk

The Royal College of Physicians of London offers a Diploma in Geriatric Medicine (DGM) Examination and a Diploma in Tropical Medicine and Hygiene run in conjunction with the London School of Tropical Medicine and Hygiene.

MEMBERSHIP
The Royal College of Physicians of London runs the MRCP(UK) Examination which is the MRCP(UK) membership examination. As the examination is run in conjunction with two other Royal Colleges of Physicians, this examination and the membership

qualification MRCP(UK) are listed in this directory under ***The Federation of Royal Colleges of Physicians***

QUALIFICATION/EXAMINATIONS

Diploma in Geriatric Medicine The Diploma in Geriatric Medicine is designed to give recognition of competence in the provision of care of older people to General Practitioner vocational trainees, staff physicians and others working in non-consultant career posts in Departments of Geriatric Medicine, and other doctors with interests in or responsibilities for the care of older people.

The Diploma in Geriatric Medicine is available to all registered doctors. It is not primarily directed towards career geriatricians, but is generally to family doctors, psycho-geriatricians and indeed any doctor involved in the care of older people.

The Diploma in Geriatric Medicine is in 2 parts, the first of which is a written examination of multiple choice (best of 5) questions, lasting 2 1/2 hours normally held twice a year at the Royal College of Physicians of London.

The second part is a Clinical Examination also held twice a year at various clinical centres in England and Wales. The clinical examination is a four station standardised examination similar to an Objective Standard Clinical Examination (OSCE).

Diploma in Tropical Medicine and Hygiene The Diploma in Tropical Medicine and Hygiene is intended to test the knowledge required of physicians who wish to practise medicine effectively in developing countries.

Candidates for the Diploma in Tropical Medicine & Hygiene must hold a primary medical qualification recognised by the Royal College of Physicians of London.

The Royal College of Physicians of London will accept applications from candidates who are in the process of completing, or have completed within the last 5 years, the Tropical Medicine courses in London, Liverpool, Sheffield and Glasgow, which are recognised as appropriate training centres for the examination. The examination is held once a year over 2 days (unless required for a viva) and is conducted in the following sections: A **Practical Section** lasting 2 hours and 30 minutes consists of a mixture of microscopy specimens, including 20 'spot' questions that are set up on a microscope for identification. Other specimens require the candidate to use the microscopes themselves. They are mainly parasitological and may include faecal, blood and haematological preparations together with some entomological specimens. A **Written Section** (3 hours and 20 minutes in total) consists of three papers. The **Clinical Paper** (1 hour) contains 18 compulsory questions. The first 16 are based on clinical pictures – usually of patients with abnormal physical signs; but occasionally laboratory slides, X-rays, or epidemiological data may be shown. There will be 2 or 3 questions on each, asking (for example) identification, diagnosis, further investigation, treatment etc. Each of these 16 questions is worth a maximum of 5 marks. The last 2 questions (17 and 18) are brief clinical cases, with 2 or 3 questions (again concentrating on diagnosis or differential diagnosis, investigation and treatment). The **Multiple Choice Question Paper** (1 hour and 20 minutes) consists of 40 multiple choice questions designed to test the knowledge of tropical medicine and hygiene over a wide area. The **Preventative Medicine Paper** (1 hour including 5 minutes reading time) consists of 10 questions of which the candidate must choose 5. Each question may have several parts, covering all aspects of preventative medicine and international community health in a tropical context.

There is also an **Oral ('Viva') Examination** for borderline candidates. The examination is conducted by 2 examiners. The first part of the examination (10 minutes) is a discussion of an illustrated clinical case history, which candidates are allowed to study for 10 minutes before the examination. The second part of the examination (10 minutes) consists of more general questions.

THE ROYAL COLLEGE OF PSYCHIATRISTS

17 Belgrave Square
London SW1X 8PG
Tel: 020 7235 2351
Fax: 020 7245 1231
E-mail: latkinson@rcpsych.ac.uk
Website: www.rcpsych.ac.uk

The RCPsych is the professional and educational body for psychiatrists in the UK and Ireland. We are committed to improving the understanding of psychiatry and mental health, and are at the forefront in setting and achieving the highest standards through education, training and research. We actively promote psychiatry as a career, and provide guidance and support to our members and associates.

MEMBERSHIP
Pre-Membership Psychiatric Trainee
New Associate
Corresponding Associate
Affiliate
Specialist Associate
Member (MRCPsych)
Fellow (FRCPsych)
Honorary Fellow
International Associate

QUALIFICATION/EXAMINATIONS
MRCPsych qualifying exams
FRCPsych qualifying exams

DESIGNATORY LETTERS
MRCPsych, FRCPsych

THE ROYAL COLLEGE OF RADIOLOGISTS

38 Portland Place
London W1B 1JQ
Tel: 020 7636 4432
Fax: 020 7323 3100
E-mail: enquiries@rcr.ac.uk
Website: www.rcr.ac.uk

The RCR is a professional body representing nearly 8,000 medical and dental practitioners worldwide that aims to advance the science and practice of clinical radiology and clinical oncology. We promote the highest standards of professional competence, undertake regular audits of training and practice, conduct examinations for Certificates and Diplomas, encourage CPD among our members, and provide information for the public.

MEMBERSHIP
Junior Member
Associate
Member
Fellow (FRCR)
Honorary Member/Fellow (Hon MRCR/Hon FRCR)

QUALIFICATION/EXAMINATIONS
Certificate of Completion of Training (in Clinical Radiology or Clinical Oncology)
First FRCR Examination
Final FRCR Examination
Diploma in Dental Radiology (DDR)

DESIGNATORY LETTERS
FRCR, Hon MRCR, Hon FRCR

THE ROYAL COLLEGE OF SURGEONS OF EDINBURGH

Nicolson Street
Edinburgh EH8 9DW
Tel: 0131 527 1600
Fax: 0131 557 6406
E-mail: information@rcsed.ac.uk
Website: www.rcsed.ac.uk

The Royal College of Surgeons of Edinburgh, which dates from 1505, is dedicated to the maintenance and promotion of the highest standards of surgical practice, through education, training and rigorous examination, and its liaison with external medical bodies. Today, with more than 17,000 Fellows and Members, we pride ourselves also on our innovation and adaptability.

MEMBERSHIP
Affiliate
Surgical Associate Member
Member (MRCSEd)
Fellow (FRCSEd)

QUALIFICATION/EXAMINATIONS
Please see the Royal College of Surgeons of Edinburgh website.

DESIGNATORY LETTERS
MRCSEd, FRCSEd

THE ROYAL COLLEGE OF SURGEONS OF ENGLAND

35–43 Lincoln's Inn Fields
London WC2A 3PE
Tel: 020 7405 3474
Fax: 020 7831 9438
E-mail: exams@rcseng.ac.uk
Website: www.rcseng.ac.uk

The Royal College of Surgeons of England is committed to enabling surgeons to achieve and maintain the highest standards of surgical practice and patient care. We examine trainees, supervise the training of and provide support and advice for surgeons, promote and support surgical research in the UK, and liaise with the DoH, health authorities, Trusts and hospitals in the UK and other medical and academic organizations worldwide.

MEMBERSHIP
Intercollegiate Member

QUALIFICATION/EXAMINATIONS
Please see the Royal College of Surgeons of England website.

THE SOCIETY OF APOTHECARIES OF LONDON

Black Friars Lane
London EC4V 6EJ
Tel: 020 7236 1180
Fax: 020 7329 3177
E-mail: registrar@apothecaries.org
Website: www.apothecaries.org

The Society of Apothecaries of London was incorporated by Royal Charter in 1617 and allowed to prepare and sell drugs for medicinal purposes, laying the foundations of the British pharmaceutical industry. Later, apothecaries were permitted to prescribe and dispense medicines, becoming the forerunners of today's GPs. Now the Society is primarily an examining body.

QUALIFICATION/EXAMINATIONS

PGDip in the Forensic and Clinical Aspects of Sexual Assault (DFCASA)
PGDip in Forensic Human Identification (DipFHID)
PGDip in Forensic Medical Sciences (DFMS)
PGDip in Genitourinary Medicine (DGUM)
PGDip in the History of Medicine (DHMSA)
PGDip in HIV Medicine
PGDip in the Medical Care of Catastrophes (DMCC)
PGDip in Medical Jurisprudence (DMJ)
PGDip in the Philosophy of Medicine (DPMSA)

METALLURGY

Membership of Professional Institutions and Associations

INSTITUTE OF CORROSION

7B High Street Mews
High Street
Vimy Road
Leighton Buzzard
Bedfordshire LU7 1EA
Tel: 01525 851771
Fax: 01525 376690
E-mail: admin@icorr.org
Website: www.icorr.org

The Institute of Corrosion has since 1959 been serving the corrosion science, technology and engineering community in the fight against corrosion, which costs the UK around 4 per cent of GNP per annum. We promote the establishment and promotion of sound corrosion management practice, the advancement of cost-effective corrosion control measures, and a sustained effort to raise corrosion awareness at all stages of design, fabrication and operation.

MEMBERSHIP

Student Member
Ordinary Member
Technical Member (TICorr)
Professional Member (MICorr)
Engineering Technician (EngTech)
Incorporated Engineer (IEng)
Chartered Engineer (CEng)
Chartered Scientist (CSci)

QUALIFICATION/EXAMINATIONS

Please see the Institute of Corrosion website.

DESIGNATORY LETTERS

TICorr, MICorr, EngTech, IEng, CEng

THE INSTITUTE OF METAL FINISHING

Exeter House
48 Holloway Head
Birmingham B1 1NQ
Tel: 01216 227387
Fax: 01216 666316
E-mail: exeterhouse@instituteofmetalfinishing.org
Website: www.uk-finishing.org.uk

The IMF, founded in 1925, provides a focus for surface engineering and finishing activities worldwide through the fulfilment of technical, educational and professional needs at all levels for individuals and companies involved in the coatings industry. We promote R&D within the industry and CPD for our members, cooperate with other institutes, and liaise with legislative bodies to influence decision-making.

MEMBERSHIP
Student
Affiliate
Associate (AssocIMF)
Technician (TechIMF)
Licentiate (LIMF)
Member (MIMF)
Fellow (FIMF)
Engineering Technician (EngTech)
Sustaining Member (company)

QUALIFICATION/EXAMINATIONS
Foundation Certificate
Technician Certificate
Advanced Technician Certificate

DESIGNATORY LETTERS
AssocIMF, TechIMF, LIMF, MIMF, FIMF, EngTech

METEOROLOGY AND CLIMATOLOGY

Membership of Professional Institutions and Associations

MET OFFICE COLLEGE

Met Office
Fitzroy Road
Exeter
Devon EX1 3PB
Tel: 01392 885680
Fax: 01392 885681
E-mail: met-training@metoffice.gov.uk
Website: www.metoffice.gov.uk

The Meteorological Office College is part of the Met Office and is located in Exeter, Devon. We provide meteorological training for our own staff and to meteorological services worldwide, as places become available on a fee-paying basis.

QUALIFICATION/EXAMINATIONS
NVQ in Meteorological Observing (Level 3)
NVQ in Meteorological Weather Forecasting (Level 4)
Forecaster Foundation Training Programme
Professional Development Programme
Specialist Forecaster Programme

ROYAL METEOROLOGICAL SOCIETY

104 Oxford Road
Reading RG1 7LL
Tel: 0118 956 8500
Fax: 0118 956 8571
E-mail: info@rmets.org
Website: www.rmets.org

The RMetS is the learned and professional society for anyone whose profession or interests are connected with weather and climate. It administers the NVQs of the profession and is the accreditation body for the status of Chartered Meteorologist. Its principal aim is the advancement of the understanding of weather and climate for the benefit of everyone.

MEMBERSHIP
Student
Associate Fellow
Fellow (FRMetS)
Honorary Member
Chartered Meteorologist (CMet)
Chartered Environmentalist (CEnv)
School Member
Corporate Member

DESIGNATORY LETTERS
FRMetS, CMet, CEnv

MICROSCOPY

Membership of Professional Institutions and Associations

THE ROYAL MICROSCOPICAL SOCIETY

Oxford OX4 1AJ
Tel: 01865 254760
Fax: 01865 791237
E-mail: info@rms.org.uk
Website: www.rms.org.uk

The RMS, which dates from 1839, is an international scientific society dedicated to advancing the science of microscopy and the interests of its 1,400 members, who range from individuals interested in microscopy to scientists and company members representing manufacturers and suppliers of microscopes, other equipment and services.

MEMBERSHIP
Ordinary Member
Fellow (FRMS)
Corporate Member

DESIGNATORY LETTERS
FRMS

MUSEUM AND RELATED WORK

Membership of Professional Institutions and Associations

MUSEUMS ASSOCIATION

24 Calvin Street
London E1 6NW
Tel: 020 7426 6955
Fax: 020 7426 6962
E-mail: cpd@museumsassociation.org
Website: www.museumsassociation.org

The MA is the oldest museums association in the world, set up in 1889 to guard the interests of museums and galleries. Today, we have 5,200 individual members, 600 institutional members and 250 corporate members. Our aim is to enhance the value of museums to society by sharing knowledge, developing skills, inspiring innovation and providing leadership.

MEMBERSHIP
Student
Volunteer
Professional Member
Associate (AMA)
Commercial Member
Institutional Member

DESIGNATORY LETTERS
AMA

MUSIC

Membership of Professional Institutions and Associations

ABRSM (ASSOCIATED BOARD OF THE ROYAL SCHOOLS OF MUSIC)

24 Portland Place
London W1B 1LU
Tel: 020 7636 5400
Fax: 020 7637 0234
E-mail: abrsm@abrsm.org
Website: www.abrsm.org

ABRSM's mission is to motivate musical achievement. We aim to support the development of learners and teachers in music education worldwide and to celebrate their achievements. We do this through authoritative and internationally recognized assessments, publications and professional development support for teachers, and through charitable donations.

MEMBERSHIP
Licentiate (LRSM)
Fellow (FRSM)

QUALIFICATION/EXAMINATIONS
Certificate of Teaching (CT ABRSM)
Diploma in Instrumental/Vocal Teaching (DipABRSM)
Diploma in Music Direction (DipABRSM)
Diploma in Music Performance (DipABRSM)

Please see the ABRSM website for details of other examinations and awards.

DESIGNATORY LETTERS
CT ABRSM, DipABRSM, LRSM, FRSM

INCORPORATED SOCIETY OF MUSICIANS

10 Stratford Place
London WIC 1AA
Tel: 020 7629 4413
Fax: 020 7408 1538
E-mail: membership@ism.org
Website: www.ism.org

The ISM, a non-profit-making organization founded in 1882, is the UK's professional body for musicians. We promote the art of music and the interests of musicians through campaigns, support and practical advice. Members also receive our monthly in-house magazine, *Music Journal*, which includes news and information on CPD.

MEMBERSHIP
Student Member
Associate Member
Full Member
Corporate Member

MUSICAL INSTRUMENT TECHNOLOGY

Membership of Professional Institutions and Associations

INCORPORATED SOCIETY OF ORGAN BUILDERS

Smithy Steads
Cragg Vale
Hebden Bridge
West Yorkshire HX7 5SQ
Fax: 0870 139 3645
E-mail: admin1@isob.co.uk
Website: www.isob.co.uk/

The ISOB was founded in 1947 to advance the science and practice of organ building, to provide a central organization for organ builders, and to provide for the better definition and protection of the profession by a system of examinations and the issue of certificates and distinctions. We hold regular meetings and conferences around the UK and overseas.

MEMBERSHIP
Student Member
Ordinary Member (MISOB)
Associate Member (AISOB)
Fellow (FISOB)
Councillor (CISOB)

DESIGNATORY LETTERS
MISOB, AISOB, FISOB, CISOB

PIANOFORTE TUNERS' ASSOCIATION

PO Box 1312
Lightwater
Woking
Surrey GU18 5UB
Tel: 0845 602 8796
E-mail: secretary@pianotuner.org.uk
Website: www.pianotuner.org.uk

The PTA is a professional body committed to improving standards, and applicants for membership must pass a theoretical and practical examination to prove their ability as a qualified piano tuner or technician. We publish a regular newsletter and hold an Annual Convention and General Meeting in different towns around Britain, to which members and aspiring non-members are invited.

MEMBERSHIP
Student
Patron
Associate
Technician Member
Member

NAVAL ARCHITECTURE

Membership of Professional Institutions and Associations

THE ROYAL INSTITUTION OF NAVAL ARCHITECTS

10 Upper Belgrave Street
London SW1X 8BQ
Tel: 020 7235 4622
Fax: 020 7259 5912
E-mail: membership@rina.org.uk
Website: www.rina.org.uk

The RINA is an internationally renowned professional institution whose members are involved at all levels in the design, construction, maintenance and operation of marine vessels and structures. Our members are widely represented in industry, universities and colleges, and maritime organizations in over 90 countries.

MEMBERSHIP
Student Member
Associate (AssocRINA)
Associate Member (AMRINA)
Member (MRINA)
Fellow (FRINA)

DESIGNATORY LETTERS
AssocRINA, AMRINA, MRINA. FRINA

NAVIGATION, SEAMANSHIP AND MARINE QUALIFICATIONS

Membership of Professional Institutions and Associations

THE NAUTICAL INSTITUTE

202 Lambeth Road
London SE1 7LQ
Tel: 020 7928 1351
Fax: 020 7401 2817
E-mail: sec@nautinst.org
Website: www.nautinst.org

The Nautical Institute is an international professional body for maritime professionals and others with an interest in maritime sciences, with 40 branches worldwide and more than 6,500 members in over 100 countries. It provides the strongest possible professional focus, dedicated to improving standards of those in control of seagoing craft while maintaining the Institute as an international centre of nautical excellence.

MEMBERSHIP
Honorary Fellow
Fellow
Associate Fellow (AFNI)
Member (MNI)
Associate Member (AMNI)

QUALIFICATION/EXAMINATIONS
Harbour Master's Certificate
Pilotage Certificate
Command Diploma

DESIGNATORY LETTERS
FNI, AFNI, MNI, AMNI

THE ROYAL INSTITUTE OF NAVIGATION

1 Kensington Gore
London SW7 2AT
Tel: 020 7591 3130
Fax: 020 7591 3131
E-mail: info@rin.org.uk
Website: www.rin.org.uk

The RIN is a learned society with charitable status. Our aims are: to unite those with a professional or personal interest in any aspect of navigation in one unique body; to further the development of navigation in every sphere; and to increase public awareness of both the art and science of navigation, how it has shaped the past, how it impacts our world today, and how it will affect the future.

MEMBERSHIP
Junior Associate Member
Student
Associate
Member (MRIN)
Associate Fellow (AFRIN)
Fellow (FRIN)
Affiliate Club
Affiliate College or University
Corporate Member

DESIGNATORY LETTERS
MRIN, AFRIN, FRIN

NON-DESTRUCTIVE TESTING

Membership of Professional Institutions and Associations

THE BRITISH INSTITUTE OF NON-DESTRUCTIVE TESTING

Newton Building
St George's Avenue
Northampton NN2 6JB
Tel: 01604 89 3811
Fax: 01604 89 3861
E-mail: info@bindt.org
Website: www.bindt.org

The BINDT was formed in 1976 from the merger of the Society of Non-Destructive Examination (SONDE) and the Society of Industrial Radiology and Allied Methods of Non-Destructive Testing, later renamed the NDT Society of Great Britain (NDTS), both formed in 1954. Our aim is to promote and advance the science and practice of non-destructive testing, condition monitoring, diagnostic engineering and all other materials and quality testing disciplines.

MEMBERSHIP
Student Member
Affiliate
Practitioner Member (PInstNDT)
Graduate Member (GInstNDT)
Member (MInstNDT)
Fellow (FInstNDT)
Engineering Technician (EngTech)
Incorporated Engineer (IEng)
Chartered Engineer (CEng)
Licensed Engineering Practitioner
Associate Member (corporate)

DESIGNATORY LETTERS
PInstNDT, GInstNDT, MInstNDT, FInstNDT, EngTech, IEng, CEng

NURSERY NURSING

Membership of Professional Institutions and Associations

COUNCIL FOR AWARDS IN CHILDREN'S CARE AND EDUCATION

Apex House
81 Camp Road
St Albans
Hertfordshire AL1 5GB
Tel: 0845 347 2123
Fax: 01727 818618
E-mail: info@cache.org.uk
Website: www.cache.org.uk

CACHE is an Awarding Body that designs courses and qualifications in the care and education of children and young people. Our courses, which are widely available, range from entry level to advanced qualifications for sector professionals. We regularly lobby the government and other agencies to raise the quality and professionalism of child care.

QUALIFICATION/EXAMINATIONS
Please see the CACHE website.

NURSING AND MIDWIFERY

Membership of Professional Institutions and Associations

THE NURSING & MIDWIFERY COUNCIL

23 Portland Place
London W1B 1PZ
Tel: 020 7333 9333
E-mail: advice@nmc-uk.org
Website: www.nmc-uk.org

The core function of the NMC is to establish standards of education, training, conduct and performance for nursing and midwifery, and to ensure that those standards are maintained, thereby safeguarding the health and well-being of the public. We work closely with partner organizations to provide quality assurance of nursing and midwifery education in the UK.

OCCUPATIONAL THERAPY

Membership of Professional Institutions and Associations

BRITISH ASSOCIATION OF OCCUPATIONAL THERAPISTS

106–114 Borough High Street
Southwark
London SE1 1LB
Tel: 020 7357 6480
Fax: 020 7450 2299
E-mail: membership@cot.co.uk
Website: www.cot.org.uk

The British Association and College of Occupational Therapists is the professional body for occupational therapy in the UK. The College has 28,000 members and represents the profession nationally and internationally.

MEMBERSHIP
Student Member
Associate
Discounted Associate
Professional Member
Discounted Professional Member
Self-employed Member
Retired Member
Overseas Member

QUALIFICATION/EXAMINATIONS
Diploma (DipCOT)

OPTICIANS (DISPENSING)

Dispensing opticians need to be registered with the General Optical Council (GOC; 41 Harley Street, London W1G 8DJ E-mail: goc@optical.org Website: www.optical.org). Qualification takes three years in total, and can be completed by combining a distance learning course or day release while working as a trainee under the supervision of a qualified and GOC-registered optician. Alternatively students can do a two-year FT course followed by one year of supervised practise with a qualified and registered optician. In the UK you can study at six GOC-approved training establishments: Association of British Dispensing Opticians (ABDO), Anglia Ruskin University, Bradford College, City and Islington College, City University and Glasgow Caledonian University. All routes are assessed by final ABDO examinations. On successful completion of training you must register with the GOC in order to practise in the UK. If you qualify as a dispensing optician and have completed training to fit contact lenses, the University of Bradford offers a career progression course that enables you to graduate with a degree in optometry in one calendar year.

ENTRY REQUIREMENTS

You will normally need to have 5 GCSEs (or equivalent) at grades C or above, including English, maths and science. For mature students and overseas/alternative/vocational courses, admission requirements will vary and may be more flexible. For further details contact the admissions tutor at the university you wish to apply to.

Membership of Professional Institutions and Associations

ASSOCIATION OF BRITISH DISPENSING OPTICIANS

199 Gloucester Terrace
London W2 6LD
Tel: 020 7298 5100
Fax: 020 7298 5111
E-mail: general@abdolondon.org.uk
Website: www.abdo.org.uk

The ABDO is the qualifying body for dispensing opticians in the UK. Our aims are to advance the science and art of dispensing optics, to further the education and training of dispensing opticians, and to support and promote the interests of the profession.

MEMBERSHIP

Student Member
Associate Member
Full Member
Fellow (FBDO)

QUALIFICATION/EXAMINATIONS

Certificate in Contact Lens Practice (Level 6)
Diploma in The Assessment & Management of Low Vision (Level 6)
Diploma in Ophthalmic Dispensing (Level 6)
Diploma in Advanced Contact Lens Practice (Level 7)
Diploma in Spectacle Lens Design (Level 7)

DESIGNATORY LETTERS

FBDO

ASSOCIATION OF CONTACT LENS MANUFACTURERS

PO Box 735
Devizes
Wiltshire SN10 3TQ
Tel: 01380 860418
Fax: 01380 860863
E-mail: secgen@aclm.org.uk
Website: www.aclm.org.uk

The ACLM was founded in 1962 to publicize the work of UK contact lens manufacturers, to develop new products and to raise standards. Today we represent the manufacturers of over 95 per cent of prescription contact lenses and lens care products in the UK, and provide a cohesive voice for our members.

MEMBERSHIP

Member

BRITISH CONTACT LENS ASSOCIATION

Walmar House
288/292 Regent Street
London W1B 3AL
Tel: 020 7580 6661
Fax: 020 7580 6669
Website: www.bcla.org.uk

The BCLA is the UK's leading supplier of information and education on contact lenses and the anterior eye, with a membership of around 1,800 in more than 40 countries. Our mission is to promote excellence in the research, manufacture and clinical practice of contact lenses and related areas. Our annual Clinical Conference and Exhibition, the world's largest, attracts more than 1,000 visitors.

MEMBERSHIP
Student Member
Member
Fellow (FBCLA)

QUALIFICATION/EXAMINATIONS
Educational activities include approved Continuing Education and Training courses and evening meetings. For details see the website.

DESIGNATORY LETTERS
FBCLA

OPTOMETRY

Careers in optometry are overseen by the General Optical Council (41 Harley Street, London W1G 8DJ E-mail: goc@optical.org Website: www.optical.org). You can study for an undergraduate optometry degree from one of eight GOC-approved institutions in the UK: Anglia Ruskin University, Aston University, the University of Bradford, Cardiff University, City University, Glasgow Caledonian University, the University of Manchester and the University of Ulster.

LENGTH OF COURSE
Usually 4 years in total (Scotland 5 years): an FT 3-yr (in Scotland 4-yr) degree course, followed by one yr's salaried pre-registration training with a practice under the guidance of a GOC-registered optometrist. This includes a series of assessments throughout the placement, which are set by the College of Optometrists.

ENTRY REQUIREMENTS
You will normally need 5 GCSEs (or equivalent) at grade C or above, one of which should be in English. You will normally be required to have 3 A Level passes/ approx. 320 UCAS tariff points from the following subjects: physics, biology, chemistry or mathematics.

Requirements vary between universities, so be sure to check the university's prospectus and/or consult the relevant admission tutors.

Membership of Professional Institutions and Associations

ASSOCIATION OF OPTOMETRISTS

61 Southwark Street
London SE1 0HL
Tel: 020 7261 9661
Fax: 020 7261 0228
E-mail: postbox@aop.org.uk
Website: www.aop.org.uk

The AOP serves its members by promoting and protecting them, providing them with relevant services, representing and supporting them, enhancing their professional and business effectiveness, and expanding the role of optometry in primary and secondary eyecare.

MEMBERSHIP
Student Member
Honorary Member
Dispensing Associate
Full Member

ORTHOPTICS

Membership of Professional Institutions and Associations

BRITISH AND IRISH ORTHOPTIC SOCIETY

4th Floor
14 Bedford Row
London WC1R 4ED
Tel: 0207 306 1135
E-mail: bios@orthoptics.org.uk
Website: www.orthoptics.org.uk

Orthoptists are AHPs, who diagnose and treat problems with visual development and binocular vision (how the eyes work together as a pair), and eye movement disorders. They are experts in childhood vision screening. Extended roles include stroke, glaucoma, reading difficulties, neurological disorders, low vision.

MEMBERSHIP
Student Members
Members

QUALIFICATION/EXAMINATIONS
Degrees in orthoptics are offered by Liverpool University (www.liv.ac.uk) and Sheffield University (www.sheffield.ac.uk)

OSTEOPATHY AND NATUROPATHY

Membership of Professional Institutions and Associations

BRITISH OSTEOPATHIC ASSOCIATION

3 Park Terrace
Manor Road
Luton
Bedfordshire LU1 3HN
Tel: 01582 488455
Fax: 01582 481533
E-mail: enquiries@osteopathy.org
Website: www.osteopathy.org

The BOA was formed in 1998 as a result of the merger of the British Osteopathic Association, the Osteopathic Association of Great Britain and the Guild of Osteopaths. We provide opportunities for individual and professional development in osteopathic practice and promote the highest standards of osteopathic education and research.

MEMBERSHIP
Student Member
1st/2nd/3rd Year Graduate Member
Full Member
Overseas Member

PATENT AGENCY

Membership of Professional Institutions and Associations

THE CHARTERED INSTITUTE OF PATENT ATTORNEYS

95 Chancery Lane
London WC2A 1DT
Tel: 020 7405 9450
Fax: 020 7430 0471
E-mail: mail@cipa.org.uk
Website: www.cipa.org.uk

CIPA is the professional, training and examining body for patent attorneys in the UK. From 2010 the IP Regulation Board, an independent body within the CIPA, sets the standards for regulation of the profession. Trainees, all technical graduates, also study for the qualification to practise before the European Patent Office.

MEMBERSHIP
Student Member
Associate
Fellow
Registered Patent Attorney (RPA)
Chartered Patent Attorney (CPA)

QUALIFICATION/EXAMINATIONS
Qualifying examination for registration as a Patent Attorney

DESIGNATORY LETTERS
RPA, CPA

PENSION MANAGEMENT

Membership of Professional Institutions and Associations

THE PENSIONS MANAGEMENT INSTITUTE

PMI House
4–10 Artillery Lane
London E1 7LS
Tel: 020 7247 1452
Fax: 020 7375 0603
E-mail: education@pensions-pmi.org.uk
Website: www.pensions-pmi.org.uk

The Pensions Management Institute is the professional body that promotes standards of excellence and lifetime learning for pensions professionals and trustees through its qualifications, membership and ongoing support services. For further details please visit our website.

MEMBERSHIP
Student Member
Ordinary Member (MPMI)
Associate Member (APMI)
Fellow (FPMI)

QUALIFICATION/EXAMINATIONS
Retirement Provision Certificate (RPC)
Advanced Diploma in Retirement Provision
Qualification in Pensions Administration (QPA)
Diploma in Pension Calculations (DPC)
Qualification in Public Sector Pensions Administration (QPSPA)
Diploma in Member Directed Pension Scheme Administration (MDPSA)
Diploma in International Employee Benefits (Dip. IEB)
The Awards in Pensions Trusteeship

DESIGNATORY LETTERS
MPMI, APMI, FPMI

PERSONNEL MANAGEMENT

Membership of Professional Institutions and Associations

CHARTERED INSTITUTE OF PERSONNEL AND DEVELOPMENT

151 The Broadway
London SW19 1JQ
Tel: 020 8612 6208
Fax: 020 8612 6201
E-mail: membershipenquiry@cipd.co.uk
Website: www.cipd.co.uk

The CIPD is Europe's largest HR and development professional body. As a globally recognized brand with over 135,000 members, we pride ourselves on supporting and developing those responsible for the management and development of people within organizations.

MEMBERSHIP
Affiliate Member
Studying Affiliate Member
Associate Member
Licentiate Member
Graduate Member
Chartered Member (MCIPD)
Chartered Fellow (FCIPD)
Chartered Companion (CCIPD)
For further information see; www.cipd.co.uk/membership

QUALIFICATION/EXAMINATIONS
We are launching a new qualifications structure in January 2010. For details of current courses see; www.cipd.co.uk/qualifications

DESIGNATORY LETTERS
MCIPD, FCIPD, CCIPD

THE INSTITUTE OF CONTINUING PROFESSIONAL DEVELOPMENT

Grosvenor Gardens House
35/37 Grosvenor Gardens
London SW1W 0BS
Tel: 020 7828 1965
Fax: 020 7828 1967
E-mail: info@cpdinstitute.org
Website: www.cpdinstitute.org

The Institute of Continuing Professional Development is part of the Continuing Professional Development Foundation, an educational charitable trust providing high-quality and broad-ranging CPD since 1981. We serve the public interest by helping to raise the effectiveness of professionals through the promotion of CPD as an important and integral element of lifelong learning.

MEMBERSHIP
Member (MInstCPD)
Fellow (FInstCPD)

DESIGNATORY LETTERS
MInstCPD, FInstCPD

UK EMPLOYEES ASSISTANCE PROFESSIONALS ASSOCIATION

3 Moors Close
Ducklington
Witney
Oxfordshire OX29 7TW
Tel: 07770 924615
Fax: 01993 772765
E-mail: info@eapa.org.uk
Website: www.eapa.org.uk

The EAPA is the professional body for Employee Assistance Programmes (EAPs). It represents the interests of professionals concerned with employee assistance, psychological health and well-being in the UK. EAPA members include external and internal EAP providers, purchasers, counsellors, consultants and trainers.

MEMBERSHIP
Individual Member
Associate Member
Retiree Member
Organizational Member
Registered External/Internal Provider

PHARMACY

Membership of Professional Institutions and Associations

ROYAL PHARMACEUTICAL SOCIETY OF GREAT BRITAIN

1 Lambeth High Street
London SE1 7JN
Tel: 020 7735 9141
Fax: 020 7735 7629
E-mail: enquiries@rpsgb.org
Website: www.rpsgb.org

The RPSGB, which dates from 1841, is the professional body for pharmacists and pharmacy technicians in England, Scotland and Wales. Our primary objectives are to lead, regulate, develop and represent the profession. We promote advancement of the science and practice of pharmacy, and pharmaceutical education and knowledge, and liaise with government and other bodies in the interests of our members.

MEMBERSHIP
Pharmacy Technician
Member (MRPharmS)
Fellow (FRPharmS)

DESIGNATORY LETTERS
MRPharmS, FRPharmS

THE COLLEGE OF PHARMACY PRACTICE

28 Warwick Row
Coventry CV1 1EY
Tel: 024 762 21359
Fax: 024 765 21110
E-mail: info@collpharm.org.uk
Website: www.collpharm.org.uk

The College of Pharmacy Practice, set up in 1981 by the Pharmaceutical Society of Great Britain, is an organization of pharmacists who share the aim of promoting and maintaining a high standard of pharmacy practice. Its mission is to promote professional and personal development through education, examination, practice and research, benefiting both patients and healthcare provision.

MEMBERSHIP
Student Member
Associate (ACPP)
Member (MCPP)
Fellow (FCPP)
Member Emeritus

DESIGNATORY LETTERS
ACPP, MCPP, FCPP

THE PHARMACEUTICAL SOCIETY OF NORTHERN IRELAND

73 University Street
Belfast BT7 1HL
Tel: 028 9032 6927
Fax: 028 9043 9919
Website: www.psni.org.uk

The Pharmaceutical Society of Northern Ireland, founded in 1925, is the regulatory and professional body for pharmacists in Northern Ireland. It maintains a register of more than 2,000 pharmacists and over 500 pharmacy premises, and sets and promotes the standards for pharmacists' admission to and remaining on the register, thereby protecting public safety.

MEMBERSHIP
Trainee
Member

QUALIFICATION/EXAMINATIONS
Registration Examination

PHOTOGRAPHY

Membership of Professional Institutions and Associations

ASSOCIATION OF PHOTOGRAPHERS (AOP)

81 Leonard Street
London EC2A 4QS
Tel: 020 7739 6669
Fax: 020 7739 8707
E-mail: general@aophoto.co.uk
Website: www.the-aop.org

The AOP was founded in 1968 to promote the highest standards throughout the industry and to improve the rights of all professional photographers based in the UK. Our membership currently comprises 1,800 photographers and photographic assistants, and we are supported by photographers' agents, printers, and manufacturers and suppliers of photographic equipment.

MEMBERSHIP
Student Member
Assistant Member
Provisional Member
Photographer (full) Member
Agent Member
College Member
Affiliated Company

BRITISH INSTITUTE OF PROFESSIONAL PHOTOGRAPHY

1 Prebendal Court
Oxford Road
Aylesbury
Buckinghamshire HP19 8EY
Tel: 01296 718530
Fax: 01296 336367
E-mail: info@bipp.com
Website: www.bipp.com

The BIPP is the qualifying body for professional photographers in the UK. We provide support, training and qualifications for photographers across all types of photography, and organize a number of regional activities and events. A not-for-profit organization, we ensure that professional standards are met and maintained.

MEMBERSHIP
Open to full- or part-time professional photographers. Join as an Affiliate (maximum of 3 years) and work towards gaining a professional qualification. Student membership is also available.

QUALIFICATION/EXAMINATIONS
Three tiers of qualification:
Licentiateship (entry level) (LBIPP)
Associateship (ABIPP)
Fellowship (FBIPP)
Full details of the qualifications criteria may be found at www.bipp.com

DESIGNATORY LETTERS
LBIPP, ABIPP, FBIPP

MASTER PHOTOGRAPHERS ASSOCIATION

Jubilee House
1 Chancery Lane
Darlington
Co Durham DL1 5QP
Tel: 01325 356555
Fax: 01325 357813
E-mail: general@mpauk.com
Website: www.mpauk.com

The MPA was founded in 1952 and is now the UK's only organization for FT, qualified professional photographers. We have more than 2,000 members, who enjoy a range of benefits, including education, qualifications, informative regional meetings, business building promotions and marketing support, and abide by the Association's Code of Conduct.

MEMBERSHIP
Licentiate (LMPA)
Associate (AMPA)
Fellow (FMPA)

QUALIFICATION/EXAMINATIONS

The Diploma in Photographic Practice (Dip.PP) is recognised by SkillSet, as a benchmark competence mapped to the Photo Imaging National Standards: it is available to all qualified members and is an assessment process of professional photographic business and personal skills.

DESIGNATORY LETTERS

LMPA, AMPA, FMPA, DipPP

THE ROYAL PHOTOGRAPHIC SOCIETY

Fenton House
122 Wells Road
Bath BA2 3AH
Tel: 01225 325733
Fax: 01225 448688
E-mail: reception@rps.org
Website: www.rps.org

The RPS, which dates from 1853, is an educational charity whose aim is to promote the art and science of photography. Membership is open to anyone and we provide information, training and advice, hold workshops on a variety of photographic topics and stage three major touring exhibitions, as well as a monthly exhibition of members' work at our headquarters in Bath.

MEMBERSHIP

Student Member
Member
Licentiate (LRPS)
Associate (ARPS)
Fellow (FRPS)

QUALIFICATION/EXAMINATIONS

Qualified Imaging Scientist and Licentiate (QIS LRPS)
Graduate Imaging Scientist and Associate (GIS ARPS)
Accredited Imaging Scientist and Associate (AIS ARPS)
Accredited Senior Imaging Scientist and Fellow (ASIS FRPS)

DESIGNATORY LETTERS

LRPS, ARPS, FRPS

PHYSICS

Membership of Professional Institutions and Associations

INSTITUTE OF PHYSICS AND ENGINEERING IN MEDICINE

Fairmount House
230 Tadcaster Road
York YO24 1ES
Tel: 01904 610821
Fax: 01904 612279
E-mail: office@ipem.org.uk
Website: www.ipem.ac.uk

The IPEM is dedicated to bringing together physical science, engineering and clinical professionals in academia, healthcare services and industry to share knowledge, advance science and technology, and inform and educate the public, with the purpose of improving the understanding, detection and treatment of disease and the management of patients.

MEMBERSHIP

Student Member
Affiliate

Associate
Medical Member (MedMIPEM)
Medical Fellow (MedFIPEM)
Incorporated Member (IIPEM)
Corporate Member (MIPEM)
Fellow (FIPEM)
Overseas Affiliate
Company Member

DESIGNATORY LETTERS
MedMIPEM, MedFIPEM, IIPEM, MIPEM, FIPEM

THE INSTITUTE OF PHYSICS

76 Portland Place
London W1B 1NT
Tel: 020 7470 4800
Fax: 020 7470 4848
E-mail: physics@iop.org
Website: www.iop.org

The IOP is a scientific charity devoted to increasing the practice, understanding and application of physics. We have a worldwide membership of over 36,000 and are a leading communicator of physics-related science to all audiences, from specialists through to government and the general public. Our publishing company, IOP Publishing, is a world leader in scientific publishing and the electronic dissemination of physics.

MEMBERSHIP
Student Member
Affiliate
Associate Member (AMInstP)
Member (MInstP)
Fellow (FInstP)
Chartered Physicist (CPhys)

DESIGNATORY LETTERS
AMInstP, MInstP, FInstP, CPhys

PHYSIOTHERAPY

Membership of Professional Institutions and Associations

THE CHARTERED SOCIETY OF PHYSIOTHERAPY

14 Bedford Row
London WC1R 4ED
Tel: 0207 306 6666
Fax: 0207 306 6611
E-mail: enquiries@csp.org.uk
Website: www.csp.org.uk

The CSP is the professional, educational and trade union body for the UK's 48,000 chartered physiotherapists, physiotherapy students and assistants. In order to become a member of the CSP it is necessary to have undertaken a qualification recognized by the Health Professions Council (HPC) – see; www.hpc-uk.org.

MEMBERSHIP
Student Member
Associate
Member (MCSP)
Fellow (FCSP)

DESIGNATORY LETTERS
MCSP, FCSP

PLASTICS AND RUBBER

Membership of Professional Institutions and Associations

LONDON METROPOLITAN POLYMER CENTRE

London Metropolitan University
166–220 Holloway Road
London N7 8DB
Tel: 020 7133 2248
Fax: 020 7133 2184
E-mail: polymers@londonmet.ac.uk
Website: www.londonmet.ac.uk/depts/polymers/

The London Metropolitan Polymer Centre is a leading UK centre for education, research and consultancy in polymer engineering, science and technology. We have a comprehensive range of modern equipment for polymer processing, testing, characterization, etc, offer courses from technician to postgraduate level, and work closely with industry, contributing to its continuing technical and commercial success.

QUALIFICATION/EXAMINATIONS
NC in Polymer Technology
HNC in Polymer Engineering
HND in Polymer Science and Engineering
BEng in Polymer Engineering
BSc in Sports Product Design
MSc in Manufacture and Design for Polymer Products
MSc in Plastics Product Design
MSc in Plastics Product Design with Management
MSc in Plastics Product Design with Marketing
MSc in Polymer Science and Engineering
MRes in Polymer Trecnology

PLUMBING

Membership of Professional Institutions and Associations

CHARTERED INSTITUTE OF PLUMBING AND HEATING ENGINEERING

64 Station Lane
Hornchurch
Essex RM12 6NB
Tel: 01708 472791
Fax: 01708 448987
E-mail: linfo@ciphe.org.uk
Website: www.ciphe.org.uk

The CIPHE, founded in 1906, is the professional body for the UK plumbing and heating industry. Our membership of around 12,000 is made up of individuals from a wide range of backgrounds and includes consultants, specifiers, designers, public health engineers, lecturers, trainers, trainees and practitioners, as well as manufacturers and distributors.

MEMBERSHIP
Trainee
Affiliate
Companion (CompCIPHE)
Associate (ACIPHE)
Member (MCIPHE)
Fellow (FCIPHE)

QUALIFICATION/EXAMINATIONS
Master Plumber Certificate (awarded jointly with the Worshipful Company of Plumbers and the City & Guilds of London Institute)

DESIGNATORY LETTERS
CompCIPHE, ACIPHE, MCIPHE, FCIPHE

PRINTING

Membership of Professional Institutions and Associations

PROSKILLS UK

Centurion Court
85b Milton Park
Abingdon
Oxfordshire OX14 4RY
Tel: 01235 833844
E-mail: info@proskills.co.uk
Website: www.proskills.co.uk

Proskills UK is the bridge between employers and Government on skills and training. Employer-led representing 9 key industries, Building Products, Coatings, Extractive and Mineral Processing, Furniture, Furnishings & Interiors, Glass & Related Industries, Glazed Ceramics, Paper, Printing and Wood industries, which make up a third of UK manufacturing sector. We help to raise the profile of the sector, set the skills standards and qualifications and ensure that the skills and funding system delivers against the current and future needs of the industries.

QUALIFICATION/EXAMINATIONS
Please see the Proskills UK website.

THE INSTITUTE OF PAPER, PRINTING AND PUBLISHING (IP3)

Runnymede Malthouse
off Hummer Road
Egham
Surrey TW20 9BD
Tel: 0870 330 8625
Fax: 0870 330 8615
E-mail: info@ip3.org.uk
Website: www.ip3.org.uk

IP3 is the professional body representing the interests of individuals within the paper, printing and publishing sector. It was formed in 2005 from the merger of the Institute of Paper, the Institute of Printing and the Institute of Publishing, and brought together more than 2,000 members and a wealth of knowledge.

MEMBERSHIP
Student
Associate (AIP3)
Member (MIP3)
Fellow (FIP3)

QUALIFICATION/EXAMINATIONS
Certificate

DESIGNATORY LETTERS
AIP3, MIP3, FIP3

PROFESSIONAL INVESTIGATION

Membership of Professional Institutions and Associations

THE INSTITUTE OF PROFESSIONAL INVESTIGATORS

Claremont House
70-72 Alma Road
Windsor
BERKS., SL4 3EZ
Tel: 0870 330 8622
Fax: 0870 330 8612
E-mail: admin@ipi.org.uk
Website: www.ipi.org.uk

The IPI was founded in 1976 as a professional body, catering primarily for the work and educational needs of professional investigators of all types and all specializations. We encourage members' CPD and require them to adhere to the Institute's strict code of ethics, and we promote the recognition of professional investigation as a profession by government, legislative bodies and the public.

MEMBERSHIP
Associate
Member (MIPI)
Fellow (FIPI)

QUALIFICATION/EXAMINATIONS
The Institute provides an interactive online Foundation Course for students and others interested in becoming part of the investigative industry, this course also provides a refresher course for those who need to update their specialisation and/or interest in other areas of investigative work.

DESIGNATORY LETTERS
MIPI, FIPI

PSYCHOANALYSIS

Membership of Professional Institutions and Associations

THE BRITISH PSYCHOANALYTICAL SOCIETY

Byron House
112a Shirland Road
London W9 2EQ
Tel: 020 7563 5000
Fax: 020 7563 5001
Website: www.psychoanalysis.org.uk

The British Psychoanalytical Society was founded in 1913 and now has 438 members and 46 candidates for membership. Our aims include: to support the development of psychoanalytical knowledge as a general theory of mind, to further the clinical and scientific standards of psychoanalysis, and to train high-quality psychoanalytical professionals in sufficient numbers to develop the profession.

MEMBERSHIP
Associate Member
Full Member

PSYCHOLOGY

Membership of Professional Institutions and Associations

BRITISH PSYCHOLOGICAL SOCIETY

St Andrews House
48 Princess Road East
Leicester LE1 7DR
Tel: 0116 254 9568
Fax: 0116 247 1314
E-mail: enquiry@bps.org.uk
Website: www.bps.org.uk

The British Psychological Society is the representative body for psychology and psychologists in the UK. Formed in 1901, it has more than 47,000 members. Through its Royal Charter, the Society has responsibility for the development, promotion and application of pure and applied psychology for the public good.

MEMBERSHIP
Student Member
Graduate Member
Associate Fellow (AFBPsS)
Fellow (FBPsS)
Honorary Fellow
Foreign Affiliate
Chartered Membership (CPsychol)

QUALIFICATION/EXAMINATIONS
Award in Educational Psychology (Scotland)
Diploma in Forensic Psychology (Stage 2)
Practioner Full Membership Qualification (PFMQ) in Clinical Neuopsychology
Qualification in Counselling Psychology (QCoP)
Qualification in Health Psychology (Stage 2)
Qualification in Occupational Psychology (QOccPsych)
Qualification in Sport & Exercise Psychology (QSEP)

DESIGNATORY LETTERS
AFBPsS, FBPsS, CPsychol

PSYCHOTHERAPY

Membership of Professional Institutions and Associations

ASSOCIATION OF CHILD PSYCHOTHERAPISTS

120 West Heath Road
London NW3 7TU
Tel: 020 8458 1609
Fax: 020 8458 1482
E-mail: contactus@childpsychotherapy.org.uk
Website: www.childpsychotherapy.org.uk

The ACP is the main professional body for psychoanalytic child and adolescent psychotherapists in the UK. Our members work with children and young people as well as their parents, families and wider networks, treating a wide range of difficulties ranging from problems with sleeping and bedwetting to eating disorders, self-harm, depression and anxiety.

MEMBERSHIP
Member

BRITISH ASSOCIATION FOR COUNSELLING AND PSYCHOTHERAPY

BACP House
15 St John's Business Park
Lutterworth
Leicestershire LE17 4HB
Tel: 01455 883300
Fax: 01455 550243
E-mail: bacp@bacp.co.uk
Website: www.bacp.co.uk

BACP is the largest and broadest body within the sector and participates in the development of counselling and psychotherapy at an international level. Our work with large and small organizations ranges from advising schools on how to set up a counselling service to assisting the NHS on service provision, working with voluntary agencies and supporting independent practitioners.

MEMBERSHIP
Student Member
Affiliate Member
Associate Member
Member (MBACP)
Accredited Member (MBACP Accred)
Fellow (FBACP)

QUALIFICATION/EXAMINATIONS
We run workshops for members and accredit individual counsellors/psychotherapists, supervisors, counselling services and training courses. For details see our website.

DESIGNATORY LETTERS
MBACP, MBACP (Accred). FBACP

BRITISH ASSOCIATION FOR COUNSELLING AND PSYCHOTHERAPY

15 St John's Business Park
Lutterworth
Leicestershire LE17 4HB
Tel: 01455 883300
Fax: 01455 550243
E-mail: bacp@bacp.co.uk
Website: www.bacp.co.uk

The British Association for Counselling and Psychotherapy welcomes applications from qualified and experienced counsellors who wish to become BACP Accredited. BACP Accreditation as a counsellor offers a direct route to Registration as an independent practitioner with the United Kingdom Register of Counsellors.

MEMBERSHIP
Student
Associate
Member (MBACP)
Fellow (FBACP)

QUALIFICATION/EXAMINATIONS
SEAs Certificate
SEAs Diploma
SEAs Professional Qualification

DESIGNATORY LETTERS
MBACP, MBACP(Accred), FBACP

BRITISH ASSOCIATION FOR THE PERSON CENTRED APPROACH

BAPCA
PO Box 143
Ross-on-Wye
Herefordshire HR9 9AH
Tel: 01989 763863
E-mail: enquires@bapca.org.uk
Website: www.bapca.org.uk

The BAPCA was founded in 1989 as a non-religious, non-profit-making organization with the aim of advancing education in Client-Centred Psychotherapy and Counselling and the Person-Centred Approach through its publications and website, and cooperation with other national and international organizations with similar goals.

MEMBERSHIP
Individual Member
Joint Member
International Member
Institutional Member

BRITISH ASSOCIATION OF PSYCHOTHERAPISTS

37 Mapesbury Road
London NW2 4HJ
Tel: 020 8452 9823
Fax: 020 8452 5182
E-mail: mail@bap-psychotherapy.org
Website: www.bap-psychotherapy.org

The BAP is one of the longest established and largest independent providers of Jungian analytic and psychoanalytic psychotherapy for adults and children in the UK. We have been training psychoanalytic and Jungian psychotherapists for nearly 60 years, and our members work in the NHS, the corporate and voluntary sectors and as private practitioners.

MEMBERSHIP
Member

QUALIFICATION/EXAMINATIONS
Certificate/Diploma/MSc in Psychodynamics of Human Development (jointly with Birkbeck College, University of London)
DPsych in Child and Adolescent Psychotherapy (jointly with Birkbeck College, University of London)

CAMBRIDGE COLLEGE OF HYPNOTHERAPY

24 Milton Road
Impington
Cambridge CB24 9NF
Tel: 01223 235127
E-mail: j.teague@ntlworld.com
Website: www.hypnotherapytraining.org.uk

The CCH offers training to become a professional hypntherapist The course is accredited by the NCH, HA, APHP and NRAH. No formal qualifications are required to enrol on the course. What is required is a willingness to learn, a sense of humour and a genuine compassion and liking for people from all paths in life. This can be a very rewarding new or second career or a supplement to your current work / lifestyle.

MEMBERSHIP
RSM, HA, NCH, NRAH, NCSAG,

QUALIFICATION/EXAMINATIONS
Diploma in Hypnotherapy

DESIGNATORY LETTERS
DipTHP

NATIONAL COLLEGE OF HYPNOSIS AND PSYCHOTHERAPY

PO Box 5779
Loughborough
Leicestershire LE12 5ZF
Tel: 0845 257 8735
E-mail: enquiries@nchp, org, uk
Website: www.hypnotherapyuk.net

The NCHP is a not-for-profit organization founded in 1977 and now offers accredited hypnotherapy training, hypnosis training and psychotherapy training at weekends in Leeds, Leicester, Liverpool, London, Manchester, Newcastle, Oxford, Glasgow and South Wales. We also provide a programme of one- and two-day workshops and seminars, and (where appropriate) distance-learning courses.

QUALIFICATION/EXAMINATIONS
Foundation Course
Certificate in Hypno-Psychotherapy (CHP(NC))
Diploma in Hypno-Psychotherapy (DHP(NC))
Advanced Diploma in Hypno-Psychotherapy (ADHP(NC))
European Certificate of Clinical Hypnosis (through the European Association for Hypno-Psychotherapy)
Hypnotherapy Practitioner Diploma

NATIONAL COUNCIL OF PSYCHOTHERAPISTS

PO Box 7219
Heanor
Derbyshire DE75 9AG
Tel: 08452 306072
Fax: 01773 711031
E-mail: ncphq@btinternet.com
Website: www.ncphq.co.uk

The National Council is a registering and accrediting body for psychotherapists, counsellors and coaches within the UK and also, through the International Council, the rest of the world.

Members can join the Council regardless of which discipline and where they completed their training.

MEMBERSHIP
Affiliate (ANCP)
Licentiate (LNCP)
Full Member (MNCP)
Fellow (FNCP)

DESIGNATORY LETTERS
ANCP, LNCP, MNCP, FNCP

THE FOUNDATION FOR PSYCHOTHERAPY AND COUNSELLING

Tel: 020 7378 2090
E-mail: office@thefoundation-uk.org
Website: www.thefoundation-uk.org

The Foundation for Psychotherapy and Counselling was formed during the 1970s as the graduate body of WPF Therapy (the largest charitable provider of counselling and psychotherapy in England) and now has some 700 fully trained and qualified members, most of whom are in private practice.

MEMBERSHIP
Member

THE NATIONAL REGISTER OF HYPNOTHERAPISTS AND PSYCHOTHERAPISTS

1st Floor
18 Carr Road
Nelson
Lancashire BB9 7JS
Tel: 01282 716839
E-mail: admin@nrhp.co.uk
Website: www.nrhp.co.uk

The NRHP (est 1985) is a professional association of qualified therapists who trained with a UKCP-accredited training organization. Members are required to adhere to a code of ethics and carry appropriate insurance. We publish a Directory of Practitioners and offer a referral service for the public via our website and the office. We are a member of the UKCP.

MEMBERSHIP
Student
Associate 1 (NRHP(Assoc 1))
Associate 2 (NRHP(Assoc 2))
Associate 3 (NRHP(Assoc 3))
Full Member (MNRHP)
Fellow (FNRHP)

DESIGNATORY LETTERS
NRHP(Assoc 1), NRHP(Assoc 2), NRHP(Assoc 3), MNRHP, FNRHP

UK COUNCIL FOR PSYCHOTHERAPY

2nd Floor Edward House
2 Wakley Street
London EC1V 7LT
Tel: 020 7014 9955
Fax: 020 7014 9977
E-mail: ukcp@psychotherapy.org.uk
Website: www.psychotherapy.org.uk

The UKCP's purpose is to promote the art and science of psychotherapy for the public benefit; to promote research and education in psychotherapy and disseminate the results of any such research; and to promote (or assist in the promotion, preservation and protection of public health by encouraging) high standards of training and practice in psychotherapy and the wider provision of psychotherapy for the public. The *National Register of Psychotherapists* is published annually, and only psychotherapists who meet the training requirements of UKCP and abide by its ethical guidelines are included.

PUBLIC ADMINISTRATION

Membership of Professional Institutions and Associations

THE INSTITUTE OF PUBLIC SECTOR MANAGEMENT

45 Cherry Tree Road
Axminster
Devon EX13 5GG
Tel: 01297 35423
Fax: 01297 35423
E-mail: info@ipsm.org.uk
Website: www.ipsm.org.uk

The IPSM is the only membership body exclusively dedicated to managers working in the public, voluntary and not-for-profit sectors. We encourage the sharing of knowledge, skills and experience between our members, provide advice and support ourselves, and as a campaigning body seek to raise public awareness and respect for public services and the role of the manager in those services.

MEMBERSHIP
Student Member
Individual (Full) Member (MIPSM)
Fellow (FIPSM)
Corporate Member

PURCHASING AND SUPPLY

Membership of Professional Institutions and Associations

THE CHARTERED INSTITUTE OF PURCHASING & SUPPLY

Easton House
Easton on the Hill
Stamford
Lincolnshire PE9 3NZ
Tel: 01780 756777
Fax: 01780 751610
E-mail: info@cips.org
Website: www.cips.org

The Chartered Institute of Purchasing & Supply (CIPS) is the leading international body representing purchasing and supply management professionals. It is the worldwide centre of excellence on purchasing and supply management issues. CIPS has almost 60,000 members in 150 different countries, including senior business people, high-ranking civil servants and leading academics. The activities of purchasing and supply chain professionals can have a major impact on the profitability and efficiency of all types of organization. CIPS also offers business solutions to companies, public and third sector.

MEMBERSHIP
Student Member
Affiliate
Certificate Member
Diploma Member
Associate Member
Full Member (MCIPS)
Fellow (FCIPS)

QUALIFICATION/EXAMINATIONS
Please see website; www.cips.org

DESIGNATORY LETTERS
MCIPS, FCIPS

QUALITY ASSURANCE

Membership of Professional Institutions and Associations

THE CHARTERED QUALITY INSTITUTE

12 Grosvenor Crescent
London SW1X 7EE
Tel: 020 7245 6722
Fax: 020 7245 6788
E-mail: info@thecqi.org
Website: www.thecqi.org

The CQI is the chartered body for quality management professionals. Established in 1919, we gained a Royal Charter in 2006 and became the CQI shortly afterwards. Our vision is to place quality at the heart of every organization: we promote the benefits of quality management to industry, disseminate quality knowledge and resources, provide qualifications and training, and assess quality competence.

MEMBERSHIP
Student
Associate Member (ACQI)
Member, Chartered Quality Professional (MCQI, CQP)
Fellow, Chartered Quality Professional (FCQI, CQP)
Company Member

QUALIFICATION/EXAMINATIONS
Certificate in Quality
Diploma in Quality

DESIGNATORY LETTERS
MCQI, CQP; FCQI, CQP

RADIOGRAPHY

Membership of Professional Institutions and Associations

THE SOCIETY OF RADIOGRAPHERS

207 Providence Square
Mill Street
London SE1 2EW
Tel: 020 7740 7200
Fax: 020 7740 7204
E-mail: info@sor.org
Website: www.sor.org

The Society of Radiographers, founded in 1920, represents more than 90 per cent of the diagnostic and therapeutic radiographers in the UK. It is responsible for their professional, educational, public and workplace interests. Together with the College of Radiographers, our charitable subsidiary, our efforts are directed towards education, research and other activities in support of the science and practice of radiography.

MEMBERSHIP
Student Member
Radiographic Assistant
Assistant Practitioner
Member

RETAIL

Membership of Professional Institutions and Associations

IGD

Grange Lane
Letchmore Heath
Watford
Hertfordshire WD25 8GD
Tel: 01923 857141
Fax: 01923 852531
E-mail: igd@igd.com
Website: www.igd.com

IGD (the Institute of Grocery Distribution) was formed in 1972 from the merger of the Institute of Charted Grocers and the Institute of Food Distribution. We provide information and practical training to the industry and now have more than 700 corporate members, covering a broad spectrum of companies and organizations across the world.

MEMBERSHIP
Corporate Member

QUALIFICATION/EXAMINATIONS
PG Cert in Food & Grocery Industry Management (validated by the University of Edinburgh)

INSTITUTE OF MASTERS OF WINE

2/3 Philpot Lane
London EC3M 8AN
Tel: 020 7621 2830
Fax: 020 7929 2302
Website: www.mastersofwine.org

The Institute of Masters of Wine is a membership body that represents the interests of its members (Masters of Wine), administers the MW Examination, and runs an education programme in preparation for the examination. We also hold a number of events throughout the year, including seminars and tastings, master classes, discussions, and, every 4 years, a symposium, most of which are open to the public.

MEMBERSHIP
Master of Wine (MW)

QUALIFICATION/EXAMINATIONS
Master of Wine Examination

DESIGNATORY LETTERS
MW

MEAT TRAINING COUNCIL

PO Box 141
Winterhill House
Snowdon Drive
Milton Keynes MK6 1YY
Tel: 01908 231062
Fax: 01908 231063
E-mail: info@meattraining.org.uk
Website: www.meattraining.org.uk

The MTC is a registered charity, limited by guarantee, working for, and with, the UK meat industry. We provide information about jobs, careers and the qualifications required to work in the red meat and poultry sector of the food business. Professional membership is administered by the Worshipful Company of Butchers via its Guild of Freemen. The qualifications awarding body is now the Food and Drink Qualifications Awarding Body (FDQ Ltd) (www.fdq.org.uk).

MEMBERSHIP
Affiliate (AffInstM)
Associate (AInstM)
Graduate Member (GMInstM)

QUALIFICATION/EXAMINATIONS
Please see the Meat Training Council's website.

DESIGNATORY LETTERS
AffInstM, AInstM, GMInstM

THE BRITISH ANTIQUE DEALERS' ASSOCIATION

20 Rutland Gate
London SW7 1BD
Tel: 020 7589 4128
Fax: 020 7581 9083
E-mail: info@bada.org
Website: www.bada.org

BADA, which was founded in 1918, is the trade association for antique dealers in Britain. Our vetted members are elected for their high business standards and expertise, and adhere to a strict code of practice; we provide safeguards for members of the public who deal with our members, including independent arbitration if a dispute arises.

MEMBERSHIP
Member

THE GUILD OF ARCHITECTURAL IRONMONGERS

8 Stepney Green
London E1 3JU
Tel: 020 7790 3431
Fax: 020 7790 8517
E-mail: info@gai.org.uk
Website: www.gai.org.uk

The GAI represents the interests of architectural ironmongers and manufacturers of architectural ironmongery. We develop, promote and protect standards of integrity and excellence, and encourage academic study relating to the industry, operating an Institute for individual members to facilitate their continuous professional development. We liaise with various bodies on matters affecting the industry.

MEMBERSHIP
Affiliate Member
Associate Member
Full Member
Registered Architectural Ironmonger (Reg AI)

QUALIFICATION/EXAMINATIONS
The GAI provides a 3-year incremental training programme. Students are examined each year and must pass each year in turn before progressing to the next. A Certificate is awarded to successful students each year, culminating in the GAI Diploma (Dip GAI) on successful completion of year 3.

DESIGNATORY LETTERS
Reg AI

THE INSTITUTE OF BUILDERS MERCHANTS

Touchwood
Oak View Rise
Harlow Wood
Mansfield
Nottinghamshire NG18 4UT
Tel: 01623 427693
E-mail: admin@instbm.co.uk
Website: www.instbm.co.uk

To improve through seminars and website articles, the technical and general knowledge of persons engaged in builders' merchants; to verify management training courses with providers; to acknowledge personal achievements and award diplomas, certificates and other distinctions; to encourage the need for knowledge, integrity and efficiency in the builders' merchants industry.

MEMBERSHIP
Student
Associate
Member
Fellow
Corporate Supporter

QUALIFICATION/EXAMINATIONS
University Degree
The Institute of Builders Merchants Business Studies Course
The Builders Merchants Federation Diploma in Merchanting
Higher National Certificate (HNC) in Business Studies
Higher National Diploma (HND) in Business Studies
NVQ Level 4
Company management programmes as approved by the Board of Governors

THE SOCIETY OF SHOE FITTERS

c/o The Anchorage
28 Admirals Walk
Hingham
Norfolk NR9 4JL
Tel: 01953 851171
Fax: 01953 851190
E-mail: secretary@shoefitters-uk.org
Website: www.shoefitters-uk.org

The Society of Shoe Fitters is a not-for-profit organization in our 50th year, set up to assist the trade and public. We disseminate shoe fitting/footwear knowledge via courses and an examination, and in turn endeavour to keep shoe fitting advice available via our website, leaflets and a helpline.

MEMBERSHIP
Student Member
Member (MSSF)
Fellow (FSSF)
Associate Member (corporate membership)

QUALIFICATION/EXAMINATIONS
One-day on-site courses – certificate only
Five- or 10-month course leading to membership qualification
Entrance examination for experienced shoe fitters leading to qualification

DESIGNATORY LETTERS
MSSF, FSSF

SECRETARIAL AND OFFICE WORK

Membership of Professional Institutions and Associations

INSTITUTE OF PROFESSIONAL ADMINISTRATORS

6 Graphite Square
Vauxhall Walk
London SE11 5EE
Tel: 020 7091 2606
Fax: 020 7091 7340
E-mail: info@inprad.org
Website: www.inprad.org

The IPA was founded in 1957 as the Institute of Qualified Professional Secretaries and is today the leading membership body for administration and office professionals. We provide our members with information, advice and guidance on suitable training and development to advance their career as well as a CPD scheme designed to meet their individual needs.

MEMBERSHIP
Student Member
Affiliate (AffIPA)
Member (MIPA)
Fellow (FIPA)
Corporate Member

DESIGNATORY LETTERS
AffIPA, MIPA, FIPA

SECURITY

Membership of Professional Institutions and Associations

THE SECURITY INSTITUTE

1 The Courtyard
Caldecote
Warwickshire CV10 0AS
E-mail: info@security-institute.org
Website: www.security-institute.org

The Institute promotes professionalism in the security world and encourages a proper understanding of the value of the security function by management. The Institute has declared its intention to progress towards chartered status. Membership of the Institute is now recognized as an employment prerequisite by many companies and government departments.

MEMBERSHIP
Affiliate/Student
Graduate
Associate

Member
Fellow (FSyI)

QUALIFICATION/EXAMINATIONS
Certificate in Security Management
Diploma in Security Management

DESIGNATORY LETTERS
FSyI

SOCIAL WORK AND PROBATION

SOCIAL WORK
The General Social Care Council (GSCC) is responsible for regulating and supporting social work education and training in England. The GSCC accredits universities who offer social work qualifications at both qualifying and post-qualifying levels, and quality-assures all social work courses. In 2003, professional qualifying training for social workers in the United Kingdom changed to a degree in social work. The diploma in social work (DipSW) and all other 'predecessor' social work qualifications will continue to be recognized as valid social work qualifications.

For further details contact the General Social Care Council: Tel: 0845 070 0630; Website: www.gscc.org.uk.

For information about social work training in Scotland, contact Scottish Social Services Council: Tel: 08456 030891; Website: www.sssc.uk.com.

For information about social work training in Wales, contact Care Council for Wales: Tel: 02920 226257; Website: www.ccwales.org.uk.

For information about social work training in Northern Ireland, contact Northern Ireland Social Care Council: Tel: 02890 417600; Website: www.niscc.n-i.nhs.uk.

Membership of Professional Institutions and Associations

THE BRITISH ASSOCIATION OF SOCIAL WORKERS

16 Kent Street
Birmingham B5 6RD
Tel: 0121 6223911
Fax: 0121 6224860
Website: www.basw.co.uk

The BASW is the largest professional association representing social work and social workers in the UK. Whether you are qualified or not, experienced or just entering the profession, we are here to help, support, advise and campaign on your behalf.

MEMBERSHIP
Student Member
Affiliate
Member (4 categories)
Retired Member
Overseas Member

SOCIOLOGY

Membership of Professional Institutions and Associations

BRITISH SOCIOLOGICAL ASSOCIATION

Bailey Suite, Palatine House
Belmont Business Park
Belmont
Durham DH1 1TW
Tel: 0191 383 0839
Fax: 0191 383 0782
E-mail: enquiries@britsoc.org.uk
Website: www.britsoc.co.uk

The BSA was founded in 1951 to represent the intellectual and sociological interests of sociologists in the UK. Our members include researchers, teachers, students and practitioners in a variety of fields. We provide a network of communication to all who are concerned with the promotion and use of sociology and sociological research.

SPEECH AND LANGUAGE THERAPY

Membership of Professional Institutions and Associations

ROYAL COLLEGE OF SPEECH AND LANGUAGE THERAPISTS

2 White Hart Yard
London SE1 1NX
Tel: 020 7378 1200
Fax: 020 7378 7254
E-mail: postmaster@rcslt.org
Website: www.rcslt.org

The RCSLT is the professional body for speech and language therapists and support workers. We set, promote and maintain high standards in education, clinical practice and ethical conduct. Our national campaigning work aims to improve services for people with speech, language, communication and swallowing needs and to influence health, education and social care policies.

MEMBERSHIP
Student Member
Newly Qualified Member
Full Member
Fellow (FRCSLT)
Honorary Fellow (Hon FRCSLT)

DESIGNATORY LETTERS
FRCSLT, Hon FRCSLT

SPORTS SCIENCE

Membership of Professional Institutions and Associations

LONDON SCHOOL OF SPORTS MASSAGE

28 Station Parade
Willesden Green
London NW2 4NX
Tel: 020 8452 8855
Fax: 020 8452 4524
E-mail: admin@lssm.com
Website: www.lssm.com

The LSSM, founded in 1989, was the first to provide specialist training in Sport & Remedial Massage. We offer vocational training for those who want to develop a professional career in massage therapy and were instrumental in setting up the Institute of Sport & Remedial Massage (ISRM), which is the professional body promoting our needs and aspirations as clinical therapists.

MEMBERSHIP
Member

QUALIFICATION/EXAMINATIONS
Introductory Massage Workshop
Professional Diploma in Clinical Sport & Remedial Massage Therapy (Level 5)

STATISTICS

Membership of Professional Institutions and Associations

THE ROYAL STATISTICAL SOCIETY

12 Errol Street
London EC1Y 8LX
Tel: 020 7638 8998
Fax: 020 7614 3905
E-mail: rss@rss.org.uk
Website: www.rss.org.uk

The RSS is the learned society and professional body for statistics and statisticians in the UK. We have over 7,000 members worldwide, and are active in a wide range of areas both directly and indirectly relating to the study and application of statistics.

MEMBERSHIP
Student Member
Fellow
Graduate Statistician (GradStat)
Chartered Statistician (CStat)

QUALIFICATION/EXAMINATIONS
Ordinary Certificate in Statistics
Higher Certificate in Statistics
Graduate Diploma in Statistics

DESIGNATORY LETTERS
GradStat, CStat

STOCKBROKING AND SECURITIES

Membership of Professional Institutions and Associations

CFA SOCIETY OF THE UK

2nd Floor
135 Canon Street
London EC4N 5BP
Tel: 020 7280 9620
Fax: 020 7280 9636
E-mail: info@cfauk.org
Website: www.cfauk.org

The CFA Society of the UK was formerly the UK Society of Investment Professionals (UKSIP) and was renamed in 2007. Our aim is to promote the development of the investment profession in the UK through the promotion of the highest standards of ethical behaviour and the provision of education, professional development, information, career support and advocacy to our members.

MEMBERSHIP
IMC Member
Candidate Member
Affiliate Member
Regular Member

QUALIFICATION/EXAMINATIONS
Investment Management Certificate (IMC)

THE CHARTERED INSTITUTE FOR SECURITIES & INVESTMENT

8 Eastcheap
London EC3M 1AE
Tel: 020 7645 0600
Fax: 020 7645 0601
Website: www.cisi.org.uk

The Chartered Institute for Securities & Investment is the largest professional body for practitioners in stockbroking, derivatives markets, investment management, corporate finance, operations and related activities, having over 38,000 members.

MEMBERSHIP
Student Member
Affiliate (ASI)
Member (MSI)
Fellow (FSI)

QUALIFICATION/EXAMINATIONS
Introduction to Investment
Islamic Finance Qualification
IT in Investment Operations
Risk in Financial Services
Investment Administration Qualification (IAQ™)
Certificate in Corporate Finance
Certificate in Investment Management (CertIM)
International Certificate in Wealth Management
Advanced Certificate in Global Securities Operations
Advanced Certificate in Investment Schemes Administration
Advanced Certificate in Operational Risk
Diploma in Investment Compliance
Diploma in Investment Operations
Master's programme

DESIGNATORY LETTERS
ASI, MSI, FSI

SURGICAL, DENTAL AND CARDIOLOGICAL TECHNICIANS

Membership of Professional Institutions and Associations

THE BRITISH INSTITUTE OF DENTAL AND SURGICAL TECHNOLOGISTS

4 Thompson Green
Shipley
West Yorkshire BD17 7PR
Tel: 0845 644 3726
E-mail: secretary@bidst.org
Website: www.bidst.org

The BIDST has been established for over 70 years and exists to provide a vehicle for the continuing education of technicians within the spheres of dental and surgical technology. It is our aim to make membership of the Institute an aspiration for all technicians, raising standards and portraying an image of professionalism which professional technicians deserve.

MEMBERSHIP
Student Associate
Associate
Licentiate (LBIDST)
Life Member
Fellow (FBIDST)

DESIGNATORY LETTERS
LBIDST, FBIDST

SURVEYING

Membership of Professional Institutions and Associations

ASSOCIATION OF BUILDING ENGINEERS

Lutyens House
Billing Brook Road
Weston Favell
Northampton NN3 8NW
Tel: 0845 126 1058
Fax: 01604 784220
E-mail: building.engineers@abe.org.uk
Website: www.abe.org.uk

The ABE is the professional body for those specialising in the technology of building and the management processes by which buildings are designed, constructed, renewed and maintained. Our objectives are to promote and advance the planning, design, construction, maintenance and repair of the built environment; to maintain a high standard of professional practice, and to encourage co-operation between professionals.

MEMBERSHIP
Student
Technician
Associate Member (ABEng)
Graduate Member (GradBEng)
Member (MBEng)
Fellow (FBEng)
Honorary Fellow (HonFBEng)

QUALIFICATION/EXAMINATIONS
Certificate in Valuation for Secured Lending (CertValSL)
Diploma in Domestic Energy Assessment (DipDEA) (Level 3)
Diploma in Display Energy Certificates (Level 3)
Diploma in Non-Domestic Energy Certificates (Level 3)

Top-up Diploma in Non-Domestic Energy Assessment (Level 4)
NVQ Construction Contracting Operations (Level 3 & 4)
NVQ Surveying Property and Maintenance (Level 3 & 4)
NVQ Construction Site Management (Level 4)
NVQ Construction Management (Level 5)
NVQ Built Environment Development and Control (Level 3 &4)
Level 3 Fire Risk Assessment

DESIGNATORY LETTERS
ABEng, GradBEng, MBEng, FBEng

SWIMMING INSTRUCTION

Membership of Professional Institutions and Associations

THE SWIMMING TEACHERS' ASSOCIATION

Anchor House
Birch Street
Walsall
West Midlands WS2 8HZ
Tel: 01922 645097
Fax: 01922 720628
E-mail: sta@sta.co.uk
Website: www.sta.co.uk

The STA is dedicated to the preservation of human life by the teaching of swimming, lifesaving and survival techniques to as many people as possible, both in the UK and internationally. We offer a range of specialist training programmes and qualifications, which are used in more than 25 countries worldwide, and liaise with other organizations concerned with swimming teaching and water safety.

MEMBERSHIP
Junior Member
Associate Member (ASTA)
Qualified Member (MSTA)
Corporate Member

QUALIFICATION/EXAMINATIONS
STA Certificate in Teaching Swimming – Beginners
STA Certificate in Teaching Swimming – Full
STA Certificate in Teaching Swimming – Primary Teacher
STA Certificate in Aquatic Teaching – Baby & Pre-School
STA Certificate in Aquatic Teaching – Special Needs (Teacher)
STA Foundation Certificate in Swimming Pool and Spa Water Treatment
STA Certificate in Swimming Pool and Spa Water Treatment
STA Certificate for the National Rescue Standard – Pool Lifeguard
STA Certificate for the National Rescue Standard – Pool Attendant
STA Certificate for the National Rescue Standard – Poolside Helper
STA Award in Emergency First Aid at Work
STA Award in Emergency First Aid for Sport

DESIGNATORY LETTERS
ASTA, MSTA

TAXATION

Membership of Professional Institutions and Associations

SOCIETY OF TRUST & ESTATE PRACTITIONERS

Artillery House (South)
11–19 Artillery Row
London SW1P 1RT
Tel: +44 (0)20 7340 0500
Fax: +44 (0)20 7340 0501
E-mail: step@step.org
Website: www.step.org

The Society of Trust and Estate Practitioners (STEP) is a unique professional body providing members with a local, national and international learning and business network focusing on the responsible stewardship of assets today and across the generations.

MEMBERSHIP
Full members of STEP are the most experienced and senior practitioners in the field of trusts and estates.

QUALIFICATION/EXAMINATIONS
STEP Diplomas and Foundation Certificates are recognized as essential qualifications and TEP's are sought after by employers. A portfolio of courses have been designed to enhance your career. STEP qualifications include the STEP Diploma for England & Wales (Trusts and Estates), STEP Diploma for Ireland, STEP Diploma for Scotland, STEP Diploma in International Trust Management, STEP Certificate for Financial Services (Trusts and Estate Planning) and many more.

DESIGNATORY LETTERS
TEP

THE ASSOCIATION OF TAXATION TECHNICIANS

1st Floor
Artillery House
11–19 Artillery Row
London SW1P 1RT
Tel: 0844 251 0830
Fax: 0844 251 0831
E-mail: info@att.org.uk
Website: www.att.org.uk

The ATT was founded in 1989 in recognition of the increasing demand for tax services and the development of tax practice as a professional activity in its own right. Our primary aim is to provide an appropriate qualification for individuals who undertake such work, and we now have more than 10,500 members, affiliates and registered students.

MEMBERSHIP
Student
Affiliate
Member

QUALIFICATION/EXAMINATIONS
Certificate of Competency in Business Compliance
Certificate of Competency in Business Taxation and Accounting Principles

DESIGNATORY LETTERS
ATT

THE CHARTERED INSTITUTE OF TAXATION

First Floor
11–19 Artillery Row
London SW1P 1RT
Tel: 020 7340 0550
Fax: 0844 579 6701
E-mail: post@tax.org.uk
Website: www.tax.org.uk

The CIOT, which dates from 1930, is the professional body for Chartered Tax Advisers and has 14,300 members. Our aims are to promote education in and the study of the administration and practice of taxation, and to achieve a better, more efficient, tax system for all affected by it – taxpayers, advisers and the authorities.

MEMBERSHIP
Associate (CTA or ATII)
Fellow (CTA or FTII)

QUALIFICATION/EXAMINATIONS
Chartered Tax Adviser (CTA) examination
Advanced Diploma in International Taxation (ADIT)

DESIGNATORY LETTERS
CTA, ATII, FTII

THE INSTITUTE OF INDIRECT TAXATION

The Stables
Station Road West
Oxted
Surrey RH8 9EE
Tel: 01883 730658
Fax: 01883 717778
E-mail: enquiries@theiit.org.uk
Website: www.theiit.org.uk

The Institute was founded in 1991 to establish a professional body of indirect tax practitioners to regulate and support its members. Membership is worldwide and includes barristers, solicitors, accountants, sole practitioners and tax specialists in commerce, the professions and government. The Institute is a member of the Confederation Fiscale Europeenne.

MEMBERSHIP
Student
Affiliate
Associate (AIIT)
Honorary Associate (AIIT(Hon))
Fellow (FIIT)
Honorary Fellow (FIIT(Hon)

QUALIFICATION/EXAMINATIONS
Associate Examination
VAT Compliance Diploma (IIT (Dip))

DESIGNATORY LETTERS
AIIT, AIIT (Hon), FIIT, FIIT (Hon)

TAXI DRIVERS

Membership of Professional Institutions and Associations

TAXI DRIVERS (LONDON)

Cab drivers and cab proprietors in the Metropolitan Police District and City of London are licensed by an Assistant Commissioner of the Metropolitan Police, through the Public Carriage Office at 15 Penton Street, Islington N1 9PU. A cab driver's licence is valid for 3 years and a cab proprietor's licence for 1 year.

TEACHING/EDUCATION

Initial Qualifications in the UK

RECOGNITION

To obtain a teaching appointment as a qualified teacher in maintained schools in England and Wales, it is necessary to have **Qualified Teacher Status (QTS)**. In order to be qualified, teachers must have satisfactorily completed an approved course of initial teacher training (ITT), and to be able to teach in maintained schools in England must have successfully completed their induction period (there are similar arrangements for teaching in Scotland, Wales and Northern Ireland).

APPROVED COURSES OF TRAINING IN ENGLAND AND WALES

Initial teacher training courses in England and Wales are provided by accredited training providers mainly through University Departments of Education. Courses available include Bachelor of Arts with QTS, Bachelor of Science with QTS for undergraduates, and Postgraduate Certificates of Education (PGCEs) for graduates.

Undergraduate training typically lasts 3 years, and a PGCE generally lasts 1 year full time. There are also some employment-based routes into teaching. The Graduate Teacher Programme is for graduates who wish to earn money while they train and are able to take on responsibilities quickly. The Registered Teacher Programme is for those without a degree but with at least two years of higher education. These employment-based routes now account for around 15 per cent of all teacher training places. In addition, Teach First is a programme enabling graduates to spend two years working in challenging secondary schools in London, the North-West, the Midlands, or Yorkshire and the Humber. The programme enables trainees to qualify as a teacher while also completing leadership training.

OTHER APPROVED COURSES OF TRAINING

A course of training leading to registration as a primary or secondary school teacher in Scotland. A course of training in Northern Ireland, approved by the Department of Education Northern Ireland, leading to recognition as a school teacher.

QUALIFICATIONS FOR ADMISSION TO TRAINING

HEIs offering undergraduate ITT courses will set admissions criteria; typically 2 good A levels (or equivalent qualifications). Entrants to PGCE and other graduate training courses will require a relevant UK bachelors degree or a recognised equivalent and be expected to demonstrate a standard equivalent to GCSE grade C in English and mathematics, and additionally a standard equivalent to GCSE grade C in a science subject for those wishing to train to teach primary school children. In order to meet all of the QTS standards in England trainees must pass professional skills tests in numeracy, literacy and ICT. These tests cover core skills that teachers need in their jobs and QTS cannot be awarded until they are passed.

THE GENERAL TEACHING COUNCILS OF THE UK

At the time of writing, the General Teaching Council for England (GTCE) is an independent professional council for teachers in England. Similar councils exist in Wales (GTCW), Scotland (GTCS) and Northern Ireland (GTCNI). These councils hold registers of qualified teachers and also act as disciplinary bodies. You can find out more from their respective websites:

GTCE; www.gtce.org.uk
GTCW; www.gtcw.org.uk
GTCS; www.gtcs.org.uk
GTCNI; www.gtcni.org.uk

APPLICATIONS

Applications for undergraduate courses are made through the University and Colleges Admission

Services (UCAS) and postgraduate applications through the Graduate Teacher Training Registry (GTTR). You can find out more about training to teach from the following websites: GTTR; www.gttr.ac.uk; UCAS; www.ucas.ac.uk; Training and Development Agency for Schools (TDA); www.tda.gov.uk and www.teach.gov.uk/recruit. You can also call the TDA's Teaching Information Line in England and Wales on 0845 6000 991992 for Welsh speakers (minicom 0117 915 8161).

Membership of Professional Institutions and Associations

TECHNICAL COMMUNICATIONS

Membership of Professional Institutions and Associations

THE INSTITUTE OF SCIENTIFIC AND TECHNICAL COMMUNICATORS (ISTC LTD)

Airport House
Purley Way
Croydon CR0 0XZ
Tel: 020 8253 4506
Fax: 020 8253 4510
E-mail: istc@istc.org.uk
Website: www.istc.org.uk

The ISTC is a non-profit-making organization and the largest UK body representing professional communicators and information designers. Our aims include improving standards of scientific and technical communication, promoting scientific and technical communication as a career, supporting our members, and consulting, cooperating and collaborating with other bodies that share out ideals.

MEMBERSHIP
Student
Associate
Junior
Member (MISTC)
Fellow (FISTC)
Business Affiliate

DESIGNATORY LETTERS
MISTC, FISTC

TEXTILES

Membership of Professional Institutions and Associations

THE TEXTILE INSTITUTE

1st Floor
Oxford Street
Manchester M1 6FQ
Tel: 01612 371188
Fax: 01612 361991
E-mail: tiihq@textileinst.org.uk
Website: www.textileinstitute.org

The Textile Institute covers all disciplines – from technology and production to design, development and marketing – relating to fibres, fabrics, clothing. footwear, and interior and technical textiles.

MEMBERSHIP
Student
Individual
Licentiate (LTI)
Associate (CText ATI)
Fellow (CText FTI)
Companion
Honorary Fellow
Corporate

DESIGNATORY LETTERS
LTI, CText ATI, CText FTI

TIMBER TECHNOLOGY

Membership of Professional Institutions and Associations

WOOD TECHNOLOGY SOCIETY

Third Floor D
Carpenters' Hall
1 Throgmorton Avenue
London EC2N 2BY
Tel: 020 7256 2700
Fax: 020 7256 2701
E-mail: info@iwsc.org.uk
Website: www.iwsc.org.uk

The Wood Technology Society (IWSc – a Division of the Institute of Materials, Minerals and Mining), formerly the Institute of Wood Science, is the professional body for the timber and allied industries. We promote and encourage a better understanding of timber, wood-based materials and associated timber processes, and are the UK examining body, awarding qualifications at Foundation, Certificate and Diploma level.

MEMBERSHIP
Student Member
Affiliate Member
Technician (TIWSc)
Licentiate (LIWSc)
Member (MIWSc)
Fellow (FIWSc)
Corporate Member

QUALIFICATION/EXAMINATIONS
Timber Studies Award (Foundation course)
Certificate
Diploma

DESIGNATORY LETTERS
TIWSc, LIWSc, MIWSc, FIWSc

TOWN AND COUNTRY PLANNING

Membership of Professional Institutions and Associations

ROYAL TOWN PLANNING INSTITUTE

41 Botolph Lane
London EC3R 8DL
Tel: 020 7929 9494
E-mail: membership@rtpi.org.uk
Website: www.rtpi.org.uk

The RTPI is the largest professional institute for planners in Europe, with over 22,000 members. As well as promoting spatial planning, we develop and shape policy affecting the built environment, work to raise professional standards and support members through continuous education, training and development.

MEMBERSHIP
Student Member
Licentiate Member
Associate Member
Legal Associate Member (LARTPI)
Technical Member (TechRTPI)
Retired Member
Honorary Member (HonMRTPI)
Chartered Member (MRTPI)
Chartered Fellow (FRTPI)

QUALIFICATION/EXAMINATIONS
Please see www.rtpi.org.uk/item/178/23/5/3 for a list of accredited training providers

DESIGNATORY LETTERS
LARTPI, TechRTPI, HonMRTPI, MRTPI, FRTPI

TRADING STANDARDS

Membership of Professional Institutions and Associations

THE TRADING STANDARDS INSTITUTE

1 Sylvan Court
Sylvan Way
Southfields Business Park
Basildon
Essex SS15 6TH
Tel: 0845 608 9400
Fax: 0845 608 9425
E-mail: institute@tsi.org.uk
Website: www.tradingstandards.gov.uk

The TSI, formed in 1881, is a not-for-profit membership association representing trading standards professionals in both the public and private sectors in the UK and overseas. TSI encourages honest enterprise and business, and helps safeguard the economic, environmental, health and social well-being of consumers.

MEMBERSHIP
Student Member
Affiliate Member
Associate Member (ASTI)
Full Member (MSTI)
Fellow (FSTI)
Corporate Affiliate

QUALIFICATION/EXAMINATIONS
The Trading Standards Qualification Framework consists of:
Certificate of Competence
Foundation Certificate in Consumer Affairs and Trading Standards
Module Certificate in Consumer Affairs and Trading Standards
Diploma in Consumer Affairs and Trading Standards
Higher Diploma in Consumer Affairs and Trading Standards

DESIGNATORY LETTERS
ASTI, MSTI, FSTI

TRANSPORT

Membership of Professional Institutions and Associations

INSTITUTE OF TRANSPORT ADMINISTRATION

The Old Studio
25 Greenfield Road
Westoning
Bedfordshire MK45 5JD
Tel: 01525 634940
Fax: 01525 750016
E-mail: director@iota.org.uk
Website: www.iota.org.uk

The primary aim of IoTA is to broaden and improve the knowledge, skills and experience of its members in the practice of efficient road, rail, air and sea transport. We are one of the few professional bodies still recognized within the terms of the Road Traffic 1968 (Statutory Instrument 78), wherein it is permitted to proffer qualified opinion as to the professional competence of its members.

MEMBERSHIP
Individual
Student
Associate (AInstTA)
Honorary Member
Corporate
Associate Member (AMInstTA)
Member (MInstTA)
Fellow (FInstTA)

DESIGNATORY LETTERS
AInstTA, AMInstTA, MInstTA, FInstTA

THE INSTITUTE OF TRAFFIC ACCIDENT INVESTIGATORS

Column House
London Road
Shrewsbury
Shropshire SY2 6NN
Tel: 08456 212066
Fax: 08456 212077
E-mail: gensec@itai.org
Website: www.itai.org

The Institute provides a means of communication, education, representation and regulation in the field of Traffic Accident Investigation. Our main aim is to provide a forum for spreading knowledge and enhancing expertise among those engaged in the discipline. Members include police officers, lecturers in higher education and private practitioners.

MEMBERSHIP
Affiliate
Associate (AITAI)
Member (MITAI)

DESIGNATORY LETTERS
AITAI, MITAI

TRAVEL AND TOURISM

Membership of Professional Institutions and Associations

CONFEDERATION OF TOURISM AND HOSPITALITY

37 Duke Street
London W1U 1LN
Tel: 020 7258 9850
Fax: 020 7258 9869
E-mail: info@cthawards.com
Website: www.cthawards.com

The Confederation of Tourism and Hospitality is an awarding body approved by Ofqual, and registered on the QCA's National Qualifications Framework. We were established in 1982 to provide recognized standards of management and vocational training appropriate to the needs of the hotel and travel industries, via our syllabuses, examinations and awards.

MEMBERSHIP
Student Member
Associate Member (AMCTH)
Professional Member (PMCTH)
Fellow (FCTH)

QUALIFICATION/EXAMINATIONS
Diploma in Hospitality and Tourism Management
Diploma in Hotel Management
Diploms in Hotel and Casino Management
Diploma in Tourism Management
Diploma in Travel Agency Management
Advanced Diploma in Hotel and Event Management
Advanced Diploma in Tourism Management
Advanced Diploma in Travel Agency Management
Graduate Diploma in Hospitality and Tourism Management
Postgraduate Diploma in Hotel Management

DESIGNATORY LETTERS
AMCTH, PMCTH, FCTH

INSTITUTE OF TRAVEL AND TOURISM

PO Box 217
Ware
Hertfordshire SG12 8WY
Tel: 0844 4995 653
Fax: 0844 4995 654
E-mail: enquiries@itt.co.uk
Website: www.itt.co.uk

The ITT, founded in 1956, is a professional membership body for individuals employed in the travel and tourism industry. We provide support and guidance for our members throughout their career and offer them CPD and training to maintain standards for the benefit of the industry as a whole.

MEMBERSHIP
Student Member
Introductory Member
Affiliate Member
Member
Member (MInstTT)
Fellow
Fellow (FInstTT)
University/College Member
Group Member
Corporate Member

DESIGNATORY LETTERS
MInstTT, FInstTT

THE TOURISM MANAGEMENT INSTITUTE

c/o CPD Co-ordinator, Cathy Guthrie, PhD, FTMI, FTS
18 Cuninghill Avenue
Inverurie
Aberdeenshire AB51 3TZ
Tel: 01467 620769
E-mail: secretary@tmi.org.uk
Website: www.tmi.org.uk

Part of the Tourism Society, the TMI is the professional body for tourism destination managers. Its network of over 300 professionals shares information via website, conferences, seminars, working groups, e-mails and newsletters. Committed to excellence, the TMI/Tourism Society Continuing Professional Development programme aims to support destination management and tourism professionals.

MEMBERSHIP
Student
Associate (ATMI)
Member (MTMI)
Fellow (FTMI)

QUALIFICATION/EXAMINATIONS
Postgraduate Certificate in Destination Management
Postgraduate Diploma in Destination Management
MSc in Destination Management
These qualifications are awarded by Leeds Metropolitan University and delivered in partnership with Bournemouth and Lancaster Universities; available as online distance learning so busy professionals can fit study around their existing schedules.

DESIGNATORY LETTERS
ATMI, MTMI, FTMI

THE TOURISM SOCIETY

Trinity Court
34 West Street
Sutton
Surrey SM1 1SH
Tel: 020 8661 4636
Fax: 020 8661 4637
E-mail: admin@tourismsociety.org
Website: www.tourismsociety.org

The Tourism Society, founded in 1977, is the professional membership body for people working in all sectors of tourism. We strive to drive up standards of professionalism and act as an advocate of tourism to the government and the public and private sectors, and liaise with other tourism professionals worldwide. We also provide advice, support and networking opportunities to our 1,200 or so members.

MEMBERSHIP
Student
Full Member (MTS)
Fellow (FTS)
Overseas/Retired Member
Group Member
Corporate Member

DESIGNATORY LETTERS
MTS, FTS

VETERINARY SCIENCE

Membership of Professional Institutions and Associations

BRITISH VETERINARY ASSOCIATION

7 Mansfield Street
London W1G 9NQ
Tel: 020 7636 6541
Fax: 020 7908 6349
E-mail: bvahq@bva.co.uk
Website: www.bva.co.uk

The BVA is the representative body for the veterinary profession in the UK and has more than 11,500 members. We promote and support the interests of our members and the animals under their care, liaise with the government and are the leading provider of veterinary information to the media and general public.

MEMBERSHIP
Student Member
Associate Member
Full Member
Overseas Member
Organizational Member

SOCIETY OF PRACTISING VETERINARY SURGEONS

The Governor's House
Cape Road
Warwick CV34 5DJ
Tel: 01926 410454
Fax: 01926 411350
E-mail: office@spvs.org.uk
Website: www.spvs.org.uk

The SPVS was founded in 1933 with the aim of promoting the interests of veterinary surgeons in private practice. We are a non-territorial division of the British Veterinary Association. Our remit is to advise on all aspects of managing the business of a clinical veterinary practice, and we hold one-day, weekend and week-long courses and an annual congress.

MEMBERSHIP
Student Member
Associate Member
Full Member
Retired Member

THE ROYAL COLLEGE OF VETERINARY SURGEONS

Belgravia House
62–64 Horseferry Road
London SW1P 2AF
Tel: 020 7222 2001
Fax: 020 7222 2004
E-mail: admin@rcvs.org.uk
Website: www.rcvs.org.uk

The RCVS is the regulatory body for veterinary surgeons in the UK. It role is to safeguard the health and welfare of animals committed to veterinary care through the regulation of the educational, ethical and clinical standards of the veterinary profession, and to act as an impartial source of informed opinion on animal health and welfare issues and their interaction with human health.

MEMBERSHIP
Member (MRCVS)
Fellow (FRCVS)

QUALIFICATION/EXAMINATIONS
Certificate in Advanced Veterinary Practice (CertAVP)
Diploma (various titles, eg Small Animal Surgery; Animal Welfare Science Ethics & Law; Equine Internal Medicine; Cattle Health & Production etc)
RCVS Recognised Specialist
Diploma in Advanced Veterinary Nursing
Diploma of Fellowship (FRCVS)

DESIGNATORY LETTERS
MRCVS, FRCVS

WASTES MANAGEMENT

Membership of Professional Institutions and Associations

CHARTERED INSTITUTION OF WASTES MANAGEMENT

9 Saxon Court
St Peter's Gardens
Marefair
Northampton NN1 1SX
Tel: 01604 620426
Fax: 01604 621339
E-mail: education@ciwm.co.uk
Website: www.ciwm.co.uk

The CIWM represents more than 7,000 waste management professionals – predominantly in the UK but also overseas. We promote education, training and research in the scientific, technical and practical aspects of waste management for the safeguarding of the environment, and set and strive to maintain high standards for individuals working in the waste management industry.

MEMBERSHIP
Student Member
Technician Member (TechMCIWM)
Associate Member (AssocMCIWM)
Graduate Member (GradMCIWM)
Licentiate (LCIWM)
Member (MCIWM)
Fellow (FCIWM)
Affiliated Organization

QUALIFICATION/EXAMINATIONS
CIWM Training Services specializes in developing and providing waste management training for individuals & organizations. Each year we organize more than 70 courses. For details see the website.

DESIGNATORY LETTERS
TechMCIWM, AssocMCIWM, GradMCIWM, LCIWM, MCIWM, FCIWM

WATCH AND CLOCK MAKING AND REPAIRING

Membership of Professional Institutions and Associations

THE BRITISH HOROLOGICAL INSTITUTE LIMITED

Upton Hall
Upton
Newark
Nottinghamshire NG23 5TE
Tel: 01636 813795
Fax: 01636 812258
E-mail: clock@bhi.co.uk
Website: www.bhi.co.uk

The BHI, which was formed in 1858 to promote horology, is a professional body with about 3,000 members worldwide. We provide education and specialist training, set recognized standards of excellence in workmanship and professional conduct, and support our members in their work making, repairing and servicing clocks and watches.

MEMBERSHIP
Student
Associate
Graduate (GradBHI)
Member (MBHI)
Fellow (FBHI)

QUALIFICATION/EXAMINATIONS
Certificate in Clock and Watch Servicing (Level 2)
Certificate in the Repair, Restoration and Conservation of Clocks/Watches (Level 3)

DESIGNATORY LETTERS
GradBHI, MBHI, FBHI

WELDING

Membership of Professional Institutions and Associations

THE WELDING INSTITUTE

Granta Park
Great Abington
Cambridge CB21 6AL
Tel: 01223 899000
Fax: 01223 894219
E-mail: twi_professional@twi.co.uk
Website: www.twiprofessional.com

The Welding Institute is the engineering institution for welding and joining professionals. We are committed to promoting the importance of welding/materials joining technology, given its importance as a key industrial technology governing the reliability and safety of many products, and to the advancement of education, training and CPD for our members.

MEMBERSHIP
Graduate (GradWeldI)
Technician (TechWeldI)

Senior Associate (SenAWeldI)
Incorporated Member (IncMWeldI)
Member (MWeldI)
Senior Member (SenMWeldI)
Fellow (FWeldI)
Honorary Fellow (HonFWeldI)
Engineering Technician (EngTech)
Incorporated Engineer (IEng)
Chartered Engineer (CEng)

QUALIFICATION/EXAMINATIONS
Certificate in Welding and Joining Technology for Students in Materials and Engineering

DESIGNATORY LETTERS
GradWeldI, TechWeldI, SenAWeldI, IncMWeldI, MWeldI, SenMWeldI, FWeldI, HonFWeldI, EngTech, IEng, CEng

WELFARE

Membership of Professional Institutions and Associations

INSTITUTE OF WELFARE

PO Box 5570
Stourbridge
West Midlands DY8 9BA
Tel: 01214 548883
Fax: 01214 547873
E-mail: info@instituteofwelfare.co.uk
Website: www.instituteofwelfare.co.uk

The Institute of Welfare was founded in 1945 and exists to promote the highest possible standards in the delivery of welfare to those who need it. We make representations to government, undertake research on welfare issues, encourage and facilitate the exchange of information, and provide opportunities for those engaged in welfare work to pursue CPD.

MEMBERSHIP
Associate Member (AMIW)
Member (MIW)
Fellow (FIW)
Companion (CIW)

DESIGNATORY LETTERS
AMIW, MIW, FIW, CIW

Part 6

Bodies Accrediting Independent Institutions

THE BRITISH ACCREDITATION COUNCIL FOR INDEPENDENT FURTHER AND HIGHER EDUCATION (BAC)

BAC is a registered charity that was established in 1984 to act as the national accrediting body for independent further and higher education. It is independent both of government and of the colleges it accredits.

A college that is accredited by BAC undergoes a thorough inspection every four years, with an interim visit after two years. Until 2000, BAC accreditation was only available to colleges in the United Kingdom, but there are now accredited colleges in Bulgaria, the Czech Republic, France, Germany, Greece, India, Lebanon, Mauritius, Pakistan, South Africa, Spain, Switzerland and the UAE. At present BAC accredits 473 colleges in the United Kingdom and 28 overseas. Lists of accredited colleges are published each year, but full details can be viewed on the BAC website.

BAC's Council includes nominees of a number of the major bodies concerned with the maintenance of standards in British education, including The Open University Validation Service, the Council of Validating Universities, Universities UK, the Association of Learning Providers, the Quality Assurance Agency for Higher Education and the United Kingdom Council for International Student Affairs (UKCISA), and observers from the Federation of Awarding Bodies, the Joint Council for Qualifications, GuildHE, the Home Office and the DfES.

Accreditation by BAC is recognized by the UK Border Agency (UKBA) of the Home Office as a qualifying requirement for institutions to enrol visa students.

Further details of the work of the BAC and a current list of accredited institutions may be obtained from The Chief Executive, BAC, 44 Bedford Row, London WC1R 4LL; Tel: 020 7447 2584, Fax: 020 7447 2585, E-mail: info@the-bac.org, Website: www.the-bac.org

THE BRITISH COUNCIL

The British Council runs the Accreditation UK scheme in partnership with English UK for the inspection and accreditation of organizations that provide courses in English as a Foreign Language (EFL) in Britain. The scheme is managed jointly by the British Council and English UK. One of its aims is to effectively promote accredited UK ELT through the British Council's network of overseas offices.

Under the terms of the scheme, institutions are inspected rigorously every four years in the areas of management, resources and environment, teaching and learning, and welfare and student services. The scheme also includes a system of random spot-checking. The management and policy of the scheme is conducted by an independent board while a separate independent committee reviews inspectors' reports.

Some 86 per cent of recognized schools are also members of English UK, which insists on British Council accreditation as a criterion for membership. In addition, all English UK members, of which there are over 400, are required to abide by the Association's Code of Practice and Regulations. English UK exists to raise the high standards of its members even further through conferences, training courses and publications. The association also represents the interests of members and students to government bodies, and promotes the teaching of English in Britain at home and overseas.

Further information on the Accreditation UK scheme may be obtained from the Accreditation Unit, British Council, Bridgewater House, 58 Whitworth Street, Manchester M1 6BB; Tel: 01619 577489, e-mail: accreditation.unit@britishcouncil.org, Website: www. britishcouncil.org/accreditation. Further information on English UK may be obtained from English UK, 219 St John Street, London EC1V 4LY; Tel: 020 7608 7960, Fax: 020 7608 7961, e-mail: info@englishuk.com, Website: www.englishuk.com

THE OPEN AND DISTANCE LEARNING QUALITY COUNCIL (ODL QC)

ODL QC was established in 1968 as the Council for the Accreditation of Correspondence Colleges, a joint initiative of the then Labour government and representatives of the sector. It is the principal accrediting body for a wide variety of providers of open and distance learning in the UK, from commercial colleges to professional and public-sector institutions. Now independent, it nevertheless continues to have the informal support of government.

ODL QC promotes quality by:

- establishing standards of education and training in open and distance learning;
- recognizing good quality provision, wherever it occurs;
- supporting and protecting the interests of learners;
- encouraging the improvement of existing methods and the development of new ones;
- linking open and distance learning with other forms of education and training;
- promoting wider recognition of the value of open and distance learning.

Accreditation includes a rigorous assessment of an educational provision, including materials, tutorial support, publicity, contractual arrangements with learners and general administrative procedures, each of which is measured against the council's published benchmark standards. If accredited, the provider is monitored on a regular basis and reassessed at least once every three years.

The council promotes those colleges that it accredits, which are by definition quality providers of ODL, and acts as honest broker in matching accredited colleges to potential markets. A list of courses offered by accredited providers is circulated widely, both in the UK and abroad, and is also included on the council's website, www.odlqc.org.uk.

The council also seeks to protect the interests of learners by promoting the importance of accreditation, and by offering advice and support directly to learners. At the same time, knowledge of good practice is disseminated more widely, and quality encouraged wherever open and distance learning occurs.

The council consists of members nominated by professional and public bodies involved in education, as well as representatives of accredited providers, and has strong links with other bodies in the sector, both in the UK and abroad.

All enquiries should be addressed to the Chief Executive, ODL QC, 44 Bedford Row, London WC1R 4LL; Tel: 020 7997 2593, e-mail: info@odlqc.org.uk, Website: www. odlqc.org.uk

THE CONFERENCE FOR INDEPENDENT FURTHER EDUCATION (CIFE)

CIFE was founded in 1973 to promote strict adherence by independent sixth-form and tutorial colleges to the highest standards of academic and professional integrity. All member colleges must be accredited by the British Accreditation Council for Independent Further and Higher Education (BAC), or optionally or as well as the Independent Schools Council (ISC) if they are registered by the Department for Education and Employment (DfEE) as schools. Candidate membership is available for up to three years for colleges that are seeking BAC or ISIC accreditation and otherwise satisfy CIFE's own exacting membership criteria. All colleges must also abide by stringent codes of conduct and practice, the character and presentation of their published exam results are subject to regulation, and the accuracy of the information must be validated by BAC as academic auditor to CIFE. Full members are subject to reinspection by their accrediting bodies. There are 17 colleges in full or candidate membership of CIFE at present, spread throughout England but with concentrations in London, Oxford and Cambridge.

CIFE colleges offer a wide range of GCSE, A and AS level courses. In addition some CIFE colleges offer English language tuition for students from overseas, and degree-level tuition. A number of the colleges offer summer holiday academic courses, and most of them also provide A level and GCSE revision courses during the Christmas and/or Easter holidays. Further information on CIFE may be obtained from the CIFE website: www.cife.org.uk, Tel: 020 8767 8666, e-mail: enquiries@cife.org.uk

Part 7

Study Associations and the 'Learned Societies'

Study associations consist of persons who wish to increase their knowledge of a particular subject or range of subjects; they may be professionals or amateurs. Some associations consist almost entirely of specialists (eg, the Royal Statistical Society); others (eg, the Royal Geographical Society and the Zoological Society of London) have a more general membership. The learned societies usually have two grades of membership, fellows or members. Some also admit group members (such as schools or libraries), which are known as corporate members, and junior associate, corresponding and overseas members, who pay lower subscriptions. Some also elect honorary fellows or members. The members of some societies may use designatory letters, but this does not mean that the holder is 'qualified' in the same sense as a doctor or a chartered accountant.

Membership of some learned societies is by election, and is commonly accepted as distinguishing the candidate by admission to an exclusive group. Candidates may be selected in respect of pre-eminence in their subject or in the public service. The chief associations of this type are the Royal Society (founded 1660 and granted Royal Charters in 1662 and 1663), the Royal Academy of Arts (founded 1768) and the British Academy (granted the Royal Charter in 1902).

The **Royal Society** was established to improve 'natural knowledge' and is mainly concerned with pure and applied science and technology. Election to Fellowship (FRS) is regarded as one of the highest distinctions. The society elects Fellows, Foreign Members and Royal Fellows (www.royalsociety.org).

The **Royal Academy** was established to cultivate and improve the arts of painting, sculpture and architecture. There are two main grades of membership: Academicians (RA), including Senior Academicians, and Associates (ARA); there are also a small number of Honorary Academicians (www.royalacademy.org.uk).

The **British Academy** is the UK's national academy for the humanities and the social sciences. It is the counterpart to the Royal Society that exists to serve the natural sciences. The Academy has Fellows (FBA), Corresponding Fellows and a small number of Honorary Fellows.

A list of learned societies and study associations can be found below.

OCCUPATIONAL ASSOCIATIONS

The occupational associations do not qualify practitioners but organize them. Some coordinate the activities of specialists (eg, the Society of Medical Officers of Health) and others promote the individual and collective interests of professionals working in a wider area. Both also seek to safeguard the public interest and to offer an educational service to their members. The latter type of association is especially numerous among teachers, who have over 20 associations (eg, the National Union of Teachers, the Educational Institute of Scotland, the National Association of Schoolmasters/Union of Women Teachers and the National Association of Head Teachers), and is represented in the medical profession by the British Medical Association.

LIST OF STUDY ASSOCIATIONS AND LEARNED SOCIETIES

This list largely excludes qualifying bodies, which are covered in Part 5. The date on the left is that of foundation or adoption of title.

Agriculture and related subjects

1926	Agricultural Economics Society
1952	British Agricultural History Society
1945	British Grassland Society
1944	British Society of Animal Science
1947	British Society of Soil Science
1921	Commonwealth Forestry Association
1927	Herb Society of Great Britain
1925	Institute of Chartered Foresters
1938	Institution of Agricultural Engineers
1947	International Fertiliser Society
1839	Royal Agricultural Society of England
1882	Royal Forestry Society of England, Wales and N Ireland
1784	Royal Highland and Agricultural Society of Scotland
1804	Royal Horticultural Society
1854	Royal Scottish Forestry Society
1904	Royal Welsh Agricultural Society
1943	Society of Dairy Technology
1945	The Soil Association

Anthropology and related subjects

1963	African Studies Association of the UK
1979	Association for the Study of Modern and Contemporary France
1982	Association for the Study of Modern Italy
1946	Association of Social Anthropologists of the UK and Commonwealth
1985	British Association for Irish Studies
1974	British Association for Japanese Studies
1972	British Association for South Asian Studies
1961	British Institute of Persian Studies
1973	British Society for Middle Eastern Studies
1981	European Association for Jewish Studies
1878	Folklore Society
1943	Hispanic and Luso Brazilian Council
1974	International Association for the Study of German Politics
1972	Japan Foundation
1891	Japan Society
1843	Royal Anthropological Institute of Great Britain and Ireland
1823	Royal Asiatic Society of Great Britain and Ireland
1868	Royal Commonwealth Society
1901	Royal Society for Asian Affairs
1936	Saltire Society
1977	Society for Caribbean Studies
1964	Society for Latin American Studies
1969	Society for Libyan Studies
1983	Society for the Promotion of Byzantine Studies
1879	Society for the Promotion of Hellenic Studies
1910	Society for the Promotion of Roman Studies
1969	University Association for Contemporary European Studies
1892	Viking Society for Northern Research

Archaeology and related subjects

1924	Ancient Monuments Society
1979	Association for Environmental Archaeology
1843	British Archaeological Association
1996	British Epigraphy Society
1948	British Institute at Ankara
1846	Cambrian Archaeological Association
1944	Council for British Archaeology
1838	Eccleriological Society
1882	Egypt Exploration Society
1855	London and Middlesex Archaeological Society
1865	Palestine Exploration Fund
1908	Prehistoric Society
1843	Royal Archaeological Institute
1967	Society for Post-Medieval Archaeology

Art and Design

1974 Association of Art Historians
1910 Contemporary Art Society
1915 Design and Industries Association
1950 International Institute for Conservation of Historic and Artistic Works
1888 National Society for Education in Art and Design
1899 Pastel Society
1768 Royal Academy of Arts
1814 Royal Birmingham Society of Artists
1883 Royal Institute of Oil-Painters
1831 Royal Institute of Painters in Watercolours
1826 Royal Scottish Academy of Art and Architecture
1754 Royal Society for the Encouragement of Arts, Manufactures and Commerce
1904 Royal Society of British Sculptors
1904 Royal Society of Marine Artists
1895 Royal Society of Miniature Painters, Sculptors and Gravers
1884 Royal Society of Painter/Printmakers
1891 Royal Society of Portrait Painters
1804 Royal Watercolours Society
1919 Society of Graphic Fine Art
1952 Society of Portrait Sculptors
1952 United Society of Artists
1955 William Morris Society

Biology and related subjects

1936 Association for the Study of Animal Behaviour
1904 Association of Applied Biologists
1968 Biomedical Engineering Society
1836 Botanical Society of Scotland
1836 Botanical Society of the British Isles
1896 British Bryological Society
1929 Freshwater Biological Association
1889 Marine Biological Association
1833 Royal Entomological Society
1931 Society for Applied Microbiology
1911 The Biochemical Society
1913 The British Ecological Society
1896 The British Mycological Society
1858 The British Ornithologists' Union
1959 The British Society for Cell Biology
1933 The British Trust for Ornithology
1937 The Systematics Association
1826 Zoological Society of London

Chemistry

1918 Oil and Colour Chemists' Association
1980 Royal Society of Chemistry
1881 Society of Chemical Industry
1897 Society of Leather Technologists and Chemists

Economics, Statistics and related subjects

1992 Association of Business Schools
1927 Economic History Society
2003 Economic Research Institute of Northern Ireland
1955 Institute of Economic Affairs
1902 Royal Economic Society
1834 Royal Statistical Society
1897 Scottish Economic Society

Engineering and related subjects

1847 Architectural Association
1966 Concrete Society
1946 Faculty of Building
1978 Institute of Concrete Technology
1997 Institute of Ergonomics and Human Factors
1976 Royal Academy of Engineering
1866 Royal Aeronautical Society

1916	Royal Incorporation of Architects in Scotland
1860	Royal Institution of Naval Architects
1916	Society of Automotive Engineers
1958	Society of Environmental Engineers
2003	The Energy Institute
1899	Town and Country Planning Association

Geography, Geology and related subjects

1963	British Cartographic Society
1949	British Geotechnical Society
1940	British Society of Rheology
1968	Council for Environmental Education
1923	English Place-Name Society
1931	Gemmological Association of Great Britain
1893	Geographical Association
1807	Geological Society of London
1858	Geologists Association
1846	Hakluyt Society
1971	Institution of Environmental Sciences
1876	Mineralogical Society of Great Britain and Ireland
1847	Palaeontographical Society
1957	Paleontological Association
1830	Royal Geographical Society
1997	Royal Institute of Navigation
1884	Royal Scottish Geographical Society

History and related subjects

1902	British Academy
1952	British Agricultural History Society
1888	British Record Society
1932	British Records Association
1947	British Society for the History of Science
1988	Centre for Metropolitan History
1864	Early English Texts Society
1964	Furniture History Society
1869	Harleian Society
1885	Huguenot Society of Great Britain and Ireland
1961	Institute of Heraldic and Genealogical Studies
1921	Institute of Historical Research
1893	Jewish Historical Society of England
1964	London Record Society
2000	Museums, Libraries and Archives Council
1920	Newcomen Society for the Study of the History of Engineering and Technology
1921	Oriental Ceramic Society
1868	Royal Historical Society
1836	Royal Numismatic Society
1869	Royal Philatelic Society, London
1953	Scottish Genealogy Society
1886	Scottish History Society
1897	Scottish Record Society
1976	Social History Society
1921	Society for Army Historical Research
1910	Society for Nautical Research
1967	Society for Renaissance Studies
1970	Society for the Social History of Medicine
1707	Society of Antiquaries of London
1780	Society of Antiquaries of Scotland
1956	Society of Architectural Historians in Great Britain
1947	Society of Archivists
1911	Society of Genealogists
1906	The Historical Association
1958	Victorian Society

Languages

1883	Alliance Française
1891	An Comunn Gaidhealach
1981	Association for French Language Studies
1932	Association for German Studies in Great Britain and Ireland
1990	Association for Language Learning
1910	Chartered Institute of Linguists
1991	Instituto Cervantes

1964	National Association for the Teaching of English
2003	National Centre for Languages
1993	University Council of Modern Languages
1988	Women in German Studies

Law

1958	British Institute of International and Comparative Law
1972	Intellectual Property Bar Association
1922	Law Society of Northern Ireland
1949	Law Society of Scotland
1920	Royal Institute of International Affairs
1965	Scottish Law Commission
1887	Selden Society

Literature and Arts

1959	Academi – Yr Academi Gymreig
1973	Alliance of Literary Societies
1969	Art Libraries Society
1970	Association for Scottish Literary Studies
1989	Association of Independent Libraries
1892	Bibliographical Society
1992	British Association for Information and Library Education and Research
1975	British Comparative Literature Association
1933	British Film Institute
1960	British Society of Aesthetics
1893	Bronte Society
1949	Cambridge Bibliographical Society
1935	Charles Lamb Society
1904	Classical Association
1902	Dickens Fellowship
1890	Edinburgh Bibliographical Society
1906	English Association
1886	Francis Bacon Society Inc
1960	H. G. Wells Society
1997	Historical Novel Society
1973	Joseph Conrad Society
1997	Leeds Philosophical and Literary Society
1906	Malone Society
1781	Manchester Literary and Philosophical Society
1995	Philip Larkin Society
1842	Philological Society
1909	Poetry Society
1820	Royal Society of Literature
1884	Society of Authors
2004	Society of College, National and University Libraries
1984	Standing Conference for the Arts and Social Sciences
1968	Thomas Hardy Society

Management

1986	British Academy of Management

Mathematics and Physics

1924	Astronomical Society of Edinburgh
1890	British Astronomical Association
1966	British Biophysical Society
1927	British Institute of Radiology
1933	British Interplanetary Society
1930	Institution of Electronics
1871	Mathematical Association
1820	Royal Astronomical Society
1850	Royal Meteorological Society

Medicine (including Psychology)

1887 Anatomical Society of GB and Ireland
1957 Association for Child and Adolescent Mental Health
1957 Association for the Study of Medical Education
1932 Association of Anaesthetists of GB and Ireland
1933 Association of British Neurologists
1953 Association of Clinical Biochemistry
1927 Association of Clinical Pathologists
1920 Association of Surgeons of GB and Ireland
1959 British Academy for Forensic Science
2003 British Association for Sexual Health and HIV
1977 British Association of Clinical Anatomists
1950 British Association of Forensic Medicine
1962 British Association of Oral Surgeons
1943 British Association of Otolaryngologists
1954 British Association of Paediatric Surgeons
1973 British Association of Surgical Oncology
1945 British Association of Urological Surgeons
1934 British Diabetic Association
1948 British Geriatrics Society
1832 British Medical Association
1950 British Neuropathological Society
1953 British Occupational Hygiene Society
1965 British Orthodontic Society
1918 British Orthopaedic Association
1925 British Osteopathic Association
1913 British Psychoanalytical Society
1901 British Psychological Society
1948 British Society for Allergy and Clinical Immunology
1962 British Society for Clinical Cytology
1937 British Society of Gastroenterology
1960 British Society for Haematology
1947 British Society for Research on Ageing
1945 British Thoracic Society
1947 Ergonomics Society
1946 Experimental Psychology Society
1950 Faculty of Homeopathy
1959 Forensic Science Society
1819 Hunterian Society
1969 Institute of Occupational Medicine
1964 Institute of Pharmacy Management
1773 Medical Society of London
1901 Medico-Legal Society
1941 Nutrition Society
1906 Pathological Society of Great Britain and Ireland
1875 Royal Environmental Health Institute of Scotland
1734 Royal Medical Society
1931 Royal Pharmaceutical Society of Great Britain
2008 Royal Society for Public Health
1805 Royal Society of Medicine
1907 Royal Society of Tropical Medicine and Hygiene
1946 Society for Endocrinology
1950 Society for Reproduction and Fertility
1884 Society for the Study of Addiction
1926 Society of British Neurological Surgeons

Music

1977 Alkan Society
1979 British Music Society
1971 Chopin Society
1932 English Folk Dance and Song Society
1882 Incorporated Society of Musicians
1888 Plainsong and Medieval Music Society
1874 Royal Musical Association
1955 Welsh Music Guild

Philosophy

1880 Aristotelian Society
2003 British Philosophical Association
1984 British Society for the History of Philosophy
1819 Cambridge Philosophical Society

1990	Friedrich Nietzsche Society
1979	Hegel Society of Great Britain
1781	Manchester Literary and Philosophical Society
1913	Philosophical Society of England
1925	Royal Institute of Philosophy
1802	Royal Philosophical Society of Glasgow

Politics

1975	British International Studies Association
1951	David Davies Memorial Institute of International Studies
1884	Electoral Reform Society
1945	Federal Trust for Education and Research
1987	Institute of Welsh Affairs
1974	International Association for the Study of German Politics
1950	Political Studies Association
1868	Royal Commonwealth Society
1920	Royal Institute of International Affairs

Science general

1924	Association for Informational Management
1831	British Science Association
1956	British Society for the History of Science
1960	British Society for the Philosophy of Science
1799	Royal Institution of Great Britain
1660	Royal Society
1783	Royal Society of Edinburgh

Theology and Religious Studies

1908	Baptist Historical Society
1954	British Association for the Study of Religions
1904	Canterbury and York Society
1904	Catholic Record Society
1961	Ecclesiastical History Society
1981	European Association for Jewish Studies
1903	Friends Historical Society
1972	United Reformed Church History Society
1893	Wesley Historical Society

General Index

Note: In addition to the abbreviations listed at the beginning of the book, the following are used throughout the index; FE – Further Education; HE – Higher Education. Universities are listed under locations eg: Aberdeen, University of

INDEX OF ADVERTISERS